What's What ®

What's What®

A Visual Glossary of the Physical World

REVISED EDITION

Reginald Bragonier Jr. and David Fisher

SMITHMARK

This edition published in 1994 by SMITHMARK Publishers Inc., 16 East 32nd Street, New York, NY 10016

SMITHMARK books are available for bulk purchase for sales promotion and premium use. For details write or call the manager of special sales, SMITHMARK Publishers, Inc., 16 East 32nd Street, New York, NY 10016; (212) 532-6600.

Library of Congress Cataloging-in-Publication Data

Bragonier, Reginald.
   What's what, a visual glossary of the physical world/Reginald Dragonier Jr., and David Fisher.—Rev. ed.
      p. cm.
      Includes index
      Summary: Pictures of common objects and their parts, each identified individually by name, are classed under such general categories as living things, transportation, and personal items.
      ISBN 0-8317-9469-0
      1. Picture dictionaries, English. [1. Picture dictionaries. 2. Vocabulary. 3. English language—Terms and phrases. 4. Technology—Dictionaries.] I. Fisher, David, 1946–   . II. Title. III. Title: What's what.
AG250.B7 1990   89-51862
031.02—dc20   CIP
                                                                                AC

Printed in the United States of America

10 9 8 7 6 5 4 3 2 1

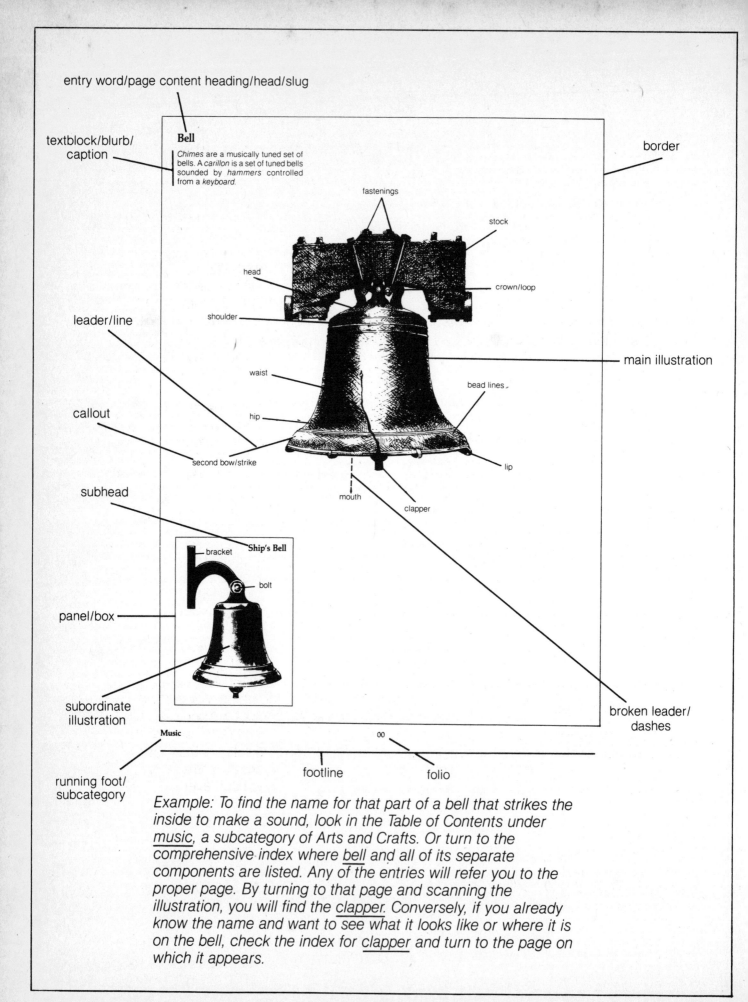

entry word/page content heading/head/slug

textblock/blurb/caption

border

Bell

Chimes are a musically tuned set of bells. A *carillon* is a set of tuned bells sounded by *hammers* controlled from a *keyboard*.

fastenings

stock

head

crown/loop

leader/line

shoulder

main illustration

waist

bead lines

callout

hip

second bow/strike

lip

subhead

mouth

clapper

Ship's Bell

bracket

bolt

panel/box

subordinate illustration

broken leader/dashes

Music

00

running foot/subcategory

footline

folio

Example: To find the name for that part of a bell that strikes the inside to make a sound, look in the Table of Contents under music, *a subcategory of Arts and Crafts. Or turn to the comprehensive index where* bell *and all of its separate components are listed. Any of the entries will refer you to the proper page. By turning to that page and scanning the illustration, you will find the* clapper. *Conversely, if you already know the name and want to see what it looks like or where it is on the bell, check the index for* clapper *and turn to the page on which it appears.*

What It Is

Until now, it has been all but impossible to find words you've forgotten or never knew to begin with. The reason for this is obvious: to use a dictionary you need to know the word in order to find it. WHAT'S WHAT® provides access to words in an entirely new way—*visually*. Readers can now find words they are seeking by turning to detailed illustrations in which all the visible parts are identified and labeled. This system of visual classification puts within verbal reach of everyone, for the first time, the words used to describe the myriad objects in our everyday world.

The objects chosen for inclusion in WHAT'S WHAT® have been selected on the basis of their usefulness to contemporary readers; and although no single volume of this kind can be encyclopedic in its coverage, WHAT'S WHAT® is both comprehensive in its scope and practical in its treatment of individual items. Thus, illustrations generally include only the visible parts of objects. However, when it is necessary or desirable to identify part of an item not actually shown, its location is indicated by a broken line. Variations and styles of objects have been presented only when the object's parts make it so distinctive that the item itself has a unique name—lorgnette, for example, which appears on the eyeglasses page. In addition, considerable use has been made of composite illustrations—nonliteral representations combining diverse elements found among similar objects.

How It Works

The book's system of classification is simple and straightforward. Since every object in the physical world is part of a larger whole, the reader can find any detail by locating the larger item. All objects fall naturally into one of the following twelve categories: *The Earth; Living Things; Shelters and Structures; Transportation; Communications; Personal Items; The Home; Sports and Recreation; Arts and Crafts; Machinery, Tools and Weapons; Uniforms, Costumes and Ceremonial Attire;* and *Signs and Symbols.*

To locate an item, turn first to the Table of Contents, where each entry is arranged by category and subcategory according to the object's nature and use. There you will readily determine in what part of the book the item is located. An automobile, for example, is listed under Transportation. An object, or the name of a part, can also be found by consulting the all-inclusive index at the back of the book. A collar stay, for example, can be located by looking under "shirt," "collar," or any other part of a shirt known to the reader, since all these entries will refer to the page on which a shirt is illustrated and all its parts are identified. Rigorous cross-referencing makes the task of finding any item or detail in the book even simpler.

And Why

WHAT'S WHAT® is far more than an ordinary reference book. Aided by well-known artists and experts in the visual-arts fields, the editors have made every effort to produce a book that is as engaging as it is informative. Its use, it is hoped, will entertain as well as enlighten.

TABLE OF CONTENTS

TABLE OF CONTENTS *(Continued)*

TABLE OF CONTENTS *(Continued)*

The Earth

This section offers various ways of looking at the earth, ranging from showing the earth as a small planet in the larger space it shares with other heavenly bodies to physical features and symbolic depictions illustrating aspects and details of the earth's surface.

Nonliteral renditions, such as the illustration of the universe, condense information visually by pulling together disparate elements for labeling. Cutaway illustrations like the one of the earth's inner layers are used only when elements considered essential to show and identify are not readily visible. The cave illustration, on the other hand, is rendered in cross section in order to show parts and details which might not be apparent in a traditional illustration.

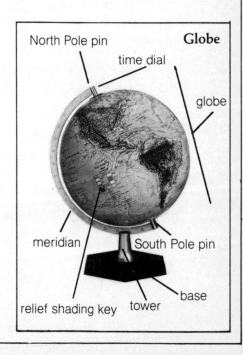

Globe

North Pole pin

time dial

globe

meridian

South Pole pin

relief shading key

tower

base

The Universe

This whimsical creation of the universe includes such bits and pieces of the entire *cosmic mass* as the *solar system*, *local galaxies* and *external galaxies*. Observable *planets* are illuminated by the light of our sun. *Meteors*, or *shooting stars*, are seen as streaks of light in the *sky* as they are vaporized on entering earth's atmosphere.

spiral galaxy

red supergiant star

side

elliptical galaxies

full face

common spiral galax

black hole

irregular galaxies

barrel spiral galaxy

asteroids/planetoids

Pluto

nebula/interstellar cloud

Neptune

stars

Uranus

doppler shift

constellation

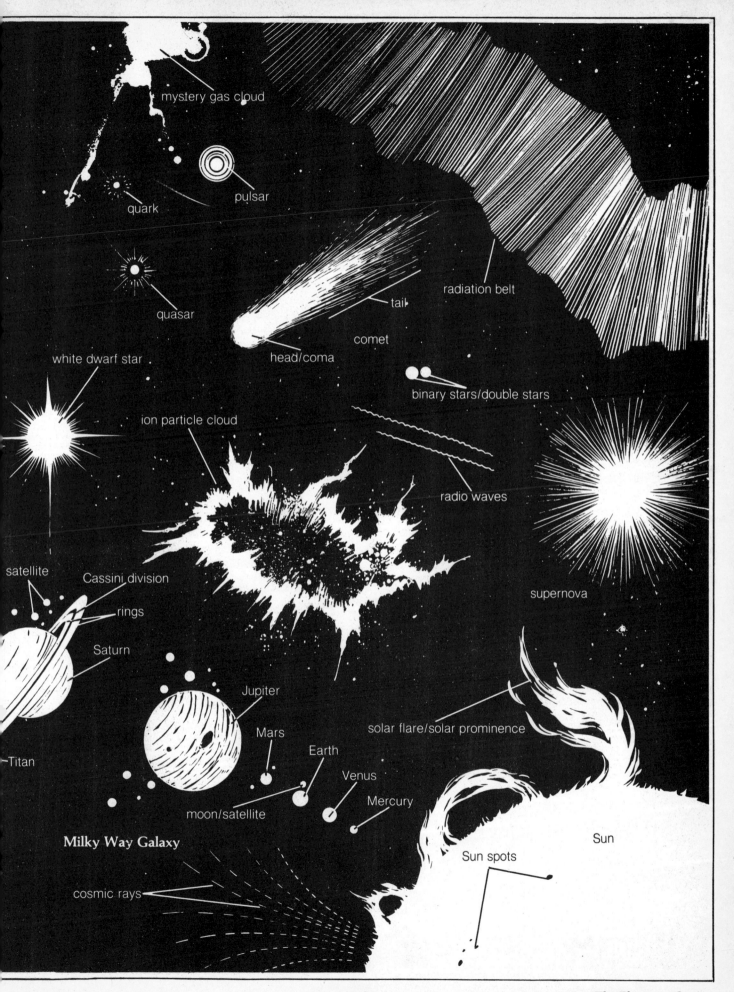

mystery gas cloud

quark

pulsar

quasar

radiation belt

tail

comet

head/coma

white dwarf star

binary stars/double stars

ion particle cloud

radio waves

supernova

satellite

Cassini division

rings

Saturn

solar flare/solar prominence

Jupiter

Mars

Titan

Earth

Venus

Mercury

moon/satellite

Milky Way Galaxy

Sun

Sun spots

cosmic rays

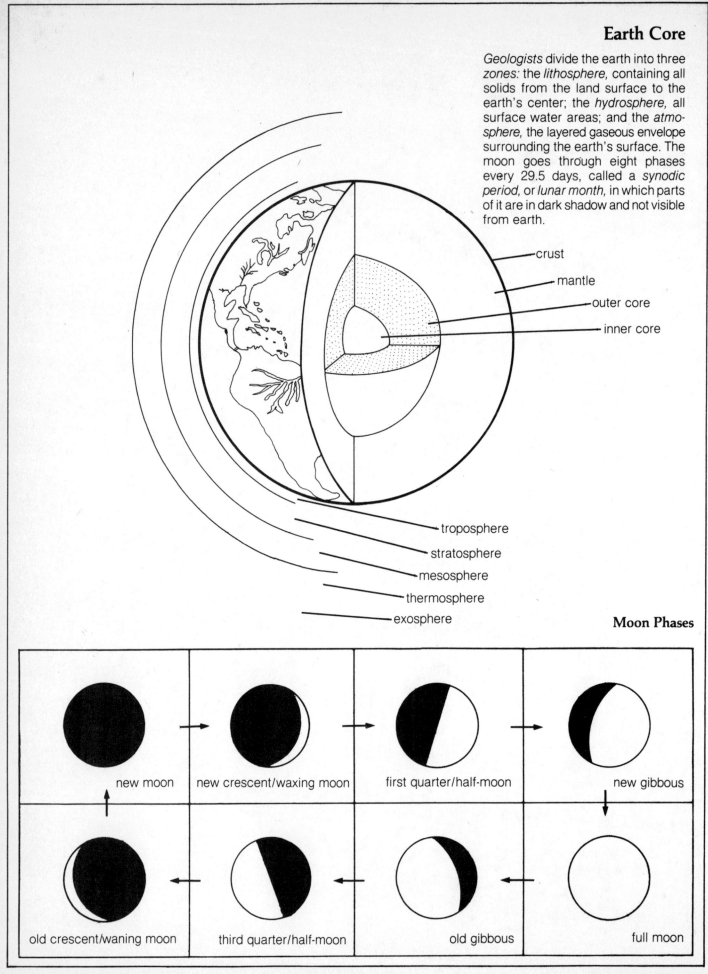

Earth Core

Geologists divide the earth into three *zones:* the *lithosphere,* containing all solids from the land surface to the earth's center; the *hydrosphere,* all surface water areas; and the *atmosphere,* the layered gaseous envelope surrounding the earth's surface. The moon goes through eight phases every 29.5 days, called a *synodic period,* or *lunar month,* in which parts of it are in dark shadow and not visible from earth.

crust

mantle

outer core

inner core

troposphere

stratosphere

mesosphere

thermosphere

exosphere

Moon Phases

new moon

new crescent/waxing moon

first quarter/half-moon

new gibbous

old crescent/waning moon

third quarter/half-moon

old gibbous

full moon

Cartographer's World

Position on the earth's *grid* can be determined by finding exact *latitude, north* or *south* of the equator, and *longitude, east* or *west* of the prime meridian. As the earth makes its daily rotation, the sun crosses every meridian once each day. When this occurs, all points on the meridian experience *noon* at the same instant. At the same time on the opposite side of the earth it is *midnight* and a new *calendar day* is beginning. There is a difference of one hour in *solar time* every 15 *degrees*. The world time zone map shows how the theoretical division of the world into 24 equal *time belts* has been modified to follow *political* or *geographical boundaries.*

pole

rhumb line

parallels of latitude/
latitude lines

meridians/
longitude lines

equator

prime meridian/
first meridian

Central
Time

Greenwich
Mean Time

Mountain
Time

Eastern
Time

Pacific
Time

Time Zones

International
Date Line

equator

Greenwich
prime meridian

The Earth

Wind and Ocean Currents

The *zonal patterns* of wind are displaced northward and southward seasonally. Those shown here prevail in winter. *Seasonal currents* change speed and direction due to seasonal winds, whereas *permanent currents* experience relatively little change.

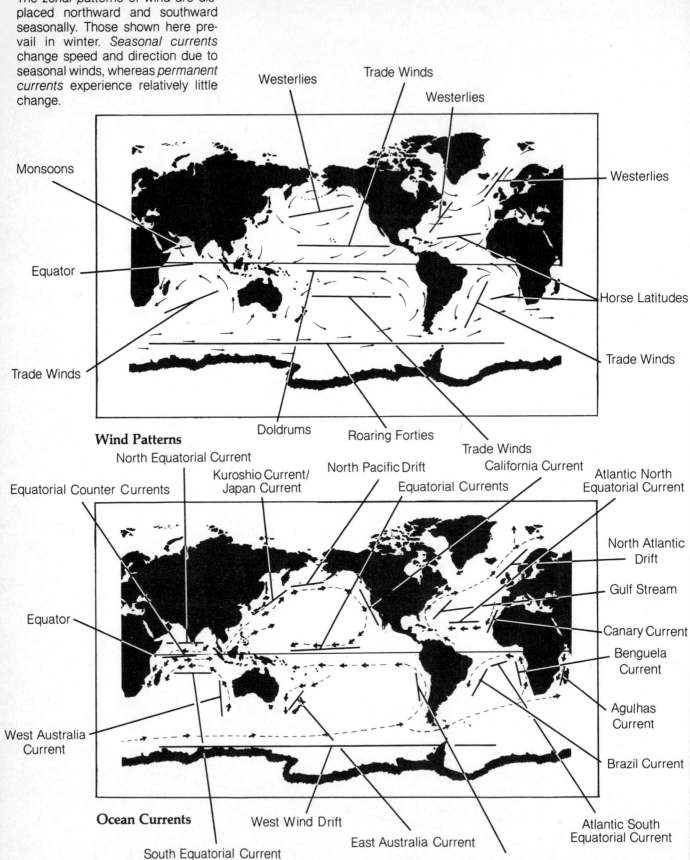

Wind Patterns

Westerlies

Trade Winds

Westerlies

Westerlies

Monsoons

Equator

Horse Latitudes

Trade Winds

Trade Winds

Doldrums

Roaring Forties

Trade Winds

Ocean Currents

North Equatorial Current

Kuroshio Current/ Japan Current

North Pacific Drift

California Current

Atlantic North Equatorial Current

Equatorial Counter Currents

Equatorial Currents

North Atlantic Drift

Gulf Stream

Equator

Canary Current

Benguela Current

West Australia Current

Agulhas Current

Brazil Current

West Wind Drift

South Equatorial Current

East Australia Current

Humboldt Current /Peru Current

Atlantic South Equatorial Current

Land Features

A part of an *ocean* or *sea* extending into the land is a *gulf*. A narrow finger of land extending into the water is a *spit*. A sand or gravel bar connecting an island with the *mainland* or another island is a *tombolo*.

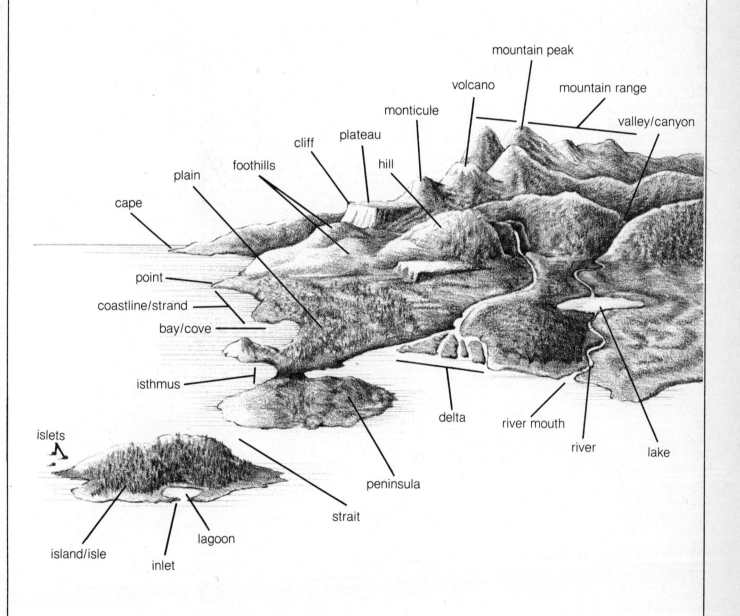

mountain peak

volcano

monticule

mountain range

valley/canyon

cliff

plateau

foothills

hill

plain

cape

point

coastline/strand

bay/cove

isthmus

islets

delta

river mouth

river

lake

peninsula

strait

island/isle

inlet

lagoon

Terrains

Mountains

A series of mountains, such as the Alpine mountains shown here, is a *range.* A circular space in mountains is a *cirque,* or *cwm.* A *kame* is a ridge or material left by a retreating *ice sheet.* An isolated hill or mountain rising abruptly from the surrounding land is a *butte.*

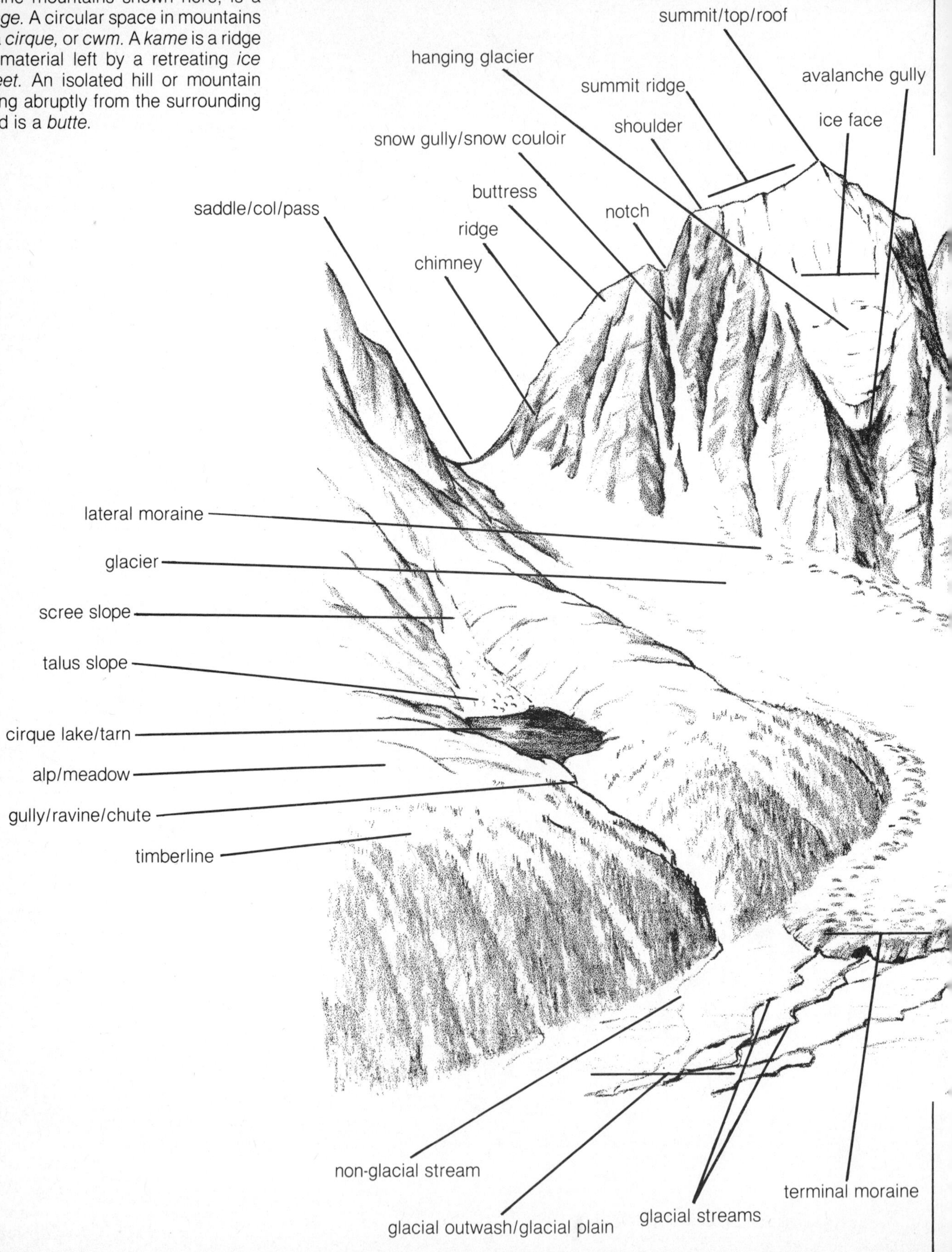

summit/top/roof

hanging glacier

avalanche gully

summit ridge

ice face

shoulder

snow gully/snow couloir

buttress

notch

saddle/col/pass

ridge

chimney

lateral moraine

glacier

scree slope

talus slope

cirque lake/tarn

alp/meadow

gully/ravine/chute

timberline

non-glacial stream

terminal moraine

glacial streams

glacial outwash/glacial plain

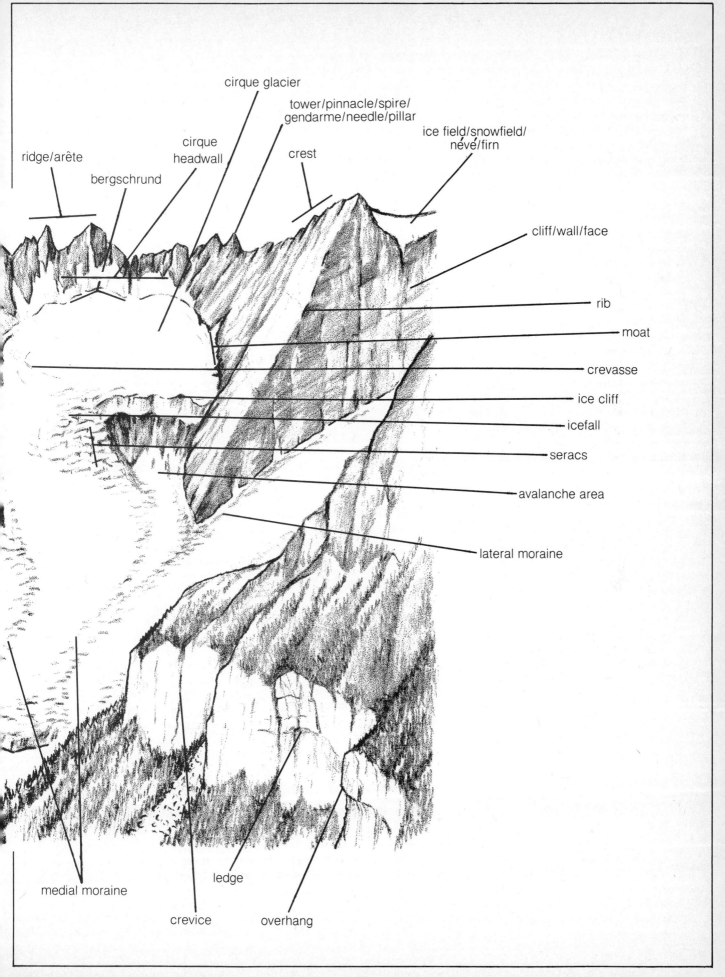

cirque glacier

tower/pinnacle/spire/
gendarme/needle/pillar

ice field/snowfield/
névé/firn

cirque
headwall

crest

ridge/arête

bergschrund

cliff/wall/face

rib

moat

crevasse

ice cliff

icefall

seracs

avalanche area

lateral moraine

medial moraine

ledge

crevice

overhang

Terrains

Volcano

In *central-vent volcanoes,* such as the one shown here, material erupts from a single pipe. *Fissure volcanoes* extrude material along extensive *fractures.*

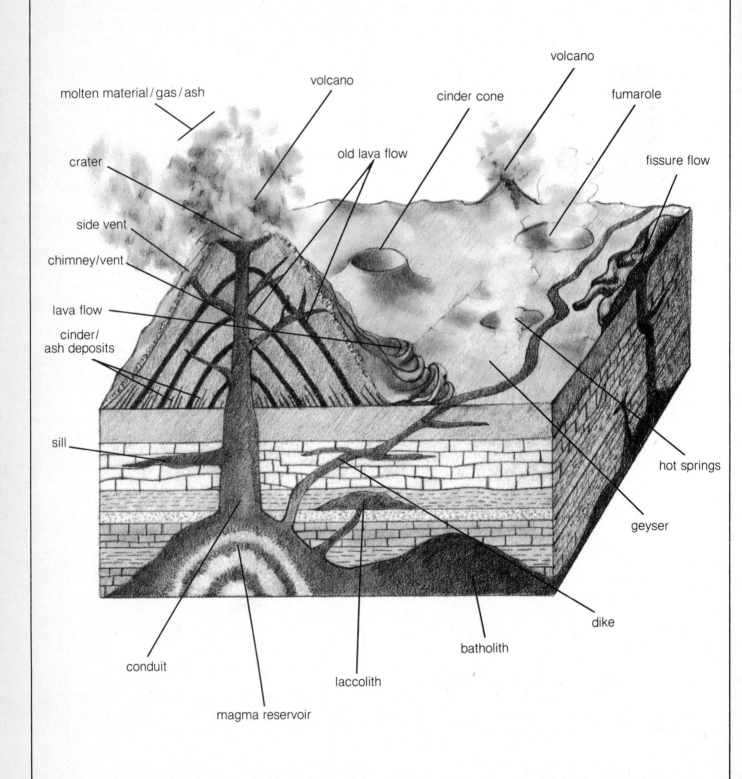

molten material / gas / ash

volcano

cinder cone

volcano

fumarole

crater

old lava flow

fissure flow

side vent

chimney/vent

lava flow

cinder/ ash deposits

sill

hot springs

geyser

dike

conduit

laccolith

batholith

magma reservoir

Cave Cross Section

The exploration of caves, or *caverns* is called *spelunking* or *caving*. The area lighted by daylight just inside a cave entrance is the *twilight zone*. An underground structure containing many *galleries, chambers* or *rooms* is a *cave system*. Anything formed inside a cave, *cavern* or *grotto*, by dripping water is *dripstone*. Knobby calcite growths often found on *walls* and *floors* of once-submerged caves are called *cave coral* or *cave popcorn*.

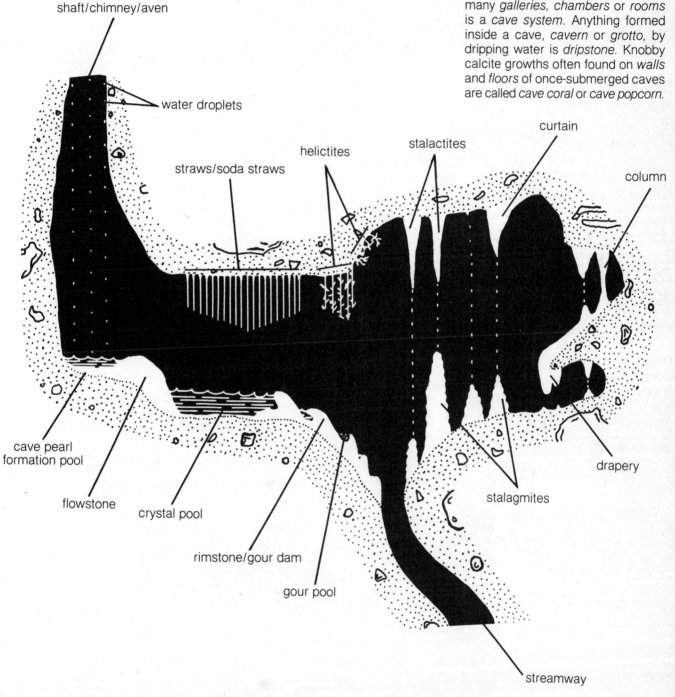

shaft/chimney/aven

water droplets

helictites

straws/soda straws

stalactites

curtain

column

cave pearl
formation pool

flowstone

crystal pool

rimstone/gour dam

gour pool

stalagmites

drapery

streamway

Terrains

Glacier

When a glacier terminates at the water's edge, sections break off, or *calve*, to form icebergs. Icebergs often break apart to form smaller, separate *bergs, bergy bits* or *bitty bergs*. Even smaller sections are called *growlers*. *Ice packs,* formed when the water surface between floating ice freezes, are called *floes*. Sections that break off are called *floebergs*.

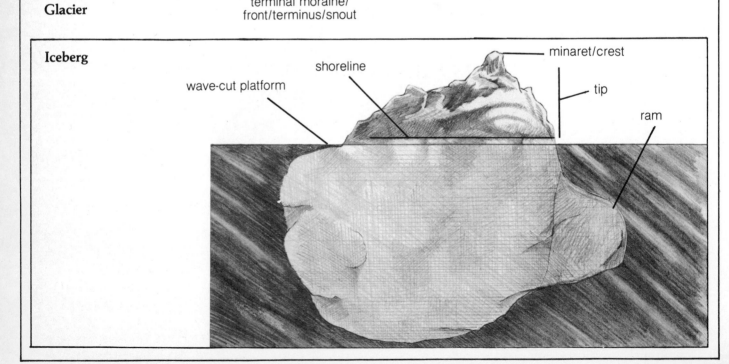

horn/spitz/peak

accumulation zone

arête

cirque glacier

snowfield

non-glaciated valley

valley glacier

lateral moraine

drumlin

medial moraine

ablation zone

terminal moraine/
front/terminus/snout

Glacier

Iceberg

minaret/crest

shoreline

tip

wave-cut platform

ram

River

A *river system* consists of the main river and its tributaries or branches. It drains from a *river basin,* and flows along a *course,* or *watercourse,* cutting a *channel* through the land. A *flood* occurs when it overflows its banks.

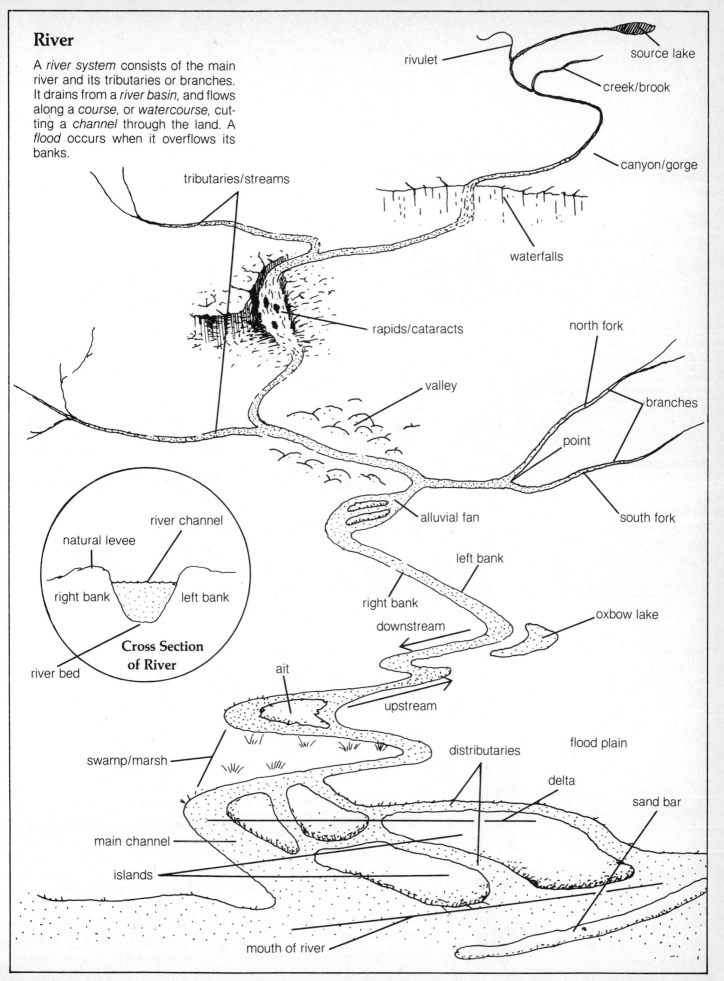

rivulet

source lake

creek/brook

canyon/gorge

tributaries/streams

waterfalls

rapids/cataracts

north fork

branches

valley

point

south fork

natural levee

river channel

right bank

left bank

alluvial fan

left bank

right bank

oxbow lake

Cross Section of River

river bed

downstream

ait

upstream

flood plain

swamp/marsh

distributaries

delta

sand bar

main channel

islands

mouth of river

13

Water Systems

Wave and Shoreline

Wavelength is the linear distance between two wave crests, *period* is the time it takes two crests to pass a given point, and *wave height* is the vertical distance measured from the trough to the crest of a wave. There are *surface waves, tidal waves, internal waves, tsunamis, storm surges* and *seiches*. Long, crestless waves are *swells*. The rapid flow of water up onto the *beach face* following the breaking of *surf* is the *uprush* or *swash*.

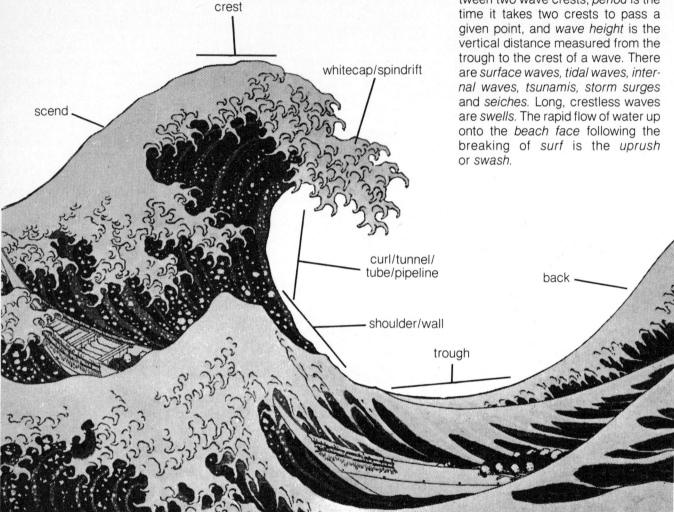

crest

whitecap/spindrift

scend

curl/tunnel/
tube/pipeline

back

shoulder/wall

trough

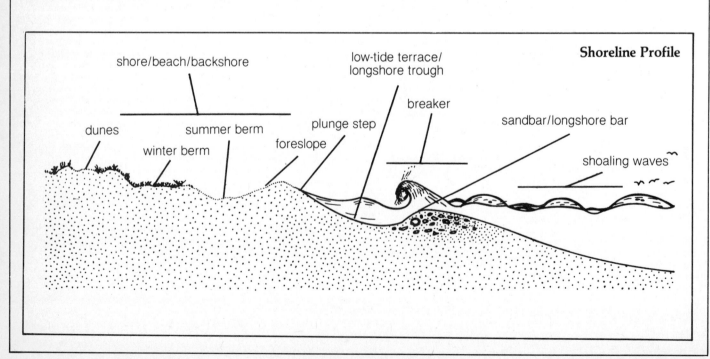

Shoreline Profile

shore/beach/backshore

low-tide terrace/
longshore trough

breaker

sandbar/longshore bar

dunes

plunge step

summer berm

foreslope

shoaling waves

winter berm

Coastline and Continental Margin

The *littoral zone* is that part of the shoreline that lies between *high* and *low tides*. The continental shelf is the submerged border of *landmasses* extending into the *ocean basin*. The *100-fathom curve* has long been used as the outer limit of the continental shelf.

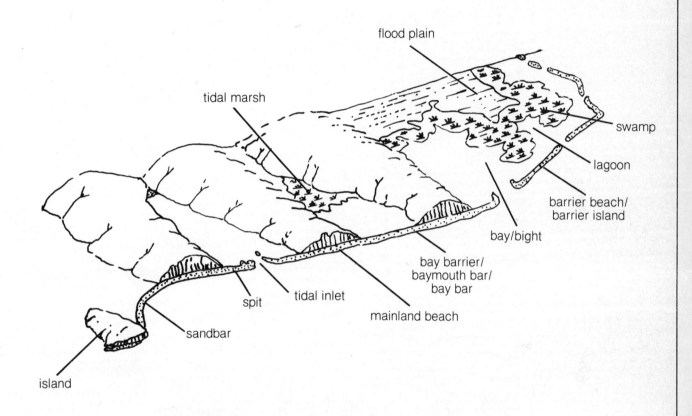

flood plain

tidal marsh

swamp

lagoon

barrier beach/
barrier island

bay/bight

bay barrier/
baymouth bar/
bay bar

mainland beach

tidal inlet

spit

sandbar

island

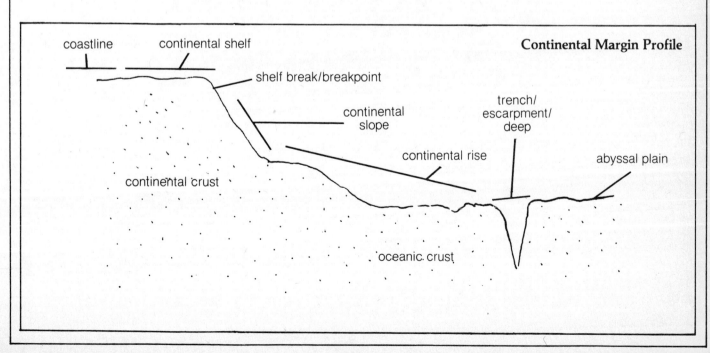

Continental Margin Profile

coastline

continental shelf

shelf break/breakpoint

continental slope

continental rise

trench/
escarpment/
deep

abyssal plain

continental crust

oceanic crust

Clouds

The name of a cloud describes both its appearance and its height above the ground. Clouds are formed from tiny droplets of water or *ice crystals* and continually change shape due to evaporation, wind and *air movements*.

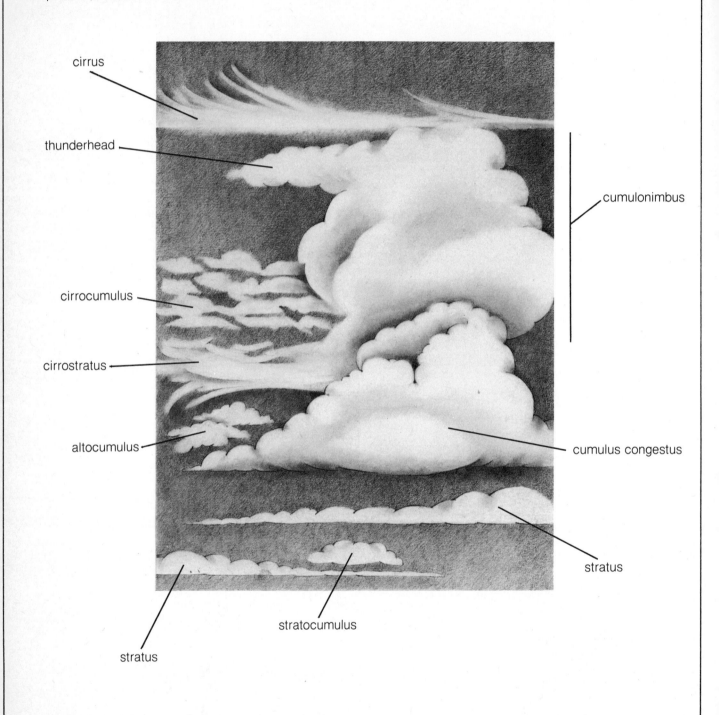

cirrus

thunderhead

cumulonimbus

cirrocumulus

cirrostratus

altocumulus

cumulus congestus

stratus

stratus

stratocumulus

Storm Systems

Thunderstorms carry the same general features: lightning, *thunder*, strong gusts of *wind*, heavy *showers*, and occasionally *hailstones*. When hurricanes occur in the Pacific, they are called *typhoons*. Tornados are also known as *twisters*.

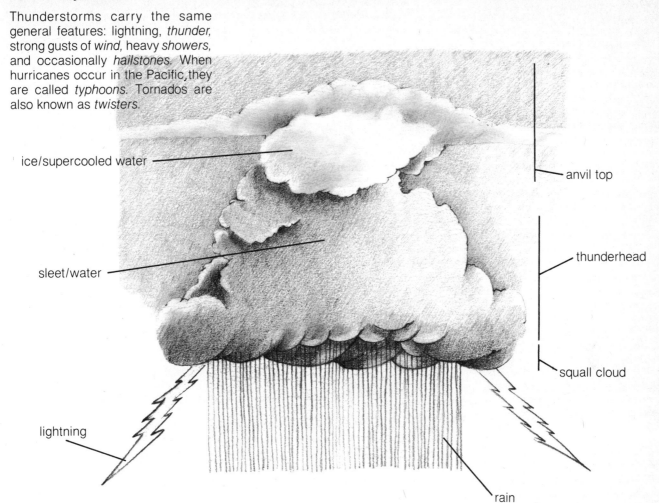

ice/supercooled water

anvil top

sleet/water

thunderhead

squall cloud

lightning

rain

Thunderstorm

Tornado

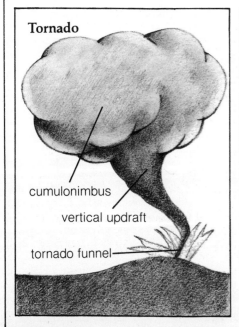

cumulonimbus

vertical updraft

tornado funnel

Cross Section of Hurricane

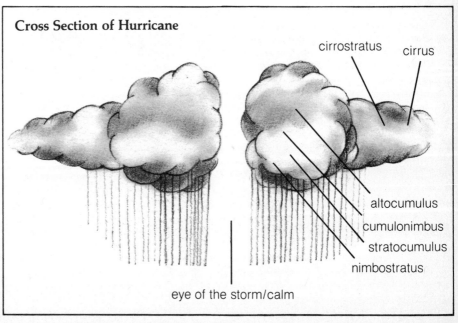

cirrostratus

cirrus

altocumulus

cumulonimbus

stratocumulus

nimbostratus

eye of the storm/calm

Weather Monitoring Equipment

Equipment, such as that shown here, helps a *meteorologist* predict weather and make *weather forecasts*.

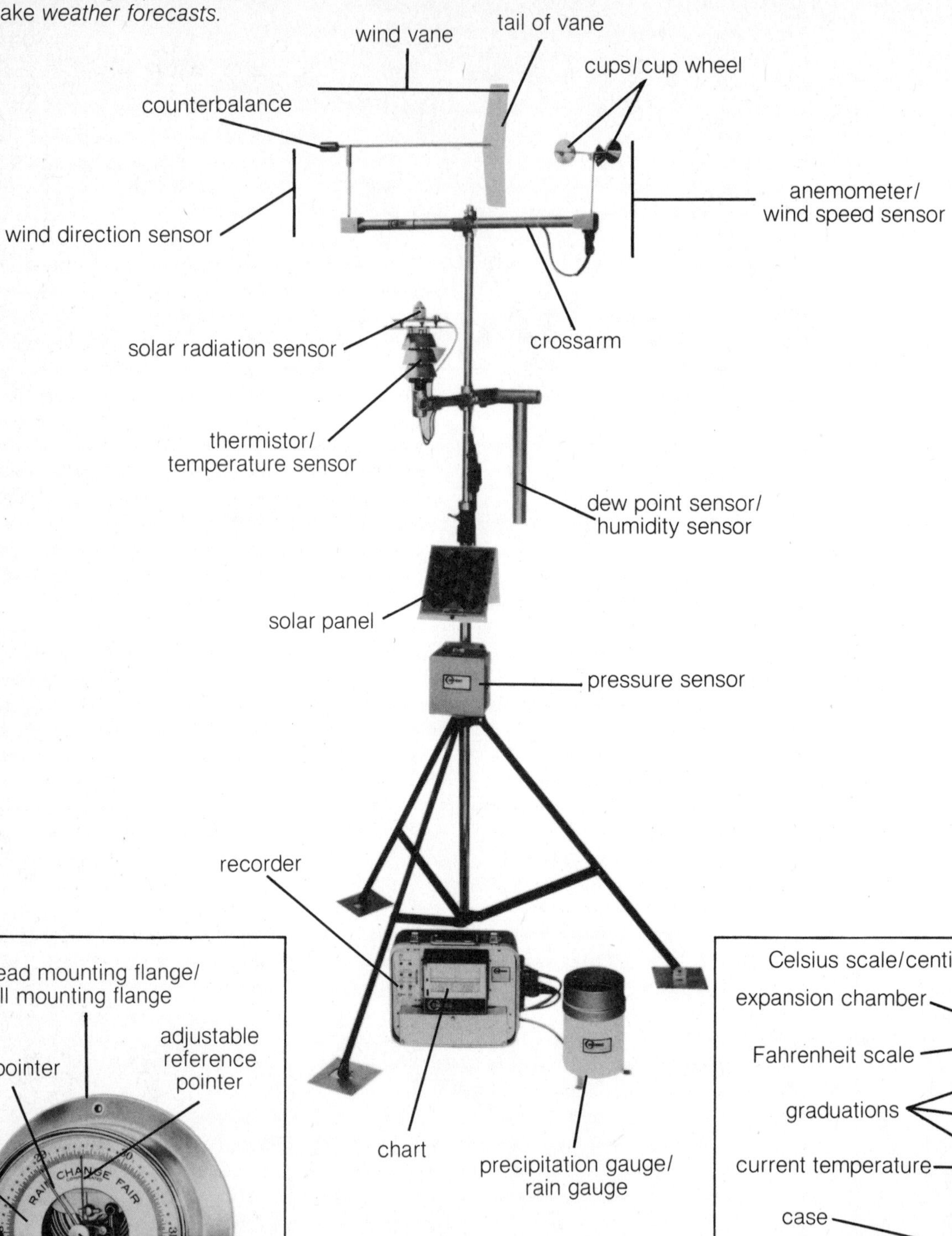

wind vane

tail of vane

cups/cup wheel

counterbalance

wind direction sensor

anemometer/ wind speed sensor

solar radiation sensor

crossarm

thermistor/ temperature sensor

dew point sensor/ humidity sensor

solar panel

pressure sensor

recorder

Aneroid Barometer

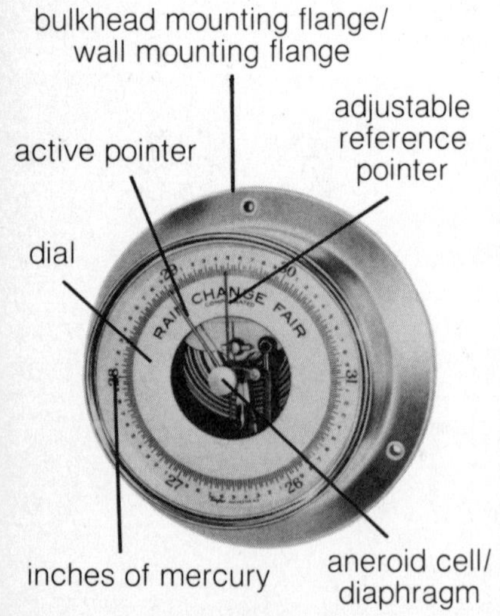

bulkhead mounting flange/ wall mounting flange

adjustable reference pointer

active pointer

dial

RAIN   CHANGE   FAIR

inches of mercury

aneroid cell/ diaphragm

chart

precipitation gauge/ rain gauge

Electronic Weather Station

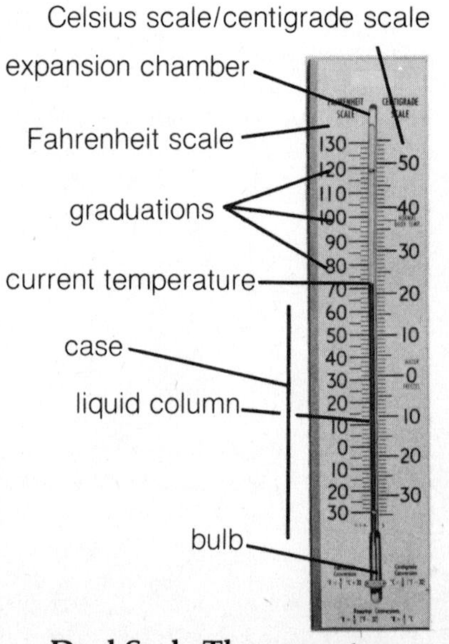

Dual Scale Thermometer

Celsius scale/centigrade scale

expansion chamber

Fahrenheit scale

graduations

current temperature

case

liquid column

bulb

130
120
110
100
90
80
70
60
50
40
30
20
10
0
10
20
30

50
40
30
20
10

10
20
30

Weather Map

This composite weather map, or *synoptic chart*, displays conditions over a broad area. The numbers around the station model indicate *temperature*, *barometric pressure* and *pressure change*.

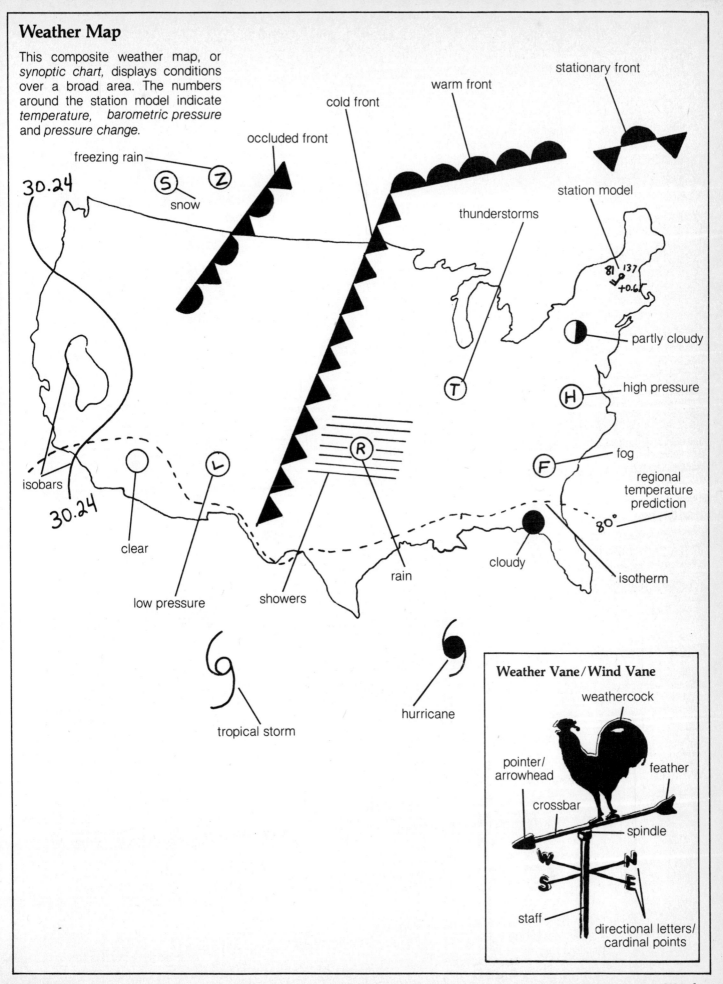

freezing rain

occluded front

cold front

warm front

stationary front

snow

30.24

thunderstorms

station model

81 137
+0.6

partly cloudy

high pressure

fog

regional temperature prediction

isobars

30.24

clear

low pressure

showers

rain

cloudy

80°

isotherm

tropical storm

hurricane

Weather Vane / Wind Vane

weathercock

pointer/ arrowhead

feather

crossbar

spindle

W N S E

staff

directional letters/ cardinal points

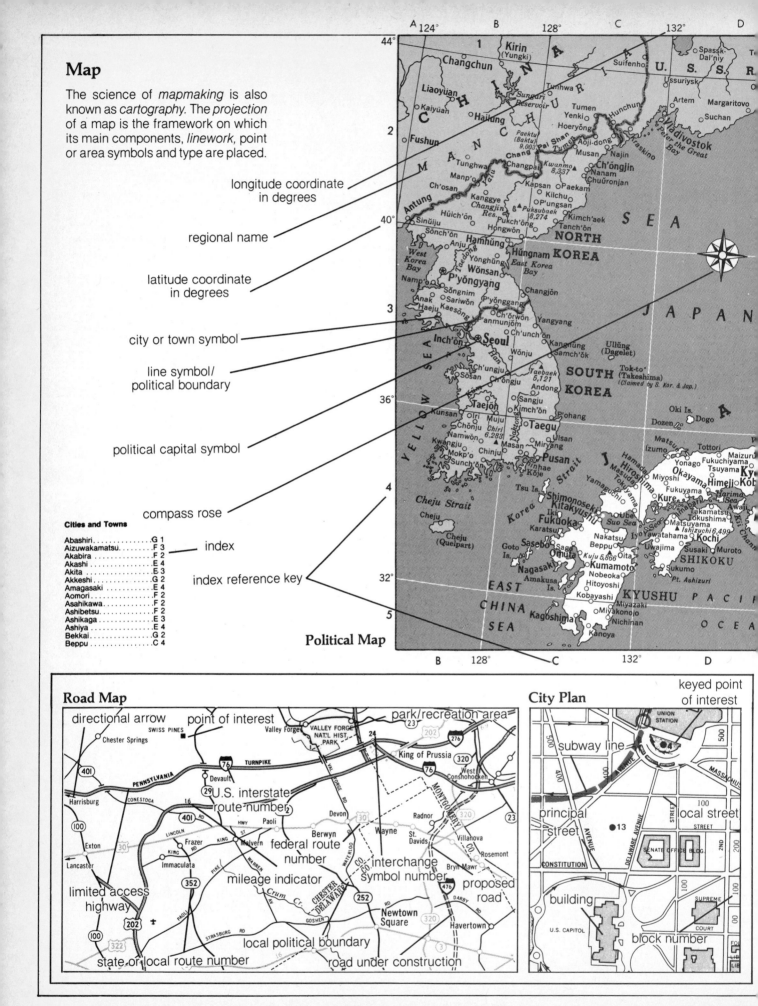

Map

The science of *mapmaking* is also known as *cartography*. The *projection* of a map is the framework on which its main components, *linework,* point or area symbols and type are placed.

longitude coordinate in degrees

regional name

latitude coordinate in degrees

city or town symbol

line symbol/ political boundary

political capital symbol

compass rose

Cities and Towns

Abashiri	G 1
Aizuwakamatsu	F 3
Akabira	F 2
Akashi	E 4
Akita	E 3
Akkeshi	G 2
Amagasaki	E 4
Aomori	F 2
Asahikawa	F 2
Ashibetsu	F 2
Ashikaga	E 3
Ashiya	E 4
Bekkai	G 2
Beppu	C 4

index

index reference key

Political Map

Road Map

directional arrow   point of interest

park/recreation area

U.S. interstate route number

federal route number

mileage indicator

limited access highway

interchange symbol number

proposed road

local political boundary

state or local route number

road under construction

City Plan

keyed point of interest

subway line

principal street

local street

building

block number

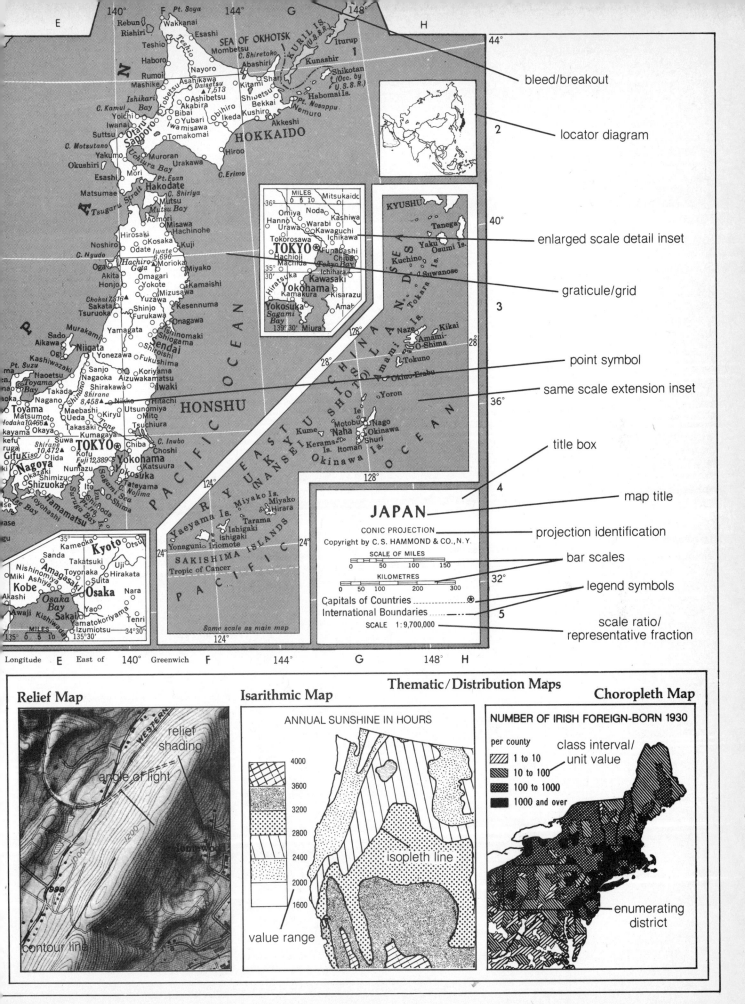

bleed/breakout

locator diagram

enlarged scale detail inset

graticule/grid

point symbol

same scale extension inset

title box

map title

projection identification

bar scales

legend symbols

scale ratio/
representative fraction

JAPAN

CONIC PROJECTION

Copyright by C.S. HAMMOND & CO., N.Y.

SCALE OF MILES

0   50   100   150

KILOMETRES

0   50   100   200   300

Capitals of Countries .... ⊗

International Boundaries ....

SCALE 1:9,700,000

Longitude   E   East of   140° Greenwich   F   144°   G   148°   H

Thematic/Distribution Maps

Relief Map

relief shading

angle of light

contour line

Isarithmic Map

ANNUAL SUNSHINE IN HOURS

4000
3600
3200
2800
2400
2000
1600

isopleth line

value range

Choropleth Map

NUMBER OF IRISH FOREIGN-BORN 1930

per county

class interval/
unit value

⬚ 1 to 10
⬚ 10 to 100
⬚ 100 to 1000
■ 1000 and over

enumerating
district

Nautical Chart and Topographic Map

On nautical charts, *sounding datum reference* is stated in the *chart title*. *Depth conversion scales* are provided to enable the mariner to work in *meters, fathoms,* or *feet.* The space outside a chart of map, used to identify and explain the map, is the *map margin.*

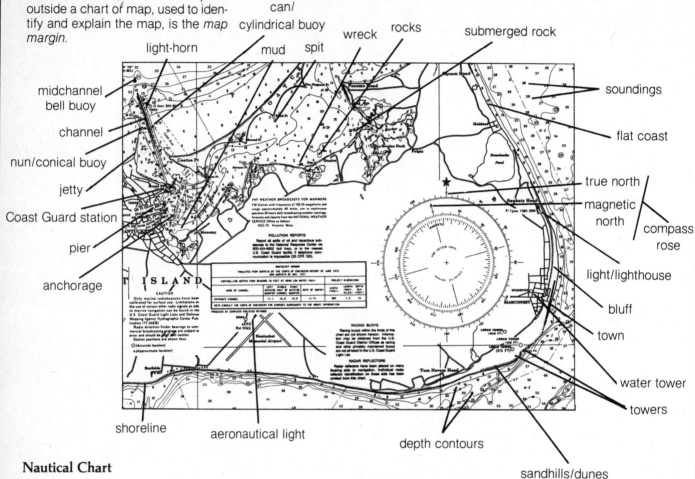

can/cylindrical buoy
light-horn
mud
spit
wreck
rocks
submerged rock
midchannel bell buoy
channel
nun/conical buoy
jetty
Coast Guard station
pier
anchorage
soundings
flat coast
true north
magnetic north
compass rose
light/lighthouse
bluff
town
water tower
towers
shoreline
aeronautical light
depth contours
sandhills/dunes

Nautical Chart

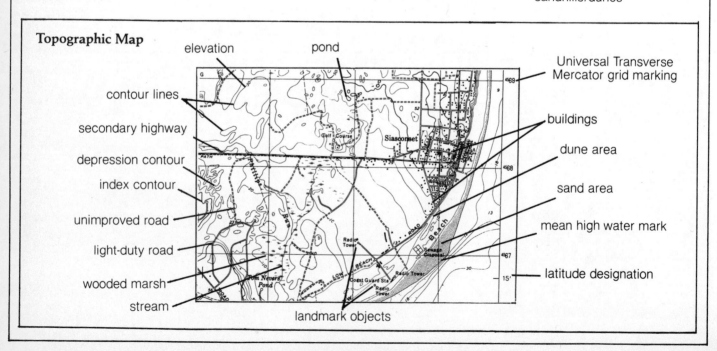

Topographic Map

elevation
pond
contour lines
secondary highway
depression contour
index contour
unimproved road
light-duty road
wooded marsh
stream
Universal Transverse Mercator grid marking
buildings
dune area
sand area
mean high water mark
latitude designation
landmark objects

Living Things

For ease of reference, this section has been divided into five subcategories: man, edible animals, domestic animals, wild animals, and plants. The animals and plants selected for inclusion within each subsection contain most of the parts common to all members of the major families they represent.

With the exception of man, examined more closely than any other subject in this section because of his obvious importance to us, only the external parts of living things have been identified. However, edible animals have been illustrated in such a way as to show those parts which supply our daily food. Domestic and wild animals, some of them grouped by habitat, are represented by single members of a species. But because there are parts which are unique to certain animals, a composite "beast" has been created to illustrate some of them.

The plant kingdom is represented from the roots up, literally, including coverage of parts of a flower, special plants, and edible portions called fruits and vegetables.

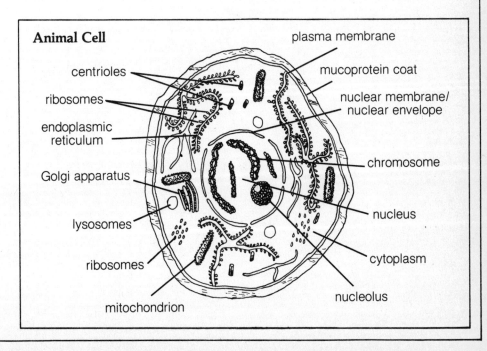

Animal Cell

plasma membrane
centrioles
mucoprotein coat
ribosomes
nuclear membrane/ nuclear envelope
endoplasmic reticulum
chromosome
Golgi apparatus
lysosomes
nucleus
ribosomes
cytoplasm
nucleolus
mitochondrion

The Human Body

The body, less the *head* and *limbs*, is referred to as the *trunk* or *torso*.

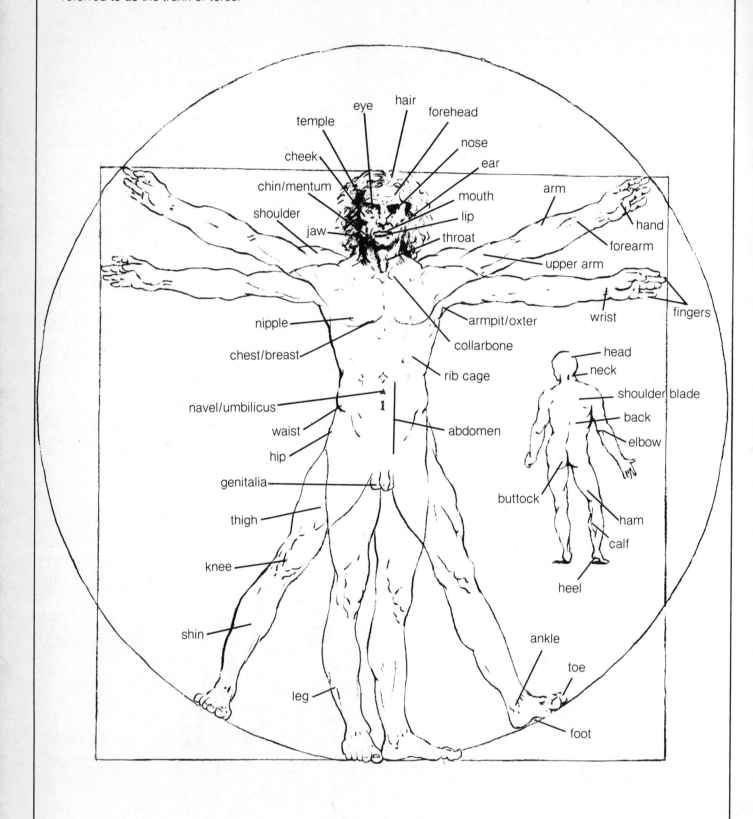

temple
eye
hair
forehead
cheek
nose
chin/mentum
ear
shoulder
mouth
jaw
lip
throat
arm
hand
forearm
upper arm
nipple
armpit/oxter
wrist
fingers
chest/breast
collarbone
navel/umbilicus
rib cage
head
neck
shoulder blade
back
elbow
waist
hip
abdomen
genitalia
buttock
thigh
ham
calf
knee
heel
shin
ankle
toe
leg
foot

Literary Anatomy

The terms used in this novel approach to descriptive male and female anatomy are derived from popular literature. *Loins* generally designate the parts of the body which should be clothed or girded. A fold of flesh is called a *collop*.

noggin/pash
mind
pate/crown
brow
orb
tress (f)/lock
Adam's apple (m)
mane
hollow of throat
cleft
gullet/gorge
button
paw
digits
bust/bosom (f)
cleavage (f)
nape of neck/scruff
heart/soul/anima/core
crook of arm
tummy/breadbasket/maw
solar plexus
spleen
flank
midriff
loin/small of back
bellybutton
Ilial crest/haunch
dimple
belly/bowels/gut/innards
pubes
funny bone
derriere/breech
groin
fist
gam (f)/limb
Achilles' heel
shank

m = male
f = female

Human Anatomy

Skeletal and Muscular System

Voluntary muscles are subject to or controlled by will, pulling on *bones* of the *skeleton* to produce movement. *Involuntary muscles*, like the heart, act independently of volition. Where one bone meets another is a *joint*. *Cartilage*, or *gristle*, is a flexible type of connective tissue. The bony structure in which the brain is housed is the *cranium*.

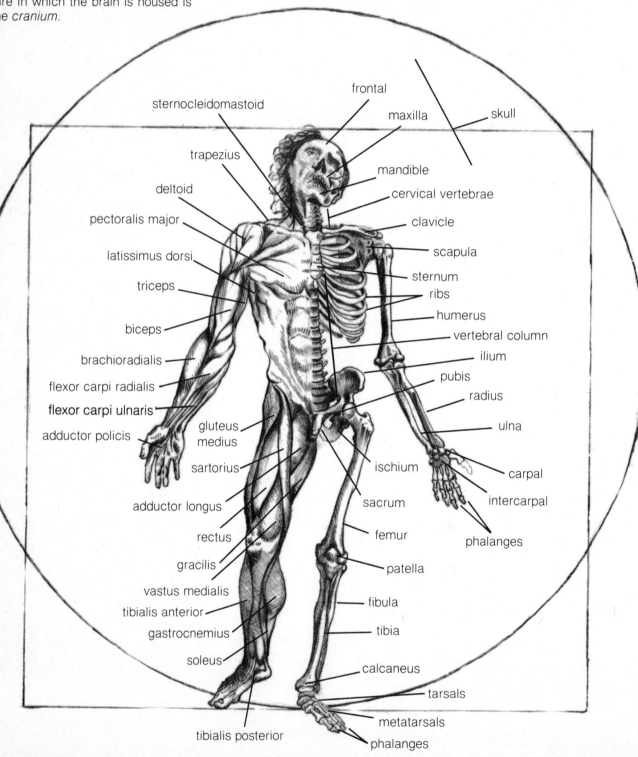

sternocleidomastoid
frontal
maxilla
skull
trapezius
mandible
deltoid
cervical vertebrae
pectoralis major
clavicle
latissimus dorsi
scapula
triceps
sternum
ribs
biceps
humerus
brachioradialis
vertebral column
ilium
flexor carpi radialis
pubis
radius
flexor carpi ulnaris
adductor policis
gluteus medius
ulna
sartorius
ischium
carpal
adductor longus
sacrum
intercarpal
rectus
femur
phalanges
gracilis
patella
vastus medialis
fibula
tibialis anterior
tibia
gastrocnemius
calcaneus
soleus
tarsals
metatarsals
tibialis posterior
phalanges

Internal Organs

The stomach and intestines are the principal organs of the *digestive system*, or *alimentary canal*, and the *pancreas*, liver and *gall bladder* all aid in the nutrition process and the elimination of wastes. The heart is the pump of the *circulatory system*, sending blood through *arteries*, *veins* and *capillaries*. The lungs are the center of the *respiratory system*.

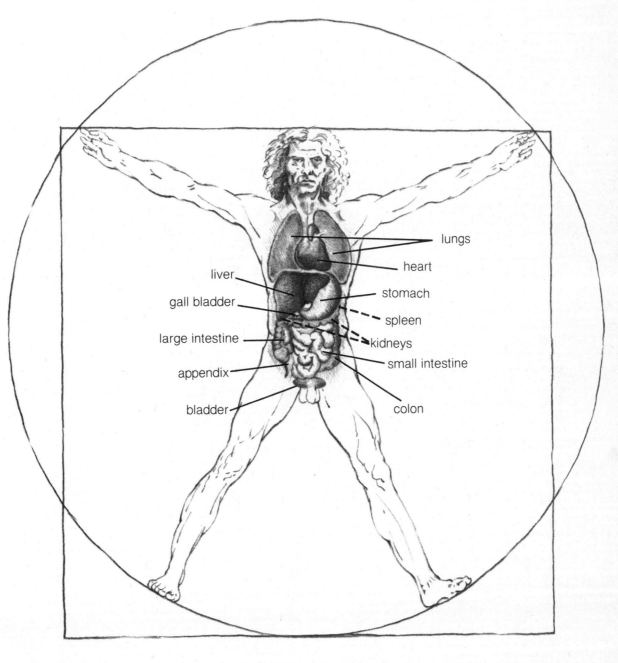

lungs

heart

liver

stomach

gall bladder

spleen

large intestine

kidneys

appendix

small intestine

bladder

colon

Human Anatomy

Circulation System and Heart

The heart pumps oxygenated and nutrient-rich blood throughout the body via arteries and their smaller branches, *arterioles*. Blood flows across body tissue through a network of small vessels, collectively called a *capillary bed*. Deoxygenated blood collects in small vessels called *venules*, which join to form veins.

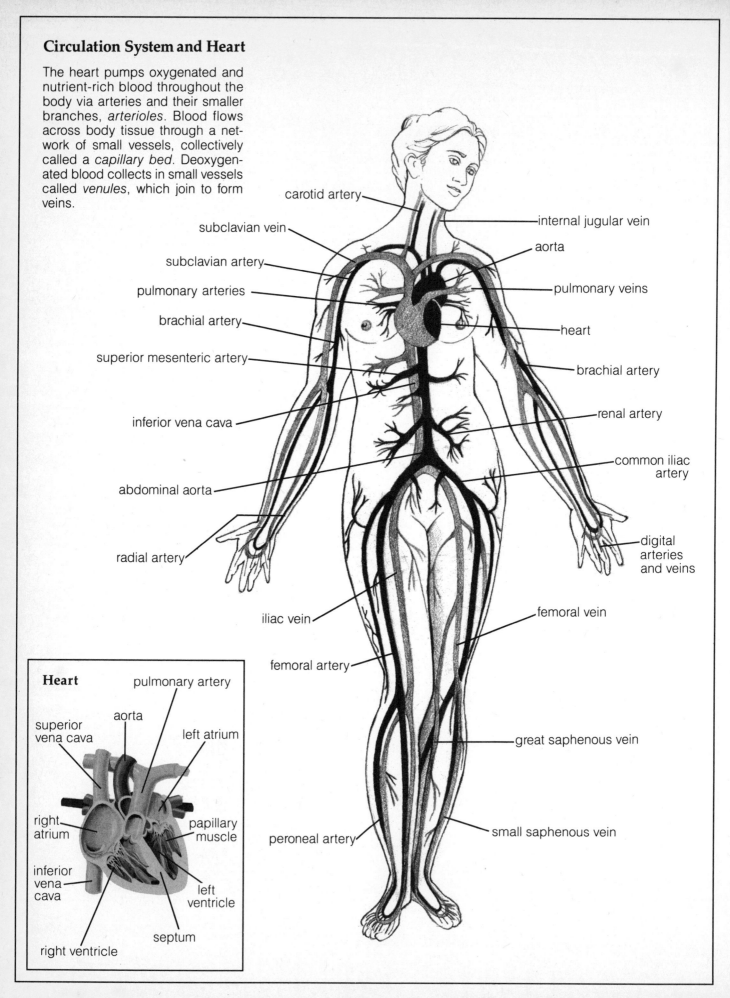

carotid artery

internal jugular vein

subclavian vein

aorta

subclavian artery

pulmonary veins

pulmonary arteries

heart

brachial artery

brachial artery

superior mesenteric artery

renal artery

inferior vena cava

common iliac artery

abdominal aorta

digital arteries and veins

radial artery

iliac vein

femoral vein

femoral artery

great saphenous vein

peroneal artery

small saphenous vein

Heart

pulmonary artery

aorta

superior vena cava

left atrium

right atrium

papillary muscle

inferior vena cava

left ventricle

septum

right ventricle

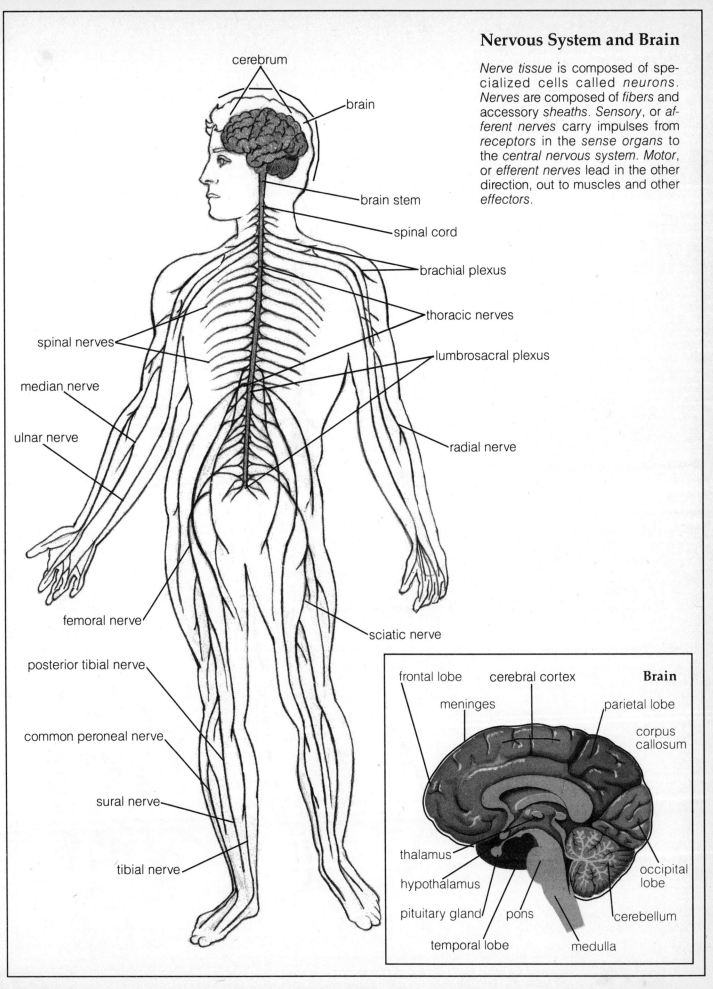

Nervous System and Brain

Nerve tissue is composed of specialized cells called *neurons*. *Nerves* are composed of *fibers* and accessory *sheaths*. *Sensory*, or *afferent nerves* carry impulses from *receptors* in the *sense organs* to the *central nervous system*. *Motor*, or *efferent nerves* lead in the other direction, out to muscles and other *effectors*.

cerebrum

brain

brain stem

spinal cord

brachial plexus

thoracic nerves

spinal nerves

lumbrosacral plexus

median nerve

ulnar nerve

radial nerve

femoral nerve

sciatic nerve

posterior tibial nerve

common peroneal nerve

sural nerve

tibial nerve

Brain

frontal lobe

cerebral cortex

meninges

parietal lobe

corpus callosum

thalamus

hypothalamus

occipital lobe

pituitary gland

pons

cerebellum

temporal lobe

medulla

Human Anatomy

Sense Organs

The eye, which is located in an *eye socket*, or *orbit*, is covered with a transparent layer called the *cornea*. The angle formed where upper and lower eyelids come together is called the *canthus*. The junction nearest the nose is the *inner canthus*, the other is the *outer canthus*. The tongue rubs against the *palate* at the top of the mouth. The *pharynx* is the beginning of the *throat*, or *gullet*.

Eye

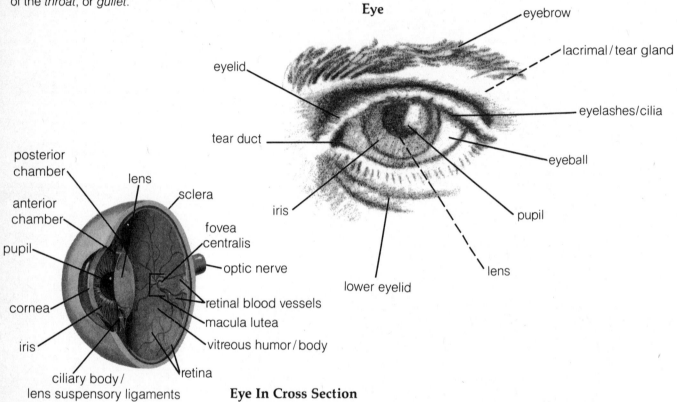

- eyebrow
- lacrimal / tear gland
- eyelashes/cilia
- eyeball
- pupil
- lens
- eyelid
- tear duct
- iris
- lower eyelid

Eye In Cross Section

- posterior chamber
- lens
- sclera
- anterior chamber
- fovea centralis
- pupil
- optic nerve
- cornea
- retinal blood vessels
- iris
- macula lutea
- vitreous humor / body
- ciliary body / lens suspensory ligaments
- retina

Nose and Mouth

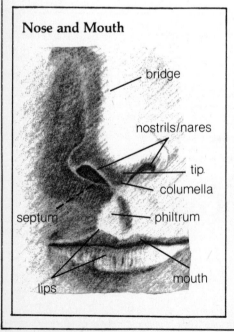

- bridge
- nostrils/nares
- tip
- columella
- septum
- philtrum
- lips
- mouth

Outer Ear / Auricle / Pinna

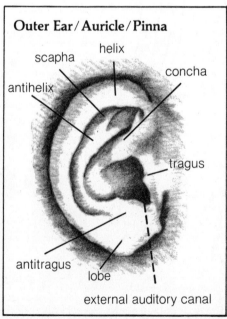

- scapha
- helix
- concha
- antihelix
- tragus
- antitragus
- lobe
- external auditory canal

Tongue

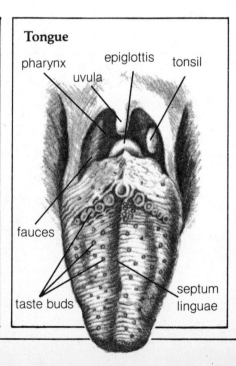

- pharynx
- epiglottis
- tonsil
- uvula
- fauces
- taste buds
- septum linguae

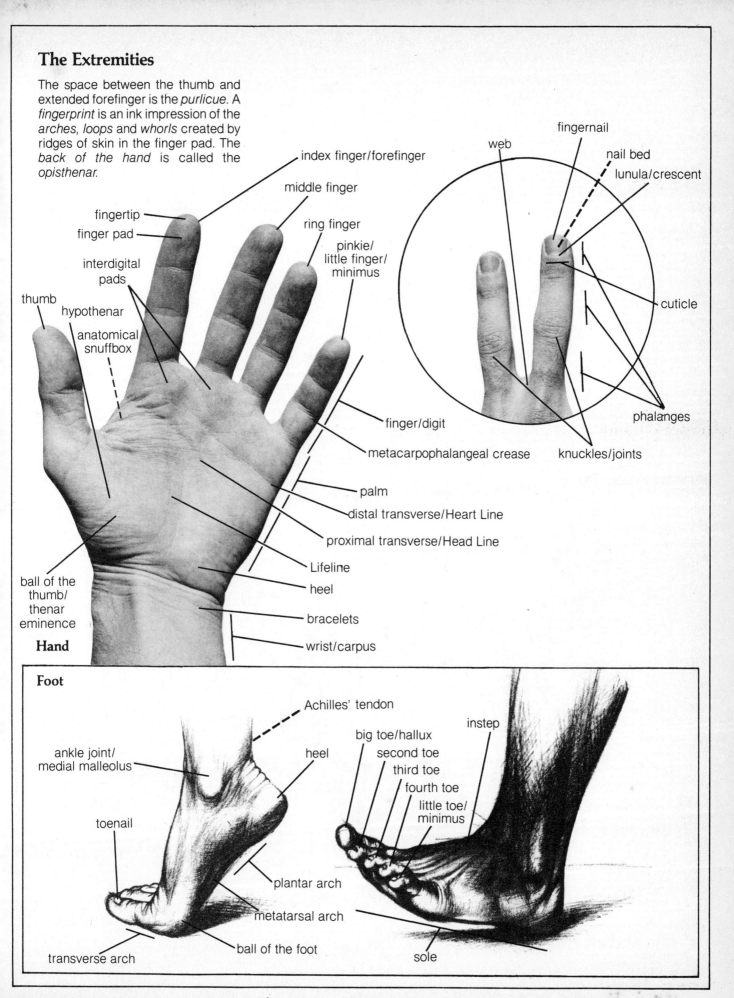

The Extremities

The space between the thumb and extended forefinger is the *purlicue*. A *fingerprint* is an ink impression of the *arches, loops* and *whorls* created by ridges of skin in the finger pad. The *back of the hand* is called the *opisthenar*.

index finger/forefinger

middle finger

ring finger

pinkie/ little finger/ minimus

fingertip

finger pad

interdigital pads

thumb

hypothenar

anatomical snuffbox

web

fingernail

nail bed

lunula/crescent

cuticle

phalanges

knuckles/joints

finger/digit

metacarpophalangeal crease

palm

distal transverse/Heart Line

proximal transverse/Head Line

Lifeline

heel

ball of the thumb/ thenar eminence

bracelets

wrist/carpus

Hand

Foot

Achilles' tendon

instep

big toe/hallux

second toe

third toe

fourth toe

little toe/ minimus

heel

ankle joint/ medial malleolus

toenail

plantar arch

metatarsal arch

ball of the foot

transverse arch

sole

Human Anatomy

Cow

Young *cattle* are *calves;* females are *heifers* until they give birth and are then cows; males are *bulls.* Castrated males, raised for *beef,* are *steers.* Castrated males, raised as draft animals, are *oxen.* The body, or *torso,* of a cow is known as the *barrel.*

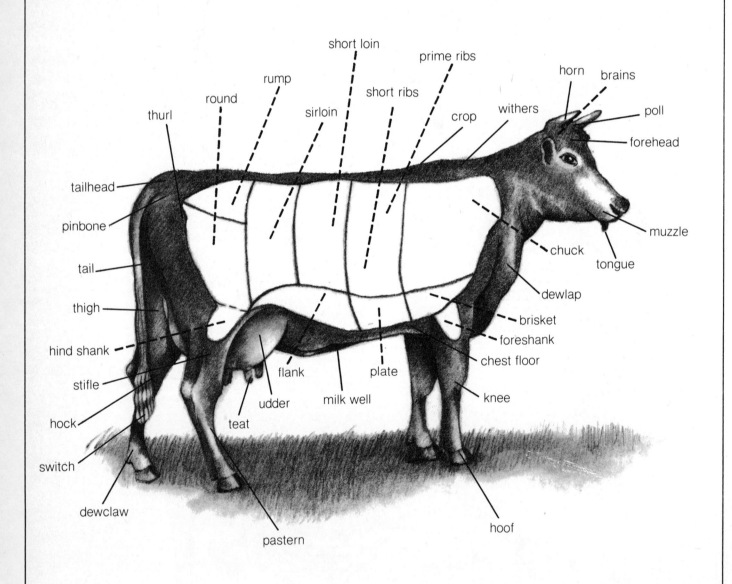

Sheep

A young sheep is called a *lamb*. An adult male is a *ram;* an adult female is a *ewe*. The meat of a young sheep is called *lamb*, while that of an animal over eighteen months old is called *mutton*.

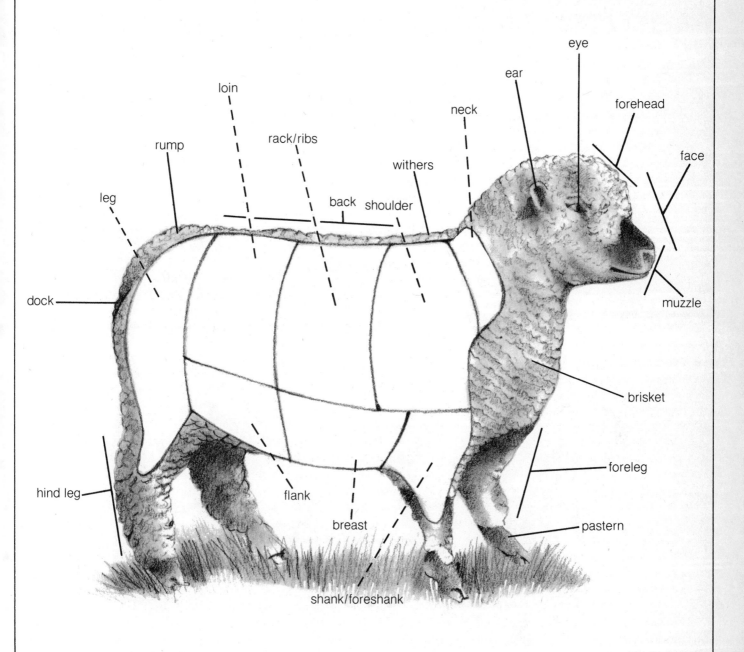

loin

rack/ribs

rump

withers

neck

ear

eye

forehead

face

leg

back   shoulder

dock

muzzle

brisket

foreleg

hind leg

flank

pastern

breast

shank/foreshank

Edible Animals

Pig

Young pigs are called *shoats*. Small or sub-adult domestic animals are *pigs* or *gruntlings*. If they weigh over 120 pounds, they are called *hogs*. Adult males are *boars*. Adult females are *sows*. Pigs, hogs, boars and sows are referred to as *swine*. Pig meat is called *pork*.

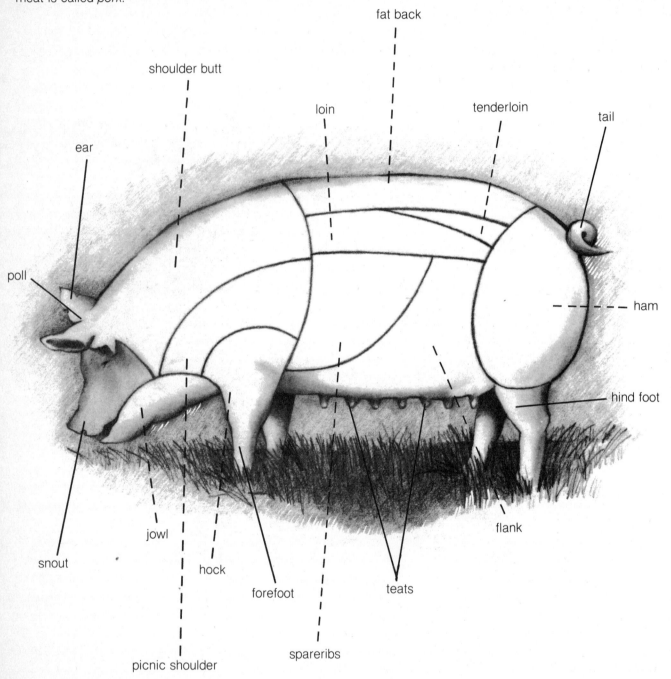

fat back

shoulder butt

loin

tenderloin

tail

ear

poll

ham

hind foot

flank

snout

jowl

hock

forefoot

teats

picnic shoulder

spareribs

Poultry

Chickens, turkeys, *ducks*, *geese* and *pheasants* are known collectively as *fowl* in the wild, as *poultry* if domesticated. A male chicken is a *rooster*; a female is a *hen*. A male turkey is a *tom*. Young chickens are *chicks*; young turkeys are *poults*. A *capon* is a male chicken that has been castrated before sexual maturity. Ducks have *webbed feet* and broad, flat *bills* with small teeth-like ridges. Among the *entrails* of a fowl, the most edible are the *giblets*: the *heart*, the *liver* and the *gizzard*.

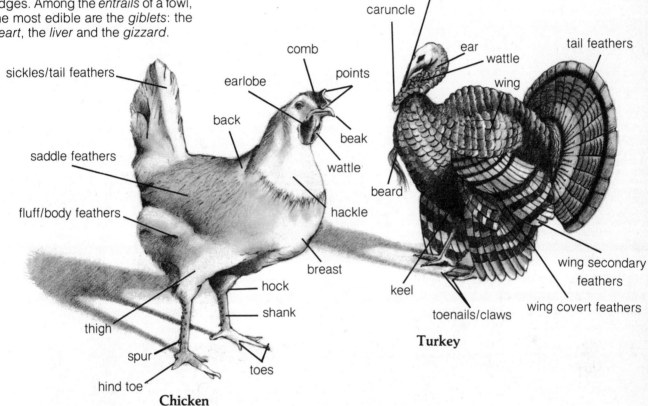

snood/dewbill
caruncle
ear
wattle
tail feathers
wing
comb
points
earlobe
back
beak
wattle
beard
hackle
keel
breast
hock
shank
thigh
spur
hind toe
toes

Chicken

sickles/tail feathers
saddle feathers
fluff/body feathers

wing secondary feathers
wing covert feathers
toenails/claws

Turkey

Poultry Parts

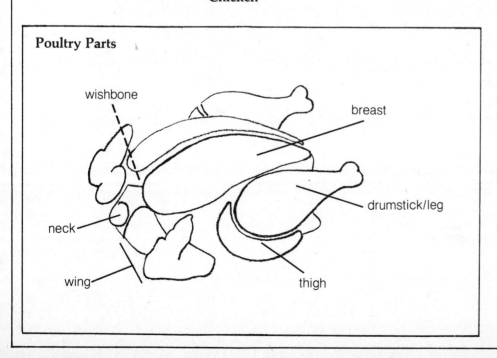

wishbone
breast
neck
drumstick/leg
wing
thigh

Dog

Dogs are digitigrade animals; they walk on what are anatomically their four *fingertips,* or pads. The fifth finger, or *thumb,* a functionless inner claw, is known as a *dewclaw,* and does not reach the ground. The bushy tail of a rough-coated dog is called a *brush.* A smooth-coated dog's tail is a *stern.*

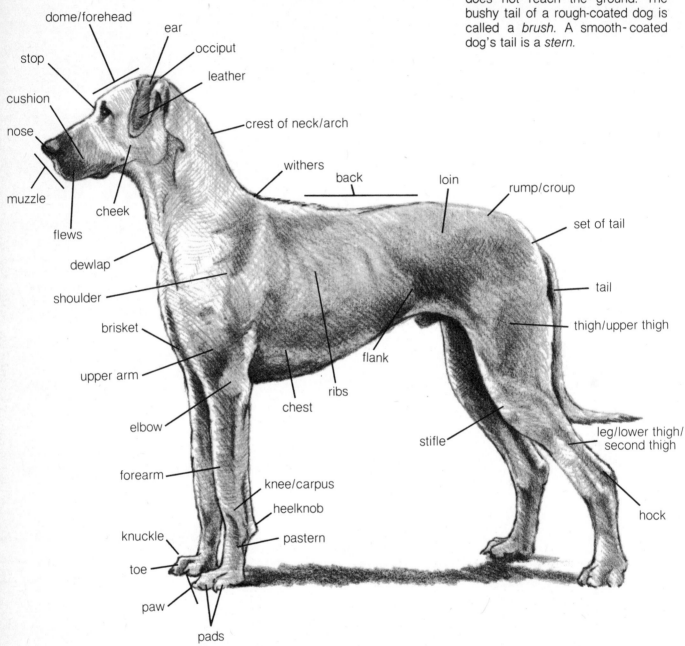

dome/forehead
ear
occiput
stop
leather
cushion
nose
crest of neck/arch
withers
back
loin
rump/croup
muzzle
set of tail
flews
cheek
tail
dewlap
thigh/upper thigh
shoulder
brisket
flank
upper arm
ribs
leg/lower thigh/
second thigh
elbow
chest
stifle
forearm
hock
knee/carpus
heelknob
knuckle
pastern
toe
paw
pads

Cat

Newborn cats are called *kittens*, adult males are *tomcats*, and adult females are *cattas*. Cats are capable of drawing their *toenails*, or *claws*, into *sheaths* located above the *pads* of their feet. A cat's *muzzle* consists of the *nose* and *jaw* sections of its face.

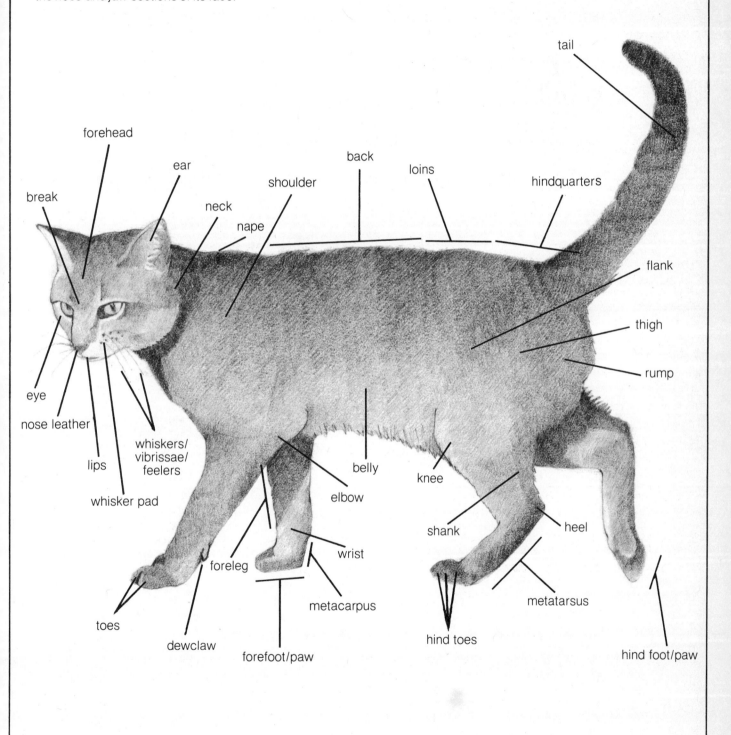

tail

forehead

ear

back

shoulder

loins

hindquarters

neck

nape

break

flank

thigh

rump

eye

nose leather

whiskers/
vibrissae/
feelers

lips

belly

knee

whisker pad

elbow

shank

heel

foreleg

wrist

toes

dewclaw

metacarpus

forefoot/paw

hind toes

metatarsus

hind foot/paw

Domestic Animals

Horse

A horse less than a year old is a *foal*. Male foals are *colts*, females are *fillies*. A mature male is a *stallion*, a female is a *mare*. In breeding, the male parent is a *sire*, the female is a *dam*. A castrated male is called a *gelding*.

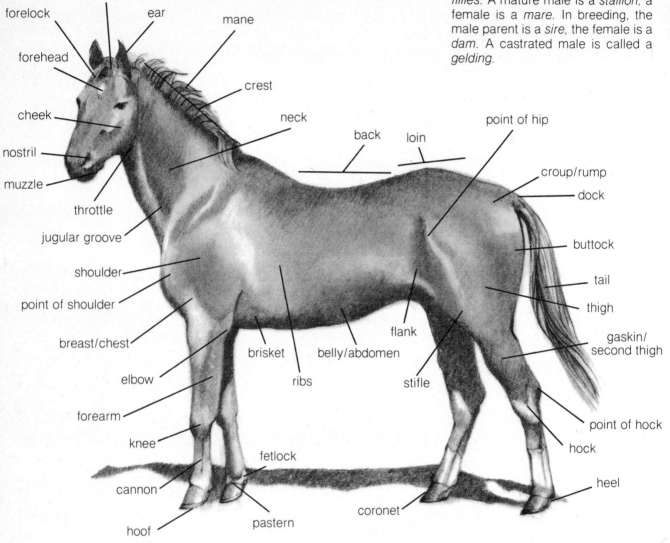

poll
forelock
ear
mane
forehead
crest
cheek
neck
nostril
muzzle
throttle
jugular groove
shoulder
point of shoulder
breast/chest
elbow
forearm
knee
cannon
hoof
fetlock
pastern
brisket
ribs
belly/abdomen
flank
stifle
coronet
back
loin
point of hip
croup/rump
dock
buttock
tail
thigh
gaskin/second thigh
point of hock
hock
heel

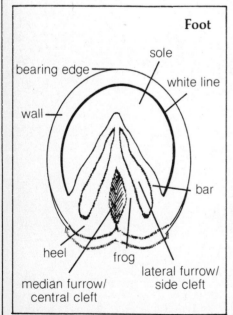

Foot

sole
bearing edge
white line
wall
bar
heel
frog
lateral furrow/side cleft
median furrow/central cleft

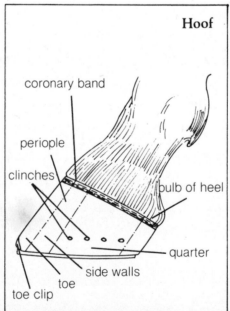

Hoof

coronary band
periople
clinches
bulb of heel
quarter
side walls
toe
toe clip

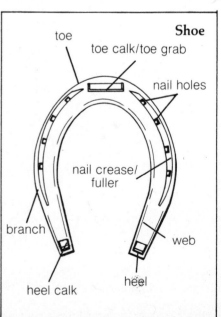

Shoe

toe
toe calk/toe grab
nail holes
nail crease/fuller
branch
web
heel calk
heel

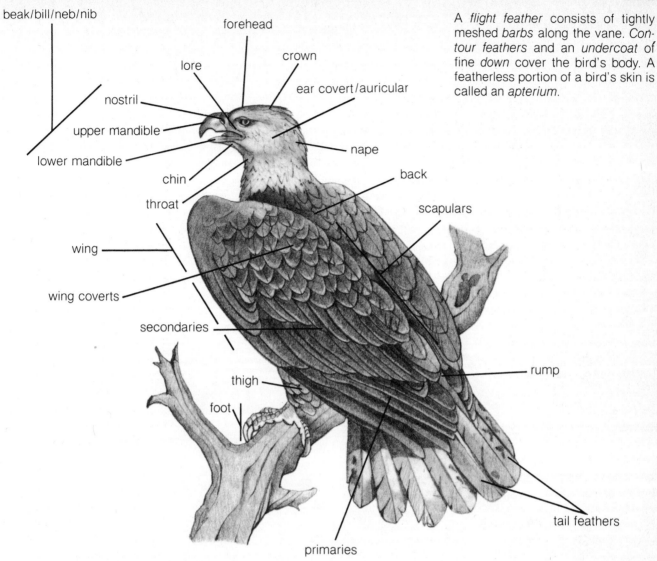

Bird

A *flight feather* consists of tightly meshed *barbs* along the vane. *Contour feathers* and an *undercoat* of fine *down* cover the bird's body. A featherless portion of a bird's skin is called an *apterium*.

beak/bill/neb/nib

forehead

crown

lore

ear covert/auricular

nostril

upper mandible

nape

lower mandible

chin

back

throat

scapulars

wing

wing coverts

secondaries

rump

thigh

foot

tail feathers

primaries

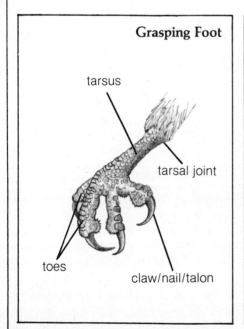

Grasping Foot

tarsus

tarsal joint

toes

claw/nail/talon

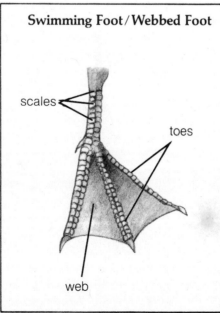

Swimming Foot/Webbed Foot

scales

toes

web

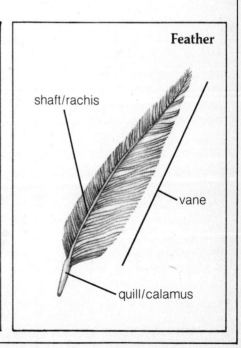

Feather

shaft/rachis

vane

quill/calamus

Wild Animals

Spider

Spiders produce *silk threads* which they use to make webs, *nests* or *parachutes* that allow the wind to carry them from one location to another. When a spider spins a web, it first constructs a *bridge* between two supports and fashions an *orb* beneath. A *scaffolding web* of dry thread is then used to lay down a *viscid spiral* of sticky thread.

pedipalpi

eyes

pedicel

coxa

trochanter

femur

patella

tibia

metatarsus

tarsus

leg

claws

scopula

spinnerets

cephalothorax

abdomen

Face

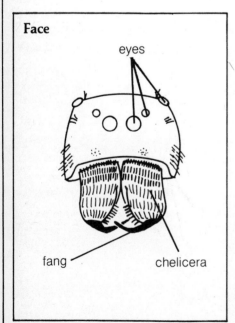

eyes

fang

chelicera

Web

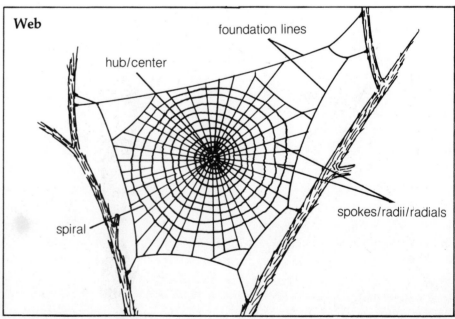

foundation lines

hub/center

spiral

spokes/radii/radials

Insects

Insects have shell-like outer coverings called *exoskeletons*. Most undergo four stages during *metamorphosis:* the *egg*, the *larva*, the *pupa*, and the *adult*.

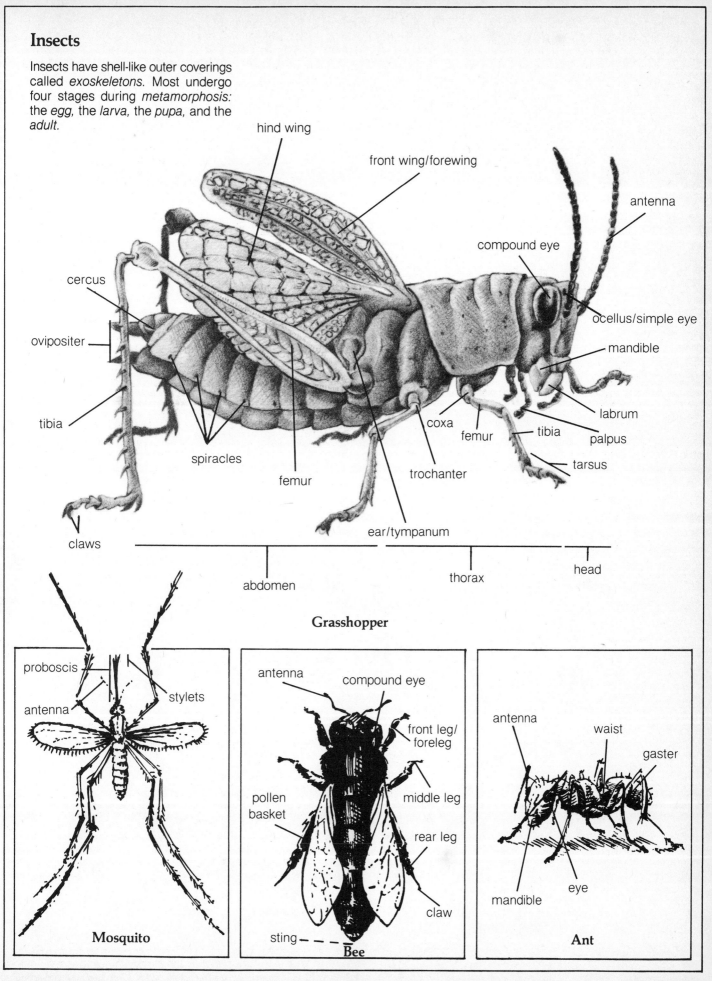

hind wing

front wing/forewing

antenna

compound eye

cercus

ocellus/simple eye

ovipositer

mandible

tibia

labrum

spiracles

coxa

femur

tibia

palpus

femur

tarsus

trochanter

claws

ear/tympanum

abdomen

thorax

head

Grasshopper

proboscis

stylets

antenna

antenna

compound eye

antenna

waist

gaster

front leg/foreleg

pollen basket

middle leg

antenna

rear leg

eye

claw

mandible

sting

Mosquito

Bee

Ant

Wild Animals

Reptiles

In addition to the reptile families represented here, there is the lizard-like *tuatara*, a leftover from the days of the *dinosaurs*, with a vestigial *third eye* on the top of its head. All *poisonous snakes* inject their prey with *venom* through fangs, but not all venomous snakes have *"hypodermic fangs,"* like the rattler shown here. The flattened swelling below a cobra's head is called the *hood*. Most land-living turtles are called *tortoises*. Turtles that live in the sea have *flippers*. Many *skinks*, which are lizards, have no legs or eyelids.

nostril

pit

poison fang sheaths

eye

fangs

tongue

teeth

lower jaw

Rattlesnake

dorsal scales

ventral scales

body

Crocodilians

nostril

horny scales

Alligator

hump

snout

Crocodile

fourth tooth

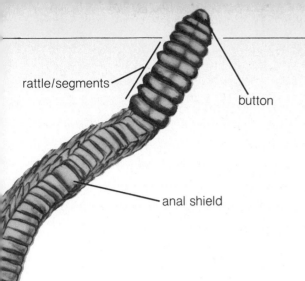

rattle/segments

button

anal shield

Dinosaurs/Extinct Reptiles

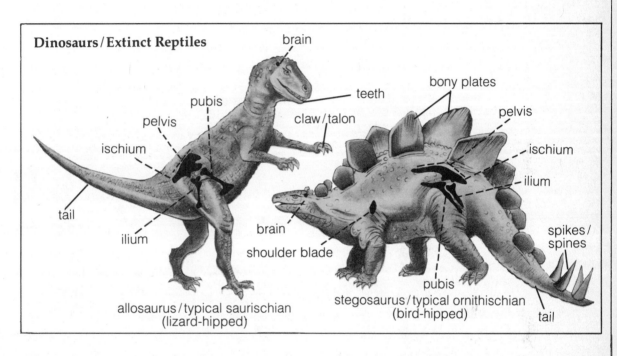

brain

pubis

pelvis

ischium

teeth

claw/talon

bony plates

pelvis

ischium

ilium

tail

ilium

brain

shoulder blade

pubis

spikes/spines

tail

allosaurus/typical saurischian
(lizard-hipped)

stegosaurus/typical ornithischian
(bird-hipped)

Turtle/Tortoise

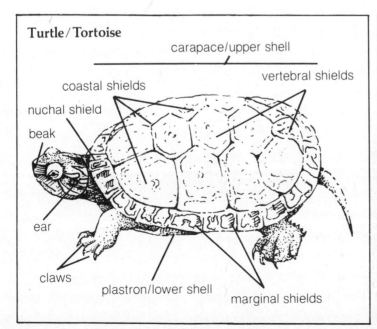

carapace/upper shell

vertebral shields

coastal shields

nuchal shield

beak

ear

claws

plastron/lower shell

marginal shields

Lizard/Iguana

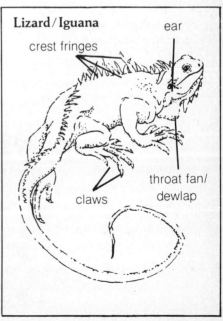

ear

crest fringes

claws

throat fan/dewlap

Wild Animals

Amphibians

Frogs and toads resemble one another closely, but toads are characteristically more terrestrial and have rougher, drier skin.

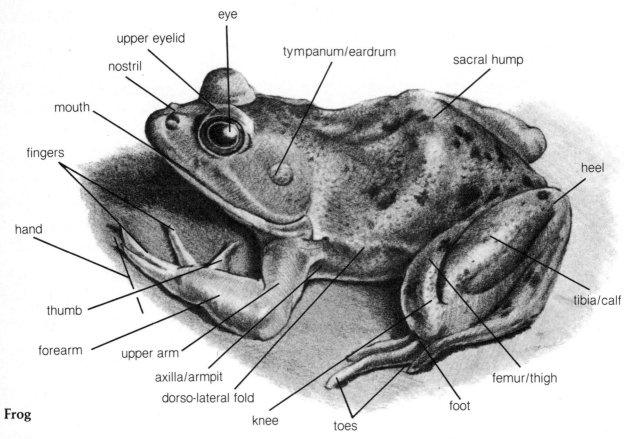

eye

upper eyelid

nostril

tympanum/eardrum

sacral hump

mouth

fingers

heel

hand

thumb

tibia/calf

forearm

upper arm

axilla/armpit

dorso-lateral fold

femur/thigh

knee

toes

foot

Frog

Tadpole / Polliwog

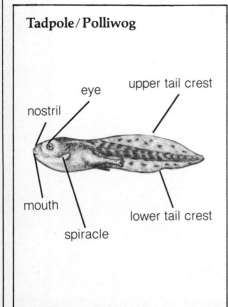

eye

upper tail crest

nostril

mouth

spiracle

lower tail crest

Toad

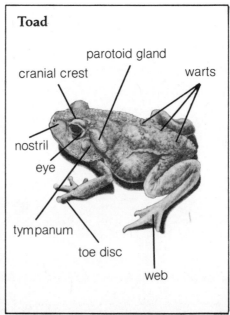

parotoid gland

cranial crest

warts

nostril

eye

tympanum

toe disc

web

Salamander

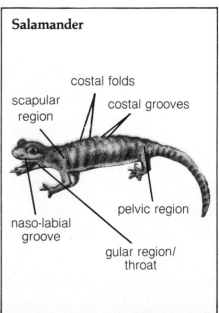

costal folds

scapular region

costal grooves

naso-labial groove

pelvic region

gular region/ throat

Marine Life

Fish often swim in groups, called *schools,* and reproduce by depositing eggs, or *spawning.* Recently hatched or small adult fish are called *fry.*

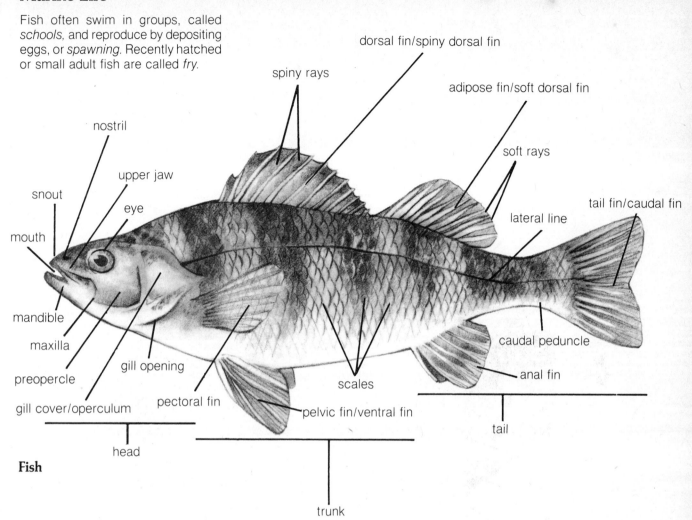

spiny rays

dorsal fin/spiny dorsal fin

adipose fin/soft dorsal fin

soft rays

nostril

upper jaw

tail fin/caudal fin

snout

eye

lateral line

mouth

mandible

maxilla

preopercle

gill cover/operculum

gill opening

pectoral fin

scales

pelvic fin/ventral fin

caudal peduncle

anal fin

head

trunk

tail

Fish

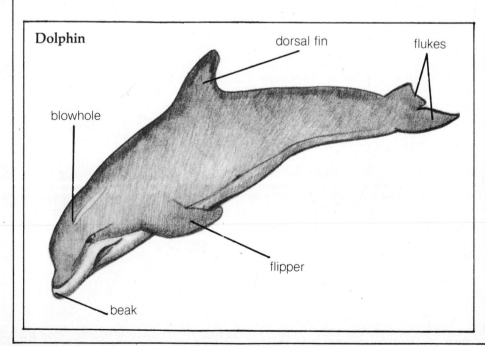

Dolphin

dorsal fin

flukes

blowhole

flipper

beak

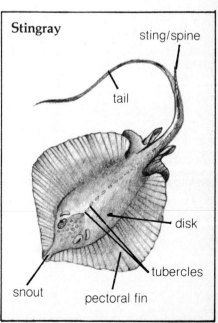

Stingray

sting/spine

tail

disk

tubercles

snout

pectoral fin

Wild Animals

Marine Life

The *mantle* of an octopus is the tough protective wrapper that covers the body and gives it shape. Octopuses and squid have *chromatophores,* or *pigment cells,* which enable them to change color, as well as *ink glands,* or *sacs,* that secrete protective *"ink."* Starfish have *mouths* on their *oral surfaces.* Coral polyps live within limestone *skeletons,* which form the basis for *coral reefs.*

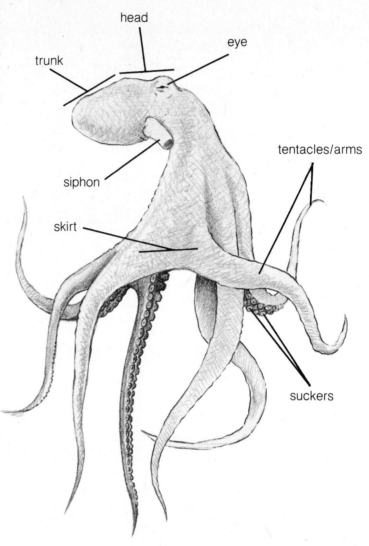

head

eye

trunk

siphon

tentacles/arms

skirt

suckers

Octopus/Devilfish

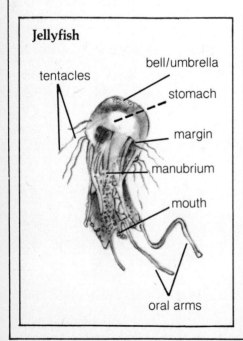

Jellyfish

tentacles

bell/umbrella

stomach

margin

manubrium

mouth

oral arms

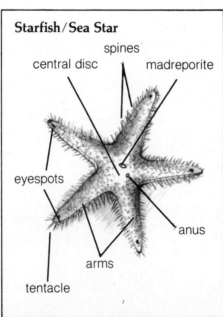

Starfish/Sea Star

spines

central disc

madreporite

eyespots

anus

arms

tentacle

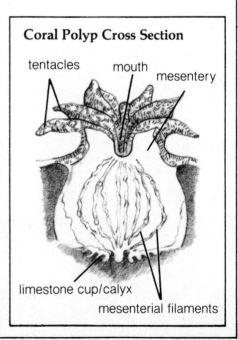

Coral Polyp Cross Section

tentacles

mouth

mesentery

limestone cup/calyx

mesenterial filaments

Shellfish

Lobsters with only one claw are called *culls,* and lobsters that have lost both claws are known as *pistols. Crustaceans*, such as lobsters, *crabs, shrimp, crayfish* and *barnacles*, are covered with a coating of *chitin*, which varies in hardness according to *lime* content. Scallops, clams, *snails, oysters* and *mussels* are *mollusks*. The study of mollusks is *malacology*. The study of shells only is *conchology*.

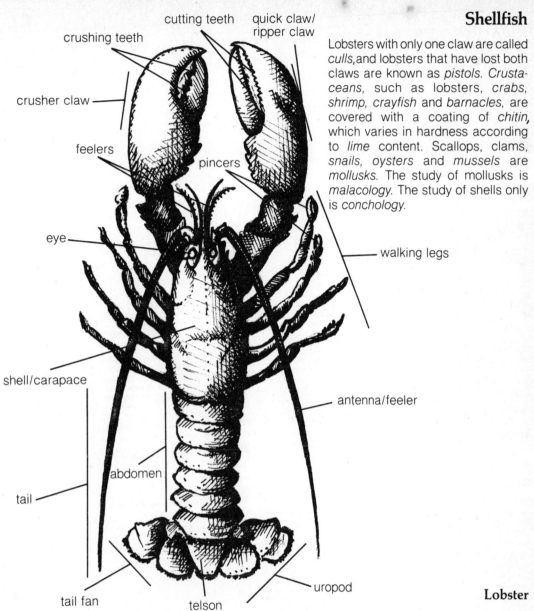

cutting teeth

quick claw/ripper claw

crushing teeth

crusher claw

feelers

pincers

eye

walking legs

shell/carapace

antenna/feeler

abdomen

tail

uropod

tail fan

telson

Lobster

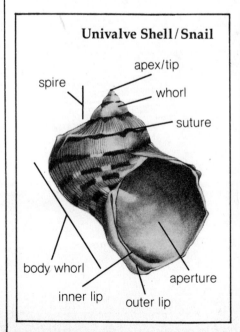

Univalve Shell / Snail

apex/tip

spire

whorl

suture

body whorl

inner lip

outer lip

aperture

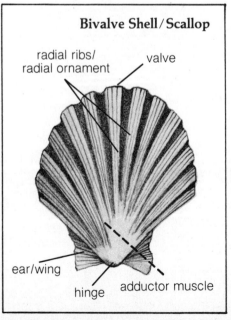

Bivalve Shell / Scallop

radial ribs/radial ornament

valve

ear/wing

hinge

adductor muscle

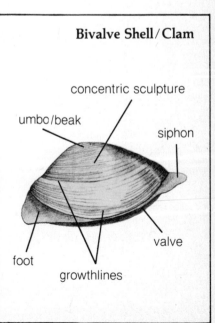

Bivalve Shell / Clam

concentric sculpture

umbo/beak

siphon

foot

growthlines

valve

Wild Animals

Ultimate Beast

This remarkable *creature* calls attention to those parts of animals which are distinctive to particular species. Missing are posterior extensions, or *tails,* which vary from long, thin tails that end in a *brush* and have a horny appendage called a *thorn* in the middle, such as a lion's, to brushy fox tails and stubby boar tails. Another composite animal is the legendary *manticore,* which combined the head of a man, the body of a lion, and the tail of a *dragon* or *scorpion.*

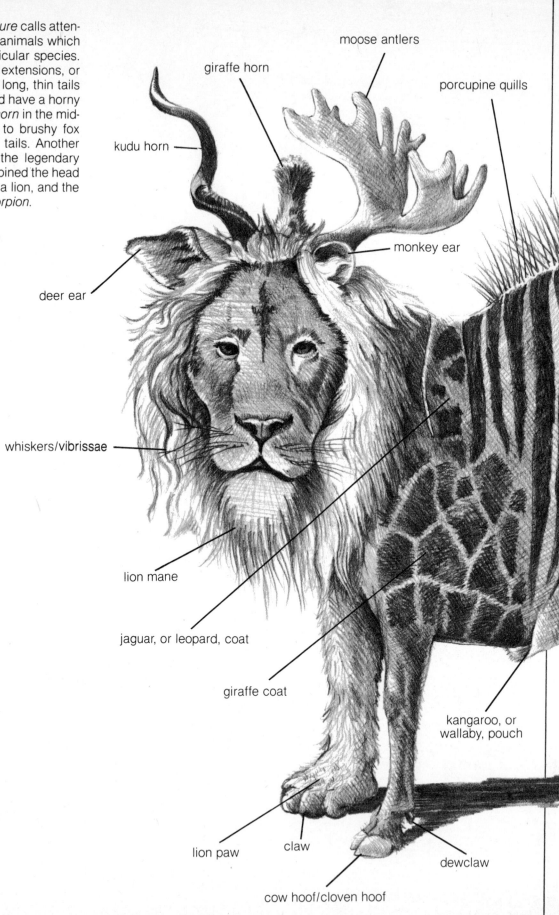

moose antlers

giraffe horn

porcupine quills

kudu horn

monkey ear

deer ear

whiskers/vibrissae

lion mane

jaguar, or leopard, coat

giraffe coat

kangaroo, or wallaby, pouch

lion paw

claw

dewclaw

cow hoof/cloven hoof

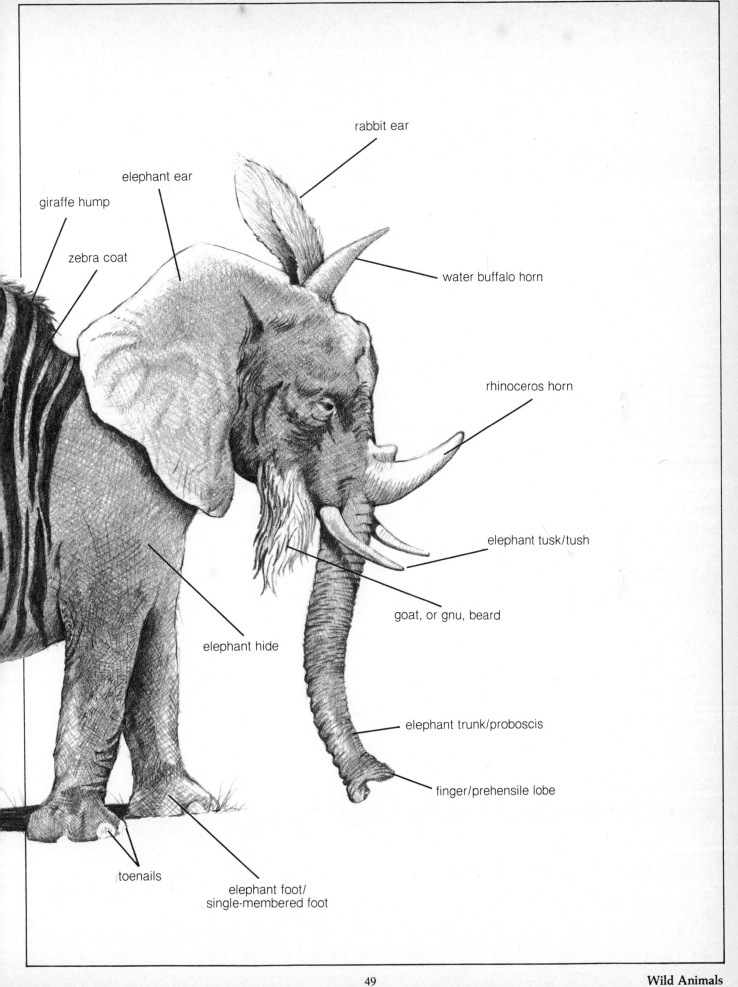

giraffe hump

zebra coat

elephant ear

rabbit ear

water buffalo horn

rhinoceros horn

elephant tusk/tush

goat, or gnu, beard

elephant hide

elephant trunk/proboscis

finger/prehensile lobe

toenails

elephant foot/
single-membered foot

Tree

When a tree is cut down, what remains attached to the *root* is called a *stump*.

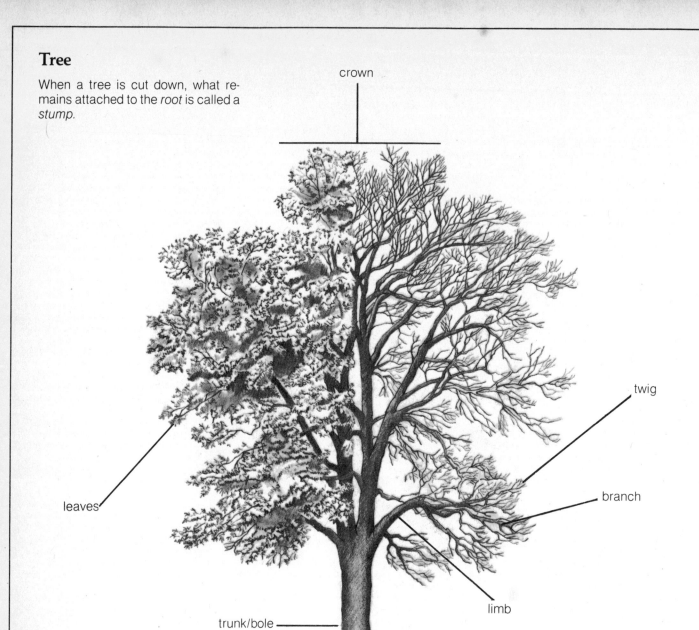

crown

twig

branch

leaves

limb

trunk/bole

Tree Trunk Cross Section

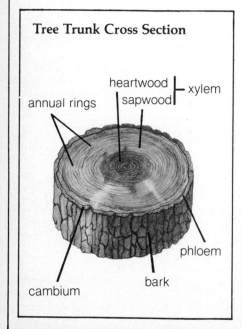

heartwood — xylem
sapwood

annual rings

phloem

cambium

bark

Twig

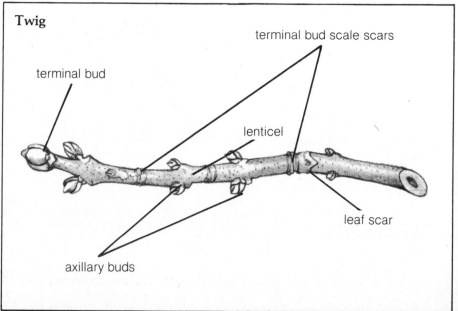

terminal bud scale scars

terminal bud

lenticel

leaf scar

axillary buds

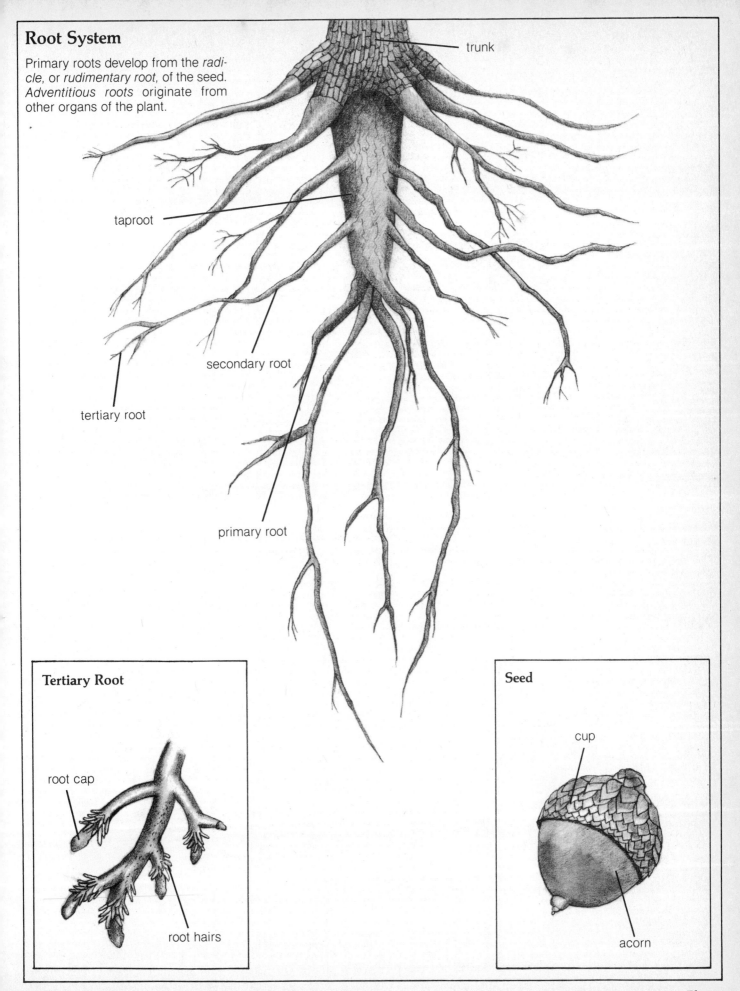

Root System

Primary roots develop from the *radicle*, or *rudimentary root*, of the seed. *Adventitious roots* originate from other organs of the plant.

trunk

taproot

secondary root

tertiary root

primary root

Tertiary Root

root cap

root hairs

Seed

cup

acorn

Plants

Leaf

The waxy layer covering the outer leaf is the *cuticle*. Tiny leaves, spines or growths at the base of a leaf stem are called *stipules*. *Compound leaves* are made up of two or more blades, or *leaflets*. The aggregate of leaves produced by one or more plants is called *foliage*.

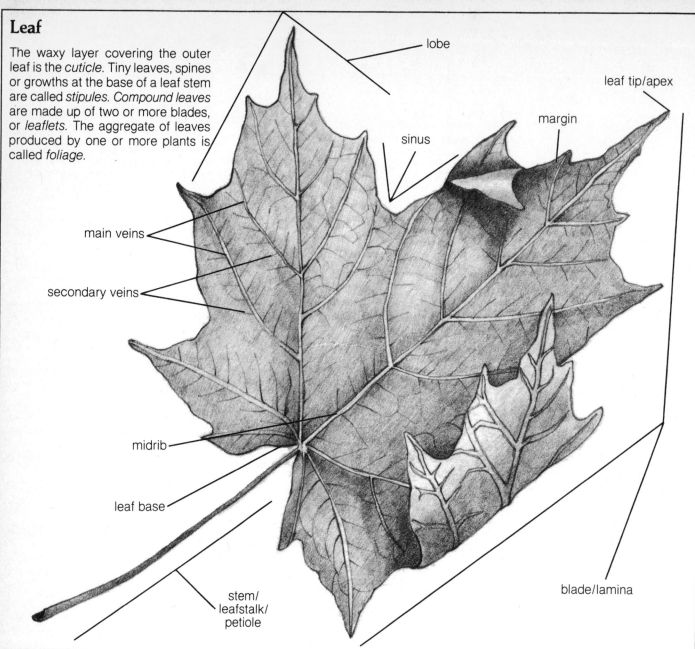

lobe

leaf tip/apex

sinus

margin

main veins

secondary veins

midrib

leaf base

stem/ leafstalk/ petiole

blade/lamina

Pine Cone

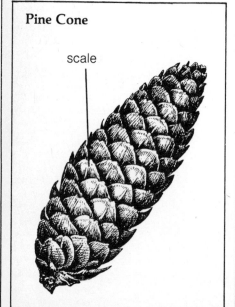

scale

Samara/Key

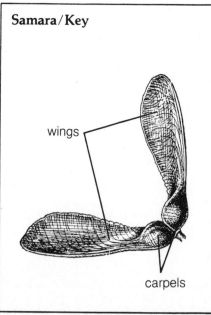

wings

carpels

Palm

crown

frond

skirt

coconut/ fruit

trunk

Plants

52

Flower

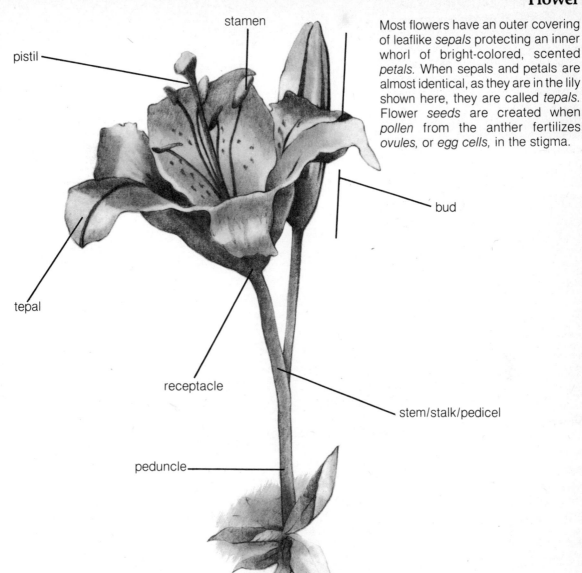

stamen

pistil

tepal

receptacle

peduncle

bud

stem/stalk/pedicel

Most flowers have an outer covering of leaflike *sepals* protecting an inner whorl of bright-colored, scented *petals*. When sepals and petals are almost identical, as they are in the lily shown here, they are called *tepals*. Flower *seeds* are created when *pollen* from the anther fertilizes *ovules*, or *egg cells,* in the stigma.

Stamen

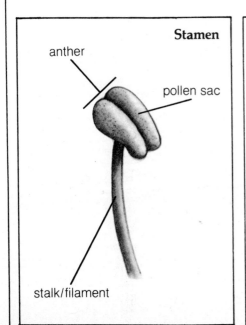

anther

pollen sac

stalk/filament

Petal

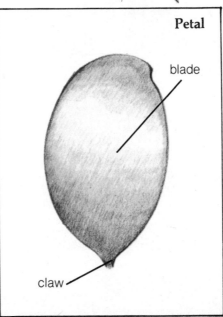

blade

claw

Pistil

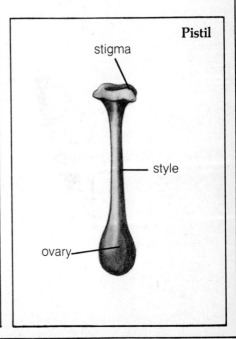

stigma

style

ovary

Plants

Vegetables

A vegetable is that part of a plant that can be eaten. The roots of carrots, beets and turnips are edible, as are asparagus stems, potato tubers, leek and onion leaf bases, cabbage, lettuce and spinach leaves, the *immature fruit,* or *ovary,* of cucumbers, peas and summer squash, and the *mature fruit* of tomatoes and winter squash.

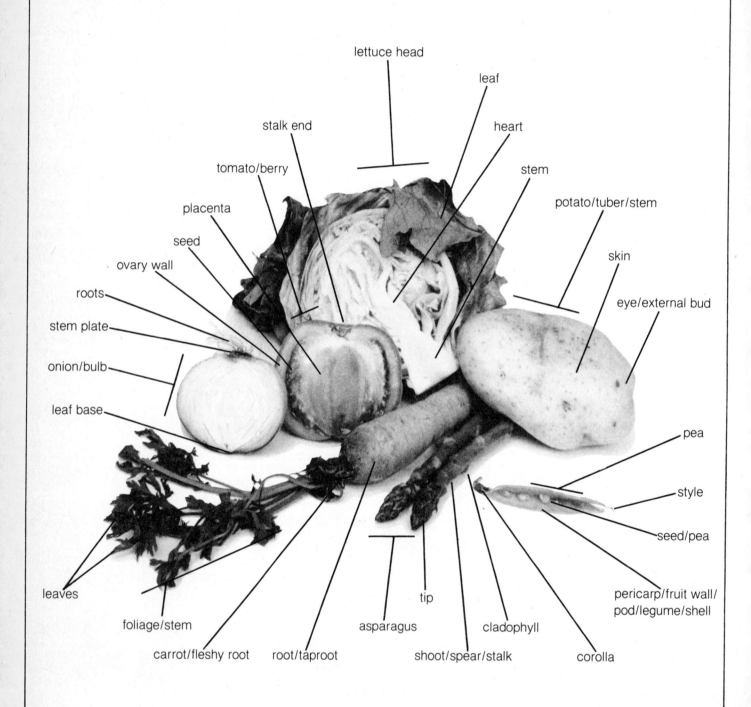

lettuce head

leaf

stalk end

heart

tomato/berry

stem

placenta

potato/tuber/stem

seed

skin

ovary wall

roots

eye/external bud

stem plate

onion/bulb

leaf base

pea

style

seed/pea

leaves

pericarp/fruit wall/ pod/legume/shell

foliage/stem

tip

carrot/fleshy root

root/taproot

asparagus

cladophyll

shoot/spear/stalk

corolla

Fruits

Nuts and crops commonly referred to as vegetables, such as tomatoes and melons, are actually *vegetable fruits.* Fruits are classed according to the number of ovaries they have: They range from simple fruits, such as peaches, to aggregate fruits, such as strawberries. Each segment of *multiple fruits,* such as pineapples and figs, is edible.

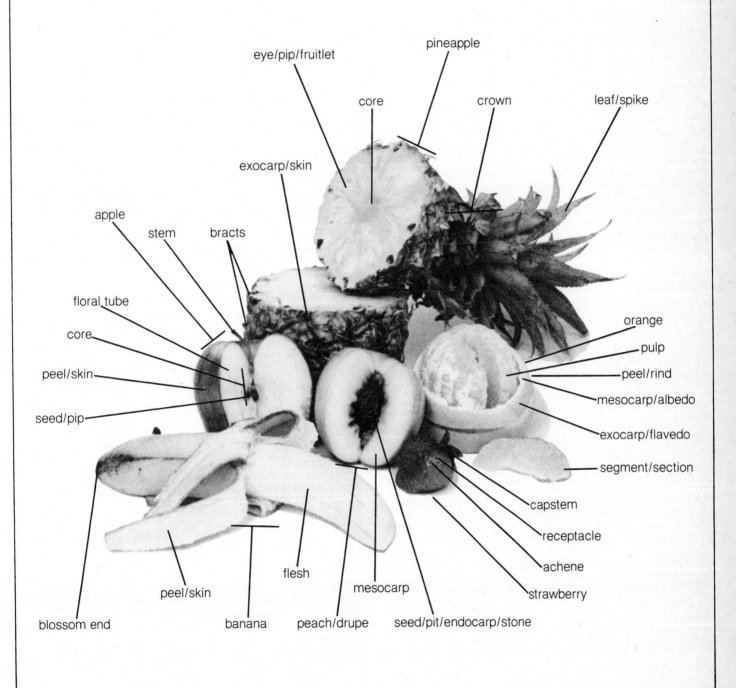

eye/pip/fruitlet

pineapple

core

crown

leaf/spike

exocarp/skin

apple

stem

bracts

floral tube

core

peel/skin

seed/pip

orange

pulp

peel/rind

mesocarp/albedo

exocarp/flavedo

segment/section

capstem

receptacle

achene

strawberry

blossom end

peel/skin

banana

flesh

peach/drupe

mesocarp

seed/pit/endocarp/stone

Succulents

Succulents are plants with *fleshy tissue* that have the ability to store moisture for long periods of time in their stem. Some cacti have protective *glochidia*, razor-sharp hairlike bristles, in addition to spines and flowers.

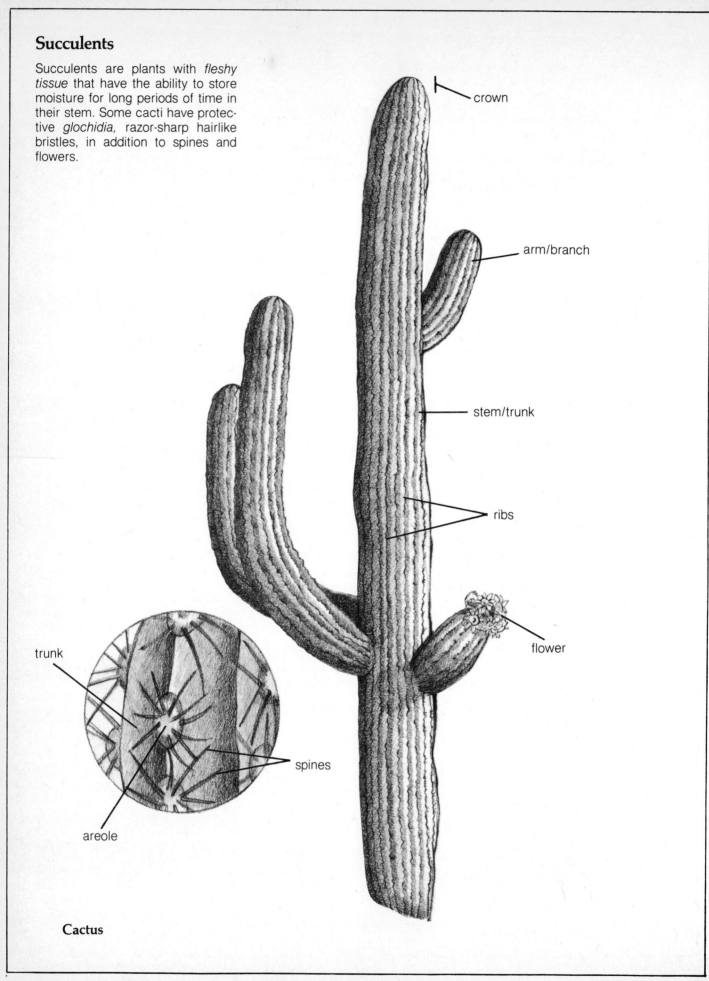

crown

arm/branch

stem/trunk

ribs

flower

trunk

spines

areole

Cactus

Toadstools are inedible mushrooms, or *fungi*. Flowerless, seedless ferns reproduce by means of *spores* carried in spore cases on the underside of the leaves. Seaweed, such as the *marine algae* shown here, attaches itself to the ocean floor by means of a *holdfast*.

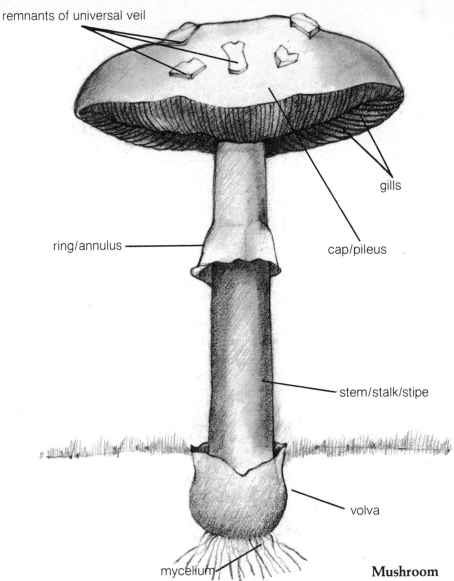

remnants of universal veil

gills

ring/annulus

cap/pileus

stem/stalk/stipe

volva

mycelium

Mushroom

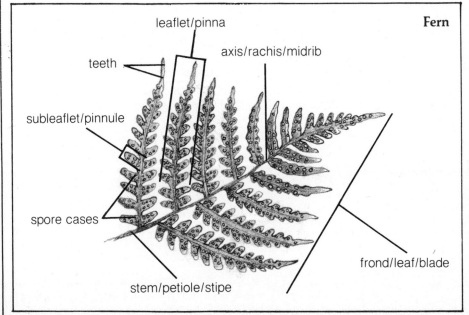

Fern

leaflet/pinna

axis/rachis/midrib

teeth

subleaflet/pinnule

spore cases

stem/petiole/stipe

frond/leaf/blade

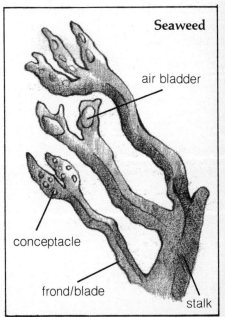

Seaweed

air bladder

conceptacle

frond/blade

stalk

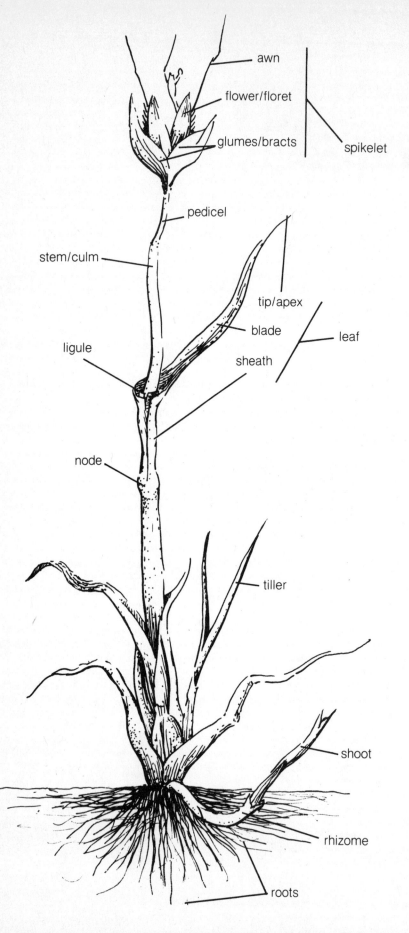

awn

flower/floret

glumes/bracts

spikelet

pedicel

stem/culm

tip/apex

blade

leaf

ligule

sheath

node

tiller

shoot

rhizome

roots

Grass

There are two parts to grass plants, the *vegetable organs* and the *floral organs*. *Cereal grasses*, such as *wheat, oat, barley* and corn, produce edible *fruit, seed* or *kernels*. Rhizomes and *stolons*, or *runners*—above-ground stems—spread out from grass plants to produce new plants. The *inflorescence*, or *flower cluster*, of grasses consists of many spikelets. Grass leaves are *parallel-veined*.

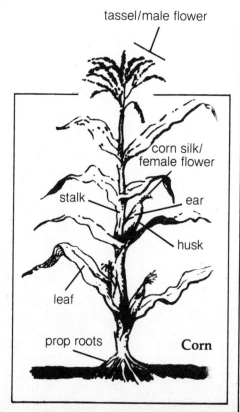

tassel/male flower

corn silk/
female flower

stalk

ear

husk

leaf

prop roots

Corn

Shelters and Structures

Since man's most basic shelter is a house, it is illustrated in a variety of ways, from foundation and frame to windows and walls.

The shelters and structures in the rest of the section are grouped in three subcategories: designs from other lands, which range from pagodas to pyramids; special-purpose buildings such as the Capitol and the White House, skyscrapers and prisons, amusement parks and airports; and other structures which bear on our everyday lives — bridges, tunnels, canals and dams.

The terms for the parts of objects found in most shelter interiors are the same as those found in a house, all of which have been illustrated. But those of a courtroom are sufficiently different to merit coverage, as are the parts of a skyscraper's elevator and escalator. In some cases floor plans and cross-section illustrations have been used to facilitate the reader's access to terms which are unique to a particular structure.

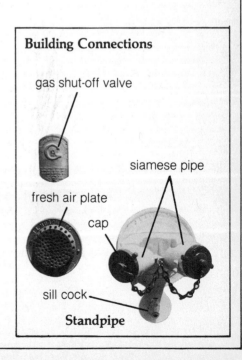

Building Connections

gas shut-off valve

fresh air plate

siamese pipe

cap

sill cock

Standpipe

Foundation

Some houses are built on sunken *posts*, or *piers*. Others are built on concrete floors, or *slabs*. The area of a house built below ground level is the *basement*. Houses without basements usually have an area between the floor joists and the ground called a *crawl space*, through which access is gained to inspect pipes.

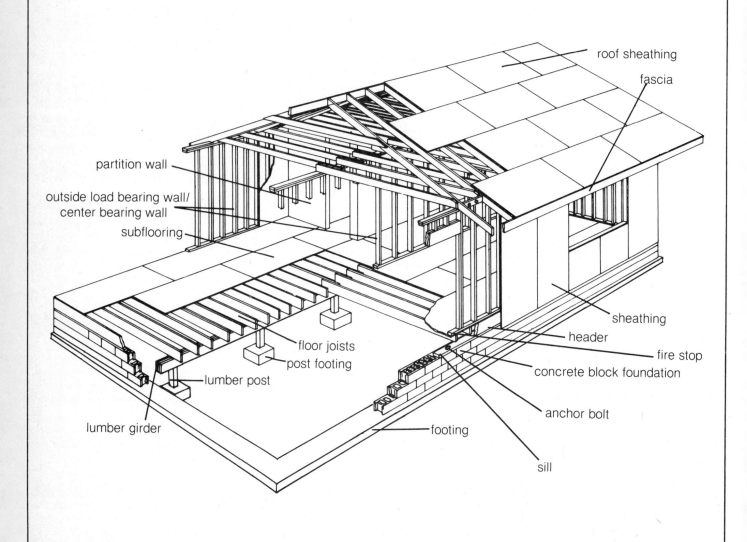

partition wall

outside load bearing wall/center bearing wall

subflooring

floor joists

post footing

lumber post

lumber girder

lumber post

footing

sill

roof sheathing

fascia

sheathing

header

fire stop

concrete block foundation

anchor bolt

Frame

Any diagonally placed piece of timber in a frame is a *brace*. A *cat* is a small piece of lumber nailed between studs for reinforcement. *Beams* are squared off pieces of timber, such as *joists*, used to support *floor* or *ceiling*, or *lintels*, horizontal *members* designed to carry loads above openings such as doors and windows.

ridgepole/ridgeboard

wood splice

collar beam

roof rafter

ceiling joist

fascia rafter

top plate

fascia

cripples

jack stud

outrigger

door bucks

header

header joist

bottom plate/sole plate

doubling

stud

corner post

anchor bolt

sill plate

rough sill

Composite Roof Truss

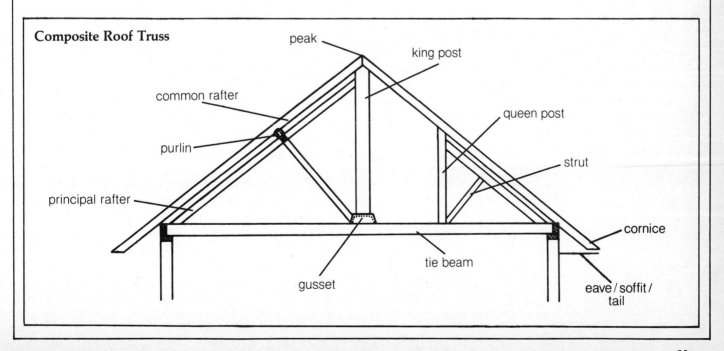

peak

king post

common rafter

queen post

purlin

strut

principal rafter

cornice

tie beam

gusset

eave / soffit / tail

House

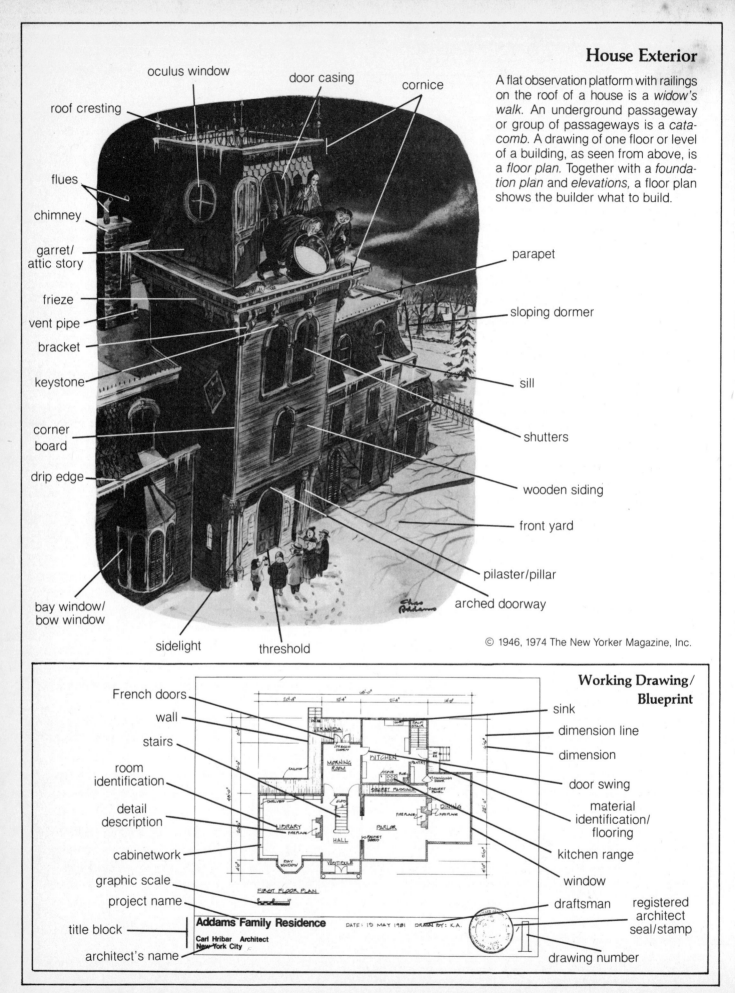

House Exterior

roof cresting

oculus window

door casing

cornice

flues

chimney

garret/ attic story

frieze

vent pipe

bracket

keystone

corner board

drip edge

bay window/ bow window

sidelight

threshold

parapet

sloping dormer

sill

shutters

wooden siding

front yard

pilaster/pillar

arched doorway

A flat observation platform with railings on the roof of a house is a *widow's walk.* An underground passageway or group of passageways is a *catacomb.* A drawing of one floor or level of a building, as seen from above, is a *floor plan.* Together with a *foundation plan* and *elevations,* a floor plan shows the builder what to build.

© 1946, 1974 The New Yorker Magazine, Inc.

Working Drawing/ Blueprint

French doors

wall

stairs

room identification

detail description

cabinetwork

graphic scale

project name

title block

architect's name

sink

dimension line

dimension

door swing

material identification/ flooring

kitchen range

window

draftsman

registered architect seal/stamp

drawing number

FIRST FLOOR PLAN

Addams Family Residence

Carl Hribar Architect
New York City

DATE: 15 MAY 1981   DRAWN BY: K.A.

House Exterior

The room or space under the roof is the *attic*. The lowest story of a house is called the *basement* if it is at least partly below ground or street level. A part of a house projecting on one side or subordinate to the main structure is called a *wing*. *Patios*, *terraces*, *decks* and *porches* adjoin a house and are used for play or relaxation. An open *gallery* alongside a house with its own roof is a *veranda*.

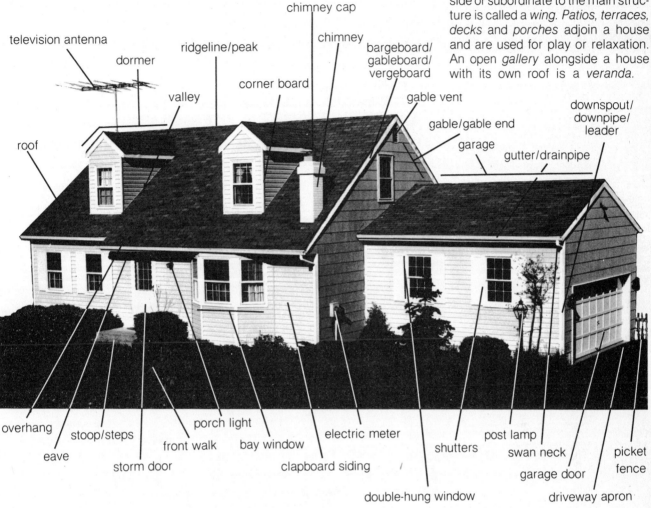

television antenna
dormer
ridgeline/peak
chimney cap
chimney
bargeboard/
gableboard/
vergeboard
valley
corner board
gable vent
gable/gable end
downspout/
downpipe/
leader
roof
garage
gutter/drainpipe

overhang
stoop/steps
porch light
electric meter
post lamp
picket
fence
eave
front walk
bay window
shutters
swan neck
storm door
clapboard siding
garage door
driveway apron
double-hung window

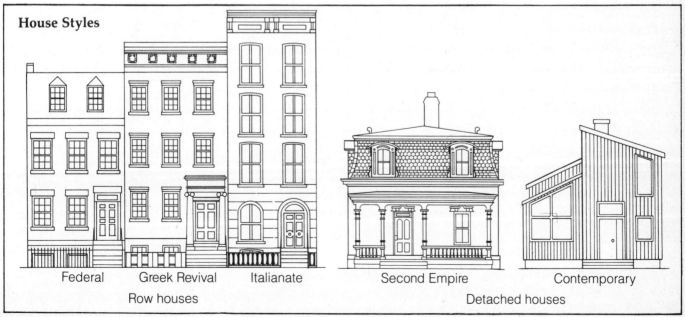

House Styles

Federal   Greek Revival   Italianate

Row houses

Second Empire   Contemporary

Detached houses

House

Door

The *sill*, *threshold*, or *saddle* is that part directly beneath the door. Entrance doors are often covered by *screendoors*. A door cut in half horizontally whose two parts can be used independently is called a *Dutch door*. A door having glass panes throughout or nearly throughout its length is a *French door*. The rubber-tipped projection attached to the wall behind an opening door to protect it from the impact is a *doorstop*.

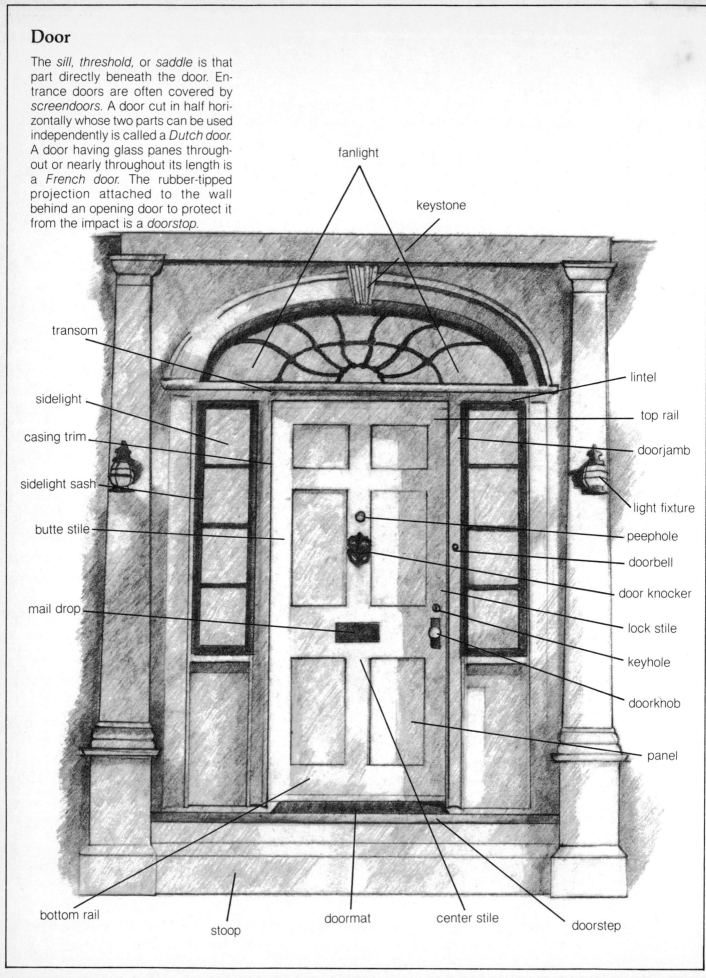

fanlight

keystone

transom

sidelight

casing trim

sidelight sash

butte stile

mail drop

lintel

top rail

doorjamb

light fixture

peephole

doorbell

door knocker

lock stile

keyhole

doorknob

panel

bottom rail

stoop

doormat

center stile

doorstep

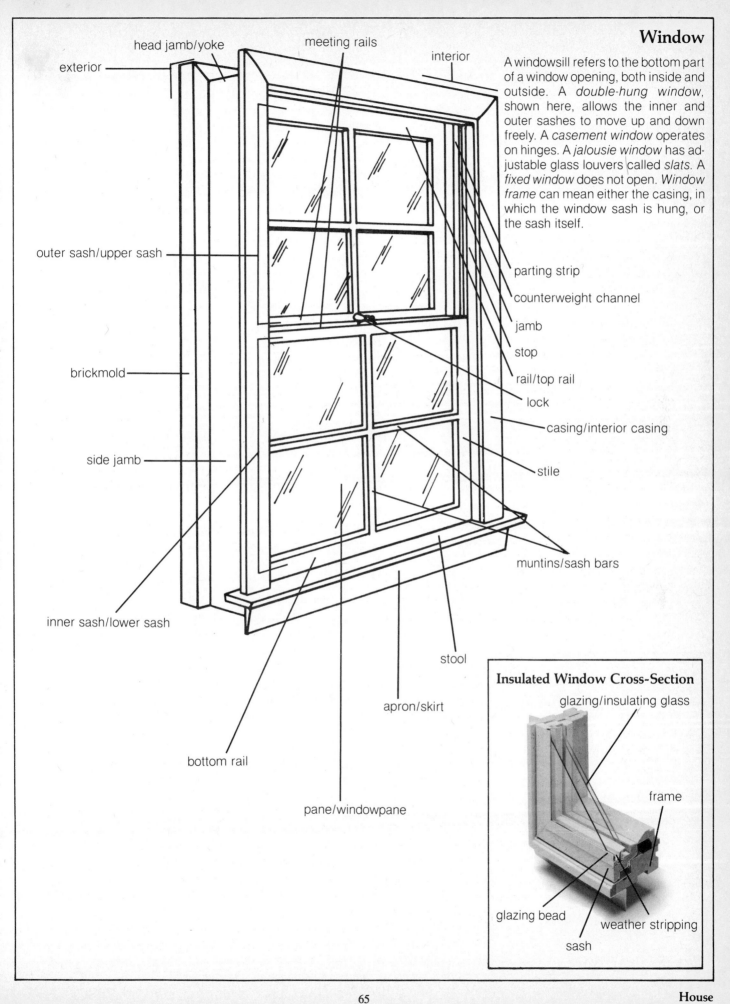

Window

exterior

head jamb/yoke

meeting rails

interior

A windowsill refers to the bottom part of a window opening, both inside and outside. A *double-hung window*, shown here, allows the inner and outer sashes to move up and down freely. A *casement window* operates on hinges. A *jalousie window* has adjustable glass louvers called *slats*. A *fixed window* does not open. *Window frame* can mean either the casing, in which the window sash is hung, or the sash itself.

parting strip

counterweight channel

jamb

stop

rail/top rail

lock

outer sash/upper sash

brickmold

casing/interior casing

side jamb

stile

inner sash/lower sash

muntins/sash bars

stool

apron/skirt

bottom rail

pane/windowpane

Insulated Window Cross-Section

glazing/insulating glass

frame

glazing bead

weather stripping

sash

65

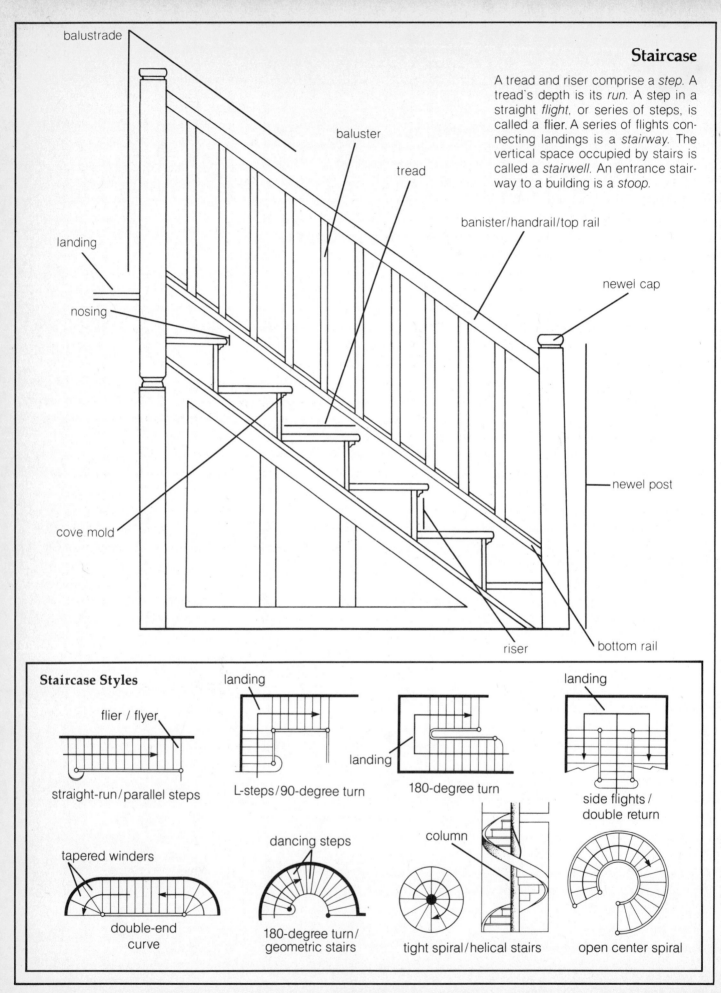

balustrade

baluster

tread

Staircase

A tread and riser comprise a *step*. A tread's depth is its *run*. A step in a straight *flight*, or series of steps, is called a *flier*. A series of flights connecting landings is a *stairway*. The vertical space occupied by stairs is called a *stairwell*. An entrance stairway to a building is a *stoop*.

banister/handrail/top rail

newel cap

landing

nosing

newel post

cove mold

riser

bottom rail

Staircase Styles

flier / flyer

straight-run/parallel steps

landing

L-steps/90-degree turn

landing

180-degree turn

landing

side flights / double return

tapered winders

double-end curve

dancing steps

180-degree turn/ geometric stairs

column

tight spiral/helical stairs

open center spiral

Fence

A solid fence can be called a *screen*. If it holds back a slope of ground it is a *retaining wall*. *Supporting members*, or *fence posts*, are anchored in foundation *postholes*. Any material used between posts is *infill*. A *weep hole* in a retaining wall allows water to seep through.

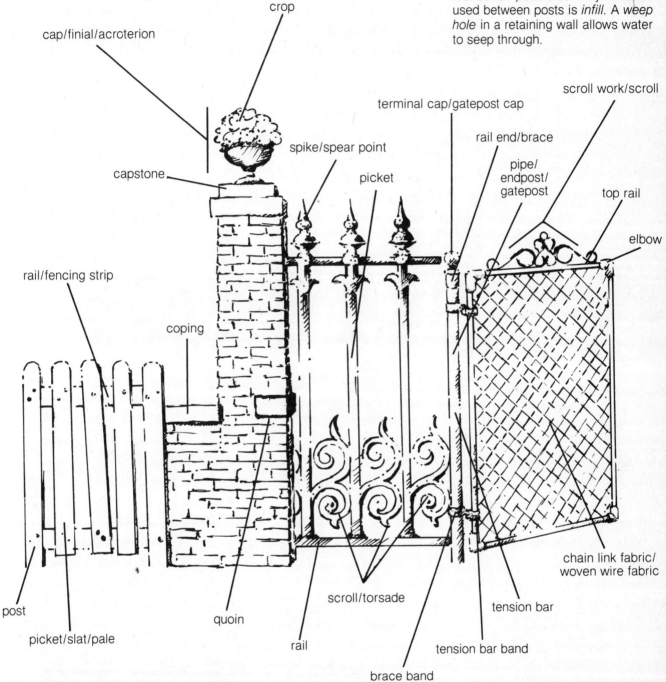

crop

cap/finial/acroterion

capstone

spike/spear point

picket

terminal cap/gatepost cap

rail end/brace

scroll work/scroll

pipe/ endpost/ gatepost

top rail

elbow

rail/fencing strip

coping

chain link fabric/ woven wire fabric

post

picket/slat/pale

quoin

scroll/torsade

rail

tension bar

tension bar band

brace band

Wood Fence   **Masonry Gate Post / Gate Pier**   **Wrought Iron Fence**   **Steel Chain Gate**

Boards are *timber,* or lumber, cut in long, flat *slabs.* When used in construction, boards are referred to as *beams,* or *balks.* When they are used to support a pitched roof, they are called *rafters.* A *plank* is thicker than a board. *Shakes* are *wooden shingles,* but cracks in wood caused by wind or frost are also called shakes. A *spall* is a chip or flaking of brick.

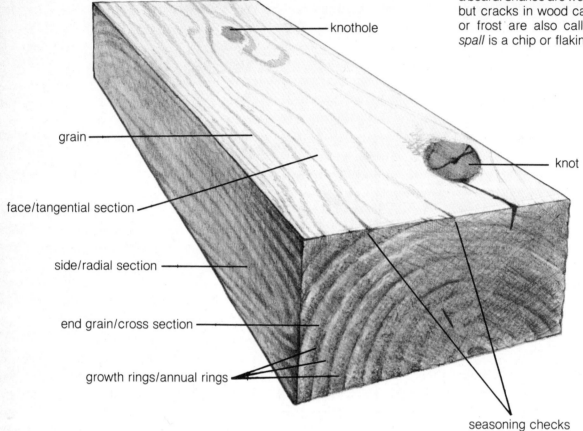

knothole

grain

knot

face/tangential section

side/radial section

end grain/cross section

growth rings/annual rings

seasoning checks

Lumber

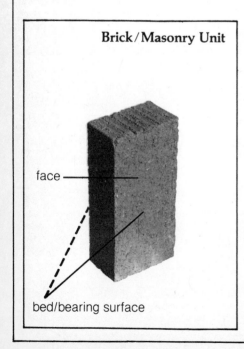

Brick/Masonry Unit

face

bed/bearing surface

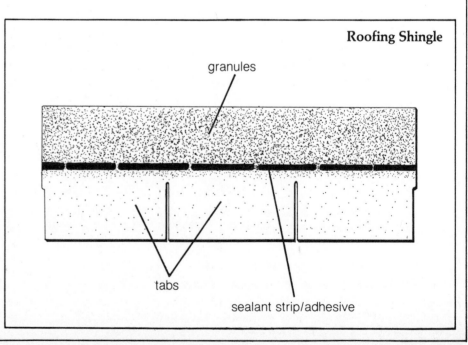

Roofing Shingle

granules

tabs

sealant strip/adhesive

Brick Wall

Bricks and brick faces take on different names, depending on where and how they are used or exposed. Structures built of *stone* or brick are called *masonry*. The pattern in which a wall is laid is its *bond*. The exposed surface is the *face*. A piece of iron or steel used to brace a wall is a *cramp,* while a recess left within for pipes or ducts is a *chase*. A *tie* is any material that holds masonry together.

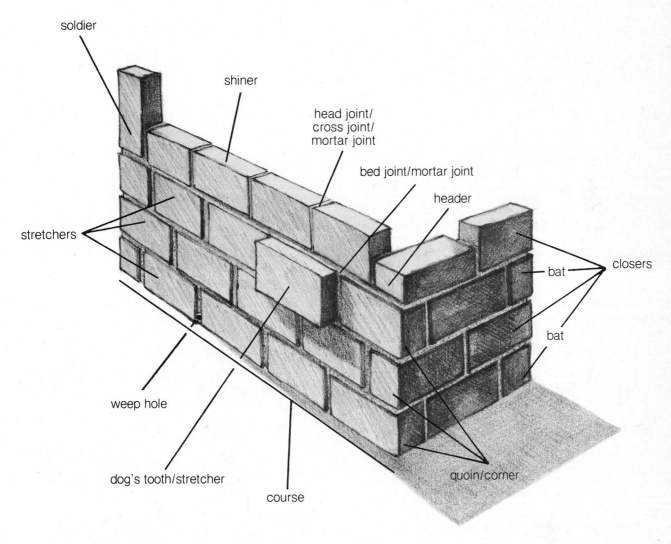

soldier

shiner

head joint/
cross joint/
mortar joint

bed joint/mortar joint

header

stretchers

closers

bat

bat

weep hole

dog's tooth/stretcher

course

quoin/corner

International Architecture

The Japanese developed the *whole-timbered building*, with *interlocking timbered joints*. Minarets, from which *criers*, or *muezzins*, call people to prayer, are normally attached or annexed to a mosque. Obelisks were often surrounded by *pillars*, or stelae, erected in honor of gods. Pyramids, *quadrilateral structures*, were used as tombs or temples. Flat-topped pyramids called *mastabas* were strictly *funerary structures*, while *ziggurats*, stepped pyramids supporting a *shrine*, were used for worship.

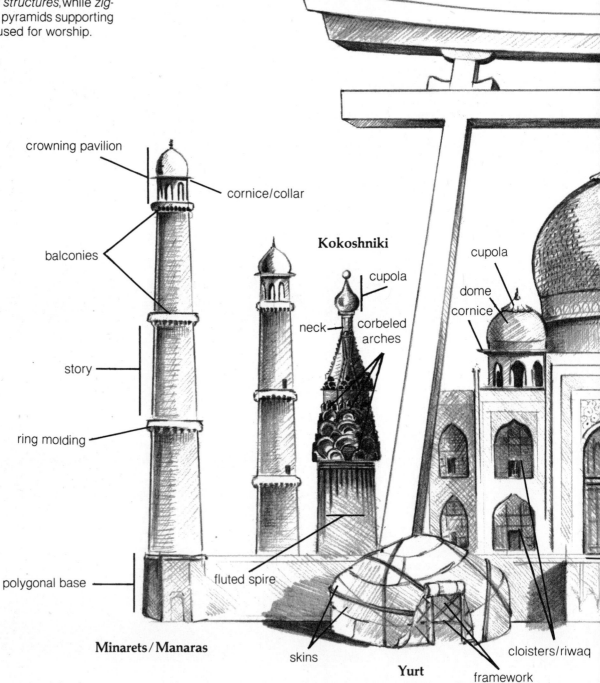

Torii/Shinto Temple Gateway

crowning pavilion

cornice/collar

balconies

Kokoshniki

cupola

neck

corbeled arches

cupola

dome

cornice

story

ring molding

polygonal base

fluted spire

Minarets/Manaras

skins

Yurt

framework

cloisters/riwaq

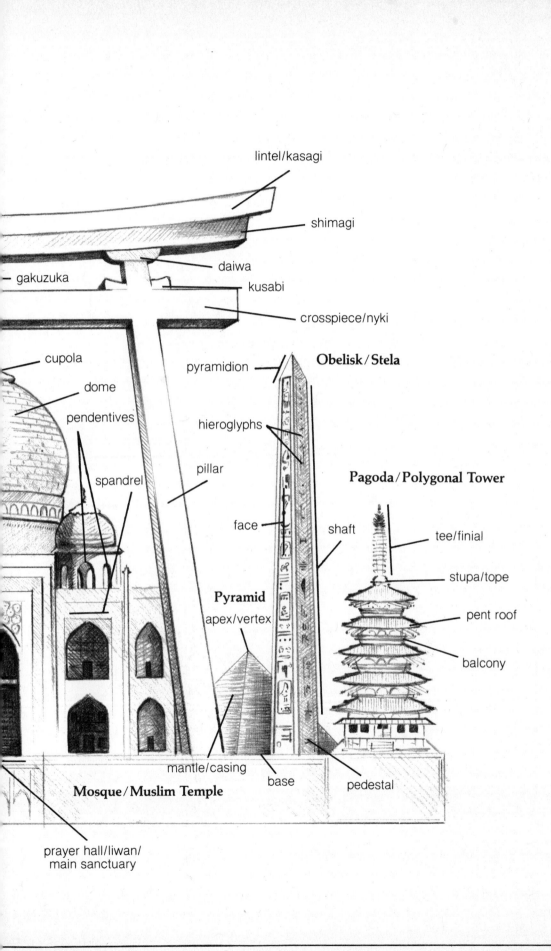

lintel/kasagi

shimagi

gakuzuka

daiwa

kusabi

crosspiece/nyki

cupola

pyramidion

Obelisk / Stela

dome

pendentives

hieroglyphs

spandrel

pillar

Pagoda / Polygonal Tower

face

shaft

tee/finial

stupa/tope

pent roof

Pyramid

apex/vertex

balcony

mantle/casing

base

pedestal

Mosque / Muslim Temple

prayer hall/liwan/
main sanctuary

Arch

The distance between the imposts is called the *span*. The *rise* is the distance between the top of the imposts and the highest point of the intrados. The *crown* is the highest point of the extrados. The area of an arch extending from the crown to the impost is the *haunch*, or *hance*.

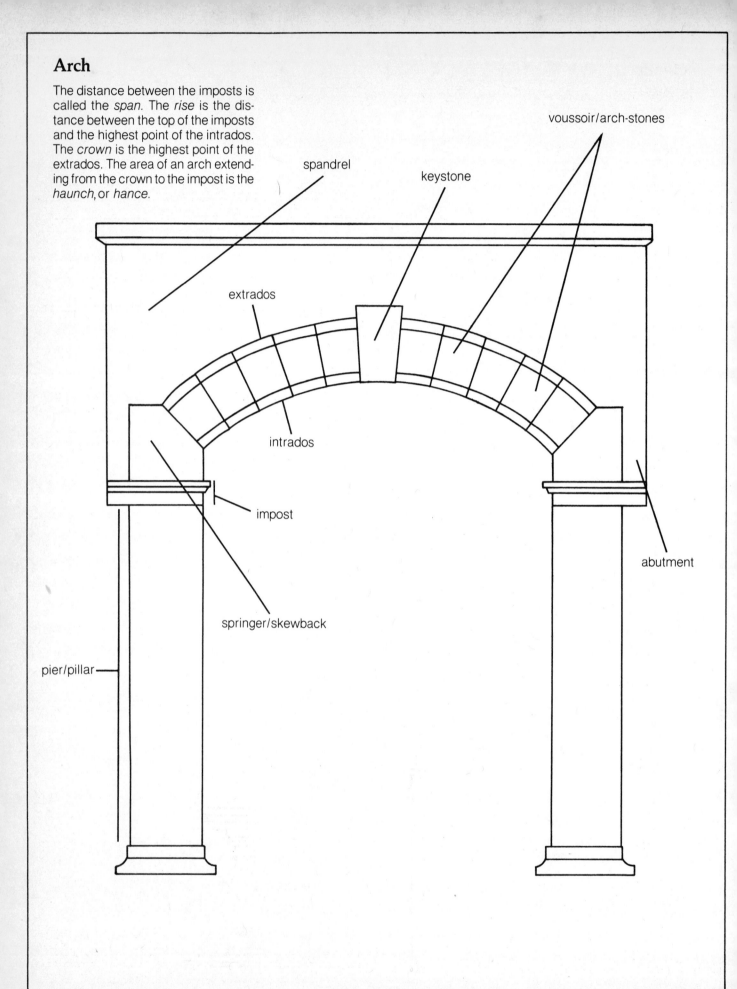

spandrel

keystone

voussoir/arch-stones

extrados

intrados

impost

abutment

springer/skewback

pier/pillar

Column

The clear space between two columns is *intercolumniation*.

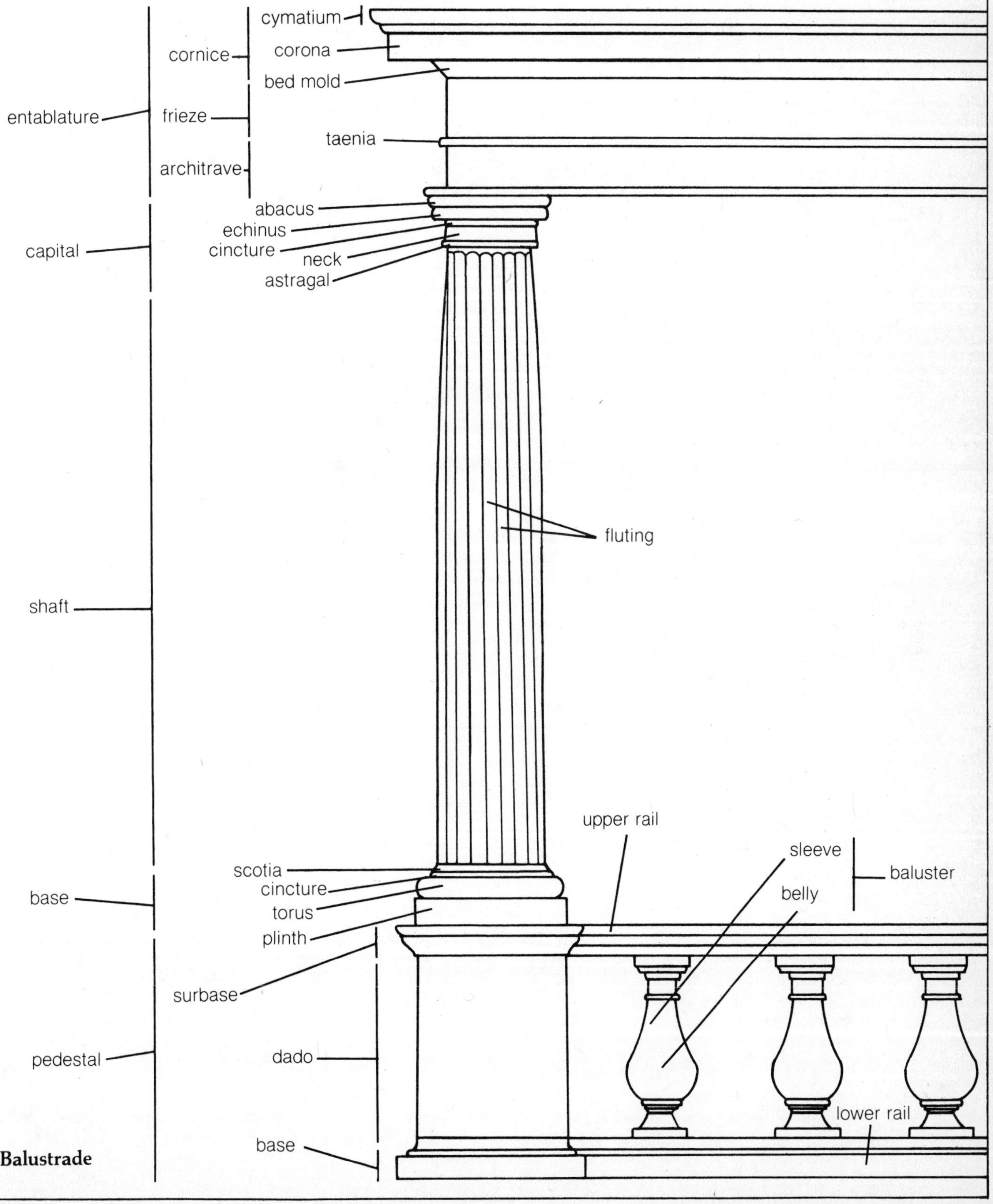

cymatium

cornice

corona

bed mold

entablature

frieze

taenia

architrave

abacus

echinus

capital

cincture

neck

astragal

fluting

shaft

upper rail

sleeve

baluster

scotia

belly

base

cincture

torus

plinth

surbase

pedestal

dado

base

lower rail

Balustrade

Architectural Designs from Other Lands

Capitol

The first floor of the Capitol contains the *Hall of Columns, House* and *Senate corridors, committee rooms, restaurants, transportation offices* and a *post office.* When the House is called to order, the *Mace of the House of Representatives* is placed on a cylindrical *pedestal* to the right of the Speaker's desk. On the Senate side is a *chandelier* with two bulbs below it. The red one indicates an executive session; the white, a regular session. Visitors to the chambers of Congress sit in *galleries.*

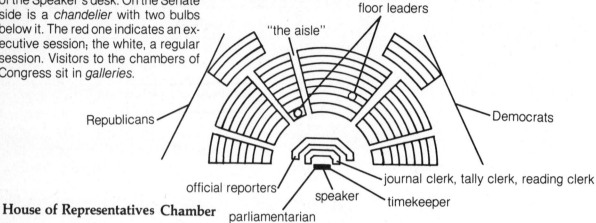

"the aisle"

floor leaders

Republicans

Democrats

official reporters

speaker

parliamentarian

timekeeper

journal clerk, tally clerk, reading clerk

House of Representatives Chamber

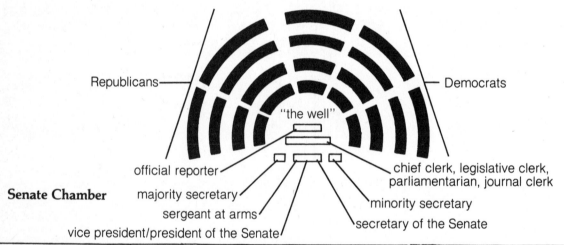

Republicans

Democrats

"the well"

official reporter

majority secretary

sergeant at arms

vice president/president of the Senate

chief clerk, legislative clerk, parliamentarian, journal clerk

minority secretary

secretary of the Senate

Senate Chamber

Capitol Building

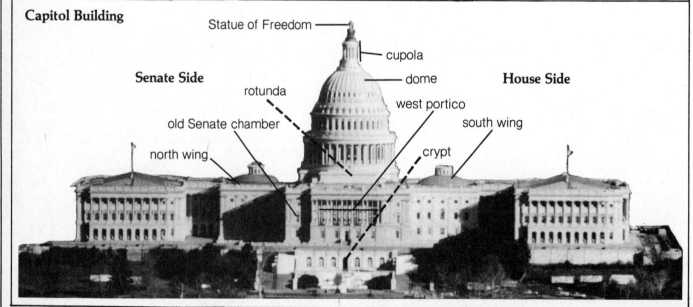

Statue of Freedom

cupola

dome

Senate Side

House Side

rotunda

west portico

old Senate chamber

south wing

north wing

crypt

White House

The White House, a historic *mansion* that serves as the President's *home* and *office,* contains *portraits, antiques* and *memorabilia.* In addition to the rooms and offices shown here, there is a bombproof *command post* in the cellar and a *helipad* on the south lawn.

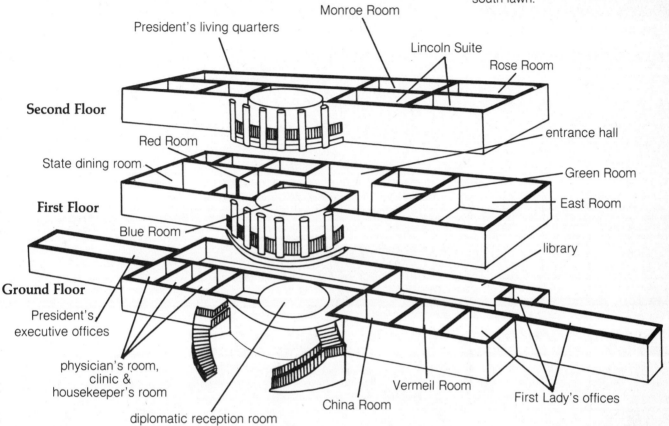

Monroe Room

President's living quarters

Lincoln Suite

Rose Room

Second Floor

Red Room

entrance hall

State dining room

Green Room

First Floor

East Room

Blue Room

library

Ground Floor

President's executive offices

physician's room, clinic & housekeeper's room

diplomatic reception room

China Room

Vermeil Room

First Lady's offices

House Plan

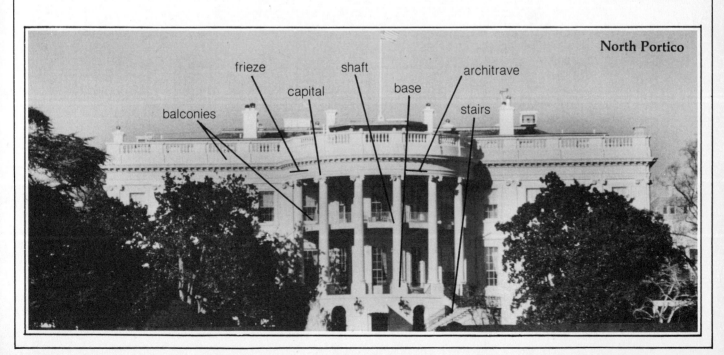

North Portico

frieze

shaft

architrave

capital

base

stairs

balconies

Special Purpose Buildings

Prison

Maximum security prisons, such as the one seen here, are characterized by high *walls*, *armed guards* and *security checkpoints*. *Minimum security prisons* may be surrounded by *chainlink fences* and have *security systems* that are largely electronic, with *doors*, *alarms*, *TV monitors* and *intercoms* monitored by *central computers*. *Prisoners*, or *inmates*, in all *correctional facilities*, including *jails*, live in *cells* with *barred doors*.

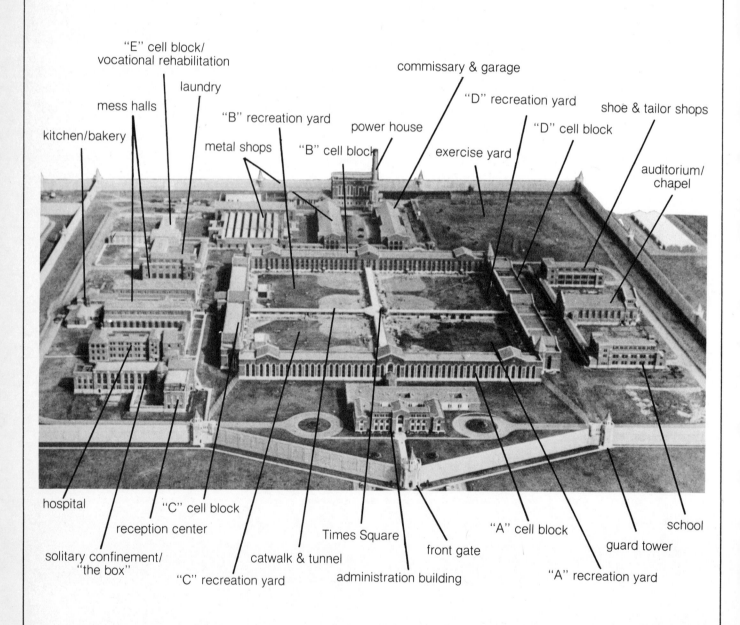

"E" cell block/ vocational rehabilitation

commissary & garage

laundry

"D" recreation yard

mess halls

shoe & tailor shops

"B" recreation yard

"D" cell block

kitchen/bakery

power house

exercise yard

metal shops

"B" cell block

auditorium/ chapel

hospital

"C" cell block

reception center

Times Square

"A" cell block

school

solitary confinement/ "the box"

catwalk & tunnel

front gate

guard tower

"C" recreation yard

administration building

"A" recreation yard

Skyscraper

A skyscraper, or *building* more than twenty stories high, is built on a *foundation* of reinforced concrete *piers* supported by *piles* driven into soil or bedrock. The center of the building, or *core,* usually contains the *elevator bank.* The machinery needed to operate the building's systems is located on the *mechanical floors.* A *cornerstone* is a stone laid at a formal inauguration ceremony.

kangaroo crane

roof

columns

beams/girders

skeleton/frame

tarpaulin cover

stories/tenant floors

skylobby/transfer to local elevators

curtainwall/ skin/facing

plaza

lobby/foyer

Under Construction

television & radio mast

fastigiated top

Completed

dirigible mooring mast

observation deck

setbacks

Special Purpose Buildings

Elevator

There is padding which makes up the *safety edges* on the *shafts,* or inner-most sides, of elevator doors. Most elevator cars have *emergency top exits* in the *canopy* or real ceiling as well as *service cabinets* which contain *fan switches, light* and *start switches.* An individual who directs people to the next available car in a *bank* of elevators is called a *starter.*

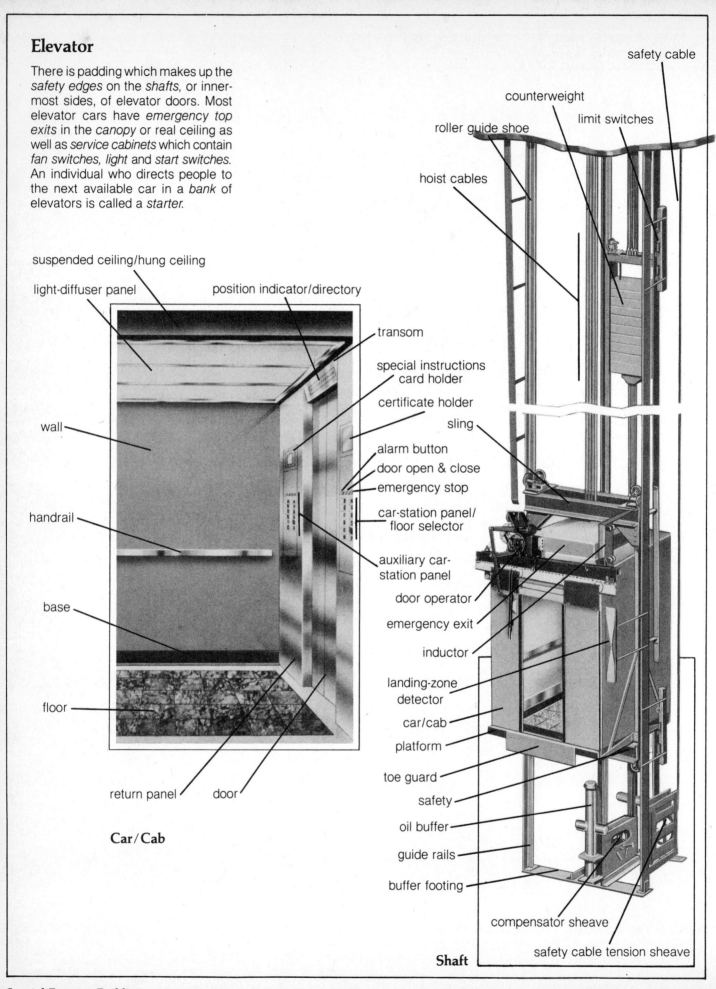

suspended ceiling/hung ceiling

light-diffuser panel

position indicator/directory

transom

special instructions card holder

certificate holder

sling

alarm button

door open & close

emergency stop

car-station panel/ floor selector

auxiliary car-station panel

door operator

emergency exit

inductor

landing-zone detector

car/cab

platform

toe guard

safety

oil buffer

guide rails

buffer footing

wall

handrail

base

floor

return panel

door

Car/Cab

safety cable

counterweight

roller guide shoe

limit switches

hoist cables

compensator sheave

safety cable tension sheave

Shaft

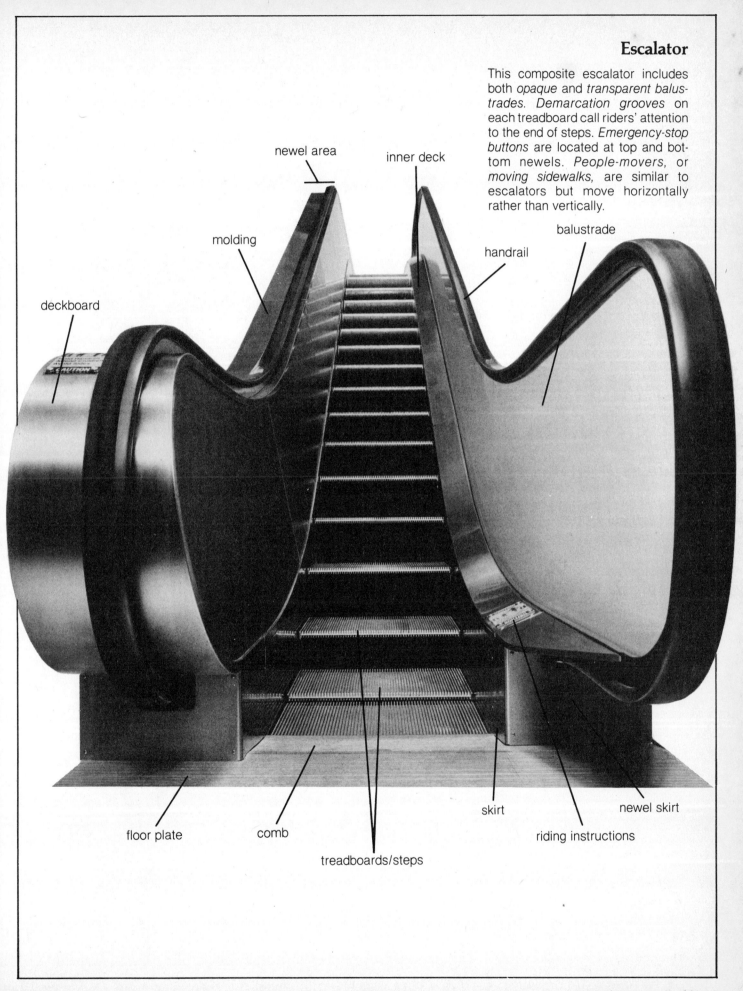

Escalator

This composite escalator includes both *opaque* and *transparent balustrades*. *Demarcation grooves* on each treadboard call riders' attention to the end of steps. *Emergency-stop buttons* are located at top and bottom newels. *People-movers*, or *moving sidewalks*, are similar to escalators but move horizontally rather than vertically.

newel area

inner deck

balustrade

handrail

molding

deckboard

skirt

newel skirt

floor plate

comb

riding instructions

treadboards/steps

Special Purpose Buildings

Castle

A castle was protected by a moat which could be crossed by a lowered *drawbridge*. Narrow openings in turret or tower floors, used to drop boiling liquids or stones on attackers, were called *machicolations*.

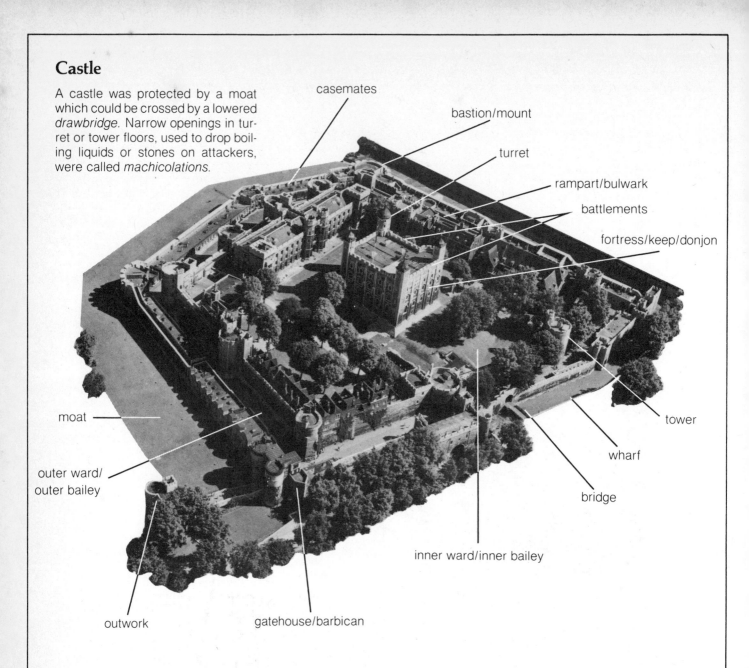

casemates

bastion/mount

turret

rampart/bulwark

battlements

fortress/keep/donjon

tower

wharf

bridge

inner ward/inner bailey

moat

outer ward/ outer bailey

outwork

gatehouse/barbican

Embattled Parapet

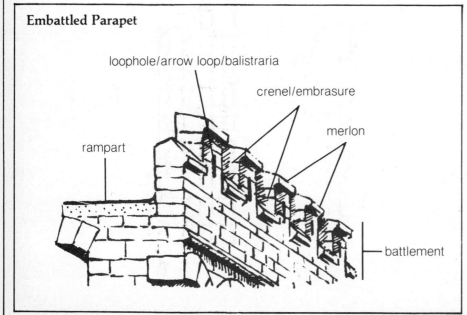

loophole/arrow loop/balistraria

crenel/embrasure

merlon

rampart

battlement

Bartizan/Turret

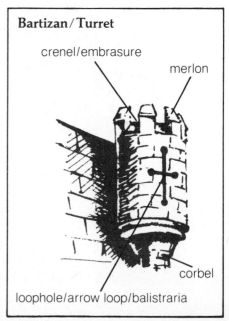

crenel/embrasure

merlon

corbel

loophole/arrow loop/balistraria

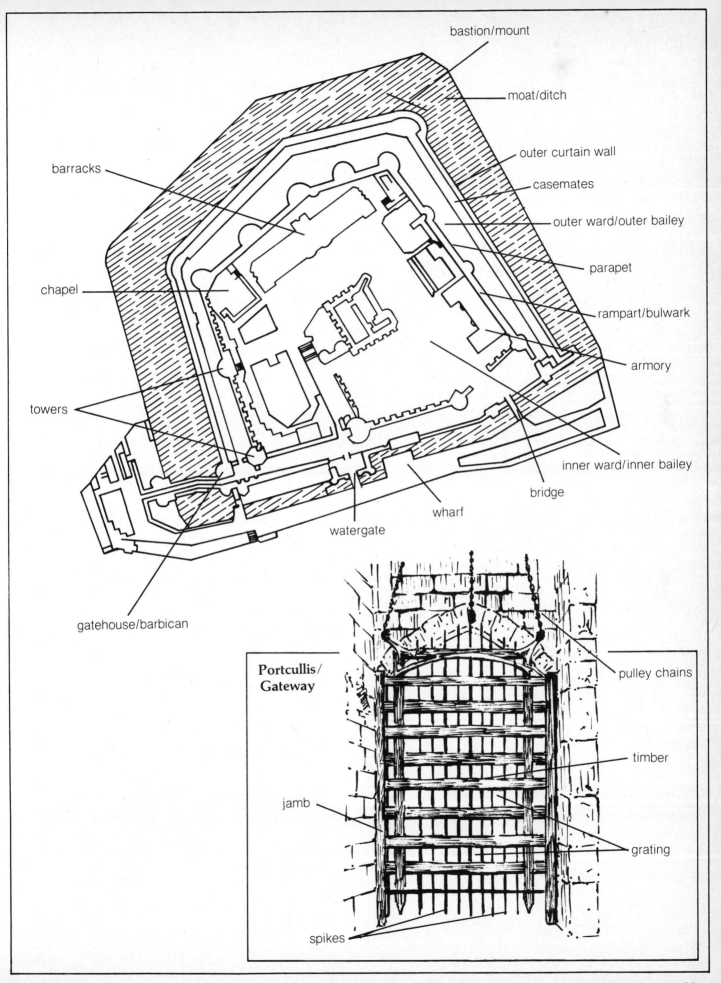

bastion/mount

moat/ditch

outer curtain wall

casemates

outer ward/outer bailey

parapet

rampart/bulwark

armory

barracks

chapel

towers

inner ward/inner bailey

bridge

wharf

watergate

gatehouse/barbican

**Portcullis/
Gateway**

pulley chains

timber

jamb

grating

spikes

Special Purpose Buildings

Fortifications

This *field fortification* or *trading post* was protected by wooden walls from behind which soldiers could fire on attackers from raised *parapets*. *Powder* and *ammunition* were stored in a building called a *magazine*.

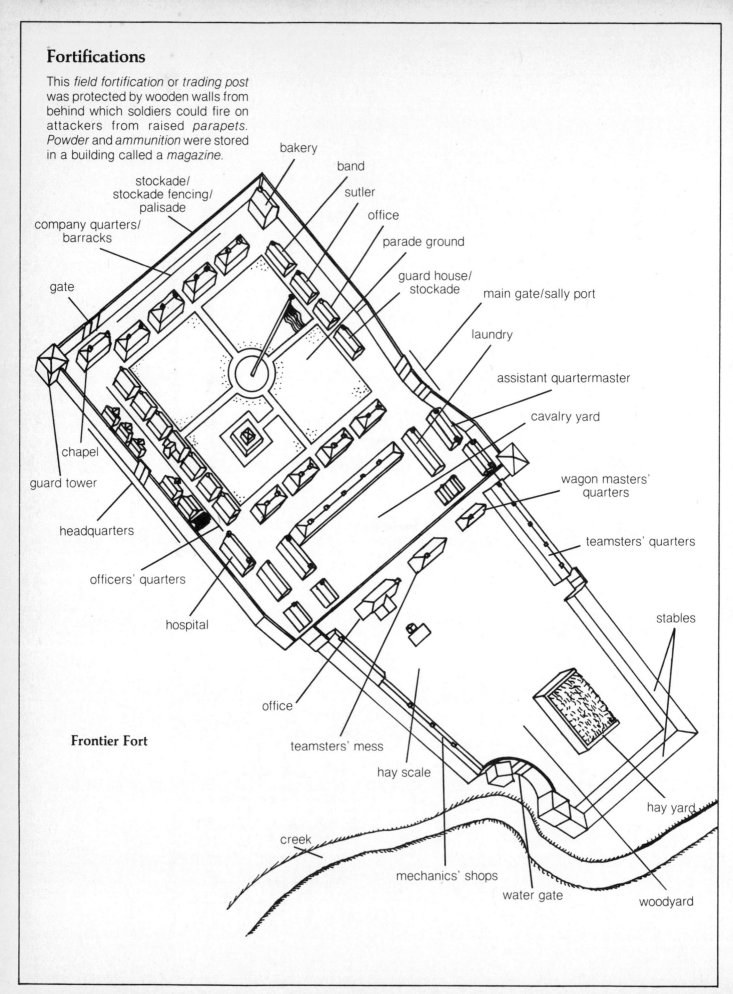

stockade/
stockade fencing/
palisade

company quarters/
barracks

gate

chapel

guard tower

headquarters

officers' quarters

hospital

office

teamsters' mess

hay scale

creek

bakery

band

sutler

office

parade ground

guard house/
stockade

main gate/sally port

laundry

assistant quartermaster

cavalry yard

wagon masters'
quarters

teamsters' quarters

stables

hay yard

woodyard

water gate

mechanics' shops

Frontier Fort

Fortifications

Permanent fortifications, such as the *point* of the star fort illustrated here, had *walls* and *slopes* made of *masonry* and earth. They often had *casemates; bombproofs*, walls impervious to explosives; *drawbridges* and *earthen breastworks*, breast-high protection for soldiers.

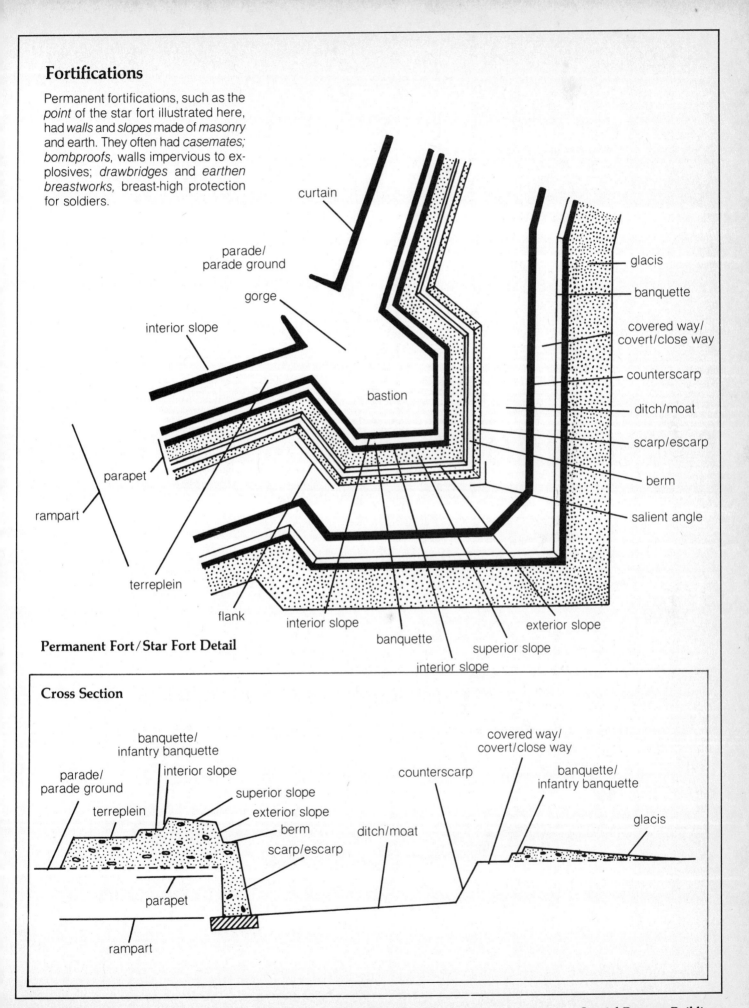

curtain

parade/ parade ground

gorge

interior slope

bastion

glacis

banquette

covered way/ covert/close way

counterscarp

ditch/moat

scarp/escarp

berm

salient angle

parapet

rampart

terreplein

flank

interior slope

banquette

superior slope

interior slope

exterior slope

Permanent Fort / Star Fort Detail

Cross Section

parade/ parade ground

banquette/ infantry banquette

interior slope

terreplein

superior slope

exterior slope

berm

scarp/escarp

parapet

rampart

counterscarp

ditch/moat

covered way/ covert/close way

banquette/ infantry banquette

glacis

Special Purpose Buildings

Tepee / Teepee / Tipi

The *pole frame* of an Indian tepee was held together at the top by a *hide rope*. It was covered with dressed buffalo *skins* and had a *fire pit* on the floor within. Other Indian dwellings included *wigwams*, rounded or oval-shaped lodges formed by poles overlaid with *bark*, *mats* or *skins*; *wickiups*, huts made of *brushwood* or covered with mats; and *hogans*, dwellings constructed of *earth* and *branches* and covered with *mud* or *sod*.

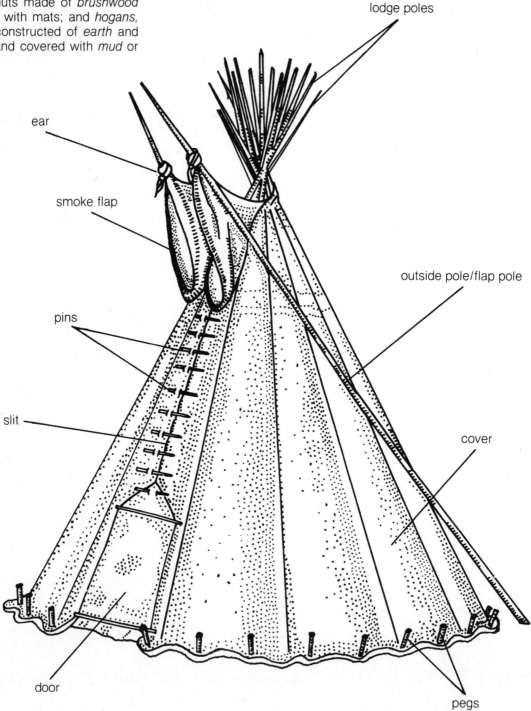

lodge poles

ear

smoke flap

outside pole/flap pole

pins

slit

cover

door

pegs

Domed Structures

Traditionally, a dome is a circular *vault* whose walls exert equal thrust in all directions, resisted by a *tension ring*. The geodesic dome consists of a *grid* of *compression* or *tension members* lying upon *great circles* running in three directions in any given area.

Igloo / Iglu

king block

snow blocks

ice window

storm igloo

air hole

tunnel/tossut

entrance

animal skin

sleeping shelf   entrance

Interior

Geodesic Dome

spoke/strut

hubs

skin/face

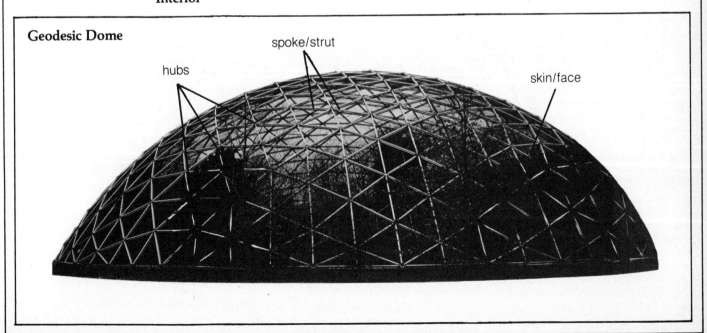

85

Church / Cathedral

A small building used for worship is called a *chapel*. Living quarters used by church clergy are the *rectory*. The office in which church business is conducted is the *chancellery*.

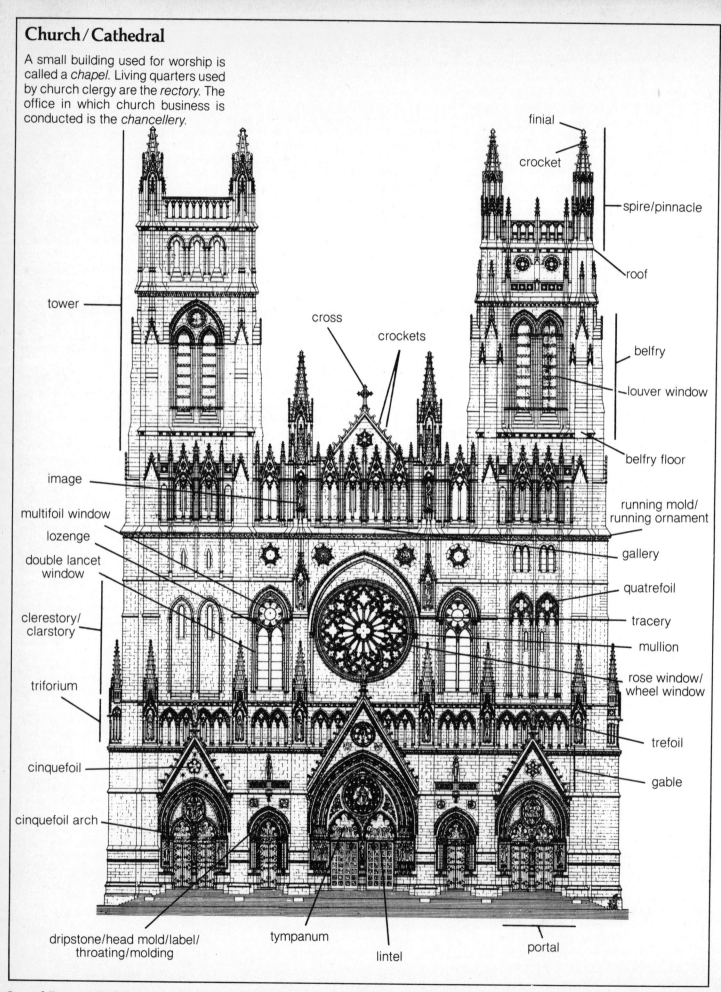

finial

crocket

spire/pinnacle

roof

tower

cross

crockets

belfry

louver window

belfry floor

image

running mold/ running ornament

multifoil window

lozenge

gallery

double lancet window

quatrefoil

tracery

clerestory/ clarstory

mullion

rose window/ wheel window

triforium

trefoil

cinquefoil

gable

cinquefoil arch

dripstone/head mold/label/ throating/molding

tympanum

lintel

portal

Church Interior

That part of a church containing the altar and seats for the clergy and choir is called the *chancel*. A *pulpit* is an elevated platform used in preaching or conducting a worship service. The *tabernacle* is a receptacle for consecrated elements of the Eucharist: the *pix*, the container in which Communion *wafers* are kept; the *paten*, a plate used to hold *Communion bread;* and the *chalice*, or *Communion cup*, used to dispense consecrated *wine*.

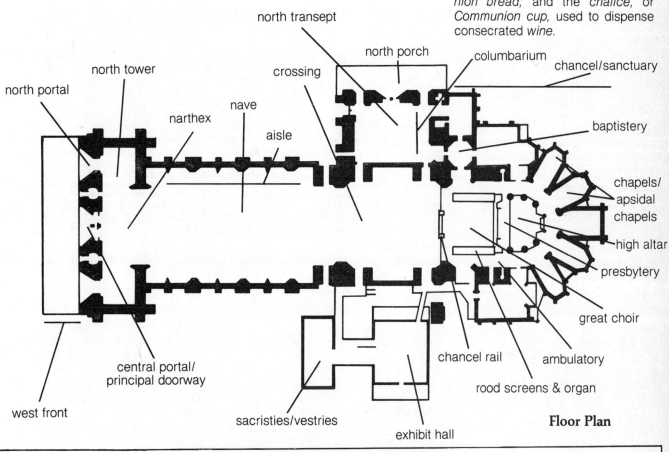

north transept

north porch

columbarium

chancel/sanctuary

crossing

north tower

north portal

narthex

nave

aisle

baptistery

chapels/ apsidal chapels

high altar

presbytery

great choir

ambulatory

chancel rail

rood screens & organ

central portal/ principal doorway

west front

sacristies/vestries

exhibit hall

Floor Plan

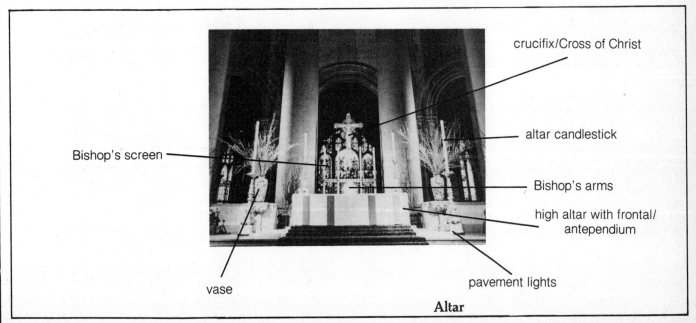

crucifix/Cross of Christ

altar candlestick

Bishop's screen

Bishop's arms

high altar with frontal/ antependium

vase

pavement lights

Altar

Special Purpose Buildings

Synagogue/Temple

The Torah is a parchment or leather *scroll* containing the first five books of the *Scriptures*, or *Pentateuch*, written in Hebrew. It is tied closed with a beltlike *wrapper*.

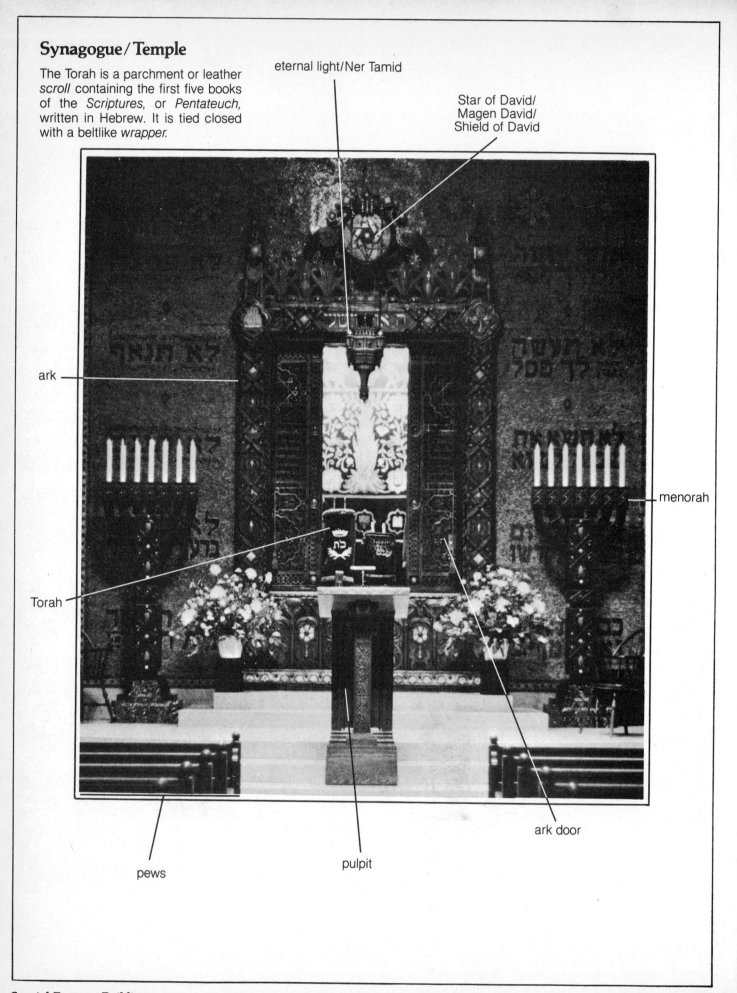

eternal light/Ner Tamid

Star of David/ Magen David/ Shield of David

ark

menorah

Torah

ark door

pews

pulpit

Courtroom

The small anteroom off the courtroom in which the *judge* changes into his *robes* and holds conferences is called the *judge's chambers*. After a *jury* has heard a case, it deliberates in a *jury room*. A judge may sometimes use a malletlike *gavel* during proceedings.

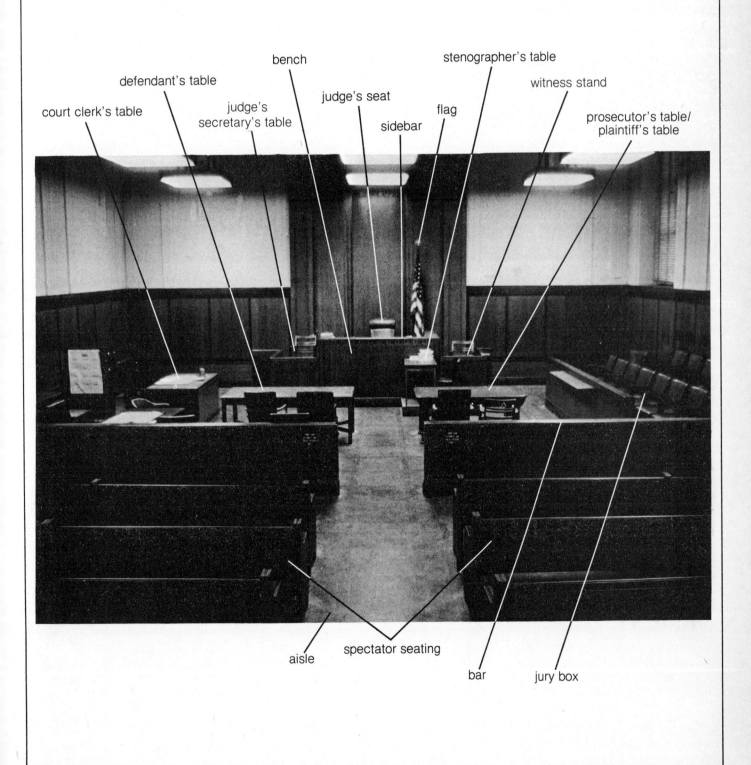

court clerk's table

defendant's table

judge's
secretary's table

bench

judge's seat

sidebar

flag

stenographer's table

witness stand

prosecutor's table/
plaintiff's table

aisle

spectator seating

bar

jury box

Special Purpose Buildings

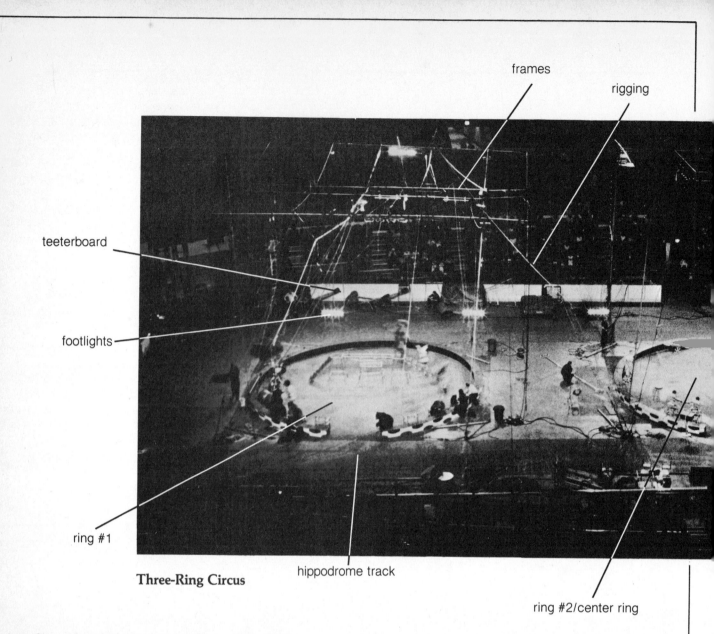

frames

rigging

teeterboard

footlights

ring #1

Three-Ring Circus

hippodrome track

ring #2/center ring

Aerialists/Flyers/Trapeze Artists

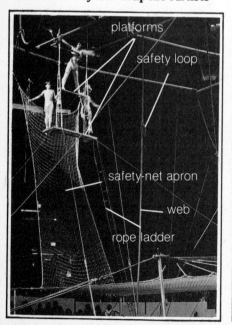

platforms

safety loop

safety-net apron

web

rope ladder

Animal Tamer

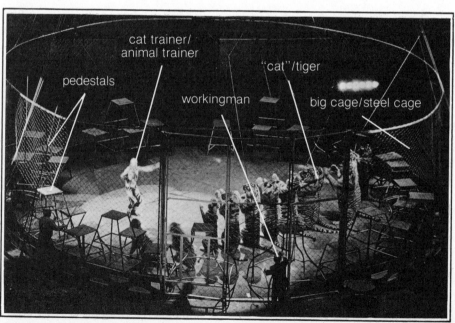

cat trainer/
animal trainer

"cat"/tiger

pedestals

workingman

big cage/steel cage

Circus

Circuses traditionally take place in tents erected by *roustabouts* and begin with a *parade* in which all the performers enter the *arena*. A *ringmaster*, usually clad in *top hat* and *tails*, announces acts, including *animal* and *clown acts; tightrope*, or *high-wire acts;* and *jugglers*. In the past, *sideshows*, which took place in an adjoining tent, featured *tattooed ladies*, *giants*, *midgets*, *sword-swallowers* and *fire-eaters*.

audience

ring curbs

animal cage

spotlight

ring #3

Circus Tent / Big Top / Top

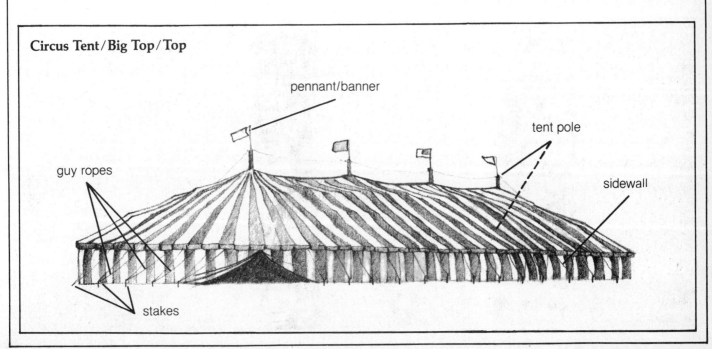

pennant/banner

tent pole

guy ropes

sidewall

stakes

Amusement Park

A roller coaster consists of *hills, straightaways* and *loops. Upstop wheels* lock roller-coaster cars to the track, *guide wheels* are used for turns and tractor wheels are used for gliding.

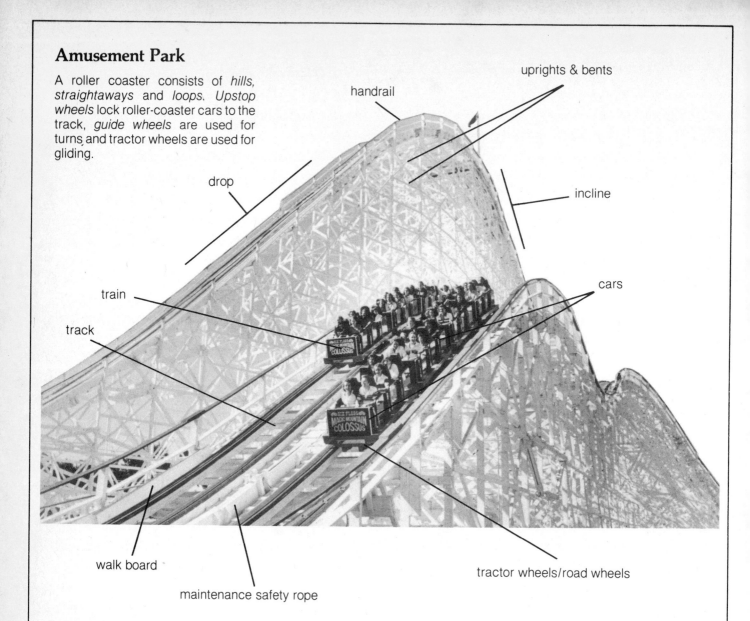

handrail

uprights & bents

drop

incline

train

cars

track

walk board

maintenance safety rope

tractor wheels/road wheels

Roller Coaster

Bumper Car/Scooter Car

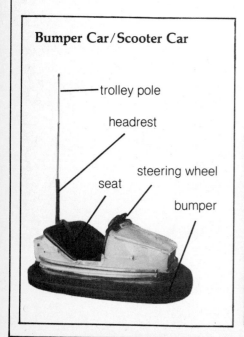

trolley pole

headrest

seat

steering wheel

bumper

Incline Track

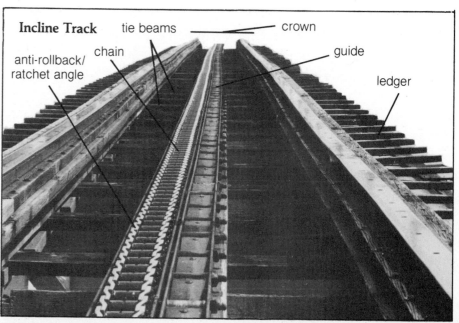

tie beams

crown

chain

anti-rollback/ratchet angle

guide

ledger

Amusement Park

Immobile carousel horses are called *gallopers*. *Jumpers* move up and down on horse rods. *Flying horses* tilt outward as the carousel picks up speed. Merry-go-round music is traditionally provided by a mechanical *band organ*, often referred to as a *calliope*.

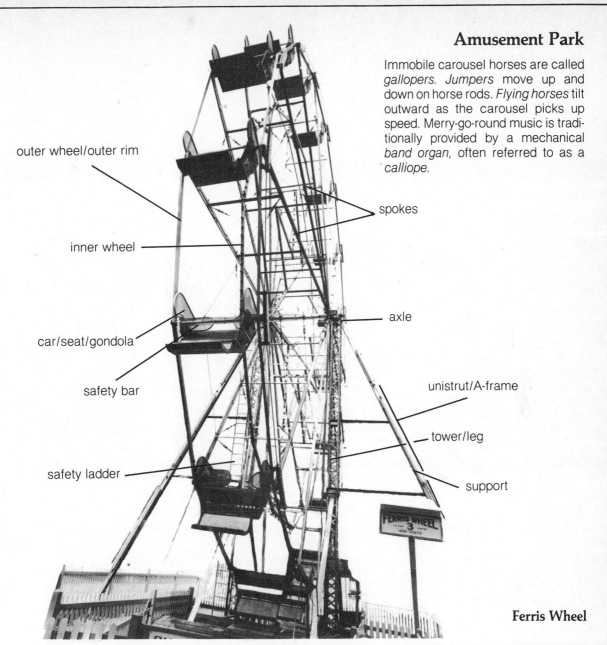

outer wheel/outer rim

inner wheel

spokes

car/seat/gondola

axle

safety bar

unistrut/A-frame

tower/leg

safety ladder

support

Ferris Wheel

Merry-Go-Round / Carousel

panel painting

rim/rounding board/cornice/shield

rotating frame

inner cornice

horse rod

horse

gondola/chariot

platform

inside drive

Special Purpose Buildings

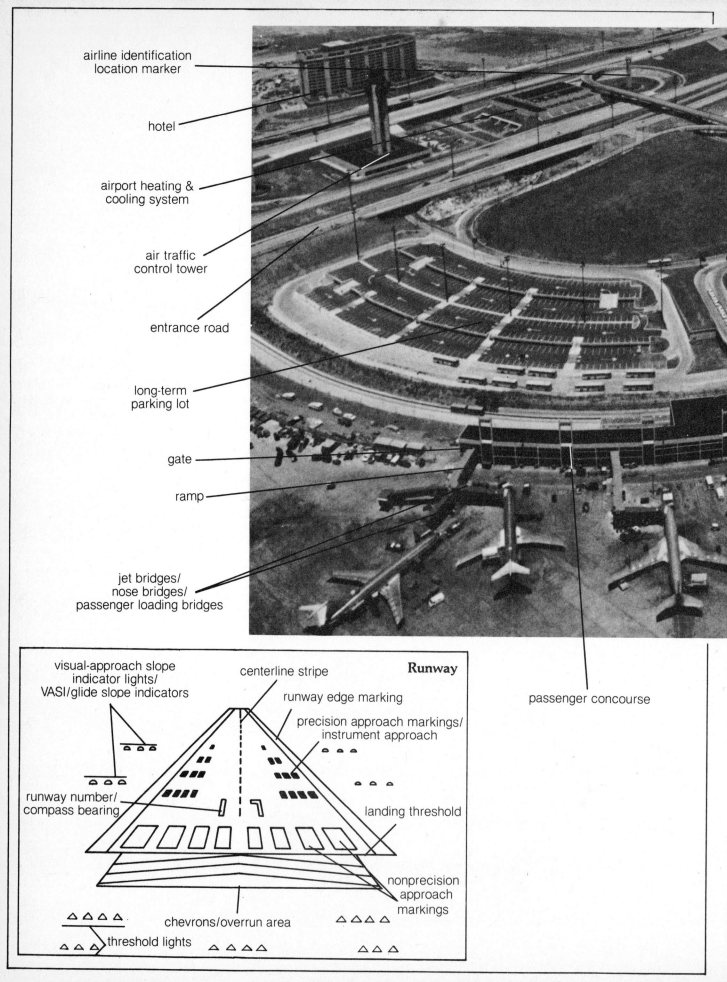

airline identification
location marker

hotel

airport heating &
cooling system

air traffic
control tower

entrance road

long-term
parking lot

gate

ramp

jet bridges/
nose bridges/
passenger loading bridges

Runway

passenger concourse

visual-approach slope
indicator lights/
VASI/glide slope indicators

centerline stripe

runway edge marking

precision approach markings/
instrument approach

runway number/
compass bearing

landing threshold

nonprecision
approach
markings

chevrons/overrun area

threshold lights

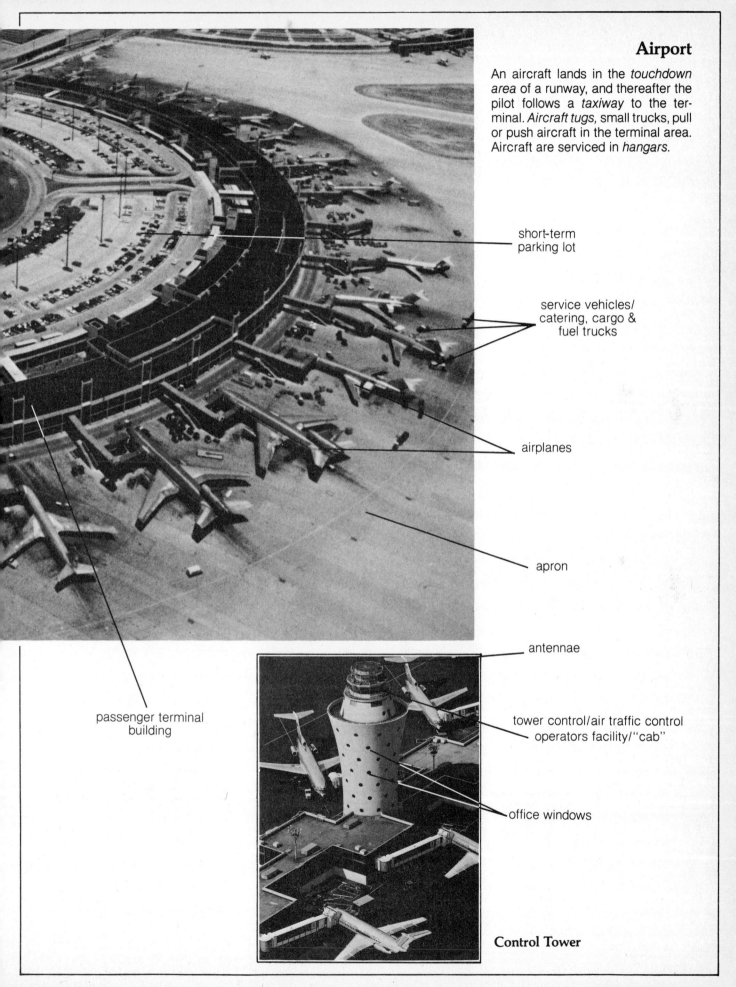

Airport

An aircraft lands in the *touchdown area* of a runway, and thereafter the pilot follows a *taxiway* to the terminal. *Aircraft tugs,* small trucks, pull or push aircraft in the terminal area. Aircraft are serviced in *hangars.*

short-term parking lot

service vehicles/catering, cargo & fuel trucks

airplanes

apron

antennae

tower control/air traffic control operators facility/"cab"

office windows

passenger terminal building

Control Tower

Special Purpose Buildings

Railroad Yard

A railroad yard, or *marshalling yard,* consists of a system of *parallel tracks, crossovers* and *switches* where *cars* are formed into *trains* and where cars, *locomotives* and other *rolling stock* are kept when not in use or awaiting repair. In *hump yards,* freight cars are pushed down a *hump* onto a *siding,* determined by a *yardmaster,* to be coupled to a forming train. *Electropneumatic retarders* control the speed of the cars as they move along the tracks.

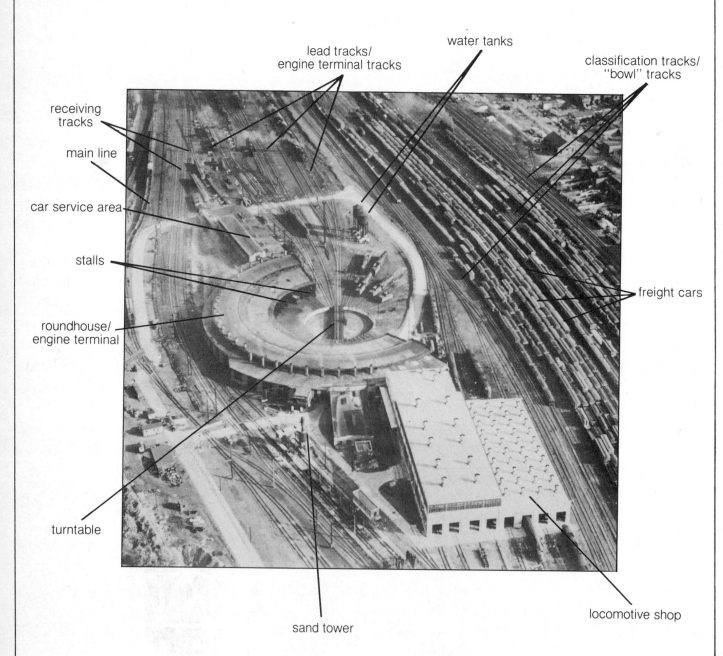

receiving tracks

main line

car service area

stalls

roundhouse/ engine terminal

turntable

lead tracks/ engine terminal tracks

water tanks

classification tracks/ "bowl" tracks

freight cars

sand tower

locomotive shop

safety rail

window

tower

A pedestrian walkway on a bridge is a *footpath*. *Fixed bridges* have no moving parts, while *movable bridges*, such as lift bridges, *drawbridges* and *bascule bridges* either lift or swing open. A *pontoon bridge* is built on *floating piers*.

main cable

stay rope

suspender cables

girder

stiffening trusses

side span

center span

tower leg

pier

Suspension Bridge

span guide

Lift Bridge

machinery tower

aviation light

main counterweight

vertical brace

elevator shaft

auxiliary counterweight

tie brace

lift span

upper chord

lower chord

roadway

span lock

shoes

gatehouse

fenders

Other Structures

Tunnel

Tunnels that take water to hydroelectric plants or to municipal waterworks and those that remove storm water and sewage are called *conduits*. Tunnels cut through rock frequently require no *lining*. Underwater tunnels can be ventilated by *shafts* leading to the surface or by *exhaust* or *booster fans* at the ends.

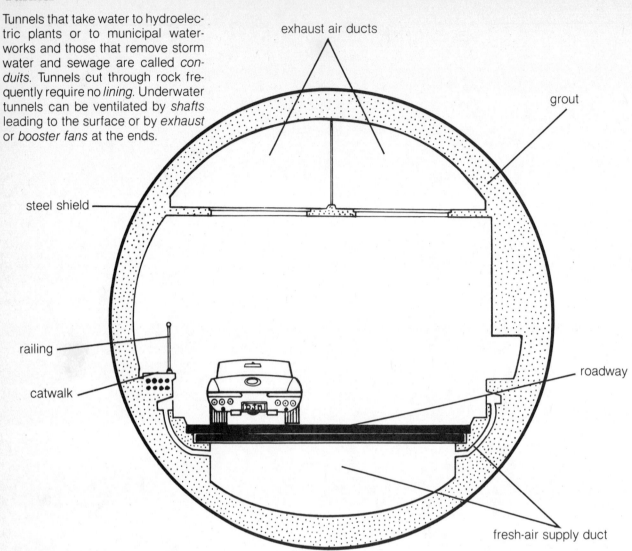

exhaust air ducts

grout

steel shield

railing

catwalk

roadway

fresh-air supply duct

Cross Section

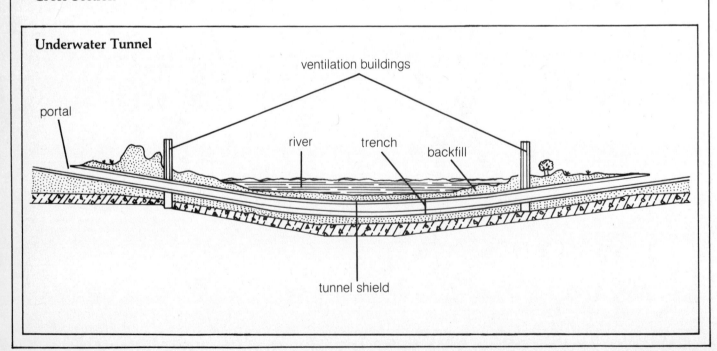

Underwater Tunnel

ventilation buildings

portal

river

trench

backfill

tunnel shield

Canal Lock

The water level in a canal lock is raised or lowered through *sluice gates* in the lock wall or *floor. Shipboard lines* or *hawsers* secured to *bollards* along the lockside hold the vessel steady while the lock is in operation. Before *electric locomotives* were used, animals would haul boats through locks following a *towpath.*

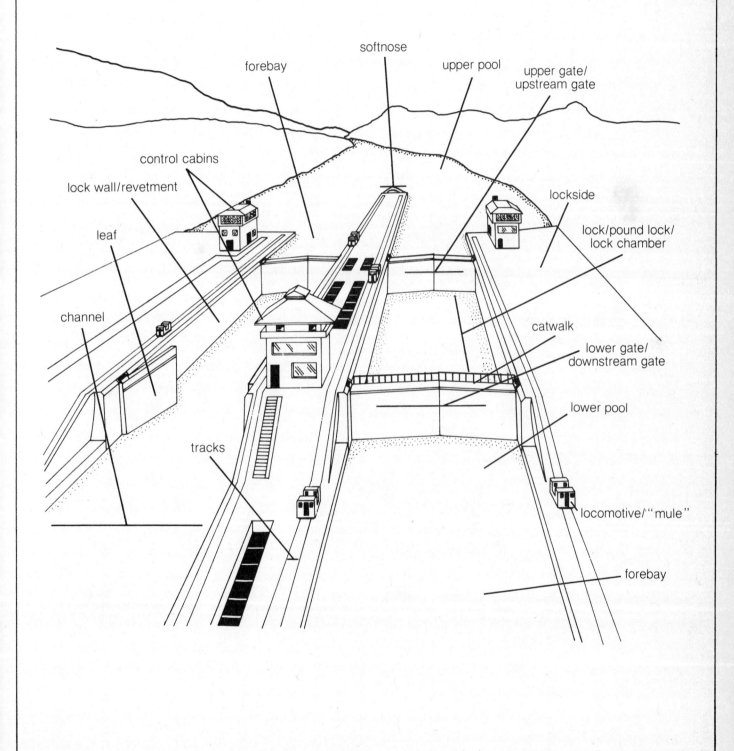

softnose

forebay

upper pool

upper gate/
upstream gate

control cabins

lock wall/revetment

lockside

leaf

lock/pound lock/
lock chamber

channel

catwalk

lower gate/
downstream gate

lower pool

tracks

locomotive/"mule"

forebay

Other Structures

Dam

Many dams have steep channels divided by partitions into pools, called *fishways* or *fish ladders,* that enable fish to swim upriver. Other dams have *log chutes* designed to allow logs to pass through. A *dike,* or *levee,* is an earthwork construction built to block water rather than to regulate its flow.

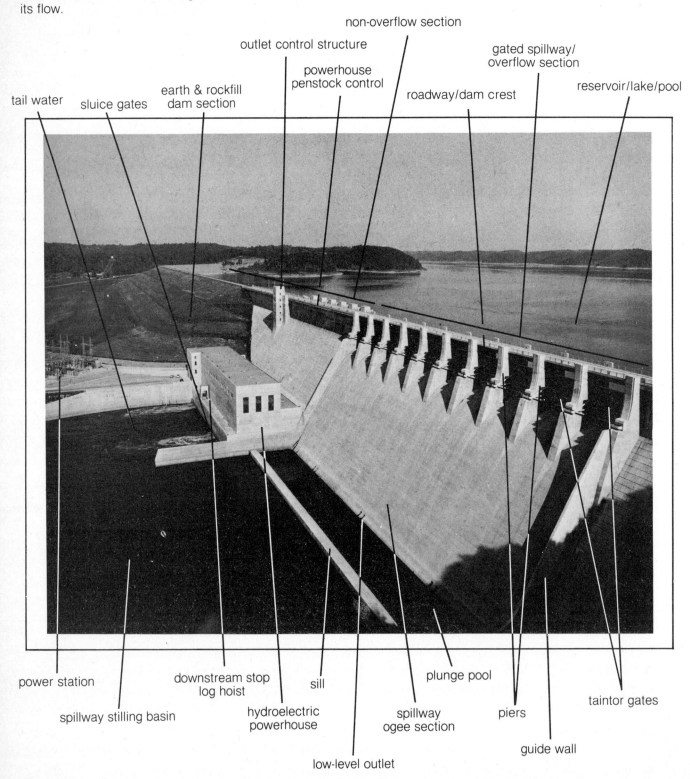

non-overflow section

outlet control structure

powerhouse penstock control

gated spillway/ overflow section

roadway/dam crest

reservoir/lake/pool

tail water

sluice gates

earth & rockfill dam section

power station

spillway stilling basin

downstream stop log hoist

hydroelectric powerhouse

sill

low-level outlet

spillway ogee section

plunge pool

piers

guide wall

taintor gates

Oil Drilling Platform/ Offshore Rig

In shallow water this *semisubmersible* rig drills in the floating position. When drilling at greater depths the motion compensator, a *hydraulic-pneumatic device,* moves up and down as the rig does in the sea to keep the *pipe* stationary in the *hole.* The "driller" controls the *drill, bit* changes and large hydraulic valves, or *blowout preventors.*

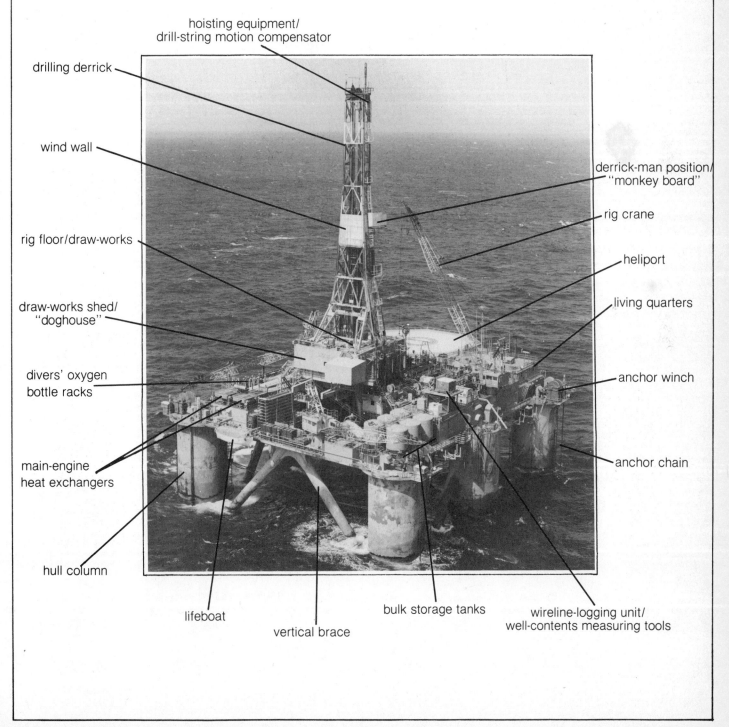

hoisting equipment/ drill-string motion compensator

drilling derrick

wind wall

rig floor/draw-works

draw-works shed/ "doghouse"

divers' oxygen bottle racks

main-engine heat exchangers

hull column

derrick-man position/ "monkey board"

rig crane

heliport

living quarters

anchor winch

anchor chain

lifeboat

vertical brace

bulk storage tanks

wireline-logging unit/ well-contents measuring tools

Other Structures

Supermarket

The representative floor plan shown here is of a typical *superstore*, or *supercombo*, a combination drug store and food store, with emphasis on *perishables* and *preprepared foods*. The supermarkets of the future will be *warehouse stores*, or *hypermarkets*.

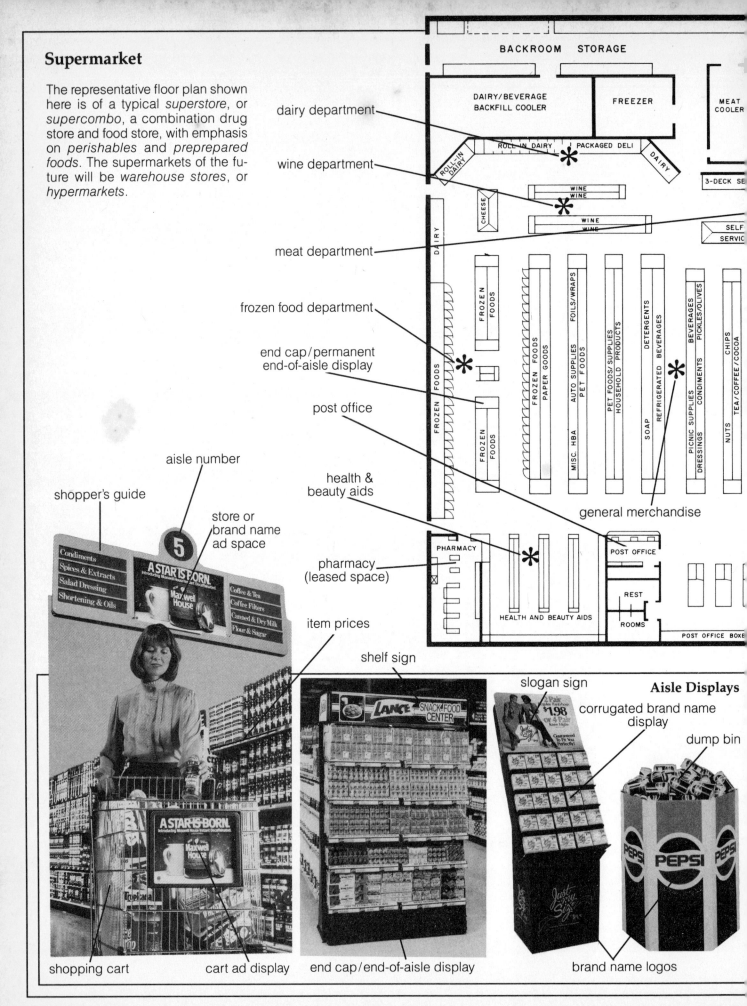

BACKROOM STORAGE

dairy department

wine department

meat department

frozen food department

end cap/permanent
end-of-aisle display

post office

aisle number

shopper's guide

store or
brand name
ad space

health &
beauty aids

pharmacy
(leased space)

item prices

shelf sign

DAIRY/BEVERAGE BACKFILL COOLER

FREEZER

MEAT COOLER

ROLL-IN DAIRY — PACKAGED DELI

ROLL-IN DAIRY

DAIRY

3-DECK SE

WINE
WINE

WINE
WINE

CHEESE

SELF
SERVIC

DAIRY

FROZEN FOODS

FROZEN FOODS

FROZEN FOODS

FROZEN FOODS

FROZEN FOODS

PAPER GOODS

FOILS/WRAPS

AUTO SUPPLIES

MISC. HBA

PET FOODS

PET FOODS/SUPPLIES

HOUSEHOLD PRODUCTS

DETERGENTS

SOAP

REFRIGERATED BEVERAGES

BEVERAGES

PICKLES/OLIVES

PICNIC SUPPLIES

CONDIMENTS

DRESSINGS

CHIPS

NUTS

TEA/COFFEE/COCOA

general merchandise

PHARMACY

POST OFFICE

REST
ROOMS

HEALTH AND BEAUTY AIDS

POST OFFICE BOXE

Aisle Displays

slogan sign

corrugated brand name
display

dump bin

Condiments
Spices & Extracts
Salad Dressing
Shortening & Oils

A STAR IS BORN.
Introducing Maxwell House Instant Decaffeinated

Maxwell House

5

Coffee & Tea
Coffee Filters
Canned & Dry Milk
Flour & Sugar

A STAR IS BORN.
Introducing Maxwell House Instant Decaffeinated

Maxwell House

LANCE SNACK FOOD CENTER

$1.98
or 4 Pair

PEPSI PEPSI PEPSI

shopping cart

cart ad display

end cap/end-of-aisle display

brand name logos

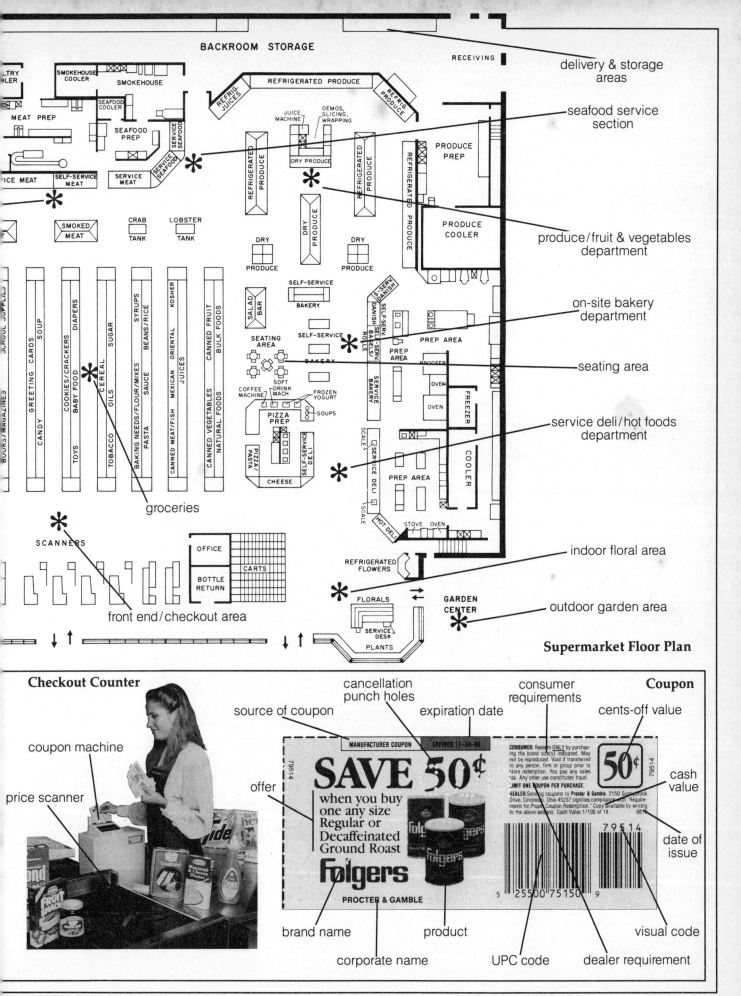

Supermarket Floor Plan

Checkout Counter

Coupon

Other Structures

Barn and Silo

A barn *floor* is divided in the center by a *feed passage* that may be lined with *stanchions* to hold cows. On either side are *manure gutters,* and on each side of these are *mangers, boxes* or *troughs,* from which horses or cattle eat. Hay is stored in a *loft,* a storage room next to the roof. Surrounding a barn is a *yard* with a *manure pit* large enough to back a wagon into. Other barnyard structures, adjoining the main barn or built nearby, include *grain pits,* or *bins; springhouses; smokehouses,* and *pigpens.*

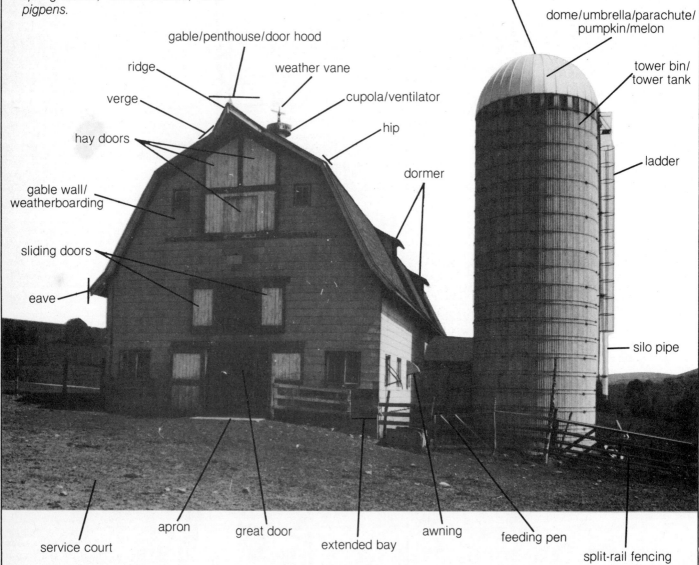

intake

dome/umbrella/parachute/ pumpkin/melon

tower bin/ tower tank

ladder

silo pipe

gable/penthouse/door hood

ridge

weather vane

verge

cupola/ventilator

hip

hay doors

dormer

gable wall/ weatherboarding

sliding doors

eave

service court

apron

great door

extended bay

awning

feeding pen

split-rail fencing

Barn

Silo

Transportation

All the major forms of transportation are incorporated in this section, beginning with the most ubiquitous mode of everyday travel—the automobile. Coverage of the car begins with an illustration of a specially built model displaying all the exterior parts that appear or have appeared on recent designs. Also included is a cutaway drawing that shows the major but often unseen interior components of a car as well as illustrations of a car engine, interior dash and traffic control devices.

The other major subcategories cover public conveyances; emergency, public service and recreational vehicles; boats and ships; aircraft and spacecraft. Vehicles used for military purposes, such as fighting ships and aircraft, are included in this section as well.

Cutaway illustrations have been used to show the reader the interior parts of an ocean liner and the cockpits of a jumbo jet, military fighter and space shuttle.

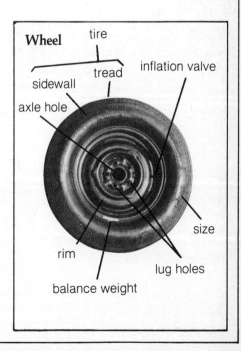

Wheel
tire
sidewall
tread
inflation valve
axle hole
size
rim
balance weight
lug holes

Automobile/Car Exterior

The *body* of this specially designed car, or *customized automobile*, rests on a *chassis* consisting of a *frame* and wheels. Older cars often had *rumble seats* instead of trunks. On *convertibles,* the entire top folds into a compartment called the *boot.* Many contemporary cars have sliding *sun roofs* or *moon roofs.* A *sedan* usually has four doors and full-width front and rear seats. A *coupe* is a smaller version of a sedan, having only two doors. A *station wagon* is a boxlike car with storage space behind the rear seat, which may have *fold-down seats* for additional passenger seating. A high-performance car with a low-slung body is a *sports car.*

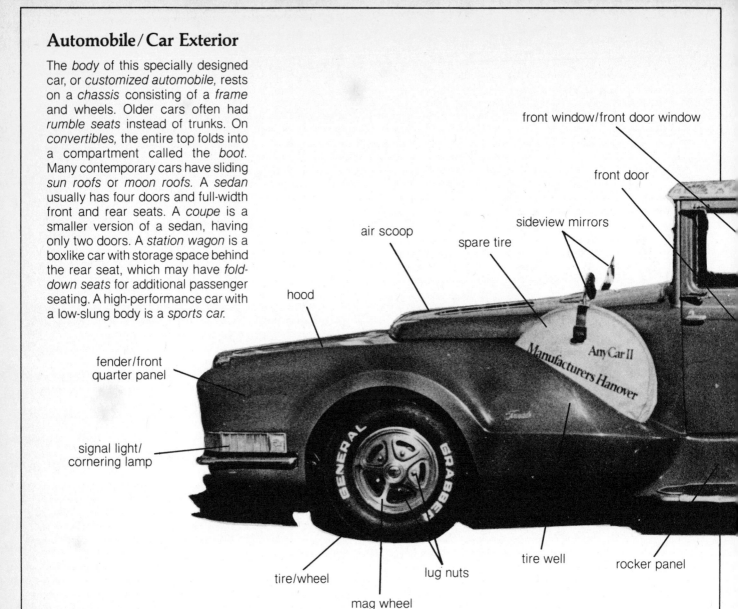

front window/front door window

front door

sideview mirrors

air scoop

spare tire

hood

AnyCar II

Manufacturers Hanover

fender/front quarter panel

signal light/ cornering lamp

GENERAL GRABBER

tire/wheel

lug nuts

mag wheel

tire well

rocker panel

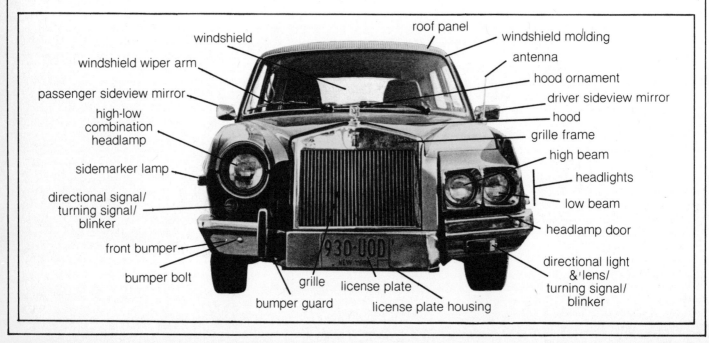

windshield

roof panel

windshield molding

windshield wiper arm

antenna

hood ornament

passenger sideview mirror

driver sideview mirror

high-low combination headlamp

hood

grille frame

high beam

sidemarker lamp

headlights

low beam

directional signal/ turning signal/ blinker

headlamp door

front bumper

directional light & lens/ turning signal/ blinker

bumper bolt

930-00D
NEW YORK

grille

license plate

bumper guard

license plate housing

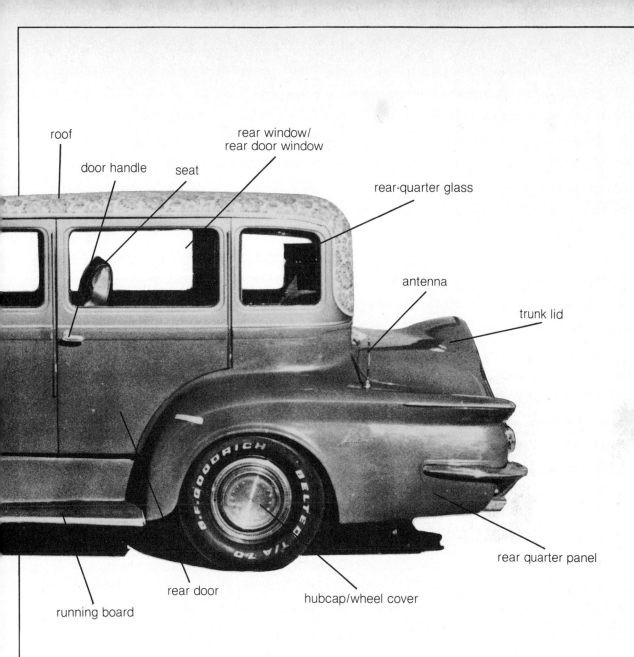

roof

door handle

seat

rear window/
rear door window

rear-quarter glass

antenna

trunk lid

rear quarter panel

running board

rear door

hubcap/wheel cover

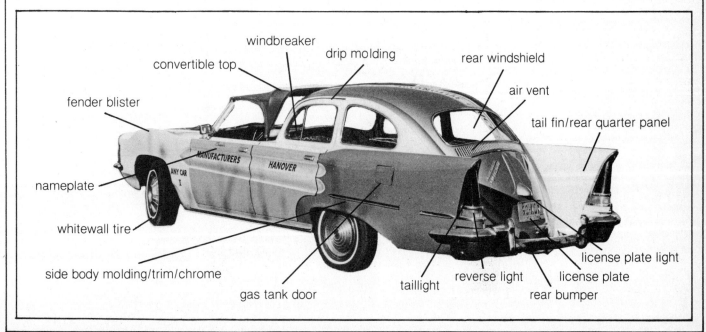

windbreaker

drip molding

convertible top

rear windshield

fender blister

air vent

tail fin/rear quarter panel

nameplate

whitewall tire

side body molding/trim/chrome

gas tank door

taillight

reverse light

license plate light

license plate

rear bumper

Automobile Cutaway

Various systems are incorporated in a car: a *power train*, which consists of *clutch*, transmission, driveshaft and rear axle; a *cooling system* designed to control engine temperature; an *electrical system* to power the engine *starter motor*, accessories and lights; a *suspension system* to provide a smooth ride; and a *braking system*.

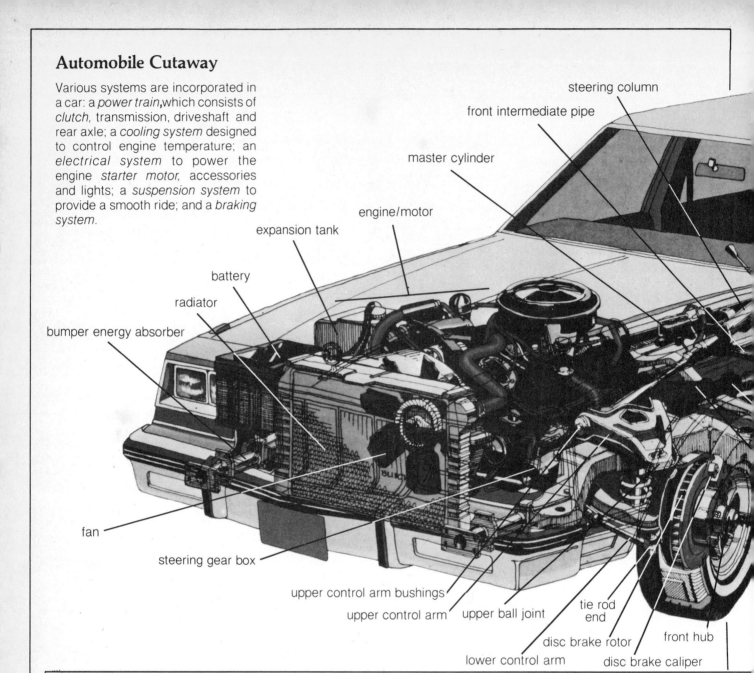

steering column

front intermediate pipe

master cylinder

engine/motor

expansion tank

battery

radiator

bumper energy absorber

fan

steering gear box

upper control arm bushings

upper control arm

upper ball joint

tie rod end

disc brake rotor

front hub

lower control arm

disc brake caliper

Passenger Car Types and Body Styles

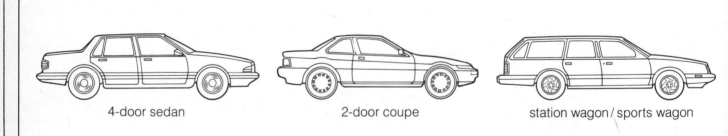

4-door sedan

2-door coupe

station wagon / sports wagon

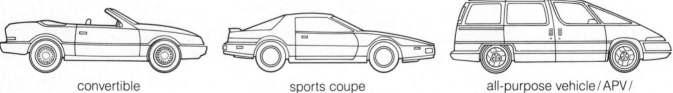

convertible

sports coupe

all-purpose vehicle / APV / minivan / vanogan

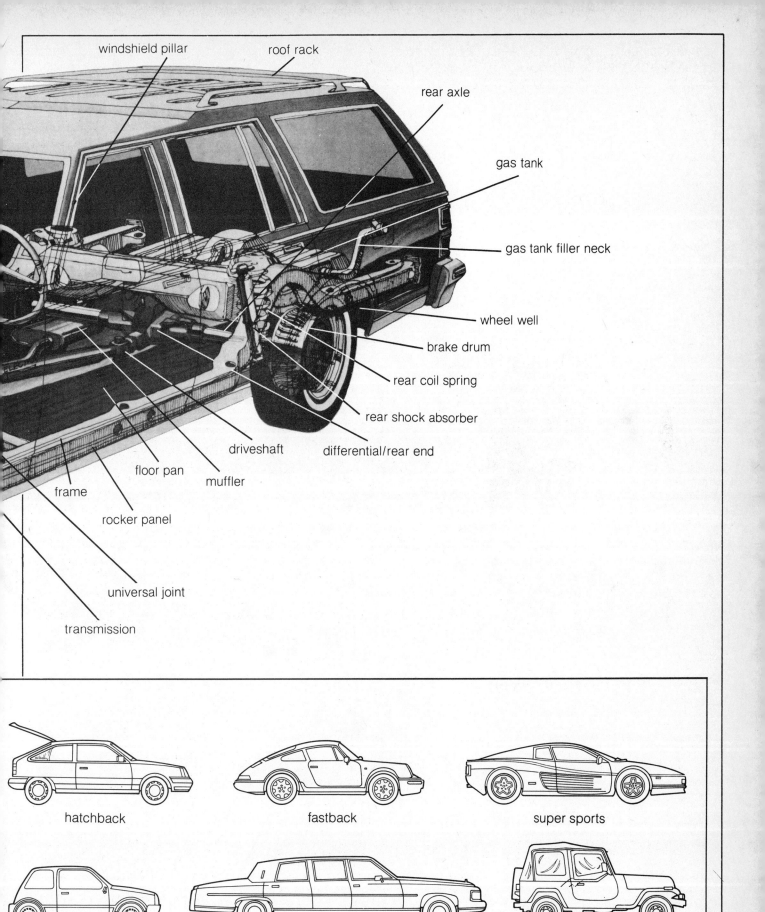

windshield pillar

roof rack

rear axle

gas tank

gas tank filler neck

wheel well

brake drum

rear coil spring

rear shock absorber

differential/rear end

driveshaft

muffler

floor pan

frame

rocker panel

universal joint

transmission

hatchback

fastback

super sports

minicar

limousine/"stretch limo"

recreational vehicle/
4 x 4/"jeep"

Automobile Interior

In addition to parts shown on this *dash*, or *dashboard*, are *headlight* and *warning light controls, hood release, engine choke* and *hand throttle, windshield wiper speed control* and *directional signal switch*. Above the dash, there is usually a *rearview mirror*. Flip-down *sun visors* are located above the windshield. Car seats are equipped with *seat belts* or *safety belts*.

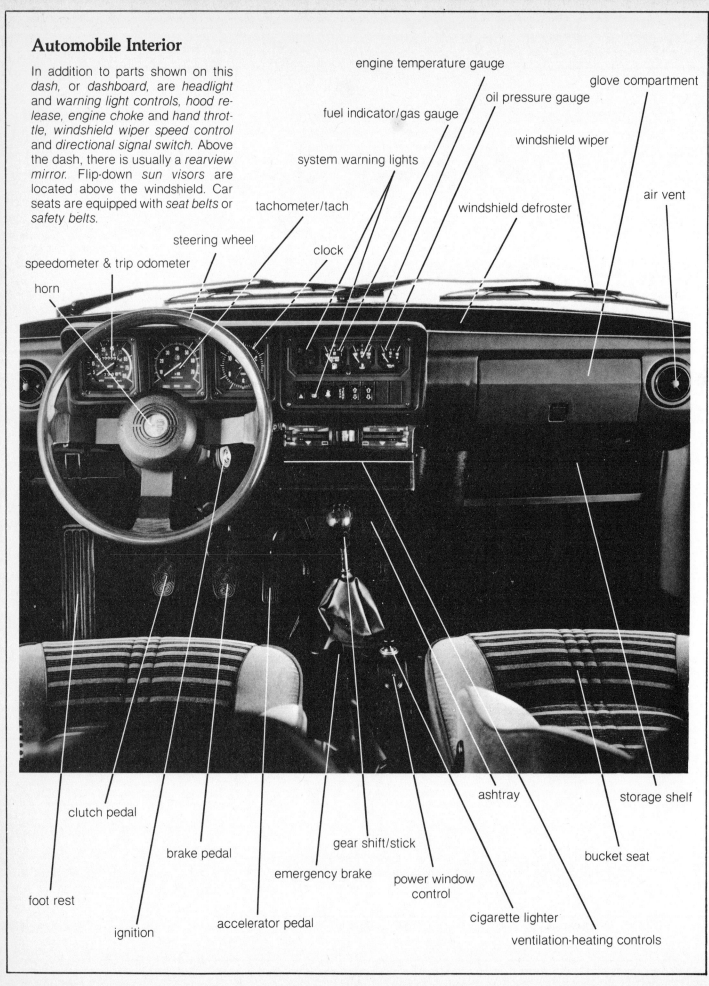

engine temperature gauge

glove compartment

oil pressure gauge

fuel indicator/gas gauge

windshield wiper

system warning lights

air vent

windshield defroster

tachometer/tach

clock

steering wheel

speedometer & trip odometer

horn

clutch pedal

storage shelf

ashtray

bucket seat

brake pedal

gear shift/stick

foot rest

emergency brake

power window control

cigarette lighter

ignition

accelerator pedal

ventilation-heating controls

Automobile Engine

The parts of an engine are fitted into or on the *engine block* or within the *head.* Common engine configurations include the *horizontally opposed,* or *flat four-cylinder;* the *in-line six;* and the *V-8.*

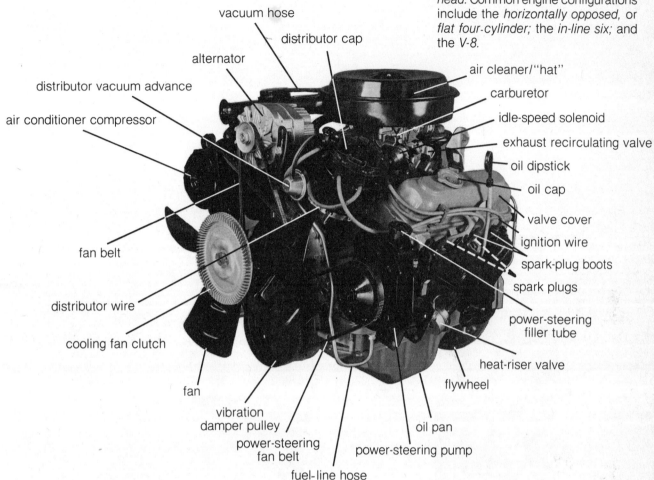

vacuum hose

distributor cap

alternator

distributor vacuum advance

air conditioner compressor

air cleaner/"hat"

carburetor

idle-speed solenoid

exhaust recirculating valve

oil dipstick

oil cap

valve cover

ignition wire

spark-plug boots

spark plugs

power-steering filler tube

heat-riser valve

flywheel

fan belt

distributor wire

cooling fan clutch

fan

vibration damper pulley

power-steering fan belt

fuel-line hose

oil pan

power-steering pump

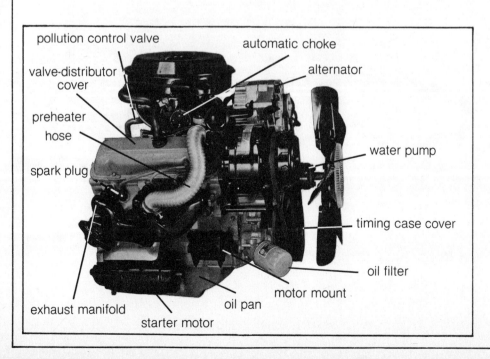

pollution control valve

valve-distributor cover

preheater hose

spark plug

automatic choke

alternator

water pump

timing case cover

oil filter

motor mount

oil pan

exhaust manifold

starter motor

Gasoline Pump

Service station islands can be *self-service* or *full-service*. Gas pumps draw supplies from underground *storage tanks*. Gasoline is purchased in different *grades* determined by *octane number*.

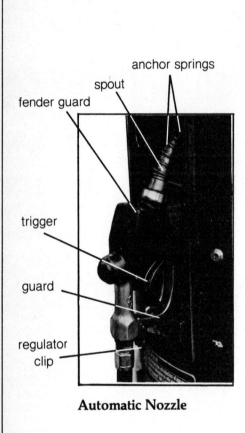

anchor springs

spout

fender guard

trigger

guard

regulator clip

Automatic Nozzle

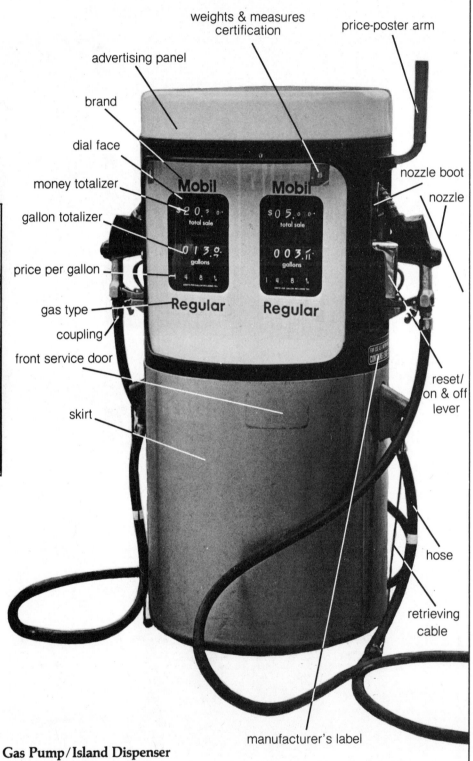

weights & measures certification

price-poster arm

advertising panel

brand

dial face

money totalizer

gallon totalizer

price per gallon

gas type

coupling

front service door

skirt

nozzle boot

nozzle

reset/ on & off lever

hose

retrieving cable

manufacturer's label

Gas Pump/Island Dispenser

Traffic Control Devices

Four-face traffic signals, or lights, are operated manually by a traffic-control official or run automatically by an electric *timer.* Parking meters, set atop *pipe standards,* contain *self-starting timers.* Jammed meters activate a *slot closer* so that additional coins cannot be inserted in the *slot block.* Some meters have a *washer detector* that allows *washers* and *slugs* to pass through without registering time on the *dial.*

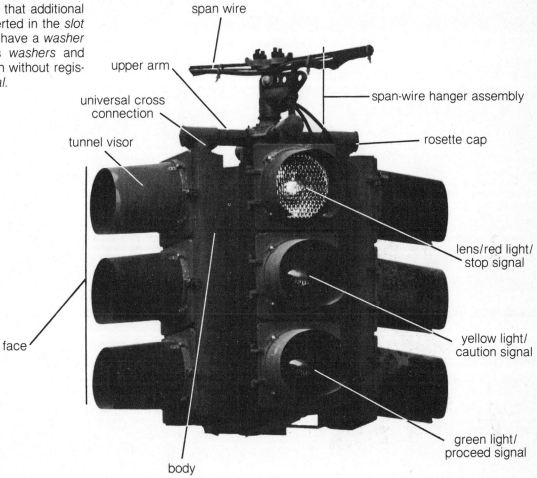

span wire

upper arm

universal cross connection

tunnel visor

span-wire hanger assembly

rosette cap

lens/red light/ stop signal

yellow light/ caution signal

green light/ proceed signal

face

body

Traffic Light

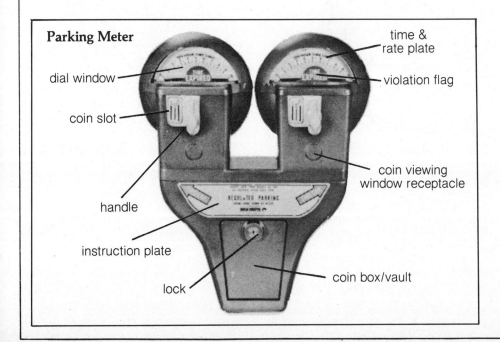

Parking Meter

time & rate plate

dial window

violation flag

coin slot

handle

coin viewing window receptacle

instruction plate

lock

coin box/vault

Highway

Energy absorbing barriers, or *impact attenuation devices,* are positioned in gore areas to reduce accidents. Some roads are lined with *guardrails,* or *railings. Milestones,* or *mile markers,* provide distance information between specific points. Many *expressways, freeways* and *thruways* have *rest areas, scenic overlooks* and *service areas.*

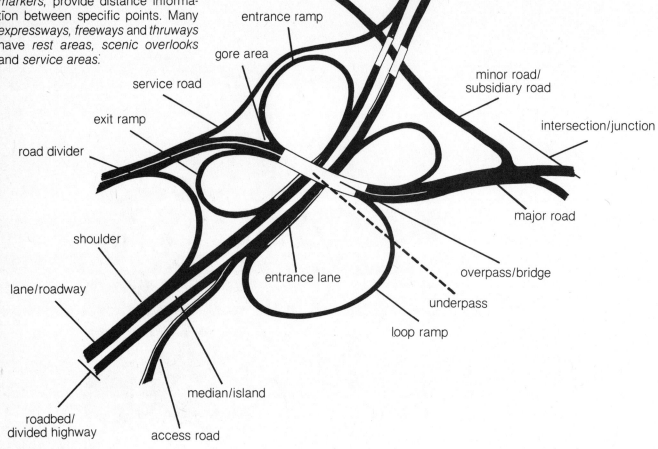

entrance ramp

gore area

service road

exit ramp

road divider

shoulder

lane/roadway

roadbed/
divided highway

access road

median/island

entrance lane

loop ramp

underpass

overpass/bridge

major road

intersection/junction

minor road/
subsidiary road

Cloverleaf / Interchange

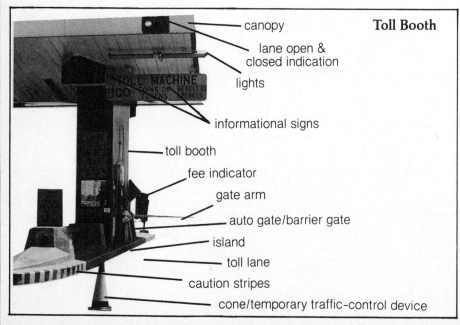

Toll Booth

canopy

lane open &
closed indication

lights

informational signs

toll booth

fee indicator

gate arm

auto gate/barrier gate

island

toll lane

caution stripes

cone/temporary traffic-control device

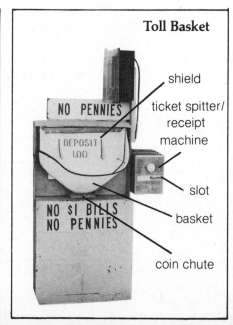

Toll Basket

shield

ticket spitter/
receipt
machine

slot

basket

coin chute

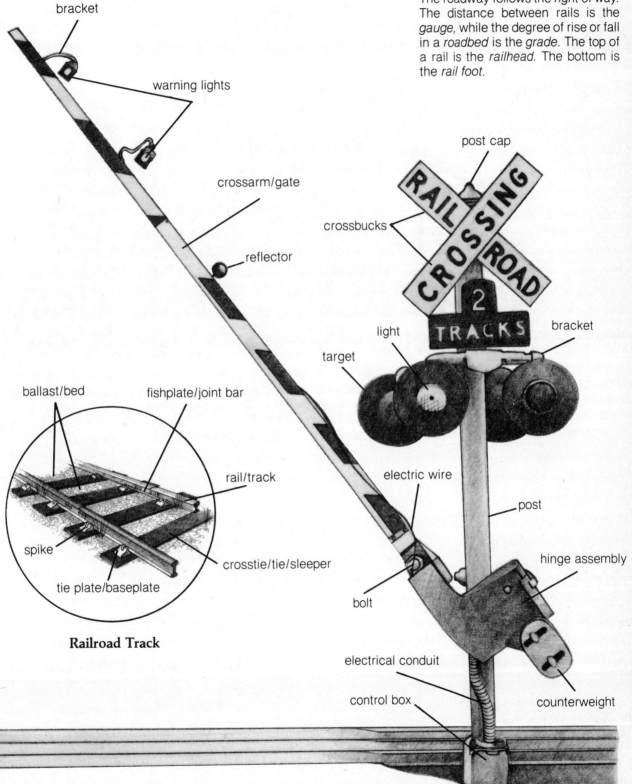

Railroad Crossing

A railroad *roadway* consists of two rails, or tracks, and all their supporting elements, including *railroad bridges, tunnels* and *embankments.* The roadway follows the *right of way.* The distance between rails is the *gauge,* while the degree of rise or fall in a *roadbed* is the *grade.* The top of a rail is the *railhead.* The bottom is the *rail foot.*

bracket

warning lights

crossarm/gate

reflector

post cap

crossbucks

RAIL CROSSING ROAD

2 TRACKS

light

target

bracket

ballast/bed

fishplate/joint bar

rail/track

spike

crosstie/tie/sleeper

tie plate/baseplate

electric wire

post

hinge assembly

bolt

electrical conduit

counterweight

control box

Railroad Track

Crossing Signal

Railroad

In addition to the locomotives shown here, there are *diesel* and *electric locomotives*. *Open-top*, *box* and *flat cars* are the principal types of *freight cars*, while *passenger trains* consist of *coaches*, *buffet* and *dining cars*, *sleeping cars*, *lounge* or *observation cars* and *baggage cars*.

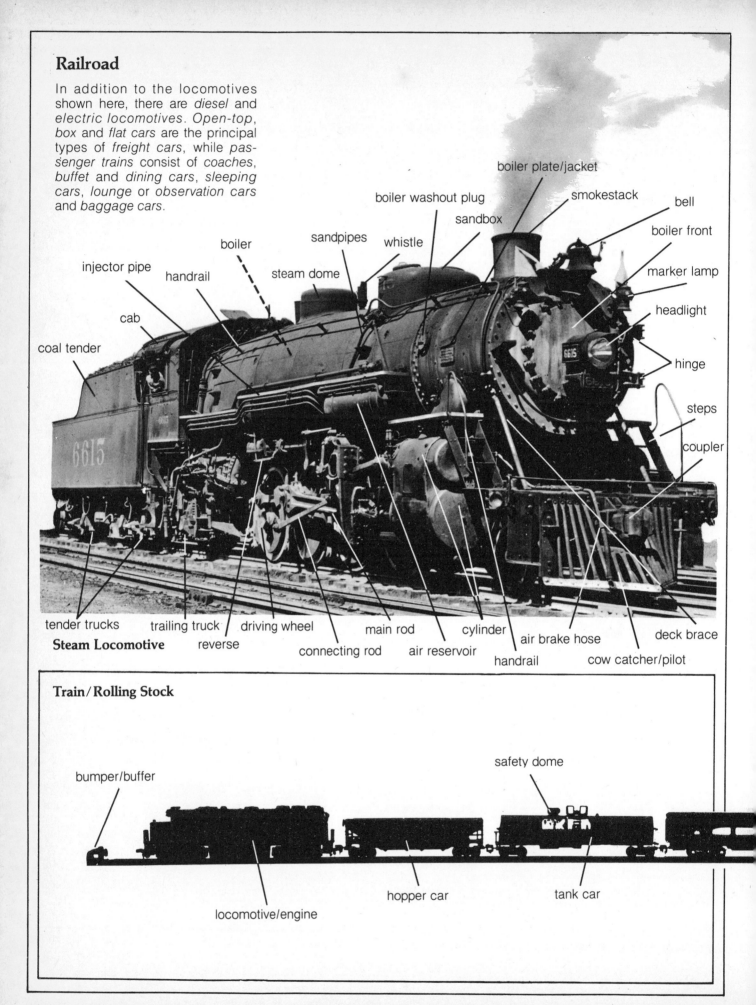

boiler plate/jacket

boiler washout plug

smokestack

bell

sandbox

boiler front

sandpipes

whistle

marker lamp

boiler

headlight

injector pipe

steam dome

handrail

hinge

cab

steps

coal tender

coupler

6615

tender trucks

trailing truck

driving wheel

main rod

cylinder

deck brace

reverse

connecting rod

air reservoir

air brake hose

cow catcher/pilot

handrail

Steam Locomotive

Train/Rolling Stock

bumper/buffer

safety dome

locomotive/engine

hopper car

tank car

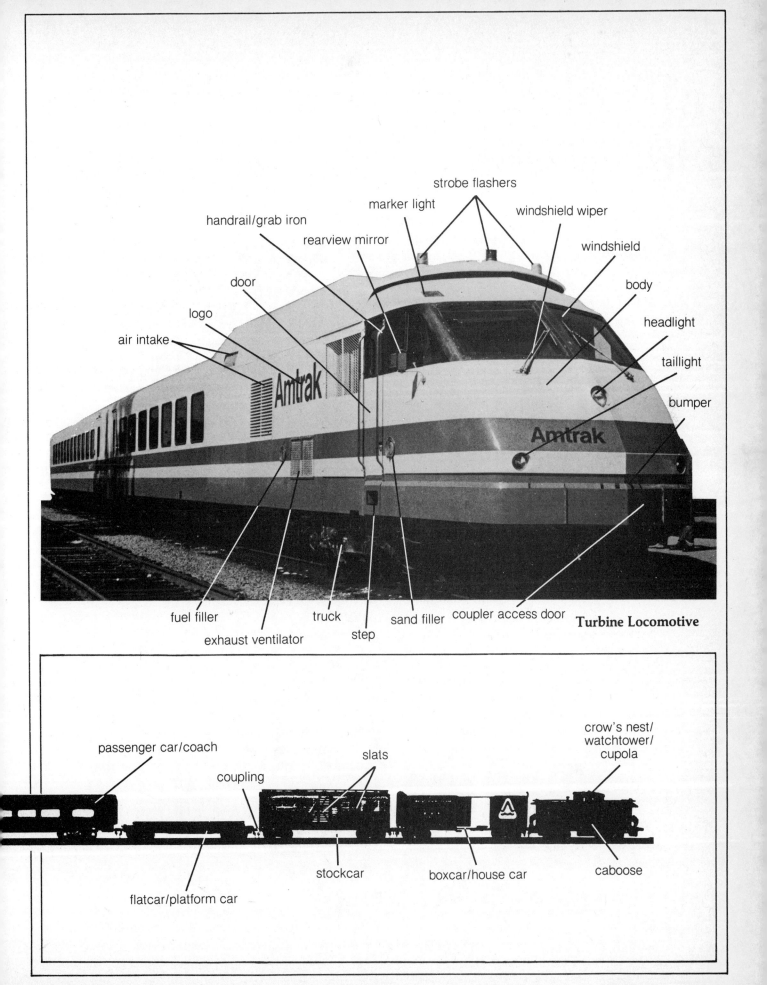

strobe flashers

marker light

windshield wiper

handrail/grab iron

rearview mirror

windshield

body

door

headlight

logo

taillight

air intake

bumper

Amtrak

Amtrak

fuel filler

truck

sand filler

coupler access door

Turbine Locomotive

exhaust ventilator

step

crow's nest/
watchtower/
cupola

passenger car/coach

slats

coupling

stockcar

boxcar/house car

caboose

flatcar/platform car

Bus

Long-distance coaches have airplanelike *reclining seats* with *overhead baggage racks* and *reading lights*. They may also have *lavatories* and *roof ventilation hatches*. *Sightseeing buses* have *transparent roofs*, at least in part, to increase the viewing area.

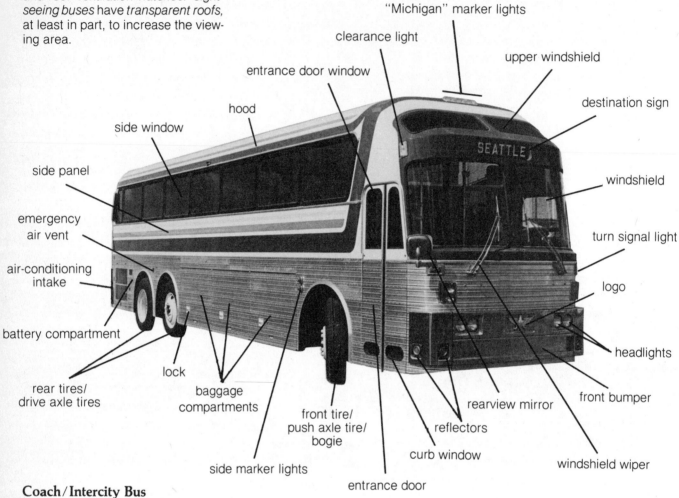

"Michigan" marker lights

clearance light

entrance door window

hood

upper windshield

destination sign

side window

windshield

side panel

turn signal light

emergency air vent

logo

air-conditioning intake

headlights

battery compartment

rear tires/ drive axle tires

lock

baggage compartments

front tire/ push axle tire/ bogie

rearview mirror

front bumper

reflectors

curb window

windshield wiper

side marker lights

entrance door

Coach/Intercity Bus

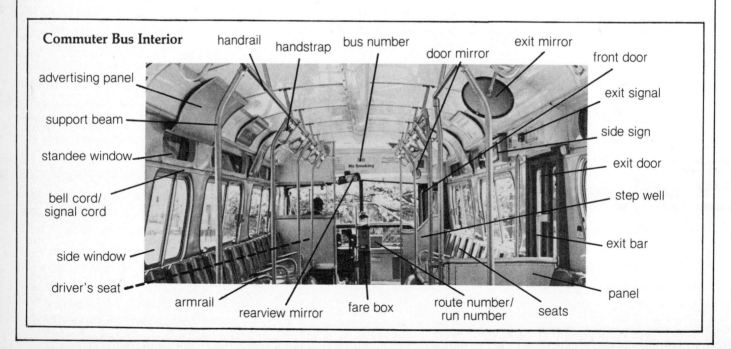

Commuter Bus Interior

handrail

handstrap

bus number

door mirror

exit mirror

front door

advertising panel

exit signal

support beam

side sign

standee window

exit door

bell cord/ signal cord

step well

side window

exit bar

driver's seat

panel

armrail

rearview mirror

fare box

route number/ run number

seats

Subway

A subway, or *rapid transit system*, usually consists of a *train* which derives its power from a *third rail*; subterranean *tunnels*, or *tubes*; *elevated tracks*; and *subway stations*, or *stops*, along each *route*.

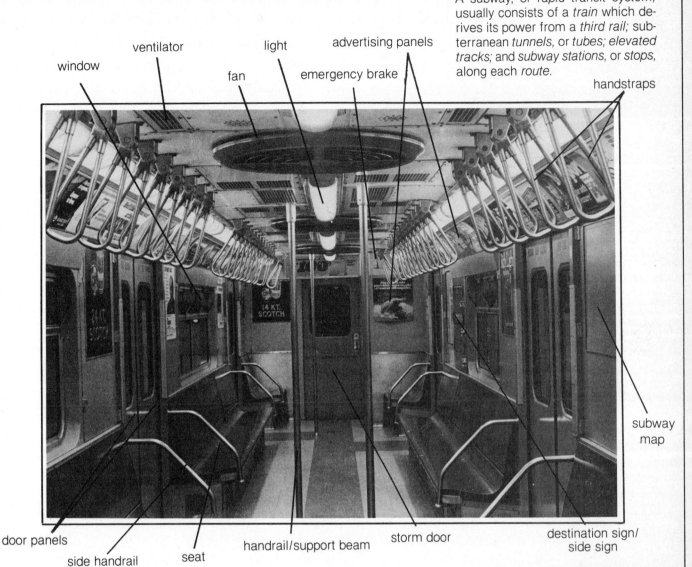

window

ventilator

light

advertising panels

fan

emergency brake

handstraps

door panels

side handrail

seat

handrail/support beam

storm door

destination sign/
side sign

subway map

Taxi Roof Light

off-duty sign

medallion number

OFF 9F8I DUTY

signal light

Motorman's Cab

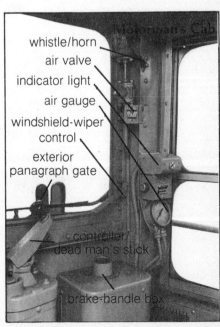

whistle/horn

air valve

indicator light

air gauge

windshield-wiper control

exterior panagraph gate

controller/
dead man's stick

brake-handle box

A *rig* consists of a tractor *coupled* with or *hooked up* to a trailer. A cab may have a partitioned section within, called a *sleeping box,* for the driver, and a *varashield,* a capelike device designed to deflect air and reduce resistance on the trailer, mounted on the roof. The *refrigeration van,* or *reefer,* shown on the opposite page, is a semi, meaning that the tractor bears some of its weight. A true trailer rests and rides on its own wheels.

vertical exhaust

windshield

cab lights

air horn

hood

rearview mirror

parking light/turn signal

assist handle

grille

bumper step

fuel tank

driving light

step

mud flap/ splash guard

tire

wheel

battery box

air compressor

lug

headlight

compressed air tanks

Tractor/Cab

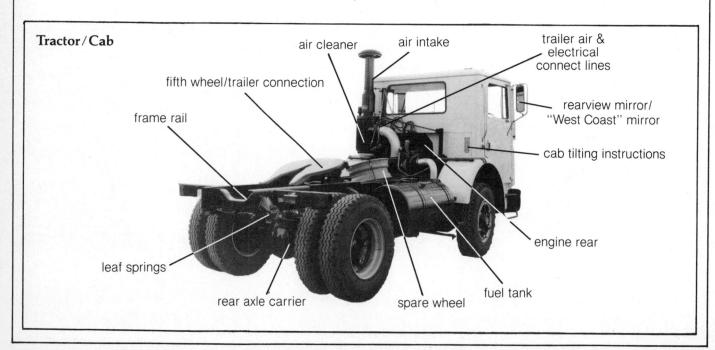

air cleaner

air intake

trailer air & electrical connect lines

fifth wheel/trailer connection

rearview mirror/ "West Coast" mirror

frame rail

cab tilting instructions

engine rear

leaf springs

rear axle carrier

spare wheel

fuel tank

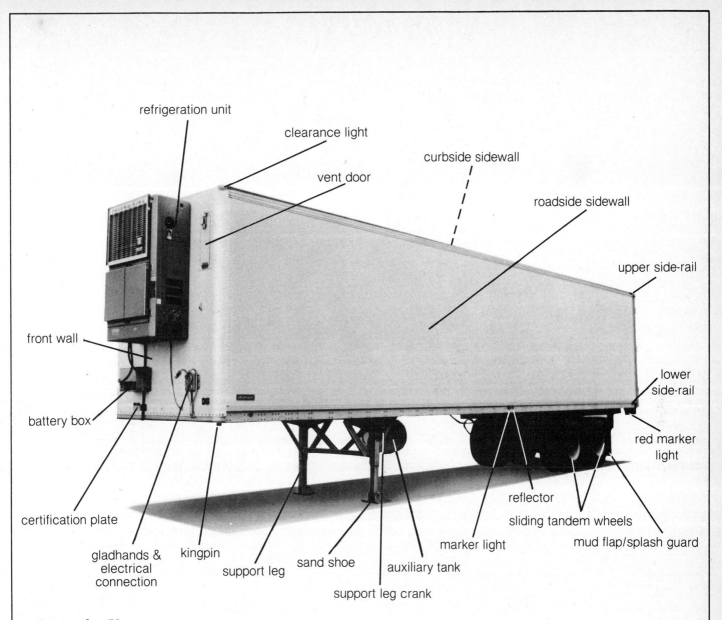

refrigeration unit

clearance light

curbside sidewall

vent door

roadside sidewall

upper side-rail

front wall

lower side-rail

battery box

red marker light

certification plate

reflector

sliding tandem wheels

mud flap/splash guard

gladhands & electrical connection

kingpin

support leg

sand shoe

auxiliary tank

marker light

support leg crank

Semitrailer / Van

Platform / Flat Bed

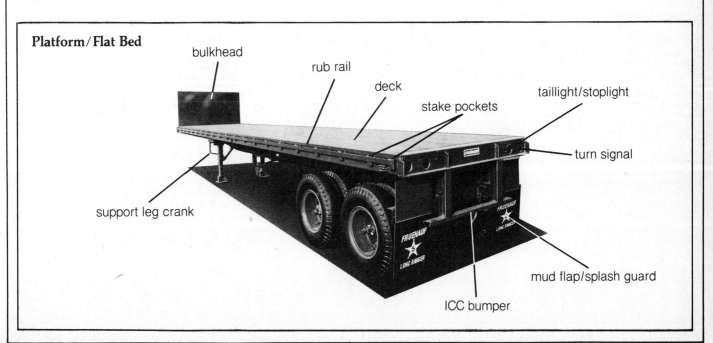

bulkhead

rub rail

deck

stake pockets

taillight/stoplight

turn signal

support leg crank

mud flap/splash guard

ICC bumper

Carriers

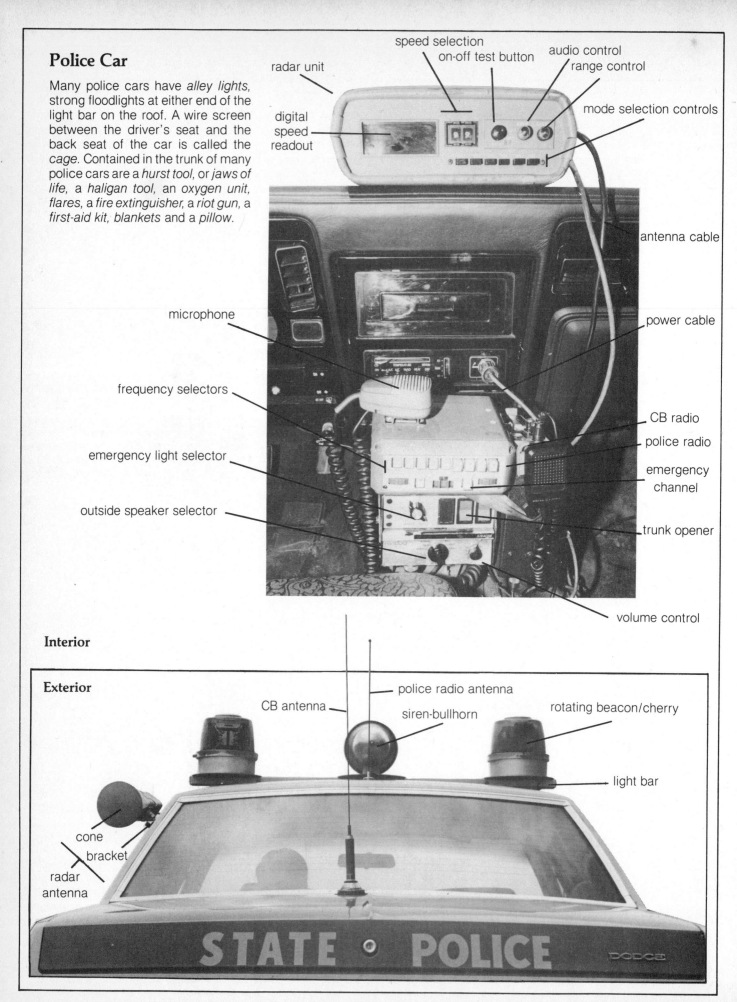

Police Car

Many police cars have *alley lights*, strong floodlights at either end of the light bar on the roof. A wire screen between the driver's seat and the back seat of the car is called the *cage*. Contained in the trunk of many police cars are a *hurst tool*, or *jaws of life*, a *haligan tool*, an *oxygen unit*, *flares*, a *fire extinguisher*, a *riot gun*, a *first-aid kit*, *blankets* and a *pillow*.

radar unit

speed selection
on-off test button

audio control
range control

mode selection controls

digital
speed
readout

antenna cable

microphone

power cable

frequency selectors

CB radio
police radio

emergency light selector

emergency
channel

outside speaker selector

trunk opener

volume control

Interior

Exterior

police radio antenna

CB antenna

siren-bullhorn

rotating beacon/cherry

light bar

cone
bracket

radar
antenna

STATE • POLICE

DODGE

Additional equipment carried inside *advanced life-support units,* such as the one shown here, are *burn sheets, gauze, emesis basins, cervical collars, neck rolls, bitee sticks, tongue blades, peroxide* and *alcohol, extension tubes,* additional *oxygen tanks, splints, sandbags* (for traction), *linens,* a *scoop stretcher* and a *carrying chair.*

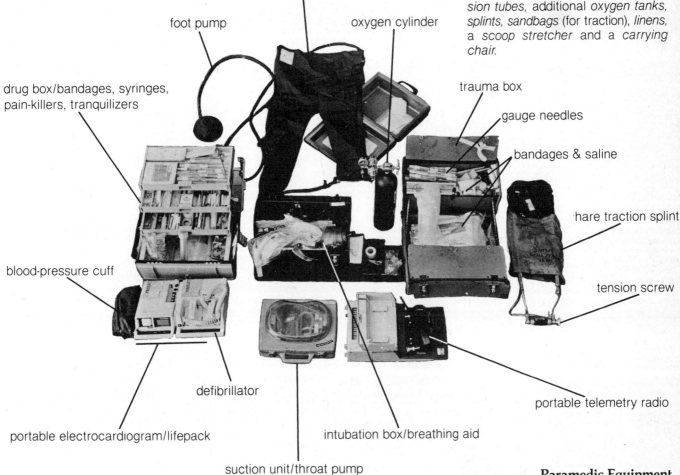

inflatable anti-shock trousers

foot pump

oxygen cylinder

trauma box

gauge needles

drug box/bandages, syringes, pain-killers, tranquilizers

bandages & saline

hare traction splint

blood-pressure cuff

tension screw

defibrillator

portable telemetry radio

portable electrocardiogram/lifepack

intubation box/breathing aid

suction unit/throat pump

Paramedic Equipment

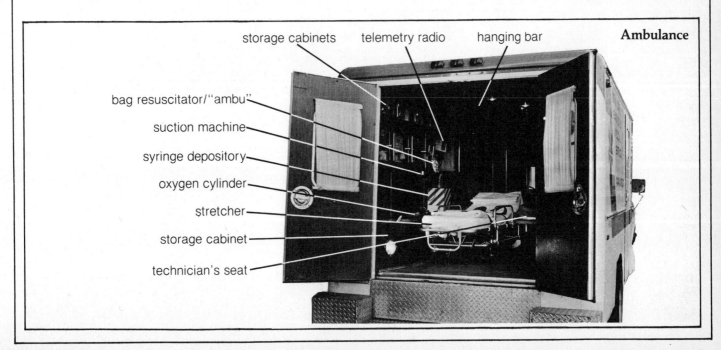

Ambulance

storage cabinets

telemetry radio

hanging bar

bag resuscitator/"ambu"

suction machine

syringe depository

oxygen cylinder

stretcher

storage cabinet

technician's seat

Emergency Vehicles

Fire Engine

On a fire truck, the entire tower ladder and control platform revolve on a *turntable*. Contained within a pumper is a water *booster tank* for fighting small fires, a *booster hose-reel*, for letting out hose line, and an *extension ladder*. Most fire fighting *apparatus* also carry *air tanks*, *lift-nets*, *EMT*, or *first aid boxes*, and *smoke ejectors*.

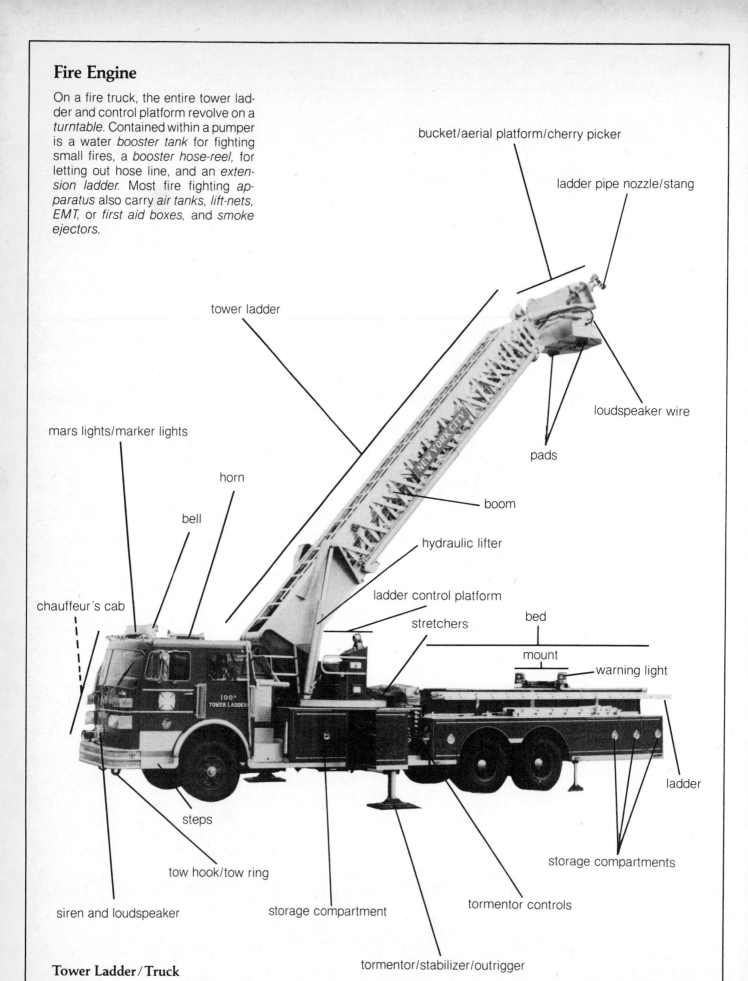

bucket/aerial platform/cherry picker

ladder pipe nozzle/stang

tower ladder

loudspeaker wire

pads

boom

mars lights/marker lights

horn

bell

hydraulic lifter

ladder control platform

bed

stretchers

mount

warning light

chauffeur's cab

steps

tow hook/tow ring

storage compartment

tormentor controls

ladder

storage compartments

siren and loudspeaker

tormentor/stabilizer/outrigger

Tower Ladder/Truck

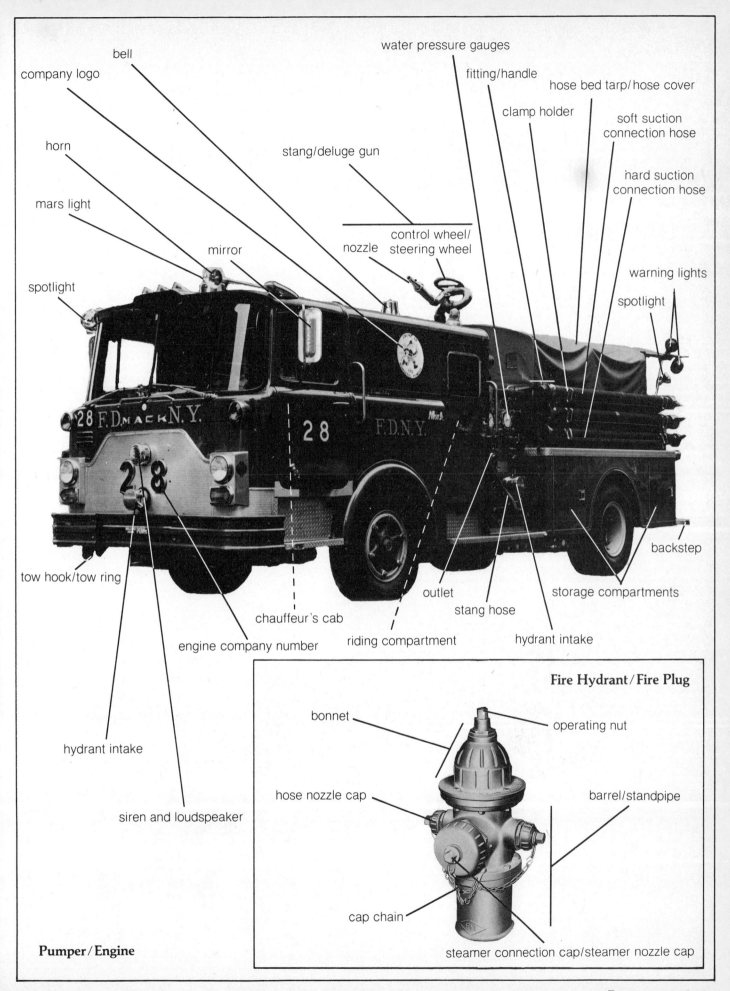

bell

company logo

horn

mars light

spotlight

mirror

stang/deluge gun

water pressure gauges

fitting/handle

clamp holder

hose bed tarp/hose cover

soft suction
connection hose

hard suction
connection hose

nozzle

control wheel/
steering wheel

warning lights

spotlight

tow hook/tow ring

chauffeur's cab

engine company number

riding compartment

outlet

stang hose

hydrant intake

storage compartments

backstep

hydrant intake

siren and loudspeaker

Fire Hydrant/Fire Plug

bonnet

operating nut

hose nozzle cap

barrel/standpipe

cap chain

steamer connection cap/steamer nozzle cap

Pumper/Engine

Emergency Vehicles

Tow Truck/Wrecker

Tow trucks, or *rigs,* that respond to accident reports are called "chasers." A fully-equipped tow truck carries *fire extinguishers, battery charger, battery jumper cables,* and a two-pronged *lockout tool* which enables the operator to open locked car doors.

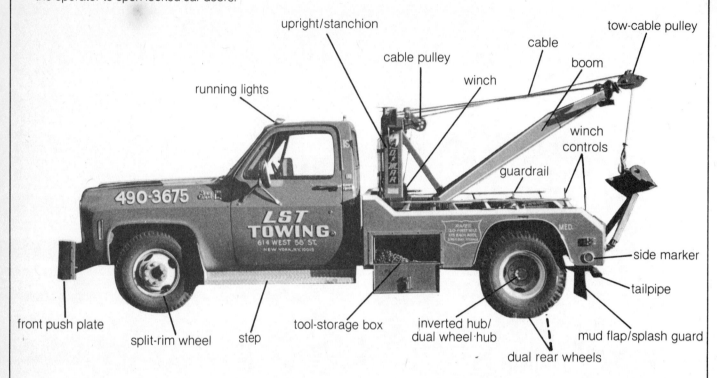

upright/stanchion

cable pulley

winch

cable

boom

tow-cable pulley

running lights

winch controls

guardrail

side marker

tailpipe

front push plate

split-rim wheel

step

tool-storage box

inverted hub/ dual wheel·hub

dual rear wheels

mud flap/splash guard

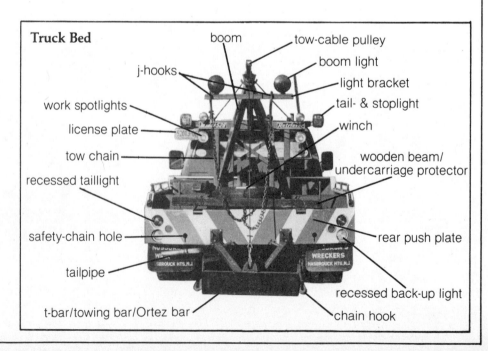

Truck Bed

boom

tow-cable pulley

j-hooks

boom light

light bracket

work spotlights

tail- & stoplight

license plate

winch

tow chain

wooden beam/ undercarriage protector

recessed taillight

safety-chain hole

rear push plate

tailpipe

recessed back-up light

t-bar/towing bar/Ortez bar

chain hook

Sanitation Vehicles

Garbage collectors, sanitation men, or *"sanmen,"* also use a large, water-carrying truck called a *flusher* to wet down and clean streets.

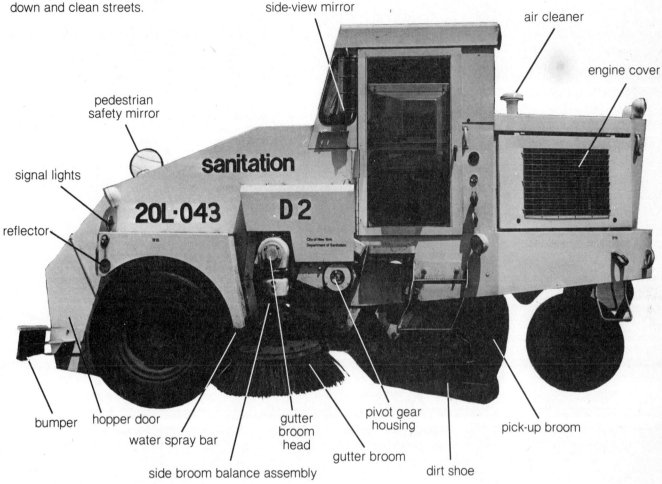

side-view mirror

air cleaner

engine cover

pedestrian safety mirror

signal lights

sanitation

20L·043

D 2

reflector

bumper

hopper door

water spray bar

side broom balance assembly

gutter broom head

gutter broom

pivot gear housing

dirt shoe

pick-up broom

Mechanical Sweeper/Street Cleaner

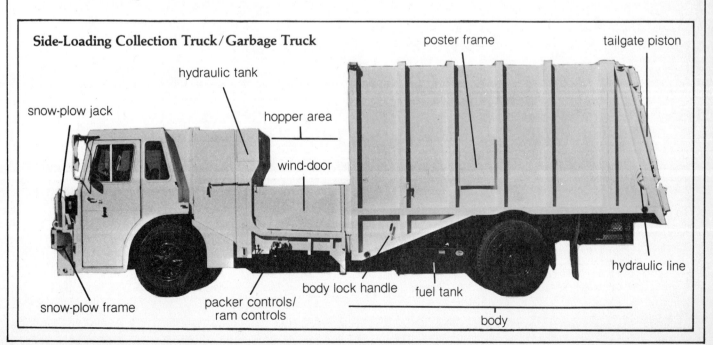

Side-Loading Collection Truck/Garbage Truck

poster frame

tailgate piston

hydraulic tank

snow-plow jack

hopper area

wind-door

snow-plow frame

packer controls/ ram controls

body lock handle

fuel tank

body

hydraulic line

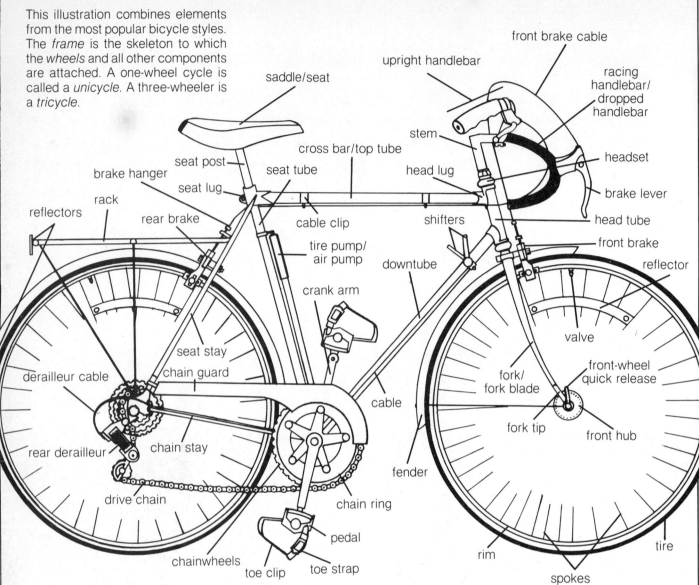

Bicycle

This illustration combines elements from the most popular bicycle styles. The *frame* is the skeleton to which the *wheels* and all other components are attached. A one-wheel cycle is called a *unicycle*. A three-wheeler is a *tricycle*.

saddle/seat

upright handlebar

front brake cable

racing handlebar/ dropped handlebar

stem

headset

cross bar/top tube

head lug

brake hanger

seat tube

seat post

brake lever

seat lug

shifters

head tube

rack

reflectors

rear brake

cable clip

front brake

reflector

tire pump/ air pump

downtube

crank arm

valve

seat stay

front-wheel quick release

derailleur cable

chain guard

fork/ fork blade

rear derailleur

chain stay

fork tip

front hub

cable

drive chain

fender

chain ring

chainwheels

pedal

toe clip

toe strap

rim

spokes

tire

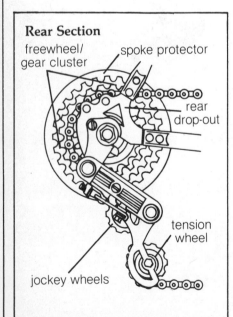

Rear Section

freewheel/ gear cluster

spoke protector

rear drop-out

rear derailleur

tension wheel

jockey wheels

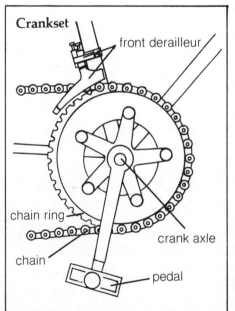

Crankset

front derailleur

chain ring

crank axle

chain

pedal

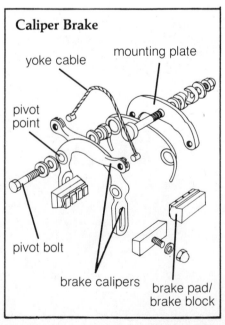

Caliper Brake

yoke cable

mounting plate

pivot point

pivot bolt

brake calipers

brake pad/ brake block

Motorcycle

Motorcycle accessories include *fairing*, a molded wind deflector, *sissy bar*, a passenger backrest, and storage containers called *saddlebags*, or *panier cases*. A motorcycle for off-the-road use is called a *trail bike* or *dirt bike*. A *sidestand*, *kickstand* or *centerstand* holds the motorcycle upright when not in use.

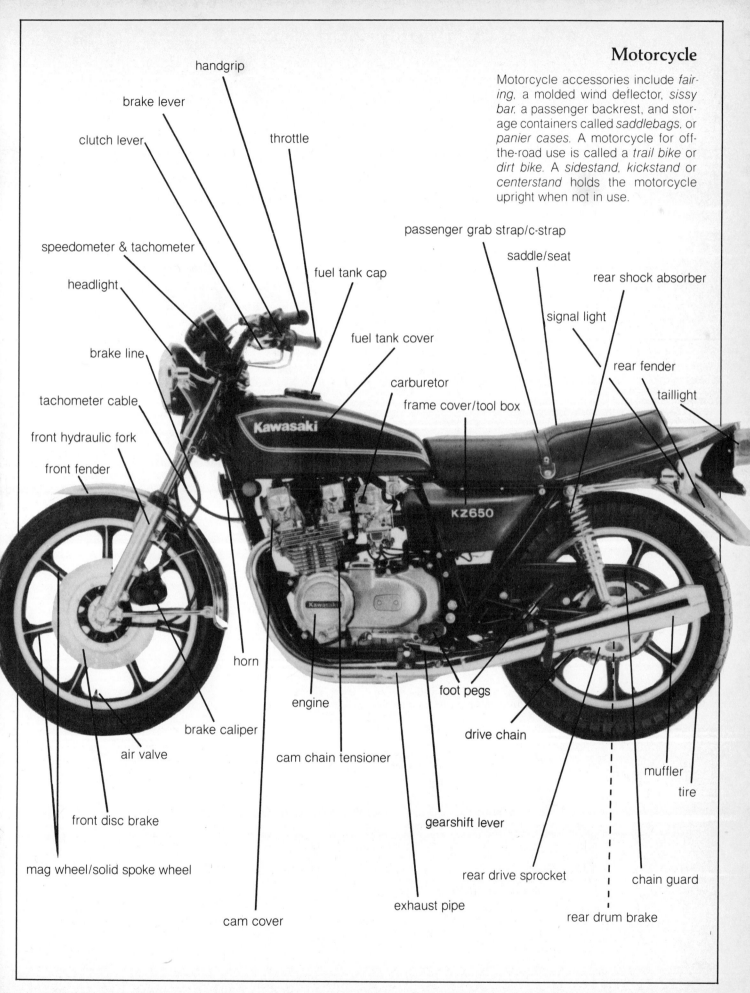

handgrip

brake lever

clutch lever

throttle

speedometer & tachometer

headlight

fuel tank cap

brake line

fuel tank cover

tachometer cable

carburetor

front hydraulic fork

frame cover/tool box

front fender

passenger grab strap/c-strap

saddle/seat

rear shock absorber

signal light

rear fender

taillight

KZ650

horn

brake caliper

air valve

engine

cam chain tensioner

front disc brake

mag wheel/solid spoke wheel

cam cover

exhaust pipe

foot pegs

drive chain

gearshift lever

rear drive sprocket

rear drum brake

chain guard

muffler

tire

Recreational Vehicles

The *heating* and *cooking units* in the rear *coach* of a camper run on *propane gas.* Unlike campers, which run under their own power, *trailers* are hitched behind a vehicle and towed. Other *off-the-road vehicles* include *four-wheel drive jeeps* and *dune buggies.*

running lights

side window

roof air conditioner

luggage rack

front window

side window

water fill

road light

sewer valve

fuel tank

power-cord compartment

hot water heater

storage compartment

Camper / Motor Home

Snowmobile

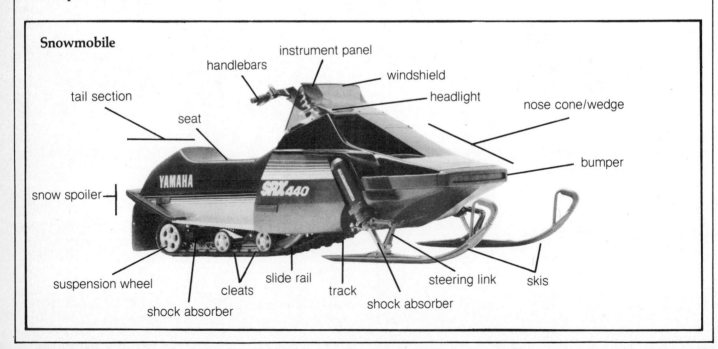

instrument panel

handlebars

windshield

headlight

nose cone/wedge

tail section

seat

bumper

snow spoiler

suspension wheel

cleats

slide rail

track

steering link

skis

shock absorber

shock absorber

Horse-drawn Carriages

Stagecoaches were drawn by teams of horses and commanded by a *driver* called the *whip*, *Charlie* or *Jehu*. Protection was provided by a *guard*, or *shotgun*. A *buggy* was four-wheeled. A *gig* had two wheels. A *buckboard* had a spring-supported seat attached to a board directly connected to the axles. A *cabriolet* was a *hackney carriage*, or *cab*, with only two wheels and a folding top.

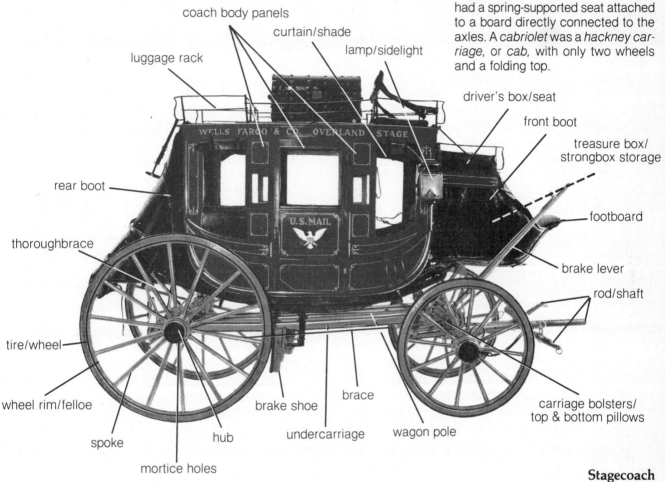

coach body panels

curtain/shade

lamp/sidelight

luggage rack

driver's box/seat

front boot

treasure box/ strongbox storage

WELLS FARGO & CO. OVERLAND STAGE

rear boot

footboard

U.S. MAIL

brake lever

thoroughbrace

rod/shaft

tire/wheel

wheel rim/felloe

brake shoe

brace

carriage bolsters/ top & bottom pillows

spoke

hub

undercarriage

wagon pole

mortice holes

Stagecoach

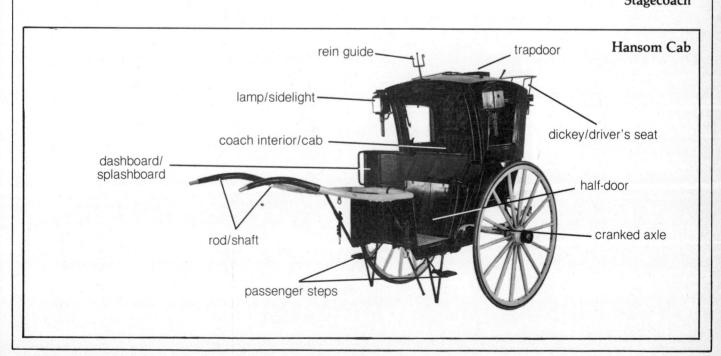

Hansom Cab

rein guide

trapdoor

lamp/sidelight

coach interior/cab

dickey/driver's seat

dashboard/ splashboard

half-door

cranked axle

rod/shaft

passenger steps

Carriages

Nautical Terminology

The outer shell of a boat is the *hull*. A hull's greatest width is the *beam*. Any line running from one side of a boat to the other is said to run *athwartships*. That part of a boat facing the direction from which the wind is blowing is called the *windward* side. The opposite side is called the *leeward* side.

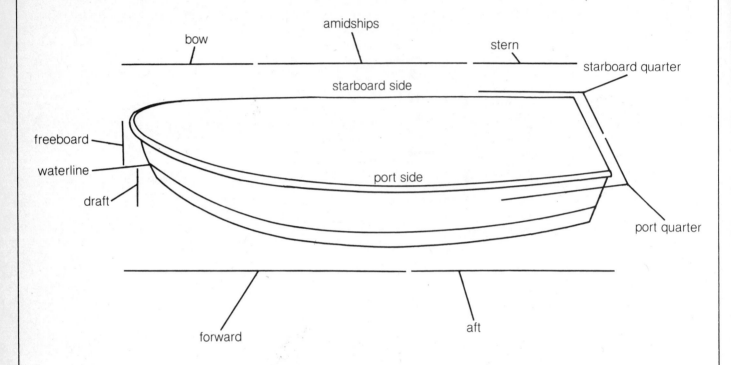

amidships

bow

stern

starboard quarter

starboard side

freeboard

waterline

port side

draft

port quarter

forward

aft

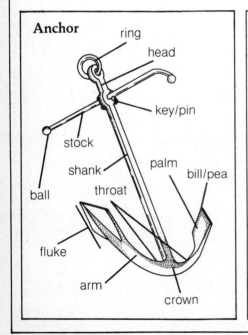

Anchor

ring

head

key/pin

stock

shank

palm

bill/pea

ball

throat

fluke

arm

crown

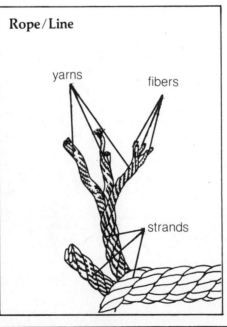

Rope/Line

yarns

fibers

strands

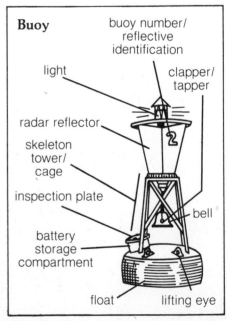

Buoy

buoy number/ reflective identification

light

clapper/ tapper

radar reflector

skeleton tower/ cage

inspection plate

bell

battery storage compartment

float

lifting eye

Rowboat

Any small *craft*, either *decked* or *open* and propelled by oars, is a rowboat, or *skiff*. If it is used to service a *yacht* or *motor cruiser*, it is called a *dinghy*, *dink* or *tender*.

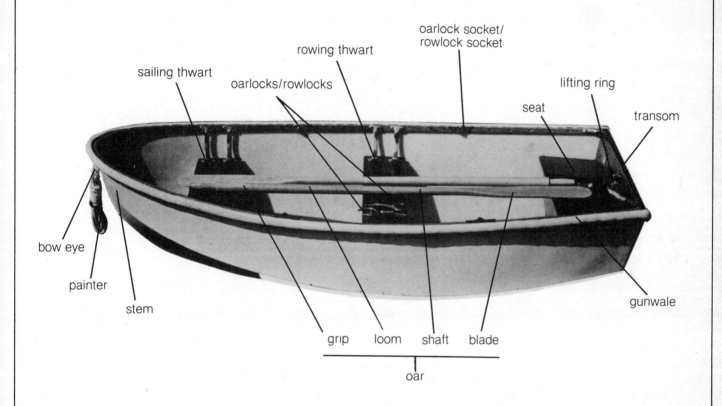

sailing thwart

oarlocks/rowlocks

rowing thwart

oarlock socket/
rowlock socket

lifting ring

seat

transom

bow eye

painter

stem

grip   loom   shaft   blade

oar

gunwale

Inflatable

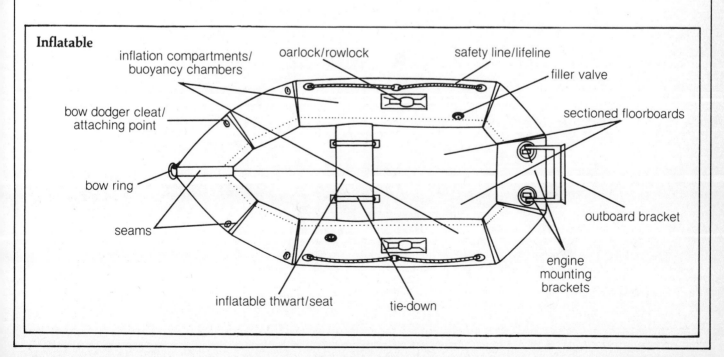

inflation compartments/
buoyancy chambers

oarlock/rowlock

safety line/lifeline

filler valve

bow dodger cleat/
attaching point

sectioned floorboards

bow ring

seams

outboard bracket

engine
mounting
brackets

inflatable thwart/seat

tie-down

Boats and Ships

Sailboat

Standing rigging, shrouds and stays, keep a sailing vessel's mast, or *spar,* upright. *Halyards* are used to hoist sails and *running rigging,* lines and *sheets,* control them. On some boats a *tiller* is used instead of a wheel to steer.

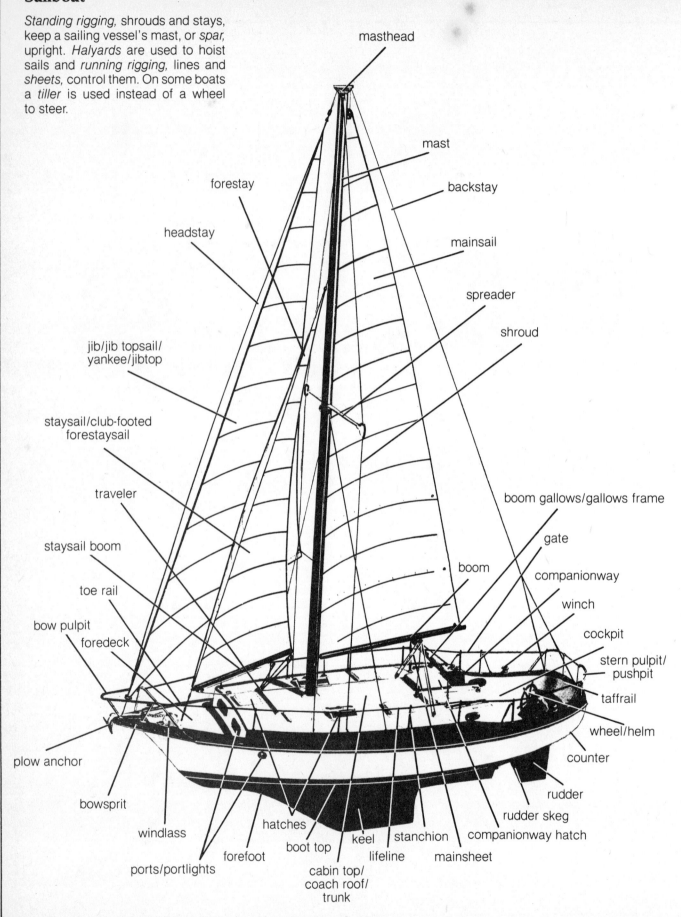

masthead

mast

backstay

forestay

mainsail

headstay

spreader

shroud

jib/jib topsail/
yankee/jibtop

staysail/club-footed
forestaysail

boom gallows/gallows frame

traveler

gate

companionway

staysail boom

boom

winch

toe rail

cockpit

bow pulpit

stern pulpit/
pushpit

foredeck

taffrail

wheel/helm

counter

plow anchor

rudder

bowsprit

rudder skeg

windlass

hatches

keel

stanchion

companionway hatch

forefoot

boot top

lifeline

mainsheet

ports/portlights

cabin top/
coach roof/
trunk

Sailboat Accommodations

The area between a vessel's cabin sole and its hull is called the *bilge*. Boats with overnight accommodations usually have a *navigator's station*, featuring a *chart table*.

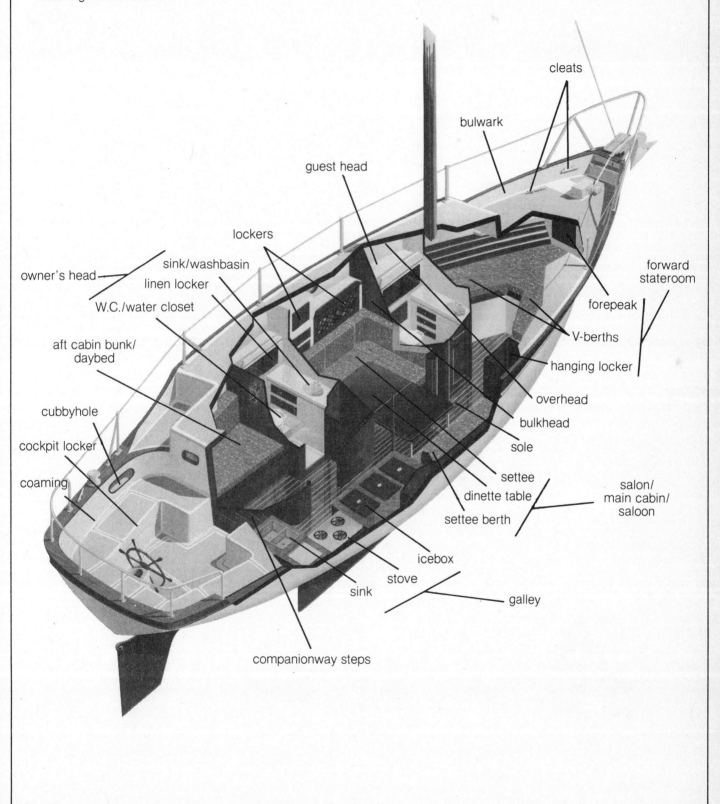

cleats

bulwark

guest head

lockers

sink/washbasin

owner's head

linen locker

W.C./water closet

aft cabin bunk/ daybed

cubbyhole

cockpit locker

coaming

forward stateroom

forepeak

V-berths

hanging locker

overhead

bulkhead

sole

settee

dinette table

settee berth

salon/ main cabin/ saloon

icebox

stove

sink

galley

companionway steps

Sail

Sails fall into two broad categories: *standing sails,* or *suits of sails,* and extras. Standing sails, such as those found on a modern *sloop,* would be mainsail and *headsail,* or *jib.* Extras, set to keep the vessel moving at optimum speed, include *spinnakers,* and, in bad weather, *trysails.* There are two types of compass: the *magnetic compass,* shown below, and the electrically-driven *gyro compass.*

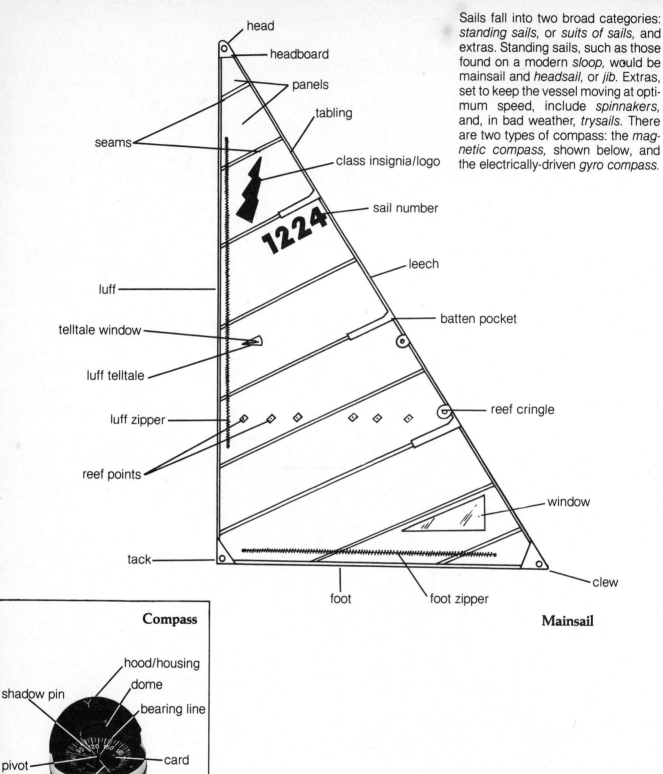

head
headboard
panels
tabling
seams
class insignia/logo
sail number
1224
leech
luff
batten pocket
telltale window
luff telltale
reef cringle
luff zipper
reef points
window
tack
clew
foot
foot zipper

Mainsail

Compass

hood/housing
dome
shadow pin
bearing line
pivot
card
lubber's line
binnacle
corrector magnet controls

Outboard Engine

Three basic types of engines are used to power vessels: outboards, *inboard-outboards,* or *sterndrives,* and *inboards.* A marine sextant, a successor to the *octant* and *quadrant,* is used to measure the angle between a celestial body and the earth's horizon to help mariners determine their position at sea.

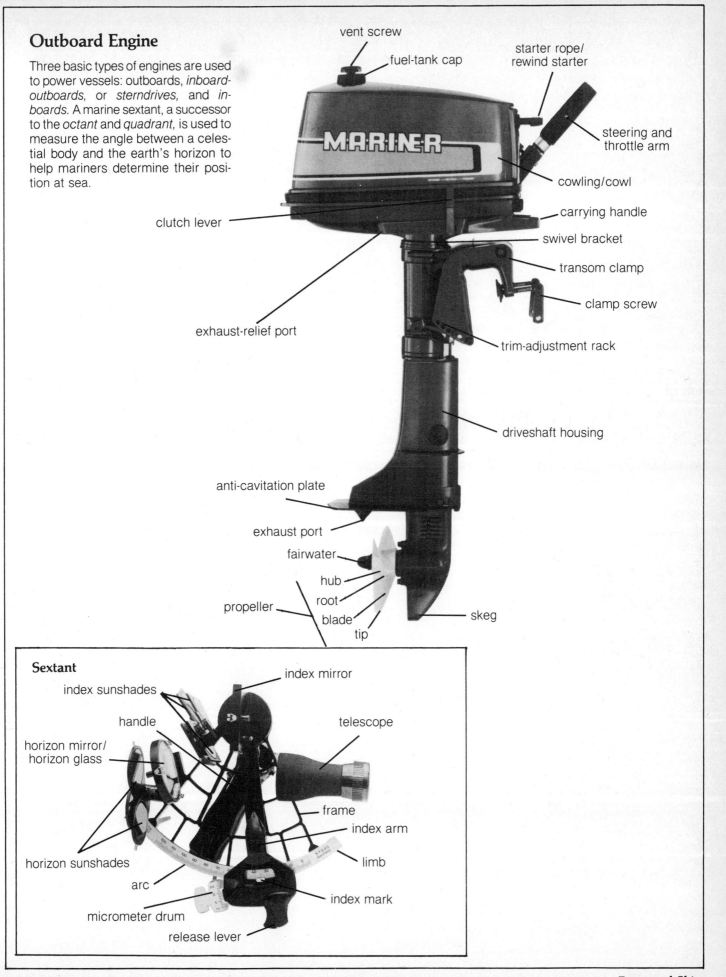

vent screw

fuel-tank cap

starter rope/ rewind starter

MARINER

steering and throttle arm

cowling/cowl

clutch lever

carrying handle

swivel bracket

transom clamp

clamp screw

exhaust-relief port

trim-adjustment rack

driveshaft housing

anti-cavitation plate

exhaust port

fairwater

hub

root

propeller

blade

skeg

tip

Sextant

index sunshades

index mirror

handle

telescope

horizon mirror/ horizon glass

frame

index arm

limb

horizon sunshades

arc

index mark

micrometer drum

release lever

Boats and Ships

Powerboat

There are basically two kinds of powerboat *hull forms: displacement* and *planing.* Within these categories there are *V-bottom, cathedral, gull-wing, flat-bottom* and *round-bottom hulls. Houseboats* are boxlike vessels designed to provide maximum living space aboard. Projecting steel fittings used to hoist and carry a dinghy on a yacht are called *davits.*

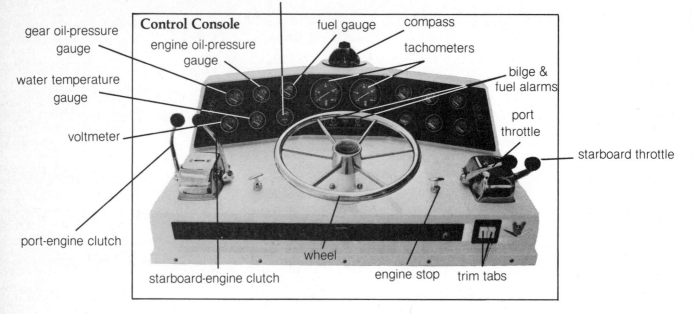

Control Console

gear oil-pressure gauge

engine oil-pressure gauge

water temperature gauge

voltmeter

port-engine clutch

starboard-engine clutch

engine hour meter

fuel gauge

compass

tachometers

bilge & fuel alarms

port throttle

starboard throttle

wheel

engine stop

trim tabs

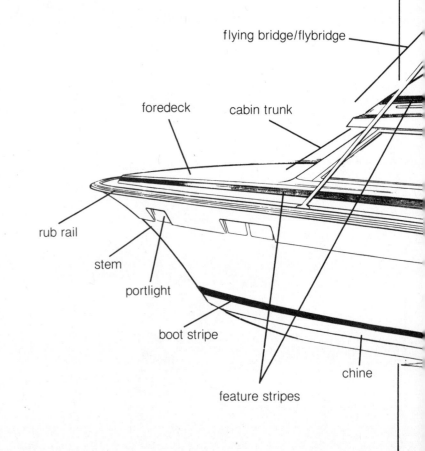

flying bridge/flybridge

foredeck

cabin trunk

rub rail

stem

portlight

boot stripe

chine

feature stripes

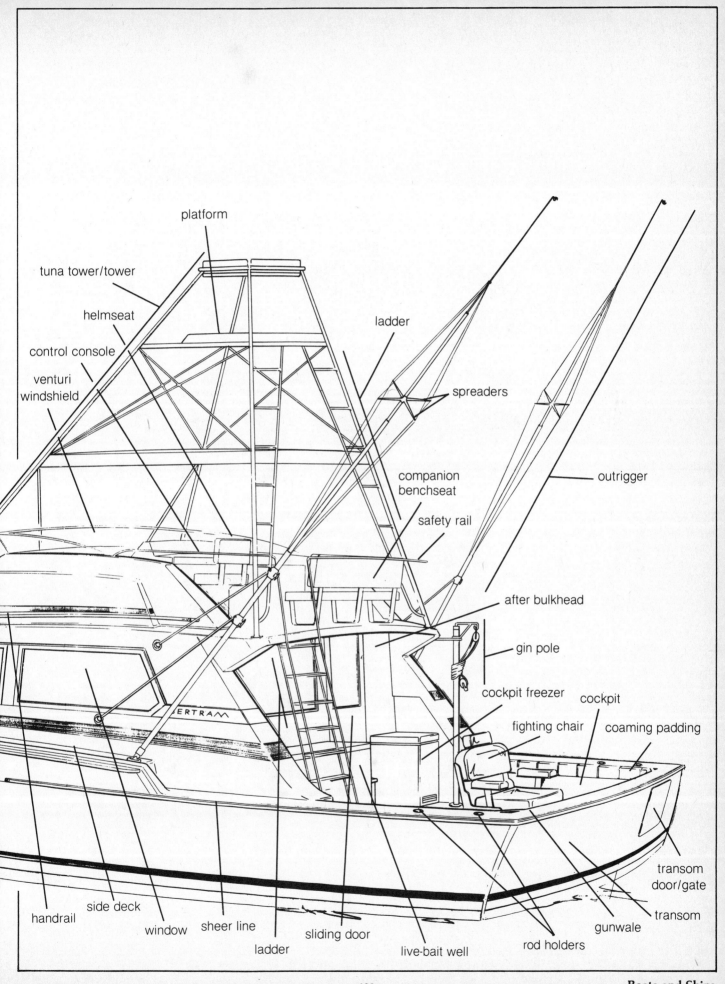

platform

tuna tower/tower

helmseat

control console

venturi
windshield

ladder

spreaders

companion
benchseat

safety rail

outrigger

after bulkhead

gin pole

cockpit freezer

cockpit

fighting chair

coaming padding

transom
door/gate

transom

handrail

side deck

window

sheer line

ladder

sliding door

live-bait well

rod holders

gunwale

Boats and Ships

Tanker

Cargo ships include *roll on-roll off ships;* *container ships;* *barge carriers;* *pallet ships;* *refrigerator ships,* or *reefers;* *dry-bulk carriers;* and *liquid-bulk carriers* such as the *super tanker* seen here. A *merchant ship* carrying *cargo* or *freight* is called a *liner* if it travels on scheduled routes at regular intervals, or a *tramp* if it does not have a fixed or scheduled route.

"catwalk"/ fore & aft gangw

foremast

"crow's nest"/ lookout area

pressure & vacuum relief valves

belowdeck storage entrance

anchor windlass & mooring winch

anchor windlass & mooring winch

radar mast & radar antennas

bridge/wheelhouse

bridge wing

wireless, telegraph & navigation aerials

king post

lifeboat

hose-handling derrick

"stowed" derrick brackets

aft superstructure/ deckhouse

pressure & vacuum relief valves

deck manifold

tank hatches

rail

foam monitors & fire-fighting stations

gas-vent lines

Passenger Ship/ Ocean Liner

Main bulkheads, steel walls running athwartships on a ship, are normally watertight. A *collision bulkhead* is a *watertight bulkhead* near the bow to prevent flooding in the event of collision. Circular windows aboard ship are called *ports* or *portholes.* A ship is boarded at the pier by a portable stairway, or *gangplank,* which fits in an opening in a ship's *rail* or *bulwark.* A metal shield on *berthing hawsers* to prevent rats from coming aboard is a *ratcatcher.*

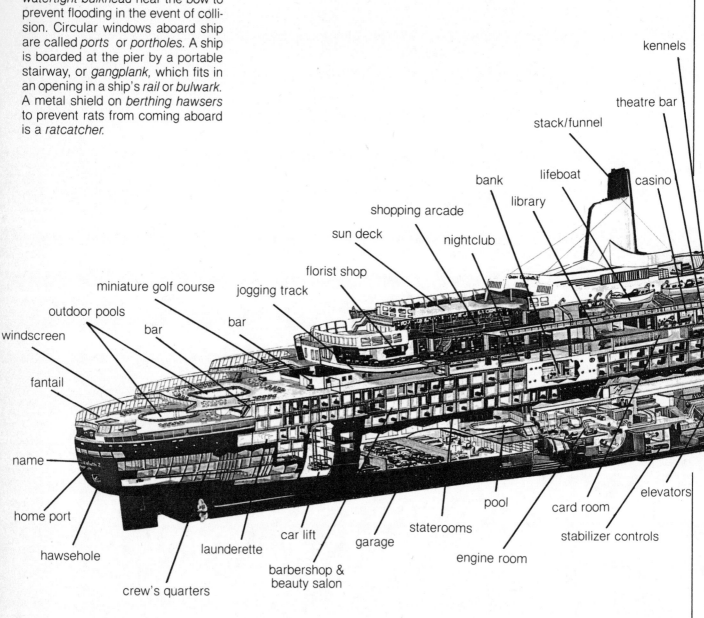

kennels

theatre bar

stack/funnel

bank

lifeboat

casino

shopping arcade

library

sun deck

nightclub

florist shop

miniature golf course

jogging track

outdoor pools

bar

bar

windscreen

fantail

name

home port

hawsehole

crew's quarters

launderette

car lift

barbershop & beauty salon

garage

staterooms

pool

engine room

card room

stabilizer controls

elevators

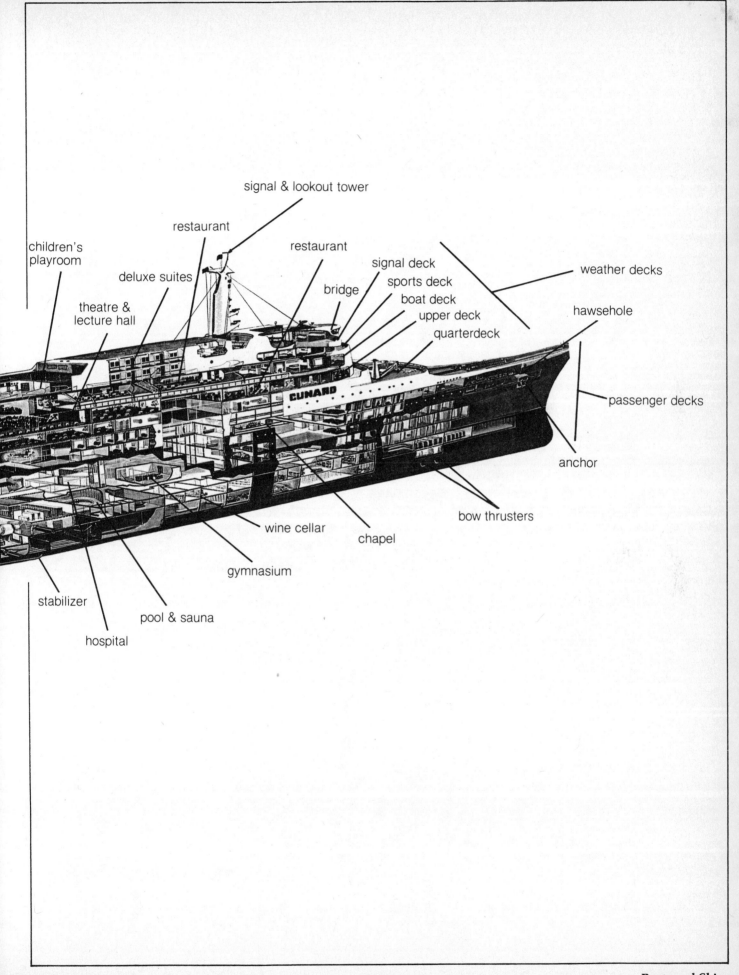

signal & lookout tower

restaurant

children's
playroom

restaurant

deluxe suites

signal deck

theatre &
lecture hall

bridge

sports deck

weather decks

boat deck

upper deck

hawsehole

quarterdeck

passenger decks

wine cellar

chapel

anchor

gymnasium

bow thrusters

stabilizer

pool & sauna

hospital

143

Boats and Ships

Tugboat and Fireboat

A *pudding fender* is a large fender made of old rope, formerly fitted to the bow of many *tugs*, or *towboats*. A *pusher tug*, also called a *pushboat*, is specially designed with a high flat bow for *barge cluster* push-towing. A fireboat is usually a tug fitted with such items as *high-pressure pumps*, *hoses* and *nozzles*.

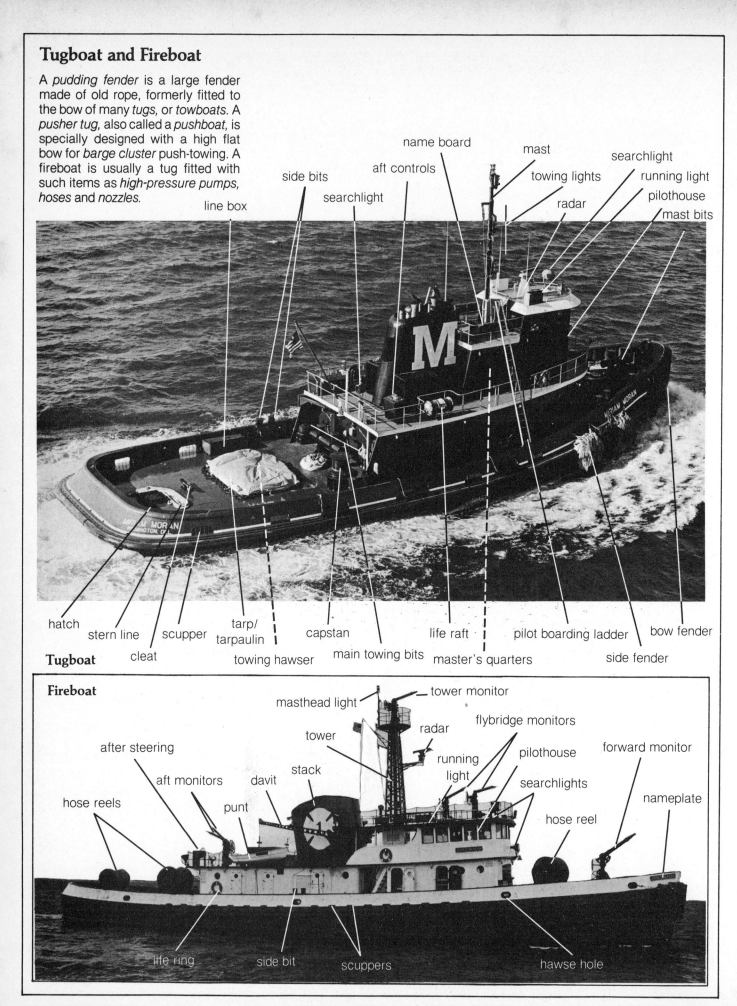

line box

side bits

searchlight

aft controls

name board

mast

towing lights

radar

searchlight

running light

pilothouse

mast bits

hatch

stern line

cleat

scupper

tarp/ tarpaulin

towing hawser

capstan

main towing bits

life raft

master's quarters

pilot boarding ladder

side fender

bow fender

Tugboat

Fireboat

masthead light

tower monitor

tower

radar

flybridge monitors

after steering

aft monitors

davit

stack

running light

pilothouse

forward monitor

hose reels

punt

searchlights

hose reel

nameplate

life ring

side bit

scuppers

hawse hole

Hovercraft and Hydrofoil

Air Cushion Vehicles *(ACV)*, or *ground-effect machines*, are *amphibious vehicles* that ride on a cushion of air blown by *lift fans* through *slots* or *jets* around the underside of the hull. There are four classes of hydrofoils: *ladder, depth-effect, surface-piercing* and *submerged foils*.

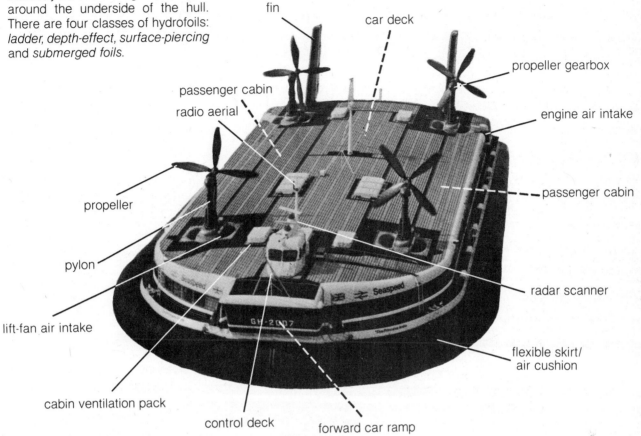

fin

car deck

propeller gearbox

passenger cabin

radio aerial

engine air intake

propeller

passenger cabin

pylon

radar scanner

lift-fan air intake

flexible skirt/ air cushion

cabin ventilation pack

control deck

forward car ramp

Hovercraft / Air Cushion Vehicle

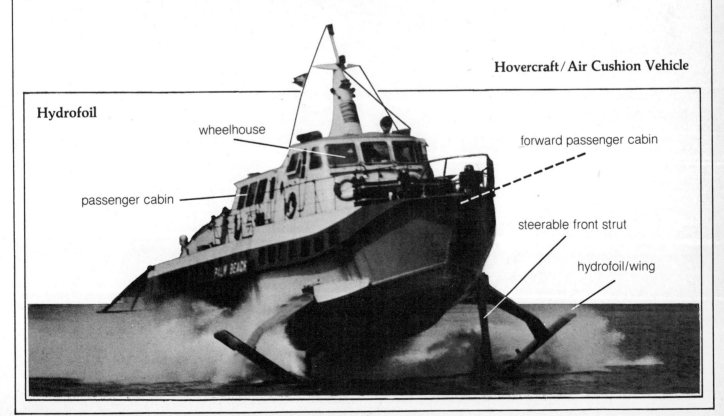

Hydrofoil

wheelhouse

forward passenger cabin

passenger cabin

steerable front strut

hydrofoil/wing

Boats and Ships

Helicopter

The main body of a helicopter, *chopper, whirlybird,* or *eggbeater,* is called the *fuselage.* The rescue helicopter shown here has an *amphibious hull.* Armed military helicopters are called *gunships.*

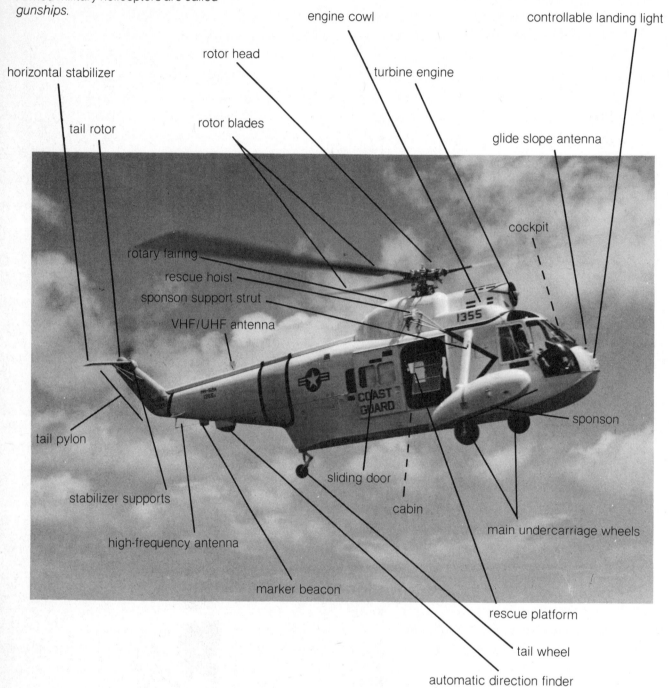

engine cowl

controllable landing light

rotor head

turbine engine

horizontal stabilizer

glide slope antenna

tail rotor

rotor blades

cockpit

rotary fairing

rescue hoist

sponson support strut

VHF/UHF antenna

1355

COAST GUARD

sponson

tail pylon

stabilizer supports

main undercarriage wheels

high-frequency antenna

sliding door

cabin

marker beacon

rescue platform

tail wheel

automatic direction finder

An aircraft's central body portion is called the *fuselage*. To land on water, an airplane uses *pontoons*. To become airborne and begin *soaring*, a glider is pulled behind a motor-driven airplane or car by a cable attached to a *tow hook*. A glider lands on either a *landing wheel* or a *skid*.

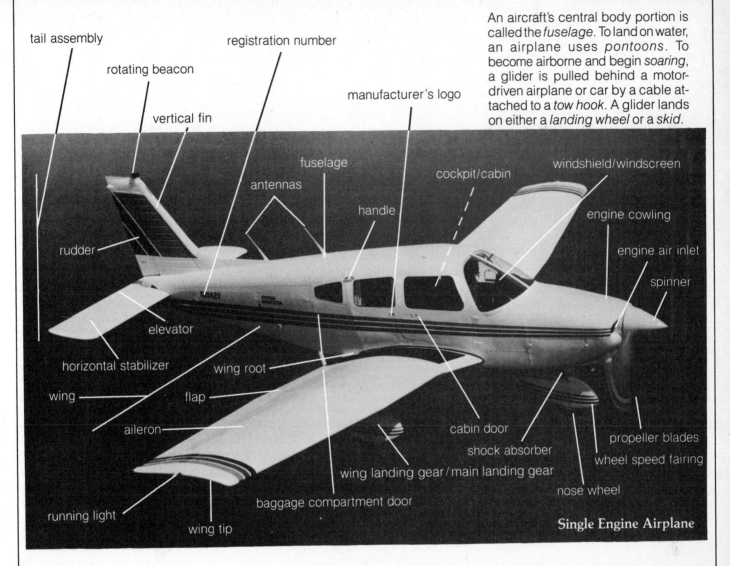

tail assembly

rotating beacon

vertical fin

registration number

manufacturer's logo

fuselage

antennas

cockpit/cabin

handle

windshield/windscreen

engine cowling

engine air inlet

spinner

rudder

elevator

horizontal stabilizer

wing root

wing

flap

aileron

cabin door

shock absorber

wing landing gear / main landing gear

propeller blades

wheel speed fairing

nose wheel

running light

wing tip

baggage compartment door

Single Engine Airplane

Glider / Sailplane

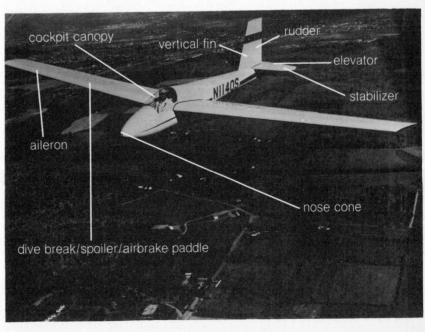

cockpit canopy

vertical fin

rudder

elevator

stabilizer

aileron

nose cone

dive break/spoiler/airbrake paddle

Civil Aircraft

The *trailing edge* of the wings on a *jumbo jet,* such as the one shown here, has small *static discharge wicks* to reduce electrical-charge buildup. Passengers store carry-on belongings in *overhead bins,* or *stowage compartments,* or in front *closets.* Aboard many aircraft, seat cushions double as *flotation devices. Life rafts* are stored in overhead ceiling compartments above the doors, and *emergency escape chutes* are folded inside the doors.

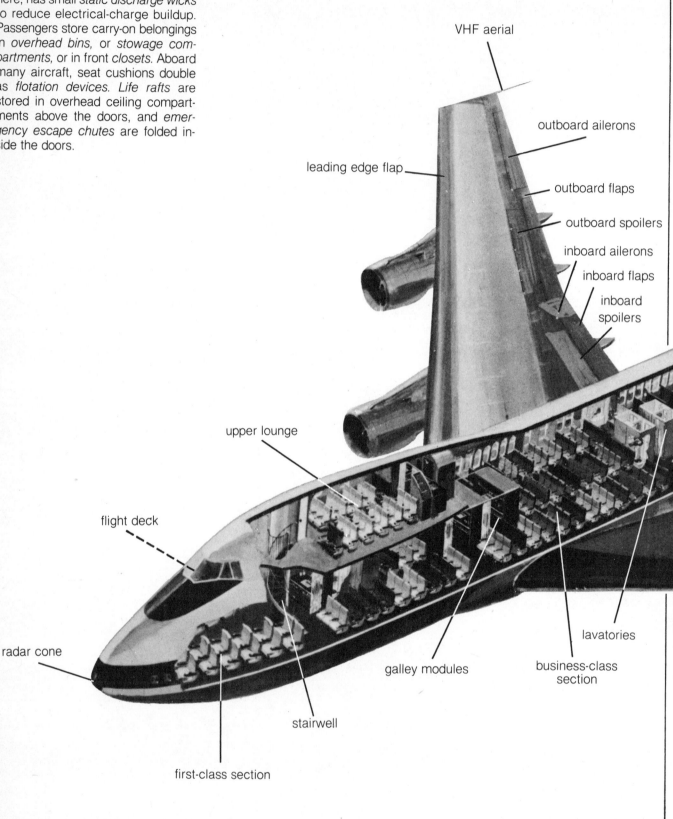

VHF aerial

outboard ailerons

leading edge flap

outboard flaps

outboard spoilers

inboard ailerons

inboard flaps

inboard spoilers

upper lounge

flight deck

radar cone

lavatories

galley modules

business-class section

stairwell

first-class section

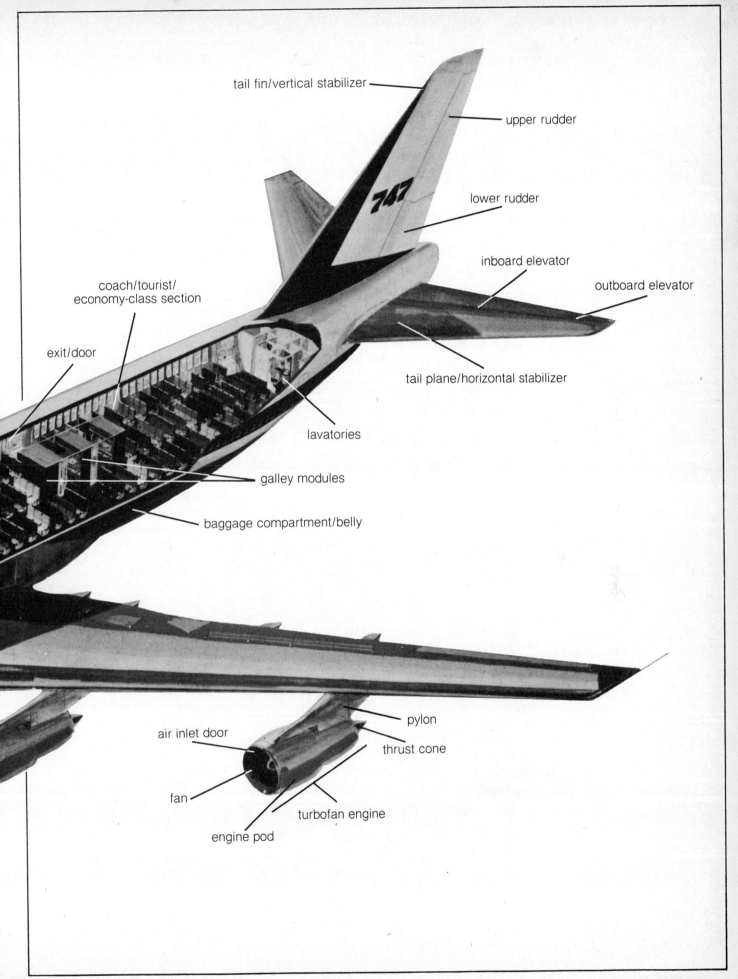

tail fin/vertical stabilizer

upper rudder

lower rudder

inboard elevator

outboard elevator

coach/tourist/
economy-class section

exit/door

tail plane/horizontal stabilizer

lavatories

galley modules

baggage compartment/belly

pylon

air inlet door

thrust cone

fan

turbofan engine

engine pod

Aircraft

747 Cockpit

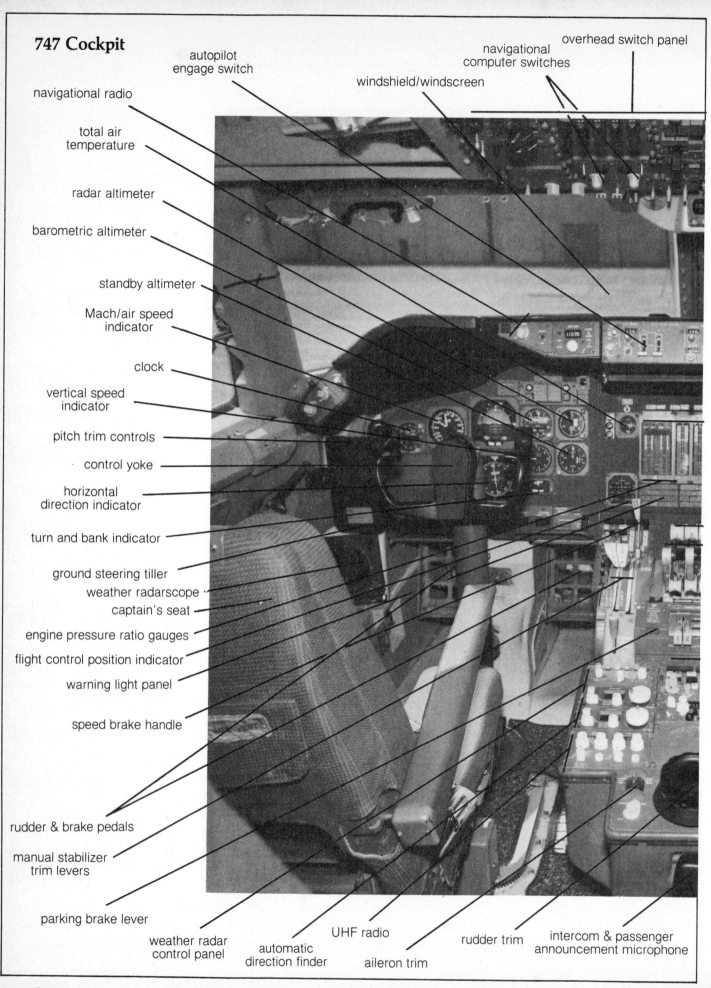

navigational radio

autopilot
engage switch

navigational
computer switches

overhead switch panel

windshield/windscreen

total air
temperature

radar altimeter

barometric altimeter

standby altimeter

Mach/air speed
indicator

clock

vertical speed
indicator

pitch trim controls

control yoke

horizontal
direction indicator

turn and bank indicator

ground steering tiller

weather radarscope

captain's seat

engine pressure ratio gauges

flight control position indicator

warning light panel

speed brake handle

rudder & brake pedals

manual stabilizer
trim levers

parking brake lever

weather radar
control panel

automatic
direction finder

UHF radio

aileron trim

rudder trim

intercom & passenger
announcement microphone

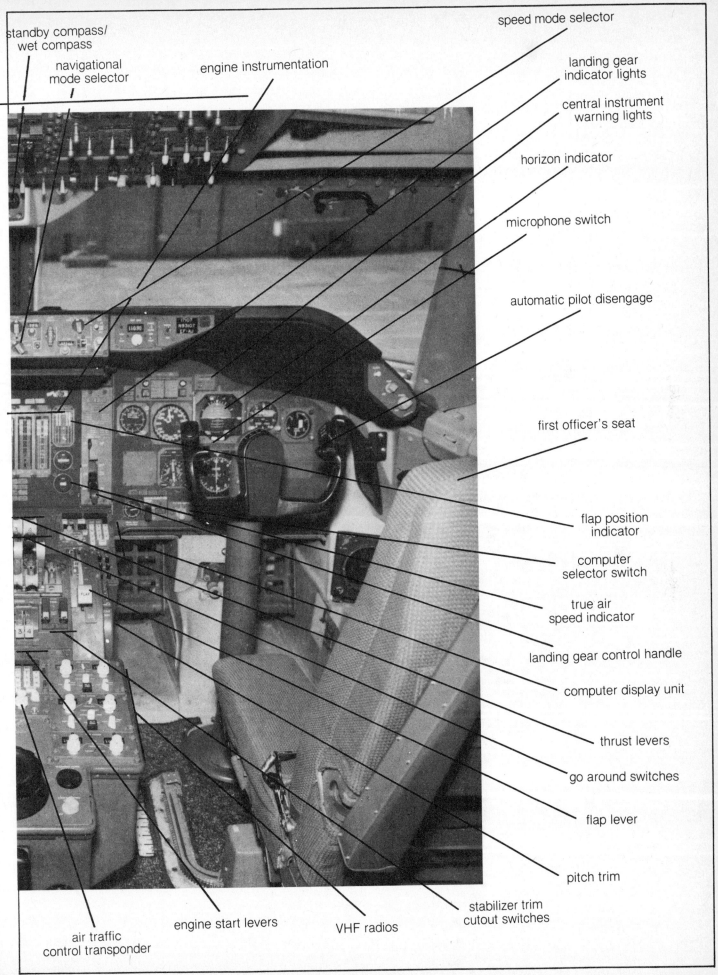

standby compass/ wet compass

navigational mode selector

engine instrumentation

speed mode selector

landing gear indicator lights

central instrument warning lights

horizon indicator

microphone switch

automatic pilot disengage

first officer's seat

flap position indicator

computer selector switch

true air speed indicator

landing gear control handle

computer display unit

thrust levers

go around switches

flap lever

pitch trim

stabilizer trim cutout switches

air traffic control transponder

engine start levers

VHF radios

Aircraft

Space Shuttle and Launch Pad

A shuttle has three main components: an orbiter, external tank and two solid-rocket boosters. Many launch pads have *flame buckets* designed to direct *fireballs* and steam away from the pad itself. A gantry is a movable structure used for erecting and servicing a rocket prior to launch.

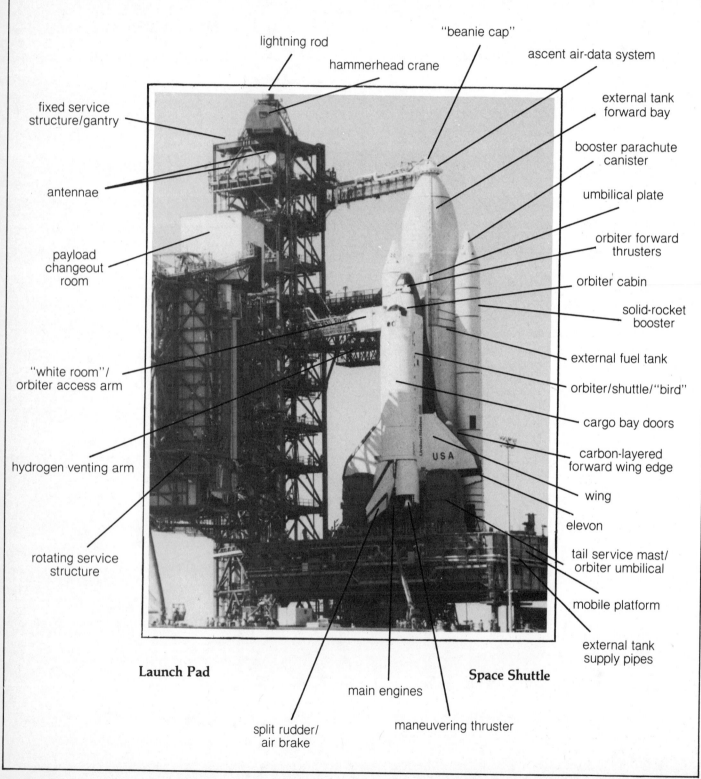

lightning rod

hammerhead crane

"beanie cap"

ascent air-data system

external tank forward bay

booster parachute canister

umbilical plate

orbiter forward thrusters

orbiter cabin

solid-rocket booster

external fuel tank

orbiter/shuttle/"bird"

cargo bay doors

carbon-layered forward wing edge

wing

elevon

tail service mast/ orbiter umbilical

mobile platform

external tank supply pipes

fixed service structure/gantry

antennae

payload changeout room

"white room"/ orbiter access arm

hydrogen venting arm

rotating service structure

Launch Pad

split rudder/ air brake

main engines

maneuvering thruster

Space Shuttle

Space Shuttle Flight Deck

Overhead controls include *circuit breakers, environmental monitors* and *fuel cell monitors.* The *orbiter* has work and living quarters for as many as seven people, including two pilots, *mission specialists* and *payload specialists.* It also features a *quad-redundant computer system,* including a fifth computer to arbitrate disputes among the first four.

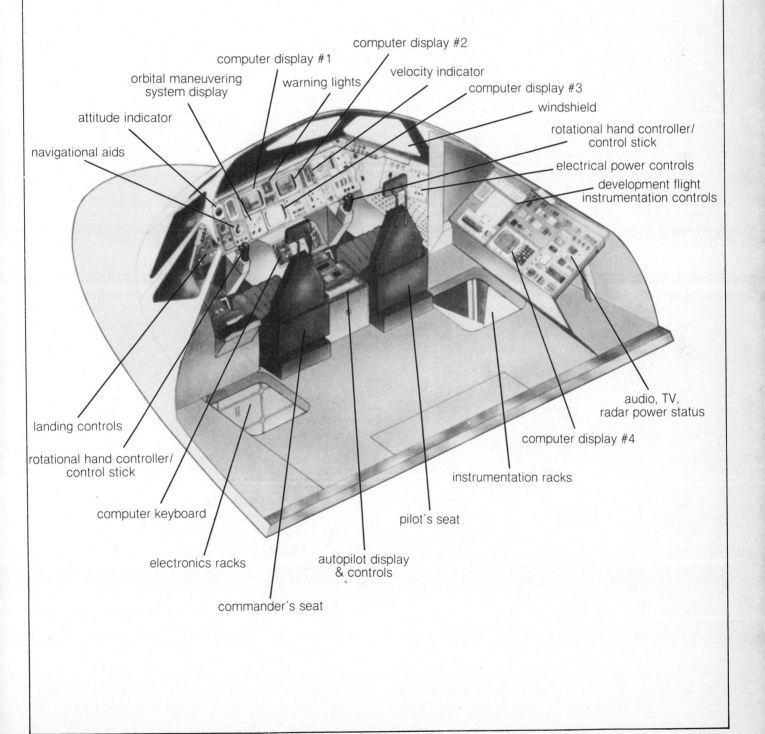

computer display #2

computer display #1

orbital maneuvering system display

warning lights

velocity indicator

computer display #3

attitude indicator

windshield

rotational hand controller/ control stick

navigational aids

electrical power controls

development flight instrumentation controls

audio, TV, radar power status

landing controls

computer display #4

rotational hand controller/ control stick

instrumentation racks

computer keyboard

pilot's seat

electronics racks

autopilot display & controls

commander's seat

Spacecraft

Lunar Lander

The *lunar module* consists of a lower *descent stage* which houses the *landing engine, exploration equipment, secondary tanks* and landing gear. The *ascent stage* contains *crew compartment* and *controls, equipment compartment, tanks* and *take-off engine,* used to rejoin the *command module.*

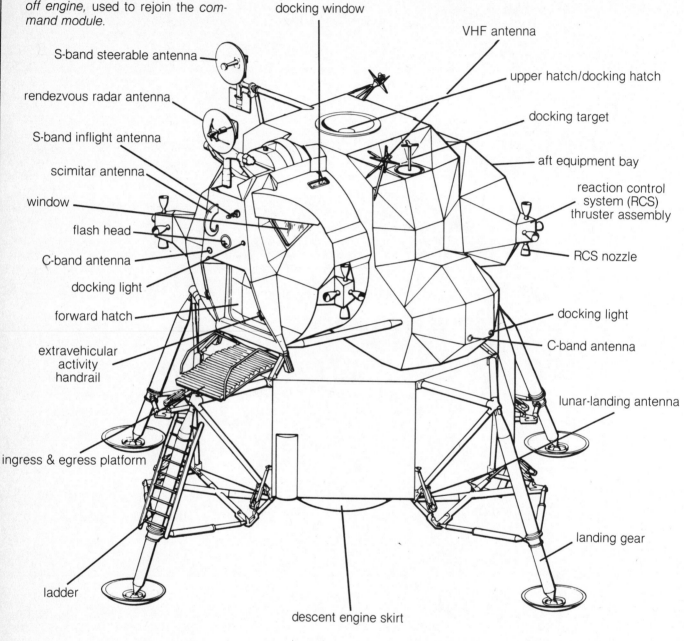

docking window

VHF antenna

upper hatch/docking hatch

S-band steerable antenna

docking target

rendezvous radar antenna

aft equipment bay

S-band inflight antenna

reaction control system (RCS) thruster assembly

scimitar antenna

window

RCS nozzle

flash head

C-band antenna

docking light

docking light

forward hatch

C-band antenna

extravehicular activity handrail

lunar-landing antenna

ingress & egress platform

landing gear

ladder

descent engine skirt

Lunar Rover

Officially called the *Lunar Roving Vehicle*, the *moon buggy* is folded in the Lunar Lander and deployed to transport astronauts and equipment on the lunar surface. The spacesuit, or *integrated thermal meteoroid garment*, is a many-layered structure laced to a *torso limb suit* which consists of an inner cloth *comfort lining*, a *bladder*, and a *restraint layer*.

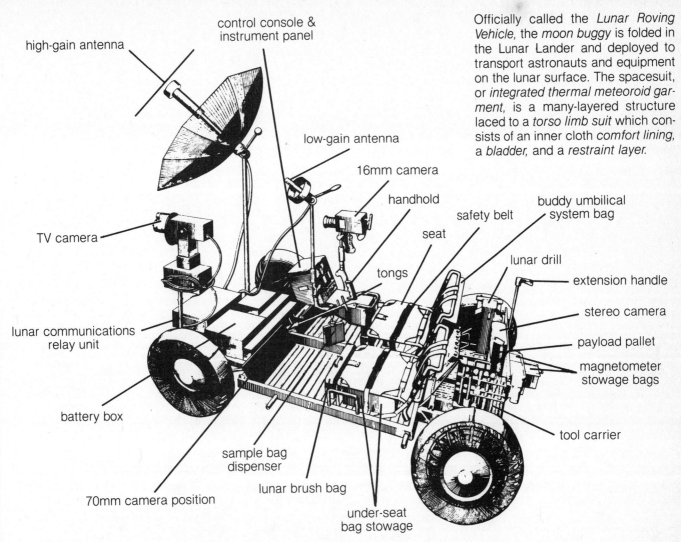

high-gain antenna

control console & instrument panel

low-gain antenna

16mm camera

handhold

safety belt

buddy umbilical system bag

seat

lunar drill

TV camera

tongs

extension handle

stereo camera

lunar communications relay unit

payload pallet

magnetometer stowage bags

battery box

tool carrier

sample bag dispenser

70mm camera position

lunar brush bag

under-seat bag stowage

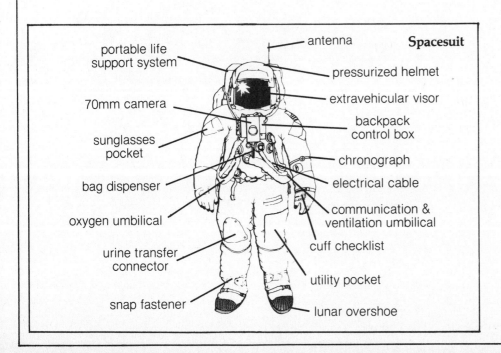

portable life support system

antenna

Spacesuit

pressurized helmet

70mm camera

extravehicular visor

sunglasses pocket

backpack control box

bag dispenser

chronograph

electrical cable

oxygen umbilical

communication & ventilation umbilical

urine transfer connector

cuff checklist

snap fastener

utility pocket

lunar overshoe

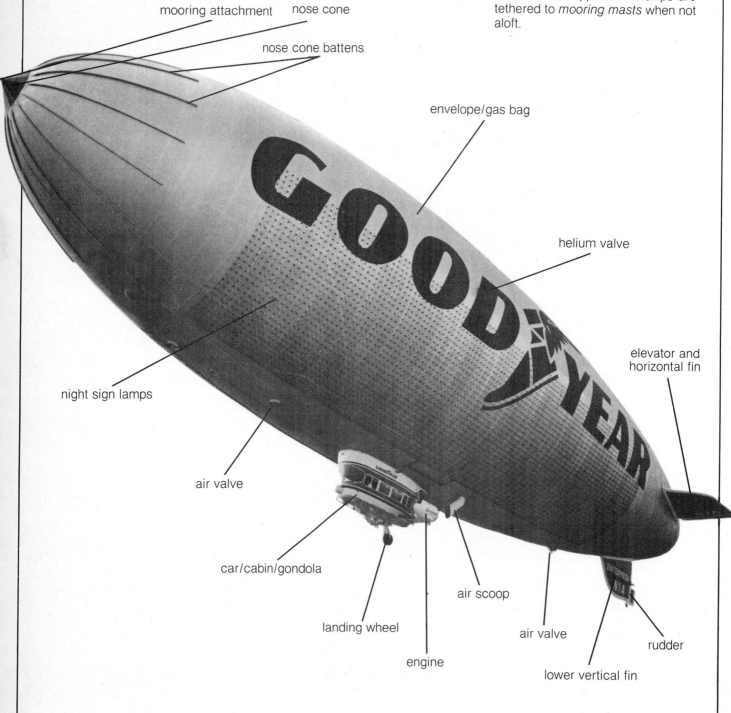

Lighter-than-air Craft

Engine-driven, steerable lighter-than-air craft are called blimps, or dirigibles. They can be *nonrigid* or *semirigid*, dependent on interior *ballonets*, or *air bags*, to maintain their shapes. *Rigid airships*, with metal *frameworks* within their *envelopes*, are referred to as *Zeppelins*. Airships are tethered to *mooring masts* when not aloft.

mooring attachment   nose cone

nose cone battens

envelope/gas bag

helium valve

elevator and horizontal fin

night sign lamps

air valve

car/cabin/gondola

air scoop

landing wheel

air valve

engine

rudder

lower vertical fin

Blimp/Dirigible

Communications

Communications ranks among the fastest-growing areas of modern life. Nevertheless, as this book is meant to demonstrate by providing visual access to language, print communications remains a vital part of the future. Print is therefore examined in some detail, up to and including a close look at the mailing label affixed to periodicals received every day by millions of subscribers.

Space limitations prevent presentation of industrial items such as transmitting stations and microwave towers, sound-recording and television studios and film-processing equipment.

But the devices used in all forms of communications—visual, aural and audiovisual—are represented by objects commonly used in most households. The single exception to this is the satellite which appears at the end of the section. It is included because of the vital role it plays in modern communications of all kinds.

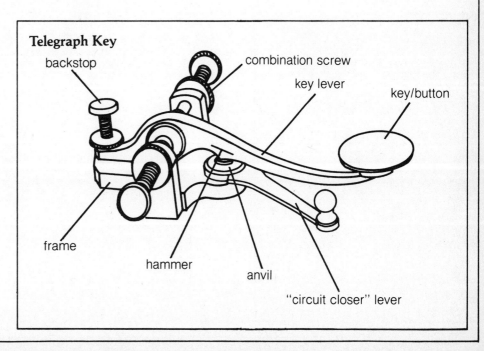

Telegraph Key

backstop

combination screw

key lever

key/button

frame

hammer

anvil

"circuit closer" lever

Pen and Pencil

In refillable *lead pencils* a *barrel cap* is turned in order to push new lead out the tip. Some fountain pens are *cartridge-loaded* but older models have a barrel, *ink reservoir* and *self-filling mechanism.* *Quills,* or *feather pens,* made from the horny, hollow barrel of bird feathers, were dipped in *ink wells.*

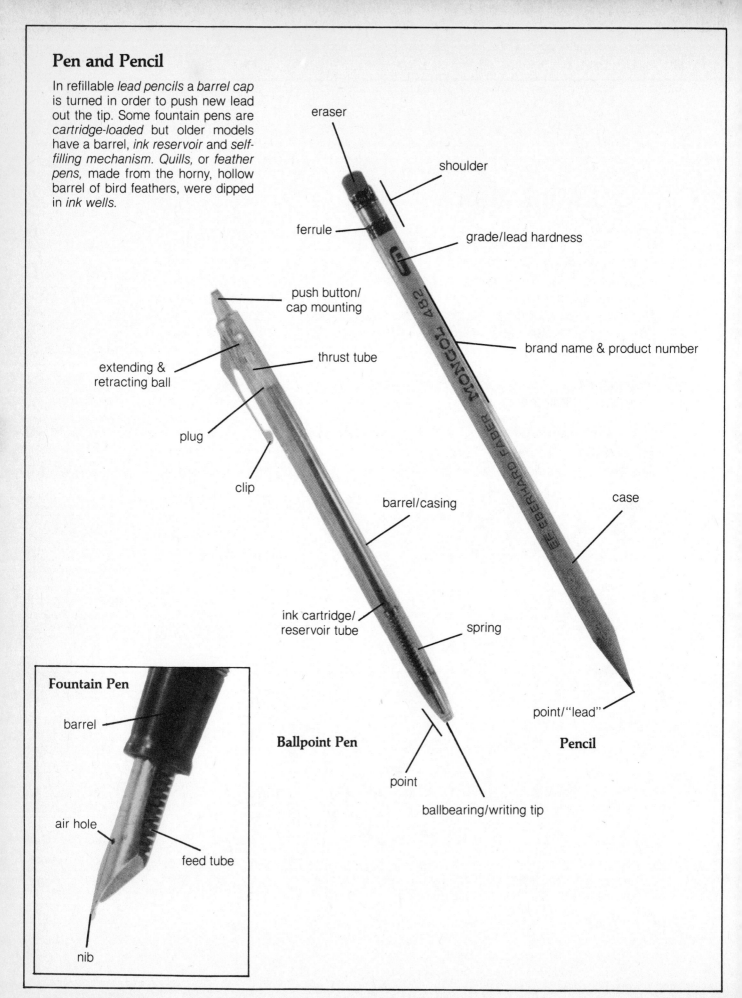

eraser

shoulder

ferrule

grade/lead hardness

push button/cap mounting

brand name & product number

extending & retracting ball

thrust tube

plug

clip

barrel/casing

case

ink cartridge/reservoir tube

spring

point/"lead"

Ballpoint Pen

Pencil

point

ballbearing/writing tip

Fountain Pen

barrel

air hole

feed tube

nib

Correspondence

A note appended to a completed letter is called a *postscript*, abbreviated as *P.S.* When items are enclosed with a letter they are indicated by the word *enclosure(s)* or *encl.* The back portion of an envelope which is glued down after a letter has been inserted is the *flap*. Postage stamps can be purchased in *books*, *strips*, *blocks*, *coils* and *sheets*, or *panes*.

letterhead

company name/logo

business/occupation

location of offices

inside address

salutation

body

typist's initials

writer's initials

distribution of copies/ "carbon copies"

stationery

heading

complimentary close

signature block

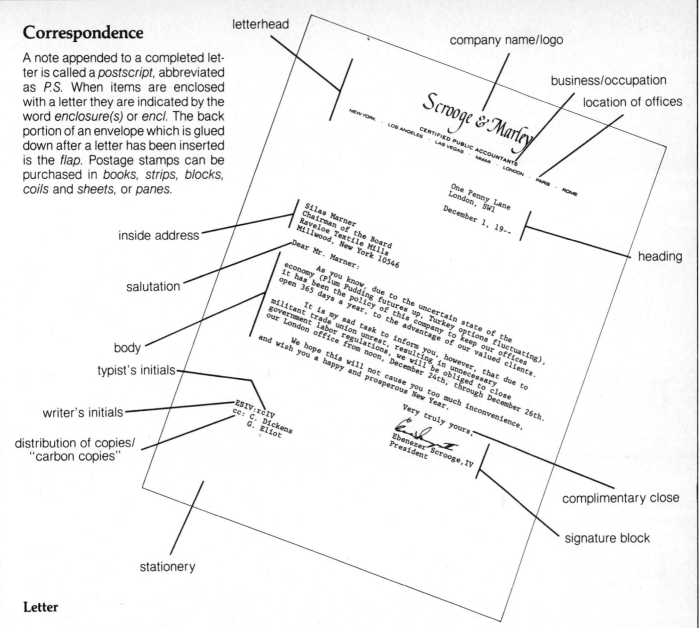

Scrooge & Marley
CERTIFIED PUBLIC ACCOUNTANTS

NEW YORK · LOS ANGELES · LAS VEGAS · MIAMI · LONDON · PARIS · ROME

One Penny Lane
London, SW1
December 1, 19--

Silas Marner
Chairman of the Board
Raveloe Textile Mills
Millwood, New York 10546

Dear Mr. Marner:

As you know, due to the uncertain state of the economy (Plum Pudding futures up, Turkey options fluctuating), it has been the policy of this company to keep our offices open 365 days a year, to the advantage of our valued clients.

It is my sad task to inform you, however, that due to militant trade union unrest, resulting in unnecessary government labor regulations, we will be obliged to close our London office from noon, December 24th, through December 26th.

We hope this will not cause you too much inconvenience, and wish you a happy and prosperous New Year.

Very truly yours,

Ebenezer Scrooge, IV
President

ESIV:rcIV
cc: C. Dickens
    G. Eliot

Letter

Envelope

return address

meter tape

postmark

stamp

postmark

cancellation

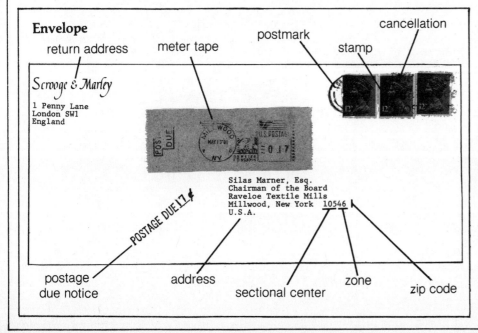

Scrooge & Marley

1 Penny Lane
London SW1
England

POSTAGE DUE 17¢

Silas Marner, Esq.
Chairman of the Board
Raveloe Textile Mills
Millwood, New York 10546
U.S.A.

postage
due notice

address

sectional center

zone

zip code

Stamp

commemorative subject

issuing government

BICENTENNIAL
EXECUTIVE BRANCH
USA 25

face value/ denomination

design

cancellation/ postmark

perforation

Print Communications

Résumé and Business Card

A summary of a job applicant's background and qualifications is called a résumé or *curriculum vitae*. In addition to brief descriptions of one's education and work experience, it may include *awards* and *honors*, *outside interests* and objectives or goals. Personal references may be listed or made available on request.

name/address

date of birth (optional)

Henry D. Thoreau
255 Main Street
Concord, Mass. 01742

RÉSUMÉ

Date of Birth
July 12, 1817

1837

Education

B.A., Harvard University
Languages -- Latin, Greek and French

education/academic career

1847 - present

Work Experience

Naturalist, writer and surveyor. Concord, Mass.
Self-employed, write magazine articles, essays and poetry, and give lectures on diverse topics; also do surveying and collect nature specimens.

1845 - 1847

Private nature study; an experiment in living. Walden Pond, Mass.

work experience/business career

1843 (8 mos.)

Private tutor. Staten Island, New York

1840 - 1844

Assistant editor, The Dial magazine. Concord, Mass.

1838 - 1840

Schoolmaster, teacher. Concord, Mass.

1837 - 1838

Pencil-maker (family business). Concord, Mass.

professional activities

Associations

Publications

Professional Activities

Member of the Transcendental Club
Poems and essays in The Dial (1840-1844)
A Week on the Concord and Merrimack Rivers (1849)
Walden; or Life in the Woods (1849)
Resistance to Civil Government (1849)

brief job description

references (optional)

References

Ralph Waldo Emerson, Concord, Mass.
Louis Agassiz, Harvard University, Cambridge, Mass.
Sam Staples, Constable, Concord, Mass.

publications

Résumé

Objective

I have been schoolmaster, surveyor, gardener, carpenter, day-laborer, pencil-maker, writer and sometimes poet. My present employment is to answer to such orders as may be expected from the above--that is, if I see fit, which is not always the case, for I have found out a way to live without what is commonly called employment or industry, attractive or otherwise. Indeed my steadiest employment, if such it can be called, is to keep myself at the top of my condition, and ready for whatever may turn up in heaven or on earth.

May 1, 1850

date of résumé

objective/career goals

Business Card

company logo

name

position/title

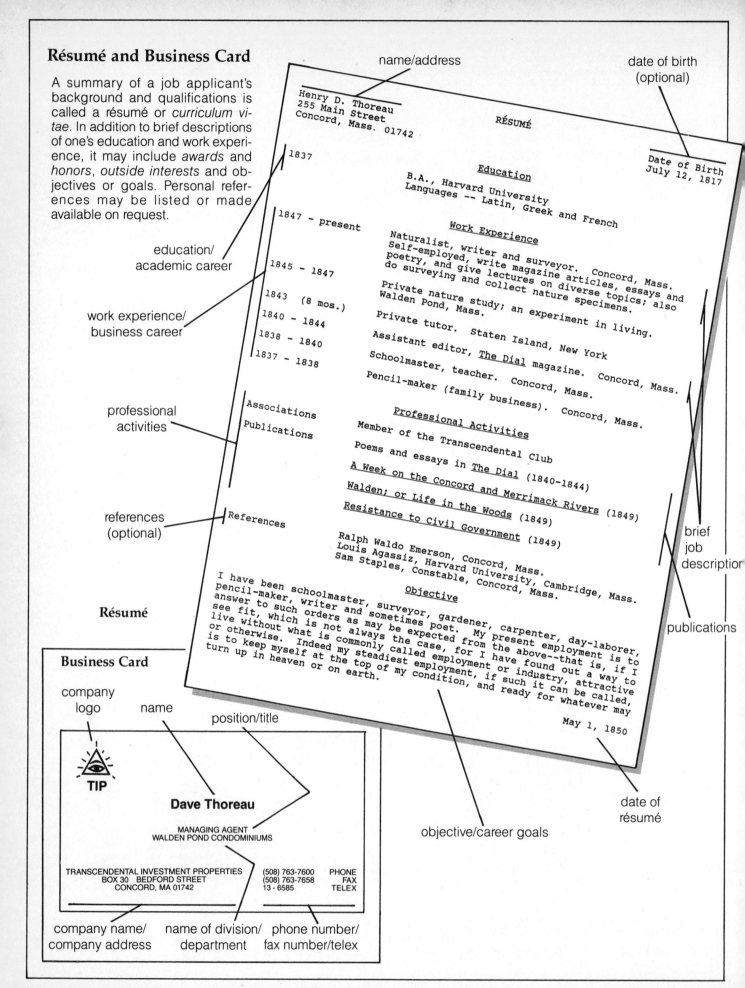

TIP

Dave Thoreau

MANAGING AGENT
WALDEN POND CONDOMINIUMS

TRANSCENDENTAL INVESTMENT PROPERTIES   (508) 763-7600   PHONE
BOX 30 BEDFORD STREET   (508) 763-7658   FAX
CONCORD, MA 01742   13 - 6585   TELEX

company name/company address

name of division/department

phone number/fax number/telex

Typewriter

On standard manual or *office type-writers,* lightweight *portables* and older *electrics,* when a key labeled with a *character* is struck, it sends the appropriate type bar toward an inked *ribbon.* On modern electric typewriters type bars in the *type basket* have been replaced with a ball.

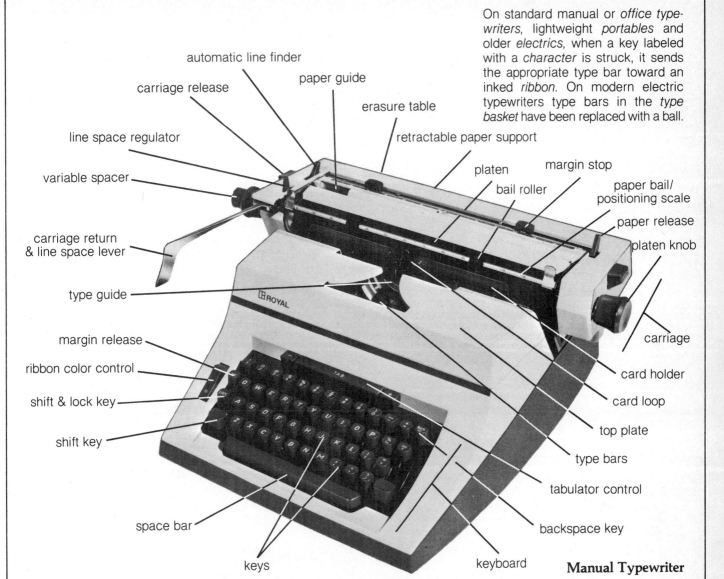

automatic line finder
carriage release
paper guide
erasure table
line space regulator
retractable paper support
variable spacer
platen
margin stop
paper bail/positioning scale
bail roller
paper release
carriage return & line space lever
platen knob
type guide
carriage
margin release
card holder
ribbon color control
card loop
shift & lock key
top plate
shift key
type bars
tabulator control
space bar
backspace key
keys
keyboard
Manual Typewriter

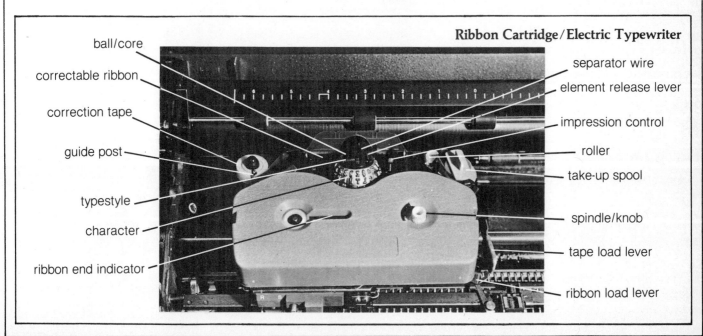

Ribbon Cartridge / Electric Typewriter

ball/core
separator wire
correctable ribbon
element release lever
correction tape
impression control
guide post
roller
typestyle
take-up spool
character
spindle/knob
ribbon end indicator
tape load lever
ribbon load lever

Print Communications

Personal Computer

A personal computer is designed to use *programs*, or instructions, written in a *language* the computer understands, that enable the *computer operator* to use the speed and sophistication of the machine's computational abilities. Programs range from *finance* and *graphics* to *word processing* and *electronic games*. A *word processor* is a computer that is designed primarily to handle writing and editing tasks.

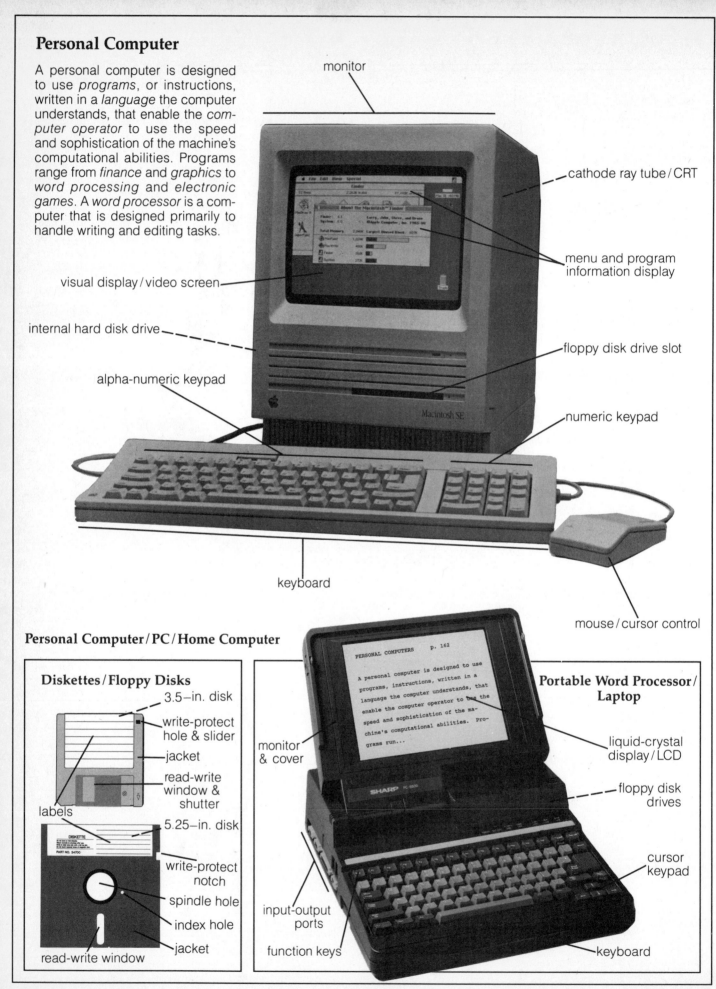

monitor

cathode ray tube / CRT

menu and program information display

visual display / video screen

internal hard disk drive

floppy disk drive slot

alpha-numeric keypad

numeric keypad

keyboard

mouse / cursor control

Personal Computer / PC / Home Computer

Diskettes / Floppy Disks

3.5–in. disk

write-protect hole & slider

jacket

read-write window & shutter

labels

5.25–in. disk

write-protect notch

spindle hole

index hole

jacket

read-write window

monitor & cover

input-output ports

function keys

Portable Word Processor / Laptop

liquid-crystal display / LCD

floppy disk drives

cursor keypad

keyboard

PERSONAL COMPUTERS   p. 162

A personal computer is designed to use programs, instructions, written in a language the computer understands, that enable the computer operator to use the speed and sophistication of the machine's computational abilities. Programs run...

Printers

Computer *output* printed on paper is called *hard copy*. The precise form this takes depends on the type of printer used. On dot matrix and laser printers, characters are built out of a series of dots, the laser's being smaller and more closely grouped to produce crisp detail. A *daisy-wheel printer* uses a wheel of type bars, similar to a typewriter's, to produce *"letter quality"* results.

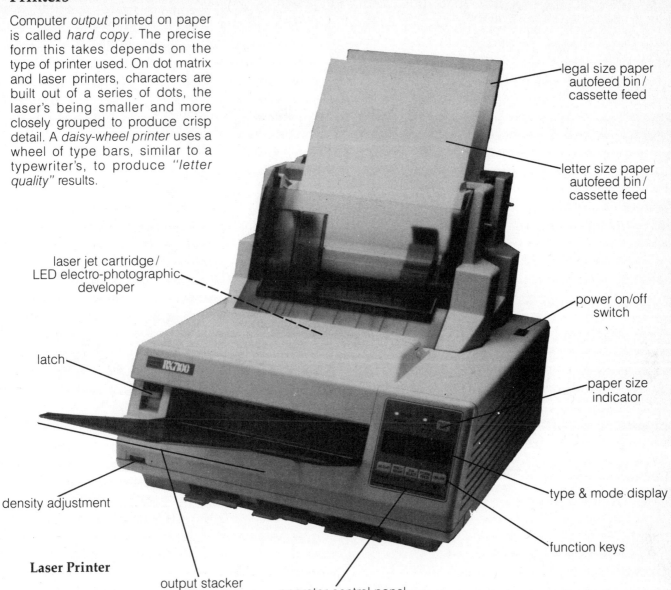

legal size paper autofeed bin/ cassette feed

letter size paper autofeed bin/ cassette feed

power on/off switch

paper size indicator

type & mode display

function keys

laser jet cartridge/ LED electro-photographic developer

latch

density adjustment

Laser Printer

output stacker

operator control panel

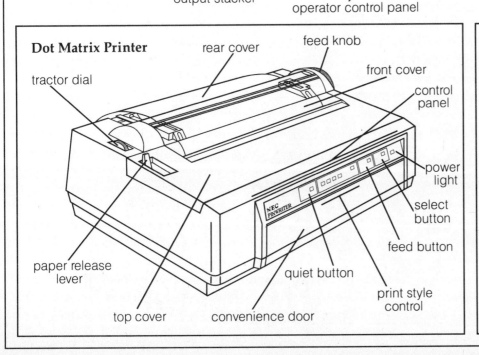

Dot Matrix Printer

rear cover

feed knob

front cover

tractor dial

control panel

power light

select button

feed button

print style control

paper release lever

top cover

convenience door

quiet button

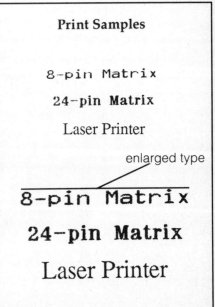

Print Samples

8-pin Matrix

24-pin Matrix

Laser Printer

enlarged type

8-pin Matrix

24-pin Matrix

Laser Printer

Print Communications

Fax Machine and Copier

Fax machines transmit clear, detailed paper *facsimilies* of documents quickly from one *terminal* to another over *telephone lines*. The fax operator may, in addition, couple the transmission with spoken conversation over the telephone handset. Copier, *answering machine, delayed transmission, unattended reception*, memory and automatic dialing capabilities may also be provided.

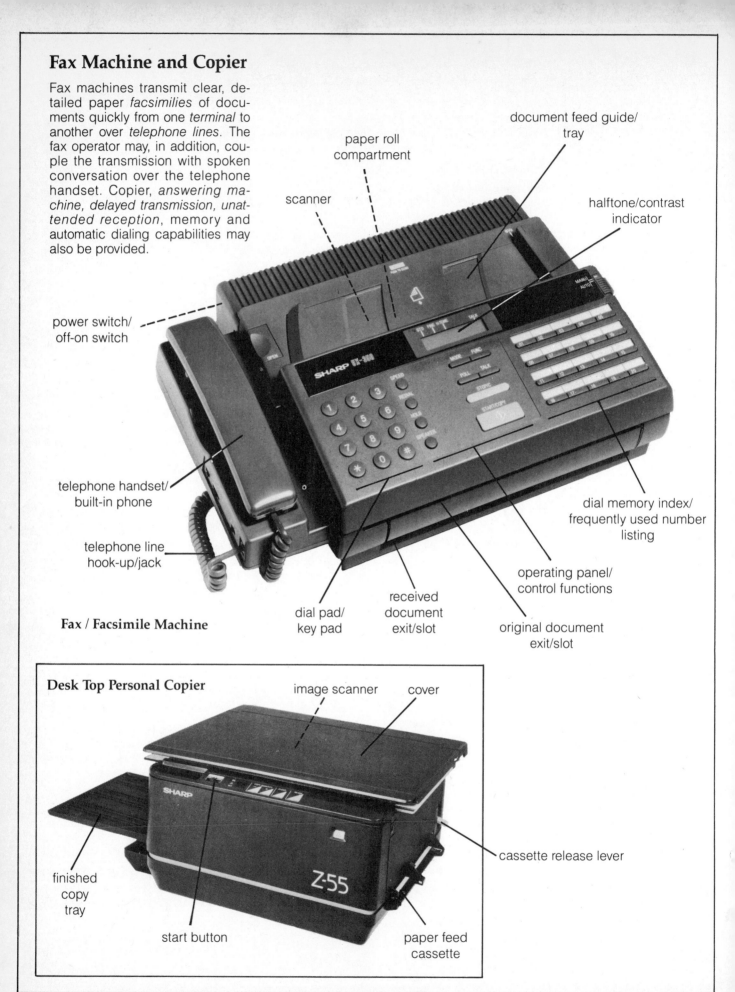

paper roll compartment

document feed guide/ tray

scanner

halftone/contrast indicator

power switch/ off-on switch

telephone handset/ built-in phone

telephone line hook-up/jack

dial memory index/ frequently used number listing

operating panel/ control functions

dial pad/ key pad

received document exit/slot

original document exit/slot

Fax / Facsimile Machine

Desk Top Personal Copier

image scanner

cover

cassette release lever

finished copy tray

start button

paper feed cassette

Typography

Type with serifs is called *book type*.
Type without serifs is *sans serif*.

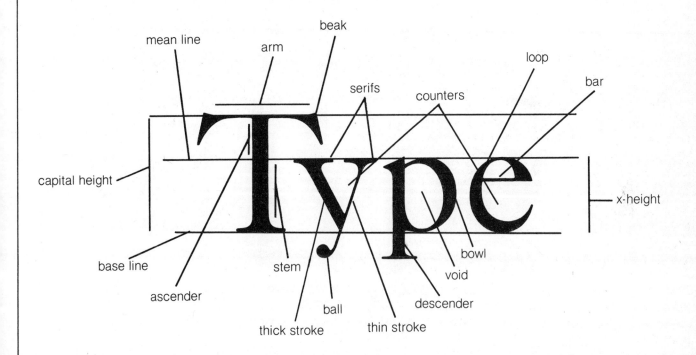

Typeface Composition

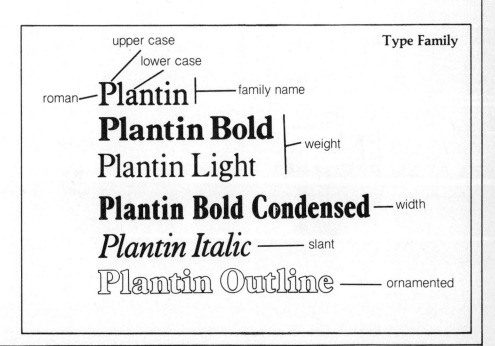

Type Family

Print Communications

All *metal type* is known collectively as *hot metal*, in contrast to *cold type*, which is produced photographically. The letterpress method of printing uses a raised surface, or *relief*, while gravure uses a depressed surface, or *intaglio*, and lithography uses a *plane*, or *flat surface*. Printing is done on sheets of paper on *sheet-fed presses* or on rolls of paper on *web-fed presses*.

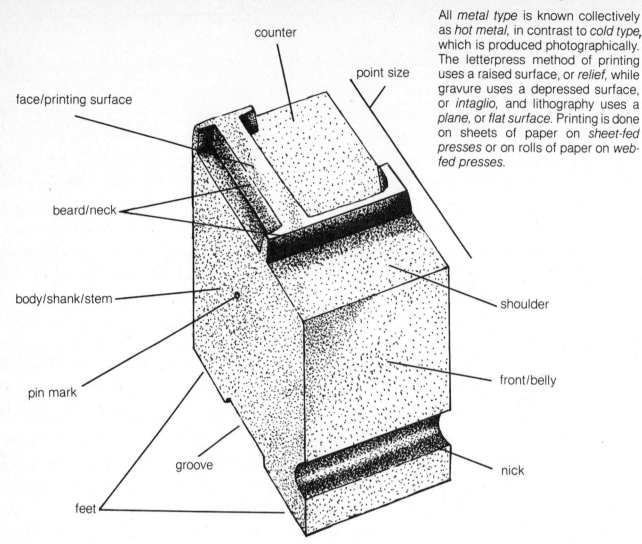

counter

point size

face/printing surface

beard/neck

body/shank/stem

pin mark

groove

feet

shoulder

front/belly

nick

Type

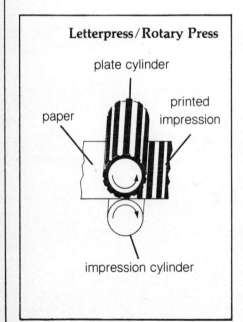

Letterpress/Rotary Press

plate cylinder

printed impression

paper

impression cylinder

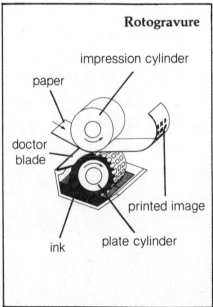

Rotogravure

impression cylinder

paper

doctor blade

printed image

ink

plate cylinder

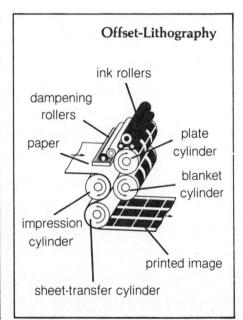

Offset-Lithography

ink rollers

dampening rollers

paper

plate cylinder

blanket cylinder

impression cylinder

printed image

sheet-transfer cylinder

Book

The *body* of a book is made up of *leaves*, each side of which is a *page*. Two facing pages form a *spread*. Pages leading up to the actual *text* are called *preliminaries* or *front matter*. Those pages following the text are *back matter, end matter* or *reference matter*. A box for a book, open at one end, is called a *slipcase* or *forel*.

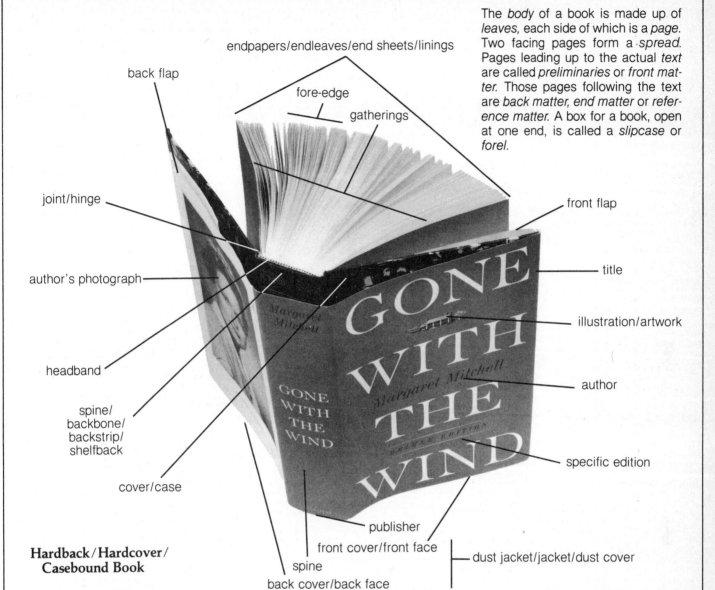

endpapers/endleaves/end sheets/linings

back flap

fore-edge

gatherings

front flap

joint/hinge

title

author's photograph

illustration/artwork

headband

author

spine/
backbone/
backstrip/
shelfback

specific edition

cover/case

publisher

front cover/front face

dust jacket/jacket/dust cover

spine

back cover/back face

**Hardback / Hardcover /
Casebound Book**

**Paperback / Softback /
Softcover / Softbound Book**

covers/wrappers   publisher

colophon/
trademark

price

spine

blurb

International
Standard
Book Number/
ISBN

order number/
inventory control
number

Spread

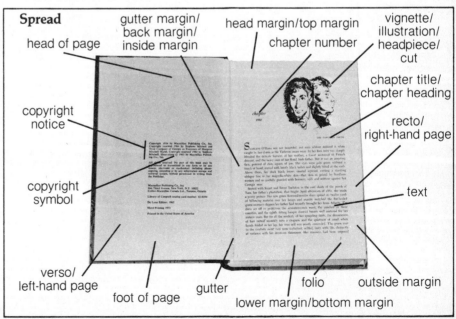

gutter margin/
back margin/
inside margin

head margin/top margin

vignette/
illustration/
headpiece/
cut

head of page

chapter number

copyright
notice

chapter title/
chapter heading

recto/
right-hand page

copyright
symbol

text

verso/
left-hand page

folio   outside margin

foot of page   gutter

lower margin/bottom margin

Newspaper

Terms vary from newspaper to newspaper. Those shown here are used at *The New York Times*. Small-size newspapers are called *tabloids*.

Labels (clockwise / as positioned):

- copyright
- nameplate/flag/logo
- issue date
- skyline
- out-of-town prices
- weather ear
- price
- dingbat
- readout dash
- agate line
- twinned stories
- credit line
- caption/cut line
- index
- hairline rule
- art
- jump line
- subhead
- body of story
- italic refer
- lead/lede
- dateline
- byline
- bar line
- deck/bank
- head
- banner headline
- folio line
- volume number
- left ear

(Newspaper front page text)

TODAY: SIX PAGES OF BICENTENNIAL ARTICLES AND PICTURES

"All the News That's Fit to Print"

The New York Times

LATE CITY EDITION
Weather: Partly cloudy and less humid today through tomorrow. Temperature range: today 64-82; Sunday 63-82. Details on page 39.

VOL. CXXV ... No. 43,262 © 1976 The New York Times Company

NEW YORK, MONDAY, JULY 5, 1976

20 CENTS

Nation and Millions in City Joyously Hail Bicentennial

ISRAELIS RETURN WITH 103 RESCUED IN UGANDA RAID

Toll Is Put at 3 Hostages, 7 Hijackers, Army Officer and 20 of Amin's Men

FORD LAUDS OPERATION

Freed Captives Are Received Joyously at Airport After Their 7-Day Ordeal

By TERENCE SMITH
Special to The New York Times

JERUSALEM, July 4—An Israeli commando unit that last night conducted a daring raid on the Entebbe airport in Uganda flew home today with the hostages it released.

Military officials said that 103 hostages had been flown to Israel. They said that four Is-

Text of the Rabin address will be found on page 2

French Officials See Signs Amin, Hijackers Colluded

PARIS, July 4 — Official...

CARTER TO BEGIN TALKS ON TICKET

Will See Muskie Today and Other Possible Running Mates Soon After

By CHARLES MOHR
Special to The New York Times

PLAINS, Ga., July 4—Jimmy Carter...

A Day of Picnics, Pomp, Pageantry and Protest

By JOHN L. HESS

The nation celebrated its 200th birthday yesterday...

PRESIDENT TALKS

Philadelphia Throngs Told U.S. Is Leader— Liberty Bell Rings

By JAMES T. WOOTEN
Special to The New York Times

PHILADELPHIA, July 4...

PANOPLY OF SAILS

Harbor Armada Led by Tall Ships in Salute to Fourth

By RICHARD F. SHEPARD

Buoyed by panoramic specta-

Preceded by a fireboat, the Coast Guard training ship Eagle leads the armada of ships past the Battery up the Hudson for the naval review

Ethnic Diversity Adds Spice to the Holiday

By FRED FERRETTI

New Yorkers and their friends poured into lower Manhattan yesterday...

President Ford waves to the crowd at Valley Forge, Pa., where he signed a bill making it a national historical site. He stands on a covered wagon that represented Michigan, his home state, in the Bicentennial wagon train.

O, Say, It Was a Glorious Patchwork Quilt of a Fourth

By McCANDLISH PHILLIPS

The Fourth of July celebration in New York City yesterday...

City Hall is the scene of street dancing and music in July 4th in Old New York festival

NEWS INDEX

Periodicals may be consumer magazines, intended for the general public; *trade* or *technical magazines*, intended for particular industries and businesses; or *journals*, published for people engaged in professions. *House organs* are distributed within a specific company. Covers may have *cover blurbs* with *selling copy*, describing inside stories, and *cover captions*.

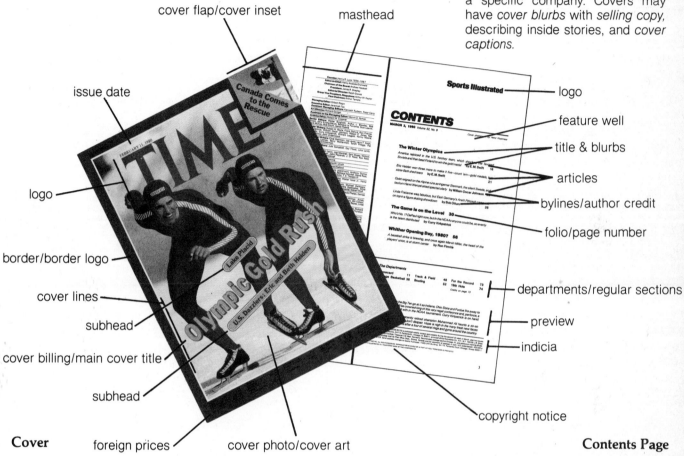

cover flap/cover inset

masthead

issue date

logo

logo

feature well

title & blurbs

articles

bylines/author credit

folio/page number

border/border logo

cover lines

subhead

departments/regular sections

preview

indicia

cover billing/main cover title

subhead

copyright notice

Cover

foreign prices

cover photo/cover art

Contents Page

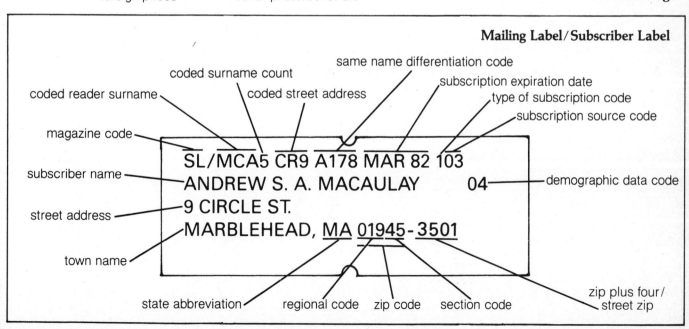

Mailing Label/Subscriber Label

same name differentiation code

subscription expiration date

coded surname count

type of subscription code

coded reader surname

coded street address

subscription source code

magazine code

SL/MCA5 CR9 A178 MAR 82 103

subscriber name

ANDREW S. A. MACAULAY   04

demographic data code

street address

9 CIRCLE ST.

town name

MARBLEHEAD, <u>MA</u> <u>01945</u>-<u>3501</u>

state abbreviation

regional code

zip code

section code

zip plus four/ street zip

The design of a magazine page is called the *layout.* In the feature shown here *dummy type* has been substituted for *text* or *copy.* Two facing pages are called a spread, *double spread,* or *double-truck.* A *sidebar* is a self-contained, boxed *article* bearing on the main feature.

frontispiece/half-title logo

head/headline/title

subhead/pullquote/deck/blurb

byline

dropped initial/set-in cap/
inset initial/descending initial

lead/lede

photo/cut/art

body copy/text

folio

Feature Spread

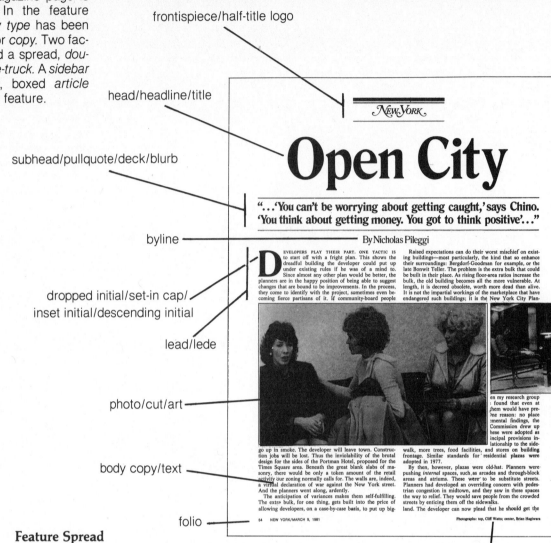

Open City

"...'You can't be worrying about getting caught,' says Chino. 'You think about getting money. You got to think positive'..."

By Nicholas Pileggi

photo credit

---

scotch rule

art/illustration

oxford rule

head

column rule

special-feature
photo treatment

sign-off

"nuts and bolts"

flush-left type

ragged-right type

running title

subhead

decorated initial

introduction

breaker

boldface/highlight

column

A page that folds out to twice the size of a regular page is called a *gatefold*. A *jump line*, or *continued line*, at the end of a page refers the reader to the remaining text of a story appearing elsewhere in the magazine. A brief descriptive headline above the main head, designed to attract the reader's attention, is a *kicker*, *teaser*, *eyebrow*, or *highline*. Subscription cards bound into a magazine are called *inserts*. Those not physically connected are called *blow-ins*.

gutter/gutter margin

italics

margin

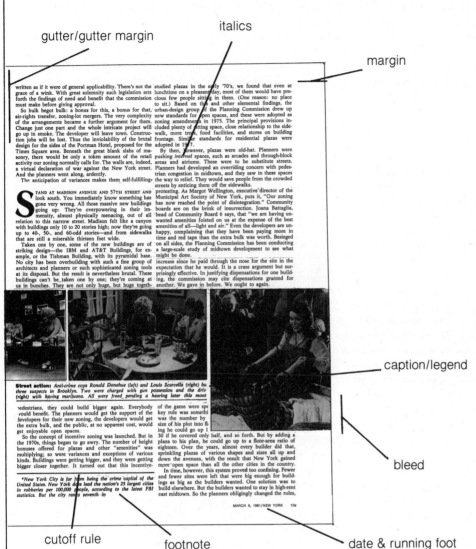

caption/legend

bleed

cutoff rule

footnote

date & running foot

Column

Back of the Book

slug

two-deck head

bold face lead-in

art

end slug/closed quad

listings

advertisement/ house ad

coupon

puzzle solutions

reader service coupon

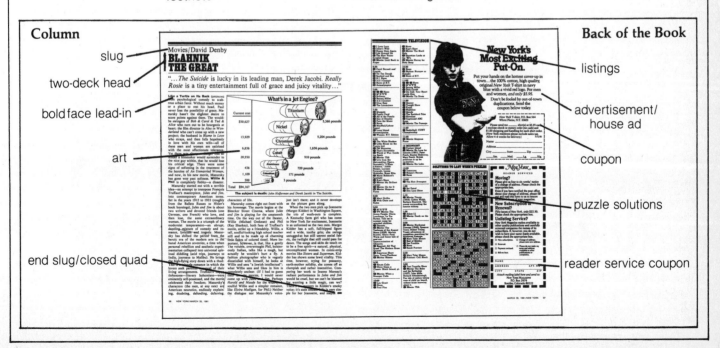

Still Camera and Film

To focus on an *image*, a photographer looks through the *viewfinder* on the back of the camera. Some cameras have *automatic focus* and *power winder* as in this model shown. Camera accessories include *interchangeable lenses—telephoto, wide-angle, zoom* and *special-purpose—lens caps* and *hoods, filters, focusing screens* and *eyecups*.

accessory shoe/ hot shoe

viewfinder

drive mode key

film speed key

exposure mode key

exposure adjustment key

data panel display

depth-of-field scale

distance scale

strap lug

aperture keys

lens-release button

focus-mode switch

on/off switch

program reset button

shutter speed keys

operating button/ shutter release

holder attaching screw

battery holder

self-timer indicator

contoured handgrip

focusing ring

attachment screw threads

lens

Single Lens Reflex/SLR/Autofocus 35 mm Camera

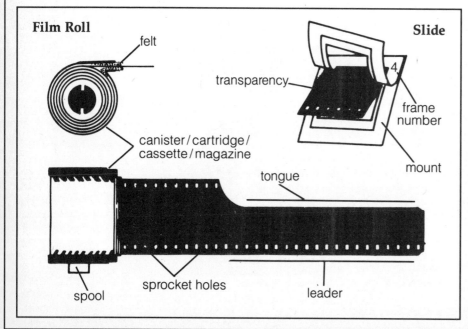

Film Roll

felt

canister/cartridge/ cassette/magazine

spool

sprocket holes

Slide

transparency

tongue

leader

frame number

mount

Zoom Lens

zoom & focus collar

distance scale

depth-of-field scale

aperture ring/ f-stops

rear lens cap

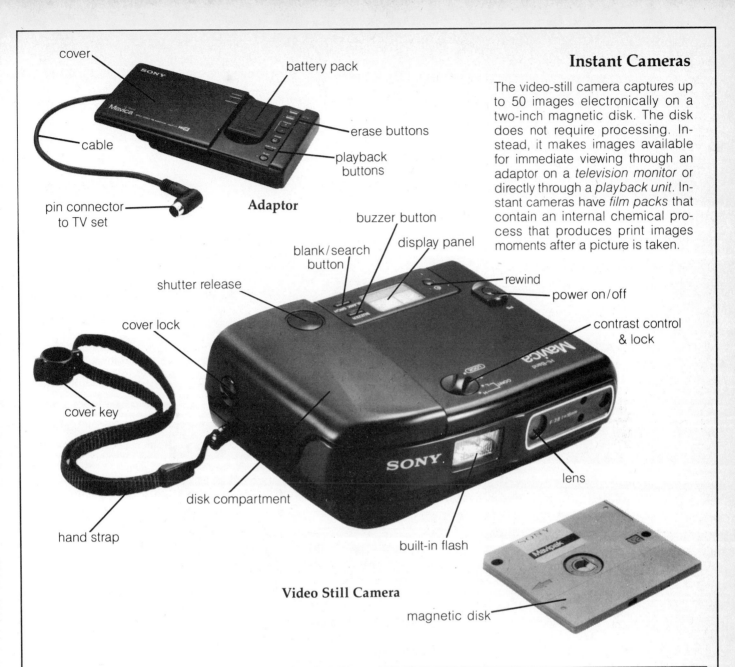

cover

battery pack

cable

erase buttons

playback buttons

pin connector to TV set

Adaptor

Instant Cameras

The video-still camera captures up to 50 images electronically on a two-inch magnetic disk. The disk does not require processing. Instead, it makes images available for immediate viewing through an adaptor on a *television monitor* or directly through a *playback unit*. Instant cameras have *film packs* that contain an internal chemical process that produces print images moments after a picture is taken.

buzzer button

blank/search button

display panel

shutter release

rewind

power on/off

cover lock

contrast control & lock

cover key

hand strap

disk compartment

built-in flash

SONY

lens

Video Still Camera

magnetic disk

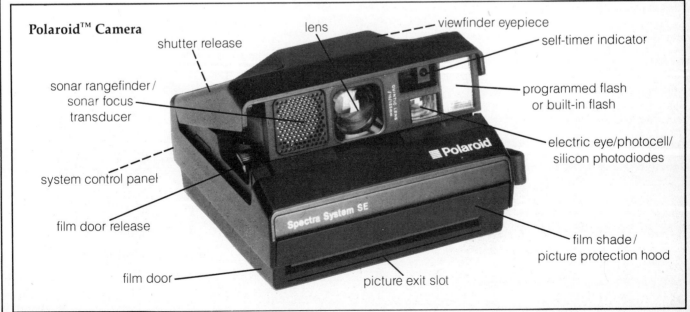

Polaroid™ Camera

shutter release

lens

viewfinder eyepiece

self-timer indicator

sonar rangefinder / sonar focus transducer

programmed flash or built-in flash

electric eye/photocell/ silicon photodiodes

system control panel

Polaroid

film door release

Spectra System SE

film door

picture exit slot

film shade / picture protection hood

Visual Communications

Movie Camera

Home-movie cameras, such as the one shown here, use film contained in *drop-in cartridges*. In large commercial models, *unexposed film* moves through the body from the *supply reel* to the *take-up reel*. The reels in these cameras are often housed in a *blimp*, a soundproof device that fits on top of the body. *Single-system sound cameras* record both *image* and *sound* on the same film. Sound tracks on film may be either *optical* or *magnetic*.

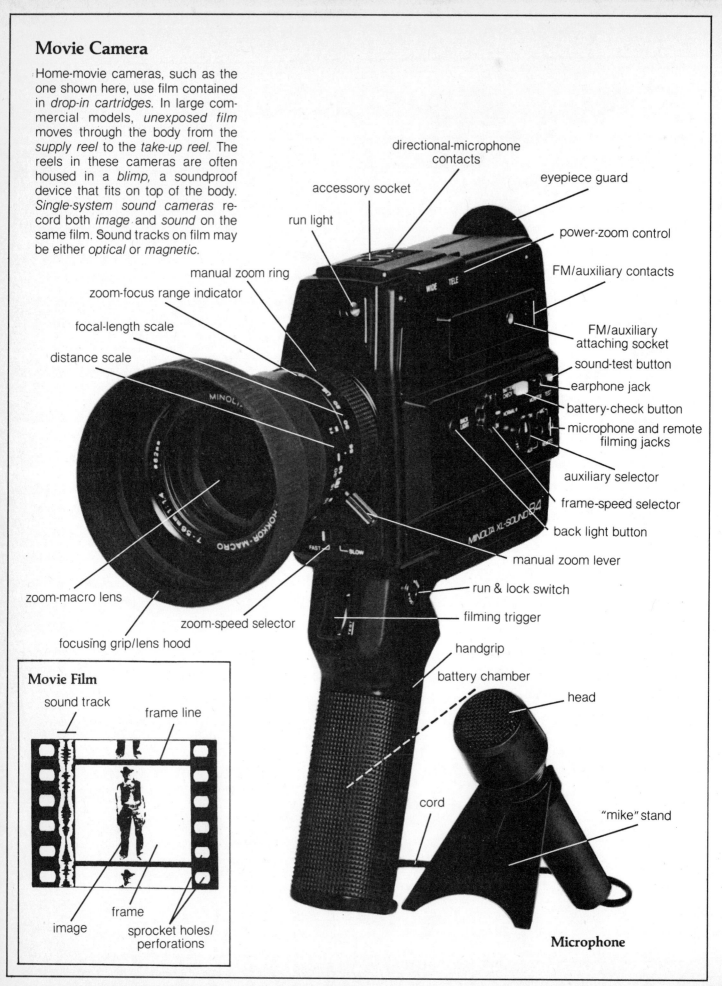

directional-microphone contacts

accessory socket

run light

eyepiece guard

power-zoom control

FM/auxiliary contacts

FM/auxiliary attaching socket

sound-test button

earphone jack

battery-check button

microphone and remote filming jacks

auxiliary selector

frame-speed selector

back light button

manual zoom lever

run & lock switch

filming trigger

handgrip

battery chamber

head

cord

"mike" stand

manual zoom ring

zoom-focus range indicator

focal-length scale

distance scale

zoom-macro lens

focusing grip/lens hood

zoom-speed selector

Microphone

Movie Film

sound track

frame line

image

frame

sprocket holes/ perforations

Projectors

The film projector shown here is a *self-threading, reel-to-reel model* with a built-in *speaker*. Slide projectors may have circular, or *carousel*, trays, *slide cubes* or *straight trays*.

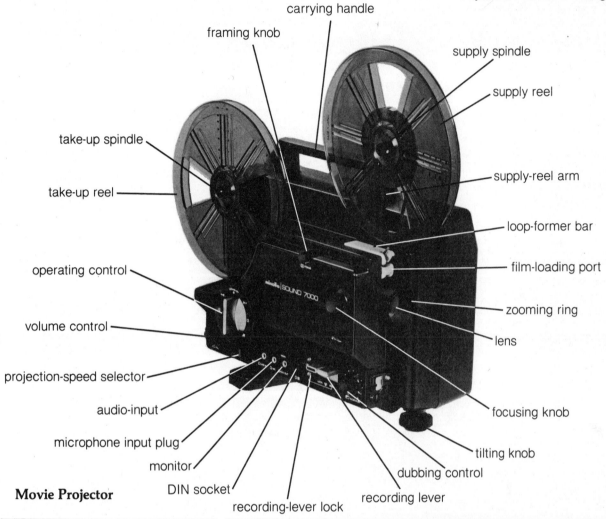

carrying handle

framing knob

supply spindle

supply reel

take-up spindle

take-up reel

supply-reel arm

loop-former bar

film-loading port

operating control

zooming ring

volume control

lens

projection-speed selector

audio-input

focusing knob

microphone input plug

tilting knob

monitor

dubbing control

DIN socket

recording lever

recording-lever lock

Movie Projector

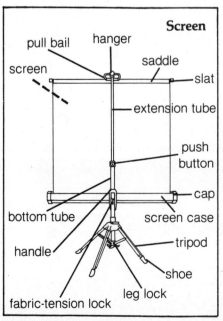

Screen

pull bail · hanger

saddle

screen

slat

extension tube

push button

cap

bottom tube

screen case

handle

tripod

shoe

leg lock

fabric-tension lock

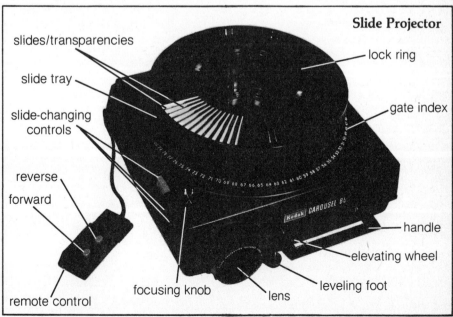

Slide Projector

slides/transparencies

lock ring

slide tray

gate index

slide-changing controls

reverse

forward

handle

remote control

focusing knob

lens

elevating wheel

leveling foot

Visual Communications

Photographic Accessories

In addition to the accessories shown here, *carrying straps, gadget bags,* and *cleaning supplies* such as *brushes, lens tissue* and *cleaning fluid* are used.

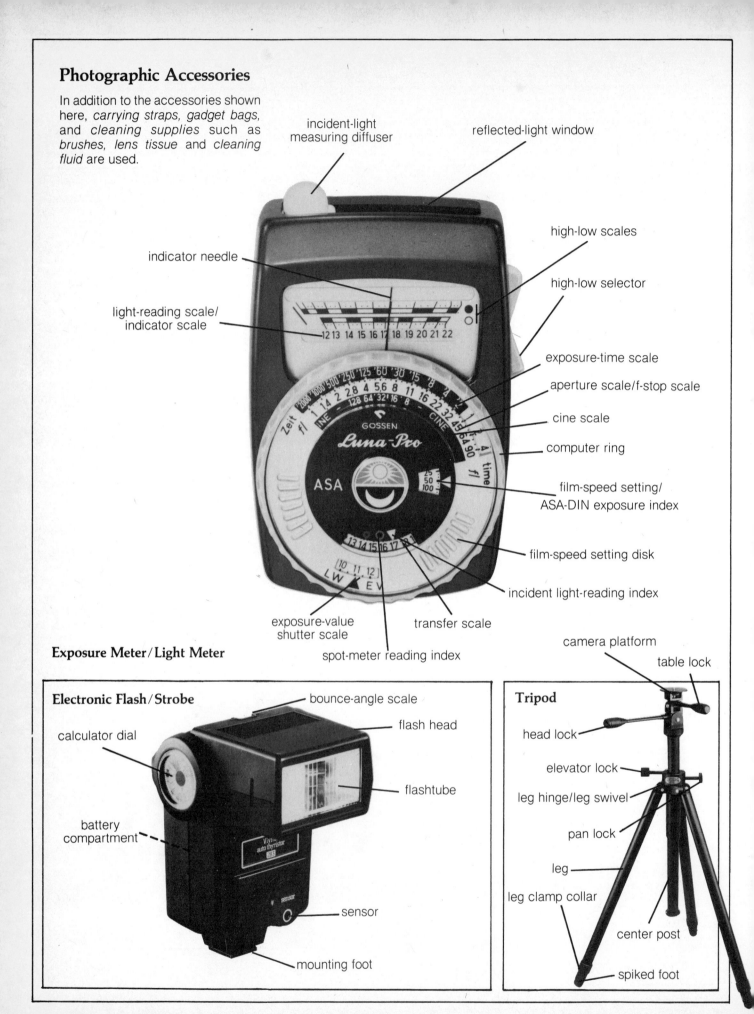

incident-light measuring diffuser

reflected-light window

indicator needle

light-reading scale/ indicator scale

high-low scales

high-low selector

exposure-time scale

aperture scale/f-stop scale

cine scale

computer ring

film-speed setting/ ASA-DIN exposure index

film-speed setting disk

incident light-reading index

exposure-value shutter scale

transfer scale

spot-meter reading index

GOSSEN

Luna-Pro

ASA

Exposure Meter/Light Meter

Electronic Flash/Strobe

bounce-angle scale

flash head

calculator dial

flashtube

battery compartment

Vivitar auto thyristor 283

sensor

mounting foot

Tripod

camera platform

table lock

head lock

elevator lock

leg hinge/leg swivel

pan lock

leg

leg clamp collar

center post

spiked foot

Tape Recorders

Sound is recorded on *magnetic tape* by passing the tape over a *recording head.* Most cassette recorders have *built-in microphones* but are designed to work with *external mikes* as well. They are *battery-powered,* have *rechargeable battery packs* or *AC power cords.*

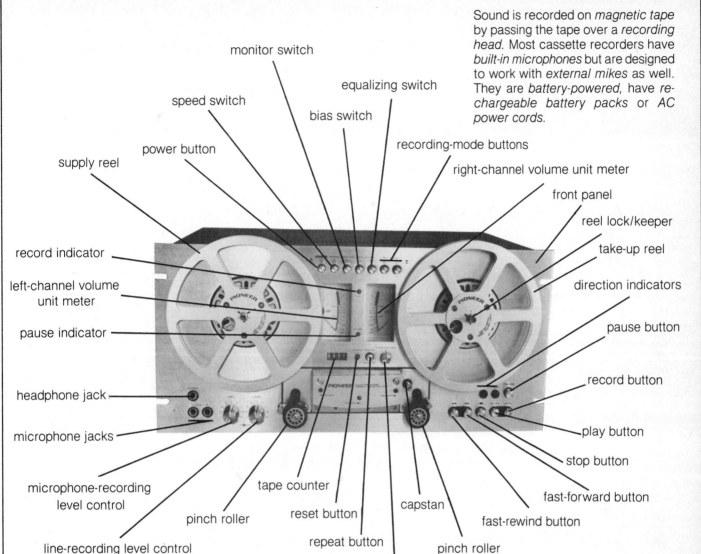

monitor switch

equalizing switch

speed switch

bias switch

power button

recording-mode buttons

supply reel

right-channel volume unit meter

front panel

reel lock/keeper

take-up reel

record indicator

direction indicators

left-channel volume unit meter

pause button

pause indicator

record button

headphone jack

microphone jacks

play button

stop button

microphone-recording level control

tape counter

fast-forward button

reset button

capstan

fast-rewind button

pinch roller

repeat button

pinch roller

line-recording level control

pitch-control dial

Reel-to-Reel Recorder and Playback Unit

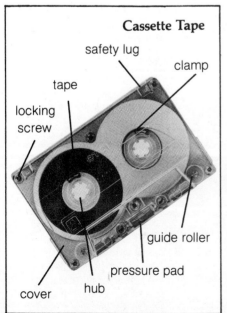

Cassette Tape

safety lug

clamp

tape

locking screw

guide roller

pressure pad

cover

hub

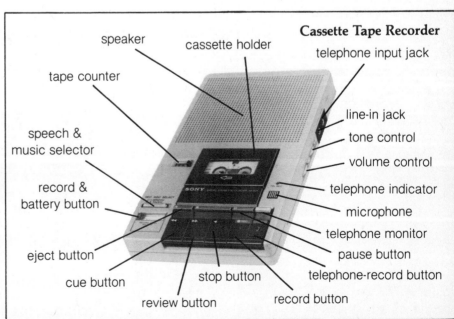

Cassette Tape Recorder

speaker

cassette holder

telephone input jack

tape counter

line-in jack

tone control

speech & music selector

volume control

record & battery button

telephone indicator

microphone

telephone monitor

eject button

pause button

cue button

telephone-record button

stop button

review button

record button

Disc and Record Players

Compact disc players use a *laser tracking system* to play or repeat selections. Multiple albums can be programmed to play in any order on a *CD changer*, while a CD player holds only one album at a time. An optional *monster cable* improves sound by eliminating disc vibration. The amount of information a player can read off a disc is measured in *bits*.

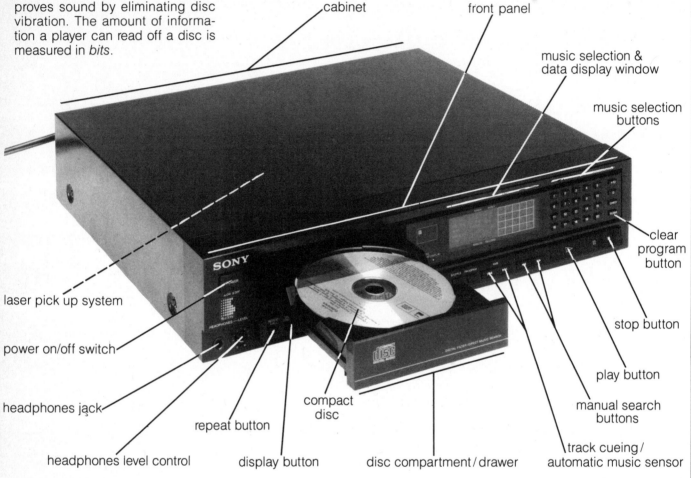

Compact Disc Player/CD Player

cabinet

front panel

music selection & data display window

music selection buttons

clear program button

stop button

play button

manual search buttons

track cueing/ automatic music sensor

disc compartment/drawer

display button

compact disc

repeat button

headphones level control

headphones jack

power on/off switch

laser pick up system

Record/Platter/Disc

lead-in groove

manufacturer

locked groove

record title & artist

grooves/ spiral

label

lead-out groove

center hole

master number

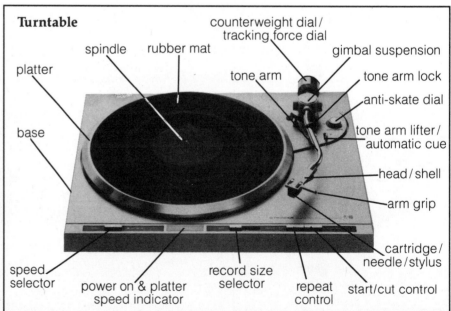

Turntable

spindle

rubber mat

counterweight dial/ tracking force dial

gimbal suspension

tone arm

tone arm lock

anti-skate dial

tone arm lifter/ automatic cue

head/shell

arm grip

cartridge/ needle/stylus

start/cut control

repeat control

record size selector

power on & platter speed indicator

speed selector

base

platter

Audio Equipment

A home audio system produces minimally distorted sound, or *high fidelity*. It is usually comprised of a *tuner*, a disc or record player, a *pre-amp*, and amplifier and speakers. Its power output is measured in *watts*.

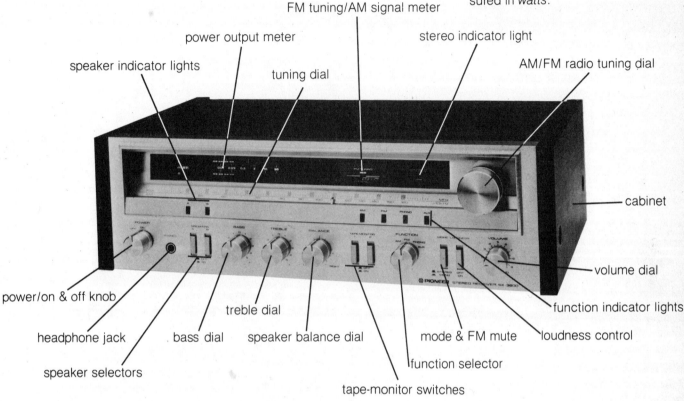

FM tuning/AM signal meter

power output meter

stereo indicator light

speaker indicator lights

tuning dial

AM/FM radio tuning dial

cabinet

volume dial

power/on & off knob

function indicator lights

headphone jack

treble dial

mode & FM mute

loudness control

bass dial

speaker balance dial

speaker selectors

function selector

tape-monitor switches

Receiver/Amplifier

Headphones

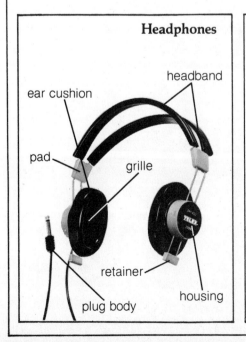

headband

ear cushion

grille

pad

grille

retainer

plug body

housing

Speakers

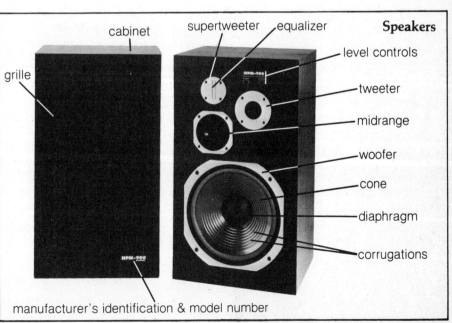

cabinet

supertweeter

equalizer

level controls

tweeter

midrange

woofer

cone

diaphragm

corrugations

manufacturer's identification & model number

Aural Communications

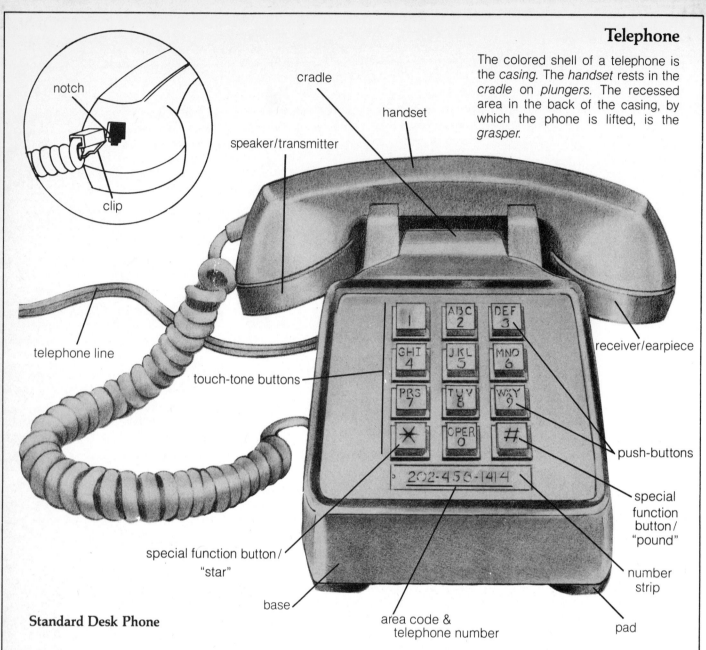

Telephone

The colored shell of a telephone is the *casing*. The *handset* rests in the *cradle* on *plungers*. The recessed area in the back of the casing, by which the phone is lifted, is the *grasper*.

notch

clip

cradle

handset

speaker/transmitter

receiver/earpiece

telephone line

touch-tone buttons

1
ABC 2
DEF 3
GHI 4
JKL 5
MNO 6
PRS 7
TUV 8
WXY 9
✳
OPER 0
#

202-456-1414

push-buttons

special function button/ "pound"

number strip

special function button/ "star"

base

area code & telephone number

pad

Standard Desk Phone

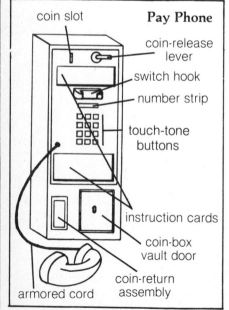

Pay Phone

coin slot

coin-release lever

switch hook

number strip

touch-tone buttons

instruction cards

coin-box vault door

coin-return assembly

armored cord

Trimline Phone

number strip

rotary dial

plunger

finger hole

base

finger stop

bell adjuster

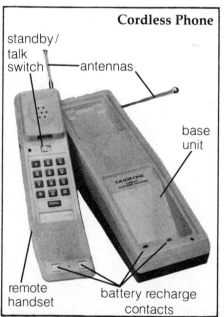

Cordless Phone

standby/ talk switch

antennas

base unit

remote handset

battery recharge contacts

Cellular Telephone

A *cell* is a circular service area of 16 mile radius, and calls are transmitted over radio waves and relayed from cell to cell over telephone wires. Available features include *memory redial* to recall numbers, *hands-off* operation, and an electronic lock to prevent unauthorized use. *Remote operation*, either with a *beeper* or *Touch-tone*™ phone, includes options like message retrieval, or leaving messages or *memos*. Many answering machines allow *call screening*, permitting calls to be heard without being answered.

antenna

liquid crystal display screen/LCD

auto redial

handset

illuminated menu keys

illuminated alpha-numeric keypad

battery pack

signal strength indicator

SIG
01 ABCDEF
1234567890

memory data

Display Screen

carrying handle

number being called

loudspeaker

Cellular Telephone/Mobile Phone

electronic lock

stand/base/case

cord

Answering Machine

message indicator lights

transfer call

telephone handset

play messages button

answer button

alpha-numeric keypad/telephone push buttons

control buttons

speakerphone

Aural Communications

Portable Radios and Cassette Players

A cassette player, or "Walkman"™, may be heard through headphones, a *built-in speaker* or *external speakers*. Portable radios often have detachable speakers. *Auto-reverse*, or *continuous play*, automatically plays both sides of a tape. *Dolby*™ sound reduces tape hiss. Some players with recording capabilities have *high-speed dubbing*, which copies tapes at faster than normal playing speed, and *synchronized dubbing*, which starts the original tape and blank tape simultaneously.

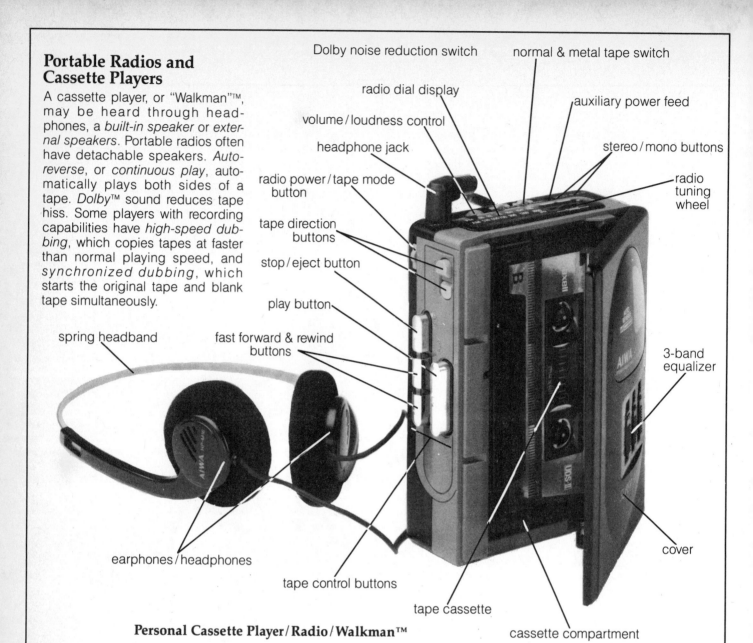

Dolby noise reduction switch

normal & metal tape switch

radio dial display

auxiliary power feed

volume/loudness control

stereo/mono buttons

headphone jack

radio power/tape mode button

radio tuning wheel

tape direction buttons

stop/eject button

play button

spring headband

fast forward & rewind buttons

3-band equalizer

earphones/headphones

cover

tape control buttons

tape cassette

cassette compartment

Personal Cassette Player/Radio/Walkman™

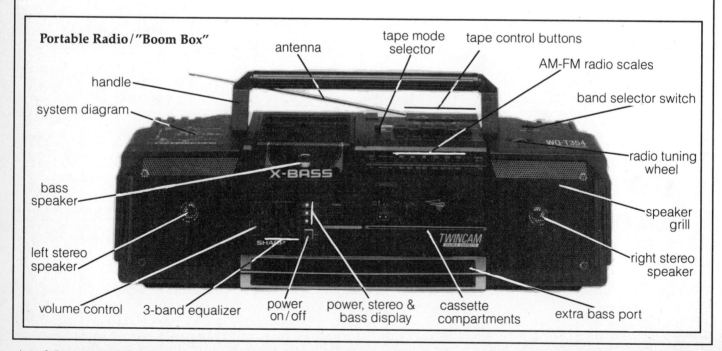

Portable Radio/"Boom Box"

antenna

tape mode selector

tape control buttons

AM-FM radio scales

handle

band selector switch

system diagram

radio tuning wheel

bass speaker

speaker grill

left stereo speaker

right stereo speaker

volume control

3-band equalizer

power on/off

power, stereo & bass display

cassette compartments

extra bass port

Transceiver

A *walkie-talkie* is a hand-held transceiver used to transmit and receive over short distances. *CBs,* or Citizens Band radios, like the one shown here, have greater but still limited range. *Amateur radio operators,* or "hams," use transceivers capable of communicating over vast distances.

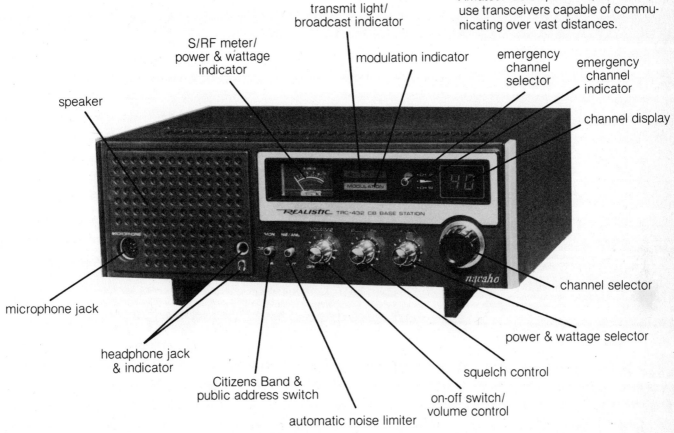

transmit light/
broadcast indicator

S/RF meter/
power & wattage
indicator

modulation indicator

emergency
channel
selector

emergency
channel
indicator

channel display

speaker

channel selector

microphone jack

power & wattage selector

headphone jack
& indicator

squelch control

Citizens Band &
public address switch

on-off switch/
volume control

automatic noise limiter

Base Station

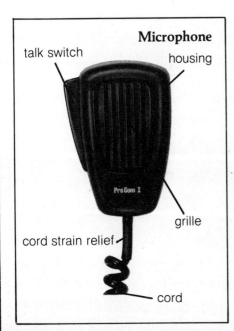

Microphone

talk switch

housing

grille

cord strain relief

cord

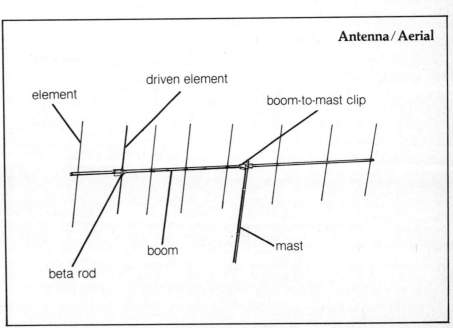

Antenna / Aerial

element

driven element

boom-to-mast clip

mast

boom

beta rod

Aural Communications

Video Recorder

Video recorders are used in conjunction with *television sets*, or *monitors*. They can be operated by hand-size *remote control units*. Some recorders use a grooveless *disc*, others use a *video cassette tape*.

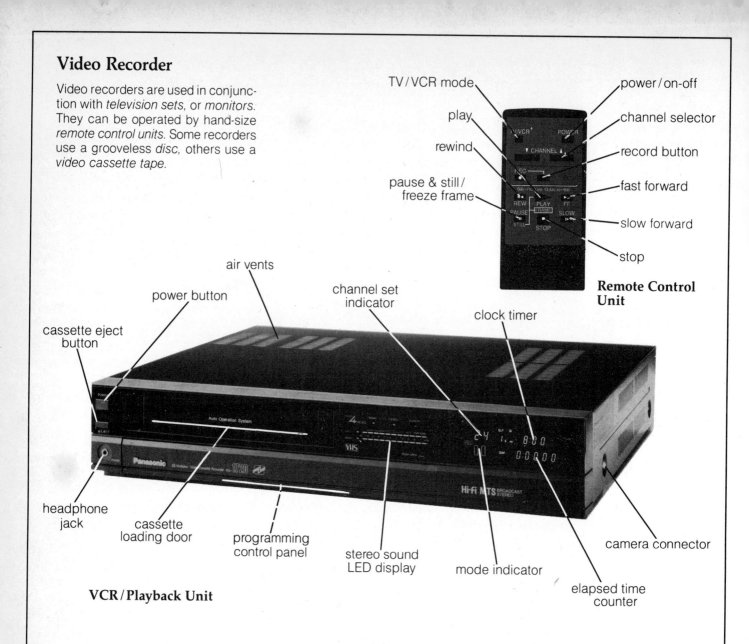

TV/VCR mode
play
rewind
pause & still / freeze frame

power/on-off
channel selector
record button
fast forward
slow forward
stop

Remote Control Unit

air vents
power button
channel set indicator
clock timer

cassette eject button

headphone jack
cassette loading door
programming control panel
stereo sound LED display
mode indicator
elapsed time counter
camera connector

VCR/Playback Unit

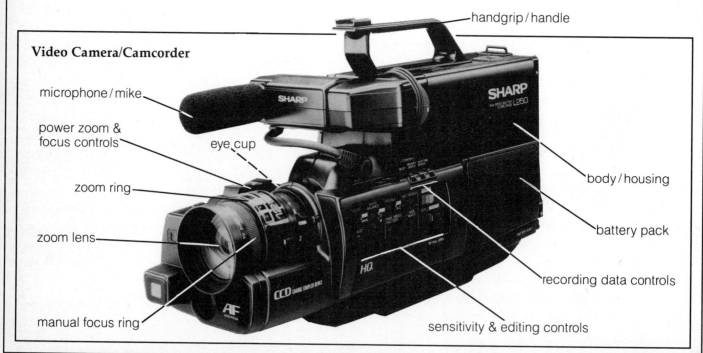

handgrip/handle

Video Camera/Camcorder

microphone/mike
power zoom & focus controls
eye cup
zoom ring
zoom lens
manual focus ring
body/housing
battery pack
recording data controls
sensitivity & editing controls

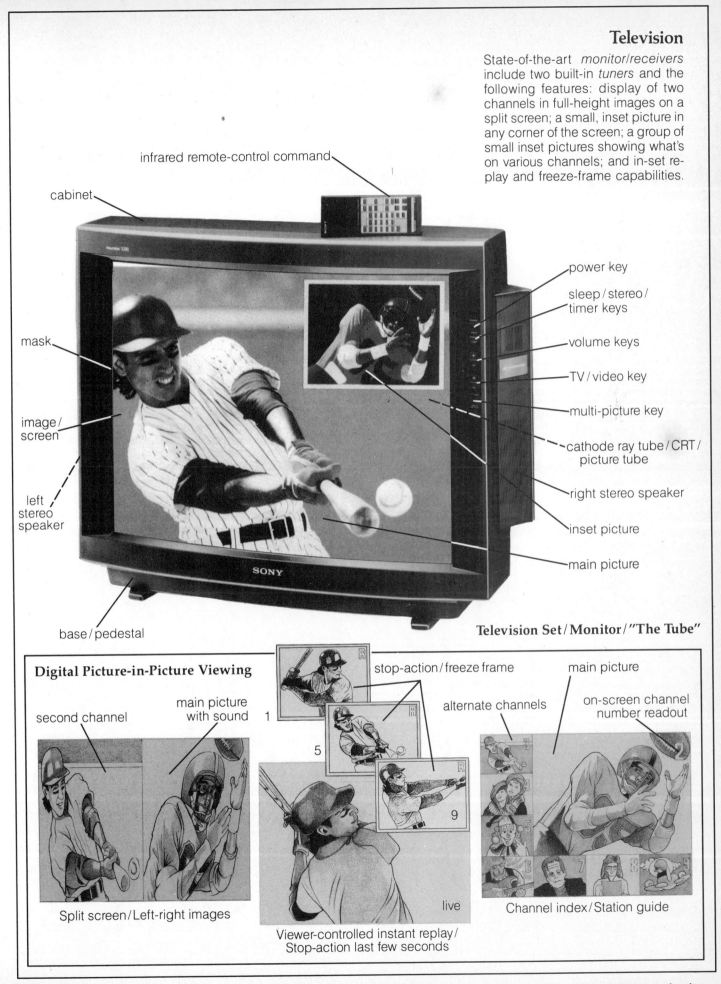

Television

State-of-the-art *monitor/receivers* include two built-in *tuners* and the following features: display of two channels in full-height images on a split screen; a small, inset picture in any corner of the screen; a group of small inset pictures showing what's on various channels; and in-set replay and freeze-frame capabilities.

infrared remote-control command

cabinet

mask

image/ screen

left stereo speaker

base/pedestal

power key

sleep/stereo/ timer keys

volume keys

TV/video key

multi-picture key

cathode ray tube/CRT/ picture tube

right stereo speaker

inset picture

main picture

Television Set/Monitor/"The Tube"

SONY

Digital Picture-in-Picture Viewing

second channel

main picture with sound

stop-action/freeze frame

main picture

alternate channels

on-screen channel number readout

1

5

9

live

Split screen/Left-right images

Viewer-controlled instant replay/ Stop-action last few seconds

Channel index/Station guide

Visual Communications

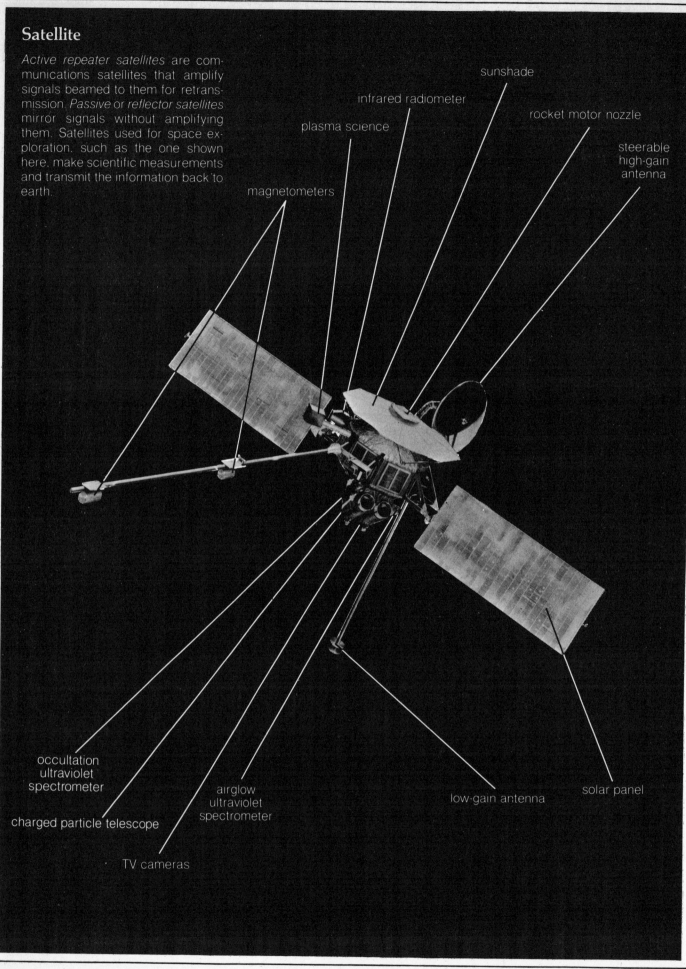

Satellite

Active repeater satellites are communications satellites that amplify signals beamed to them for retransmission. *Passive* or *reflector satellites* mirror signals without amplifying them. Satellites used for space exploration. such as the one shown here. make scientific measurements and transmit the information back to earth.

magnetometers

plasma science

infrared radiometer

sunshade

rocket motor nozzle

steerable high-gain antenna

occultation ultraviolet spectrometer

charged particle telescope

airglow ultraviolet spectrometer

TV cameras

low-gain antenna

solar panel

Personal Items

This section includes items people are likely to wear, carry or use in the course of their everyday lives. Thus, coverage includes clothing, hats, shoes, jewelry and money.

Wherever men's and women's apparel differ appreciably, items have been separated. But in the case of items such as sweaters and overcoats, articles worn by both sexes, only one version has been presented. Liberal use has been made to show the variations possible on single objects. However trendy clothing fashions or hairstyles may be, they share the same basic parts and details shown in the illustrations on the pages that follow.

Because cosmetics, grooming, hairstyles and jewelry are an important part of everyday life, they have been included in this section, as have such items as eyeglasses, handbags and wallets, timepieces and smoking materials. And because on rainy days an umbrella is essential to carry, it, too, appears here.

Identification Bracelet

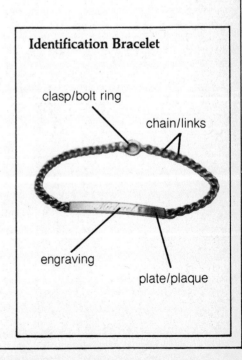

clasp/bolt ring

chain/links

engraving

plate/plaque

Jacket and Vest

A jacket, or *coat*, can be *single* or *double-breasted*. A *handkerchief pocket* or *breast pocket* is usually found on the upper left front panel. The pouch-like attachment inside a side pocket is called a *change pocket*. Most jackets have a *vent* or *double vent* cut into the hem in the back panel. Vests have an adjustable *backstrap* in the back.

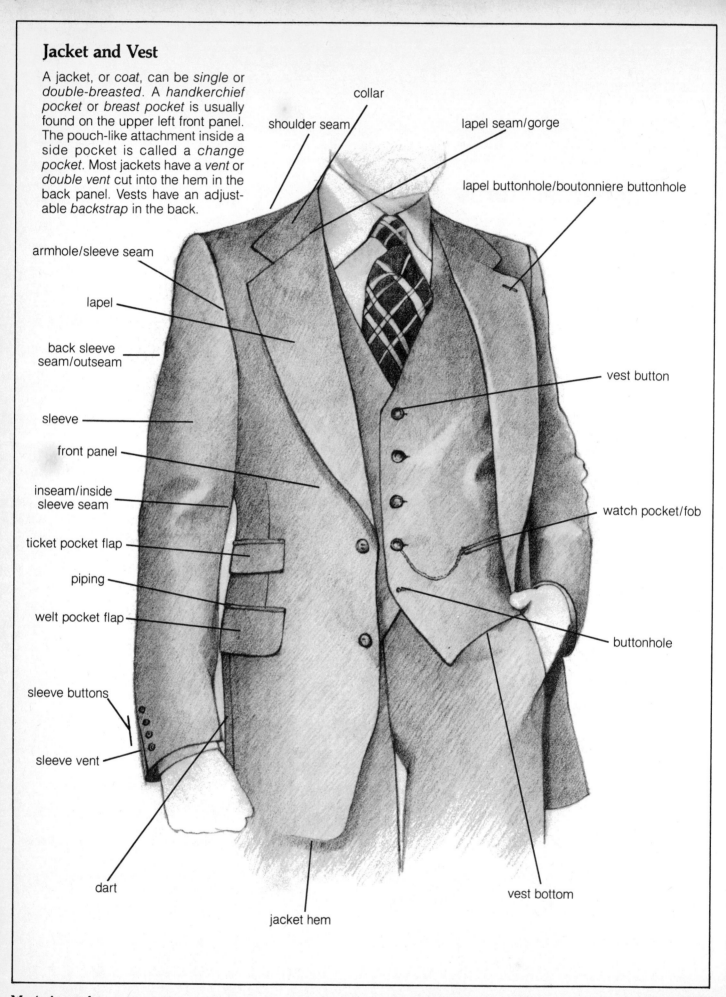

collar

shoulder seam

lapel seam/gorge

lapel buttonhole/boutonniere buttonhole

armhole/sleeve seam

lapel

back sleeve seam/outseam

sleeve

front panel

inseam/inside sleeve seam

ticket pocket flap

piping

welt pocket flap

sleeve buttons

sleeve vent

dart

jacket hem

vest button

watch pocket/fob

buttonhole

vest bottom

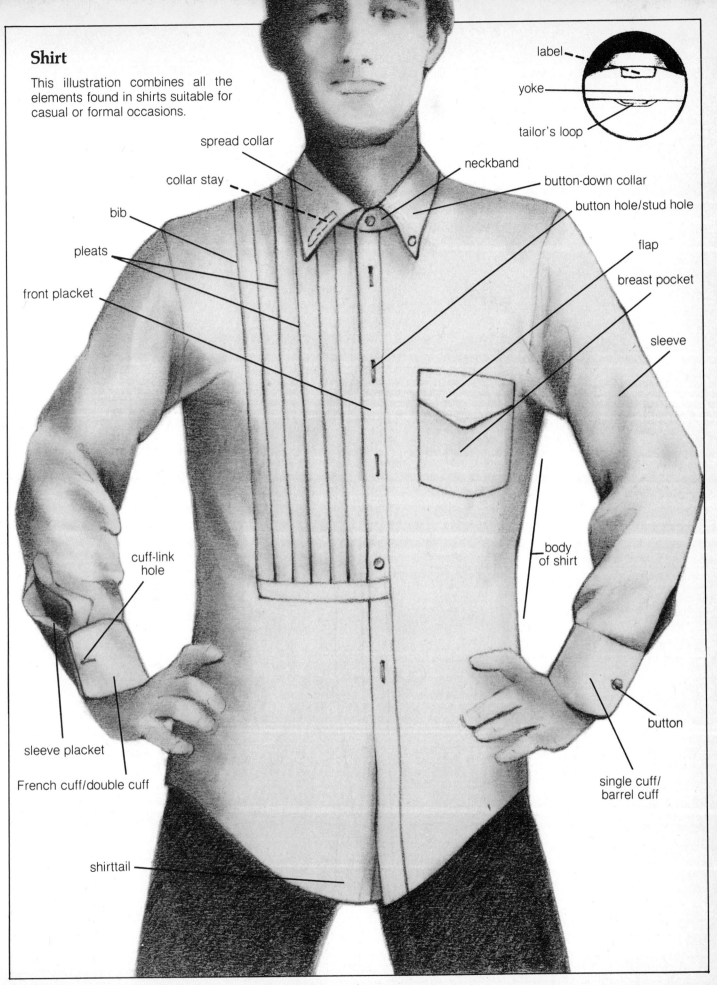

Shirt

This illustration combines all the elements found in shirts suitable for casual or formal occasions.

label

yoke

tailor's loop

spread collar

collar stay

bib

pleats

front placket

neckband

button-down collar

button hole/stud hole

flap

breast pocket

sleeve

cuff-link hole

body of shirt

sleeve placket

French cuff/double cuff

button

single cuff/barrel cuff

shirttail

Men's Apparel

Belt and Suspenders

Large, often elaborately engraved buckles are called *plaque buckles*. *Military buckles*, or *ratchet buckles*, are adjusted by pushing a *tension rod* inside the *frame*. Some belts come with reinforcing *eyelets* in the punch holes. The composite pair of suspenders shown here are *fireman's*, *policeman's*, or *working man's suspenders*. They all have a single elastic band at the back, whereas *dress suspenders* have crossed bands.

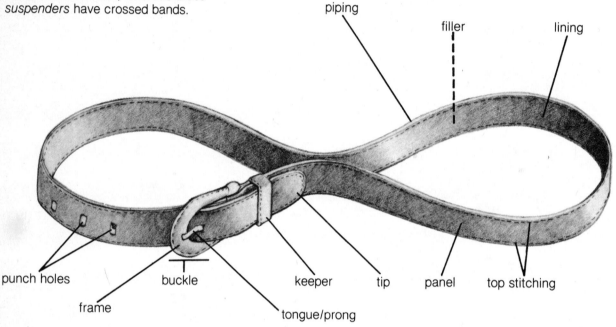

piping

filler

lining

punch holes

frame

buckle

tongue/prong

keeper

tip

panel

top stitching

Belt

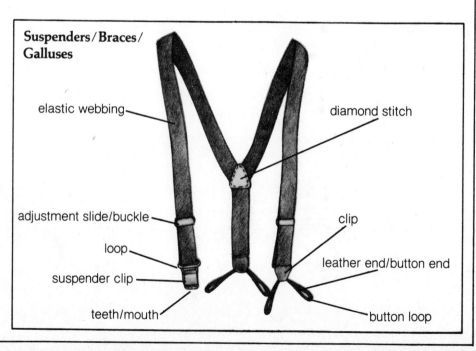

Suspenders / Braces / Galluses

elastic webbing

diamond stitch

adjustment slide/buckle

clip

loop

leather end/button end

suspender clip

teeth/mouth

button loop

Pants

The back of a *pair of pants* is called the *seat*. Mid-thigh or knee length pants are *shorts*. *Jeans* often have pockets and seams reinforced with *rivets*. *Waistband closures* on pants are secured with *button tab closings* or metal *hook and eye closings*.

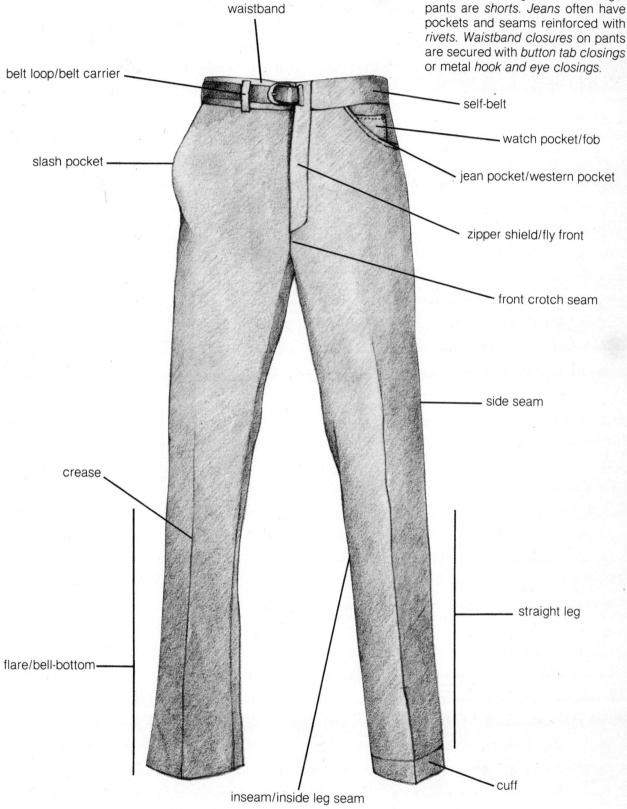

waistband

belt loop/belt carrier

self-belt

watch pocket/fob

slash pocket

jean pocket/western pocket

zipper shield/fly front

front crotch seam

side seam

crease

straight leg

flare/bell-bottom

cuff

inseam/inside leg seam

Trousers/Slacks

Men's Apparel

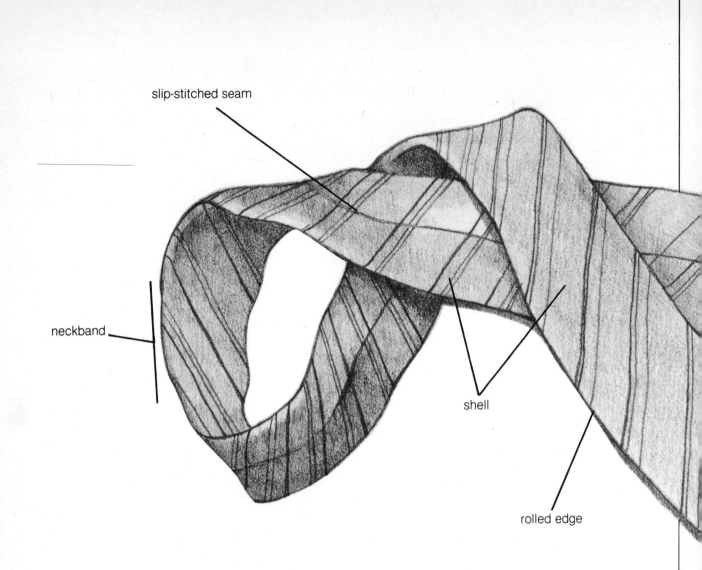

slip-stitched seam

neckband

shell

rolled edge

Necktie/Four-in-Hand

Bow Tie/Butterfly Tie

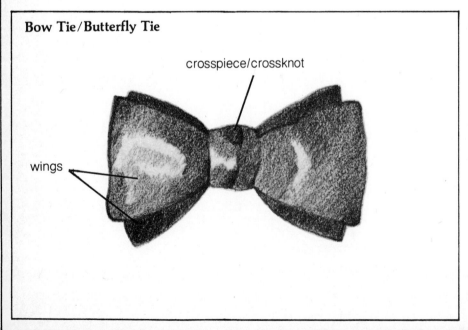

crosspiece/crossknot

wings

String Tie/Bolo Tie

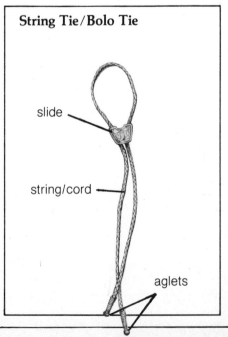

slide

string/cord

aglets

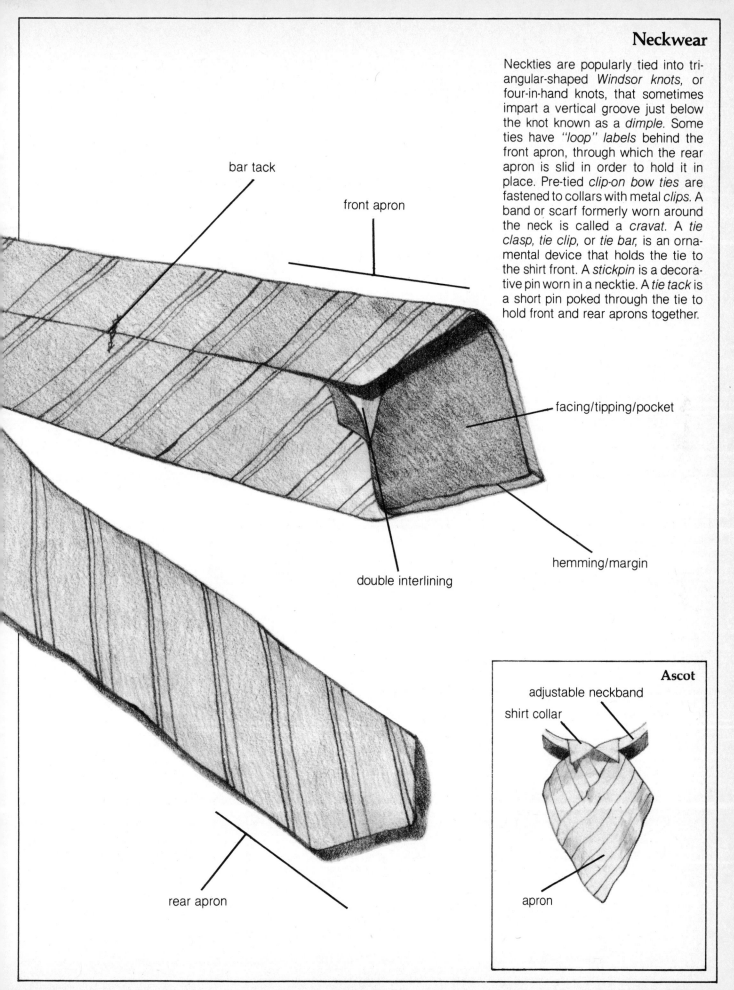

Neckwear

Neckties are popularly tied into tri-angular-shaped *Windsor knots*, or four-in-hand knots, that sometimes impart a vertical groove just below the knot known as a *dimple*. Some ties have *"loop" labels* behind the front apron, through which the rear apron is slid in order to hold it in place. Pre-tied *clip-on bow ties* are fastened to collars with metal *clips*. A band or scarf formerly worn around the neck is called a *cravat*. A *tie clasp, tie clip,* or *tie bar,* is an ornamental device that holds the tie to the shirt front. A *stickpin* is a decorative pin worn in a necktie. A *tie tack* is a short pin poked through the tie to hold front and rear aprons together.

bar tack

front apron

facing/tipping/pocket

hemming/margin

double interlining

rear apron

Ascot

adjustable neckband

shirt collar

apron

Men's Apparel

Underwear

A *T-shirt* has short sleeves rather than shoulder straps. Loose-fitting *boxer shorts* have short, trouserlike legs rather than leg openings. Some athletic supporters, or *jockstraps*, have pockets in the pouch to accommodate rubber-lined *protective cups.*

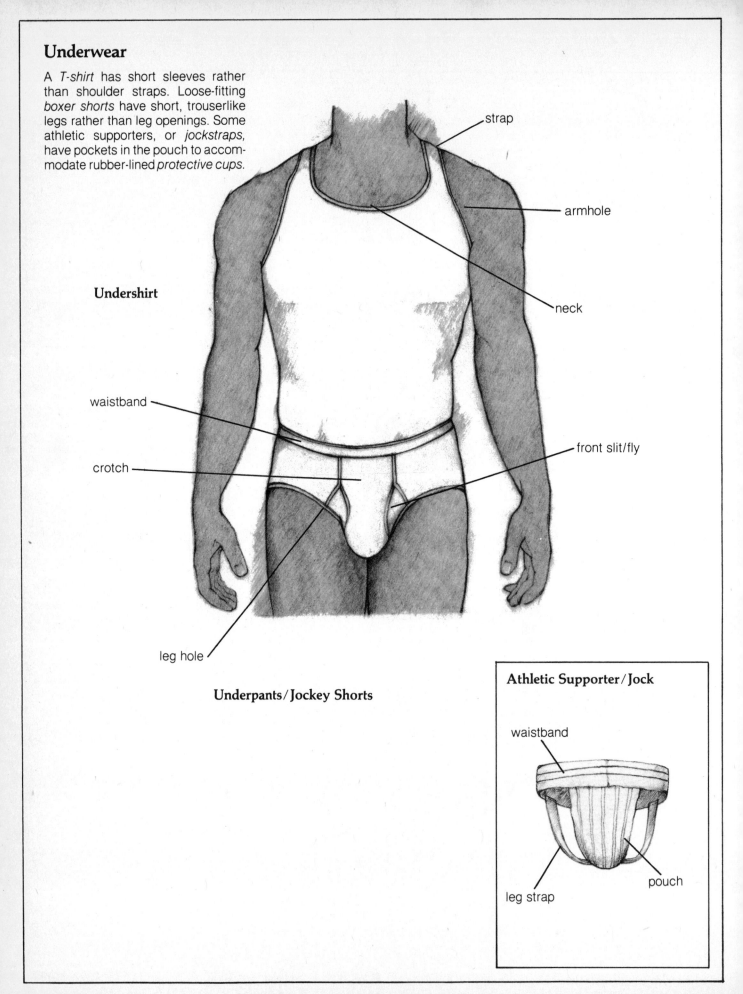

strap

armhole

Undershirt

neck

waistband

front slit/fly

crotch

leg hole

Underpants/Jockey Shorts

Athletic Supporter/Jock

waistband

pouch

leg strap

Foundation Garments

Most *bras* are secured with *hook-and-eye closures* either on a *back-strap* or in the front of the garment. Many have *underwiring* and/or *side-bones* for added support. *Cup padding* is another optional element. Girdles are sometimes stiffened with *spiral bones* or *stays*. *Corsets* are similar to girdles.

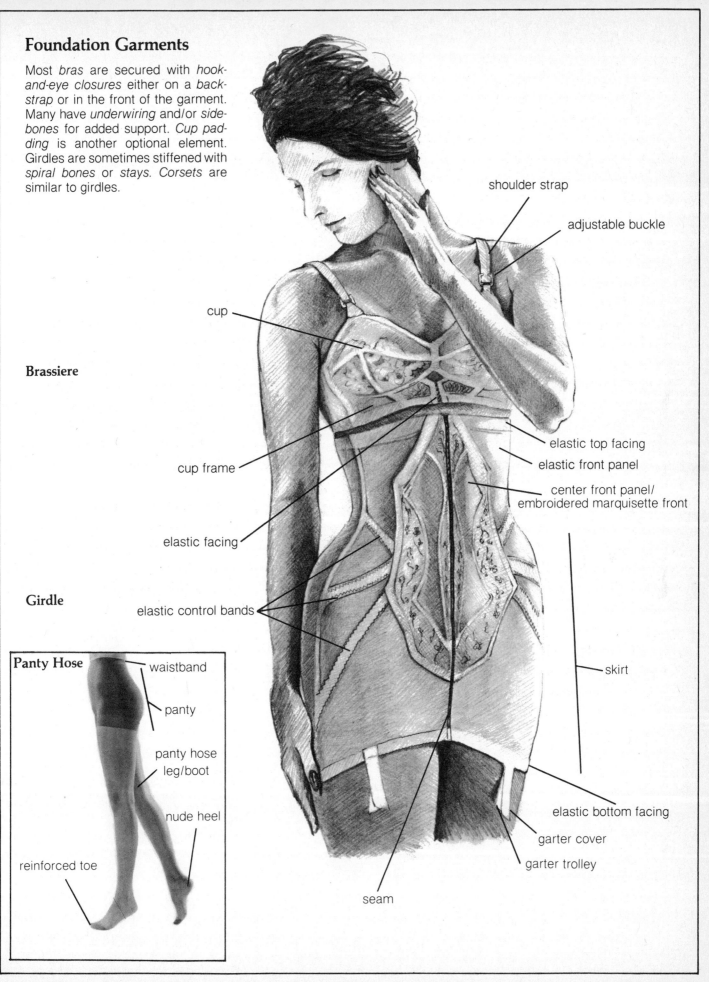

Brassiere

shoulder strap

adjustable buckle

cup

cup frame

elastic facing

elastic top facing

elastic front panel

center front panel/
embroidered marquisette front

Girdle

elastic control bands

skirt

Panty Hose

waistband

panty

panty hose leg/boot

nude heel

reinforced toe

elastic bottom facing

garter cover

garter trolley

seam

Women's Apparel

Jacket and Pants

Facing material is used on the underside of a lapel. *Lining* is used on the inside of a garment to cover up seamwork and provide body. A pair of lined pants has inside material from cuff to waist. In half-lined pants, the material stretches from waist to knee. In unlined garments, *seams* are clean finished with *bias tape,* or bias binding, sewn on a diagonal to provide stretch and support and to protect fabric from raveling.

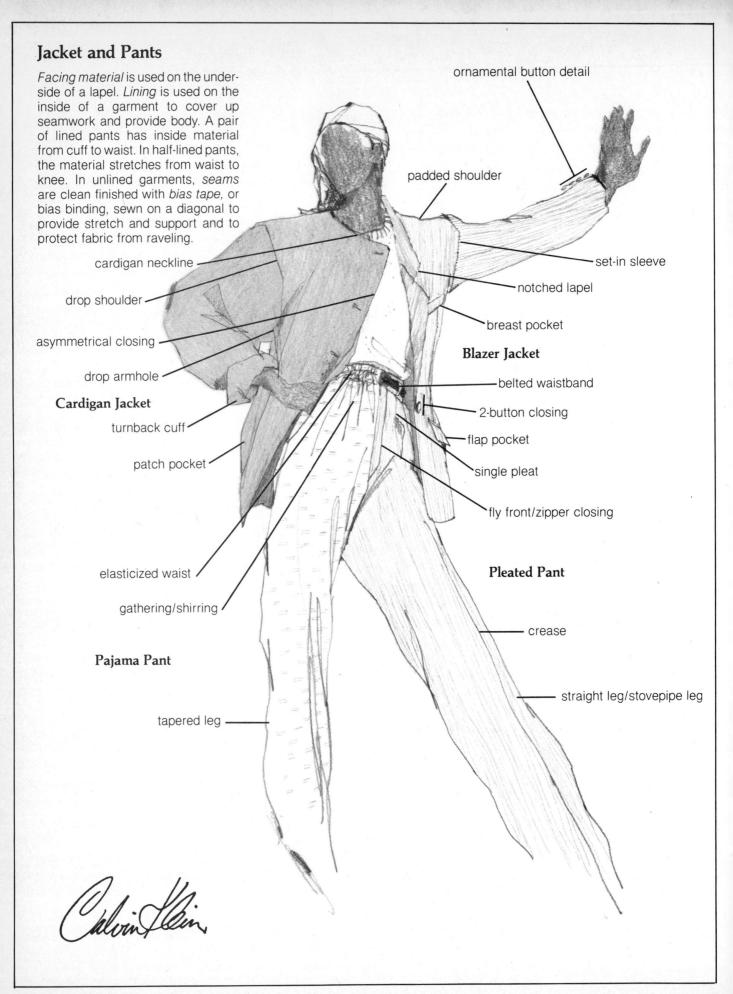

ornamental button detail

padded shoulder

cardigan neckline

drop shoulder

asymmetrical closing

drop armhole

set-in sleeve

notched lapel

breast pocket

Blazer Jacket

Cardigan Jacket

turnback cuff

patch pocket

belted waistband

2-button closing

flap pocket

single pleat

fly front/zipper closing

elasticized waist

gathering/shirring

Pleated Pant

crease

Pajama Pant

straight leg/stovepipe leg

tapered leg

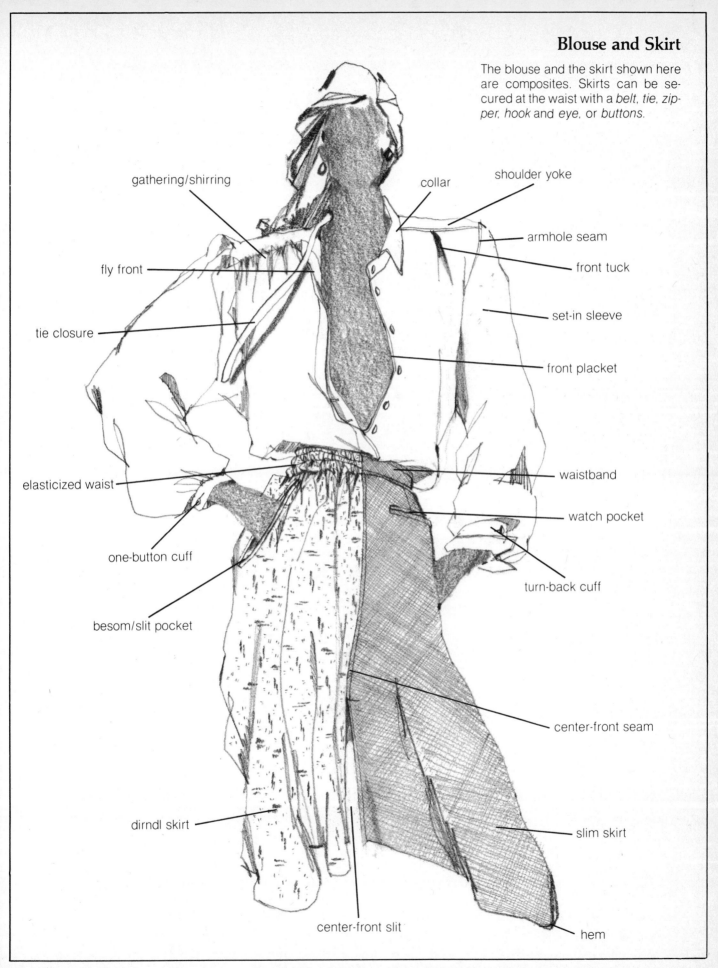

Blouse and Skirt

The blouse and the skirt shown here are composites. Skirts can be secured at the waist with a *belt, tie, zipper, hook* and *eye,* or *buttons.*

gathering/shirring

collar

shoulder yoke

armhole seam

front tuck

fly front

set-in sleeve

tie closure

front placket

waistband

elasticized waist

watch pocket

one-button cuff

turn-back cuff

besom/slit pocket

center-front seam

dirndl skirt

slim skirt

center-front slit

hem

Women's Apparel

Dress

This composite dress, or *gown,* has a *camisole top.* A dress hanging straight from the shoulders is a *chemise.* Some dresses have a fitted or shaped piece at the shoulder called a *yoke. Bratelles* are ornamental suspenderlike straps. Dresses are stored on hangers by means of *keepers, carriers, riders, loops* or *hangers.*

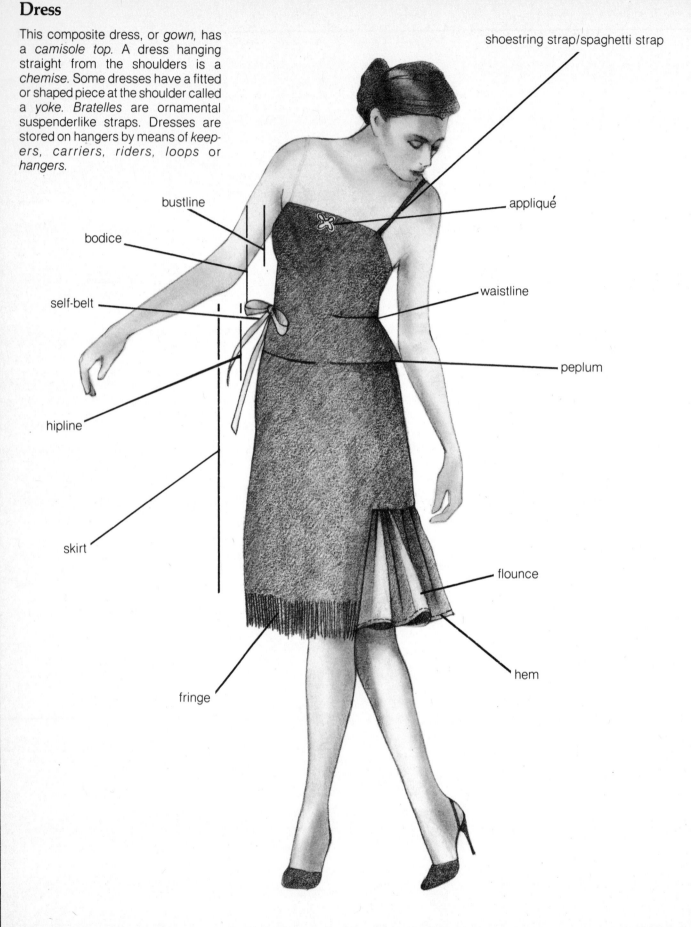

shoestring strap/spaghetti strap

bustline

bodice

appliqué

self-belt

waistline

peplum

hipline

skirt

flounce

fringe

hem

Sweater

A *crew neck sweater* is a pullover with a high, round neck. A *turtleneck* has a high neck that turns back over itself. A sweater with a neck opening that stretches from shoulder to shoulder is a *boat neck,* or *bateau neck.* A sweater without arms is a *vest,* or *knit vest.*

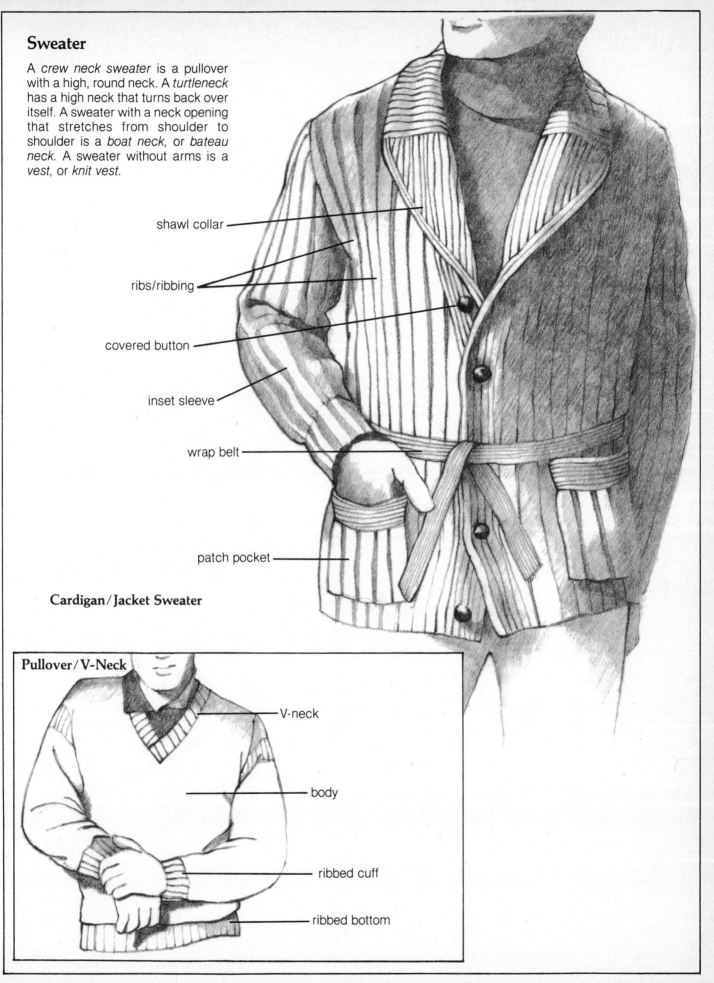

shawl collar

ribs/ribbing

covered button

inset sleeve

wrap belt

patch pocket

Cardigan/Jacket Sweater

Pullover/V-Neck

V-neck

body

ribbed cuff

ribbed bottom

Outerwear

The type of combination *overcoat* and *raincoat* shown here usually has a *button-out* or *zip-out robe lining* which provides warmth in cold weather. It also has a *storm shield* on the back, ornamental *'D' rings* hanging from the back of the belt and sometimes a *throat latch* strap around the collar.

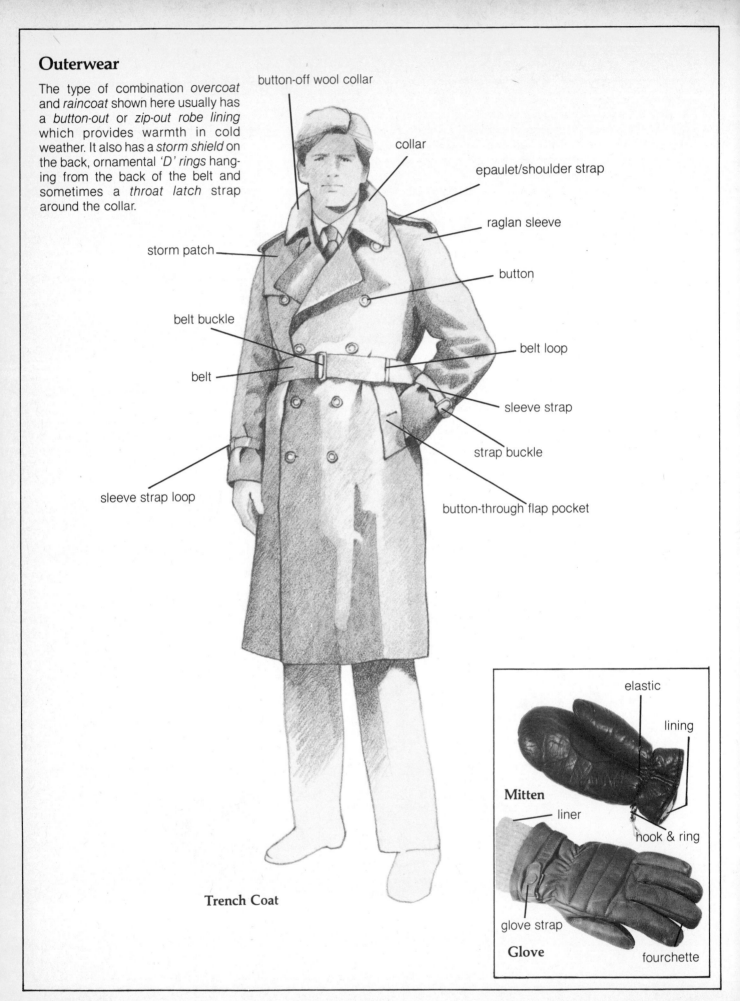

button-off wool collar

collar

epaulet/shoulder strap

raglan sleeve

button

storm patch

belt buckle

belt loop

belt

sleeve strap

strap buckle

sleeve strap loop

button-through flap pocket

Trench Coat

elastic

lining

Mitten

liner

hook & ring

glove strap

Glove

fourchette

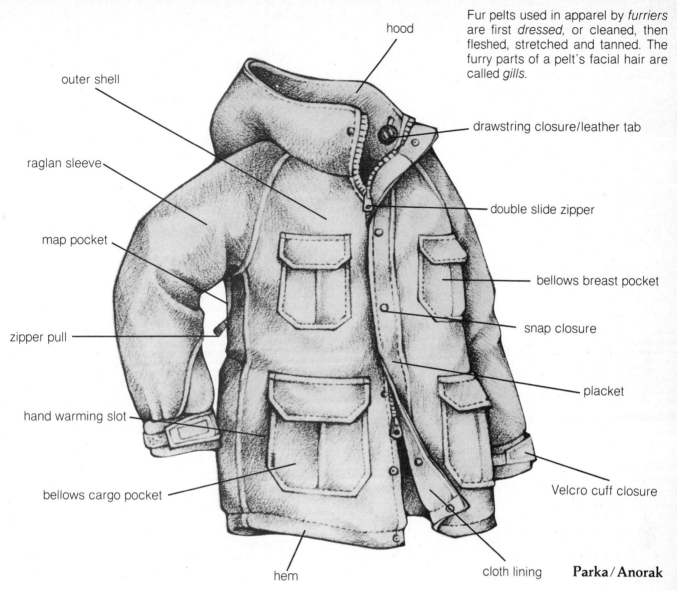

Outerwear

Fur pelts used in apparel by *furriers* are first *dressed,* or cleaned, then fleshed, stretched and tanned. The furry parts of a pelt's facial hair are called *gills.*

hood

outer shell

raglan sleeve

map pocket

zipper pull

hand warming slot

bellows cargo pocket

hem

drawstring closure/leather tab

double slide zipper

bellows breast pocket

snap closure

placket

Velcro cuff closure

cloth lining

Parka/Anorak

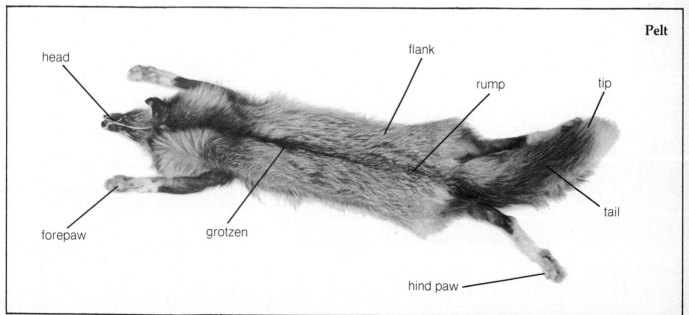

Pelt

flank

head

rump

tip

forepaw

grotzen

tail

hind paw

Men's Hats

Hats are *styled,* or *blocked,* by a *hat-maker* or *hatter.* Hats that have not been creased have an *open crown.* Some hats have *plastic linings.*

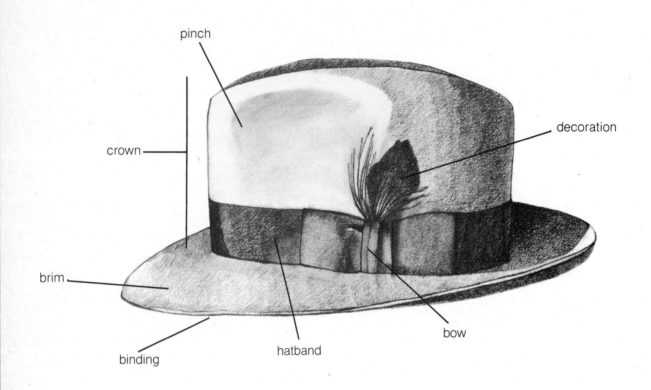

pinch

crown

decoration

brim

binding

hatband

bow

Cowboy Hat / Ten-Gallon Hat

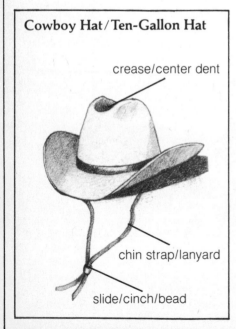

crease/center dent

chin strap/lanyard

slide/cinch/bead

Beret

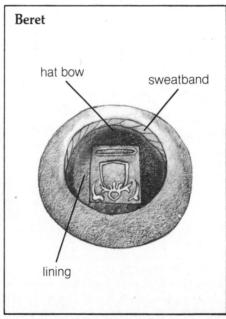

hat bow

sweatband

lining

Cap

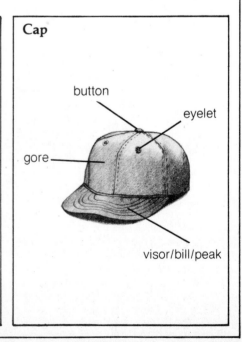

button

eyelet

gore

visor/bill/peak

Women's Hats

Women's hats are designed, made and sold by *milliners*. *Malines*, or stiff, fine *netting*, is often used as a veil. *Buckles*, *sequins*, *plastic fruit*, *fabric flowers*, *buttons*, *tassels* and *braids* are among the many items used as decorative *trimming*. Brimless, close-fitting hats include a *toque*, a *cloche*, and a *turban*. A *picture hat* has a broad flexible brim and is often decorated with trimming. A shallow, round hat with vertical sides is a *pillbox*. A netlike hat or part of a hat or the fabric that holds or covers the back of a woman's hair is a *snood*.

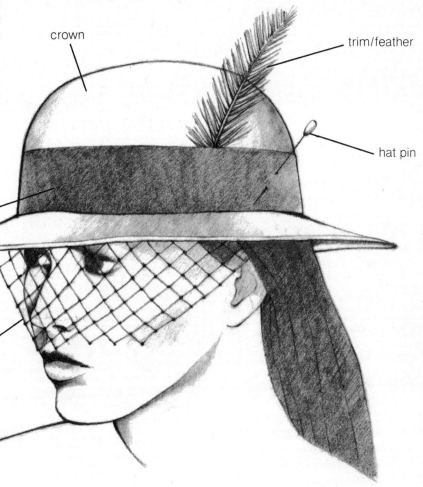

crown

trim/feather

hat pin

hatband

brim

veil

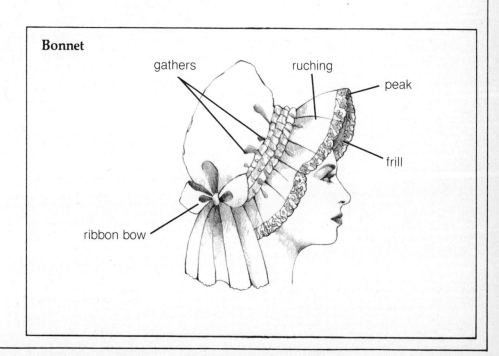

Bonnet

gathers

ruching

peak

frill

ribbon bow

Man's Shoe

A shoe consists of a *bottom,* or heel and sole, an *inner sole,* or *insole,* and an *upper.* Shoes like the one shown here, in which the flaps fold over the tongue or vamp, are *bluchers.* Shoes without this construction are *barrels.* A step-in shoe without laces is a *loafer,* whereas a *moccasin* has neither laces nor a heel. The fringed leather decoration on some shoes that covers the laces is the *kiltie.*

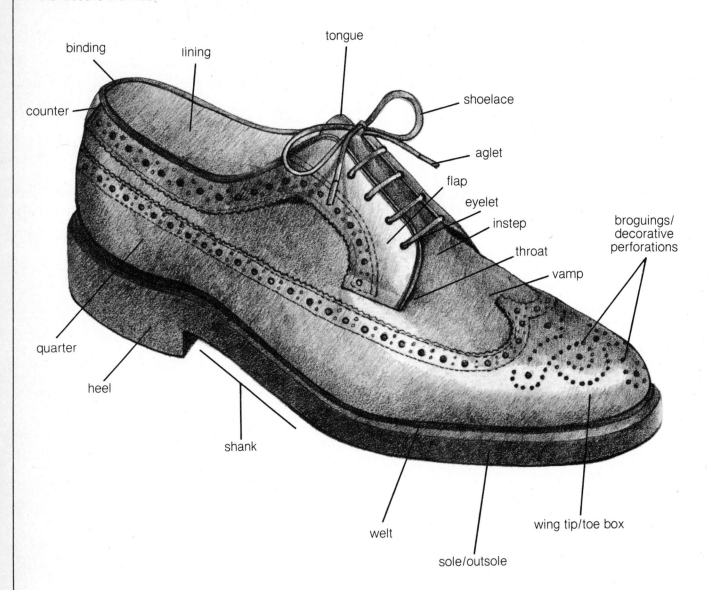

binding

lining

tongue

counter

shoelace

aglet

flap

eyelet

instep

broguings/
decorative
perforations

throat

vamp

quarter

heel

shank

welt

wing tip/toe box

sole/outsole

Woman's Shoe

A shoe with an open front is an *open-toed shoe,* whereas a shoe with an open back, held on by a strap, is a *slingback,* or *sling shoe.* The *high-heel shoe* seen here is similar to a *pump* in that it grips both the toe and the heel. A high, thin heel is a *spiked,* or *stiletto, heel.* A shoe with a thick layer between the *inner sole* and the outsole is a *platform.*

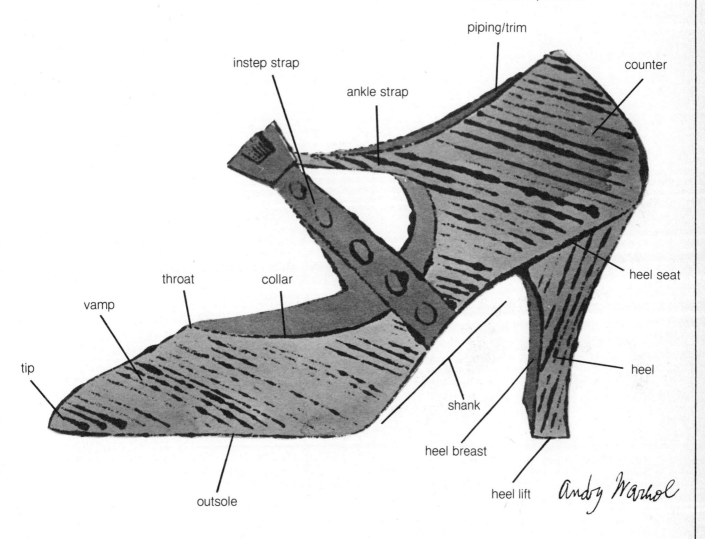

piping/trim

counter

instep strap

ankle strap

heel seat

throat

collar

vamp

heel

tip

shank

heel breast

heel

outsole

heel lift

Andy Warhol

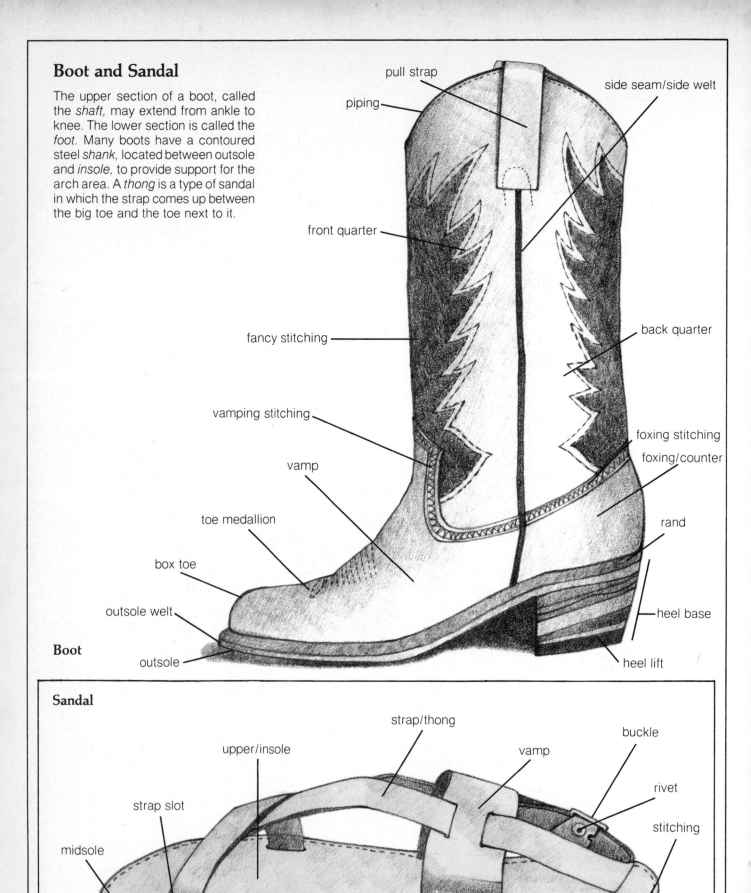

Boot and Sandal

The upper section of a boot, called the *shaft*, may extend from ankle to knee. The lower section is called the *foot*. Many boots have a contoured steel *shank*, located between outsole and insole, to provide support for the arch area. A *thong* is a type of sandal in which the strap comes up between the big toe and the toe next to it.

pull strap

piping

side seam/side welt

front quarter

fancy stitching

back quarter

vamping stitching

foxing stitching

foxing/counter

vamp

rand

toe medallion

box toe

heel base

outsole welt

heel lift

Boot

outsole

Sandal

strap/thong

buckle

upper/insole

vamp

rivet

strap slot

stitching

midsole

crepe sole

arch cookie/scaphoid pad

Shoe Accessories

Shoes can be protected in wet weather by *rubbers, rain boots* or *galoshes.* Socks, or *hose,* which extend to the ankle are *ankle socks,* whereas *knee socks* reach to the knee. *Support* hose have a higher *denier,* or mesh count, than regular hose, which provides additional support for the foot and leg. *Peds* are liners that cover the toes, sole and heel. *Boot hooks,* which fit into *boot loops,* help pull boots on, while V-shaped *bootjacks* hold the boot heel for easier removal. *Athletic socks,* or *sweat socks,* absorb perspiration. Shapeless *tube socks* mold to any foot shape.

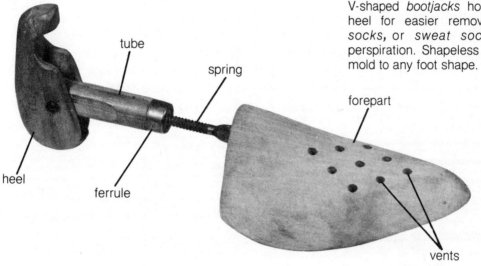

tube

spring

forepart

heel

ferrule

vents

Shoe Tree

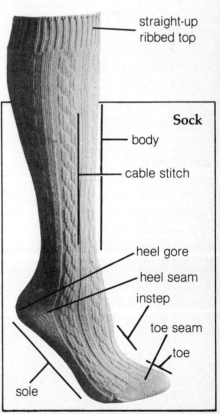

straight-up ribbed top

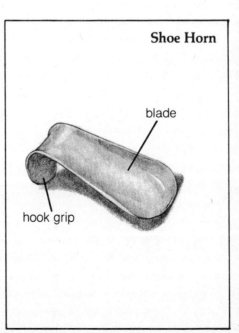

Shoe Horn

blade

hook grip

Sock

body

cable stitch

heel gore

heel seam

instep

toe seam

toe

sole

Fasteners

Heavy-duty hook-and-eye closures are called *hook and bars*. In a *cinch fastener*, a *strap* is pulled through two *rings* then back through the second ring to fasten. A *frog* consists of an intricately knotted *cord loop* through which a button is hooked.

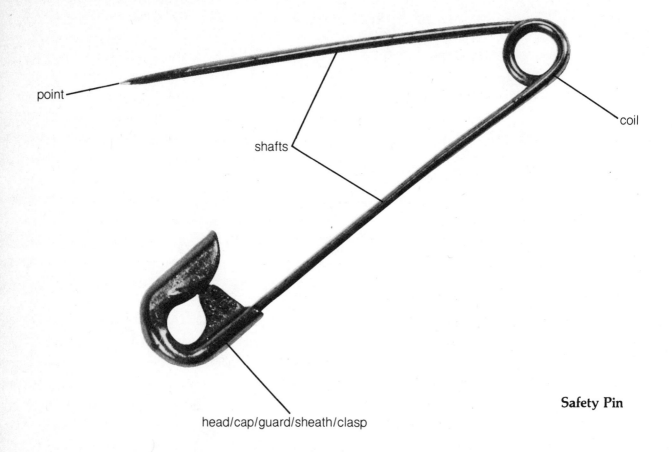

point

shafts

coil

head/cap/guard/sheath/clasp

Safety Pin

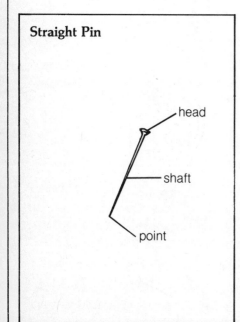

Straight Pin

head

shaft

point

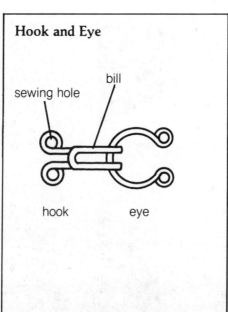

Hook and Eye

sewing hole

bill

hook

eye

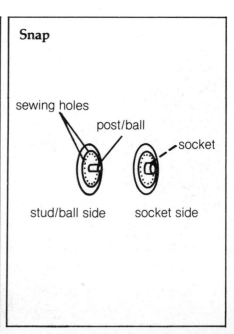

Snap

sewing holes

post/ball

socket

stud/ball side

socket side

A *divider* within the zipper slide separates teeth when it is moved downward. Some zippers have a *synthetic coil* rather than teeth. A *pull ring* is occasionally attached to the slide for decorative purposes. A *two-way zipper* can be opened from either end, while an *invisible zipper* is concealed when closed and appears to be a *seam*.

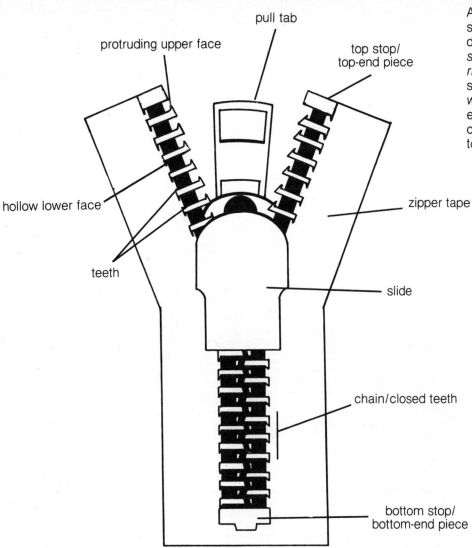

protruding upper face

pull tab

top stop/ top-end piece

hollow lower face

zipper tape

teeth

slide

chain/closed teeth

bottom stop/ bottom-end piece

Zipper/Slide Fastener

Velcro®

hook tape

loop tape

pile

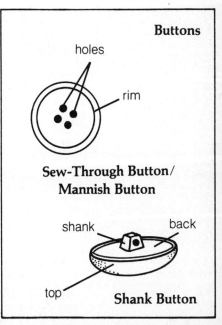

Buttons

holes

rim

Sew-Through Button/ Mannish Button

shank

back

top

Shank Button

Shavers

A *straight razor* has a single, long blade which folds into a *handle*. It is sharpened on a long strip of leather called a *strop*. Other, older barbering equipment includes *shaving brushes* and *shaving mugs*. A *safety razor* has two *wings* on the *head* which are opened by a screw at the base of the handle. Bleeding from shaving cuts or nicks can be stopped with a *styptic pencil*.

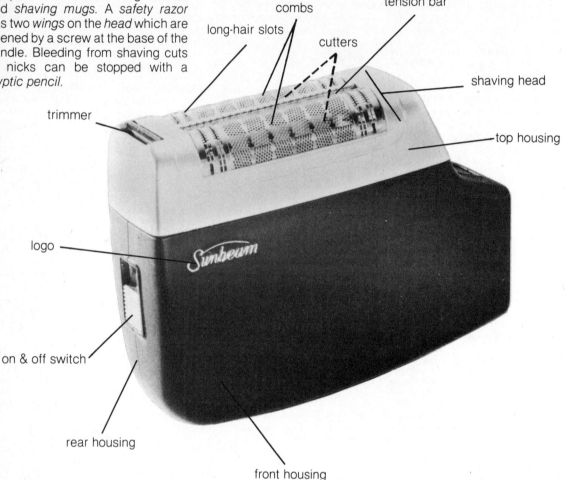

combs

tension bar

long-hair slots

cutters

shaving head

trimmer

top housing

logo

on & off switch

rear housing

front housing

Electric Razor

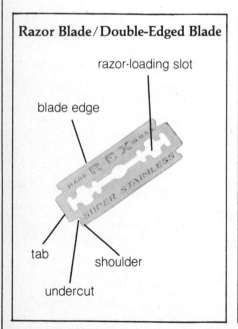

Razor Blade/Double-Edged Blade

razor-loading slot

blade edge

tab

shoulder

undercut

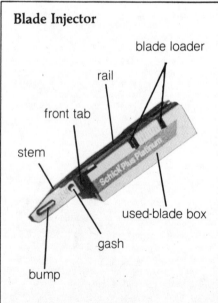

Blade Injector

blade loader

rail

front tab

stem

gash

bump

used-blade box

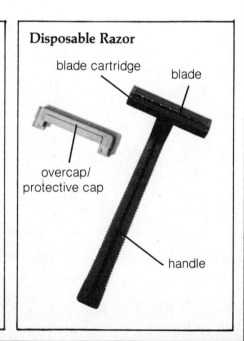

Disposable Razor

blade cartridge

blade

overcap/ protective cap

handle

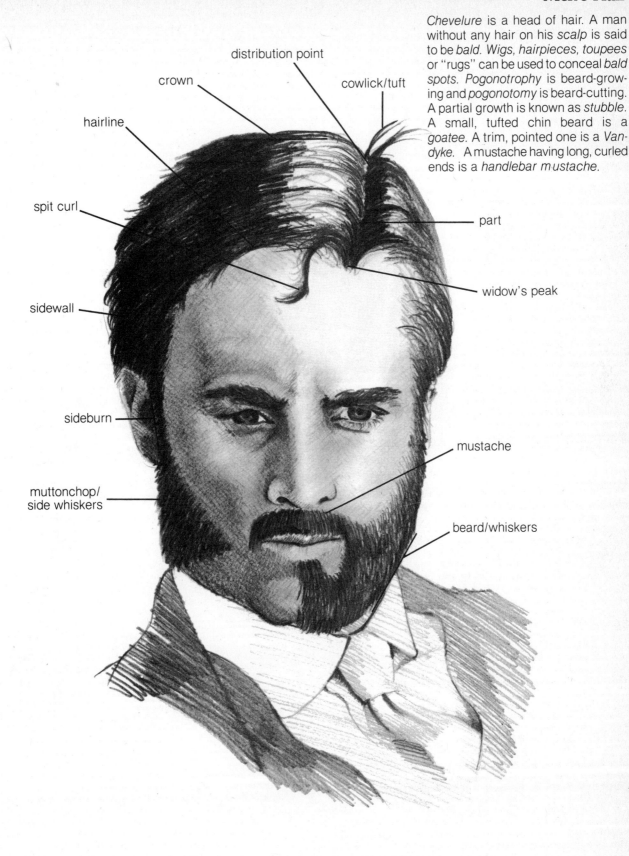

Men's Hair

Chevelure is a head of hair. A man without any hair on his *scalp* is said to be *bald*. *Wigs, hairpieces, toupees* or "rugs" can be used to conceal *bald spots. Pogonotrophy* is beard-growing and *pogonotomy* is beard-cutting. A partial growth is known as *stubble*. A small, tufted chin beard is a *goatee*. A trim, pointed one is a *Van-dyke*. A mustache having long, curled ends is a *handlebar mustache*.

distribution point

crown

cowlick/tuft

hairline

spit curl

part

sidewall

widow's peak

sideburn

mustache

muttonchop/ side whiskers

beard/whiskers

Hairstyles and Facial Hair

Hair Grooming Implements

Among other attachments available for use with a *pro-style dryer* are combs, brush and an *air-flow nozzle*, to limit the amount of hot air.

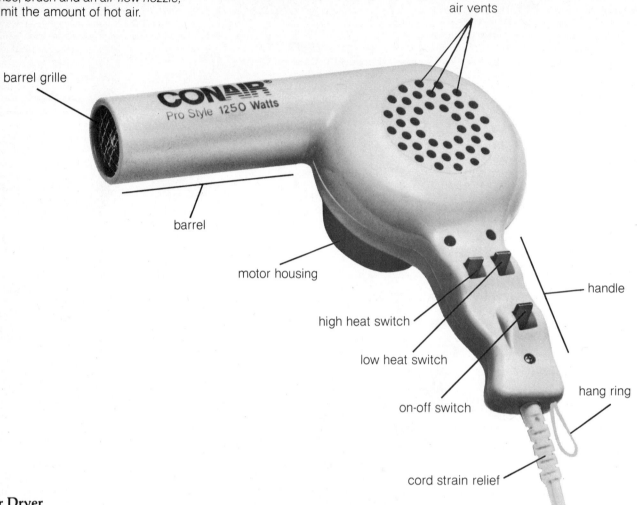

air vents

barrel grille

barrel

motor housing

handle

high heat switch

low heat switch

on-off switch

hang ring

cord strain relief

Hair Dryer

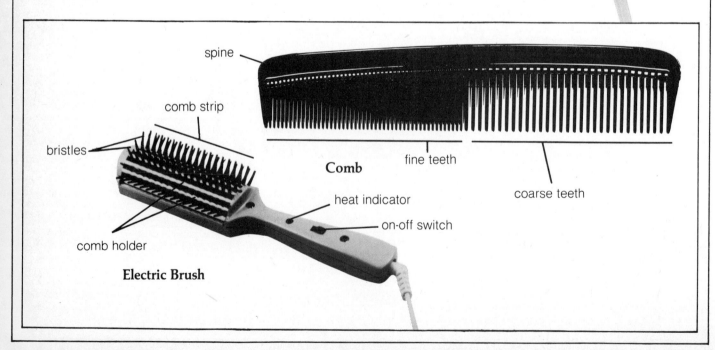

spine

comb strip

bristles

fine teeth

Comb

coarse teeth

comb holder

heat indicator

on-off switch

Electric Brush

Women's Hair

A small portion of hair in a woman's *hairdo*, or *coiffure*, is a *lock*. *Bouffant* is a puffed-out hairdo. *Teased*, or *back-combed*, *hair* is achieved by taking hold of a strand and pushing the short hairs toward the scalp with a comb. A braid on the back of the head is a *pigtail*. Hair that turns inward at the end, rather than outward, is a *pageboy*. A long piece of store-bought hair clipped to real hair is a *fall*.

knot/bun/beehive/chignon

kiss curl

bangs

eyebrow

eyelashes

flip

strand/wisp

ponytail

curl

braid/plait/tress

tendril/ringlet

Hairstyles and Facial Hair

Hairstyling Implements

A curling iron is used to curl a *strand* of hair or to straighten it. Hair clips and bobby pins, which may be long or short, can be used to secure a roller while hair is being set. The roller shown here, however, is *self-clasping*. *Barrettes, combs, hair ribbons, headbands* and *hair bands* hold hair in place or serve as decorative *hair ornaments*. Professional *hairdressers* use *permanent rods* and *papers, applicator bottles* filled with *permanent lotion, setting lotion, rinse* or *dye*, plastic *caps, dryers* and *infrared lamps* to treat and style *hairdos*.

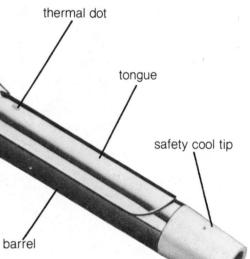

power cord

on-off switch

thumb press

strain relief

thermal dot

tongue

main housing

safety cool tip

stand

barrel

Curling Iron

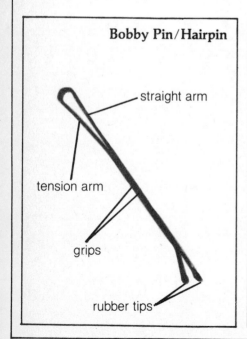

Bobby Pin/Hairpin

straight arm

tension arm

grips

rubber tips

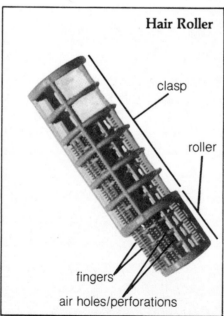

Hair Roller

clasp

roller

fingers

air holes/perforations

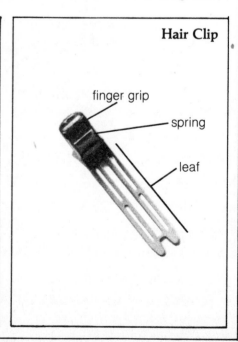

Hair Clip

finger grip

spring

leaf

Toothbrush

The stimulator tip on a toothbrush fits in what is called a *hang-up hole*. Teeth can also be cleaned with *dental floss*, a waxed string, and *high-pressure water-spray units*. Nails can be smoothed with an *emery board*, a cardboard strip covered with *powdered emery*, or a *nail file*.

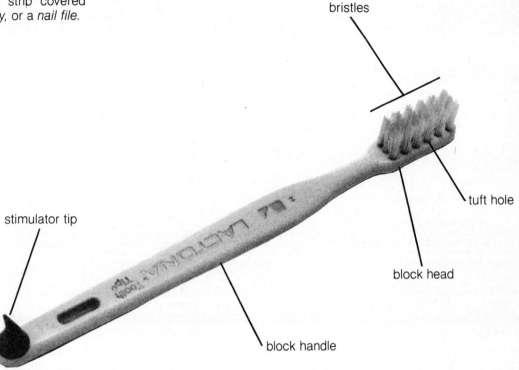

stimulator tip

bristles

tuft hole

block head

block handle

Toothbrush

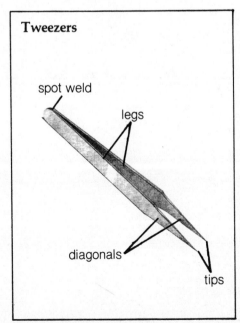

Tweezers

spot weld

legs

diagonals

tips

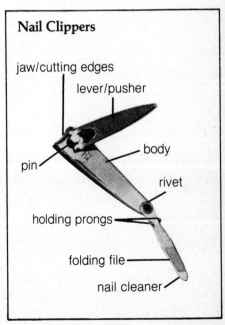

Nail Clippers

jaw/cutting edges

lever/pusher

body

pin

rivet

holding prongs

folding file

nail cleaner

Cosmetics

Makeup

A skin-colored *concealer*, or *coverup*, can be used to cover blemishes or undesirable shadows under the eyes. *Pancake makeup* is a thick face powder used by actors and actresses as a foundation. Makeup can be removed with a *cleansing cream* or *cold cream*.

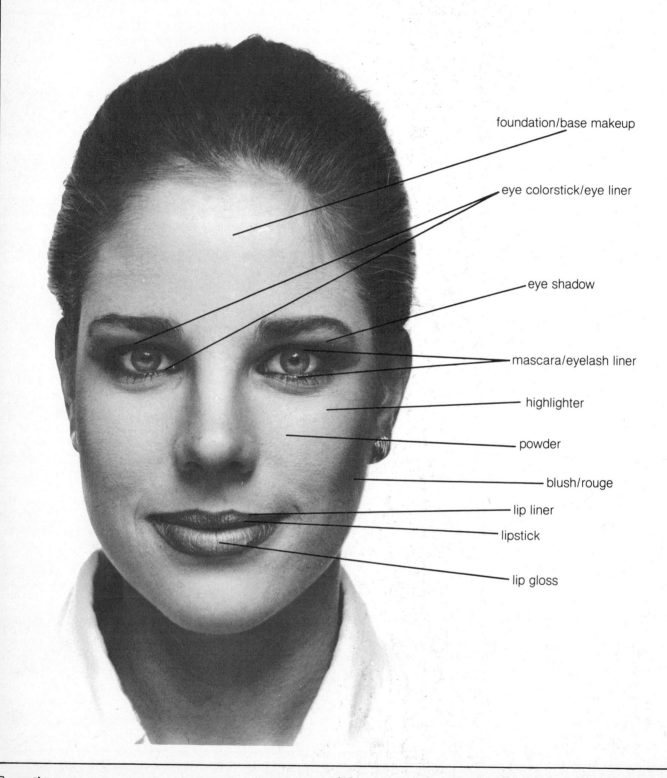

foundation/base makeup

eye colorstick/eye liner

eye shadow

mascara/eyelash liner

highlighter

powder

blush/rouge

lip liner

lipstick

lip gloss

Colored *nail polish* is often used to "paint" fingernails and toenails. In addition to those beauty products shown here, there are *scents,* such as *perfume,* applied by women to *pulse points; bath oils; body oils; moisturizers* and *lotions.* Men use *colognes* or *after-shave lotions.*

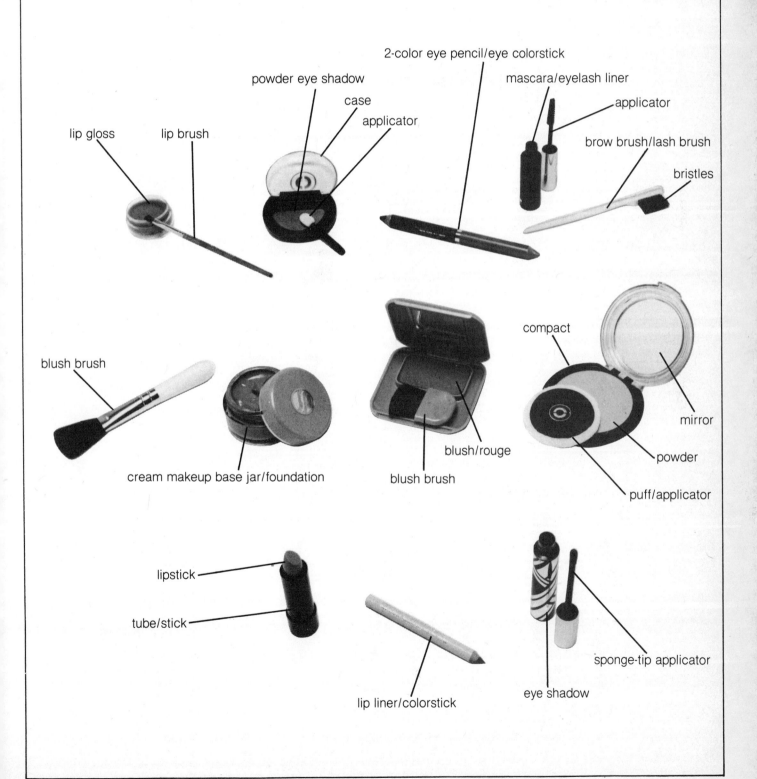

2-color eye pencil/eye colorstick

powder eye shadow

mascara/eyelash liner

case

applicator

applicator

lip gloss

lip brush

brow brush/lash brush

bristles

compact

blush brush

mirror

cream makeup base jar/foundation

blush/rouge

powder

blush brush

puff/applicator

lipstick

tube/stick

sponge-tip applicator

lip liner/colorstick

eye shadow

Gemstone

The shades of color a gemstone gives off are called *fire*. A matched set of jewelry, or *parure*, often includes a necklace, earrings and a *brooch*. A *cameo* is a gem on which a relief carving has been made. Nonprecious *costume jewelry* is made to simulate its precious counterparts. The end of a *cuff link* that is passed through the buttonhole and fastened is called a *wing-back*, or *airplane-back*.

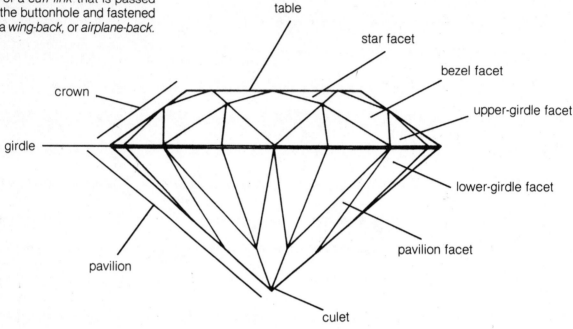

Cut Gemstone

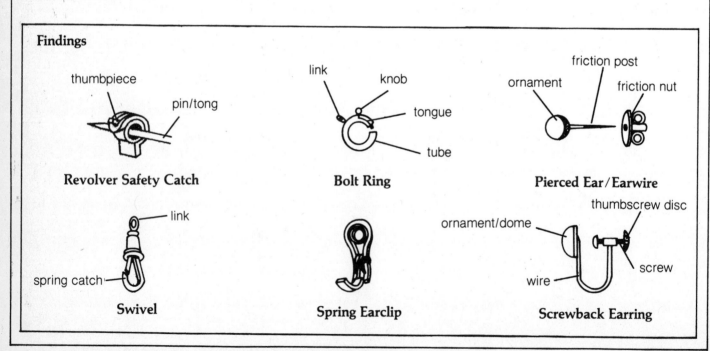

Revolver Safety Catch

Bolt Ring

Pierced Ear/Earwire

Swivel

Spring Earclip

Screwback Earring

Findings

Ring

A *lavaliere* is a pendant worn on a chain as a necklace. A *charm* is a trinket worn on a bracelet or necklace, often having personal or symbolic meaning. An *ouch* is a brooch or a setting for a precious stone. *Spangles* are glittering pieces of metal used on clothing for decoration. A *riviere* is a multi-stringed necklace containing many precious stones.

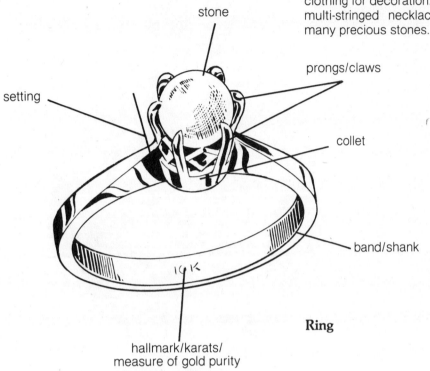

stone

prongs/claws

setting

collet

band/shank

hallmark/karats/ measure of gold purity

Ring

Pendant

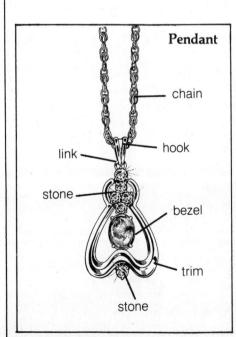

chain

hook

link

stone

bezel

trim

stone

Pieces

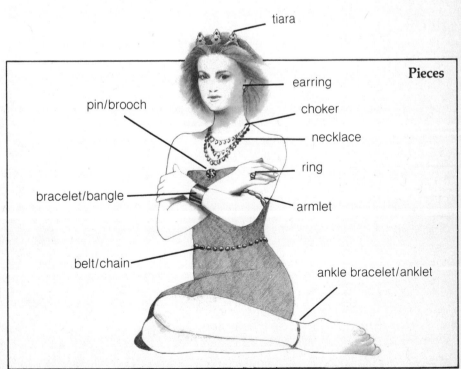

tiara

earring

pin/brooch

choker

necklace

ring

bracelet/bangle

armlet

belt/chain

ankle bracelet/anklet

Jewelry

Watches

The digital display on this watch can indicate date, seconds, time in a different time zone, and it can perform *stopwatch* functions. An extremely accurate timepiece is called a *chronometer*. A watchband, or *strap*, is attached to the case by *push-pins*, or *spring-bars*.

link

watchband/bracelet

zero mark

dial/face

case

hour hand

minute hand

protective shoulder

Liquid Crystal Display (LCD)

crown

LCD second time zone display control

LCD second and date display control

elapsed time bezel

luminous indices/markers

Chronosport U D T

SEA QUARTZ

00:00

Wristwatch

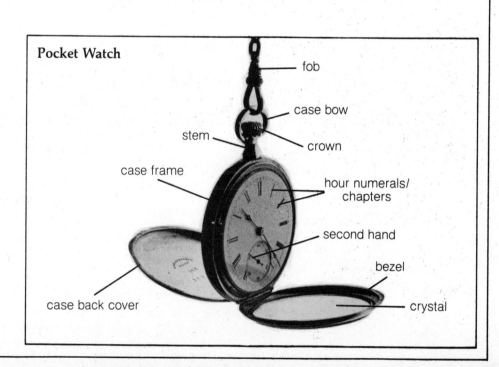

Pocket Watch

fob

case bow

stem

crown

case frame

hour numerals/chapters

second hand

bezel

case back cover

crystal

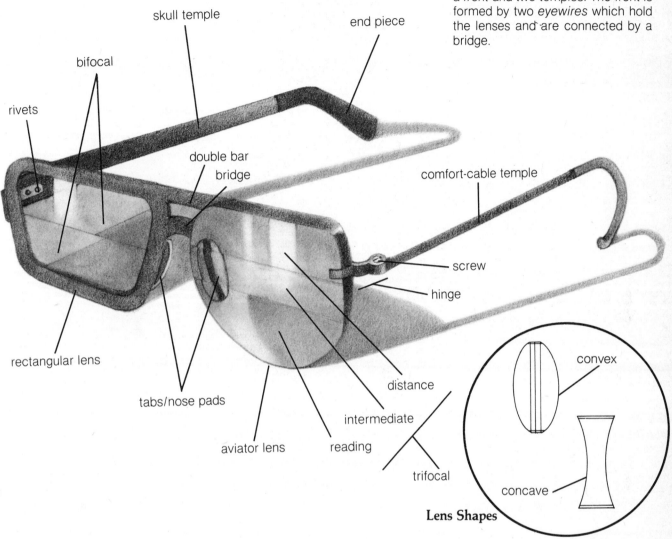

Eyeglasses

This is a composite pair of eyeglasses, or *spectacles*. The *frame* consists of a *front* and two temples. The front is formed by two *eyewires* which hold the lenses and are connected by a bridge.

skull temple

end piece

bifocal

rivets

double bar

bridge

comfort-cable temple

screw

hinge

rectangular lens

tabs/nose pads

distance

intermediate

aviator lens

reading

trifocal

convex

concave

Lens Shapes

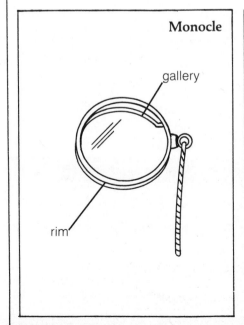

Monocle

gallery

rim

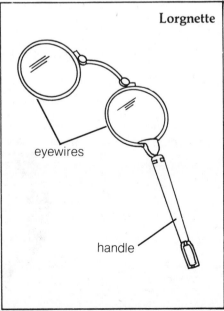

Lorgnette

eyewires

handle

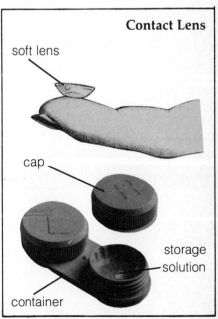

Contact Lens

soft lens

cap

storage
solution

container

221

Handbag

A handbag can also be referred to as a *pocketbook* or *purse*. A bag with no handles is a *clutch*. *East-west* describes a handbag which is wider than it is long. A *north-south* bag has a long, narrow shape. The metal ornaments and closures on bags are collectively called *hardware* or *fittings*.

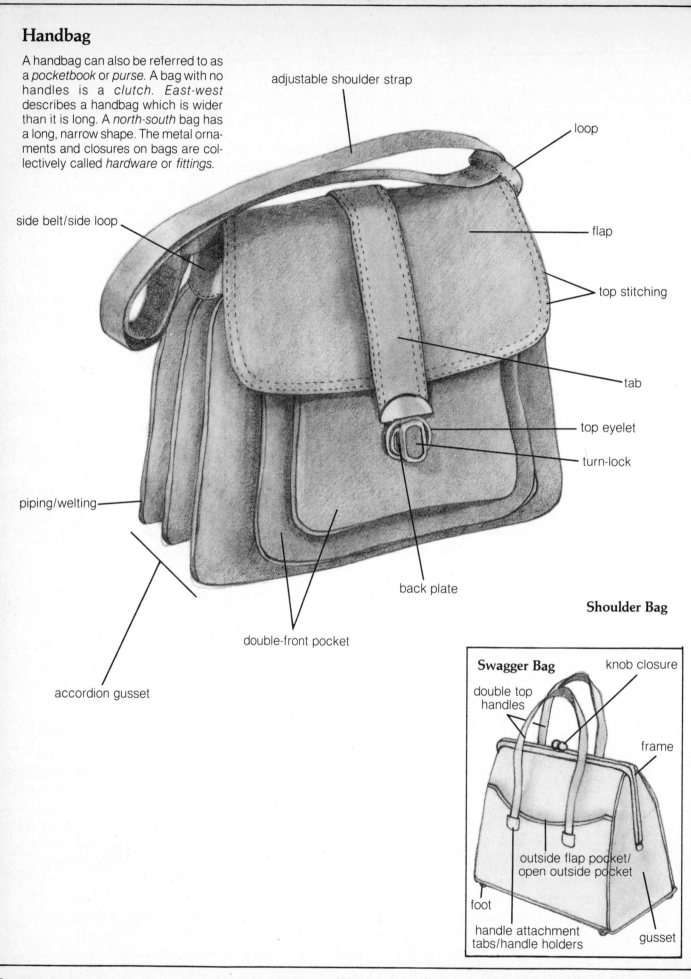

adjustable shoulder strap

loop

flap

top stitching

tab

top eyelet

turn-lock

side belt/side loop

back plate

piping/welting

double-front pocket

accordion gusset

Shoulder Bag

Swagger Bag

double top handles

knob closure

frame

outside flap pocket/ open outside pocket

foot

handle attachment tabs/handle holders

gusset

Wallet/Billfold

A wallet's exterior covering is called the *cover*. Women's wallets often have a *coin purse* within and a *tab closing* on the outside. *Photo holders* that unfold and become a long strip are called *accordion windows*.

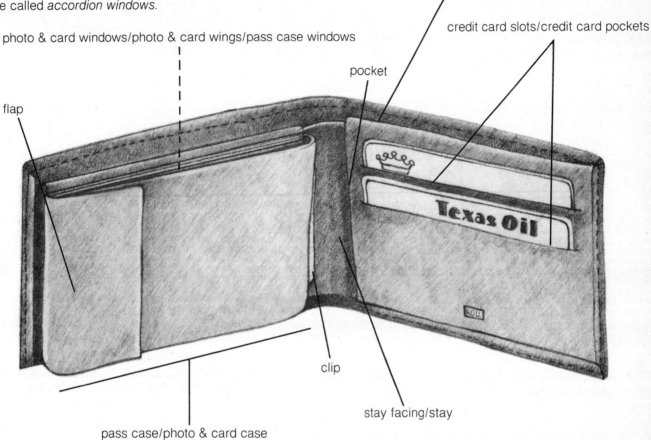

bill compartment/currency pocket

credit card slots/credit card pockets

pocket

photo & card windows/photo & card wings/pass case windows

flap

Texas Oil

clip

stay facing/stay

pass case/photo & card case

Checkbook Clutch

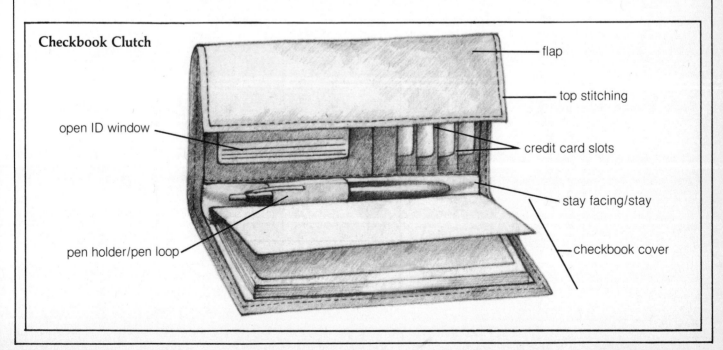

flap

top stitching

open ID window

credit card slots

stay facing/stay

checkbook cover

pen holder/pen loop

Money

United States paper currency in circulation today consists primarily of *Federal Reserve Notes* or "greenbacks" bearing a green seal, and a few *United States Notes* (mainly $100 bills) bearing a red seal. Other types of paper money, such as *Silver Certificates*, have been withdrawn from circulation. *Bills* are printed from *engraved plates* on paper containing colored *fibers*. Notes damaged during printing are replaced by *star notes*. Money printed illegally and passed off as *legal tender* is called *counterfeit money*.

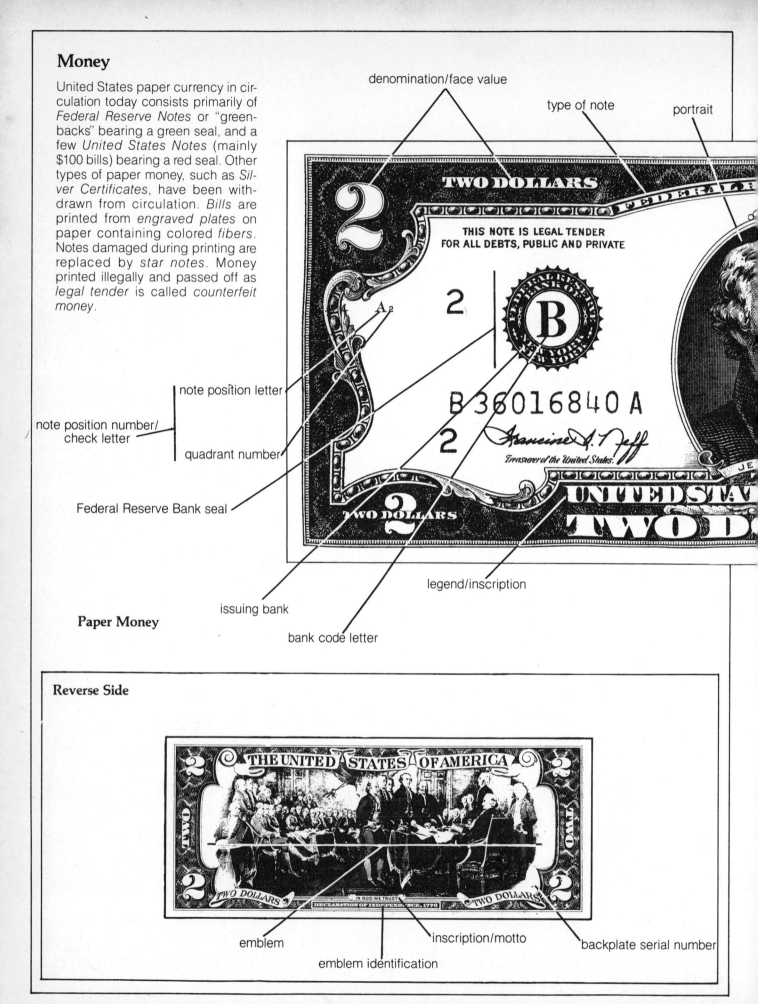

denomination/face value

type of note

portrait

THIS NOTE IS LEGAL TENDER
FOR ALL DEBTS, PUBLIC AND PRIVATE

note position letter

note position number/
check letter

quadrant number

Federal Reserve Bank seal

B 36016840 A

Francine I. Neff
Treasurer of the United States.

issuing bank

bank code letter

legend/inscription

Paper Money

Reverse Side

THE UNITED STATES OF AMERICA

TWO DOLLARS

IN GOD WE TRUST

DECLARATION OF INDEPENDENCE, 1776

TWO DOLLARS

emblem

emblem identification

inscription/motto

backplate serial number

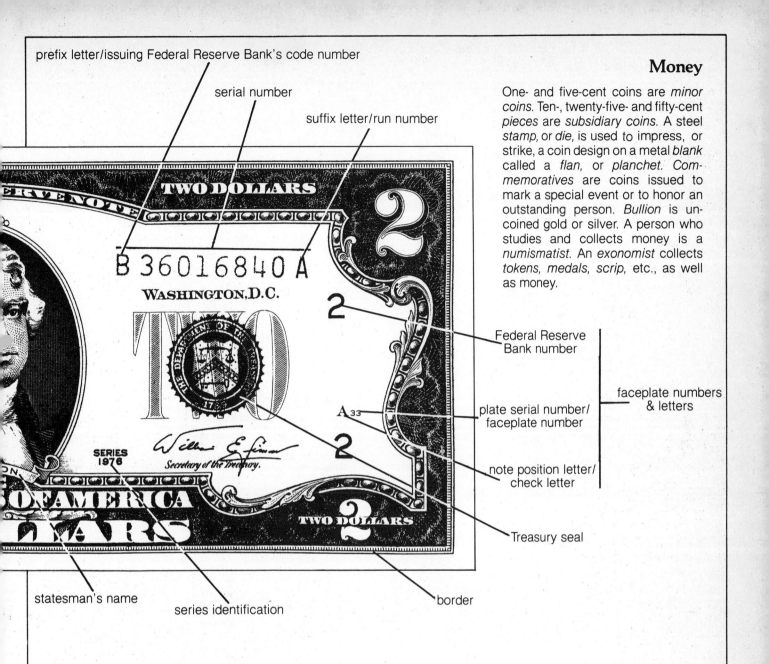

prefix letter/issuing Federal Reserve Bank's code number

serial number

suffix letter/run number

TWO DOLLARS

2

B 36016840 A

WASHINGTON, D.C.

TWO

THE DEPARTMENT OF THE 1789

SERIES 1976

Secretary of the Treasury.

2

2

A₃₃

OF AMERICA

LLARS

TWO DOLLARS

2

One- and five-cent coins are *minor coins*. Ten-, twenty-five- and fifty-cent *pieces* are *subsidiary coins*. A steel *stamp*, or *die*, is used to impress, or strike, a coin design on a metal *blank* called a *flan*, or *planchet*. *Commemoratives* are coins issued to mark a special event or to honor an outstanding person. *Bullion* is uncoined gold or silver. A person who studies and collects money is a *numismatist*. An *exonomist* collects *tokens*, *medals*, *scrip*, etc., as well as money.

Federal Reserve Bank number

faceplate numbers & letters

plate serial number/ faceplate number

note position letter/ check letter

Treasury seal

border

statesman's name

series identification

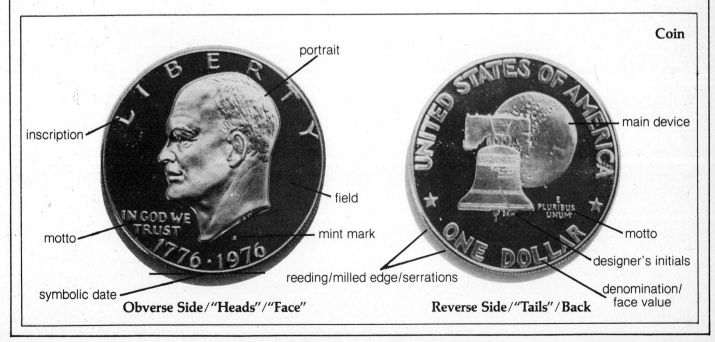

portrait

LIBERTY

inscription

field

mint mark

motto

IN GOD WE TRUST

1776 · 1976

symbolic date

reeding/milled edge/serrations

Obverse Side/"Heads"/"Face"

UNITED STATES OF AMERICA

E PLURIBUS UNUM

ONE DOLLAR

main device

motto

designer's initials

denomination/ face value

Reverse Side/"Tails"/Back

Personal Banking

A check must be signed by the maker, and *endorsed* on the back by the payee to be valid. Banking at an automatic teller machine requires a bank card and a *Personal Identification Number*, or *PIN* number. *Cash machines* allow withdrawals and deposits to be made, while *banking centers* permit most banking functions to be performed.

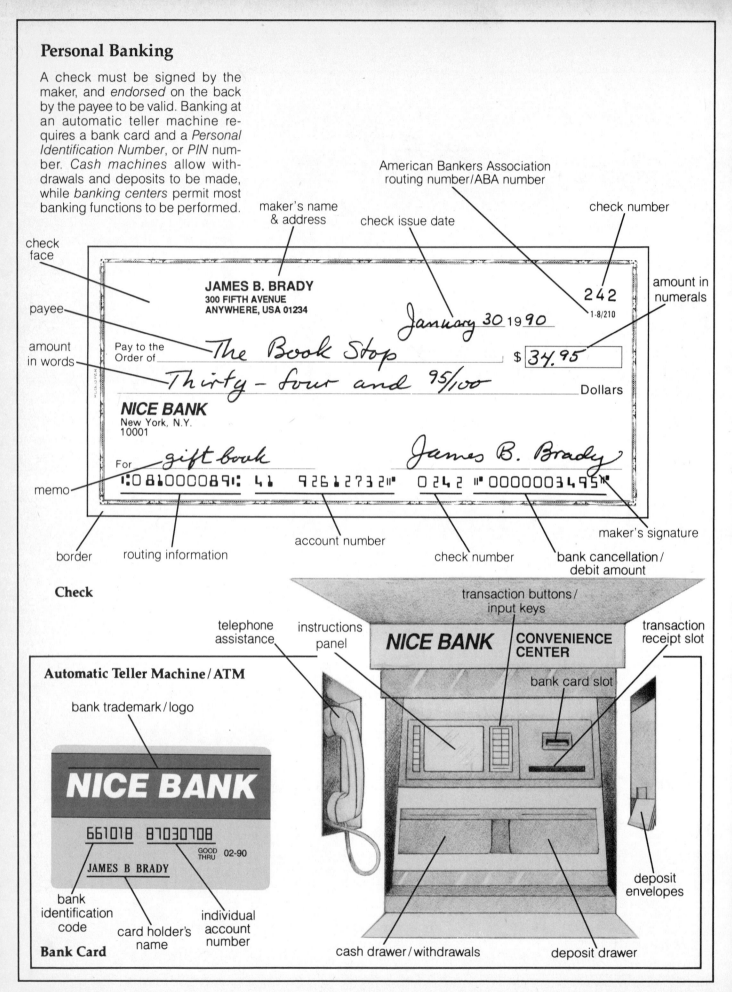

American Bankers Association routing number/ABA number

check issue date

maker's name & address

check number

check face

payee

amount in words

memo

border

routing information

amount in numerals

242
1-8/210

JAMES B. BRADY
300 FIFTH AVENUE
ANYWHERE, USA 01234

January 30 19 90

Pay to the Order of _The Book Stop_ $ 34.95

Thirty - four and 95/100 Dollars

NICE BANK
New York, N.Y.
10001

For _gift book_ _James B. Brady_

⑈081000089⑈ 41 926127321⑈ 0242 ⑈000000349⑈

account number

check number

maker's signature

bank cancellation/ debit amount

Check

transaction buttons/ input keys

telephone assistance

instructions panel

NICE BANK CONVENIENCE CENTER

transaction receipt slot

bank card slot

Automatic Teller Machine/ATM

bank trademark/logo

NICE BANK

661018 87030708

GOOD THRU 02-90

JAMES B BRADY

bank identification code

card holder's name

individual account number

Bank Card

cash drawer/withdrawals

deposit drawer

deposit envelopes

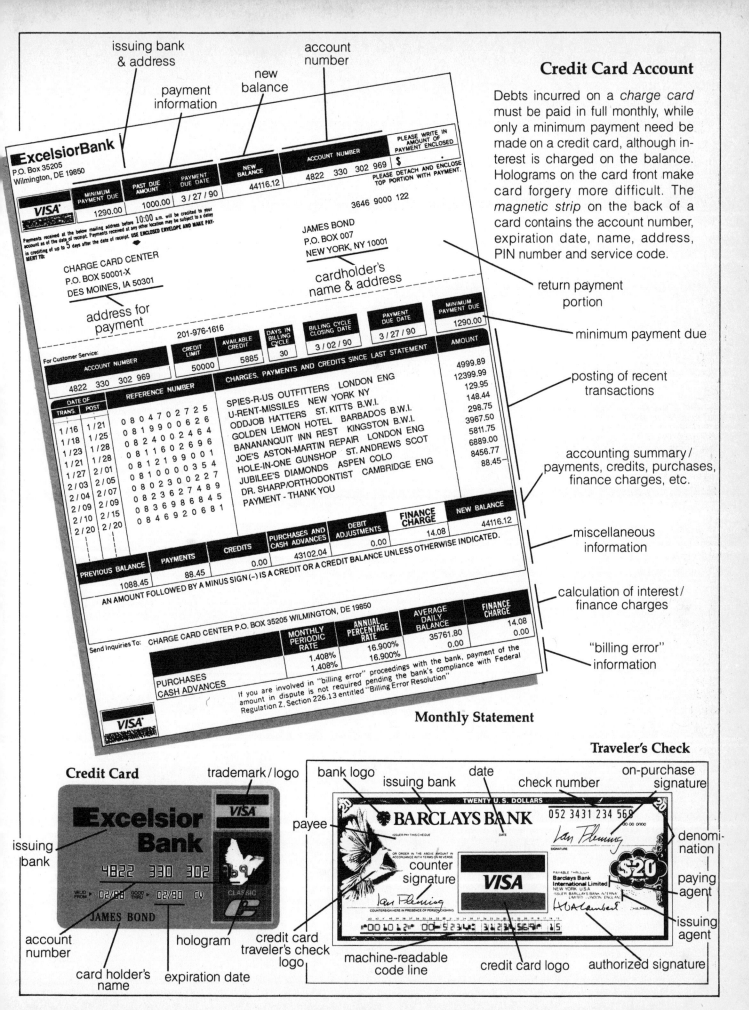

Credit Card Account

Debts incurred on a *charge card* must be paid in full monthly, while only a minimum payment need be made on a credit card, although interest is charged on the balance. Holograms on the card front make card forgery more difficult. The *magnetic strip* on the back of a card contains the account number, expiration date, name, address, PIN number and service code.

issuing bank & address

payment information

new balance

account number

ExcelsiorBank
P.O. Box 35205
Wilmington, DE 19850

PLEASE WRITE IN AMOUNT OF PAYMENT ENCLOSED

ACCOUNT NUMBER

NEW BALANCE — 44116.12

4822 330 302 969 $

PLEASE DETACH AND ENCLOSE TOP PORTION WITH PAYMENT.

MINIMUM PAYMENT DUE	PAST DUE AMOUNT	PAYMENT DUE DATE
1290.00	1000.00	3 / 27 / 90

3646 9000 122

Payments received at the below mailing address before 10:00 a.m. will be credited to your account as of the date of receipt. Payments received at any other location may be subject to a delay in crediting of up to 5 days after the date of receipt. USE ENCLOSED ENVELOPE AND MAKE PAYMENT TO:

CHARGE CARD CENTER
P.O. BOX 50001-X
DES MOINES, IA 50301

JAMES BOND
P.O. BOX 007
NEW YORK, NY 10001

cardholder's name & address

return payment portion

address for payment

201-976-1616

For Customer Service:

	CREDIT LIMIT	AVAILABLE CREDIT	DAYS IN BILLING CYCLE	BILLING CYCLE CLOSING DATE	PAYMENT DUE DATE	MINIMUM PAYMENT DUE
	50000	5885	30	3 / 02 / 90	3 / 27 / 90	1290.00

minimum payment due

ACCOUNT NUMBER		AMOUNT
4822 330 302 969	CHARGES, PAYMENTS AND CREDITS SINCE LAST STATEMENT	

posting of recent transactions

DATE OF		REFERENCE NUMBER		
TRANS	POST			
1/16	1/21	0 8 0 4 7 0 2 7 2 5	SPIES-R-US OUTFITTERS LONDON ENG	4999.89
1/18	1/25	0 8 1 9 9 0 0 6 2 6	U-RENT-MISSILES NEW YORK NY	12399.99
1/23	1/28	0 8 2 4 0 0 2 4 6 4	ODDJOB HATTERS ST. KITTS B.W.I.	129.95
1/21	1/28	0 8 1 1 6 0 2 6 9 6	GOLDEN LEMON HOTEL BARBADOS B.W.I.	148.44
1/27	2/01	0 8 1 2 1 9 9 0 0 1	BANANANQUIT INN REST LONDON ENG	298.75
2/03	2/05	0 8 1 0 0 0 0 3 5 4	JOE'S ASTON-MARTIN REPAIR ST. ANDREWS SCOT	3967.50
2/04	2/07	0 8 0 2 3 0 0 2 2 7	HOLE-IN-ONE GUNSHOP ST. ANDREWS SCOT	5811.75
2/09	2/09	0 8 2 3 6 2 7 4 8 9	JUBILEE'S DIAMONDS ASPEN COLO	6889.00
2/10	2/15	0 8 3 6 9 8 6 8 4 5	DR. SHARP/ORTHODONTIST CAMBRIDGE ENG	8456.77
2/20	2/20	0 8 4 6 9 2 0 6 8 1	PAYMENT - THANK YOU	88.45—

accounting summary / payments, credits, purchases, finance charges, etc.

PREVIOUS BALANCE	PAYMENTS	CREDITS	PURCHASES AND CASH ADVANCES	DEBIT ADJUSTMENTS	FINANCE CHARGE	NEW BALANCE
	88.45	0.00	43102.04	0.00	14.08	44116.12
1088.45						

miscellaneous information

AN AMOUNT FOLLOWED BY A MINUS SIGN (–) IS A CREDIT OR A CREDIT BALANCE UNLESS OTHERWISE INDICATED.

calculation of interest / finance charges

Send Inquiries To: CHARGE CARD CENTER P.O. BOX 35205 WILMINGTON, DE 19850

	MONTHLY PERIODIC RATE	ANNUAL PERCENTAGE RATE	AVERAGE DAILY BALANCE	FINANCE CHARGE
PURCHASES	1.408%	16.900%	35761.80	14.08
CASH ADVANCES	1.408%	16.900%	0.00	0.00

"billing error" information

If you are involved in "billing error" proceedings with the bank, payment of the amount in dispute is not required pending the bank's compliance with Federal Regulation Z, Section 226.13 entitled "Billing Error Resolution".

Monthly Statement

Credit Card

trademark/logo

Excelsior Bank

VISA

issuing bank

4822 330 302 369 1

VALID FROM 02/88 GOOD THRU 02/90 CV

CLASSIC

JAMES BOND

account number

card holder's name

hologram

expiration date

credit card traveler's check logo

Traveler's Check

bank logo

issuing bank

date

check number

on-purchase signature

payee

TWENTY U.S. DOLLARS

BARCLAYS BANK

052 3431 234 569

ISSUER PAY THIS CHEQUE

Ian Fleming

SIGNATURE

OR ORDER IN THE ABOVE AMOUNT IN ACCORDANCE WITH TERMS ON REVERSE

counter signature

VISA

PAYABLE THROUGH
Barclays Bank International Limited
NEW YORK, U.S.A.
ISSUER BARCLAYS BANK INTERNATIONAL LIMITED, LONDON, ENGLAND

$20

denomination

paying agent

Ian Fleming

COUNTERSIGN HERE IN PRESENCE OF PERSON CASHING

H.O.A. Lambert

CHAIRMAN

issuing agent

⑈00 6012⑈ 00⑆5234⑆ 3123⑆5684⑈ 15

machine-readable code line

credit card logo

authorized signature

Cigar and Cigarette

The cigar wrapper, as well as the interior *binder,* is a spirally-rolled *leaf.* Cigars, or *"stogies,"* are stored in *humidors* to insure freshness. The residue of smoked tobacco is *ash.* The remains of a smoked cigar or cigarette is the *butt.* The abrasive striking surface or *friction strip* on which matches are struck is on the *back cover* of a matchbook.

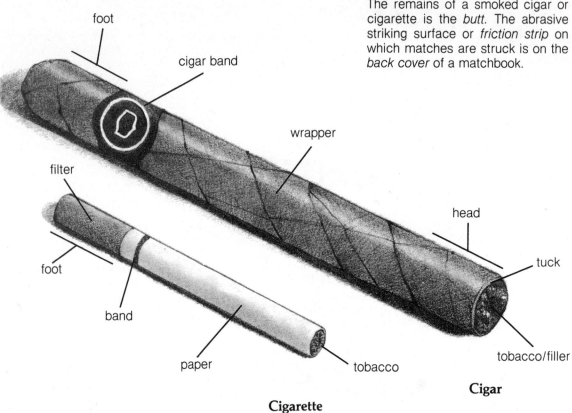

foot

cigar band

wrapper

head

tuck

tobacco/filler

Cigar

filter

foot

band

paper

tobacco

Cigarette

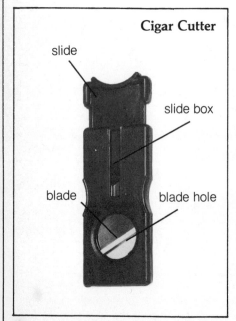

Cigar Cutter

slide

slide box

blade

blade hole

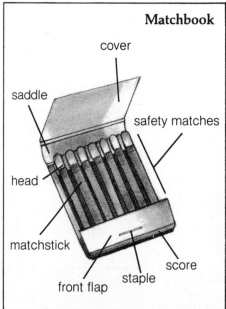

Matchbook

cover

saddle

safety matches

head

matchstick

front flap

staple

score

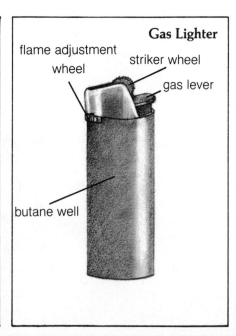

Gas Lighter

flame adjustment wheel

striker wheel

gas lever

butane well

Pipe

Pipe smoke is also called *lunt,* and unsmoked tobacco in the bottom of the bowl after smoking is called *dottle.* The pliable, tufted rod used to clean the inside of a pipe's stem is a *pipe cleaner.* Pipe tobacco is kept in a *pouch.* Some bowls are covered with a *pipe umbrella* or *bowl lid.* An Eastern pipe with a long, flexible tube by which the smoke is drawn through a jar of water and thus cooled is a *water pipe, hookah,* or *hubble-bubble.*

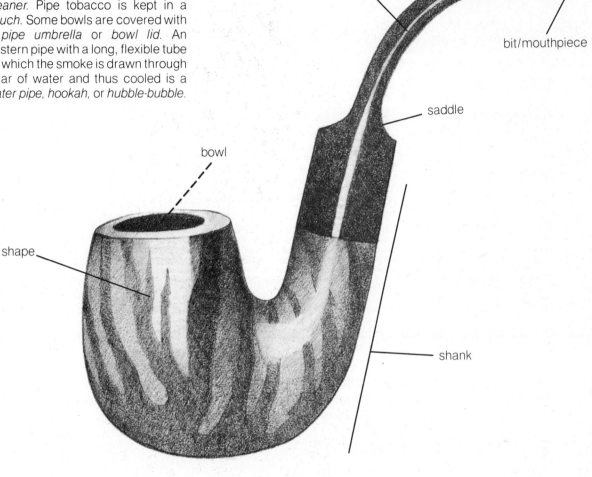

stem

bit/mouthpiece

saddle

bowl

shape

shank

Pipe Tool

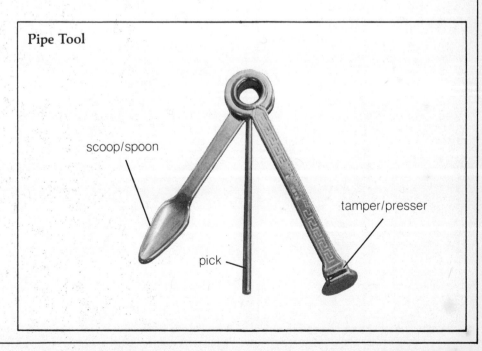

scoop/spoon

pick

tamper/presser

Smoking Materials

Umbrella

An umbrella's water-repellent *fabric* is attached to a *frame,* or *skeleton.* The specific points where the fabric is sewn to the skeleton are called *tacks.*

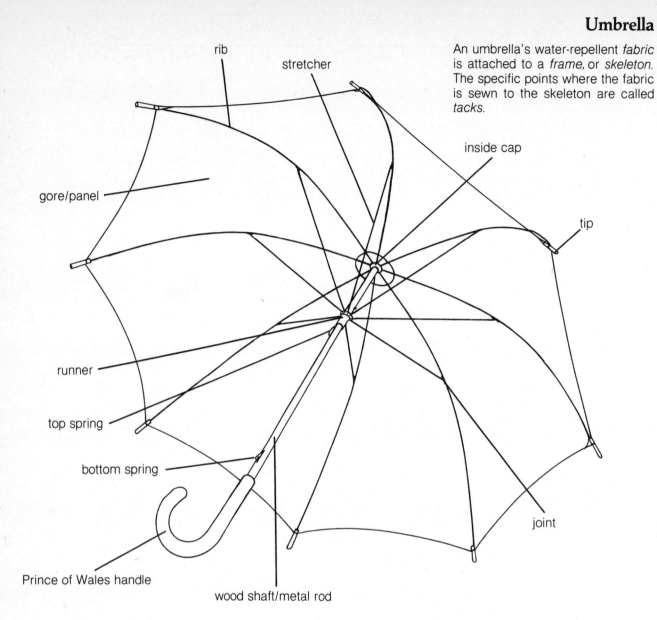

rib

stretcher

inside cap

gore/panel

tip

runner

top spring

bottom spring

joint

Prince of Wales handle

wood shaft/metal rod

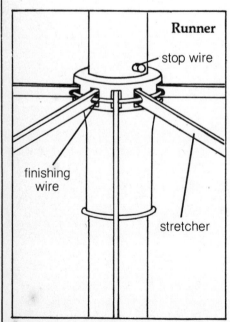

Runner

stop wire

finishing wire

stretcher

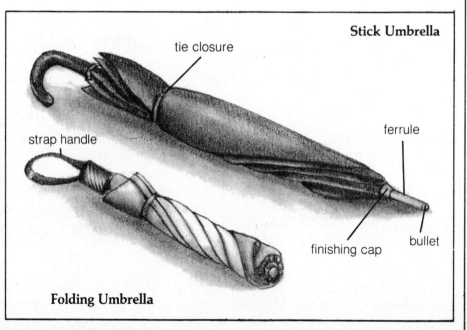

Stick Umbrella

tie closure

ferrule

strap handle

finishing cap

bullet

Folding Umbrella

The Home

To facilitate locating items found in the home, the objects in this section have been grouped according to where they are most likely to be encountered: living room, dining room, kitchen, bedroom, bathroom, playroom, utility room or yard.

The kitchen subsection, for example, includes implements for preparing food as well as appliances that make food preparation easier. In addition to identifying the parts of containers used to bring groceries into the kitchen, coverage includes all the terms used in the designing and packaging of food and kitchenware. Knowing the names for these components will surely change how the reader views his or her cereal box at the breakfast table in the future.

The terms for details of desk equipment, found in the playroom/utility room subsection, apply as well to office furnishings. The seven parts of a paper clip, for example, are valid wherever this unique little device is used.

Although a nursery is not included as a subsection, objects used for or by children—stroller, car seat, playpen, and swings—have been incorporated in the subcategory of yard equipment.

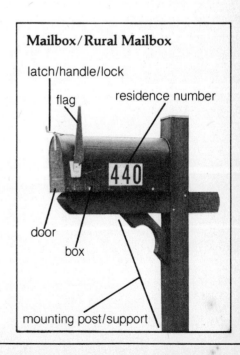

Mailbox / Rural Mailbox

latch/handle/lock

flag

residence number

440

door

box

mounting post/support

Fireplace

Many fireplaces have glass and metal *fire screens* to prevent heat loss and to keep sparks from flying into the room. Others have a low metal *fender* between the inner and outer hearth. A metal cover, used to shield a banked or dying fire, is called a *curfew*. Fireplace accessories include air-blowing *bellows, coal hods* and *wood carriers,* and *grates* or *heat exchangers* which can be used instead of andirons. A *firebrand* is a piece of burning wood.

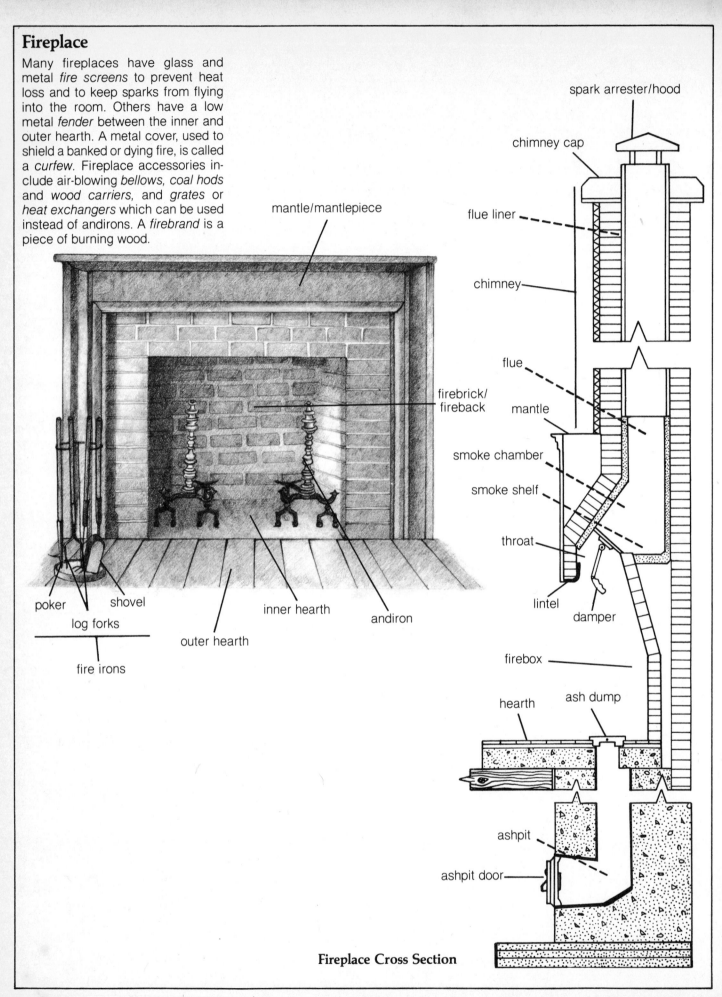

mantle/mantlepiece

firebrick/ fireback

poker

shovel

log forks

fire irons

outer hearth

inner hearth

andiron

spark arrester/hood

chimney cap

flue liner

chimney

flue

mantle

smoke chamber

smoke shelf

throat

lintel

damper

firebox

hearth

ash dump

ashpit

ashpit door

Fireplace Cross Section

Clock

A *pendulum clock* tall enough to stand on the floor, either a grandfather or the shorter *grandmother clock*, is called a *tall-case clock*. The machinery or *movement* within is called the *clockworks*. A *rating*, the length of a pendulum swing, can be adjusted by a *rating nut*, usually found beneath the bob.

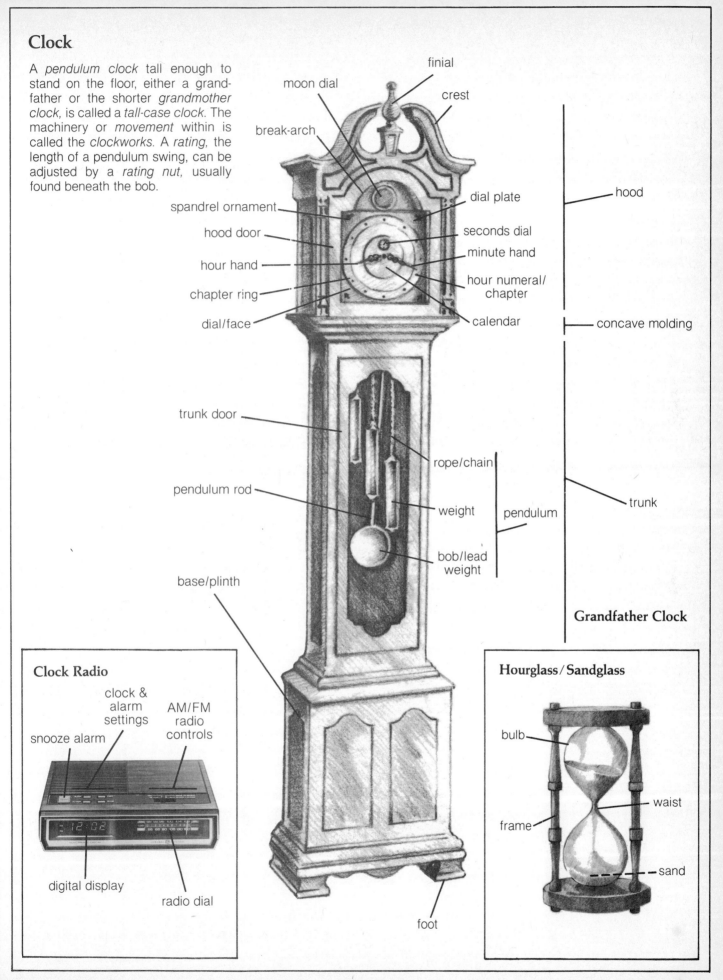

finial

moon dial

crest

break-arch

dial plate

spandrel ornament

seconds dial

hood door

minute hand

hour hand

chapter ring

hour numeral/chapter

dial/face

calendar

hood

concave molding

trunk door

rope/chain

pendulum rod

weight

pendulum

trunk

bob/lead weight

base/plinth

Grandfather Clock

Clock Radio

clock & alarm settings

AM/FM radio controls

snooze alarm

digital display

radio dial

Hourglass/Sandglass

bulb

waist

frame

sand

foot

Chair

A single broad center upright used in place of spindles in a seat back is called a *splat*. Horizontal members across the seat back are called *slats*, or *crosspieces*. *Braces* are two spindles that form a "V" at the back of a chair seat. The crest of a chair may have a shape called a *handgrip, roll top* or *pillow*. A *slip seat* is a seat that is fitted into a molding and can be removed and covered with fabric, then replaced. An extended arm with a flat surface is called a *writing arm*.

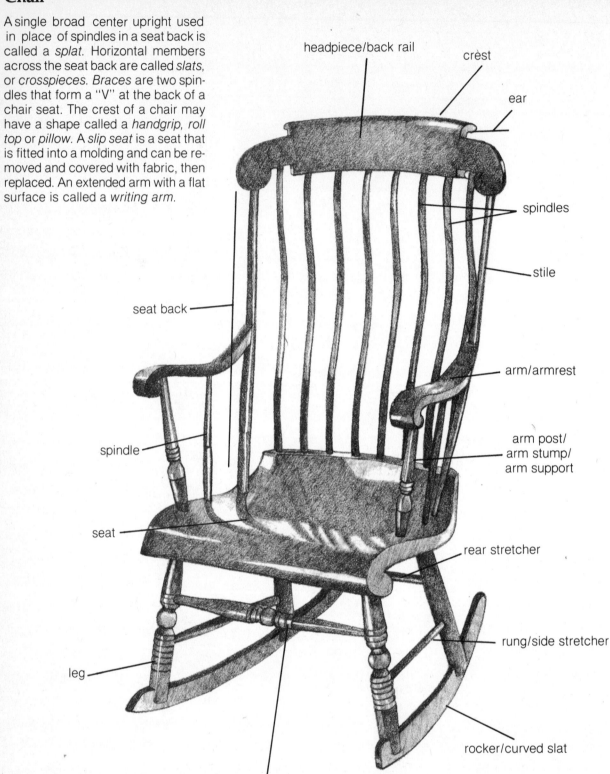

headpiece/back rail

crest

ear

spindles

stile

seat back

arm/armrest

spindle

arm post/
arm stump/
arm support

seat

rear stretcher

leg

rung/side stretcher

front stretcher

rocker/curved slat

Rocking Chair/Rocker

Lounger

When the backrest of this *recliner*, or *Barcalounger*, is pushed back, the *footrest* rises to seat level. The term *ottoman*, or *pouf*, is often used to refer to an overstuffed *footstool*. An *arm pad* on an *easy chair* is also called a *manchette*.

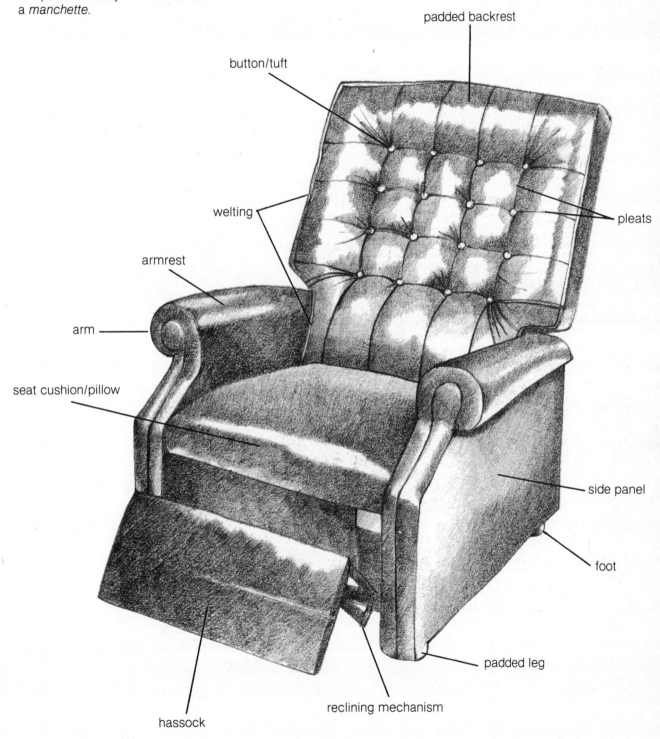

padded backrest

button/tuft

welting

pleats

armrest

arm

seat cushion/pillow

side panel

foot

padded leg

reclining mechanism

hassock

Living Room

Sofa

A sofa is an upholstered *couch* with a back and two arms or raised ends. If it is composed of several independent sections that can be arranged individually or in various combinations, it is a *sectional*. A *davenport* or *convertible* can be converted into a bed for nighttime use, whereas a *divan* is a large couch without back or arms that is often used as a bed. A sofa for two is a *loveseat,* or *courting seat.* Cylindrical pillows, or *bolsters,* and *fitted* or *tailored pillows* or *cushions* are often used on sofas.

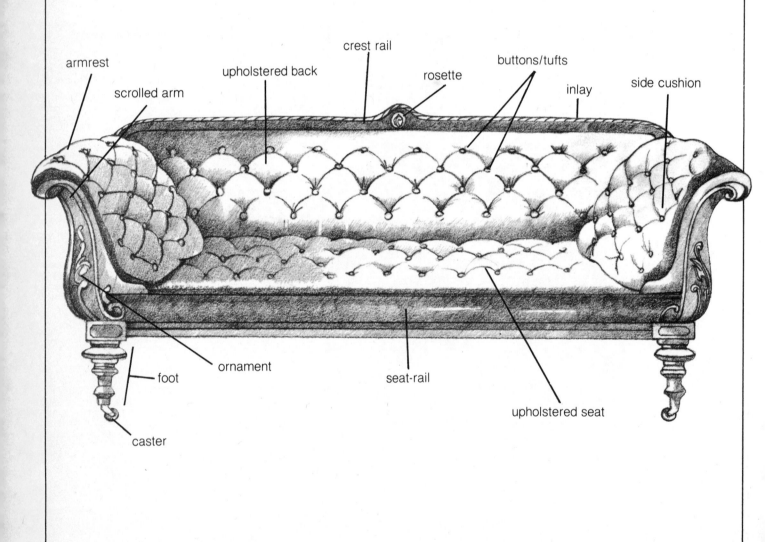

armrest

crest rail

scrolled arm

upholstered back

rosette

buttons/tufts

inlay

side cushion

ornament

foot

seat-rail

upholstered seat

caster

Candle and Candelabrum

Candles, or *tapers*, are made of *tallow*, *wax* or *paraffin*. Most are *dripless*. A collar placed at the top of a candle is a *burner*. The charred or partly consumed portion of a candle-wick, or *snaste*, is the *snuff*, formerly referred to as the *snot*. The remains of a used candle is the *stub*. Many candlesticks have a pointed *pricket* on which a candle is impaled, rather than a socket. Small candles used for religious purposes are called *devotionals* or *votive candles*.

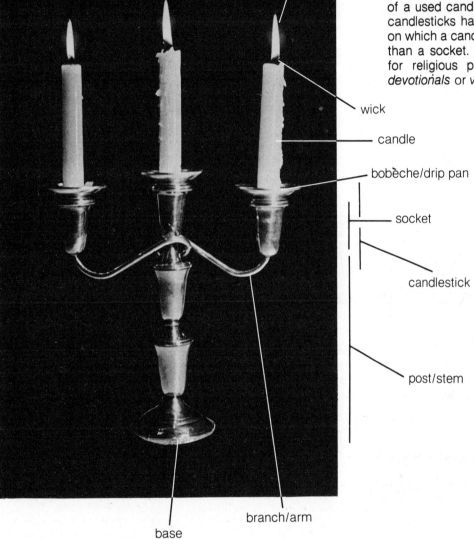

flame

wick

candle

bobèche/drip pan

socket

candlestick

post/stem

branch/arm

base

Candle Snuffer/Extinguisher

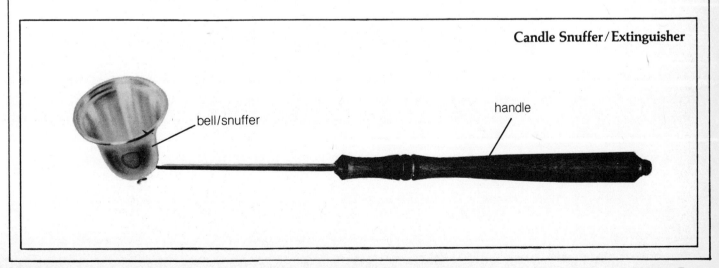

bell/snuffer

handle

Living Room

Lamps and Lighting

Light output, measured in *lumens*, depends on the amount of electricity used by a bulb. *Long-life bulbs* have heavier filaments. *Three-way bulbs* have two filaments, used separately for two of the light levels and together for the third. Two general types of bulb glass are soft, or *lime glass*, and hard, or *heat-resistant glass*. Lamp shades come in *drum, empire* and *bell* shapes. Lighting fixtures suspended from the ceiling are called *chandeliers*. The ceiling cap that covers the *junction box* for hanging lighting fixtures is the *canopy*.

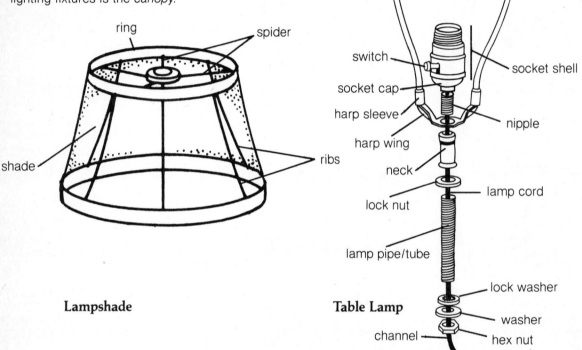

finial

harp

switch

socket cap

harp sleeve

harp wing

neck

lock nut

lamp pipe/tube

socket shell

nipple

lamp cord

lock washer

washer

channel

hex nut

power cord

ring

spider

shade

ribs

Lampshade

Table Lamp

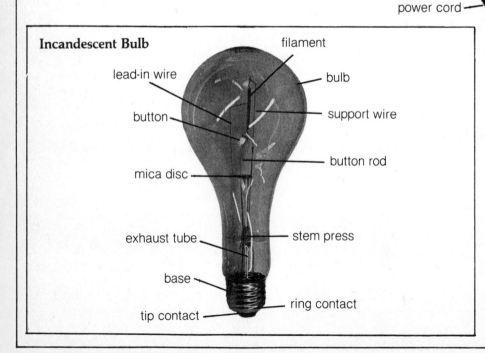

Incandescent Bulb

filament

lead-in wire

button

mica disc

exhaust tube

base

tip contact

bulb

support wire

button rod

stem press

ring contact

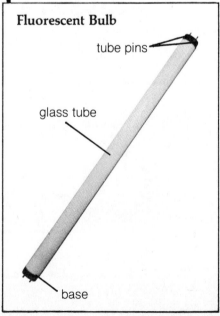

Fluorescent Bulb

tube pins

glass tube

base

Lamps and Lighting

Adjustable lamps, such as the one seen here, have an *inner reflector* around the bulb to help ventilate the shade. *Gooseneck lamps* have flexible shafts which permit the shade to be turned in any direction. *High-intensity* lamps produce a strong beam of light that illuminates only a small area.

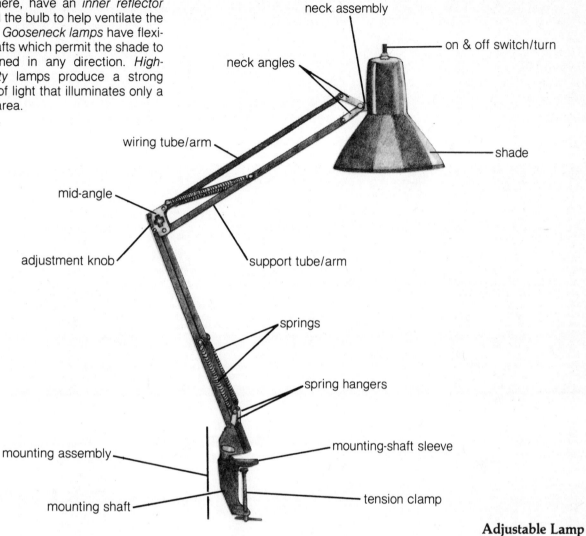

neck assembly

on & off switch/turn

neck angles

wiring tube/arm

shade

mid-angle

adjustment knob

support tube/arm

springs

spring hangers

mounting assembly

mounting-shaft sleeve

mounting shaft

tension clamp

Adjustable Lamp

Track Lighting

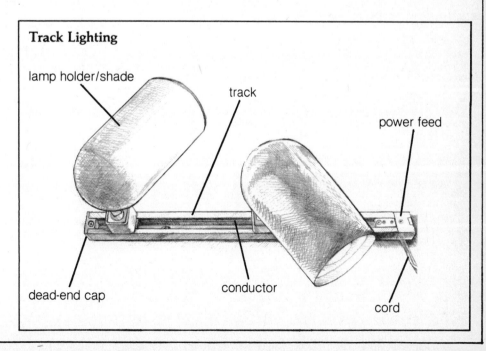

lamp holder/shade

track

power feed

dead-end cap

conductor

cord

Living Room

Window Coverings

The gathering of material at the top of draperies, hidden by the valance in this illustration, is called the *heading*. A *curtain rod* is a simple metal or wooden rod on which curtains are hung and moved by hand, without aid of pulley mechanisms. A curtain *panel* is a vertical section of fabric. *Cafe curtains* are suspended from rings and cover only part of a window.

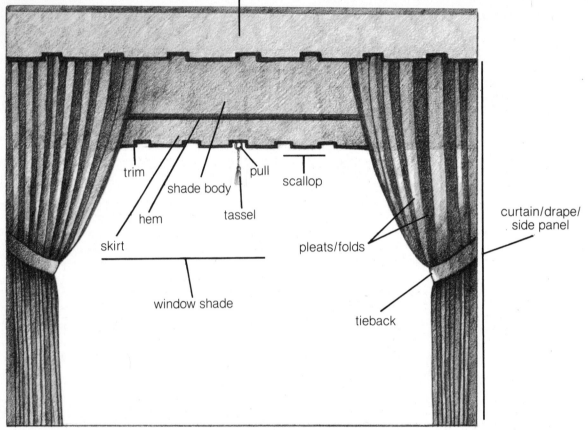

valance/cornice

trim

shade body

pull

scallop

hem

tassel

skirt

pleats/folds

curtain/drape/side panel

window shade

tieback

Curtains/Draperies and Shade

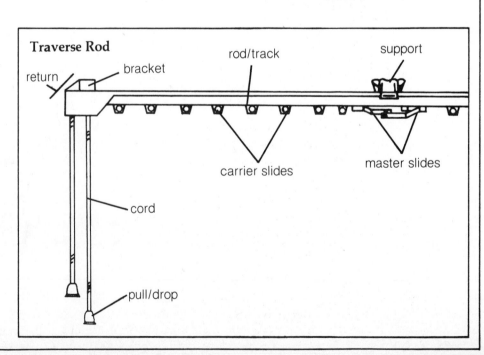

Traverse Rod

return

bracket

rod/track

support

carrier slides

master slides

cord

pull/drop

Window Coverings

Braided ladders are used in place of ladder tapes on some venetian blinds, and tubular *wands* are sometimes used instead of tilt cords. In *roll-up blinds*, slat tilt cannot be adjusted. A shutter consists of *panels*, each one of which contains louvers within a frame.

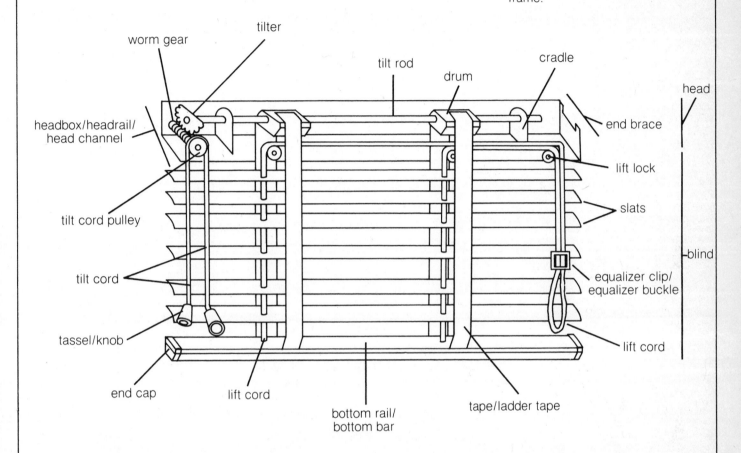

worm gear
tilter
tilt rod
drum
cradle
head
headbox/headrail/ head channel
end brace
lift lock
tilt cord pulley
slats
tilt cord
equalizer clip/ equalizer buckle
blind
tassel/knob
lift cord
end cap
lift cord
tape/ladder tape
bottom rail/ bottom bar

Venetian Blinds

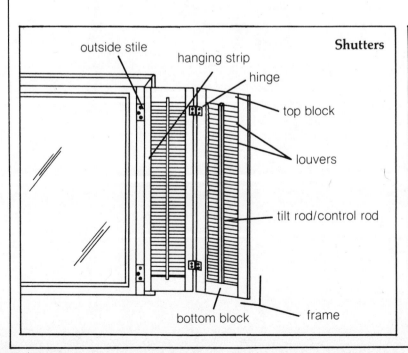

Shutters

outside stile
hanging strip
hinge
top block
louvers
tilt rod/control rod
bottom block
frame

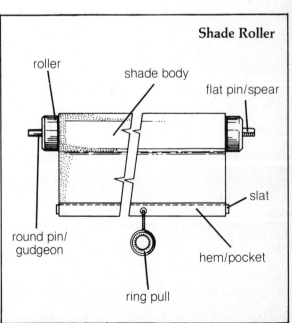

Shade Roller

roller
shade body
flat pin/spear
round pin/ gudgeon
slat
hem/pocket
ring pull

Living Room

Table

A drop-leaf table is any table with a leaf that drops down to the side, such as a *gateleg* or a *butterfly table*. In a butterfly table, which has *splayed legs,* wooden wing-shaped *brackets* support the leaves. *Pedestal tables* rest on a single *base* rather than on legs. Some tables have an *apron,* wooden slats that run along the sides just beneath the top, to provide additional support. *Card tables,* or *bridge tables,* are lightweight, portable tables with folding *frames.*

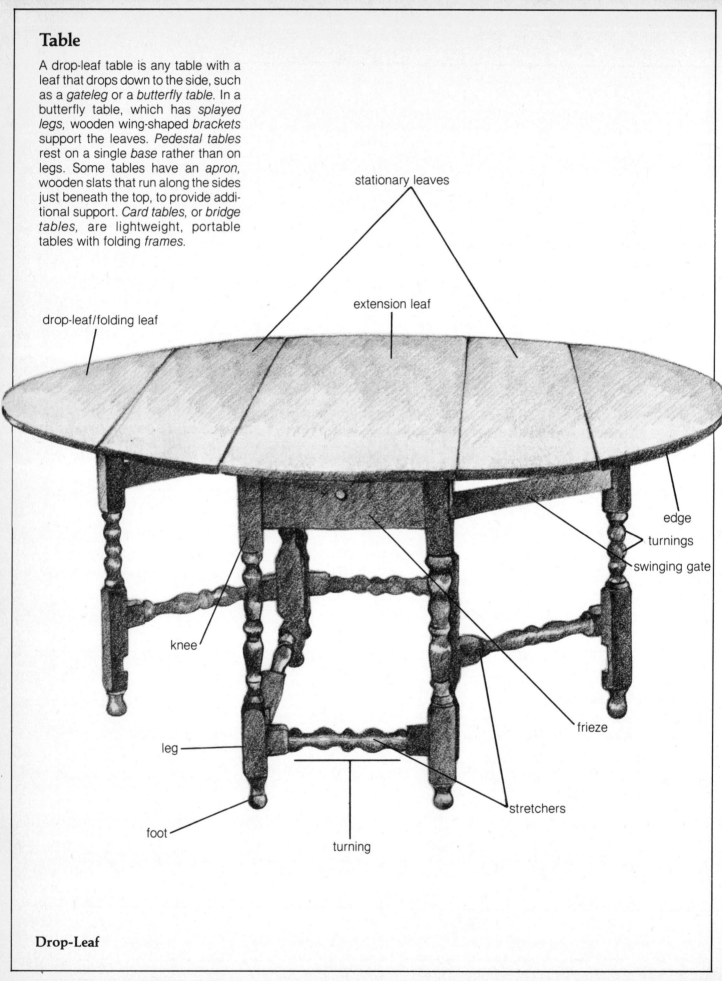

stationary leaves

extension leaf

drop-leaf/folding leaf

edge

turnings

swinging gate

knee

frieze

leg

stretchers

foot

turning

Drop-Leaf

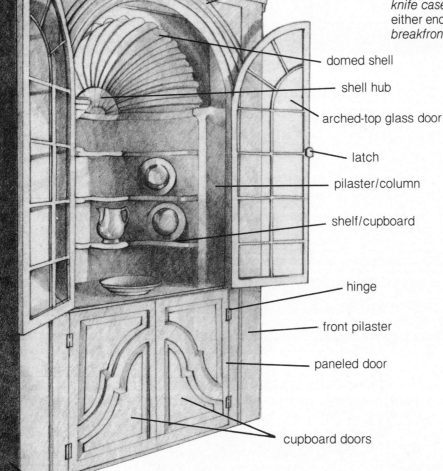

cornice

keystone

rosette

molding

Storage cabinets and receptacles are known as *casework* furniture. Some sideboards have *candle slides*, which are boards that slide out to support candlesticks. *Knife boxes*, or *knife cases*, sit atop the sideboard at either end. Other side pieces include *breakfronts*, *hutches* and *dry sinks*.

domed shell

shell hub

arched-top glass door

latch

pilaster/column

shelf/cupboard

hinge

front pilaster

paneled door

cupboard doors

return end

Corner Cupboard/China Cabinet

Sideboard/Buffet

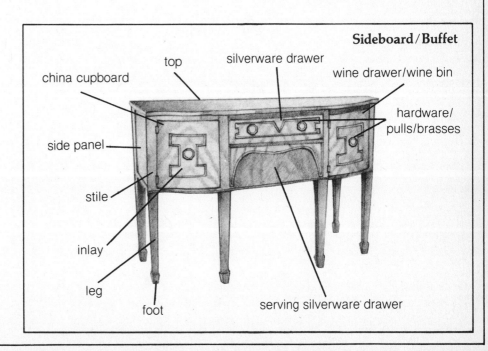

china cupboard

top

silverware drawer

wine drawer/wine bin

hardware/
pulls/brasses

side panel

stile

inlay

leg

foot

serving silverware drawer

243

Dining Room

Place Setting

There is no universally accepted way of setting a table. The elements and their proper position vary. The arrangement shown here is based on that used by the White House on formal occasions.

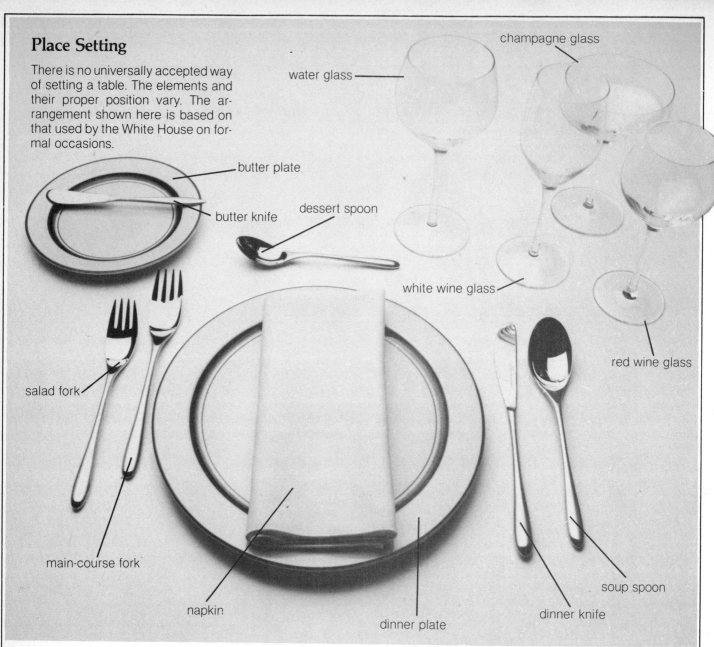

champagne glass

water glass

butter plate

butter knife

dessert spoon

white wine glass

red wine glass

salad fork

main-course fork

napkin

dinner plate

dinner knife

soup spoon

Flatware/Silverware

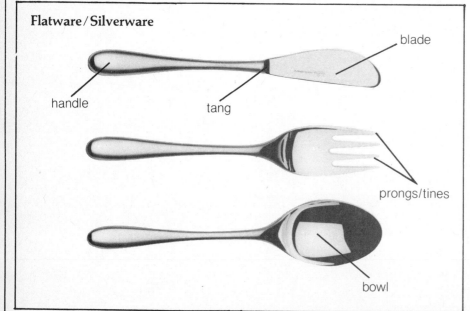

blade

handle

tang

prongs/tines

bowl

Stemware

rim/lip

head

bowl

stem

foot

Dessert Setting

Among other plates used for serving dessert and sweets are multi-tiered *terrace servers, serving trays, cake plates, fruit bowls* called *centerpieces,* and *compotes.* After-dinner drinks are often poured from ornamental glass bottles called *decanters.*

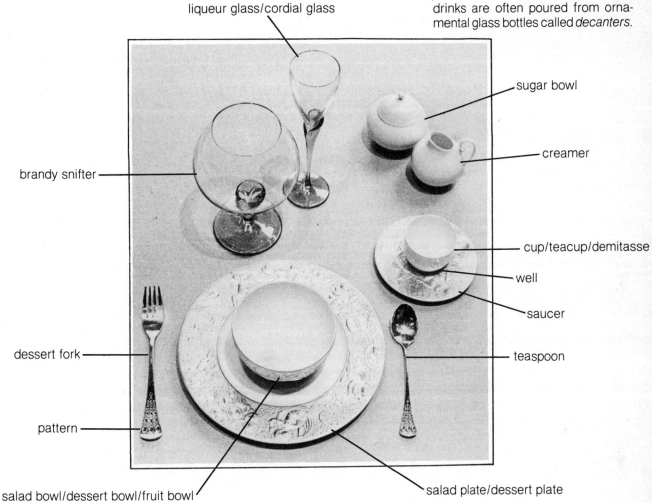

liqueur glass/cordial glass

sugar bowl

creamer

brandy snifter

cup/teacup/demitasse

well

saucer

dessert fork

teaspoon

pattern

salad bowl/dessert bowl/fruit bowl

salad plate/dessert plate

Chafing Dish

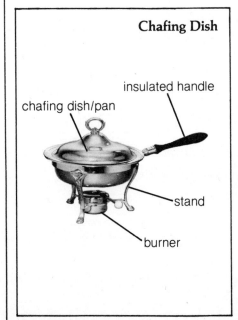

insulated handle

chafing dish/pan

stand

burner

Tea Set / Tea Service and Kettle

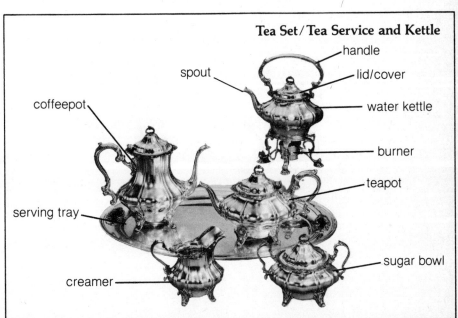

handle

spout

lid/cover

coffeepot

water kettle

burner

teapot

serving tray

sugar bowl

creamer

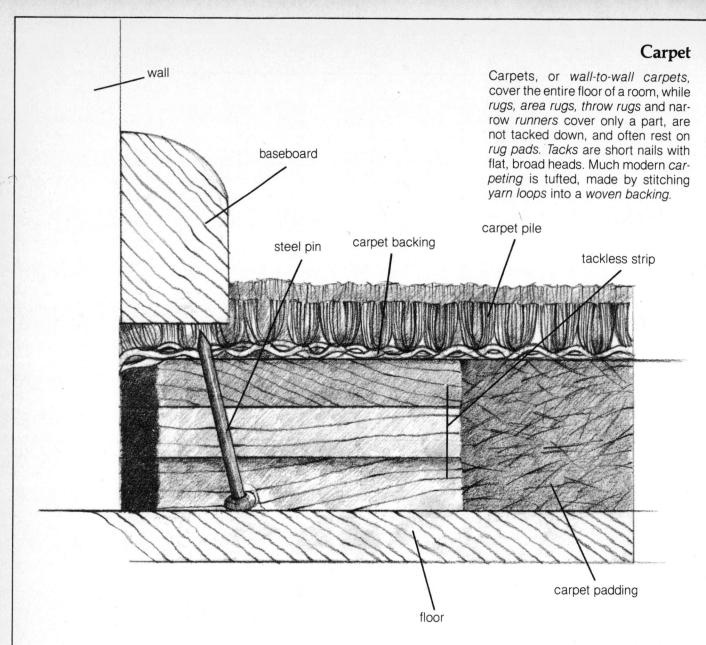

Carpet

Carpets, or *wall-to-wall carpets*, cover the entire floor of a room, while *rugs, area rugs, throw rugs* and narrow *runners* cover only a part, are not tacked down, and often rest on *rug pads. Tacks* are short nails with flat, broad heads. Much modern *carpeting* is tufted, made by stitching *yarn loops* into a *woven backing*.

wall

baseboard

steel pin

carpet backing

carpet pile

tackless strip

carpet padding

floor

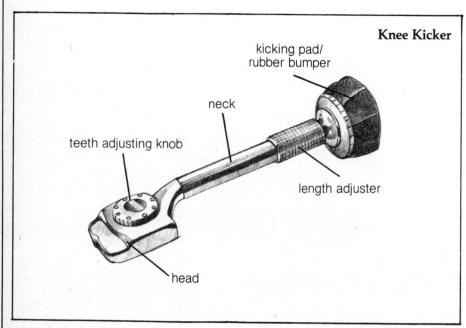

Knee Kicker

kicking pad/
rubber bumper

neck

teeth adjusting knob

length adjuster

head

Sink and Compactor

The hardware in a sink, the faucet handles and spout, are known as *fixtures*. Sink drains usually have perforated *drain baskets* which trap debris but allow water to pass through. Many baskets are two-piece units that form a watertight seal when the *inner basket* is twisted. *Instant hot-water devices* mounted on the spout of some sinks have a constantly heated coil that produces small amounts of hot water on demand.

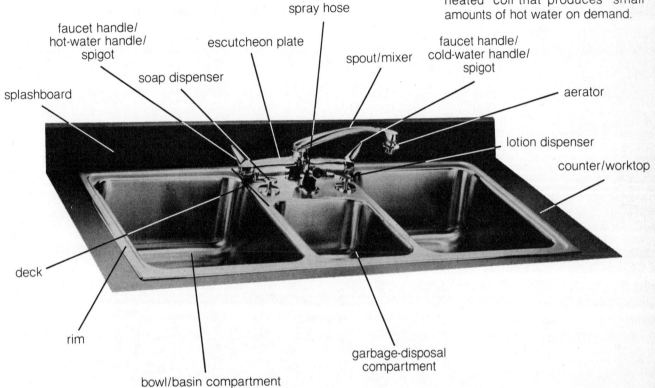

spray hose

faucet handle/
hot-water handle/
spigot

escutcheon plate

soap dispenser

spout/mixer

faucet handle/
cold-water handle/
spigot

splashboard

aerator

lotion dispenser

counter/worktop

deck

rim

garbage-disposal
compartment

bowl/basin compartment

Kitchen Sink

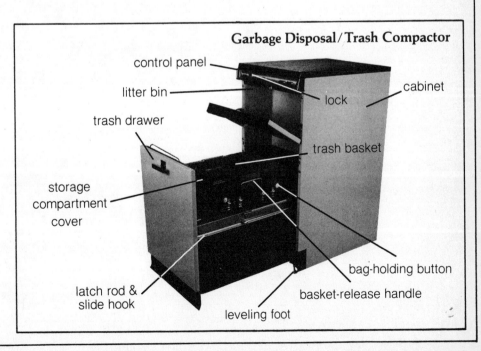

Garbage Disposal/Trash Compactor

control panel

litter bin

lock

cabinet

trash drawer

trash basket

storage
compartment
cover

latch rod &
slide hook

leveling foot

bag-holding button

basket-release handle

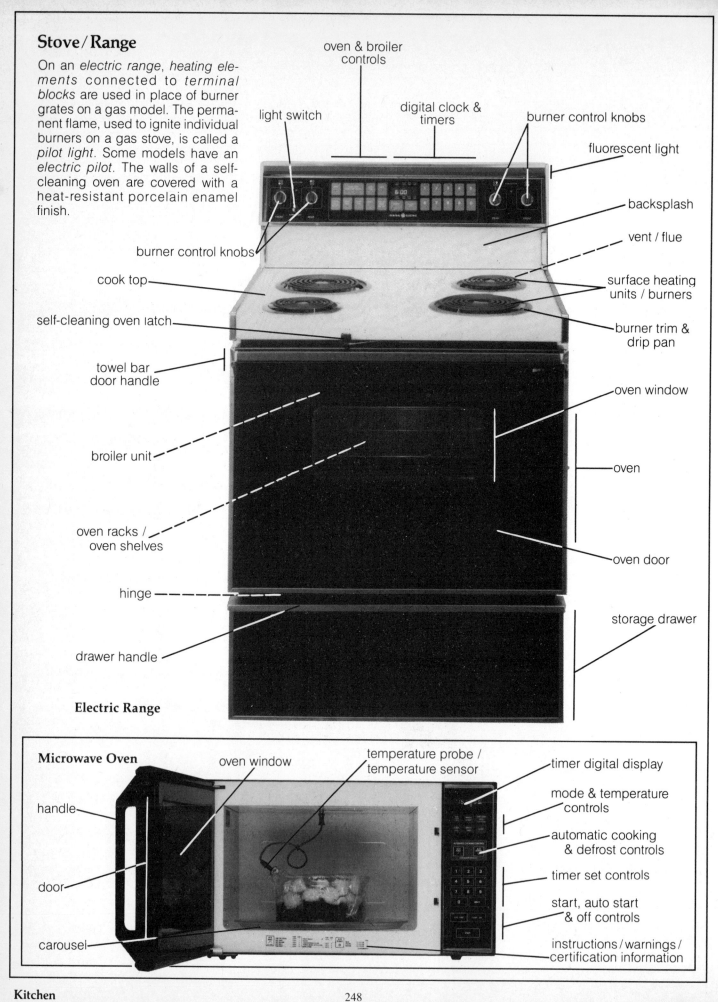

Stove/Range

On an *electric range*, *heating elements* connected to *terminal blocks* are used in place of burner grates on a gas model. The permanent flame, used to ignite individual burners on a gas stove, is called a *pilot light*. Some models have an *electric pilot*. The walls of a self-cleaning oven are covered with a heat-resistant porcelain enamel finish.

oven & broiler controls

light switch

digital clock & timers

burner control knobs

fluorescent light

burner control knobs

backsplash

vent / flue

cook top

surface heating units / burners

self-cleaning oven latch

burner trim & drip pan

towel bar door handle

oven window

broiler unit

oven

oven racks / oven shelves

oven door

hinge

storage drawer

drawer handle

Electric Range

Microwave Oven

oven window

temperature probe / temperature sensor

timer digital display

handle

mode & temperature controls

automatic cooking & defrost controls

door

timer set controls

start, auto start & off controls

carousel

instructions / warnings / certification information

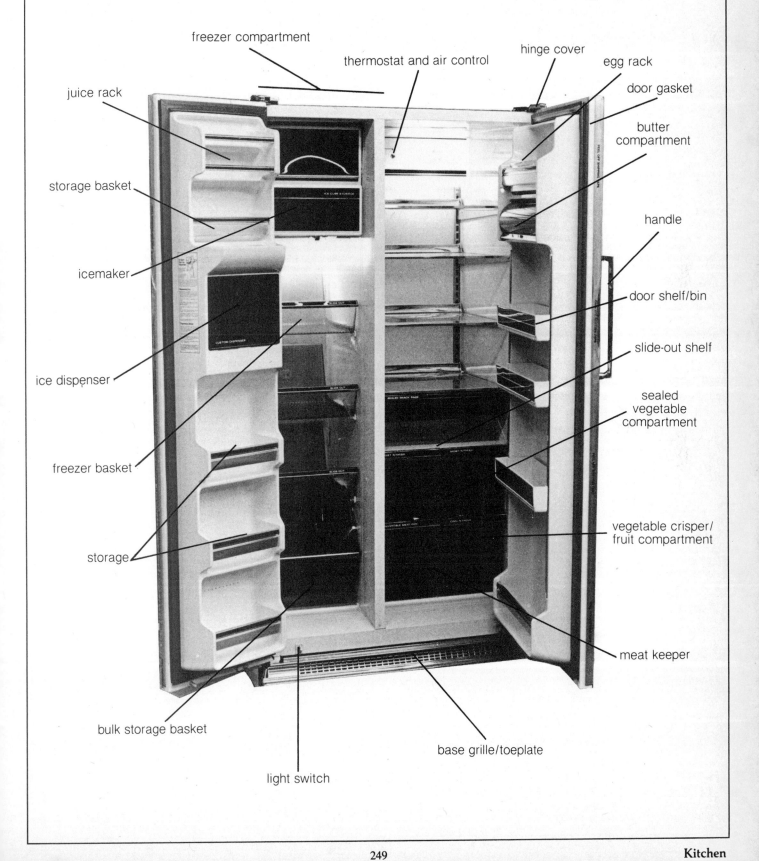

Refrigerator

Some refrigerators, or *iceboxes*, have an *ice dispenser* in the freezer section. Others have *ice trays*. A *frostfree*, or *no-frost*, model does not require defrosting.

freezer compartment

thermostat and air control

hinge cover

egg rack

door gasket

juice rack

butter compartment

storage basket

handle

icemaker

door shelf/bin

slide-out shelf

ice dispenser

sealed vegetable compartment

freezer basket

storage

vegetable crisper/ fruit compartment

meat keeper

bulk storage basket

base grille/toeplate

light switch

Dishwasher

The *cycle-selector control panel* and *timer* are located on the outside of the door of this built-in dishwasher. The machine will operate only when the *external door switch,* or latch, is engaged.

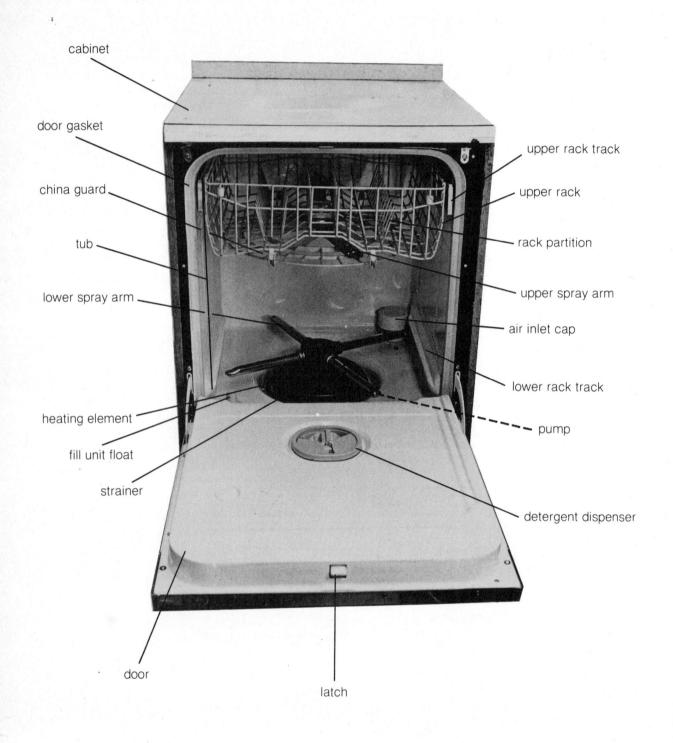

cabinet

door gasket

china guard

tub

lower spray arm

heating element

fill unit float

strainer

door

upper rack track

upper rack

rack partition

upper spray arm

air inlet cap

lower rack track

pump

detergent dispenser

latch

Openers

With manual openers, the can rim is held between a *cutting blade* and a *turning gear,* with pressure applied by squeezing two *handles* and the can rotated with a winged *key.* The blade and handle device used by military personnel to open food ration cans is called a *"John Wayne."* The corkscrew shown below is used by *sommeliers,* or *wine stewards.*

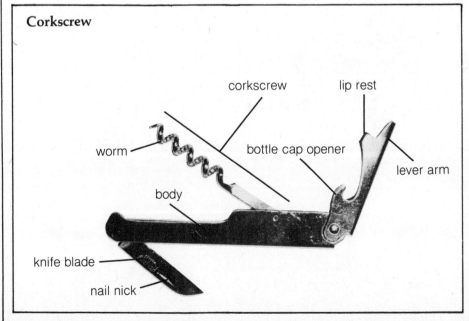

cutting lever

release knob

blade shaft

cutting blade/plow

pivot pin

magnetic lid lifter

drive wheel

motor housing

nameplate

shaft

can ledge

front housing

base

Electric Can Opener

Corkscrew

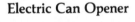

corkscrew

lip rest

worm

bottle cap opener

body

lever arm

knife blade

nail nick

"Church Key" / Can Piercer

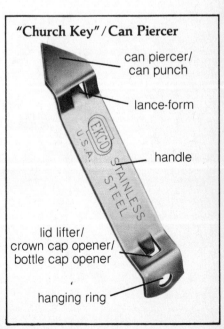

can piercer/
can punch

lance-form

handle

lid lifter/
crown cap opener/
bottle cap opener

hanging ring

Kitchen

Coffee Makers

Coffee is *brewed* by passing boiling water through *ground coffee* beans. *Espresso* is brewed by forcing steam through roasted beans. *Cappuccino* consists of espresso and steamed milk.

brew control

fill opening

filter basket

water reservoir

lid

brew starter/automatic timer

handle

carafe/decanter

on-off switch

warming unit/hot plate

indicator light/signal light

cup level scale

Drip Coffee Maker

Percolator

dome

spout

lid

pot/body

plug outlet

brewing & warming element

brew selector

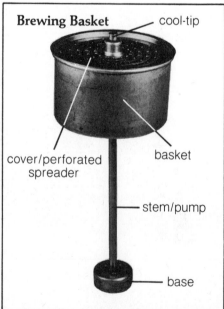

Brewing Basket

cool-tip

cover/perforated spreader

basket

stem/pump

base

Infusion Maker

knob/plunger

lip/spout

rod

frame

filter assembly

beaker/carafe/jug

Many toasters have removable *crumb trays*. The heating elements in toasters are flat *nichrome wires*. Toasters have either a spring-and-cylinder *dash-pot* or a simple spring device to pop toast up once it is browned. Toaster ovens have removable *baking trays*.

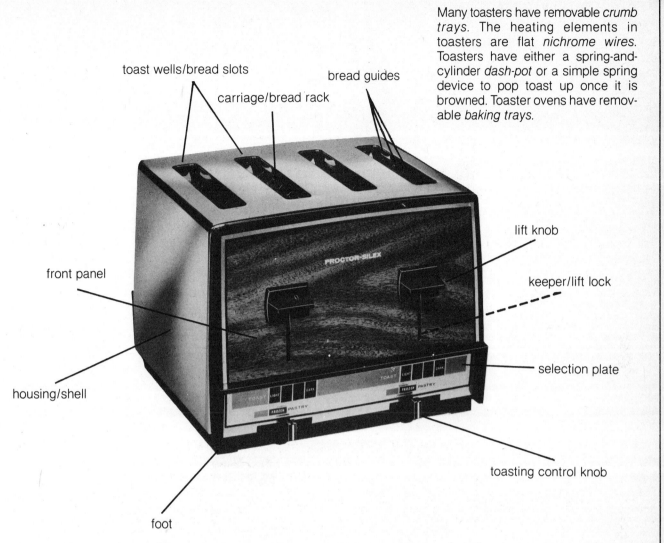

toast wells/bread slots

carriage/bread rack

bread guides

lift knob

keeper/lift lock

front panel

selection plate

housing/shell

toasting control knob

foot

Toaster

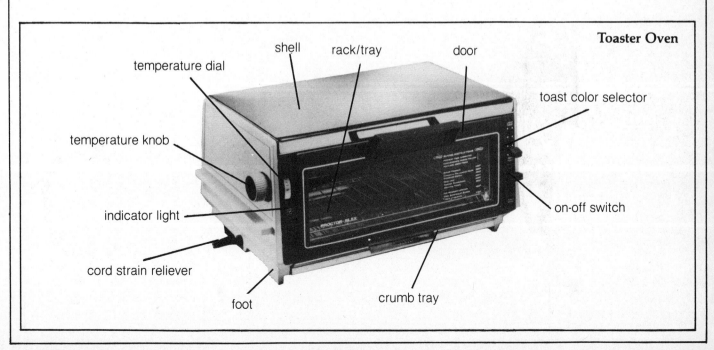

Toaster Oven

shell

rack/tray

door

temperature dial

toast color selector

temperature knob

indicator light

on-off switch

cord strain reliever

foot

crumb tray

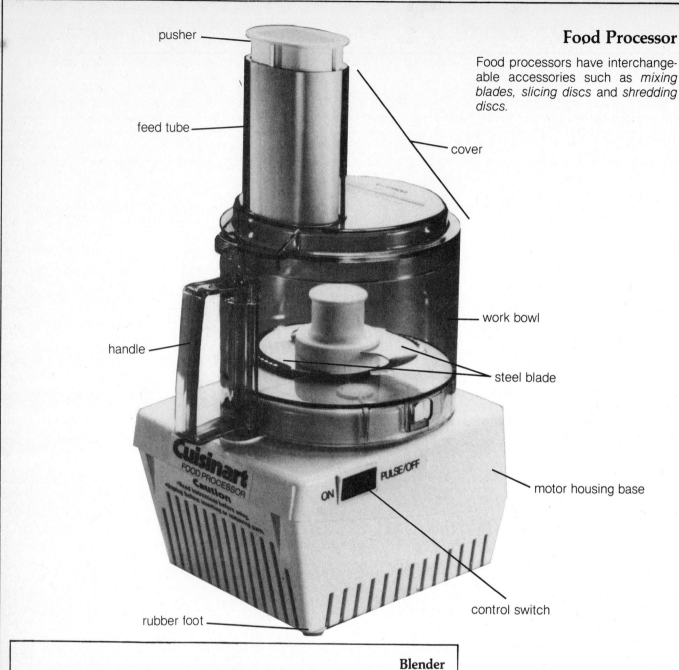

Food Processor

Food processors have interchange-able accessories such as *mixing blades, slicing discs* and *shredding discs.*

pusher

feed tube

cover

handle

work bowl

steel blade

motor housing base

control switch

rubber foot

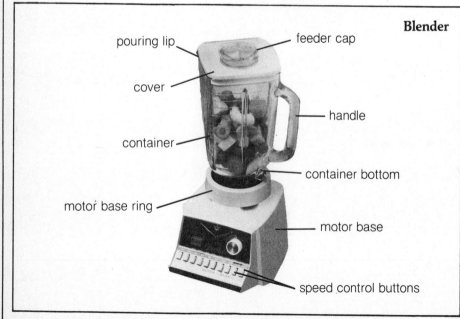

Blender

pouring lip

feeder cap

cover

handle

container

container bottom

motor base ring

motor base

speed control buttons

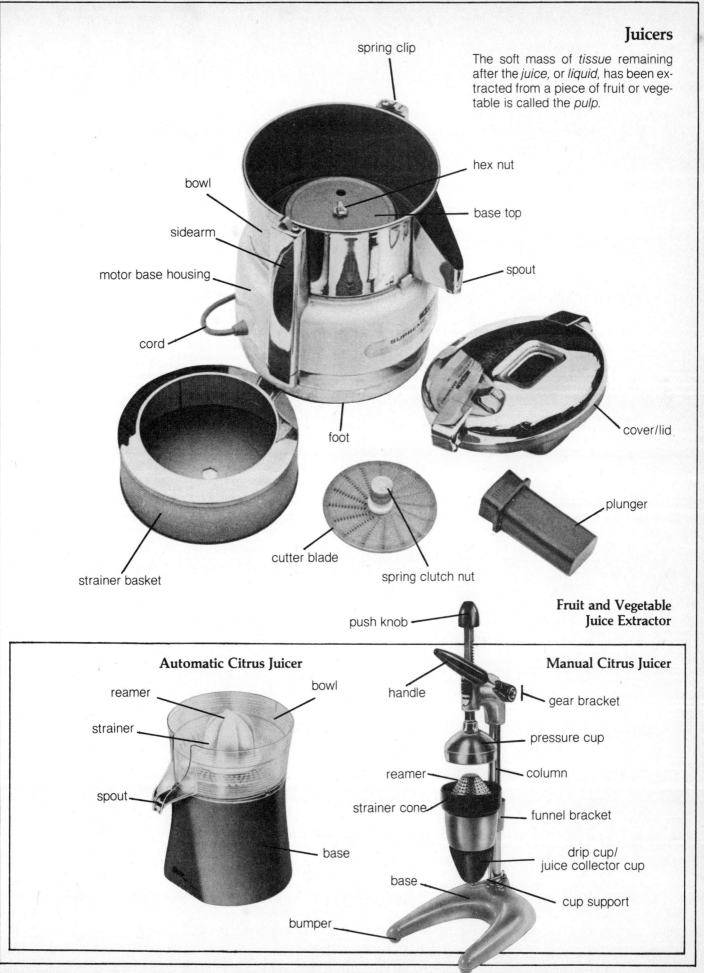

Juicers

The soft mass of *tissue* remaining after the *juice,* or *liquid,* has been extracted from a piece of fruit or vegetable is called the *pulp.*

spring clip

hex nut

bowl

base top

sidearm

motor base housing

spout

cord

cover/lid

foot

plunger

strainer basket

cutter blade

spring clutch nut

Fruit and Vegetable Juice Extractor

push knob

Automatic Citrus Juicer

Manual Citrus Juicer

reamer

bowl

handle

gear bracket

strainer

pressure cup

reamer

column

spout

strainer cone

funnel bracket

base

drip cup/ juice collector cup

base

cup support

bumper

Knife

The part of a knife blade that extends into the handle is called the *tang,* and the blade's formation is known as the *grind.* In a *flat grind,* the sides of the blade are smooth. In a *hollow grind* there is a marked curve or bevel along the length of the blade.

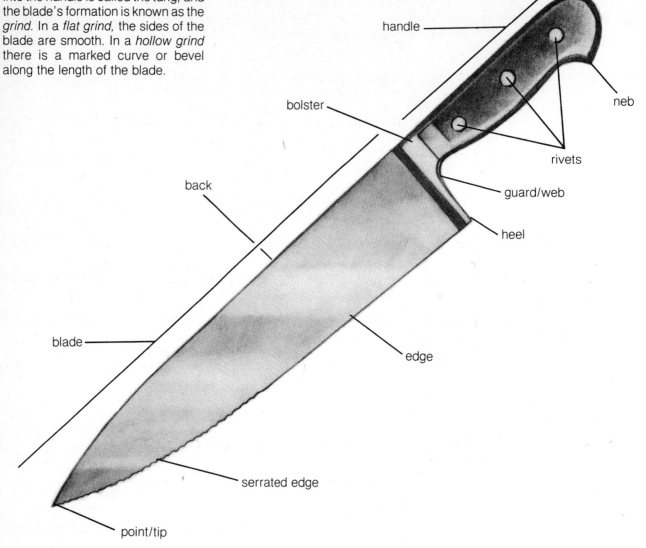

handle

neb

bolster

rivets

guard/web

back

heel

blade

edge

serrated edge

point/tip

Peeler

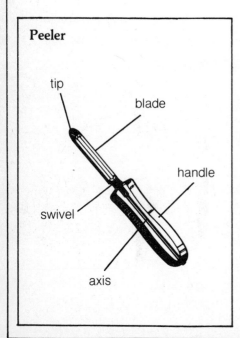

tip

blade

handle

swivel

axis

Sharpening Steel

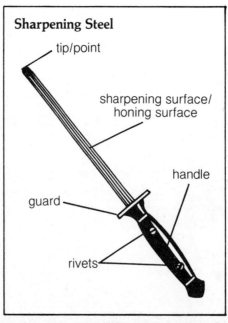

tip/point

sharpening surface/ honing surface

handle

guard

rivets

Cheese Plane/Cheese Slicer

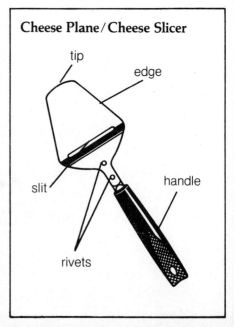

tip

edge

slit

handle

rivets

Pots and Pans

Pots and pans are often described by their function—for example, a *boiler* or *steamer. Crockpots* are pots made of earthenware. *Casseroles* are earthenware, glass or cast-iron pots in which food can be both baked and served. A *pipkin* is a small saucepan with a long handle used to melt butter.

knob

cover/lid

handle

Stock Pot/Stew Pot

rim

lift-out stem

perforated panel

Steamer Basket

leg/foot

Saucepan

side

tang

bottom

hanging ring

handle

Skillet/Frying Pan

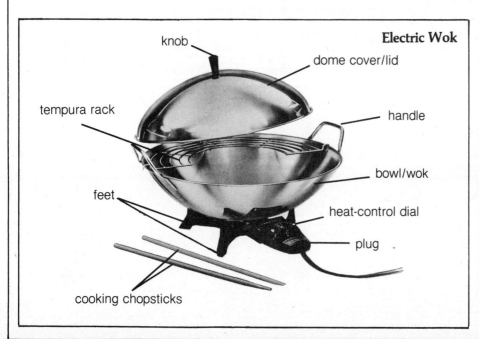

Electric Wok

knob

dome cover/lid

tempura rack

handle

bowl/wok

feet

heat-control dial

plug

cooking chopsticks

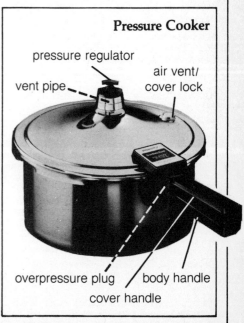

Pressure Cooker

pressure regulator

vent pipe

air vent/ cover lock

overpressure plug

body handle

cover handle

Mixing and Measuring Tools

In addition to the *meat,* or *rapid-response thermometer,* seen here, well-equipped kitchens have *oven* and *freezer thermometers, deep-frying thermometers, scales* and *funnels.*

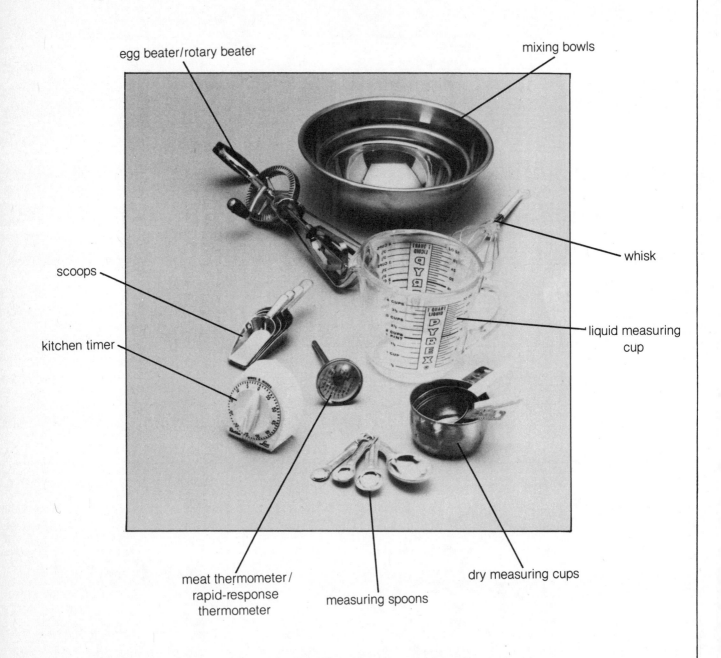

egg beater/rotary beater

mixing bowls

whisk

scoops

liquid measuring cup

kitchen timer

meat thermometer/ rapid-response thermometer

measuring spoons

dry measuring cups

Additional preparation implements include *molding scoops,* for soft foods, wooden *spaghetti spoons* with long *prongs* to wrap pasta and lift it from boiling water, *basting ladles* with an egg-shaped *bowl* for easy pouring, and cylindrical one-piece *pastry pins.*

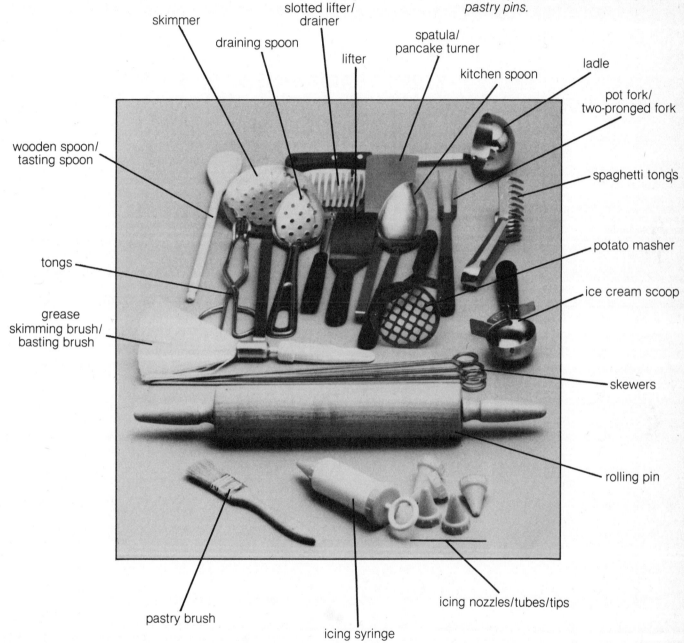

skimmer

slotted lifter/ drainer

draining spoon

lifter

spatula/ pancake turner

kitchen spoon

ladle

pot fork/ two-pronged fork

wooden spoon/ tasting spoon

spaghetti tongs

tongs

potato masher

grease skimming brush/ basting brush

ice cream scoop

skewers

rolling pin

pastry brush

icing syringe

icing nozzles/tubes/tips

Strainers and Drainers

Clean dishes, vegetables and fruits may be left on a *draining rack,* or *dish rack,* to dry. *Cooling racks* are used in conjunction with baked foods. A *sieve* has a mesh bottom for straining. A *food mill,* or *food foley,* is a heavy colander through which food is pressed by means of a flat *plate* attached to a *rotating handle.*

colander

strainer

sifter

tea ball/ tea infuser

tea and coffee strainer

deep frying basket

lettuce dryer/salad shaker

dredger/sugar and flour shaker

A *potato peeler* has a swivel blade for following contours and a sharp tip for gouging. Hand-cranked *meat grinders* chop meats and other foods. A *zester* is a tool that shaves the thin surface off fruits.

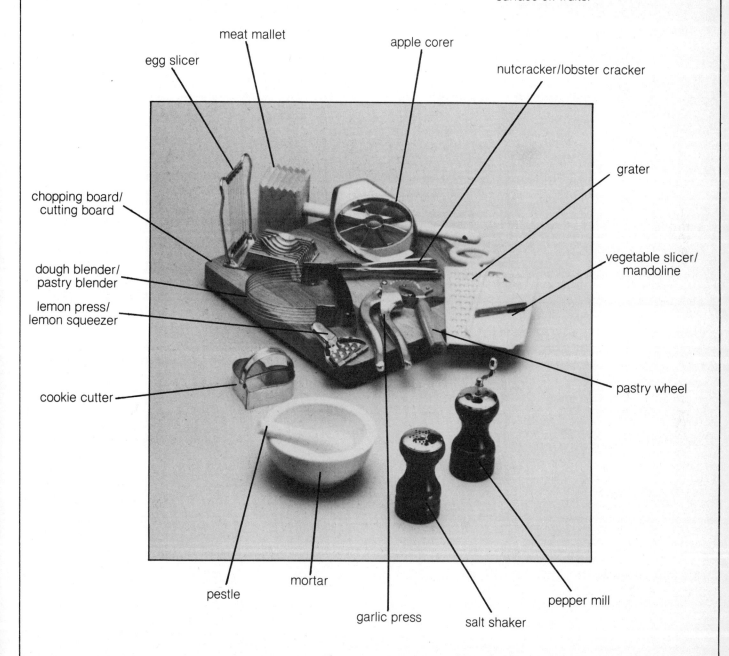

egg slicer

meat mallet

apple corer

nutcracker/lobster cracker

grater

chopping board/ cutting board

dough blender/ pastry blender

lemon press/ lemon squeezer

vegetable slicer/ mandoline

cookie cutter

pastry wheel

pestle

mortar

garlic press

salt shaker

pepper mill

Raw Ingredients

On *lettuce*, the entire mass of leaves is called the *head*, while the center leaves are the *heart*. A small slice of meat is a *collop*. A *peppercorn* is a dried berry of black pepper.

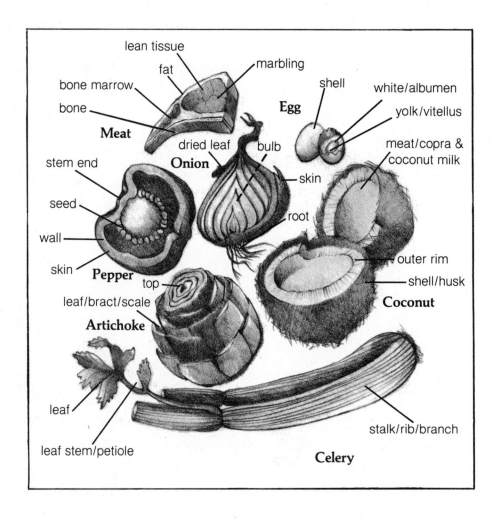

Appetizers, or *hors d'oeuvres*, are served before the main *course*, or *entree*. An ingredient, such as a *condiment*, *spice* or *herb*, added to food for the savor it imparts, is *seasoning*. Cheese is made by separating the *curd*, milk solids, from the *whey*, milk liquids. *Crumb* refers to both the soft inner portion of bread and any tiny piece that flakes off the loaf or a slice.

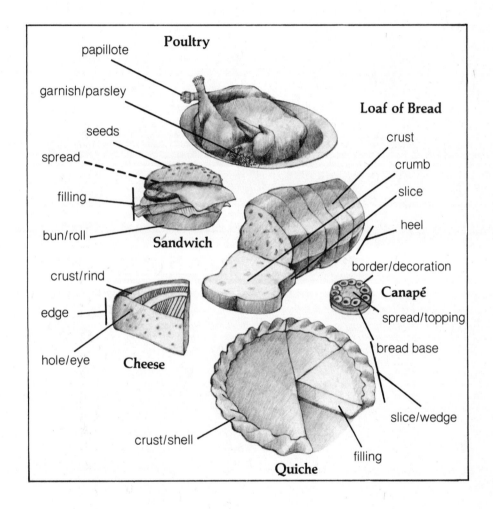

Poultry

papillote

garnish/parsley

seeds

spread

filling

bun/roll

Sandwich

crust/rind

edge

hole/eye

Cheese

crust/shell

Quiche

Loaf of Bread

crust

crumb

slice

heel

border/decoration

Canapé

spread/topping

bread base

slice/wedge

filling

Kitchen

Desserts

Baked desserts, or *sweet goods,* made of dough or having a crust made of enriched dough, such as *pies,* tarts and *turnovers,* are *pastries.* A *parfait* is similar to a sundae but may have layers of fruit and be frozen.

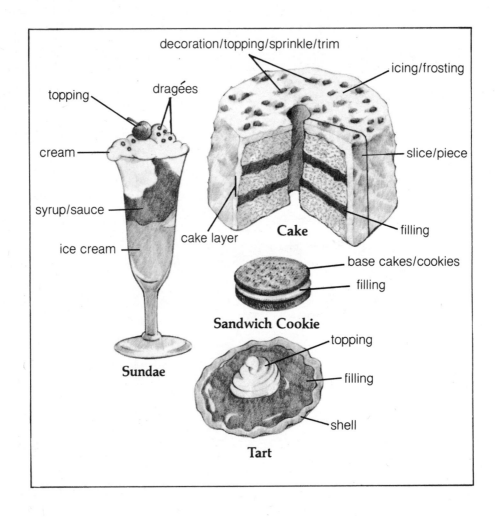

Snack Foods

Ice cream scoops are also put in flat-bottomed *wafer cones* and topped with other *fixings,* including *nuts* and *cherries.* When ice cream melts and drips down the cone, it forms *lickings.* The part of a hot dog roll that remains attached after the roll is sliced is the *hinge. Smoked sausages* are larger than franks and often include additional *seasonings.* Among other pizza toppings are *anchovies, extra cheese, pepperoni* and *onions.*

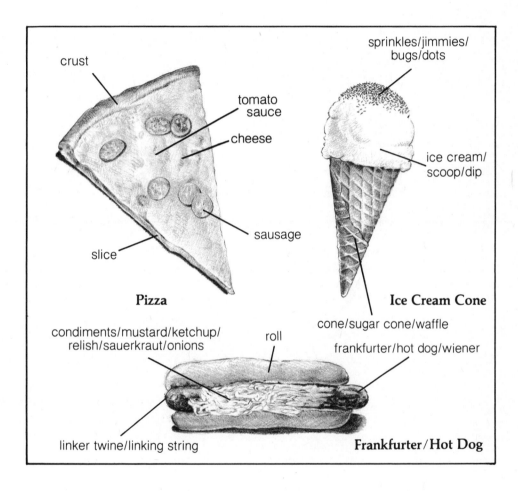

crust

tomato sauce

cheese

sausage

slice

Pizza

sprinkles/jimmies/bugs/dots

ice cream/scoop/dip

Ice Cream Cone

cone/sugar cone/waffle

condiments/mustard/ketchup/relish/sauerkraut/onions

roll

frankfurter/hot dog/wiener

linker twine/linking string

Frankfurter/Hot Dog

Kitchen

Containers

Most baskets are made by weaving individual *strands* or *rods* in front of one *stake* of the *frame* and behind the next. Some baskets have a border, or *foot,* on the bottom, just above the *base,* as well as a *cover,* or *lid,* which often rests on an inside *ledge.* A small, oblong veneer basket with rounded ends, the kind used for mushrooms, is a *climax basket,* and a little wooden paillike container with one stave extending up for a handle is a *piggin.*

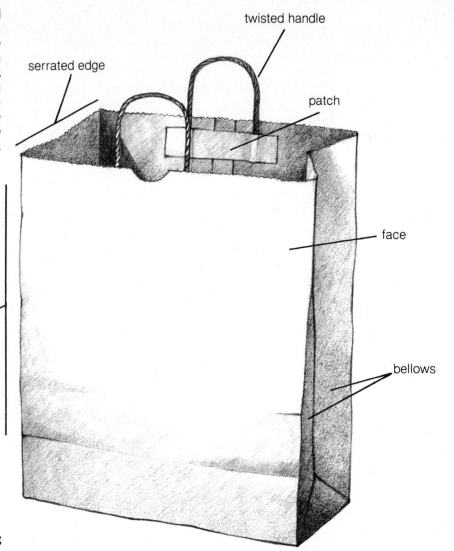

serrated edge

twisted handle

patch

face

body

bellows

Paper Bag

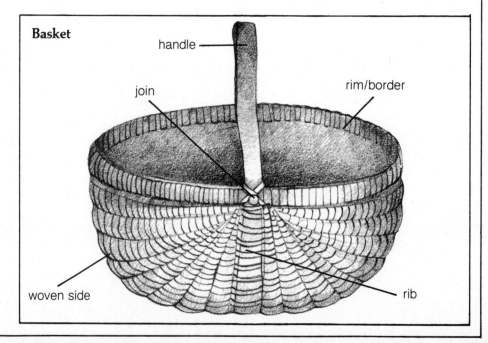

Basket

handle

join

rim/border

woven side

rib

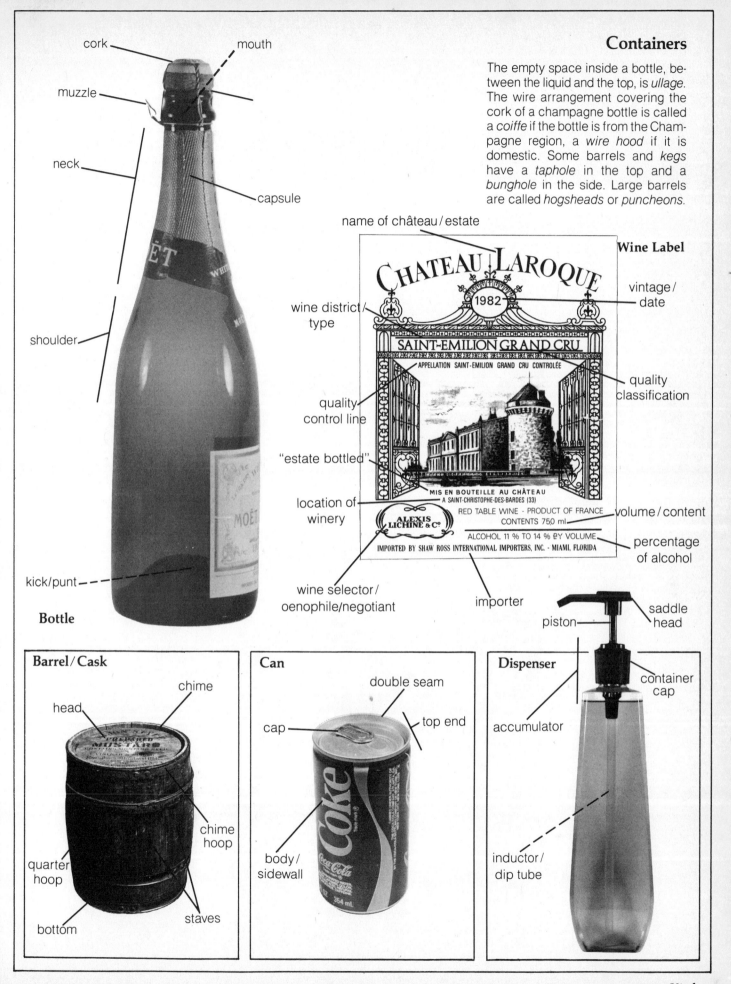

Containers

cork

mouth

muzzle

neck

capsule

shoulder

The empty space inside a bottle, between the liquid and the top, is *ullage*. The wire arrangement covering the cork of a champagne bottle is called a *coiffe* if the bottle is from the Champagne region, a *wire hood* if it is domestic. Some barrels and *kegs* have a *taphole* in the top and a *bunghole* in the side. Large barrels are called *hogsheads* or *puncheons*.

name of château / estate

Wine Label

CHATEAU LAROQUE

1982

wine district / type

vintage / date

SAINT-EMILION GRAND CRU

APPELLATION SAINT-EMILION GRAND CRU CONTROLÉE

quality classification

quality control line

"estate bottled"

MIS EN BOUTEILLE AU CHÂTEAU
A SAINT-CHRISTOPHE-DES-BARDES (33)

location of winery

ALEXIS LICHINE & Cº

RED TABLE WINE - PRODUCT OF FRANCE
CONTENTS 750 ml

volume / content

ALCOHOL 11 % TO 14 % BY VOLUME

percentage of alcohol

IMPORTED BY SHAW ROSS INTERNATIONAL IMPORTERS, INC. - MIAMI, FLORIDA

kick/punt

wine selector / oenophile/negotiant

importer

Bottle

piston

saddle head

accumulator

container cap

inductor / dip tube

Barrel / Cask

chime

head

chime hoop

quarter hoop

bottom

staves

Can

double seam

top end

cap

body / sidewall

Dispenser

Labeling and Packaging

Sketches or pictures on labels are called *vignettes*. When letters or vignettes on labels are raised, they are *embossed*. When they are recessed they are *debossed*. A seal of clear plastic that conforms to a product's shape is a *shrinkwrap*. A *promotional,* or *spot label,* often applied over the regular label, is a *tip-on*.

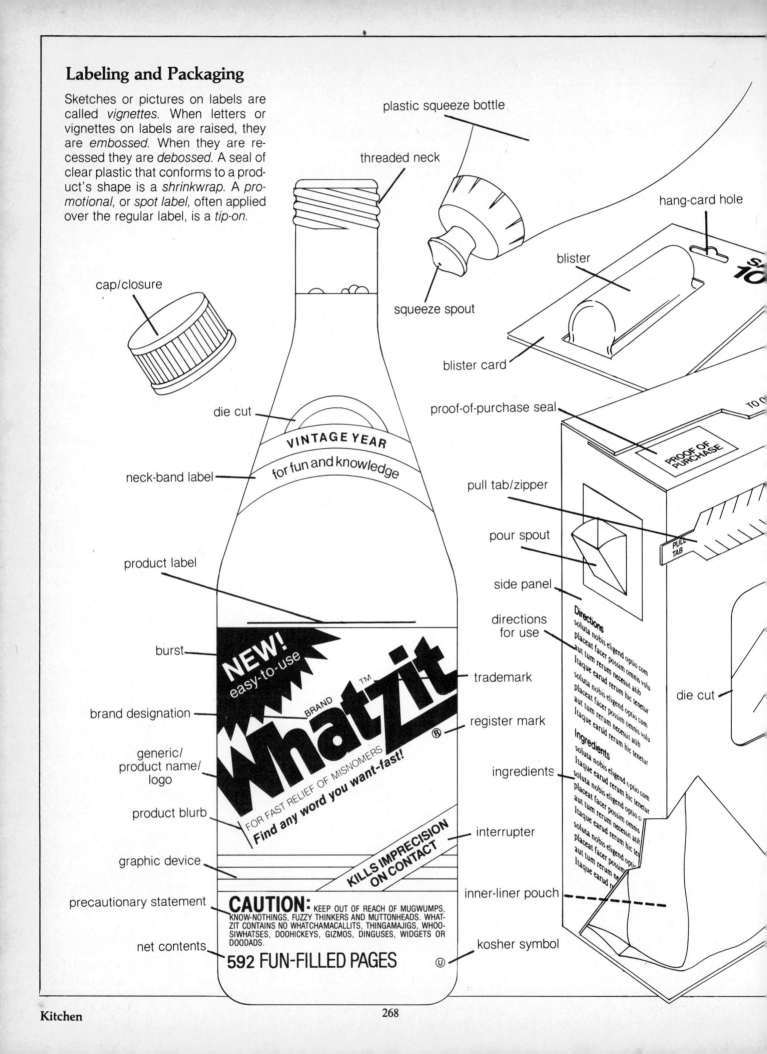

plastic squeeze bottle

threaded neck

hang-card hole

blister

squeeze spout

blister card

cap/closure

proof-of-purchase seal

die cut

VINTAGE YEAR

for fun and knowledge

neck-band label

pull tab/zipper

pour spout

side panel

product label

directions for use

NEW! easy-to-use

burst

BRAND

Whatzit ™

trademark

brand designation

register mark

generic/ product name/ logo

FOR FAST RELIEF OF MISNOMERS

®

Find any word you want-fast!

ingredients

product blurb

KILLS IMPRECISION ON CONTACT

interrupter

graphic device

inner-liner pouch

precautionary statement

CAUTION: KEEP OUT OF REACH OF MUGWUMPS, KNOW-NOTHINGS, FUZZY THINKERS AND MUTTONHEADS. WHATZIT CONTAINS NO WHATCHAMACALLITS, THINGAMAJIGS, WHOOSIWHATSES, DOOHICKEYS, GIZMOS, DINGUSES, WIDGETS OR DOODADS.

net contents

kosher symbol

592 FUN-FILLED PAGES

Ⓤ

die cut

Directions

soluta nobis eligend optio com placeat facer possim omnis volu aut tum rerum necessit atib Itaque earud rerum hic tenetur soluta nobis eligend optio com placeat facer possim omnis volu aut tum rerum necessit atib Itaque earud rerum hic tenetur

Ingredients

soluta nobis eligend optio com Itaque earud rerum hic tenetur soluta nobis eligend optio c placeat facer possim omnis aut tum rerum necessit Itaque earud rerum hic te soluta nobis eligend opti placeat facer possim aut tum rerum possi Itaque earud r

PROOF OF PURCHASE

PULL TAB

TO O

S 10

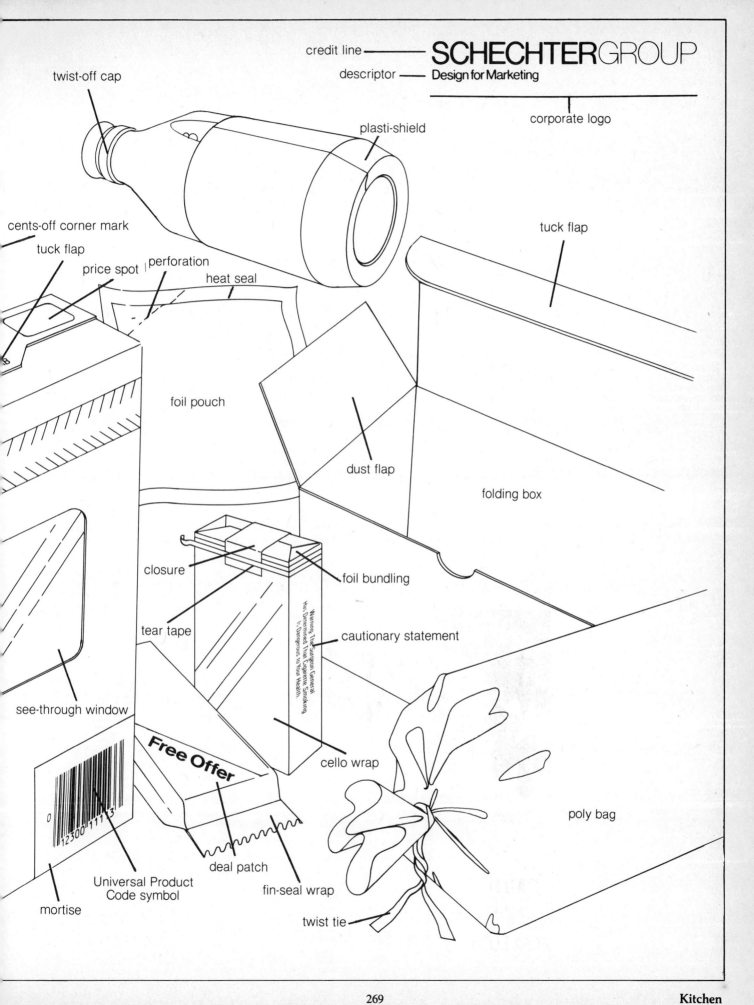

twist-off cap

plasti-shield

corporate logo

cents-off corner mark

tuck flap

tuck flap

price spot

perforation

heat seal

foil pouch

dust flap

folding box

closure

foil bundling

tear tape

cautionary statement

Warning The Surgeon General Has Determined That Cigarette Smoking Is Dangerous to Your Health.

see-through window

cello wrap

Free Offer

poly bag

Universal Product
Code symbol

deal patch

fin-seal wrap

mortise

twist tie

0 12300 11113

Bed and Bedding

A bedstead or *bed frame* consists of *side rails*, or *bedrails*, which connect the headboard to the *footboard*. A *twin bed* is a single bed, or one of a matching pair or beds, while a *double bed* is large enough to sleep two adults. A *comforter* is a small, thick quilt, while a *throw* is a bedspread with a short *side drop* rather than long *skirts*.

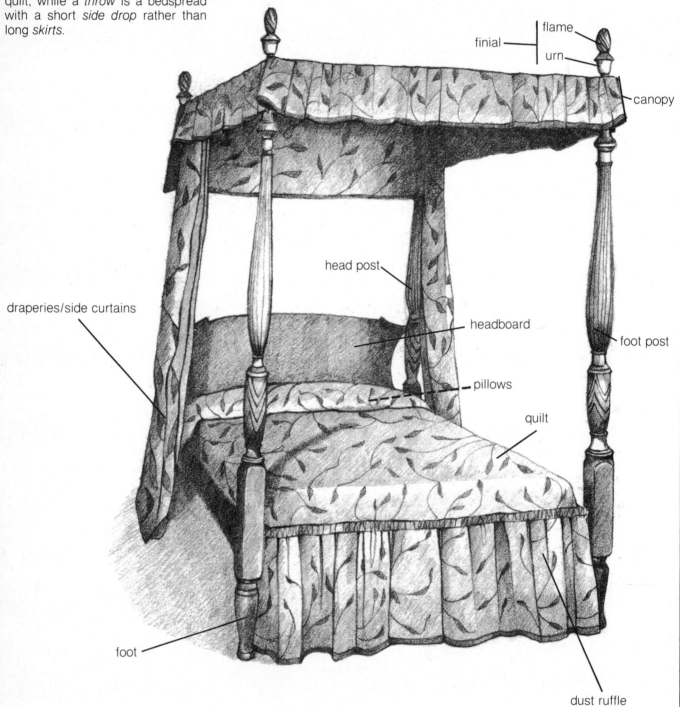

flame

finial

urn

canopy

head post

draperies/side curtains

headboard

foot post

pillows

quilt

foot

dust ruffle

Four-Poster/Canopy Bed

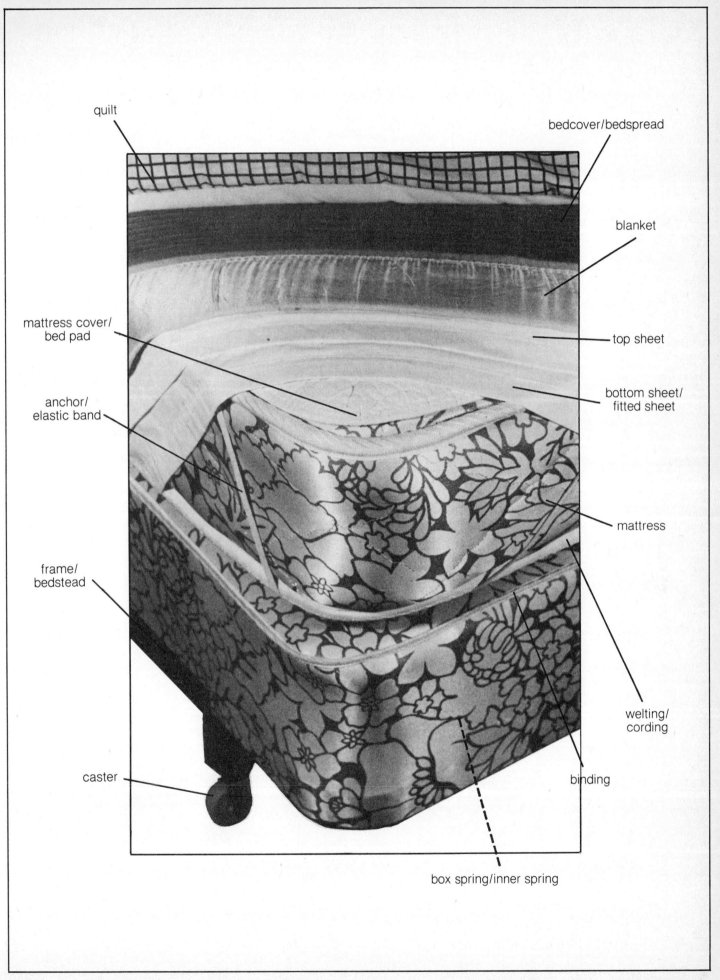

quilt

bedcover/bedspread

blanket

mattress cover/
bed pad

top sheet

anchor/
elastic band

bottom sheet/
fitted sheet

mattress

frame/
bedstead

welting/
cording

caster

binding

box spring/inner spring

Bedroom

Dressers

A dresser without the drawers in it is called the *main body,* or *carcass.* The thin plywood sheets between drawers, to keep *drawer cases* rigid, are *dust panels.* An *armoire,* or *wardrobe,* is a tall, movable closet in which to hang clothes. A *chiffonier* is a high, narrow chest of drawers.

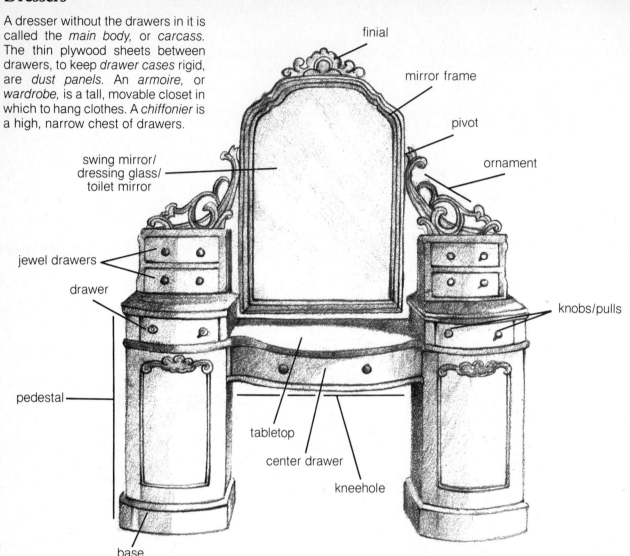

finial

mirror frame

pivot

ornament

swing mirror/
dressing glass/
toilet mirror

jewel drawers

drawer

knobs/pulls

pedestal

tabletop

center drawer

kneehole

base

Dressing Table/Vanity

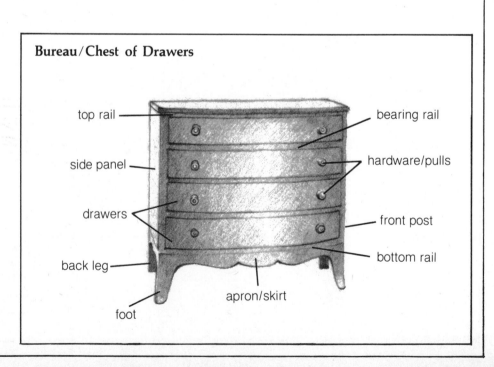

Bureau/Chest of Drawers

top rail

bearing rail

side panel

hardware/pulls

drawers

front post

back leg

bottom rail

foot

apron/skirt

Faucet and Sink

Some basins have *rubber plug* and *chain stoppers* to hold water, and *splash rims* or *lips* to prevent water from overflowing.

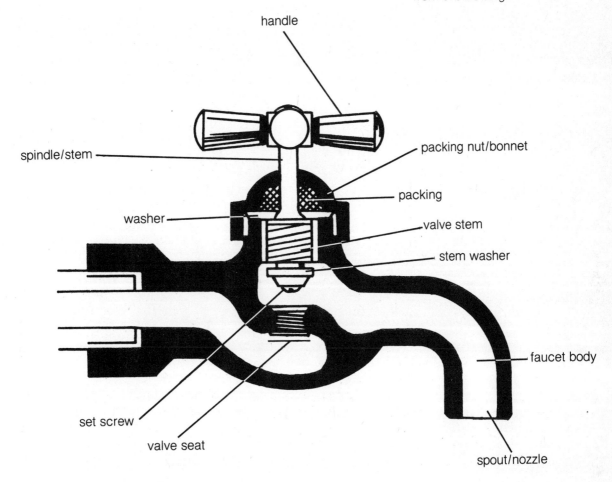

handle

spindle/stem

packing nut/bonnet

packing

washer

valve stem

stem washer

set screw

valve seat

faucet body

spout/nozzle

Faucet / Spigot / Tap / Bibcock

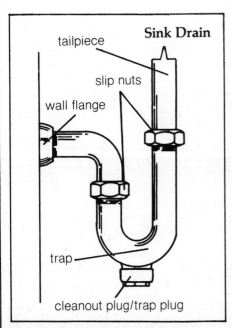

Sink Drain

tailpiece

slip nuts

wall flange

trap

cleanout plug/trap plug

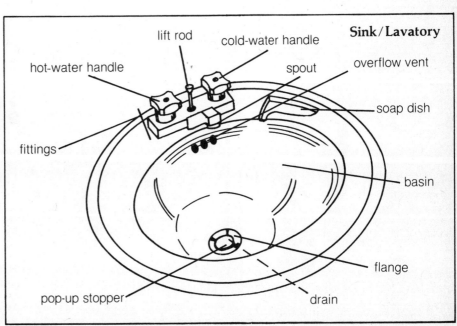

Sink / Lavatory

lift rod

cold-water handle

hot-water handle

spout

overflow vent

soap dish

fittings

basin

pop-up stopper

flange

drain

Bathroom

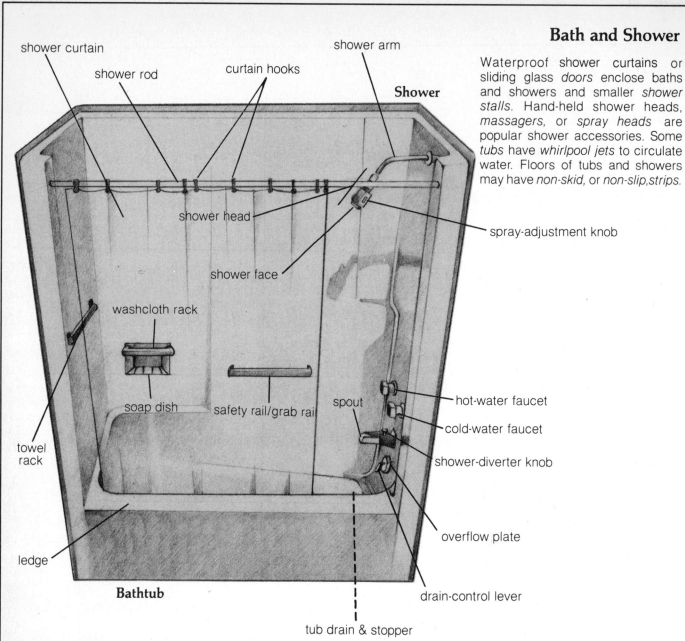

shower curtain

shower rod

curtain hooks

shower arm

Shower

shower head

shower face

Bath and Shower

Waterproof shower curtains or sliding glass *doors* enclose baths and showers and smaller *shower stalls*. Hand-held shower heads, *massagers*, or *spray heads* are popular shower accessories. Some *tubs* have *whirlpool jets* to circulate water. Floors of tubs and showers may have *non-skid*, or *non-slip, strips*.

spray-adjustment knob

washcloth rack

soap dish

safety rail/grab rail

spout

hot-water faucet

cold-water faucet

shower-diverter knob

towel rack

overflow plate

ledge

drain-control lever

Bathtub

tub drain & stopper

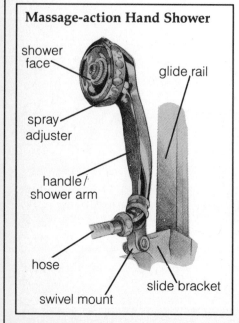

Massage-action Hand Shower

shower face

glide rail

spray adjuster

handle/ shower arm

hose

slide bracket

swivel mount

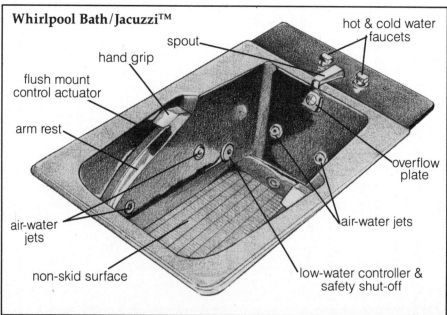

Whirlpool Bath/Jacuzzi™

spout

hand grip

flush mount control actuator

arm rest

air-water jets

non-skid surface

hot & cold water faucets

overflow plate

air-water jets

low-water controller & safety shut-off

Bathroom

274

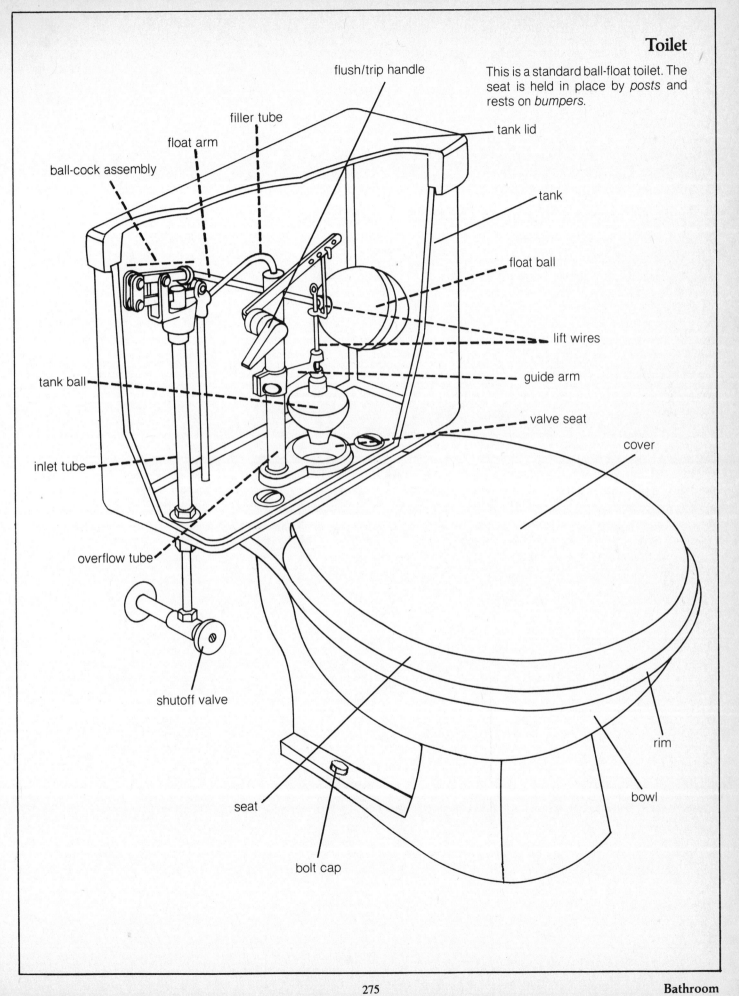

Toilet

This is a standard ball-float toilet. The seat is held in place by *posts* and rests on *bumpers*.

flush/trip handle

filler tube

float arm

ball-cock assembly

tank lid

tank

float ball

lift wires

guide arm

tank ball

valve seat

cover

inlet tube

overflow tube

shutoff valve

rim

bowl

seat

bolt cap

Bathroom

Desk

A *rolltop* or *cylinder desk* has a *sliding cover* that covers the desk's *writing area* when not in use. In *slant-front, falling-front* or *drop-lid desks,* the *front* flips down to offer a writing area which is supported by two *slide-out supports.* Some modern office desks have *elevator platforms* that can be raised and locked in place to hold a business machine, or lowered and closed behind a *cabinet door.*

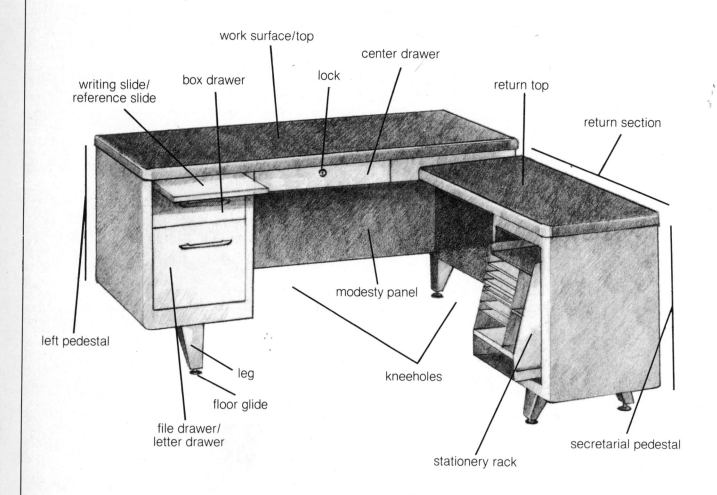

work surface/top

center drawer

box drawer   lock

writing slide/
reference slide   return top

return section

left pedestal

modesty panel

leg

floor glide   kneeholes

file drawer/
letter drawer   stationery rack   secretarial pedestal

Strips of staples are loaded into a stapler's *channel*. Pencils are sharpened in a *carrier* which holds two grooved cylinders called *cutters*. A paper clip is a piece of bessemer stock wire given three *twists*.

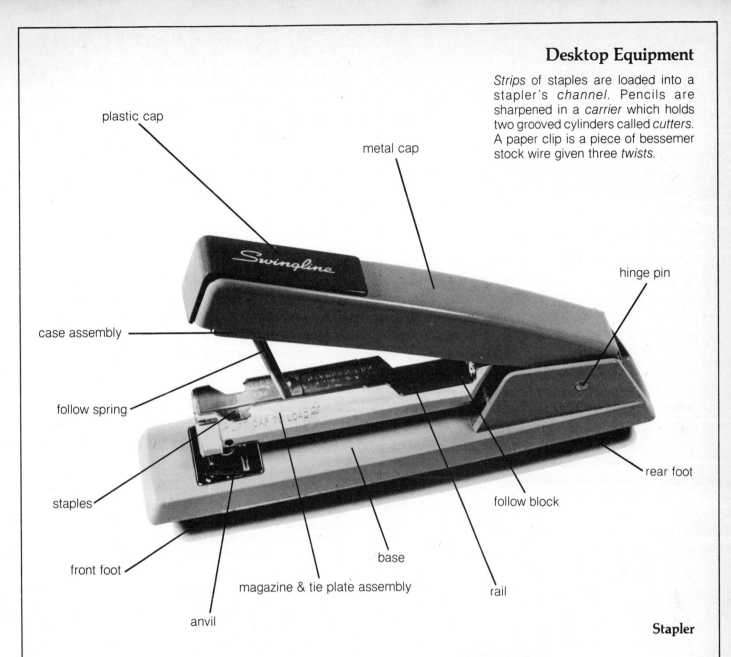

plastic cap

metal cap

hinge pin

case assembly

follow spring

rear foot

staples

follow block

front foot

base

magazine & tie plate assembly

rail

anvil

Stapler

Paper Clip/Gem Clip

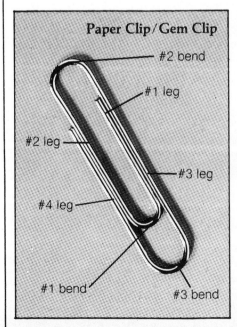

#2 bend

#1 leg

#2 leg

#3 leg

#4 leg

#1 bend

#3 bend

Pencil Sharpener

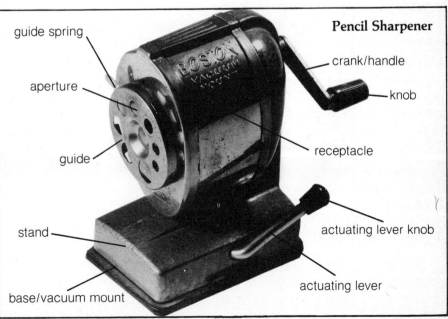

guide spring

crank/handle

aperture

knob

guide

receptacle

stand

actuating lever knob

base/vacuum mount

actuating lever

Sewing Machine

The standard presser foot can be replaced by a variety of special attachments, including a *zipper foot, hemmer foot* and *roller foot.* Some machines have a *slide plate* as well as a needle plate that opens to provide access to the bobbin case.

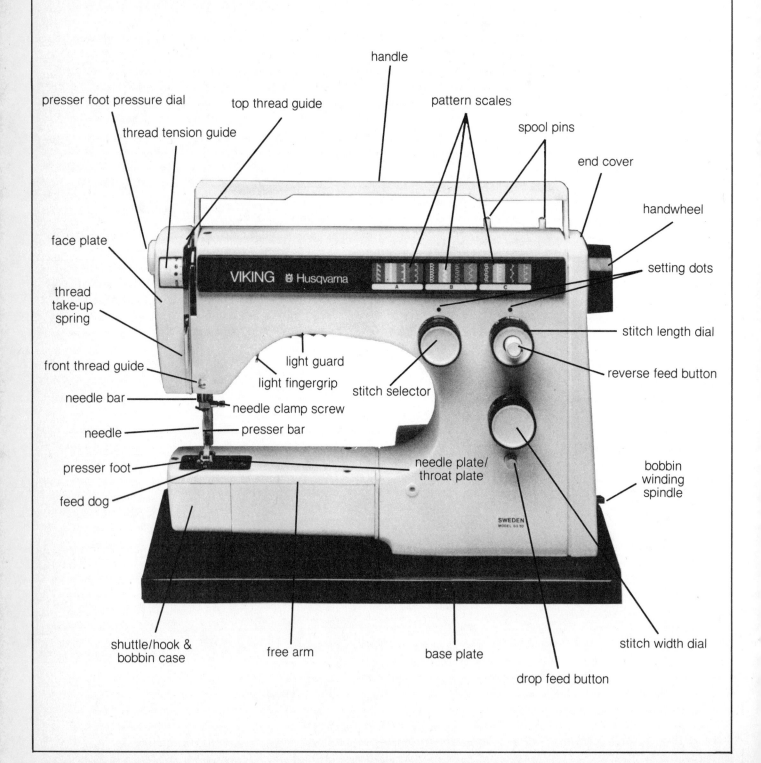

handle

pattern scales

spool pins

end cover

handwheel

presser foot pressure dial

top thread guide

thread tension guide

face plate

thread take-up spring

front thread guide

needle bar

needle

presser foot

feed dog

setting dots

stitch length dial

reverse feed button

light guard

light fingergrip

stitch selector

needle clamp screw

presser bar

needle plate/throat plate

bobbin winding spindle

shuttle/hook & bobbin case

free arm

base plate

drop feed button

stitch width dial

VIKING ☒ Husqvarna

SWEDEN
MODEL 6570

The *steam-and-dry iron*, or *flatiron*, shown here has *steam vents*, or *steam ports*, in the soleplate. Some irons have *front spray nozzles* as well.

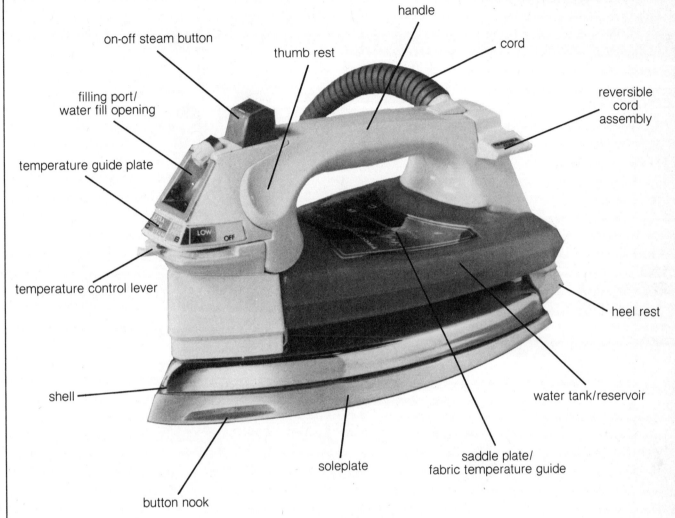

handle

on-off steam button

thumb rest

cord

filling port/water fill opening

reversible cord assembly

temperature guide plate

temperature control lever

heel rest

shell

water tank/reservoir

button nook

soleplate

saddle plate/fabric temperature guide

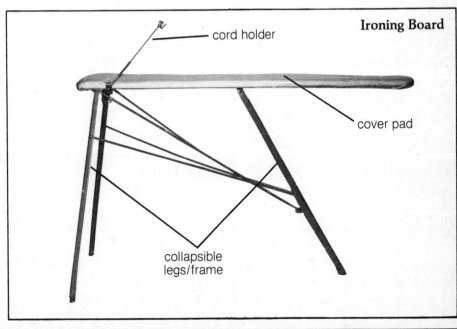

Ironing Board

cord holder

cover pad

collapsible legs/frame

Washing and Drying

Formerly, clothes were washed in a *washtub* with a *scrubboard* and *wringer* before being hung out to dry on *clotheslines,* or *washlines,* with clothespins. Wash-and-wear shirts are still air-dried on hangers. In automatic *top-loading washing machines* and *front-loading washers,* the basket, which has *drain holes* inside it, is contained within a metal *tub.* Some washers and dryers have a *window* in the *door* and a *tub light.*

gripping hole

spring slot

claw end

pinwood

handle

spring

Clothespin

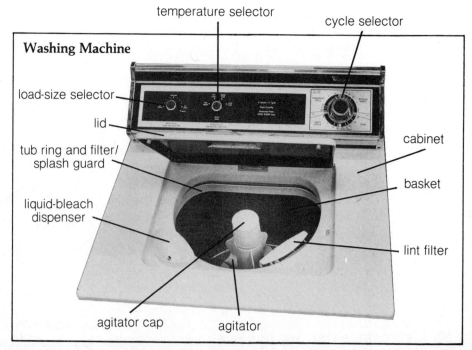

temperature selector

cycle selector

Washing Machine

load-size selector

lid

tub ring and filter/ splash guard

liquid-bleach dispenser

cabinet

basket

lint filter

agitator cap

agitator

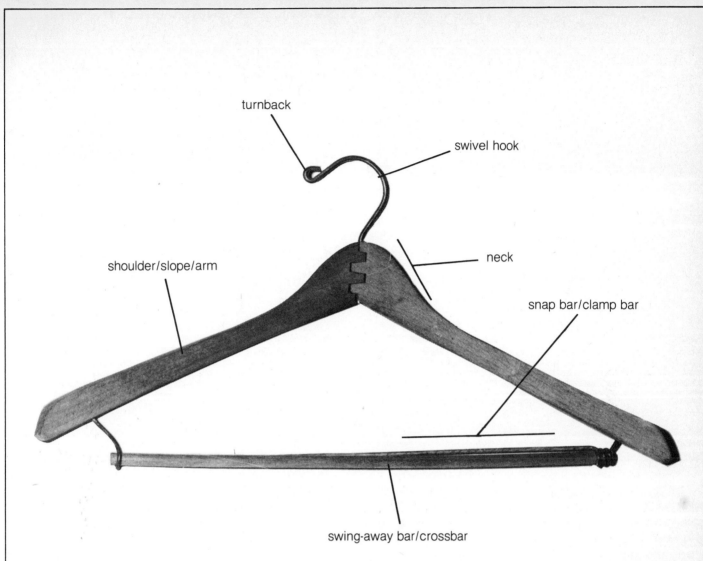

turnback

swivel hook

shoulder/slope/arm

neck

snap bar/clamp bar

swing-away bar/crossbar

Suit Hanger

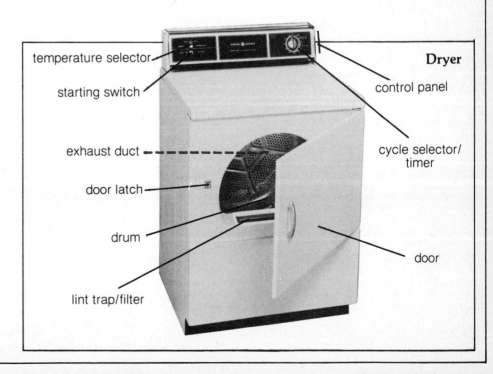

temperature selector

starting switch

exhaust duct

door latch

drum

lint trap/filter

Dryer

control panel

cycle selector/
timer

door

Playroom/Utility Room

Household Cleaning Equipment

A conventional mop has absorbent *strands* rather than a sponge. An *electric broom* is a lightweight vacuum cleaner on a handle. A *carpet sweeper* contains two revolving brushes in a box at the end of a pushing handle.

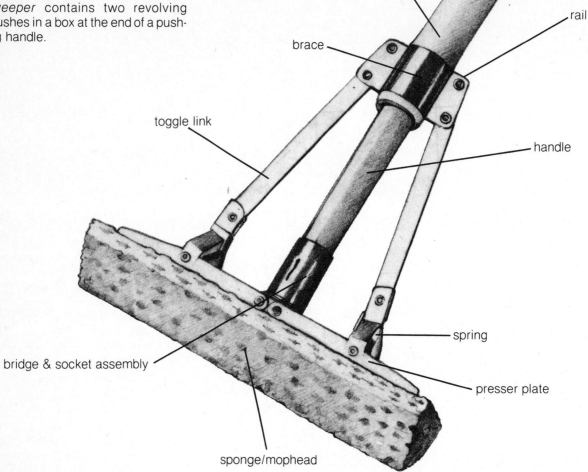

sleeve

rail

brace

handle

toggle link

spring

bridge & socket assembly

presser plate

sponge/mophead

Sponge Mop

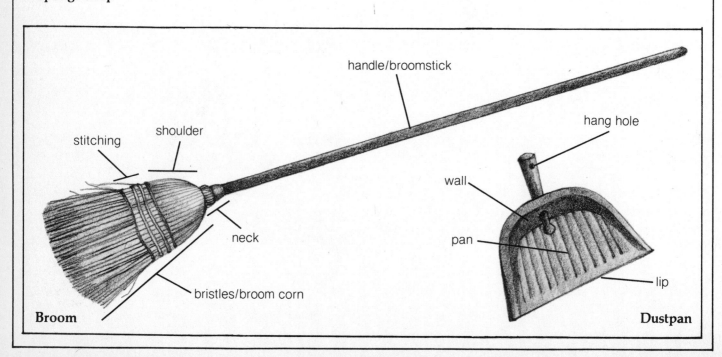

handle/broomstick

hang hole

shoulder

stitching

wall

neck

pan

lip

bristles/broom corn

Broom

Dustpan

Vacuum Cleaners

In an *upright vacuum cleaner,* shown here, *spiral brushes* under the hood and *beater bars* stir up dust and dirt. A *fan* blows these into a *disposable bag.* In a *cylinder model,* all the cleaning components are mounted horizontally. Dirt is sucked directly from the *intake tube* into a *vacuum bag,* or *dust bag.*

handle grip

manual operation button

handle

dust bag jacket

motor housing

handle release pedal/ height adjustment pedal

nozzle adjustment lever

wheel

bumper/furniture guard

hood

Upright Vacuum Cleaner

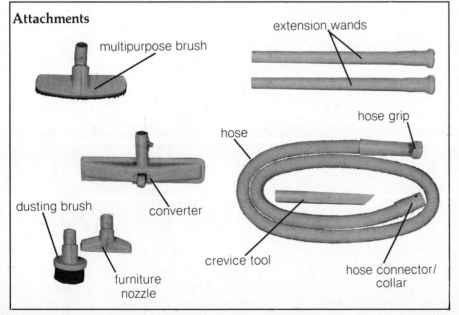

Attachments

multipurpose brush

extension wands

hose grip

hose

dusting brush

converter

crevice tool

furniture nozzle

hose connector/ collar

Minivacuum

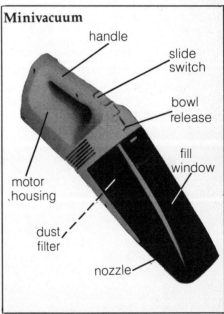

handle

slide switch

bowl release

fill window

motor housing

dust filter

nozzle

Firefighting Devices

Dry chemical extinguishers, containing chemicals and gas under pressure, are activated by squeezing or twisting the handle. *Soda-acid extinguishers*, inverted to mix the contents, produce a smothering *foam*.

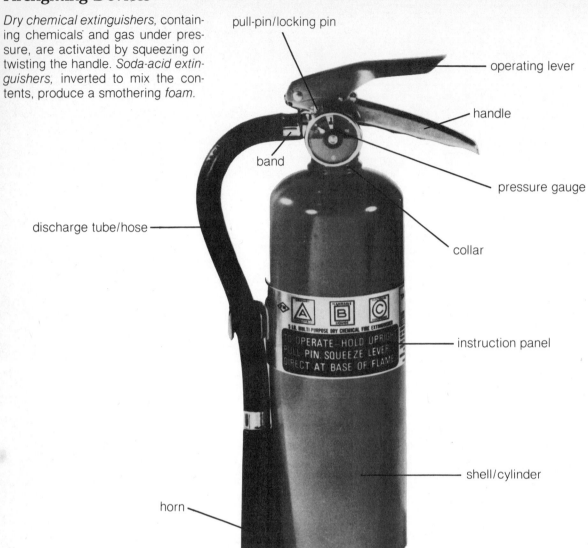

pull-pin/locking pin

operating lever

handle

band

pressure gauge

discharge tube/hose

collar

instruction panel

shell/cylinder

horn

Fire Extinguisher

Smoke Alarm/Smoke Detector

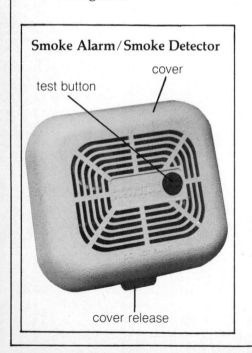

test button

cover

cover release

Pail/Bucket

bail/handle

ear

rim/curl

body

Luggage

The exterior parts of a *suitcase* or *bag* are identical to those of an attaché case. A suitcase that unfolds to be hung up is called a *garment bag*. Briefcases sometimes have zippered *file folders* or *portfolios* as well as paper storage *pockets*.

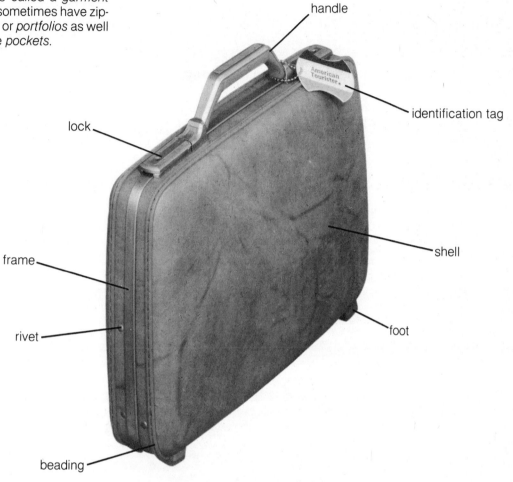

handle

identification tag

lock

shell

frame

rivet

foot

beading

Attaché Case/Briefcase

Overnight Bag

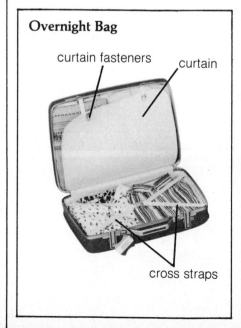

curtain fasteners

curtain

cross straps

Cosmetic Case

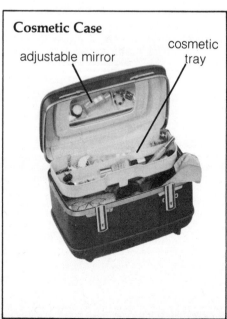

adjustable mirror

cosmetic tray

Two-Suiter

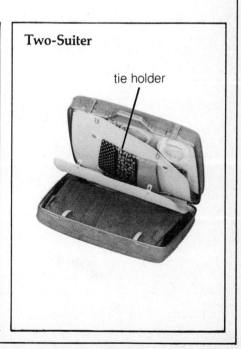

tie holder

Modern strollers have largely replaced more elaborate *baby carriages,* or *perambulators.* A portable, basketlike infant bed, often with a *hood* at one end, is called a *bassinet.* An indoor *baby chair,* or *high chair,* has long legs, a *footrest* and a *serving tray.*

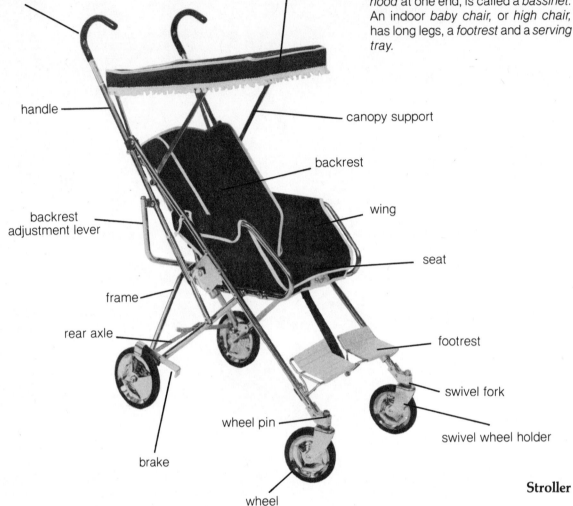

handle grip

canopy

handle

canopy support

backrest

backrest adjustment lever

wing

seat

frame

rear axle

footrest

swivel fork

wheel pin

swivel wheel holder

brake

wheel

Stroller

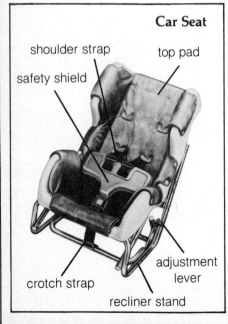

Car Seat

shoulder strap

top pad

safety shield

crotch strap

adjustment lever

recliner stand

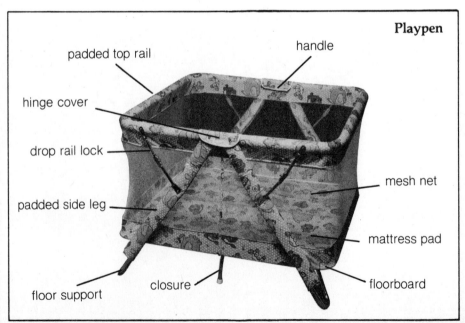

Playpen

padded top rail

handle

hinge cover

drop rail lock

mesh net

padded side leg

mattress pad

floor support

closure

floorboard

Backyard Equipment

Other popular backyard and *playground* equipment includes *seesaws,* or *teeter-totters; jungle gyms,* or *monkey bars; climbing nets; overhead ladders* and *sandboxes.*

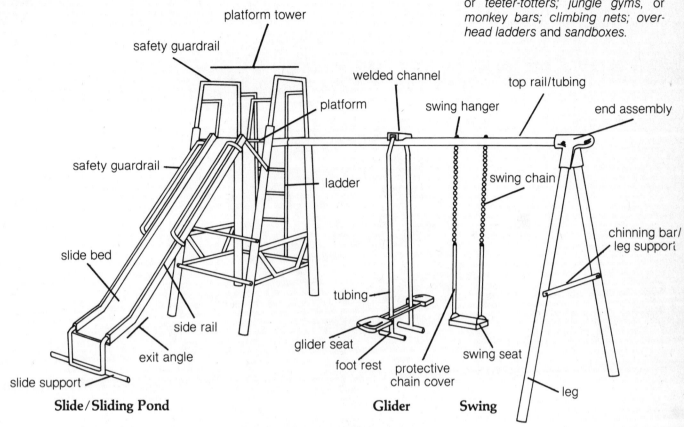

platform tower

safety guardrail

welded channel

swing hanger

top rail/tubing

end assembly

platform

safety guardrail

ladder

swing chain

chinning bar/ leg support

slide bed

side rail

exit angle

tubing

glider seat

foot rest

protective chain cover

swing seat

leg

slide support

Slide/Sliding Pond

Glider   **Swing**

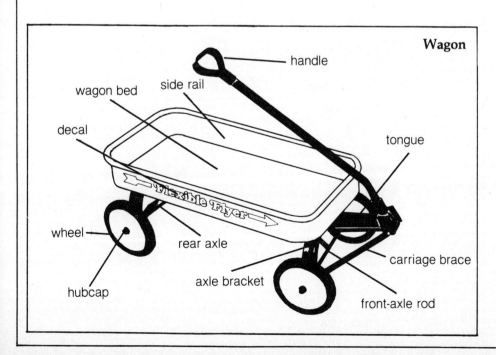

Wagon

handle

side rail

wagon bed

decal

tongue

wheel

rear axle

carriage brace

hubcap

axle bracket

front-axle rod

Flexible Flyer

Patio Accessories

On regular grills and *braziers,* food is cooked over *charcoal briquettes* resting in a *fire bowl,* whereas on gas and electric models food is grilled over *volcanic rock.* Other grills include *hibachis* and *kettle grills* featuring *damper controls, adjustable grills,* and *ash catchers.* On some outdoor lounges and *settees,* small springs, or *helicals,* connect the frame to metal supporting straps.

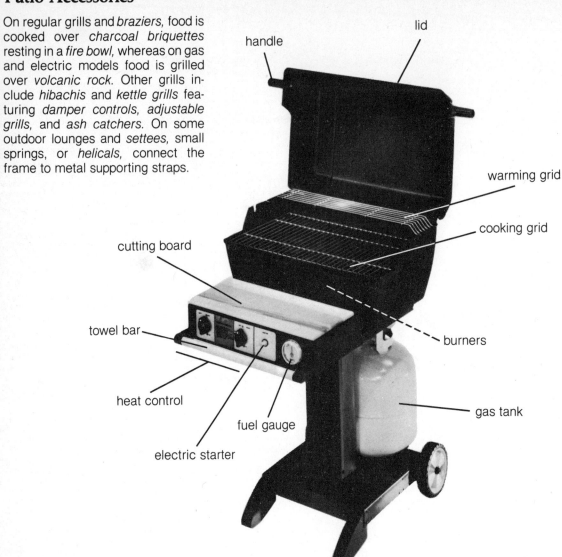

handle

lid

warming grid

cooking grid

cutting board

towel bar

heat control

fuel gauge

electric starter

burners

gas tank

Barbecue Grill/Gas Barbecue

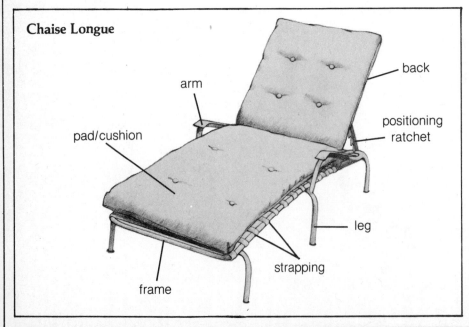

Chaise Longue

arm

back

pad/cushion

positioning ratchet

leg

strapping

frame

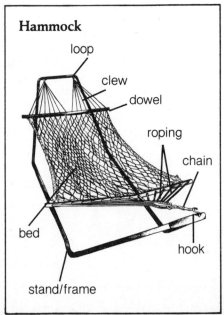

Hammock

loop

clew

dowel

roping

chain

bed

hook

stand/frame

Sports and Recreation

Emphasis in this section is given to major sports and forms of recreational activity which involve gear and equipment. Word and picture games, for example, have been omitted, since the nomenclature involved is so limited.

In order to enable the reader to find particular items quickly, recreational activities have been grouped in the following way: team sports, competitive sports, individual sports, equestrian sports, automobile racing, outdoor sports, bodybuilding, board games and casino games.

Because playing areas involved in team and competitive sports are an integral part of the activity, fields, courts and rinks have been diagramed with all the vital areas, lines and demarcations identified.

And to show the parts of clothing and equipment used by players, real athletes rather than models have been photographed: batter Rod Carew, football running back Bruce Harper, basketball guard Mike Glenn, hockey defenseman Ken Morrow and goalie Billy Smith.

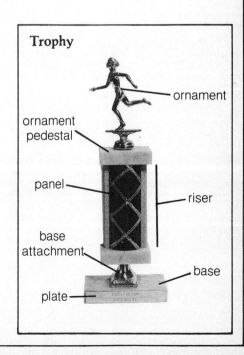

Trophy

ornament

ornament pedestal

panel

riser

base attachment

base

plate

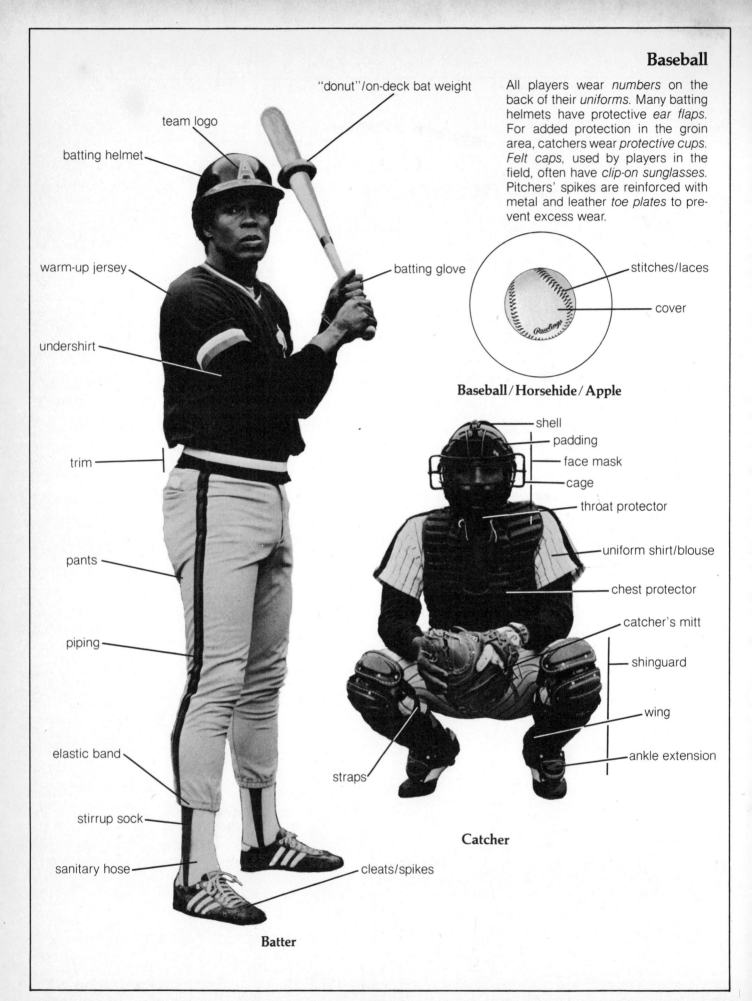

Baseball

All players wear *numbers* on the back of their *uniforms*. Many batting helmets have protective *ear flaps*. For added protection in the groin area, catchers wear *protective cups*. *Felt caps*, used by players in the field, often have *clip-on sunglasses*. Pitchers' spikes are reinforced with metal and leather *toe plates* to prevent excess wear.

"donut"/on-deck bat weight

team logo

batting helmet

warm-up jersey

undershirt

trim

pants

piping

elastic band

stirrup sock

sanitary hose

batting glove

stitches/laces

cover

Baseball/Horsehide/Apple

shell

padding

face mask

cage

throat protector

uniform shirt/blouse

chest protector

catcher's mitt

shinguard

wing

ankle extension

straps

cleats/spikes

Catcher

Batter

Baseball

Artificial turf has replaced natural *grass* in the outfield and certain portions of the infield in many *stadiums,* or *ballparks.*

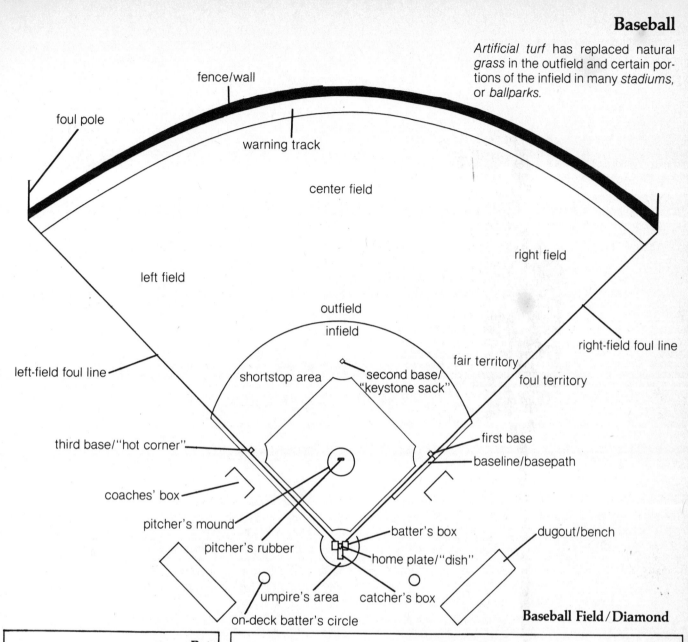

fence/wall

foul pole

warning track

center field

right field

left field

outfield

infield

right-field foul line

left-field foul line

fair territory

shortstop area

second base/ "keystone sack"

foul territory

third base/"hot corner"

first base

baseline/basepath

coaches' box

pitcher's mound

batter's box

dugout/bench

pitcher's rubber

home plate/"dish"

umpire's area

catcher's box

on-deck batter's circle

Baseball Field/Diamond

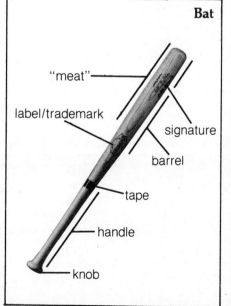

Bat

"meat"

label/trademark

signature

barrel

tape

handle

knob

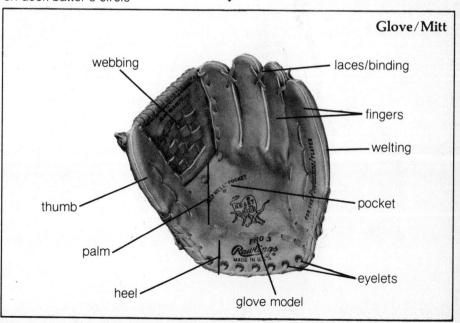

Glove/Mitt

webbing

laces/binding

fingers

welting

thumb

pocket

palm

heel

glove model

eyelets

Team Sports

Football

Protective equipment worn on the upper body is covered with a *numbered jersey*. A *tear-away jersey* is loosely sewn and meant to rip apart when grabbed by an opponent. Helmets are manufactured with different *suspension systems*, some of which are air-inflated. Football covers have a rough *pebble finish* and an air-retaining *bladder* which is filled by inserting an *inflation needle* in the valve.

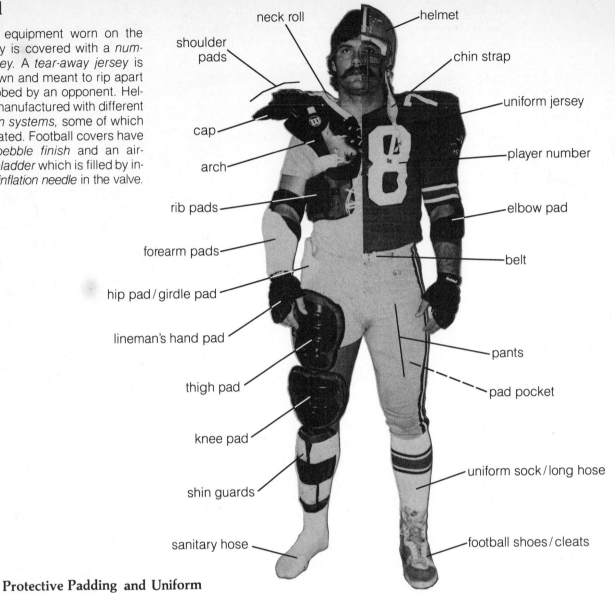

- neck roll
- shoulder pads
- cap
- arch
- rib pads
- forearm pads
- hip pad / girdle pad
- lineman's hand pad
- thigh pad
- knee pad
- shin guards
- sanitary hose
- helmet
- chin strap
- uniform jersey
- player number
- elbow pad
- belt
- pants
- pad pocket
- uniform sock / long hose
- football shoes / cleats

Protective Padding and Uniform

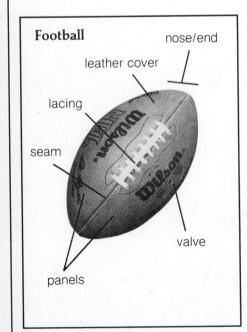

Football

- nose/end
- leather cover
- lacing
- seam
- panels
- valve

Helmet

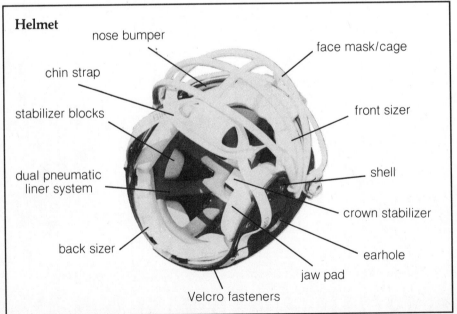

- nose bumper
- chin strap
- stabilizer blocks
- dual pneumatic liner system
- back sizer
- Velcro fasteners
- face mask/cage
- front sizer
- shell
- crown stabilizer
- earhole
- jaw pad

Football

A *down marker* is used to mark the exact location of the ball on the field between downs. The *flip chart* at the top of the down marker has *flip panels* to indicate what down is about to be played. Yard lines cross the field every five yards. *Flags* are located at the junction of the goal line and sideline to mark in bounds. Small, rubber inverted V-shaped *yard markers* are placed at five-yard intervals along the sidelines.

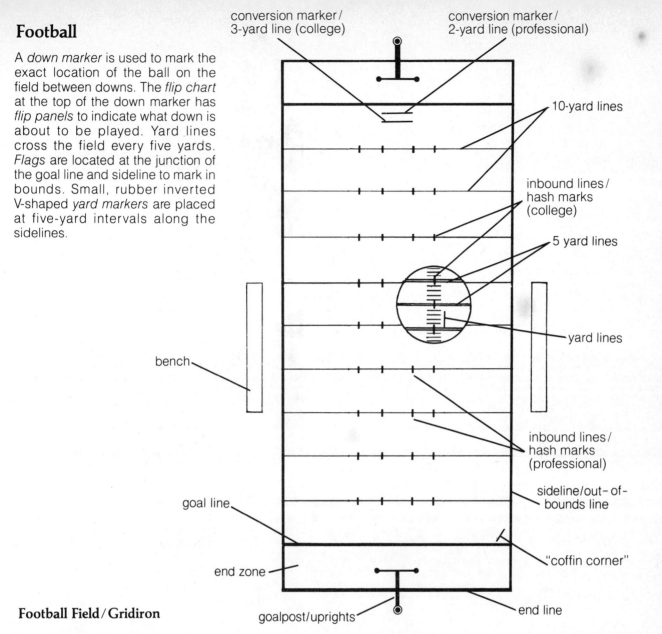

conversion marker/ 3-yard line (college)

conversion marker/ 2-yard line (professional)

10-yard lines

inbound lines/ hash marks (college)

5 yard lines

yard lines

bench

inbound lines/ hash marks (professional)

sideline/out-of-bounds line

goal line

"coffin corner"

end zone

end line

goalpost/uprights

Football Field / Gridiron

Field Equipment

Goalpost/Uprights

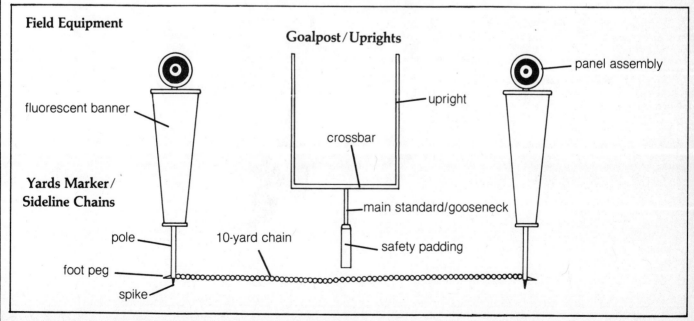

panel assembly

fluorescent banner

upright

crossbar

Yards Marker/ Sideline Chains

main standard/gooseneck

pole

10-yard chain

safety padding

foot peg

spike

Team Sports

Ice Hockey

Hockey players' pants are held up by *suspenders*. Socks are attached to a *garter belt*. The angle between the shaft of a hockey stick and the blade is called the *lie*. The game is played with a black vulcanized rubber *puck*. A blinking *red light* atop the goal judge's box indicates a goal.

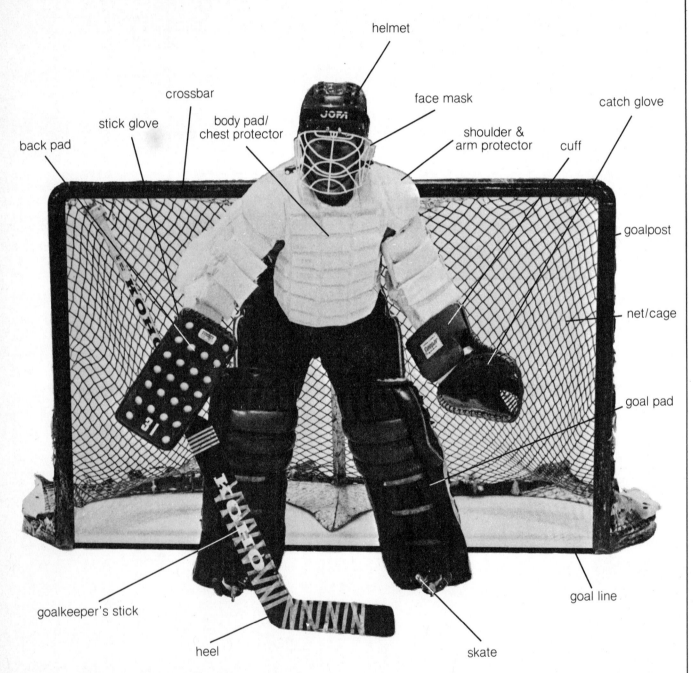

helmet

crossbar

stick glove

body pad/ chest protector

back pad

face mask

catch glove

shoulder & arm protector

cuff

goalpost

net/cage

goal pad

goalkeeper's stick

heel

skate

goal line

Goal and Goalie/Goalkeeper/Goaler

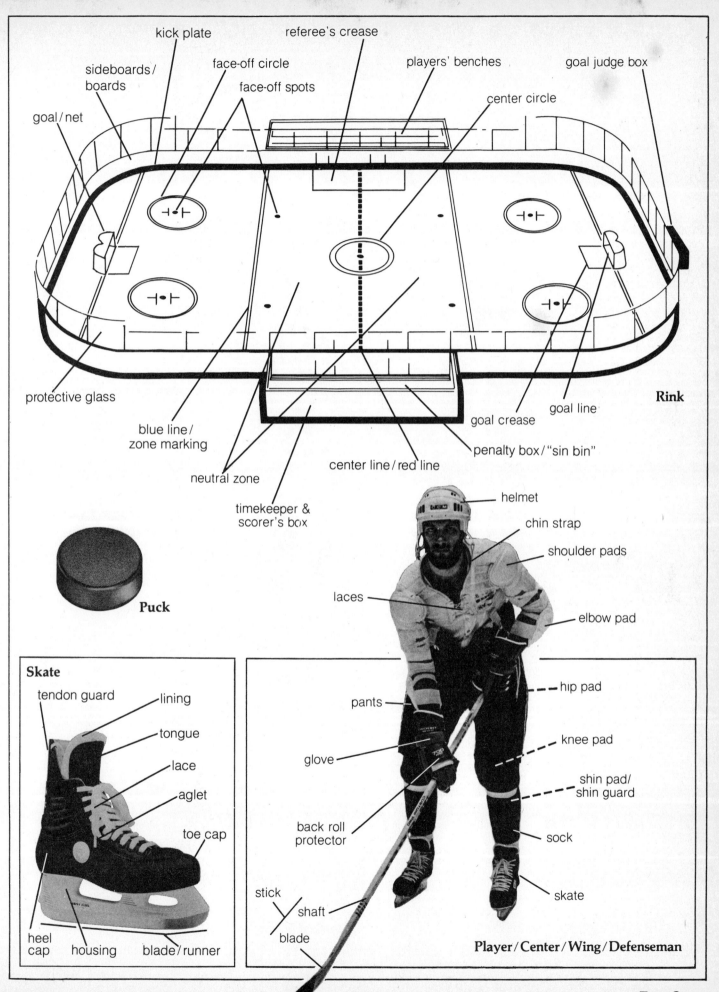

Rink

goal / net

sideboards / boards

kick plate

face-off circle

face-off spots

referee's crease

players' benches

goal judge box

center circle

protective glass

blue line / zone marking

neutral zone

timekeeper & scorer's box

center line / red line

goal crease

penalty box / "sin bin"

goal line

Puck

Skate

tendon guard

lining

tongue

lace

aglet

toe cap

heel cap

housing

blade / runner

helmet

chin strap

shoulder pads

laces

elbow pad

hip pad

knee pad

shin pad / shin guard

sock

skate

pants

glove

back roll protector

stick

shaft

blade

Player / Center / Wing / Defenseman

Basketball

The offensive team advances from its own *backcourt* into the *forecourt*. The area at the top of the free-throw lane, usually patrolled by the *center* (as opposed to one of two *guards* or two *forwards*), is called the *pivot*. Many players wear *kneepads* and *elbow pads* for protection, and *warm-up suits* prior to games.

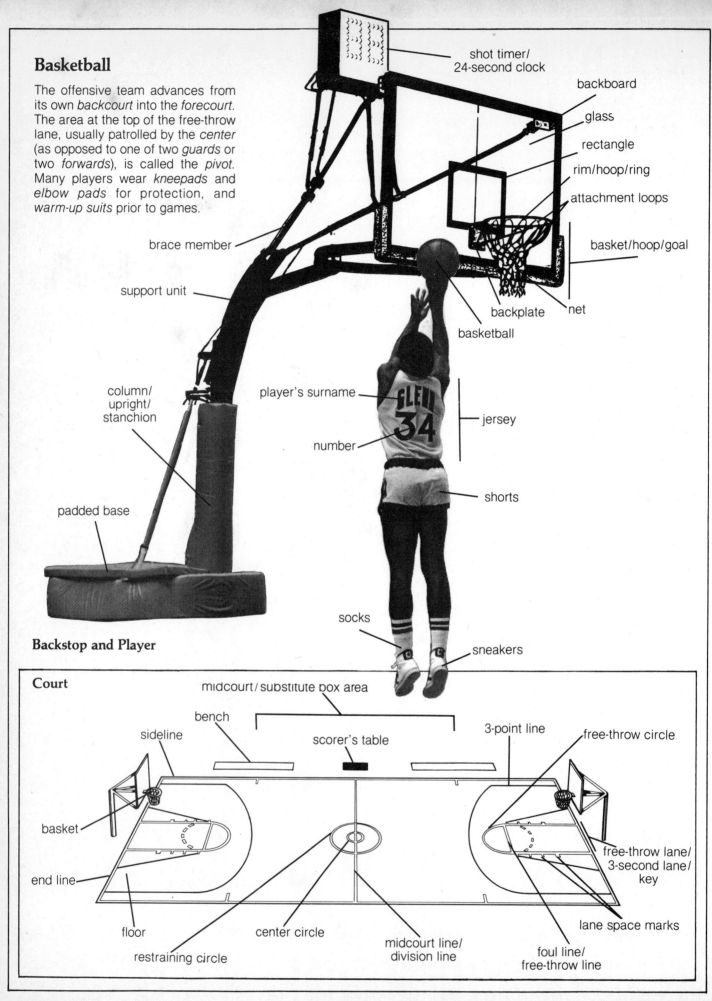

shot timer/ 24-second clock

backboard

glass

rectangle

rim/hoop/ring

attachment loops

basket/hoop/goal

brace member

support unit

backplate

net

basketball

player's surname

jersey

column/ upright/ stanchion

number

shorts

padded base

socks

sneakers

Backstop and Player

Court

midcourt/ substitute box area

bench

scorer's table

3-point line

free-throw circle

sideline

basket

free-throw lane/ 3-second lane/ key

end line

floor

center circle

midcourt line/ division line

lane space marks

restraining circle

foul line/ free-throw line

Soccer

Football, or *association football*, as soccer is known in most of the world, is played by two teams of 11 players. If a *match* is tied after two 45-minute *halves*, the game is decided by a *sudden-death overtime*, in which the first team to score wins, or a *shootout*, in which each team is given several free kicks.

Footballers / Players

jersey / shirt

wristband

team / club insignia

shorts

sock / stocking

shin pad

player number

shoe / boot

color panel

Ball

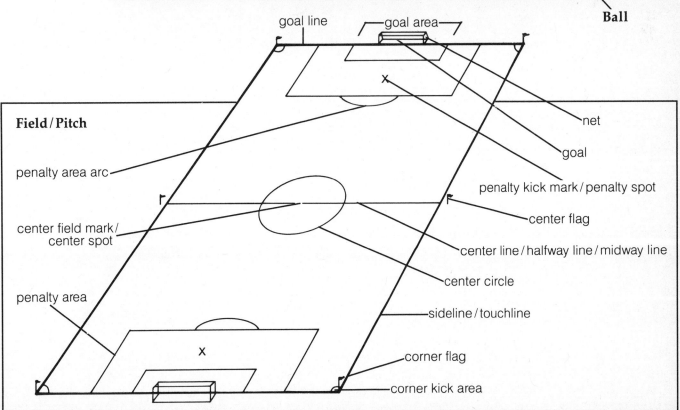

goal line

goal area

net

goal

Field / Pitch

penalty area arc

penalty kick mark / penalty spot

center flag

center field mark / center spot

center line / halfway line / midway line

center circle

penalty area

sideline / touchline

corner flag

corner kick area

Lacrosse

Lacrosse is a *contact sport*, meaning that *blocking* and other physical contact is legal. Defensive players use their sticks or bodies to *check* a *possession player* carrying the ball. Illegal body checks or slashing players with a stick are *personal fouls*; the offending player is sent to a penalty box for 1 to 3 minutes.

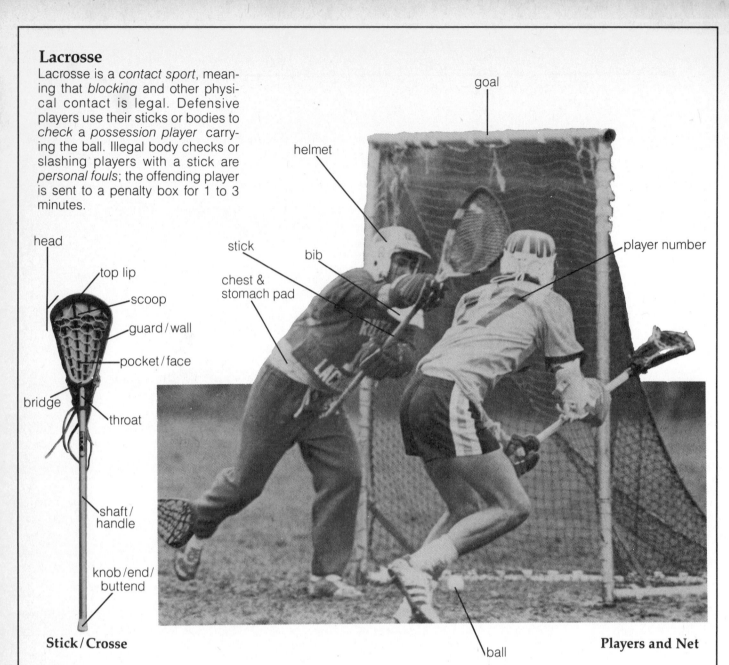

head
top lip
scoop
guard / wall
pocket / face
bridge
throat
shaft / handle
knob / end / buttend

Stick / Crosse

goal
helmet
stick
bib
chest & stomach pad
player number
ball

Players and Net

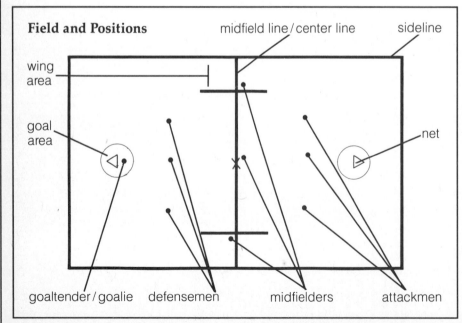

Field and Positions

midfield line / center line
sideline
wing area
goal area
net
goaltender / goalie   defensemen   midfielders   attackmen

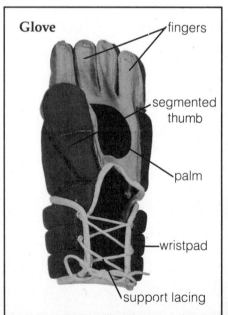

Glove

fingers
segmented thumb
palm
wristpad
support lacing

Polo

Polo is played on horseback by two teams of four players each. A *match* consists of eight seven-minute periods, or *chukkas*. Players ride a *string*, or several ponies, during play. The match is officiated by two mounted *umpires* and a *referee* on the sideline.

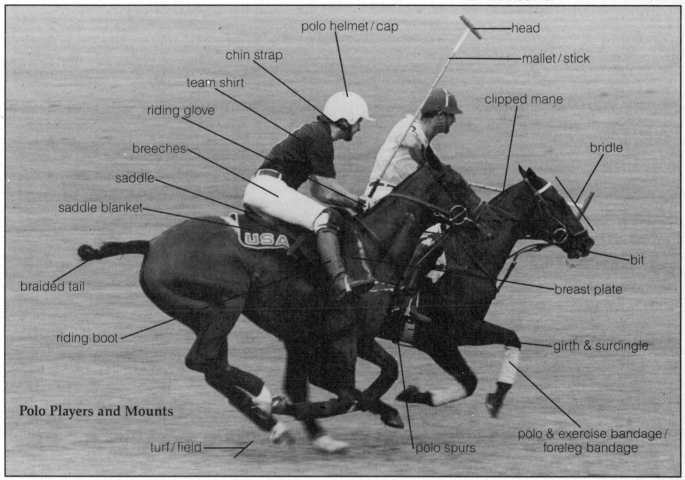

polo helmet / cap
chin strap
team shirt
riding glove
breeches
saddle
saddle blanket
braided tail
riding boot
head
mallet / stick
clipped mane
bridle
bit
breast plate
girth & surcingle
polo & exercise bandage / foreleg bandage
polo spurs
turf / field

Polo Players and Mounts

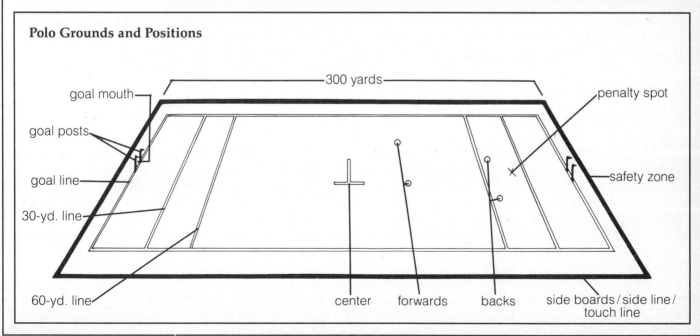

Polo Grounds and Positions

300 yards
goal mouth
penalty spot
goal posts
goal line
safety zone
30-yd. line
60-yd. line
center
forwards
backs
side boards / side line / touch line

Track and Field

Track-and-field events take place on a *running track* and the enclosed *field* within. Besides *jumping events* and *throwing events*, there are *footraces*, including *walking races*, *hurdle races*, *steeplechase*, *relay races*, *medley relays*, *runs* and the *marathon*. The *decathlon* is a ten-event contest, while the *pentathlon* consists of five events.

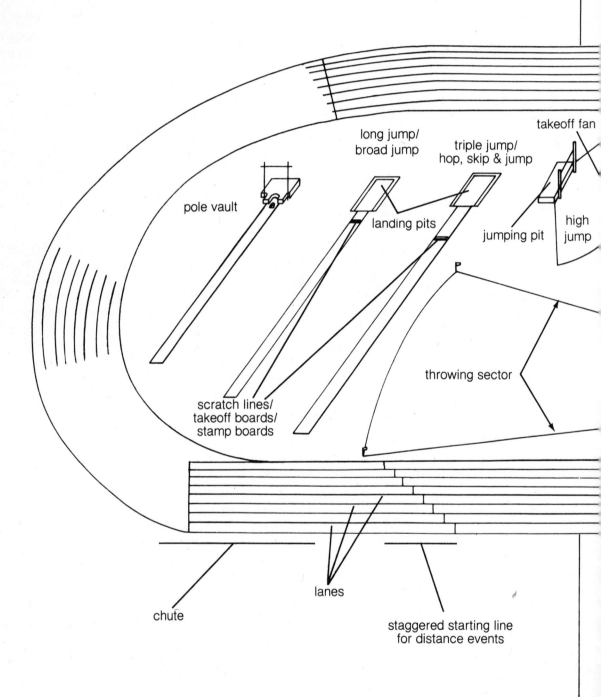

long jump/ broad jump

triple jump/ hop, skip & jump

takeoff fan

pole vault

landing pits

jumping pit

high jump

throwing sector

scratch lines/ takeoff boards/ stamp boards

lanes

chute

staggered starting line for distance events

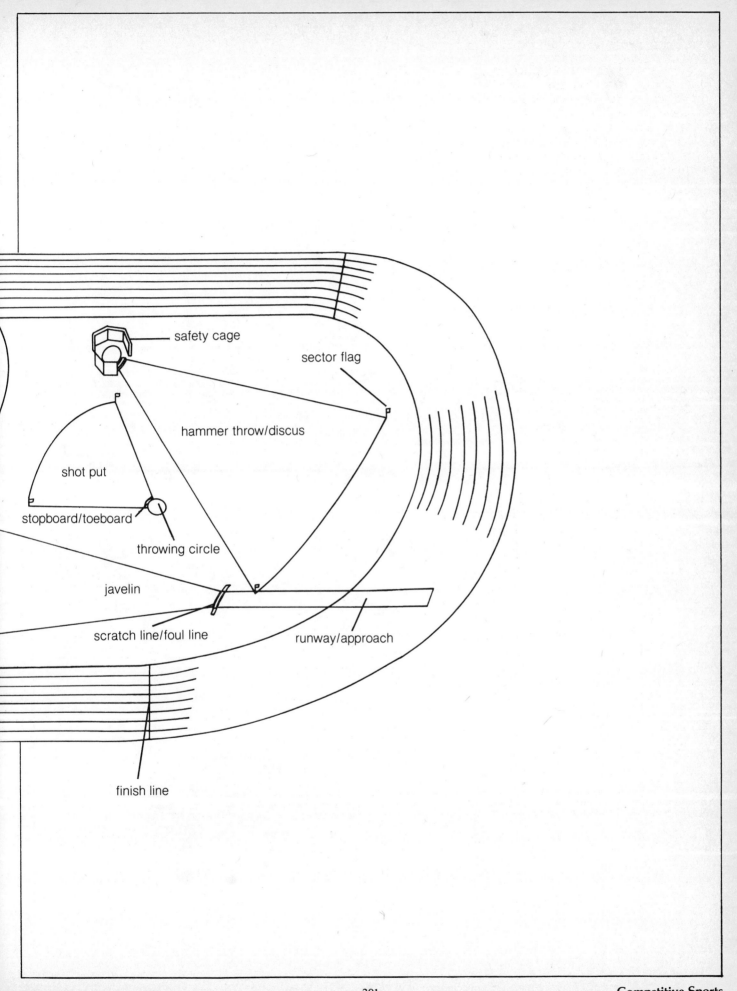

safety cage

sector flag

hammer throw/discus

shot put

stopboard/toeboard

throwing circle

javelin

scratch line/foul line

runway/approach

finish line

Running Shoe

These *training shoes,* or *trainers,* are more durable than lighter-weight *racing flats.* Lightweight running shoes are worn by *joggers* or *distance runners* in long races such as *marathons.* *Track shoes,* shoes with *spikes,* are used for most track-and-field events.

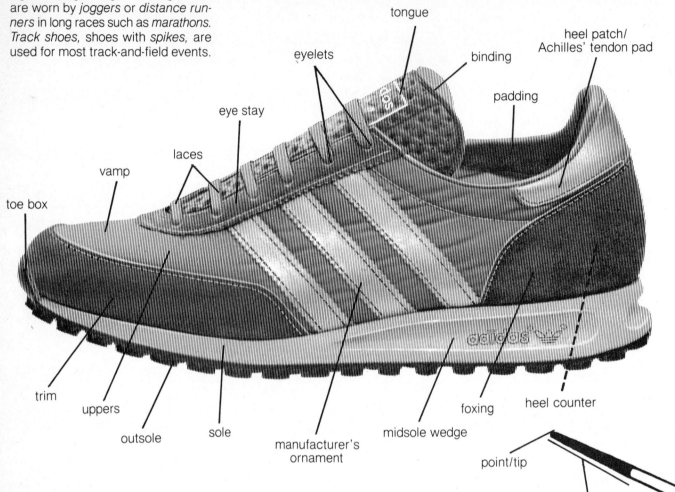

tongue

heel patch/ Achilles' tendon pad

binding

padding

eyelets

eye stay

laces

vamp

toe box

trim

uppers

outsole

sole

manufacturer's ornament

midsole wedge

foxing

heel counter

point/tip

head

Tread

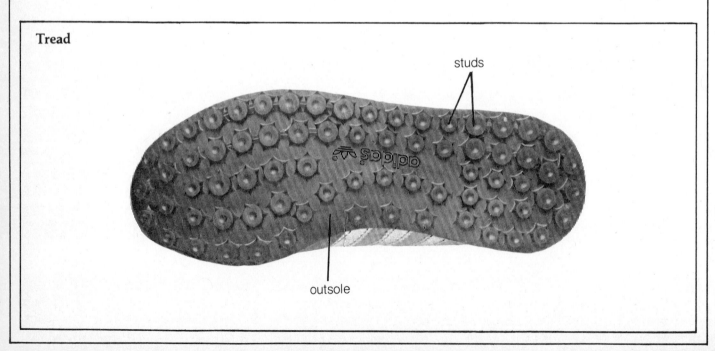

studs

outsole

Field Events Equipment

In addition to the equipment shown here, a round metal ball called a *shot put,* or *shot,* is also used in field events. Hammer throwers often wear *gloves* with padded palms.

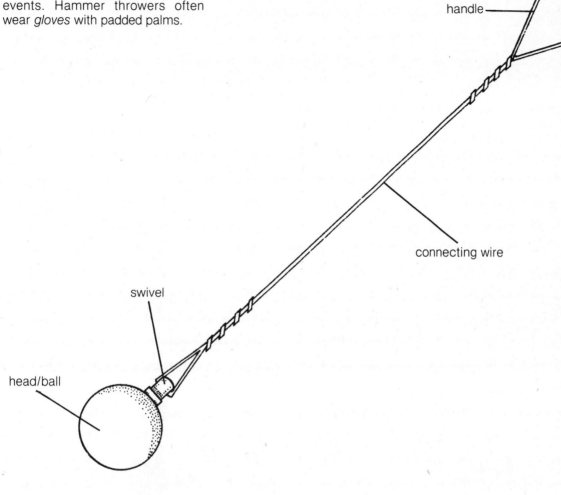

grip

handle

connecting wire

swivel

head/ball

Hammer

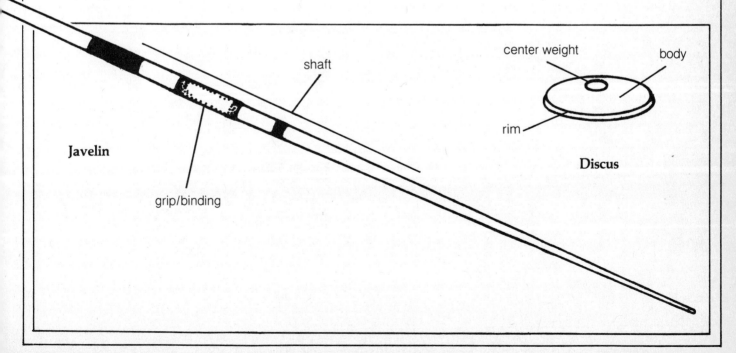

shaft

center weight

body

rim

Javelin

grip/binding

Discus

Competitive Sports

Hurdle

The height of hurdles can be adjusted for use in *high, intermediate* and *low hurdle* events. Base weights can also be adjusted to provide the proper *pull-over,* or *flipover,* the force required to knock them over. *Fixed hurdles* are used in a *steeplechase race,* an event that includes *water hazards.* Roller, or notched *lever locks* permit runners to adjust the slant on starting blocks, and a *plunger snap lock* allows them to position the blocks individually on the rail.

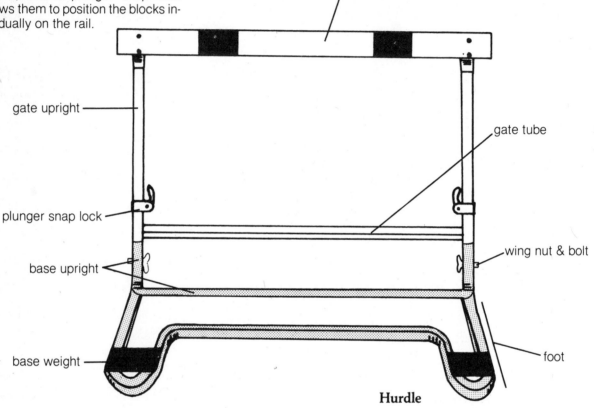

gatebar/top bar

gate upright

gate tube

plunger snap lock

base upright

wing nut & bolt

base weight

foot

Hurdle

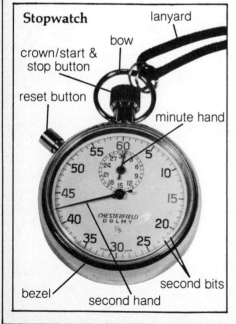

Stopwatch

lanyard

bow

crown/start & stop button

reset button

minute hand

second bits

bezel

second hand

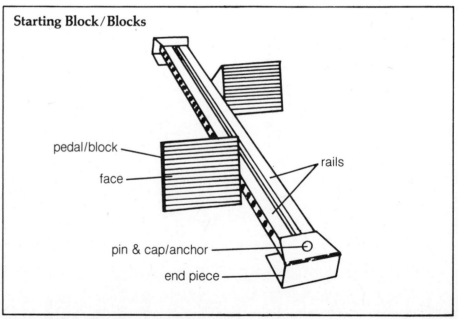

Starting Block/Blocks

pedal/block

face

rails

pin & cap/anchor

end piece

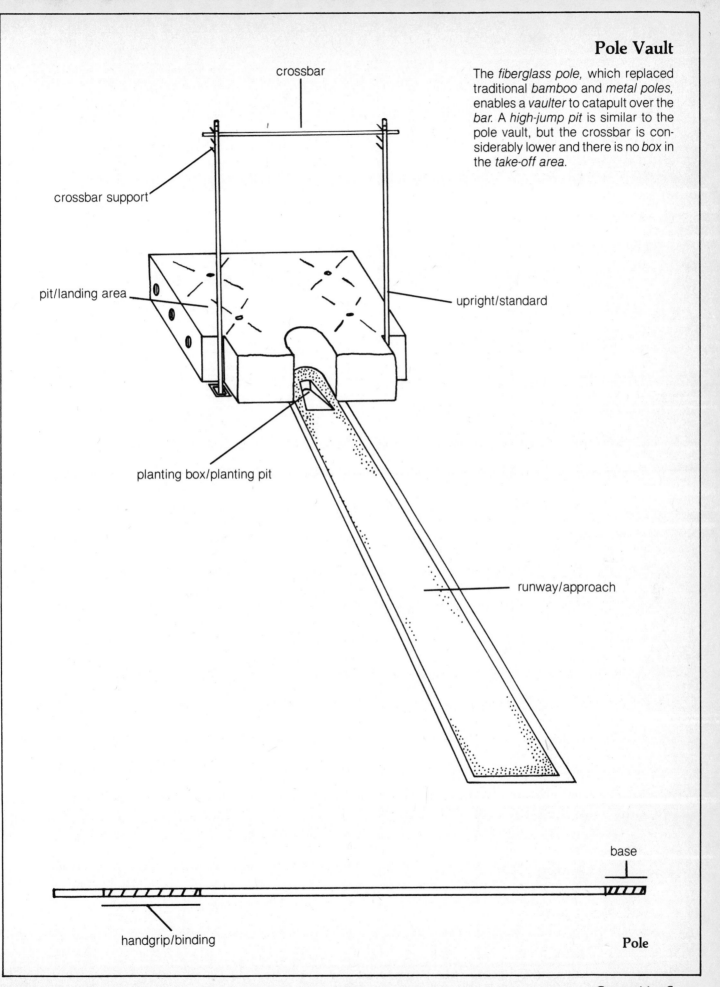

Pole Vault

The *fiberglass pole,* which replaced traditional *bamboo* and *metal poles,* enables a *vaulter* to catapult over the *bar.* A *high-jump pit* is similar to the pole vault, but the crossbar is considerably lower and there is no *box* in the *take-off area.*

crossbar

crossbar support

pit/landing area

upright/standard

planting box/planting pit

runway/approach

base

handgrip/binding

Pole

Gymnastics

Protective *landing mats* are placed around each piece of gymnastic equipment when it is in use. In addition, during practice sessions, assistants called *spotters* stand by to aid the *gymnast*. Gymnastic competition called *floor exercises* takes place on lined *floor exercise mats*.

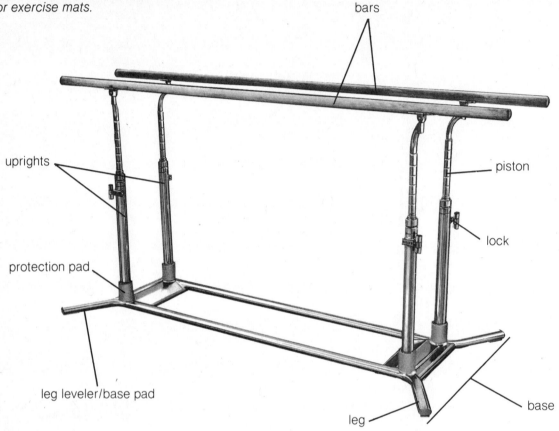

bars

uprights

piston

lock

protection pad

leg leveler/base pad

leg

base

Parallel Bars

Horizontal Bar/High Bar

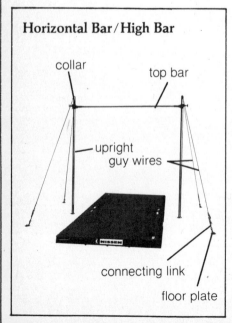

collar

top bar

upright
guy wires

connecting link

floor plate

Uneven Parallel Bars

top bar

guy brace

low bar

Balance Beam

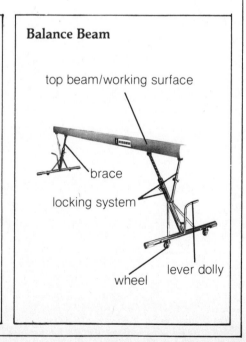

top beam/working surface

brace

locking system

wheel

lever dolly

Some pommel horses, or *side horses,* can be converted into *vaulting,* or *long, horses* by removing the pommels and plugging the holes they fit in. *Vaulting boards,* or *springboards,* are used by *vaulters* to gain height when mounting the apparatus.

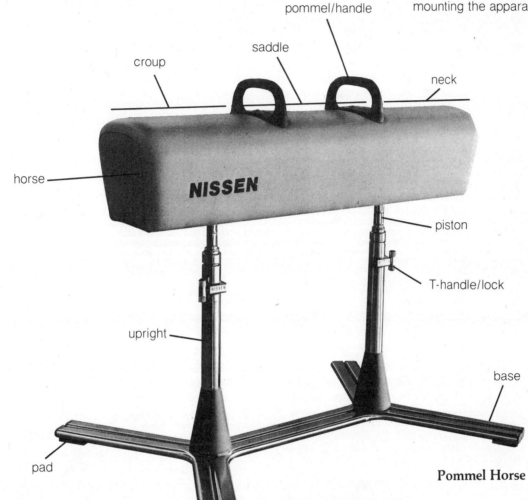

pommel/handle

saddle

croup

neck

horse

NISSEN

piston

T-handle/lock

upright

base

pad

Pommel Horse

Stationary Rings

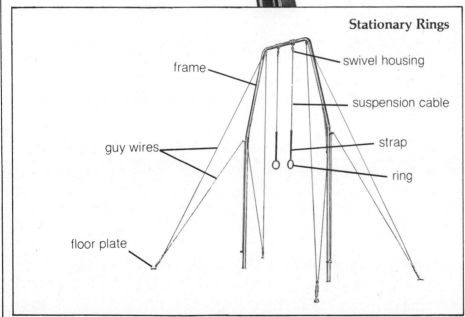

frame

swivel housing

suspension cable

guy wires

strap

ring

floor plate

Trampoline

Trampolining, trampoline tumbling, or *rebound tumbling* is performed on the canvas or elastic-webbing bed. Smaller *trampolets* are often used as *springboards* for mounting gymnastic apparatus.

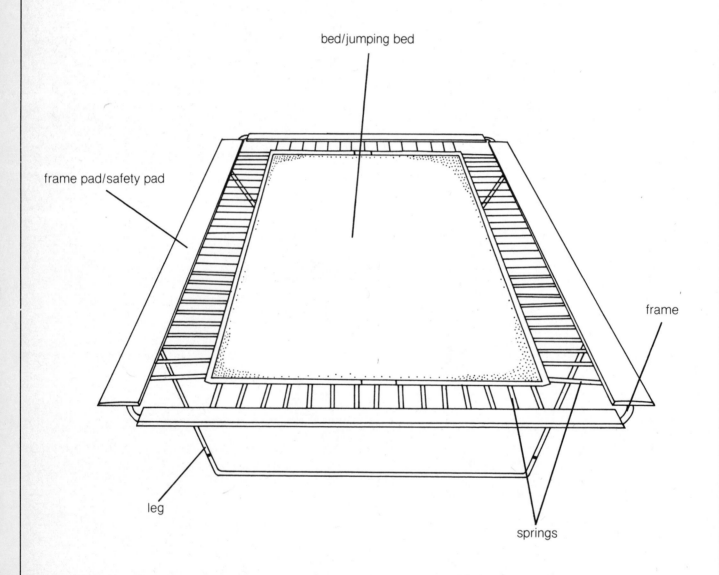

bed/jumping bed

frame pad/safety pad

frame

leg

springs

Boxing

In addition to the *sparring,* or practice, equipment shown here, *boxers* use a *mouthpiece* or *mouthguard* for protection of teeth. A *bell* at *ringside* is used to indicate the beginning and end of each *round.* Boxers rest on *stools* placed in their corners by assistants, or *handlers,* between rounds. Corners not used by fighters during these periods are called *neutral corners.*

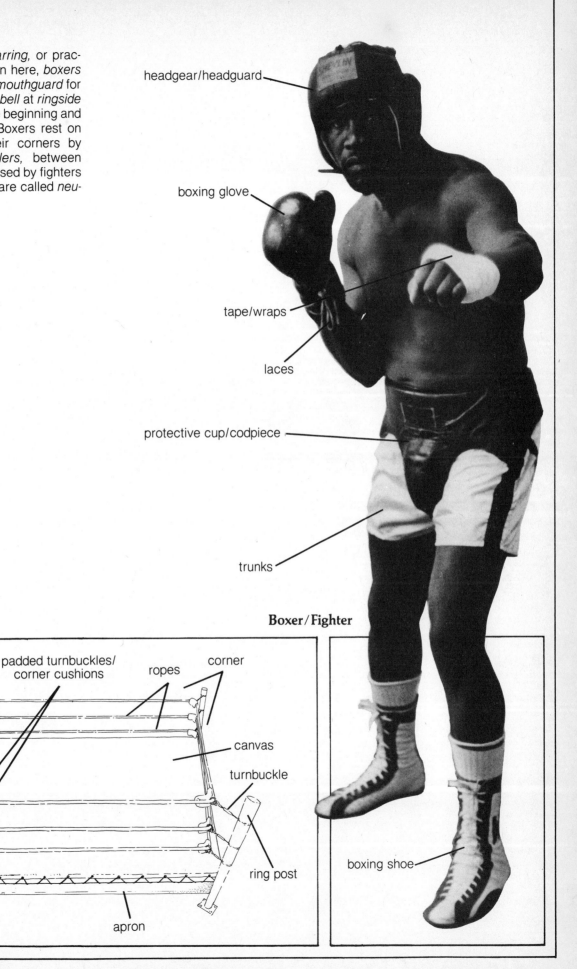

headgear/headguard

boxing glove

tape/wraps

laces

protective cup/codpiece

trunks

Boxer/Fighter

Boxing Ring

padded turnbuckles/
corner cushions

ropes

corner

canvas

turnbuckle

ring post

apron

boxing shoe

Competitive Sports

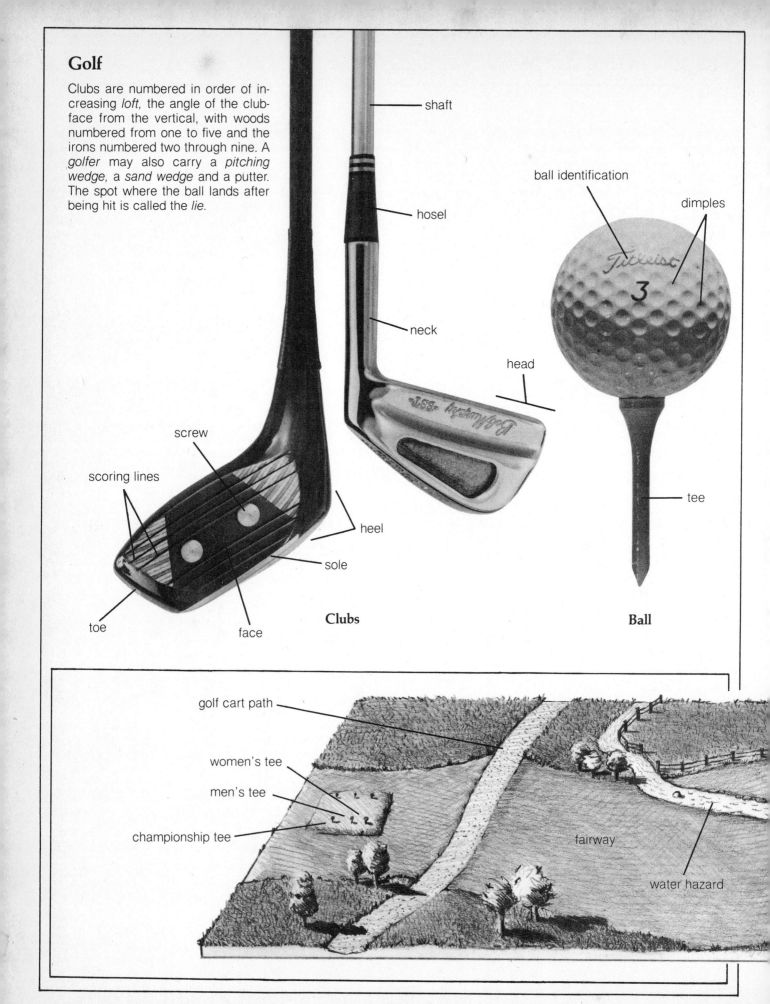

Golf

Clubs are numbered in order of increasing *loft*, the angle of the clubface from the vertical, with woods numbered from one to five and the irons numbered two through nine. A *golfer* may also carry a *pitching wedge*, a *sand wedge* and a putter. The spot where the ball lands after being hit is called the *lie*.

shaft

hosel

neck

head

ball identification

dimples

screw

scoring lines

heel

sole

toe

face

tee

Clubs

Ball

golf cart path

women's tee

men's tee

championship tee

fairway

water hazard

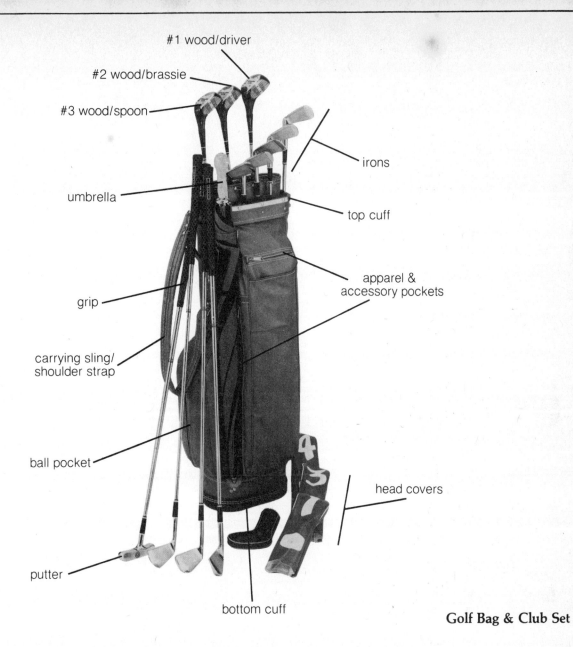

#1 wood/driver

#2 wood/brassie

#3 wood/spoon

irons

umbrella

top cuff

apparel &
accessory pockets

grip

carrying sling/
shoulder strap

ball pocket

head covers

putter

bottom cuff

Golf Bag & Club Set

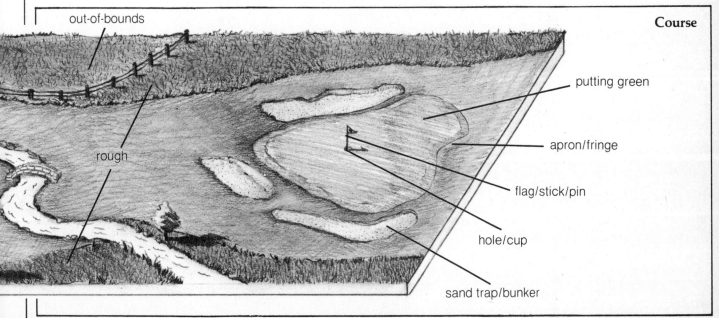

Course

out-of-bounds

putting green

rough

apron/fringe

flag/stick/pin

hole/cup

sand trap/bunker

Tennis

Some rackets have an interchangeable handle, or *pallet*, and a replaceable *throatpiece*, or *yoke*. The "sweet spot" is the prime hitting area of a racket *face*.

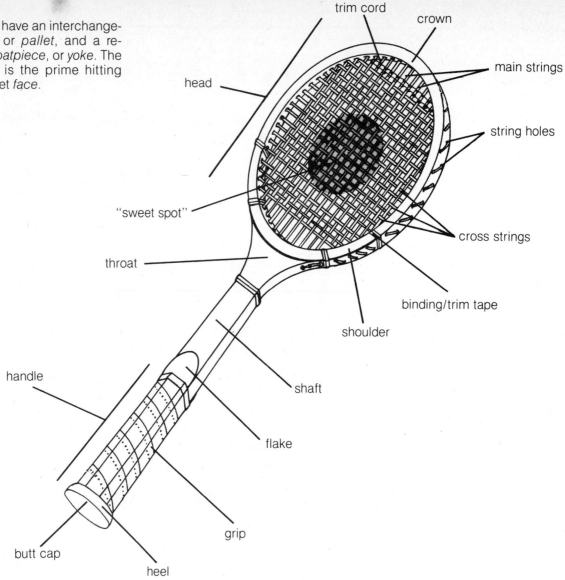

trim cord

crown

main strings

head

string holes

"sweet spot"

cross strings

throat

binding/trim tape

shoulder

handle

shaft

flake

butt cap

grip

heel

Racket

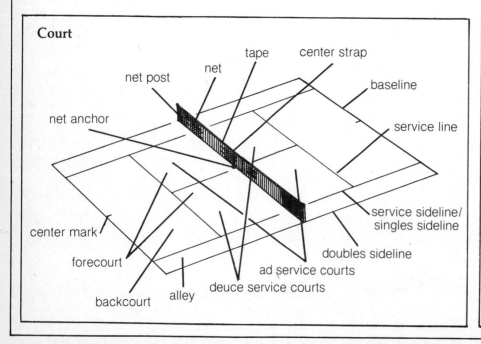

Court

center strap

tape

baseline

net post

net

service line

net anchor

center mark

service sideline/
singles sideline

forecourt

doubles sideline

ad service courts

backcourt

alley

deuce service courts

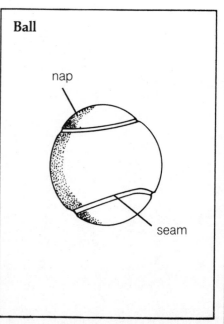

Ball

nap

seam

Handball and Squash Courts

The composite court shown here includes both handball and squash rackets terms. In each case, the court is entered through a small *door* in the *back wall*. In handball, players alternately hit a hard black *ball* with their hands, whereas in squash a soft rubber ball is hit with a *racket*.

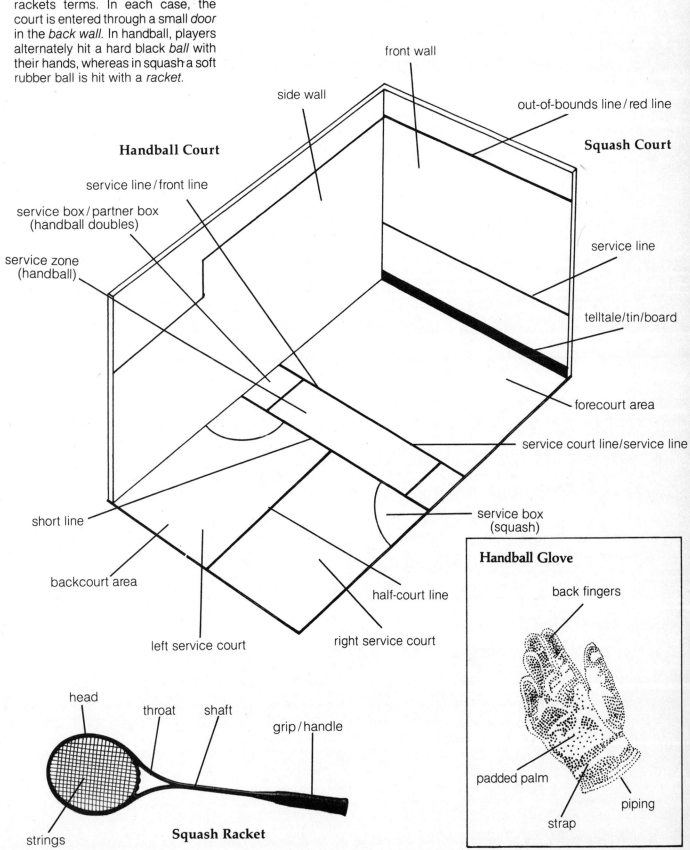

front wall

side wall

out-of-bounds line / red line

Squash Court

Handball Court

service line / front line

service line

service box / partner box
(handball doubles)

service zone
(handball)

telltale / tin / board

forecourt area

service court line / service line

short line

service box
(squash)

backcourt area

half-court line

left service court

right service court

Handball Glove

back fingers

head

throat   shaft

grip / handle

padded palm

piping

strings

strap

Squash Racket

Jai Alai / Pelota

Jai alai is played in a *fronton,* an auditorium that includes the court, a tiered spectator seating area, and *parimutuel betting* facilities. A clear-vision mesh *screen* separates the spectators from the playing area.

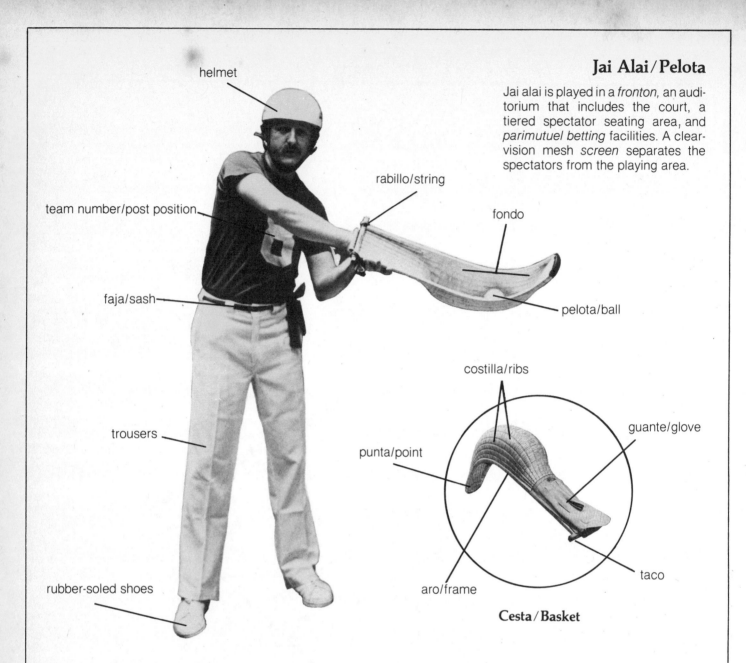

helmet

rabillo/string

team number/post position

fondo

faja/sash

pelota/ball

trousers

costilla/ribs

guante/glove

punta/point

rubber-soled shoes

aro/frame

taco

Cesta / Basket

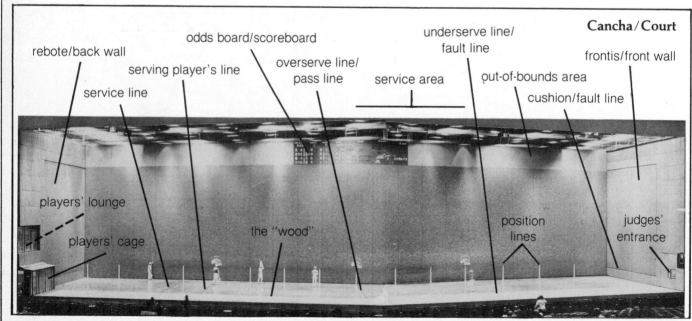

Cancha / Court

rebote/back wall

odds board/scoreboard

underserve line/ fault line

frontis/front wall

serving player's line

overserve line/ pass line

out-of-bounds area

service line

service area

cushion/fault line

players' lounge

players' cage

the "wood"

position lines

judges' entrance

Fencing

Foils, *sabres* or *épées,* which differ slightly in weight and design, are used in fencing *matches* or *bouts.* Each *fencer* must wear a chest-protecting *plastron* under his jacket, and women must also wear *breast protectors.* Four *judges* and a *director,* or *president,* referee *dry* or *nonelectric* matches.

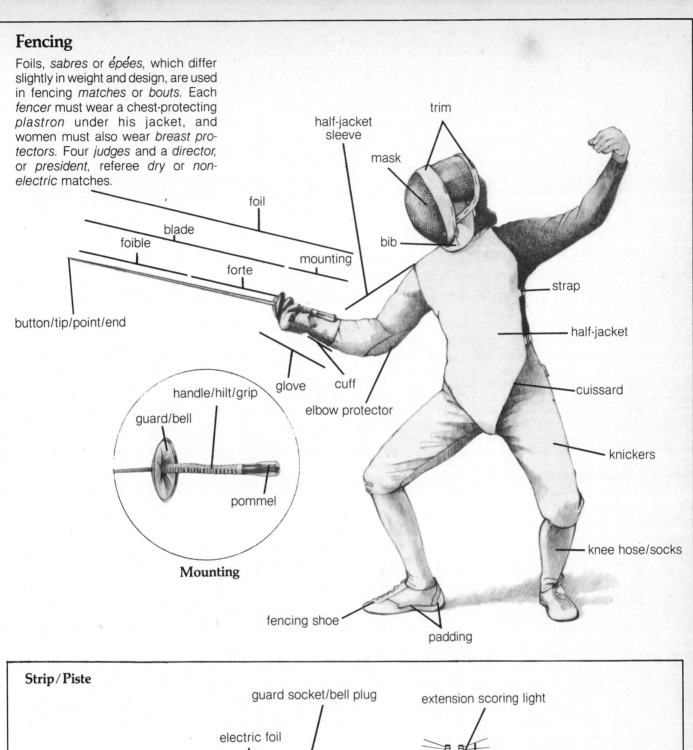

trim

half-jacket sleeve

mask

bib

foil

blade

foible

forte

mounting

button/tip/point/end

strap

half-jacket

cuissard

knickers

handle/hilt/grip

guard/bell

glove

cuff

elbow protector

pommel

Mounting

knee hose/socks

fencing shoe

padding

Strip / Piste

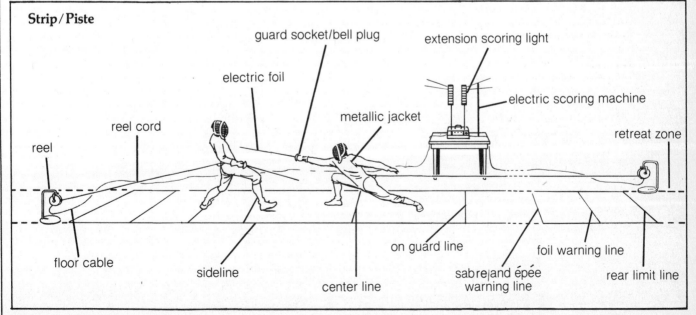

guard socket/bell plug

extension scoring light

electric foil

electric scoring machine

reel cord

metallic jacket

reel

retreat zone

floor cable

sideline

on guard line

foil warning line

center line

sabre and épée warning line

rear limit line

Competitive Sports

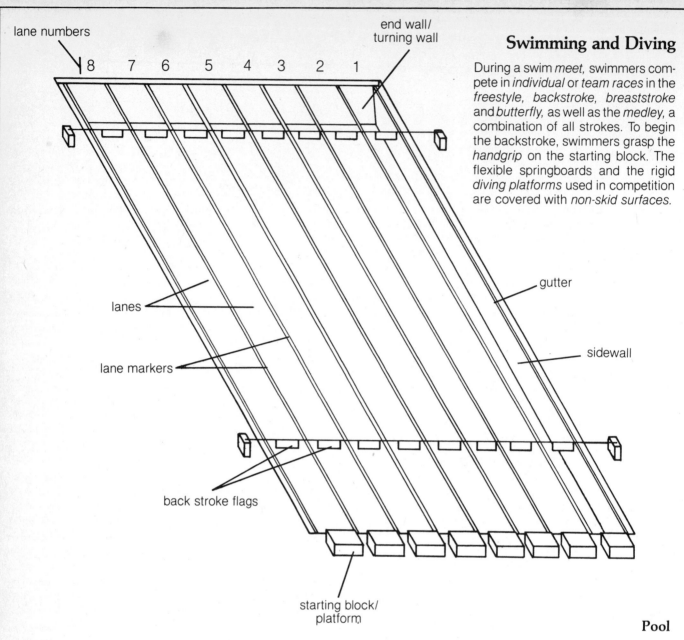

lane numbers

8 7 6 5 4 3 2 1

end wall/
turning wall

Swimming and Diving

During a swim *meet,* swimmers compete in *individual* or *team races* in the *freestyle, backstroke, breaststroke* and *butterfly,* as well as the *medley,* a combination of all strokes. To begin the backstroke, swimmers grasp the *handgrip* on the starting block. The flexible springboards and the rigid *diving platforms* used in competition are covered with *non-skid surfaces.*

gutter

sidewall

lanes

lane markers

back stroke flags

starting block/
platform

Pool

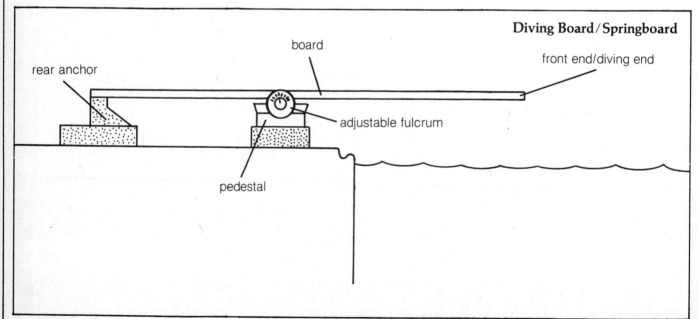

Diving Board/Springboard

rear anchor

board

front end/diving end

adjustable fulcrum

pedestal

Bowling

The strike pocket opposite to the hand delivering the ball is called the *Brooklyn pocket* or *Jersey pocket*. Pins are reset by a mechanical *pinsetter* or *pinspotter*. *Duckpins* and *candlepins* are forms of bowling in which differently shaped pins and lighter, smaller balls are used.

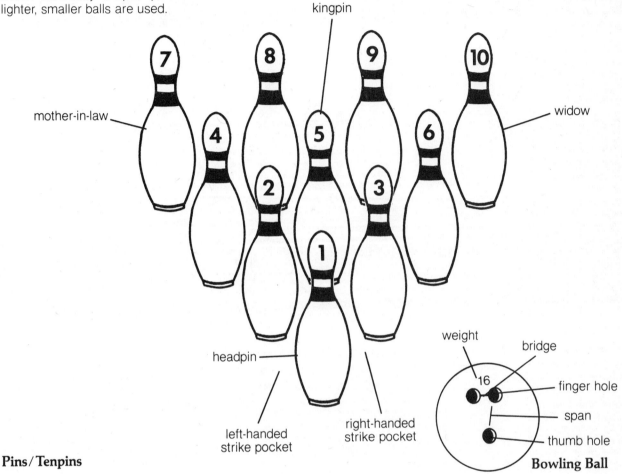

kingpin

mother-in-law

widow

headpin

left-handed strike pocket

right-handed strike pocket

weight

bridge

finger hole

span

thumb hole

16

Pins / Tenpins

Bowling Ball

Lane / Alley

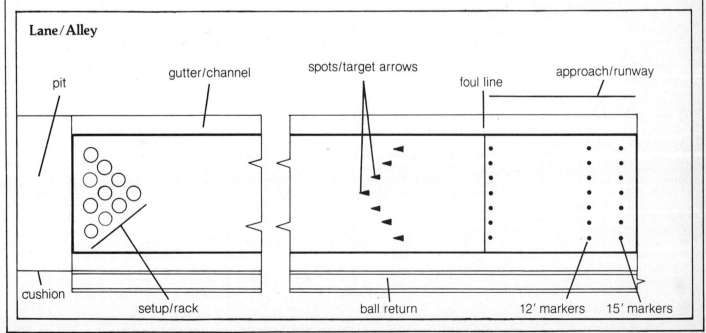

pit

gutter/channel

spots/target arrows

foul line

approach/runway

cushion

setup/rack

ball return

12′ markers

15′ markers

Competitive Sports

Shuffleboard and Croquet

A shuffleboard game may begin at either end of a *court*. That end is designated the *head*. The opposite end is the *foot*. In croquet, *strikers* start at the *home stake* and return to it after going through wickets and hitting the *turning stake*.

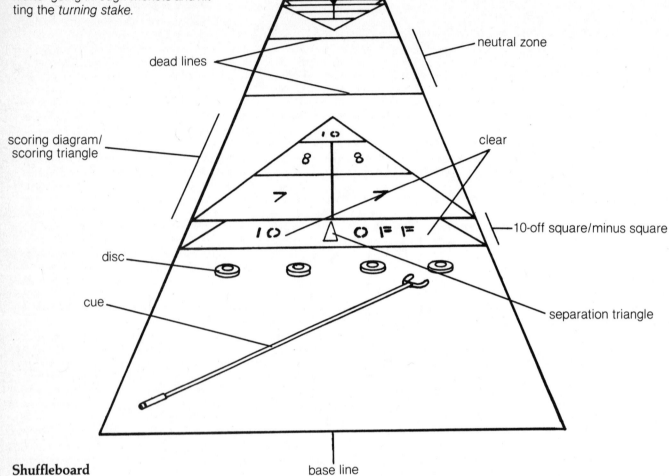

dead lines

neutral zone

scoring diagram/ scoring triangle

clear

10-off square/minus square

disc

separation triangle

cue

Shuffleboard

base line

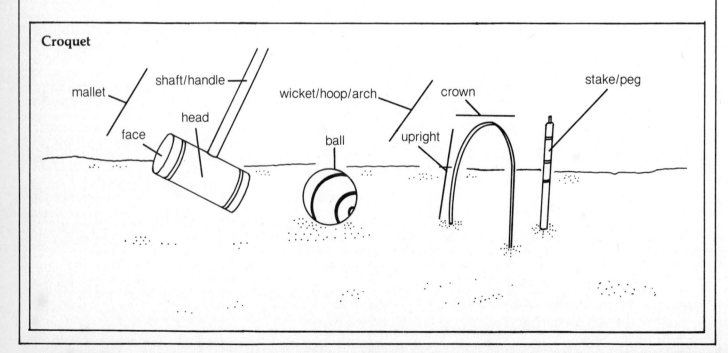

Croquet

mallet

shaft/handle

wicket/hoop/arch

crown

stake/peg

head

face

ball

upright

Volleyball and Badminton

In volleyball, an inflated ball hit sharply is called a *spike* or *kill*. Badminton is played with a *racket* or *bat* whose parts are similar to those of a tennis racket. Some badminton shuttles have nylon *skirts* rather than feathers.

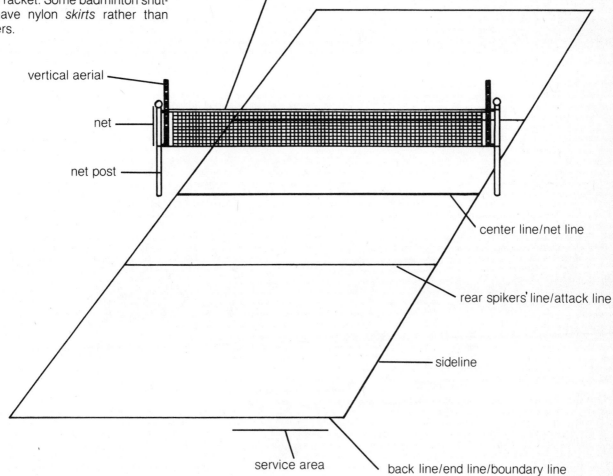

tape

vertical aerial

net

net post

center line/net line

rear spikers' line/attack line

sideline

service area

back line/end line/boundary line

Volleyball Court

Badminton Court

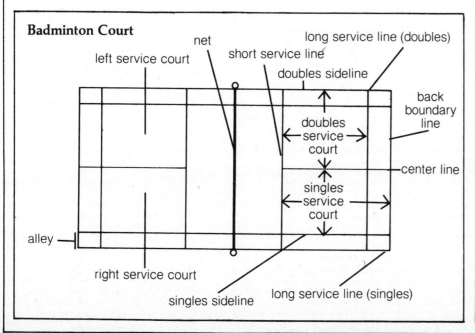

net

left service court

short service line

long service line (doubles)

doubles sideline

back boundary line

doubles service court

center line

singles service court

alley

right service court

singles sideline

long service line (singles)

Shuttlecock / Bird / Shuttle

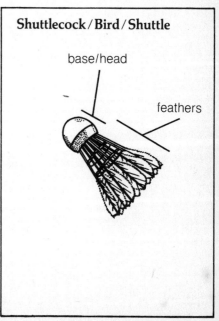

base/head

feathers

Competitive Sports

Billiards and Pool

Billiard and pool tables are usually covered with a dark green cloth called *felt*, or *bed cloth*. A triangular *rack* is used to position object balls at the beginning of a pool or *snooker* game. *Chalk* is used on cue tips. A point scored in billiards is called a *carom*.

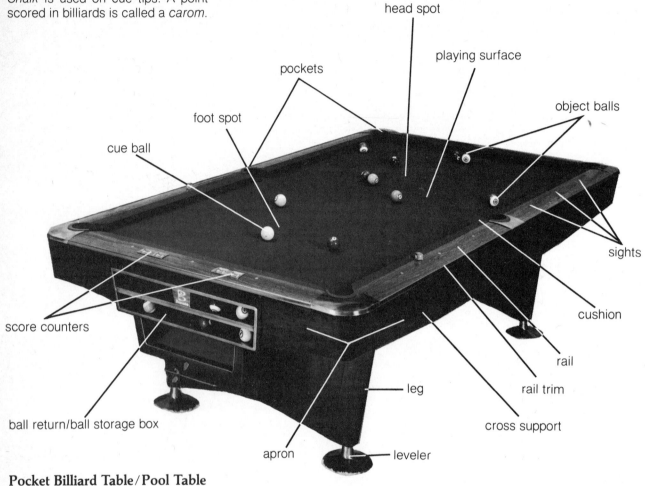

head spot

playing surface

pockets

object balls

foot spot

cue ball

sights

cushion

score counters

rail

rail trim

leg

cross support

ball return/ball storage box

apron

leveler

Pocket Billiard Table/Pool Table

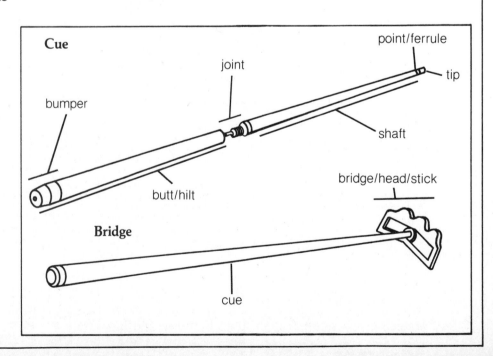

Cue

point/ferrule

joint

tip

bumper

shaft

butt/hilt

bridge/head/stick

Bridge

cue

Ping-Pong/Table Tennis

Paddles have two types of grips, *shake-hands grips* and *penhold grips,* and two types of faces, *rubber* and *sponge.* The game is played with a ping-pong *ball.*

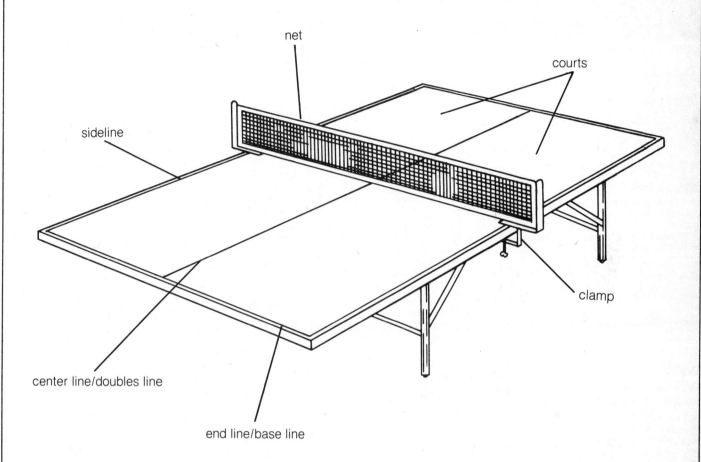

net

courts

sideline

clamp

center line/doubles line

end line/base line

Ping-Pong Table

Racket/Paddle/Bat

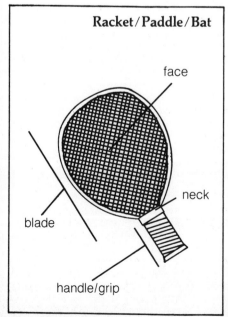

face

neck

blade

handle/grip

Net

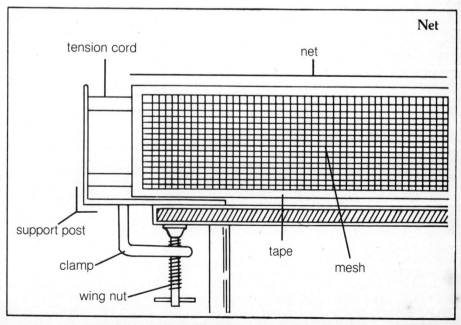

tension cord

net

support post

clamp

wing nut

tape

mesh

Table Games

Darts

Darts, or *darting*, is played by two *dartists* or teams of from two to eight. Darts are scored on *point of entry* on the board *face*. Of the *clock-face games, tournament darts* is the most popular. Other games include *round-the-clock, all-fives, baseball, high score, cricket, 51-in-5's, 14-stop, killer, Mulligan, 301, sudden death,* and *Shanghai.*

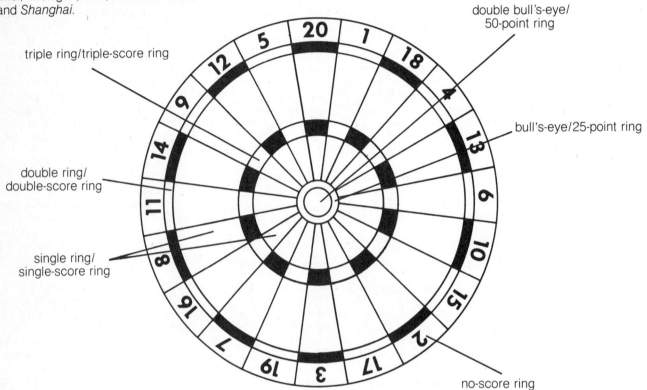

triple ring/triple-score ring

double bull's-eye/ 50-point ring

bull's-eye/25-point ring

double ring/ double-score ring

single ring/ single-score ring

no-score ring

Dart Board/English Clock

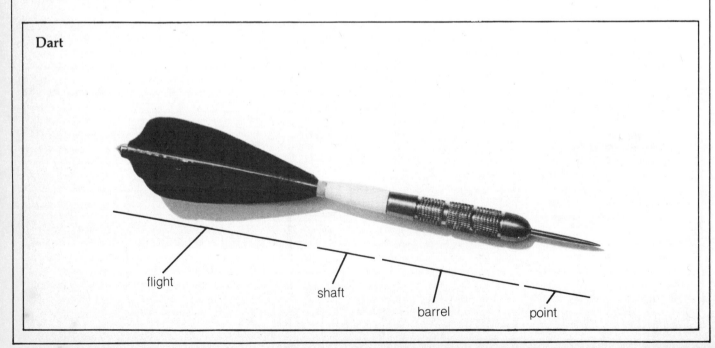

Dart

flight

shaft

barrel

point

Kites

Bridle lines are attached to the spine through holes in the front cover. They are shown here on the rear of the kite only for illustrative purposes. Among the limitless varieties of kites, there are six major categories: flat, *plane*, or *two-stick kites; bowed kites*, sometimes known by their classic example, the *Eddy;* box, or *cellular*, kites; *compound kites*, represented by the *Conyne kite; semiflexible kites*, such as *delta-keels;* and *Rogallos*, or *flexible*, kites. *Fighting kites* have two flying lines.

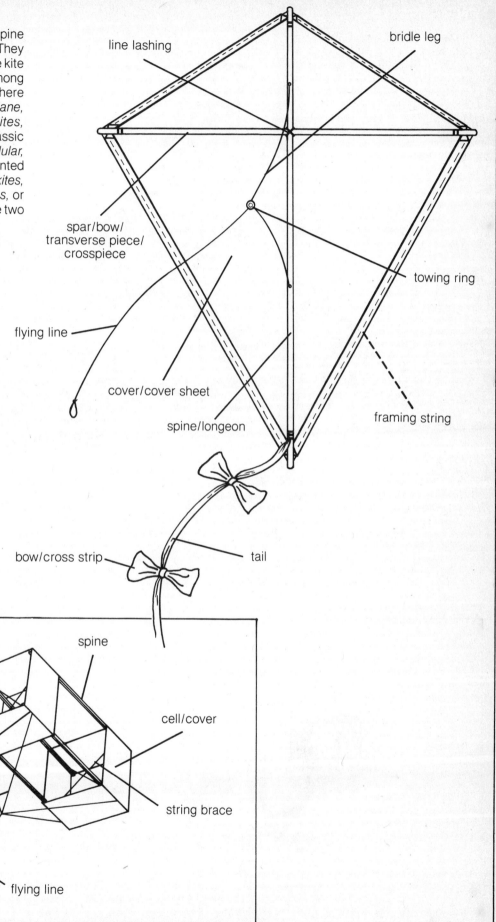

line lashing

bridle leg

spar/bow/
transverse piece/
crosspiece

towing ring

flying line

cover/cover sheet

spine/longeon

framing string

bow/cross strip

tail

Flat Kite

Box Kite/"Flying Crate"

spine

crosspiece

cell/cover

keels

string brace

bridle legs

flying line

Roller Skating and Skateboarding

On the skateboard seen here, the raised tail is called a *kicktail*. The degree to which a board bends is its *flex*. Auxiliary roller sports equipment includes *helmet*, *kneepads* and *elbow pads*.

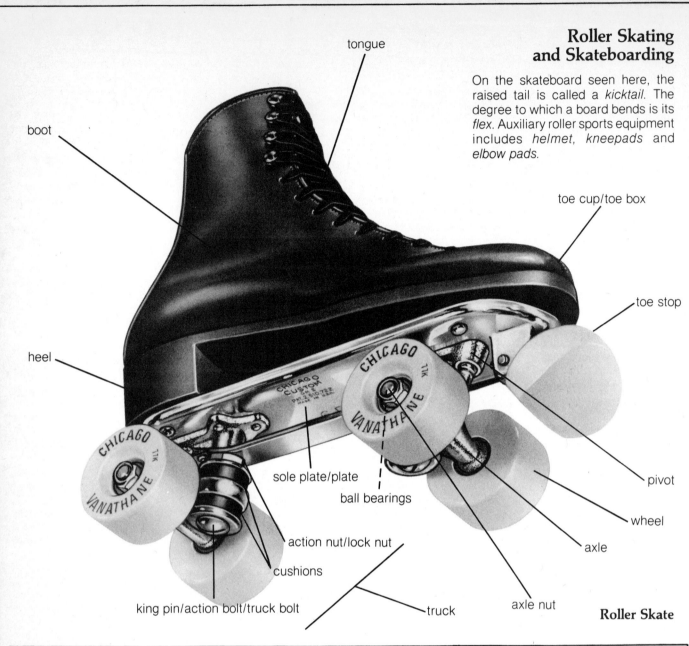

tongue

boot

toe cup/toe box

toe stop

heel

sole plate/plate

ball bearings

pivot

wheel

action nut/lock nut

cushions

axle

king pin/action bolt/truck bolt

axle nut

truck

Roller Skate

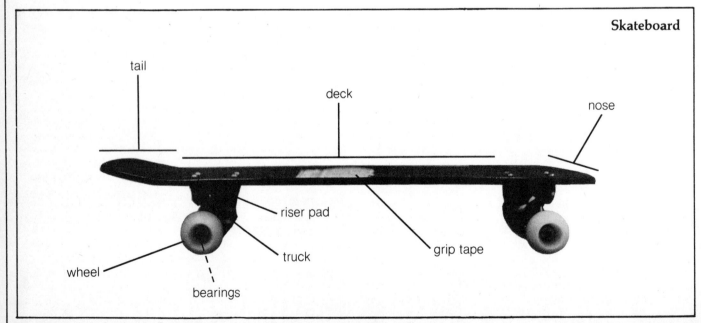

Skateboard

tail

deck

nose

riser pad

truck

grip tape

wheel

bearings

Ice Skates

Uppers refer to the area of a skate above the sole. *Inserts* can be used to reinforce the uppers and tighten the heel, and *lunge pads* provide extra protection in the toe area. Hockey skates often have L-shaped *ankle guards* built into the boot. *Skate guards* or *blade booties* protect skate blades when not in use.

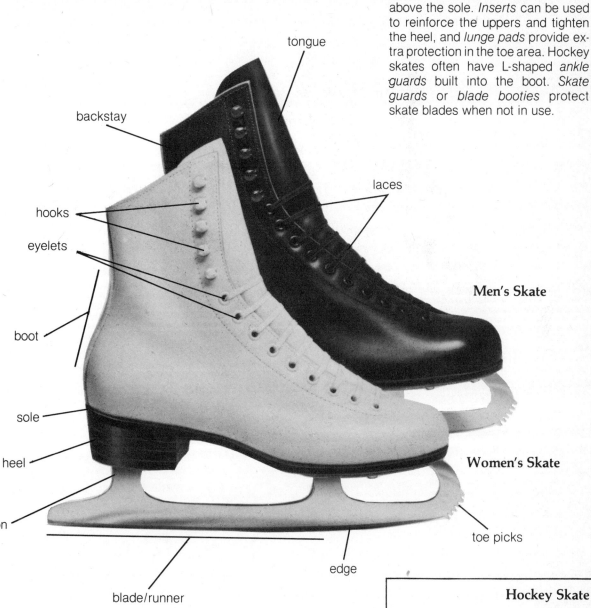

tongue

backstay

laces

hooks

eyelets

boot

sole

heel

stanchion

blade/runner

edge

toe picks

Men's Skate

Women's Skate

Figure Skates

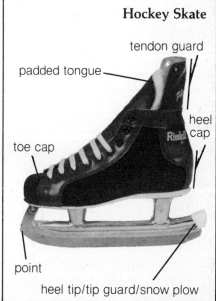

Hockey Skate

tendon guard

padded tongue

heel cap

toe cap

point

heel tip/tip guard/snow plow

Individual Sports

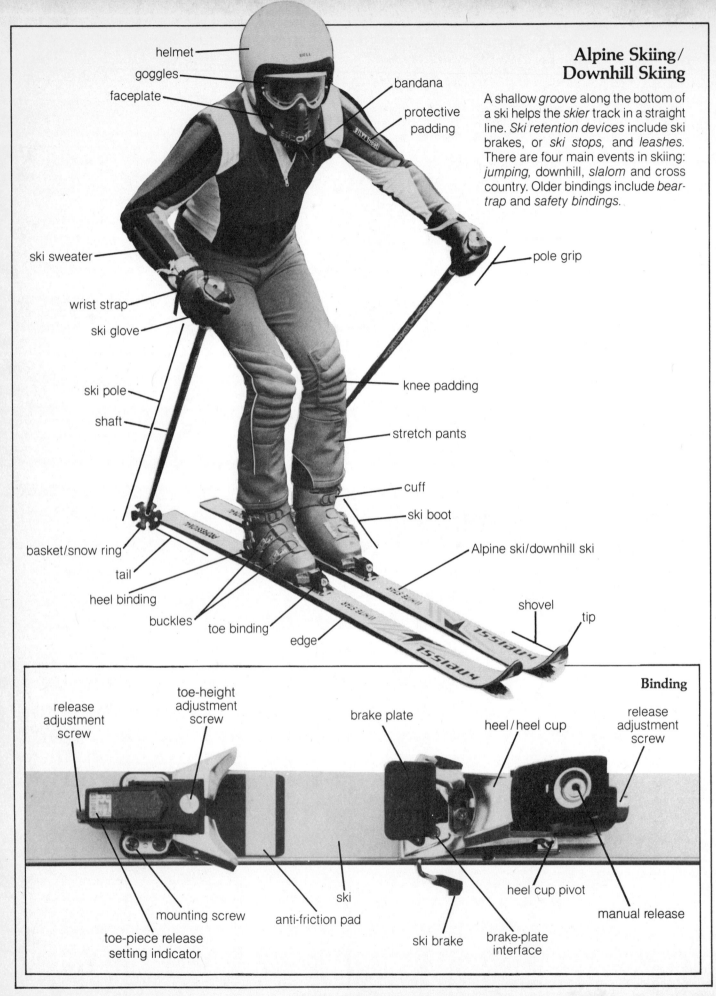

Alpine Skiing/ Downhill Skiing

A shallow *groove* along the bottom of a ski helps the *skier* track in a straight line. *Ski retention devices* include ski brakes, or *ski stops,* and *leashes.* There are four main events in skiing: *jumping,* downhill, *slalom* and cross country. Older bindings include *bear-trap* and *safety bindings.*

helmet

goggles

faceplate

bandana

protective padding

ski sweater

pole grip

wrist strap

ski glove

ski pole

shaft

knee padding

stretch pants

cuff

ski boot

basket/snow ring

Alpine ski/downhill ski

tail

heel binding

buckles

toe binding

edge

shovel

tip

Binding

release adjustment screw

toe-height adjustment screw

brake plate

heel/heel cup

release adjustment screw

mounting screw

toe-piece release setting indicator

anti-friction pad

ski

ski brake

brake-plate interface

heel cup pivot

manual release

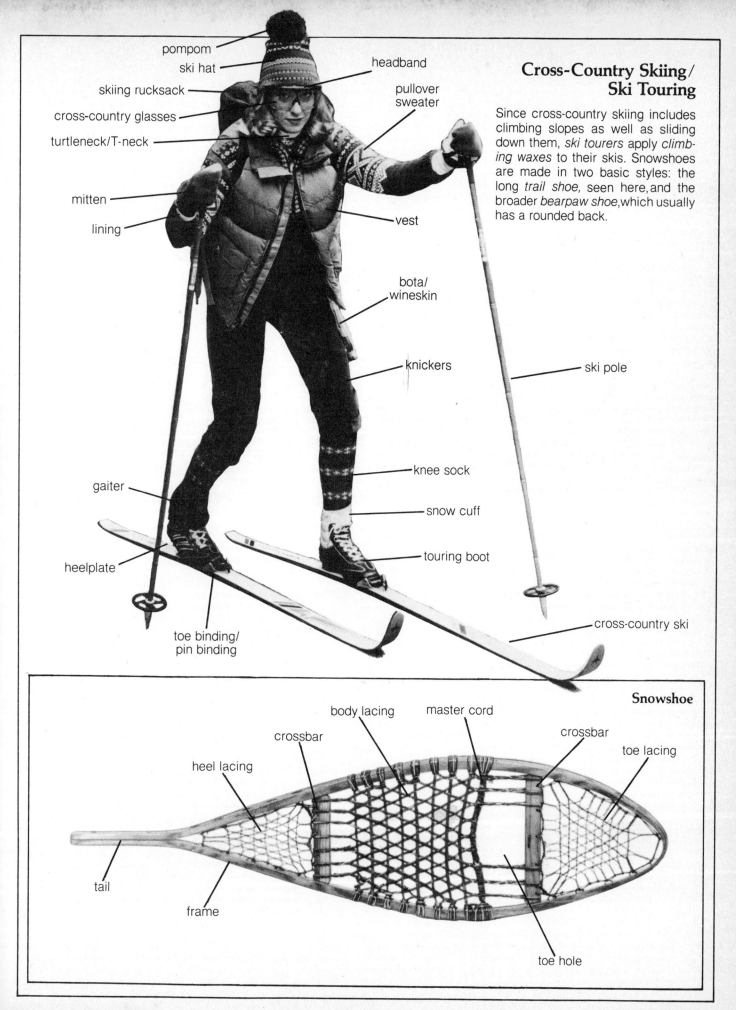

pompom

ski hat

skiing rucksack

cross-country glasses

turtleneck/T-neck

mitten

lining

headband

pullover sweater

vest

bota/wineskin

knickers

knee sock

snow cuff

touring boot

gaiter

heelplate

toe binding/pin binding

ski pole

cross-country ski

Cross-Country Skiing/ Ski Touring

Since cross-country skiing includes climbing slopes as well as sliding down them, *ski tourers* apply *climbing waxes* to their skis. Snowshoes are made in two basic styles: the long *trail shoe,* seen here, and the broader *bearpaw shoe,* which usually has a rounded back.

Snowshoe

body lacing

master cord

crossbar

crossbar

toe lacing

heel lacing

tail

frame

toe hole

Sledding and Tobogganing

Bobsleds, driven by two- or four-man crews, have a racing *cowl* and toothed metal *brake.* Small racing sleds called *luges* are controlled by reclining drivers using their feet and *hand ropes.*

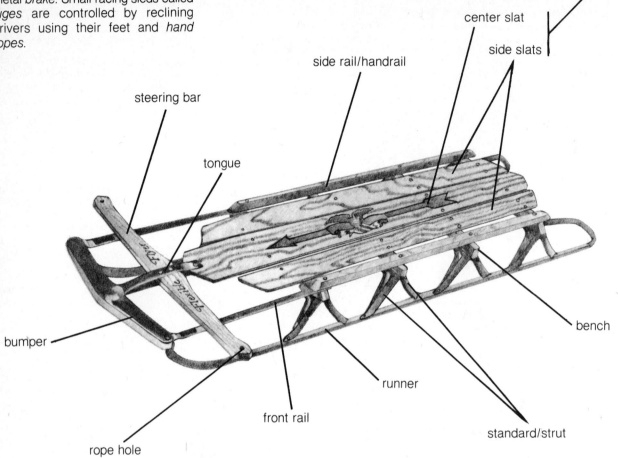

deck

center slat

side slats

side rail/handrail

steering bar

tongue

bumper

rope hole

front rail

runner

standard/strut

bench

Sled

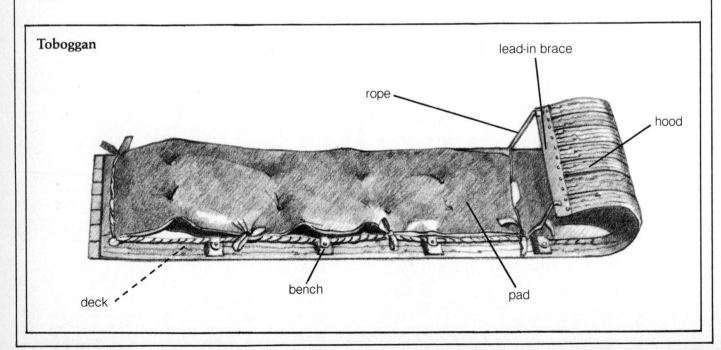

Toboggan

lead-in brace

rope

hood

deck

bench

pad

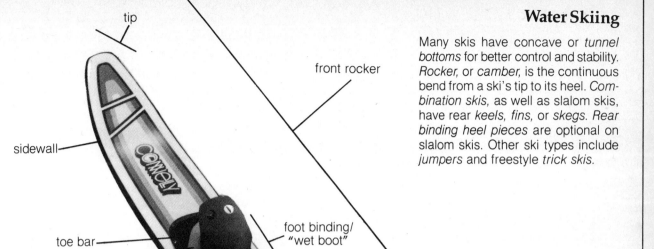

tip

front rocker

sidewall

Water Skiing

Many skis have concave or *tunnel bottoms* for better control and stability. *Rocker,* or *camber,* is the continuous bend from a ski's tip to its heel. *Combination skis,* as well as slalom skis, have rear *keels, fins,* or *skegs. Rear binding heel pieces* are optional on slalom skis. Other ski types include *jumpers* and freestyle *trick skis.*

toe bar

toepiece

foot binding/ "wet boot"

heel piece/ heel flap

rear toe binder

heel glide

tail rocker

trigger

heel plate

drop-through fin cover

tail

Slalom Ski

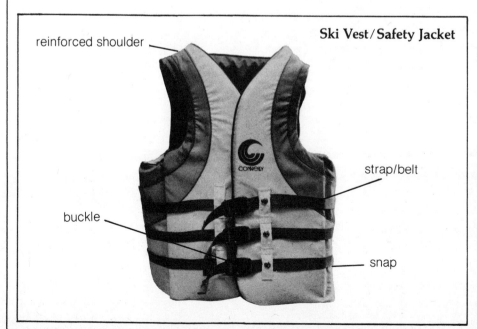

Ski Vest/Safety Jacket

reinforced shoulder

strap/belt

buckle

snap

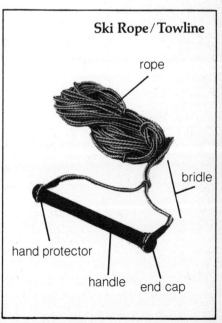

Ski Rope/Towline

rope

bridle

hand protector

handle

end cap

329

Surfing

A windsurfer, or *sailboard,* is equipped with a *free-rotating mast* and *loose-footed sail*, or *free-sail system*. Surfboards range in size from heavy *big guns* to smaller *hotdogging boards*. A *pig board* or *tear drop* is a board shaped like a pie wedge.

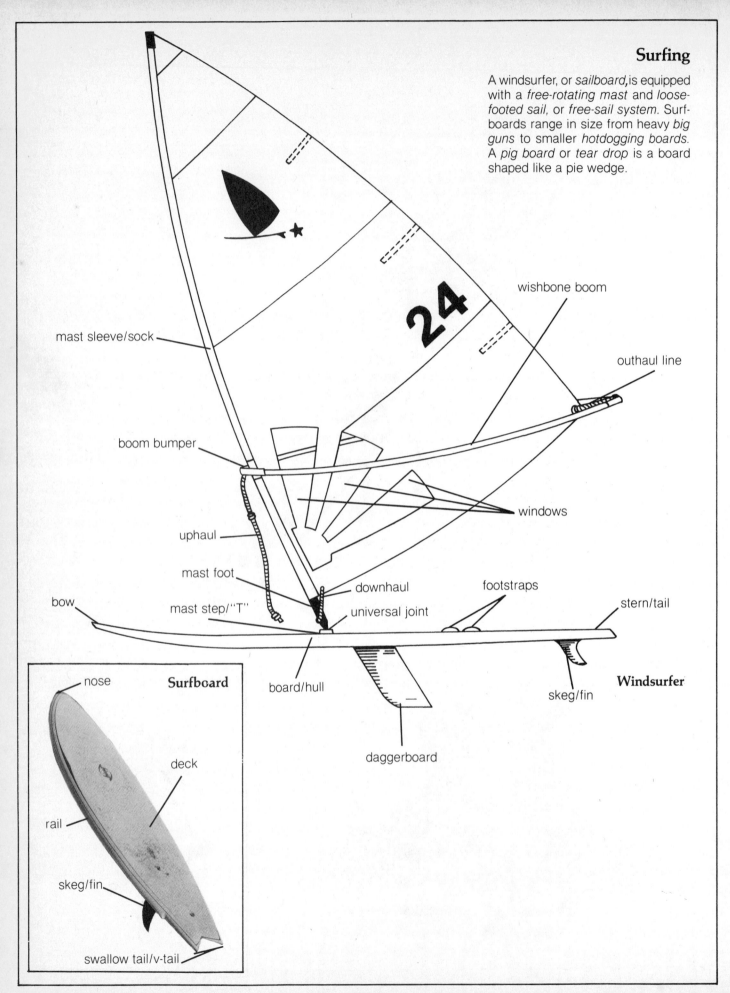

wishbone boom

outhaul line

mast sleeve/sock

windows

boom bumper

uphaul

mast foot

downhaul

footstraps

stern/tail

bow

mast step/"T"

universal joint

skeg/fin

Windsurfer

board/hull

daggerboard

Surfboard

nose

deck

rail

skeg/fin

swallow tail/v-tail

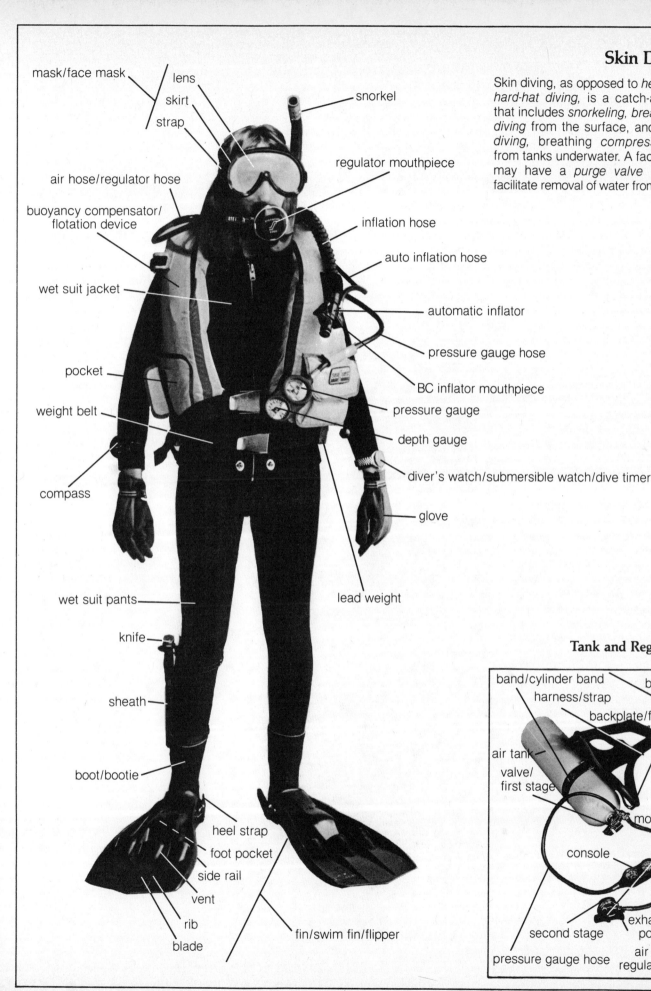

mask/face mask

lens

skirt

strap

snorkel

air hose/regulator hose

regulator mouthpiece

buoyancy compensator/ flotation device

inflation hose

auto inflation hose

wet suit jacket

automatic inflator

pressure gauge hose

pocket

BC inflator mouthpiece

weight belt

pressure gauge

depth gauge

compass

diver's watch/submersible watch/dive timer

glove

lead weight

wet suit pants

knife

sheath

boot/bootie

heel strap

foot pocket

side rail

vent

rib

blade

fin/swim fin/flipper

Skin diving, as opposed to *helmet* or *hard-hat diving*, is a catch-all term that includes *snorkeling, breath-hold diving* from the surface, and *scuba diving*, breathing *compressed air* from tanks underwater. A face mask may have a *purge valve* in it to facilitate removal of water from within.

Tank and Regulator

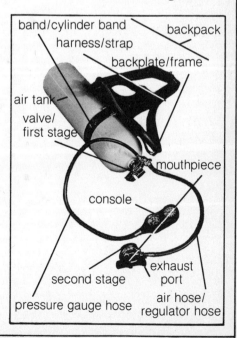

band/cylinder band

backpack

harness/strap

backplate/frame

air tank

valve/ first stage

mouthpiece

console

second stage

exhaust port

pressure gauge hose

air hose/ regulator hose

Individual Sports

Hot Air Balloon

A balloon, or *montgolfier,* rises when *ballast,* usually water or *sandbags,* is jettisoned. A *drag,* or *trail rope,* hangs from the balloon to give it stability in flight and slow it down upon landing. To deflate the balloon a *ripping panel,* or *rip panel,* near the top is opened.

parachute valve/
parachute vent

envelope/bag

registration number/
"N" number

envelope
graphic

panel seams

gore seams

load cords

panels

bottom girdle

skirt

skirt band

burner

suspension rope

load ring

padding

basket handle

mouth

valve line

burner support

basket/carriage

scuff leather

tether line

Parachuting and Hang Gliding

Unless attached to a *static line,* which automatically opens a *chute* once a *jumper* has cleared the *jump plane,* a *sky diver* can *free-fall* before pulling his *rip cord.*

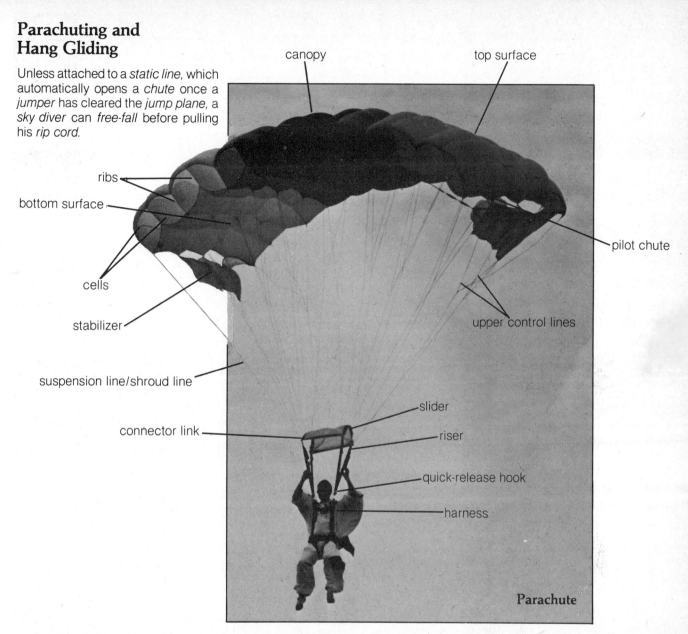

canopy

top surface

ribs

bottom surface

cells

stabilizer

suspension line/shroud line

connector link

pilot chute

upper control lines

slider

riser

quick-release hook

harness

Parachute

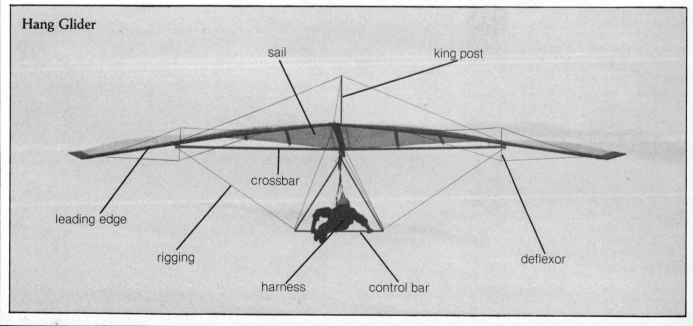

Hang Glider

sail

king post

crossbar

leading edge

rigging

harness

control bar

deflexor

Mountain Climbing

Mountaineers use nylon webbing for *shoulder slings* and *swami belts*. Carabiners, either oval- or D-shaped, have spring-loaded *gates* for connecting various pieces of climbing equipment. Unlike *pitons*, which are hammered into cracks, nuts are wedged into cracks and easily removed. *Icescrews*, ring-topped threaded tubes, are actually screwed into the ice for protection.

- hardware sling
- carabiners
- climbing harness
- tape
- chocks & nuts
- climbing rope
- rand
- smooth-soled climbing shoe/ klettershoe/PA

Ice Climbing Boot

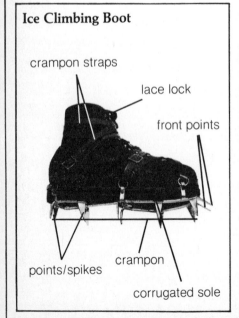

- crampon straps
- lace lock
- front points
- points/spikes
- crampon
- corrugated sole

Ice Tools

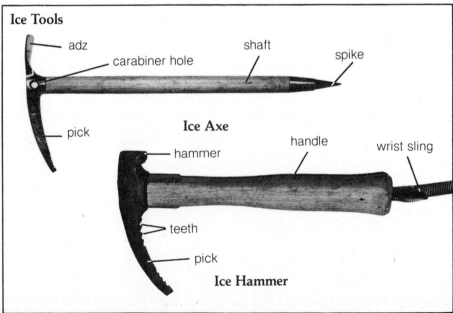

- adz
- carabiner hole
- shaft
- spike
- pick

Ice Axe

- hammer
- handle
- wrist sling
- teeth
- pick

Ice Hammer

Riding Equipment

A saddle is built on a frame called a *saddle tree*. A *saddle blanket* or *saddle pad* is placed between horse and saddle. Metal stirrups, or *stirrup irons*, are attached to the saddle by *stirrup leathers*. *Saddlebags* fit over the back of the saddle.

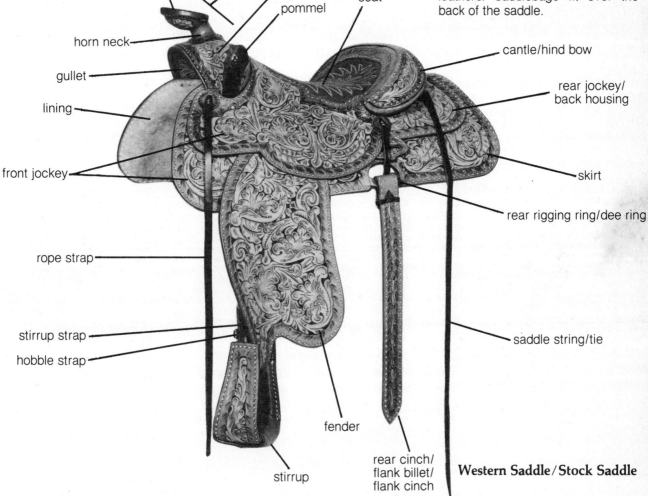

horn cap

horn

fork/swell

pommel

seat

horn neck

gullet

lining

cantle/hind bow

rear jockey/ back housing

front jockey

skirt

rear rigging ring/dee ring

rope strap

saddle string/tie

stirrup strap

hobble strap

fender

stirrup

rear cinch/ flank billet/ flank cinch

Western Saddle / Stock Saddle

English Saddle

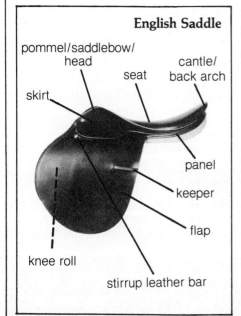

pommel/saddlebow/ head

seat

cantle/ back arch

skirt

panel

keeper

flap

knee roll

stirrup leather bar

Stirrup

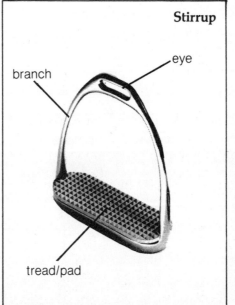

branch

eye

tread/pad

Spur

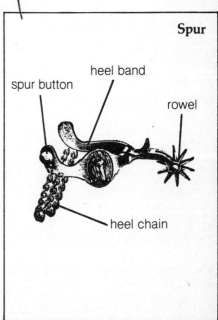

spur button

heel band

rowel

heel chain

Equestrian Sports

Flat Racing

The equipment used on a racehorse is called the *tack*. *Thoroughbreds* start from a fixed *starting gate*, while harness racers start from a car-pulled *moving gate*. The most desirable *post position* in a race is gate number one, the *pole position* closest to the *rail*. Bettors pick horses to finish first, second and third, or *win*, *place* and *show*. Picking all three finishers in the right order is called a *trifecta*.

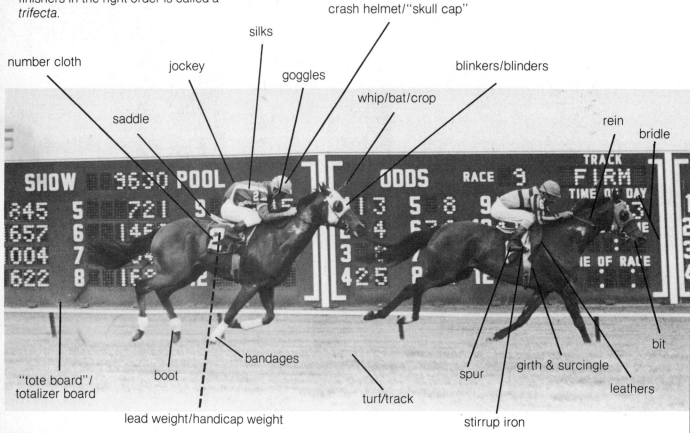

number cloth · silks · jockey · goggles · crash helmet/"skull cap" · whip/bat/crop · blinkers/blinders · saddle · rein · bridle · bit · "tote board"/totalizer board · boot · bandages · turf/track · spur · girth & surcingle · leathers · stirrup iron · lead weight/handicap weight

Racing Program Entry

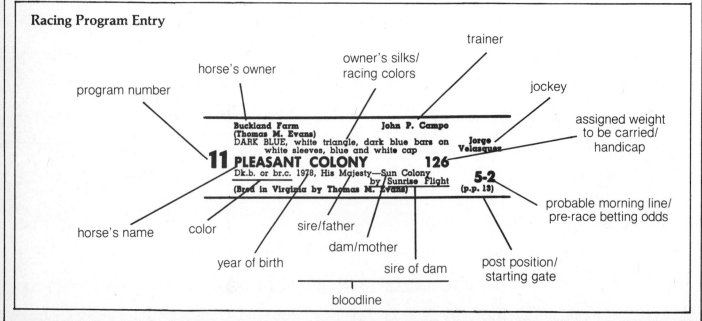

program number · horse's owner · owner's silks/racing colors · trainer · jockey · assigned weight to be carried/handicap · horse's name · color · year of birth · sire/father · dam/mother · sire of dam · post position/starting gate · probable morning line/pre-race betting odds · bloodline

Harness Racing

Trotters and pacers race in *harness.* Trotters move front and opposing rear legs in unison, *laterally gaited,* while pacers move front and rear legs on the same side in unison, *diagonally gaited.* Horses are assembled, saddled and paraded in the *paddock area.*

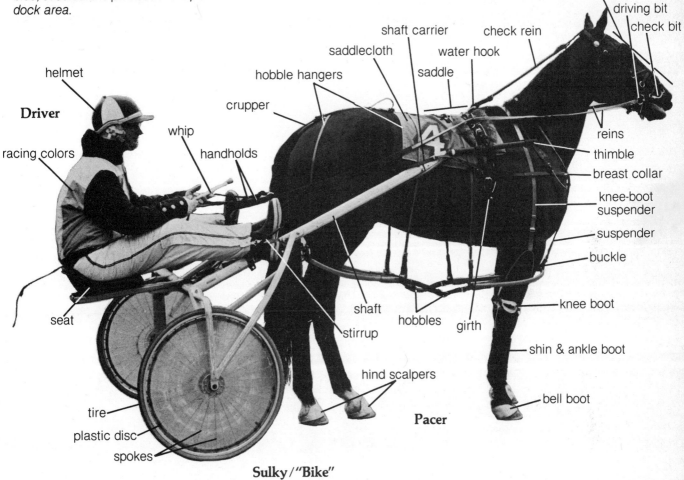

Driver

helmet

racing colors

whip

handholds

crupper

hobble hangers

saddlecloth

shaft carrier

saddle

water hook

check rein

bridle

driving bit

check bit

reins

thimble

breast collar

knee-boot suspender

suspender

buckle

knee boot

shin & ankle boot

bell boot

shaft

stirrup

hobbles

girth

hind scalpers

Pacer

seat

tire

plastic disc

spokes

Sulky/"Bike"

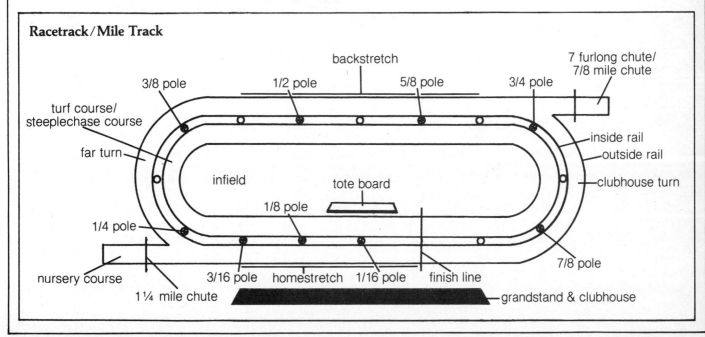

Racetrack/Mile Track

backstretch

3/8 pole

1/2 pole

5/8 pole

3/4 pole

7 furlong chute/ 7/8 mile chute

turf course/ steeplechase course

far turn

infield

tote board

inside rail

outside rail

clubhouse turn

1/4 pole

1/8 pole

nursery course

3/16 pole

homestretch

1/16 pole

finish line

7/8 pole

1¼ mile chute

grandstand & clubhouse

Equestrian Sports

Grand Prix Racing

International *road racing* takes place on *closed-circuit tracks* laid out through the countryside, as opposed to *speedway racing,* which takes place on banked, oval-shaped *race tracks. Formulas* primarily limit engine size and car weight, and range from *Super-Vee* to *Formula One,* used in Grand Prix racing.

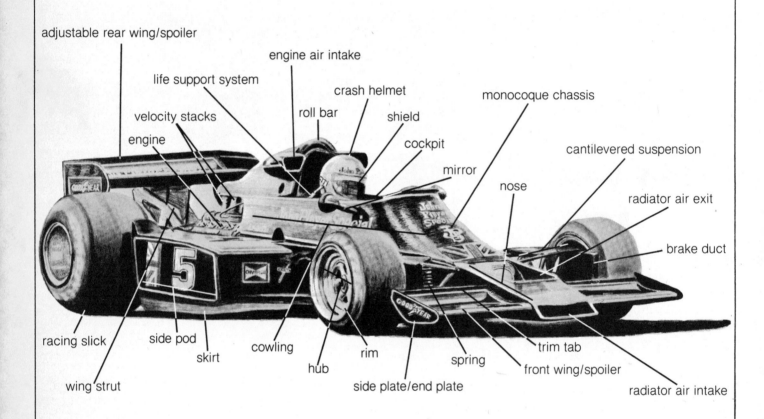

Formula One Racing Car

Drag Racing

Each drag racing *event,* or *acceleration contest,* involves two-car *heats,* the winner of which is deemed the *eliminator.* Vehicles include *slingshot dragsters* and *funny cars* whose mismatched bodies, or *"hulls,"* and *chassis* give them an unusual appearance. The Christmas Tree is situated in the middle of a divided, two-lane *straight-line course, drag strip* or *dragway. Elapsed time,* or *"ET,"* is computed from the moment a car breaks a *light beam* at the *starting line* until it breaks a similar beam at the *finish.* A car leaving the starting line prematurely, in either *handicap* or *heads-up racing,* is said to be *"red-lighting."*

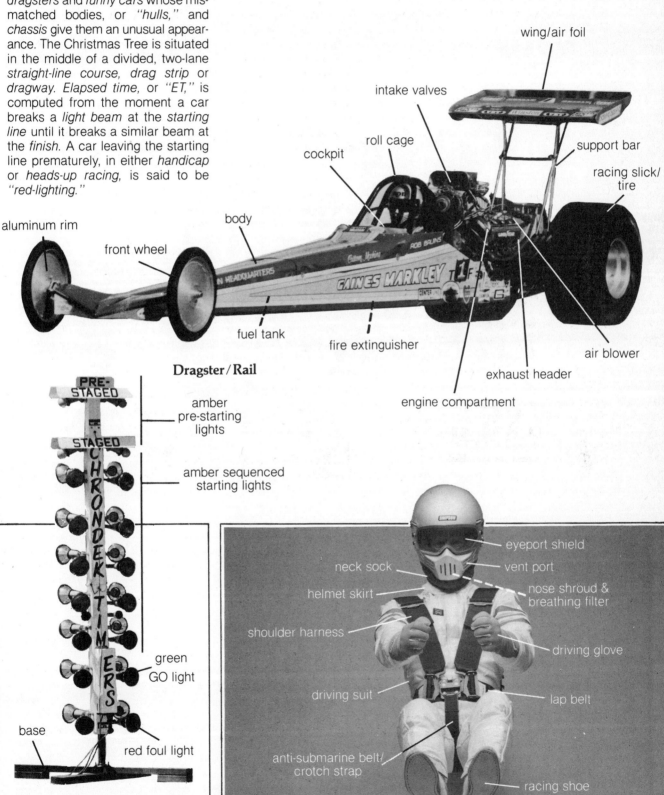

wing/air foil

intake valves

roll cage

cockpit

support bar

racing slick/ tire

aluminum rim

front wheel

body

fuel tank

fire extinguisher

air blower

exhaust header

engine compartment

Dragster/Rail

amber pre-starting lights

amber sequenced starting lights

PRE-STAGED

STAGED

CHRONDEK TIMERS

green GO light

base

red foul light

Starting Lights/Christmas Tree

eyeport shield

neck sock

vent port

helmet skirt

nose shroud & breathing filter

shoulder harness

driving glove

driving suit

lap belt

anti-submarine belt/ crotch strap

racing shoe

Driver's Fire Suit

handle

foot/pole mount

leg/reel stem

crank handle

trip/dog

bail/pick-up arm

spool skirt

spool

anti-reverse lever

PENN
750SS

3 BALL BEARINGS
SKIRTED SPOOL

rear bearing

gear housing

bearing cover

silent
anti-reverse
housing

drag-adjustment knob/
drag knob

line roller/line guide

Reel/Spinning Reel

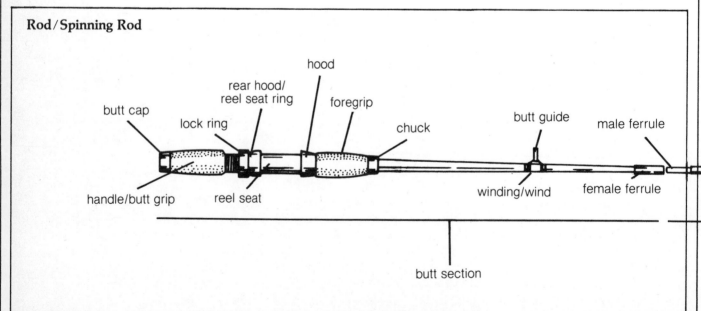

Rod/Spinning Rod

hood

rear hood/
reel seat ring

foregrip

butt cap

lock ring

chuck

butt guide

male ferrule

handle/butt grip

reel seat

winding/wind

female ferrule

butt section

Fishing

Fishermen, or anglers, use a variety of tackle, from simple cane rods, or bank rods, to sophisticated fly rods and trolling gear. Sinkers hold bait underwater, while floats, or bobbers, keep it suspended from the surface. A gaff or landing net is used to land fish.

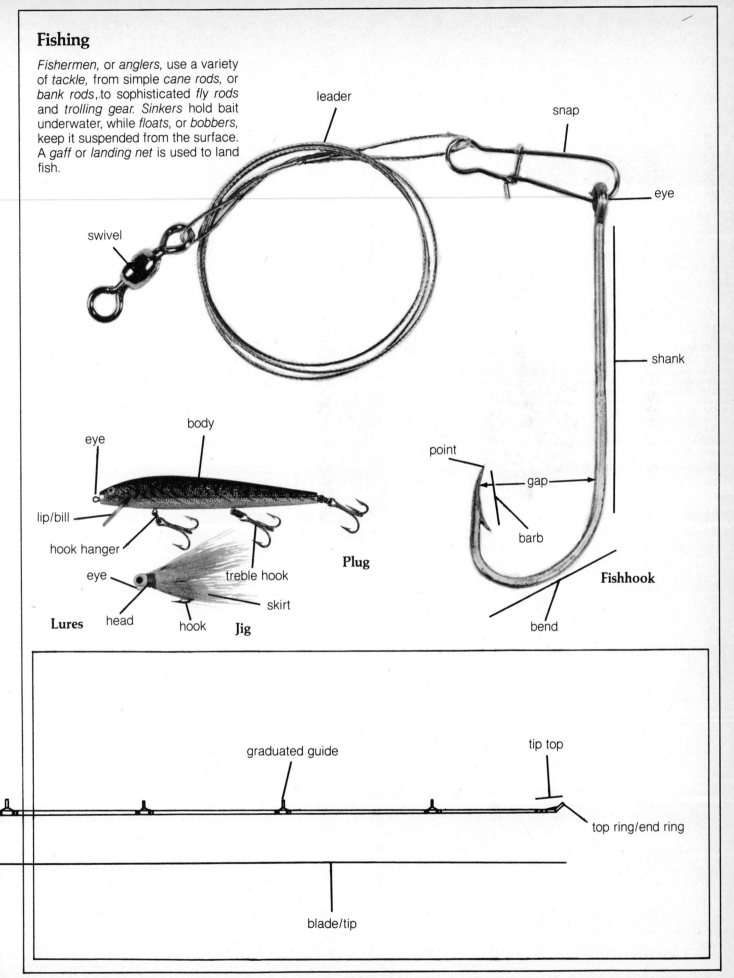

leader

snap

eye

swivel

shank

body

eye

point

gap

lip/bill

barb

hook hanger

treble hook

Plug

eye

skirt

Fishhook

Lures

head

hook

Jig

bend

graduated guide

tip top

top ring/end ring

blade/tip

Camping

Wall tents and pup tents are held up by tent poles. Many modern tents have *exterior frame* construction. Features in all the above-mentioned tents include *lap-felled* or *French seams*, which provide four layers for keeping out water, webbed–tape *backing* and pressed-on *grommets* or sewn-in *rings* for *ropes* secured to the ground with *pegs* or *stakes*, and sewn-in *flooring*. A lantern is primed by pumping the *pump valve* and lit by a match placed in the *lighting hole*.

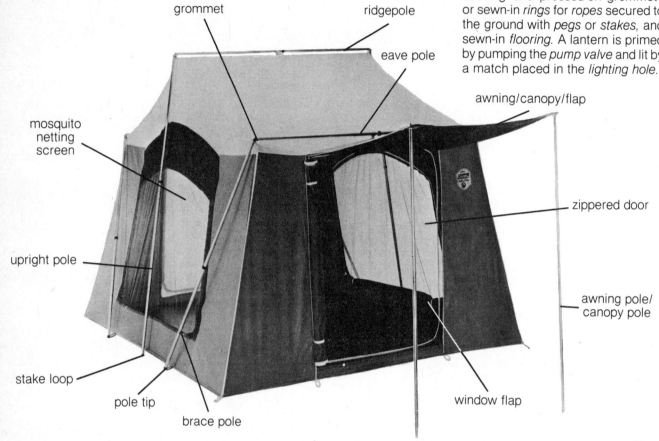

grommet

ridgepole

eave pole

mosquito netting screen

awning/canopy/flap

zippered door

upright pole

awning pole/ canopy pole

stake loop

pole tip

brace pole

window flap

Tent

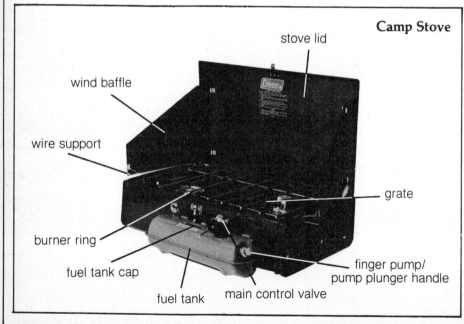

Camp Stove

stove lid

wind baffle

wire support

grate

burner ring

fuel tank cap

fuel tank

main control valve

finger pump/ pump plunger handle

Lantern

ventilator

bail

mantle

globe

heat shield

fuel valve

base rest

tank/fount

fuel cap

Loft is the trade term for fluffiness in sleeping bags. *Bonded insulation filling* eliminates the need for *quilting* and reduces "cold spots." The various pockets of backpacks, *knapsacks* or *rucksacks,* are called *local organizers.* Small camping items are packed in *stuffsacks,* which are then put inside a hiker's *pack.*

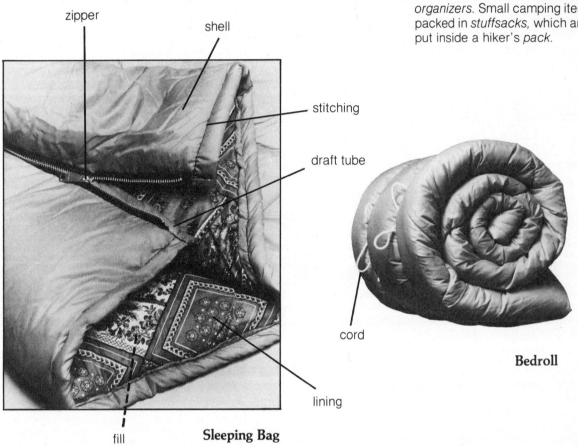

zipper

shell

stitching

draft tube

cord

lining

fill

Bedroll

Sleeping Bag

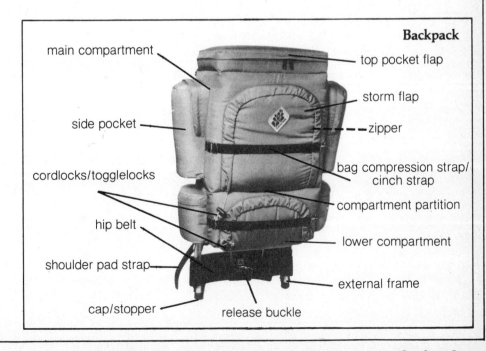

Backpack

main compartment

top pocket flap

storm flap

side pocket

zipper

cordlocks/togglelocks

bag compression strap/ cinch strap

compartment partition

hip belt

lower compartment

shoulder pad strap

external frame

cap/stopper

release buckle

Body Building

Among other *stations* in the universal gym, designed to improve muscle development through *isotonic exercises*, are *dead lift* and *low pulley*. Muscle-building and toning equipment includes *dumbbells, hand grips, or hand flexors, scissor grips, tone-up wheels, power twisters, exercise bikes, neck developers, ankle* and *wrist weights, triceps exercisers* and *waist trimmers.*

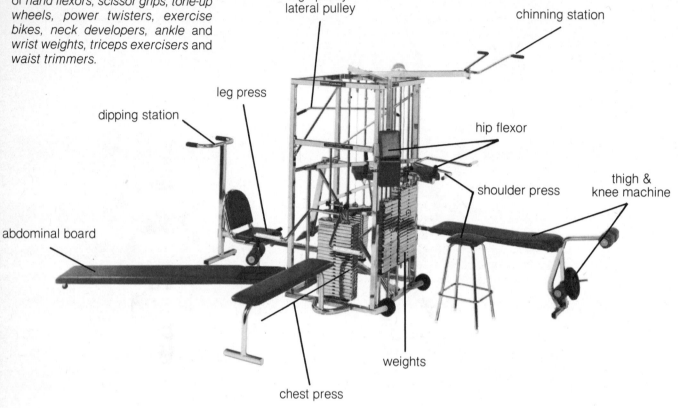

high pulley/ lateral pulley

chinning station

leg press

dipping station

hip flexor

shoulder press

thigh & knee machine

abdominal board

weights

chest press

Universal Gym

Jump Rope/Skip Rope

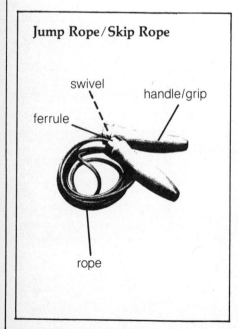

swivel

handle/grip

ferrule

rope

Chest Pull

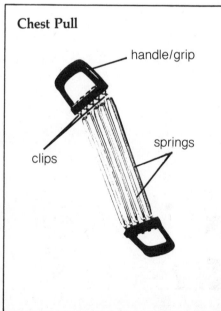

handle/grip

springs

clips

Barbell

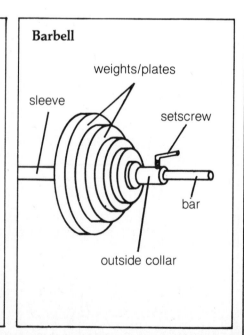

weights/plates

sleeve

setscrew

bar

outside collar

Chess, Checkers, Backgammon and Tile Games

When chessmen and checkers are arranged at the start of a game, they are positioned in a *setup*. A chessboard's horizontal rows are called *ranks*. Vertical rows are *files*. In backgammon, a player increases the stakes by turning a dicelike *doubling cube*. A single backgammon piece on a point is called a *blot*. Two or more on a point make a *block*. In dominos, pieces with identical numbers on both ends are called *doubles* or *spinners*. Dominos that have been played form a *layout*. In mah-jongg, tiles are arranged in a *wall* to begin a game.

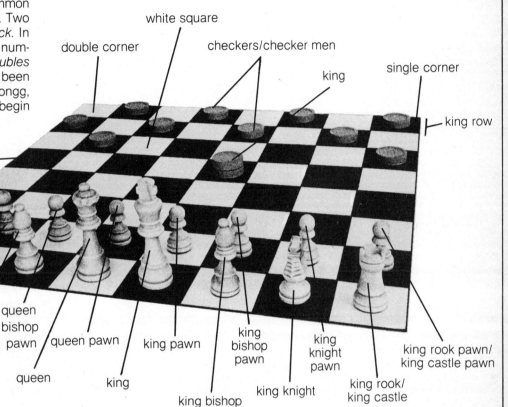

double corner
white square
checkers/checker men
king
single corner
king row
black square
chessmen/ chess pieces
queen rook/ queen castle
queen rook pawn/ queen castle pawn
queen knight
queen bishop pawn
queen bishop
queen knight pawn
queen pawn
queen
king pawn
king
king bishop pawn
king bishop
king knight pawn
king knight
king rook/ king castle
king rook pawn/ king castle pawn

Chessboard/Checkerboard

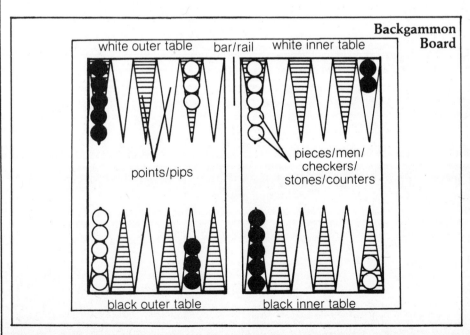

Backgammon Board

white outer table
bar/rail
white inner table
points/pips
pieces/men/ checkers/ stones/counters
black outer table
black inner table

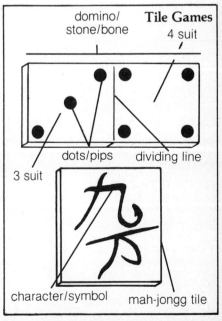

Tile Games

domino/ stone/bone
4 suit
3 suit
dots/pips
dividing line
character/symbol
mah-jongg tile

Gambling Equipment

A roulette wheel is operated by a *croupier*. Bets are placed on a *layout*. Slots are divided into *red* and *black* for betting purposes. Dice players bet either with the person rolling the dice, the *shooter*, or with the casino, or *house*. The blackjack dealer pushes money won by the house into a double-locked *drop box* below the betting table. Other casino games include *baccarat*, *chemin de fer*, *wheel of fortune*, and *chuck-a-luck*, a game played with three dice.

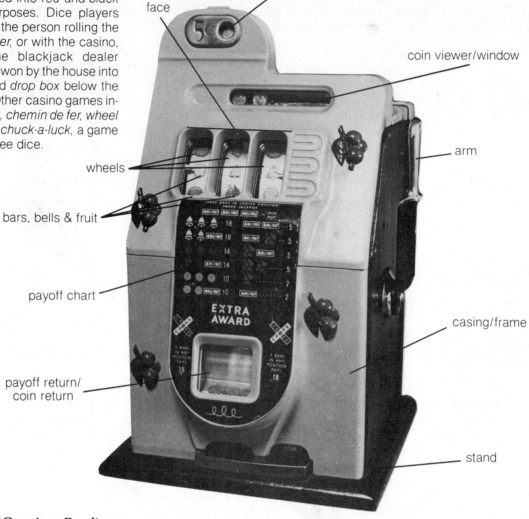

coin slot

face

coin viewer/window

arm

wheels

bars, bells & fruit

payoff chart

casing/frame

payoff return/
coin return

stand

Slot Machine/One-Arm Bandit

Roulette Wheel

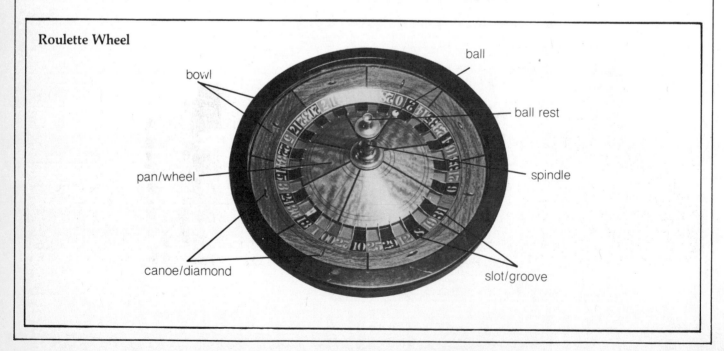

bowl

ball

ball rest

pan/wheel

spindle

canoe/diamond

slot/groove

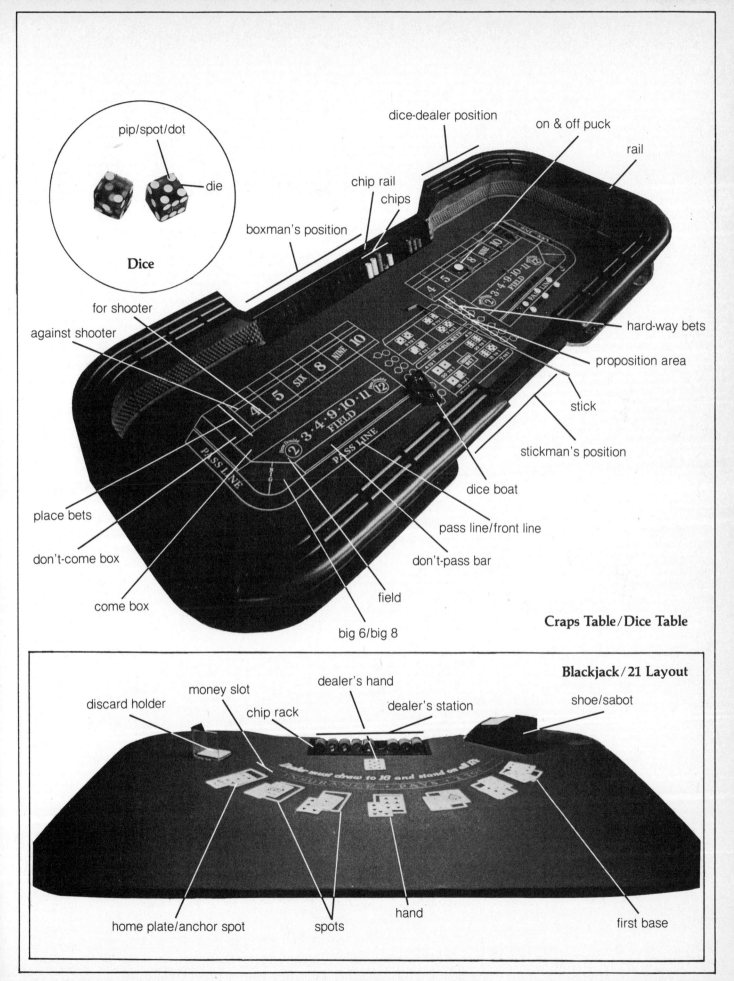

pip/spot/dot

die

Dice

dice-dealer position

on & off puck

rail

chip rail

chips

boxman's position

for shooter

against shooter

hard-way bets

proposition area

stick

stickman's position

place bets

don't-come box

dice boat

pass line/front line

come box

don't-pass bar

field

Craps Table/Dice Table

big 6/big 8

4 5 SIX 8 NINE 10

2·3·4·9·10·11·12 FIELD

PASS LINE

PASS LINE

Blackjack/21 Layout

discard holder

money slot

dealer's hand

chip rack

dealer's station

shoe/sabot

Dealer must draw to 16 and stand on all 17

INSURANCE PAYS 2 to 1

home plate/anchor spot

spots

hand

first base

Casino Games

Playing Cards

There are 52 cards in a *deck* or *pack*. The *aces*, shown below, and cards numbered two through ten, are called *spot cards* or *pip cards*. An additional card, the *joker*, or *mistigris*, is used in *card games* requiring a *wild card*. A *marked deck* is one in which the card *backs* have been altered slightly to allow a player to read their *values* illegally.

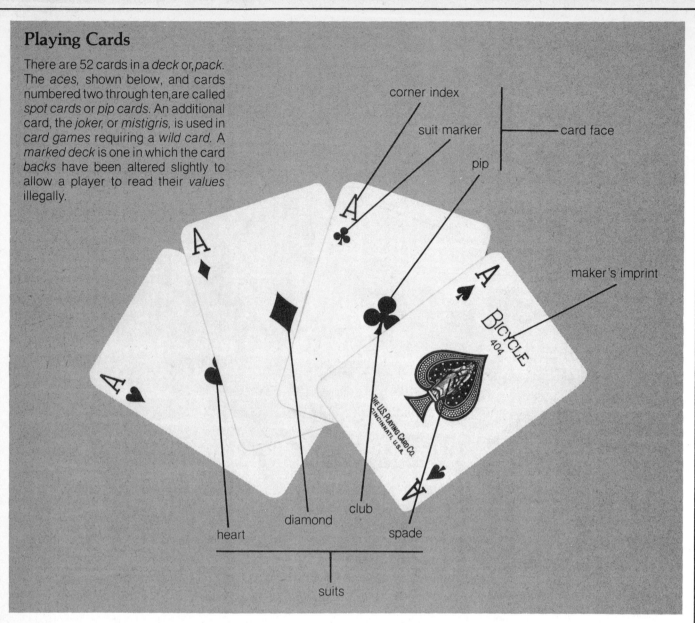

corner index

suit marker

pip

card face

maker's imprint

heart

diamond

club

spade

suits

Picture Cards/Court Cards/Face Cards

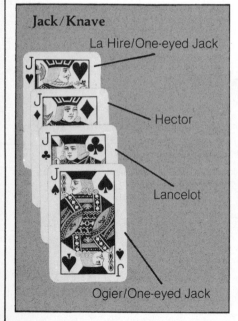

Jack/Knave

La Hire/One-eyed Jack

Hector

Lancelot

Ogier/One-eyed Jack

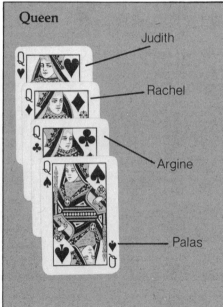

Queen

Judith

Rachel

Argine

Palas

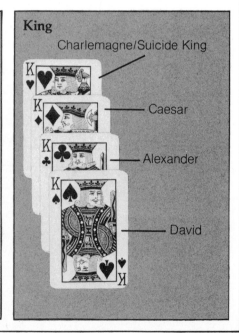

King

Charlemagne/Suicide King

Caesar

Alexander

David

Arts and Crafts

The main subsections here include the platforms on which the performing arts take place; coverage of the music field, ranging from the symbols that appear on sheet music to the parts of various musical instruments; the fine arts and crafts.

In the fine arts subsection an effort has been made to identify the terms for elements of style, rather than to cover styles themselves. The equipment used in everything from painting and sculpting to relief arts and stained glass are also illustrated and their parts labeled. The crafts subsection covers decorative stitching, knitting and weaving, and also includes the terms used to identify a sewing pattern.

Cartooning has a subsection all to itself. Here, for the first time, the reader will be able to identify everything from the beads of fear on a comic character (plewds) to the meaning of double XX's on a cartoon bottle (boozex). In addition the reader will henceforth be able to recognize the difference between a thought balloon, a speech balloon and an idea balloon in a cartoon panel.

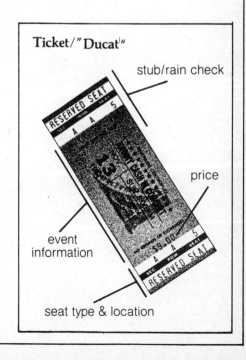

Ticket/"Ducat"

stub/rain check

price

event information

seat type & location

Stage

Also found on many stages are *tormentors,* or *legs* which frame the stage to narrow the acting area, a *trapdoor,* or *scruto,* an *elevator,* and a fabric backdrop, or *scrim.* Everything used on stages, or *boards,* are *props,* or *properties.* The arrangement of scenery, furniture and properties is called a set.

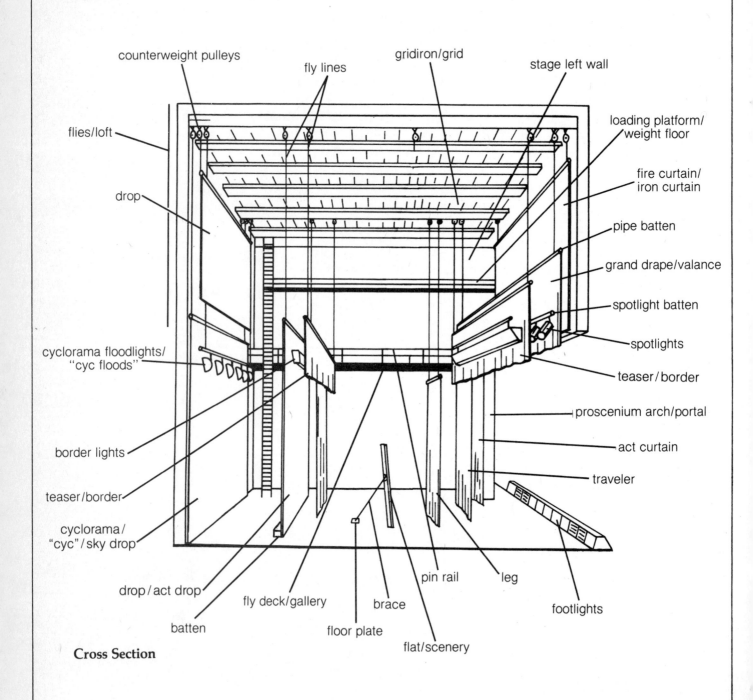

counterweight pulleys

fly lines

gridiron/grid

stage left wall

flies/loft

loading platform/weight floor

fire curtain/iron curtain

drop

pipe batten

grand drape/valance

spotlight batten

spotlights

cyclorama floodlights/"cyc floods"

teaser/border

proscenium arch/portal

border lights

act curtain

teaser/border

traveler

cyclorama/"cyc"/sky drop

pin rail

leg

footlights

drop/act drop

fly deck/gallery

brace

batten

floor plate

flat/scenery

Cross Section

In a *performance hall*, the orchestra sits in a sunken *orchestra pit* between the audience and the stage. For some shows a *runway*, or *ramp*, extends from the stage into the *center aisle*. The seating area above the orchestra is the *balcony*. In theaters with more than one balcony, the lowest one is the *mezzanine*, the front section of which is the loge.

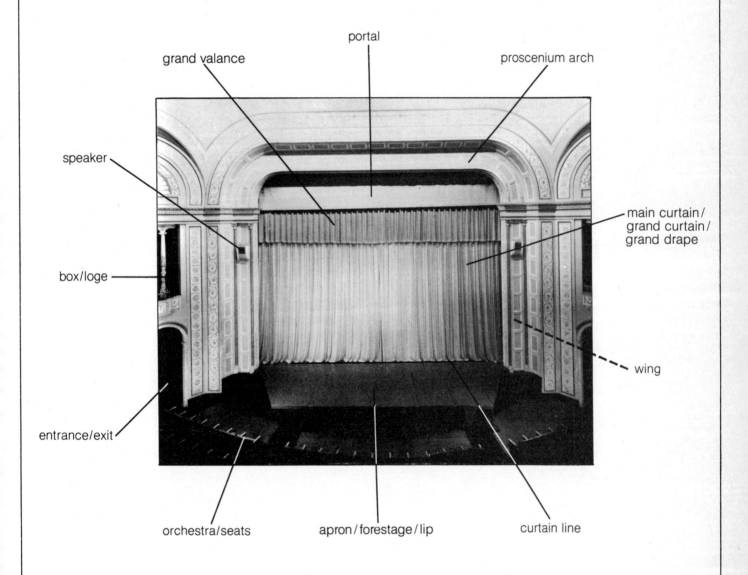

portal

grand valance

proscenium arch

speaker

main curtain/
grand curtain/
grand drape

box/loge

wing

entrance/exit

orchestra/seats

apron/forestage/lip

curtain line

Sheet Music Notations

Words to be sung, or *lyrics,* appear below the staff on sheet music. The notation ' is a *breath mark* indicating that the singer or musician should briefly pause. A combination of tones that blend harmoniously is a *chord.* Sharps, flats and naturals appearing directly in front of specific notes are called *accidentals.* A *quasihemidemisemiquaver* is a 128th note.

Lines and Spaces/Staff Degrees

Note

Orchestra

In symphony orchestras, string, woodwind and brass parts are performed by many *musicians.* In *chamber music ensembles,* each part is usually played by a single *player. Bands* do not normally include stringed instruments. *Marching bands* generally use no oboes or bassoons, and flutes are replaced with piccolos or *fifes. Dance bands* and *jazz bands* are loosely structured.

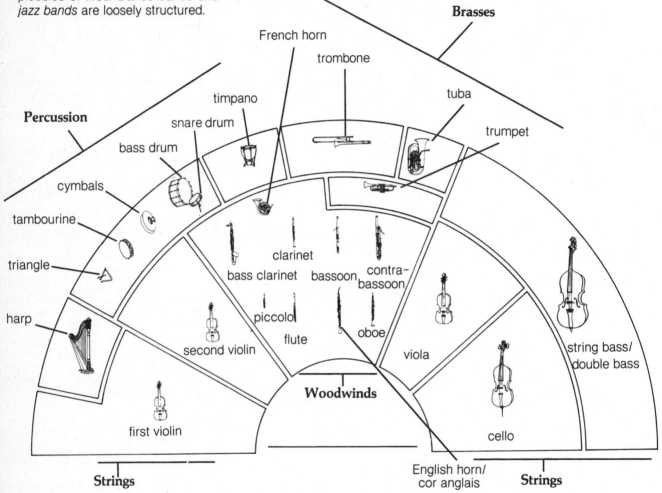

Brasses

French horn

trombone

tuba

Percussion

timpano

snare drum

trumpet

bass drum

cymbals

tambourine

clarinet

bass clarinet

bassoon

contra-bassoon

triangle

piccolo

oboe

harp

flute

viola

second violin

Woodwinds

string bass/double bass

first violin

cello

English horn/cor anglais

Strings

Strings

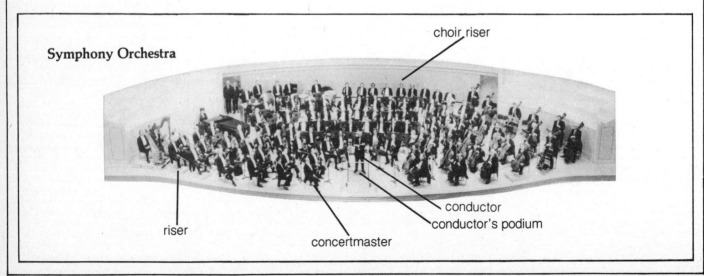

Symphony Orchestra

choir riser

conductor

conductor's podium

riser

concertmaster

Violin

Stringed instruments produce tones when a bow is drawn across the strings (*arco*) or they are finger-plucked (*pizzicato*). The sympathetic vibration produced between the instrument's belly and *back* adds *resonance* and *volume* to the sound.

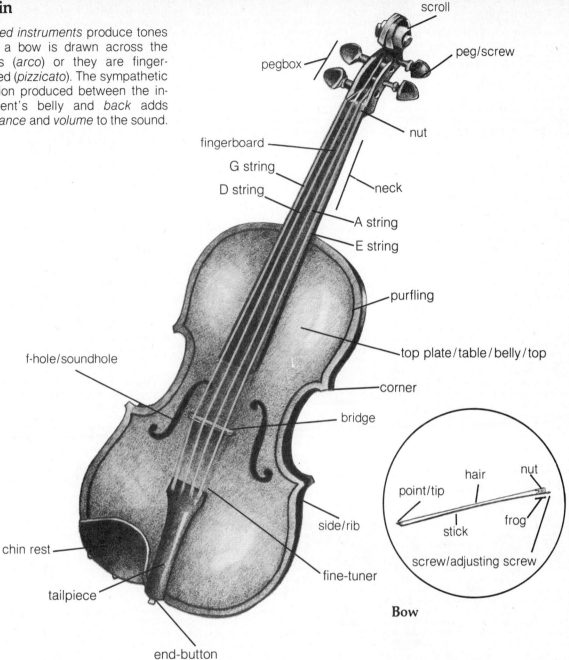

scroll

peg/screw

pegbox

nut

fingerboard

G string

D string

neck

A string

E string

purfling

top plate / table / belly / top

corner

f-hole/soundhole

bridge

point/tip

hair

nut

side/rib

stick

frog

chin rest

fine-tuner

screw/adjusting screw

tailpiece

Bow

end-button

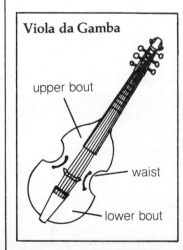

Viola da Gamba

upper bout

waist

lower bout

Cello / Violoncello

endpin

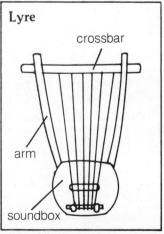

Lyre

crossbar

arm

soundbox

Double Bass/Bass/ Bass Fiddle

E string

A string

D string

G string

Music

Woodwinds

Woodwinds produce *tones* by the vibration of one or two reeds of pliant cane in the mouthpiece or by the passing of air across a blow hole.

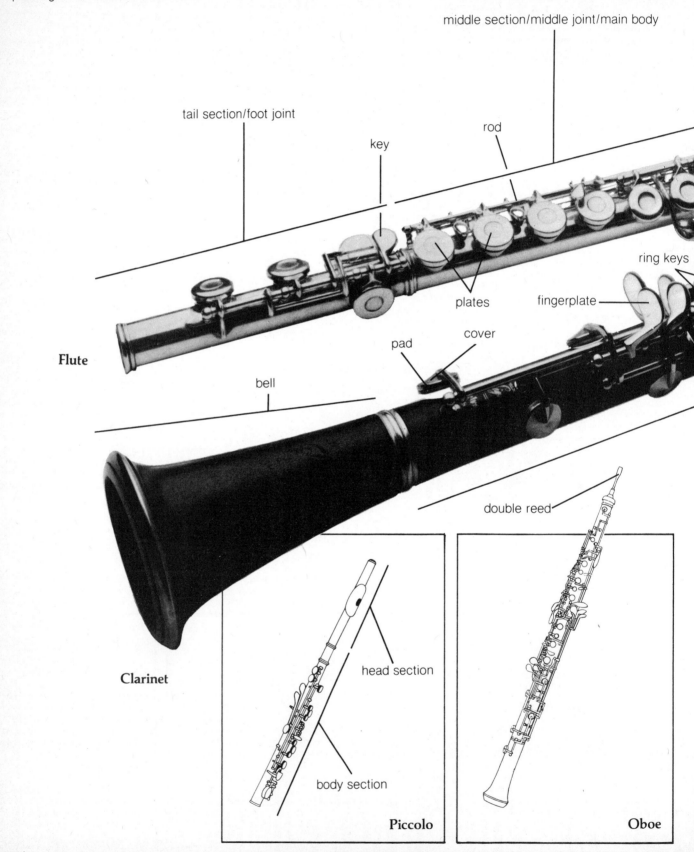

middle section/middle joint/main body

tail section/foot joint

rod

key

ring keys

fingerplate

plates

pad

cover

Flute

bell

double reed

Clarinet

head section

body section

Piccolo

Oboe

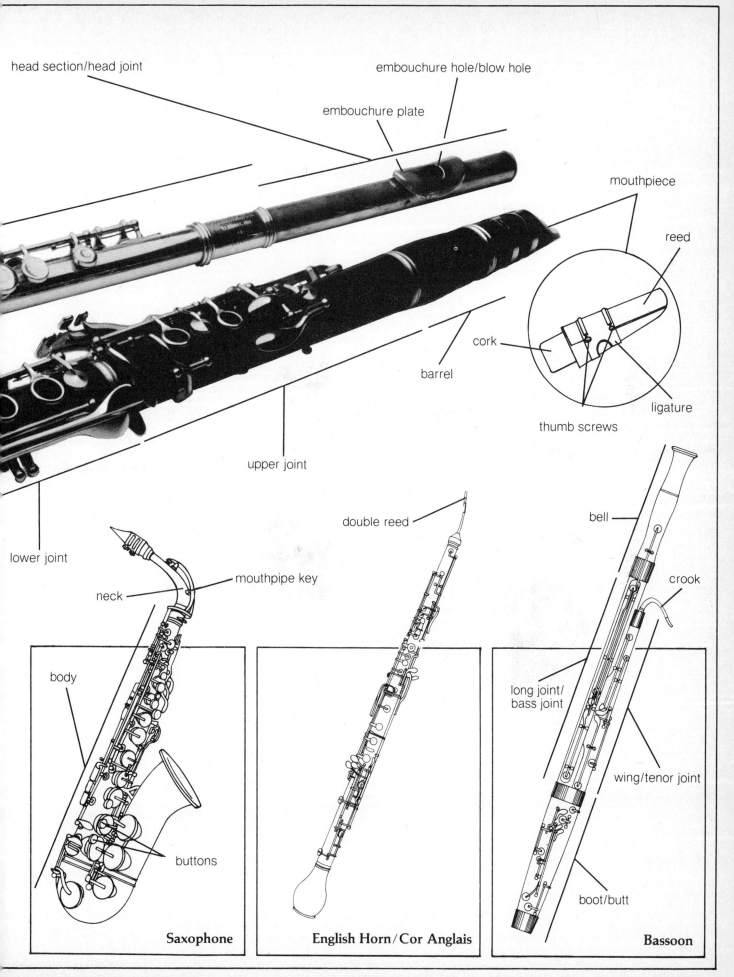

head section/head joint

embouchure hole/blow hole

embouchure plate

mouthpiece

reed

cork

barrel

ligature

thumb screws

upper joint

lower joint

double reed

bell

crook

neck

mouthpipe key

body

long joint/
bass joint

wing/tenor joint

buttons

boot/butt

Saxophone

English Horn/Cor Anglais

Bassoon

Music

Brasses

Brasses are *wind instruments* that produce *tones* when lips are buzzed against the mouthpiece. The range of brass instruments is increased by added lengths of tubing called *crooks* or *shanks*.

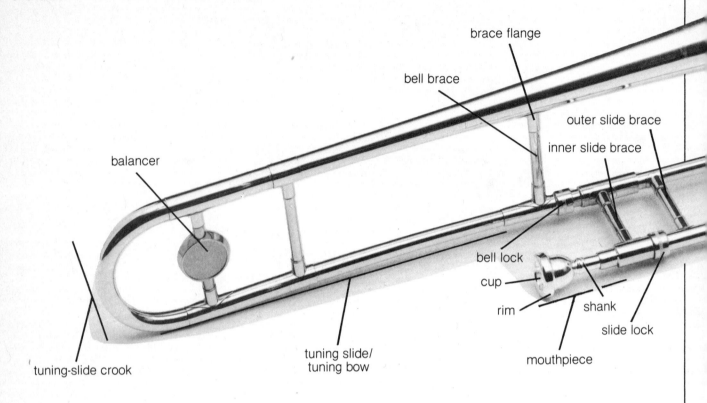

brace flange

bell brace

outer slide brace

inner slide brace

balancer

bell lock

cup

rim

shank

slide lock

mouthpiece

tuning slide/
tuning bow

tuning-slide crook

Trombone

Sousaphone

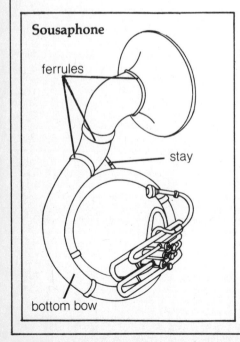

ferrules

stay

bottom bow

Tuba

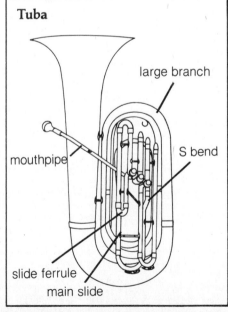

large branch

mouthpipe

S bend

slide ferrule

main slide

French Horn

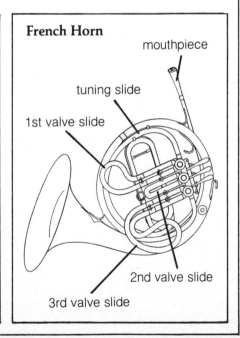

mouthpiece

tuning slide

1st valve slide

2nd valve slide

3rd valve slide

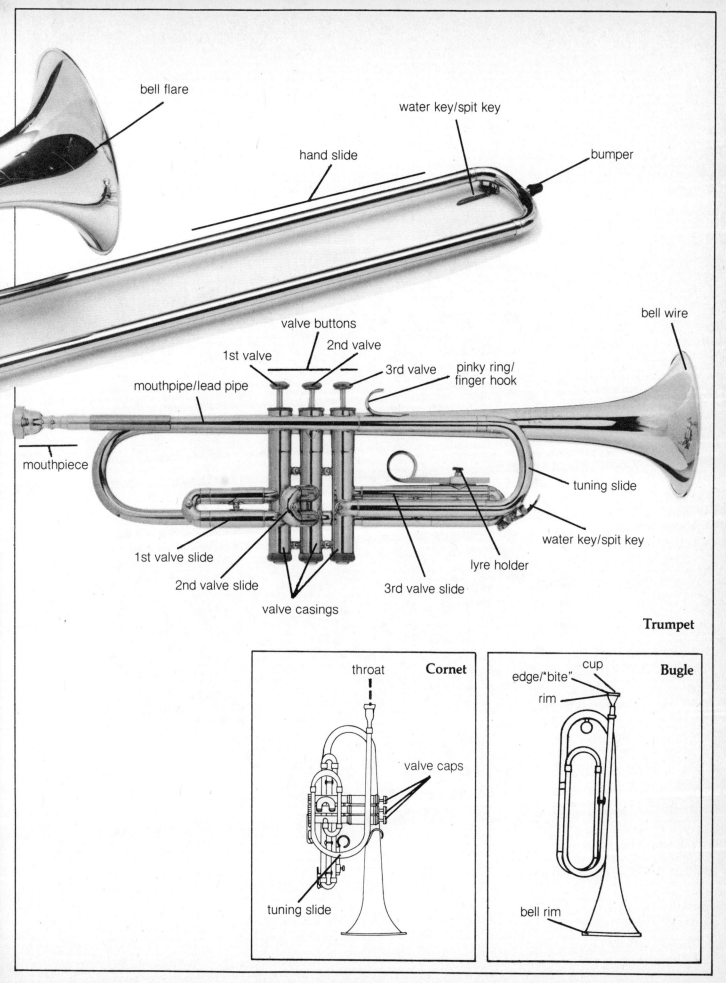

bell flare

water key/spit key

hand slide

bumper

bell wire

valve buttons

2nd valve

1st valve

3rd valve

pinky ring/
finger hook

mouthpipe/lead pipe

mouthpiece

tuning slide

water key/spit key

1st valve slide

lyre holder

2nd valve slide

3rd valve slide

valve casings

Trumpet

throat

Cornet

cup

edge/"bite"

Bugle

rim

valve caps

tuning slide

bell rim

Organ

The keyboards, or *manuals*, and pedal board, contained in a *console* or *keydesk*, as shown here, together with a number of *organ pipes,* separate from the console, comprise a pipe organ. Music is produced when air, sent into a *wind chest* by *bellows*, is directed into a selection of the organ's many pipes. An *electric organ* produces tones mechanically; an *electronic organ* uses integrated circuits and speakers to make *sounds*.

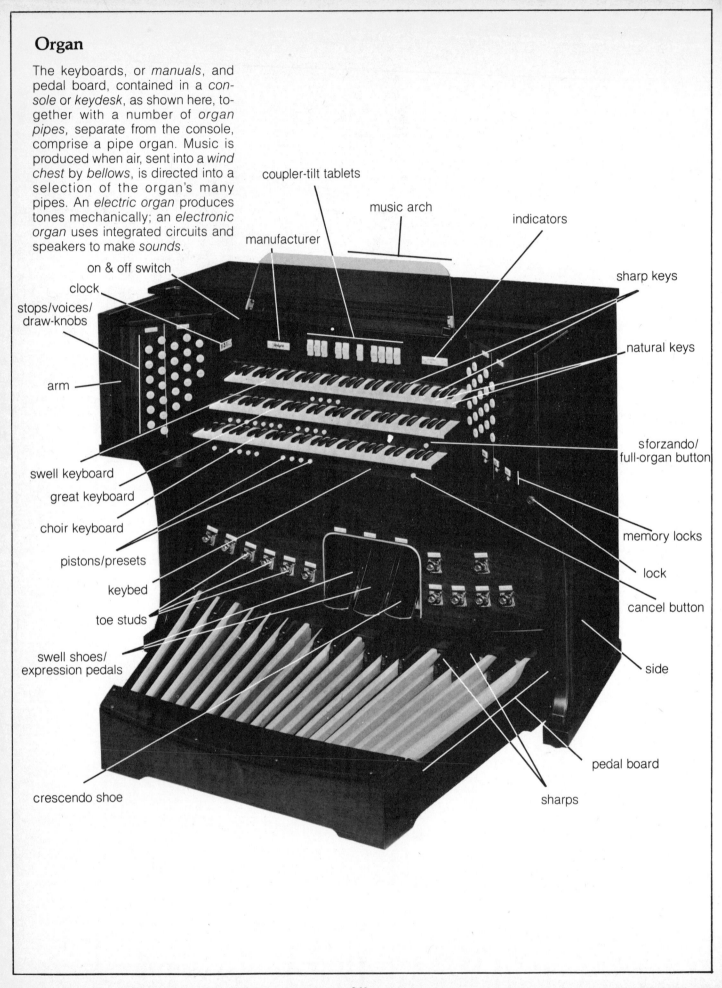

coupler-tilt tablets

music arch

indicators

manufacturer

on & off switch

clock

stops/voices/draw-knobs

sharp keys

natural keys

arm

sforzando/full-organ button

swell keyboard

great keyboard

choir keyboard

memory locks

pistons/presets

lock

keybed

toe studs

cancel button

swell shoes/expression pedals

side

crescendo shoe

sharps

pedal board

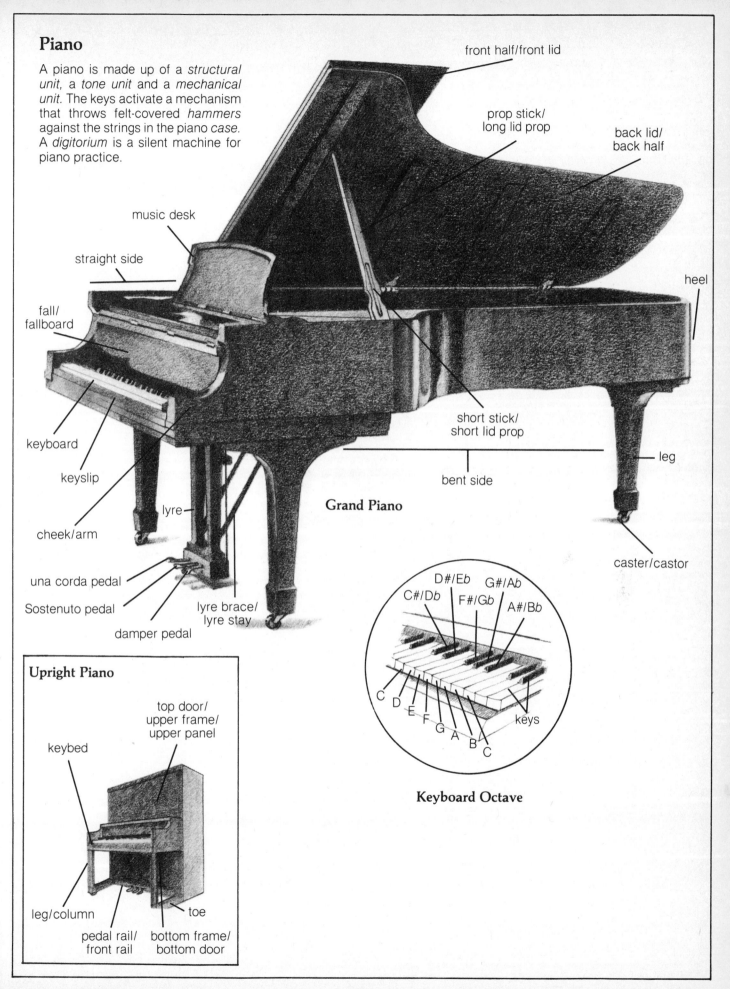

Piano

A piano is made up of a *structural unit*, a *tone unit* and a *mechanical unit*. The keys activate a mechanism that throws felt-covered *hammers* against the strings in the piano *case*. A *digitorium* is a silent machine for piano practice.

front half/front lid

prop stick/
long lid prop

back lid/
back half

heel

music desk

straight side

fall/
fallboard

keyboard

keyslip

cheek/arm

lyre

short stick/
short lid prop

bent side

Grand Piano

leg

caster/castor

una corda pedal

Sostenuto pedal

damper pedal

lyre brace/
lyre stay

C#/Db

D#/Eb

F#/Gb

G#/Ab

A#/Bb

keys

C

D

E

F

G

A

B

C

Keyboard Octave

Upright Piano

top door/
upper frame/
upper panel

keybed

leg/column

pedal rail/
front rail

toe

bottom frame/
bottom door

Guitar

These *chordophones,* or *stringed instruments,* are members of the lute family. They are played by plucking or strumming the strings with the fingers or with a stiff *plectrum* or *pick.* A movable device attached to a guitar neck, used to raise the pitch of the strings, is a *capo.* There are *sympathetic strings* inside the hollow neck of a sitar that vibrate in response to the drone or melody strings.

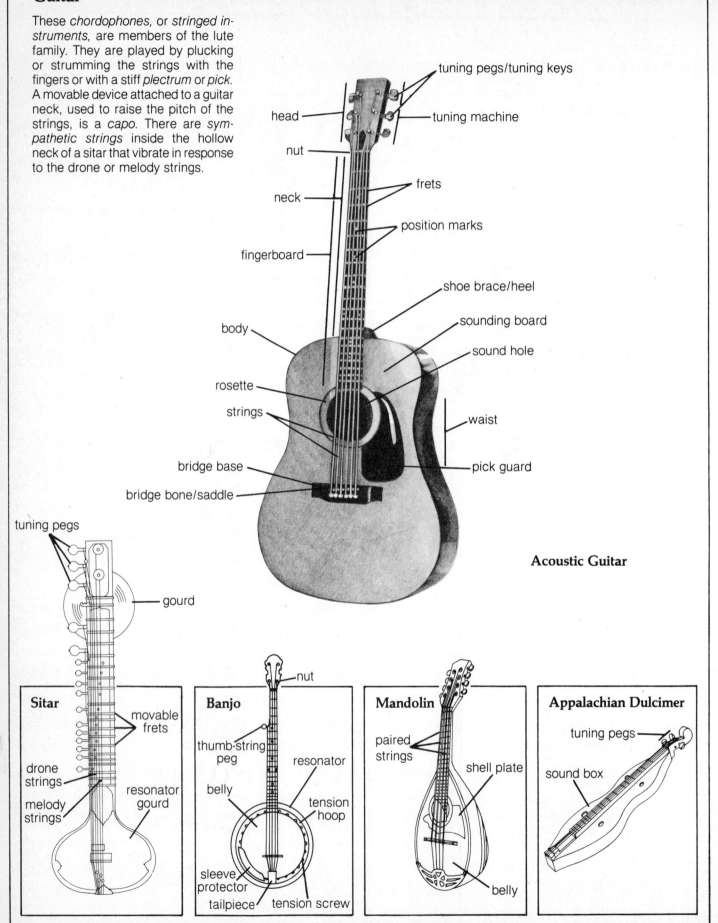

tuning pegs/tuning keys

head

tuning machine

nut

frets

neck

position marks

fingerboard

shoe brace/heel

sounding board

body

sound hole

rosette

strings

waist

bridge base

pick guard

bridge bone/saddle

Acoustic Guitar

tuning pegs

gourd

Sitar

movable frets

drone strings

melody strings

resonator gourd

Banjo

nut

thumb-string peg

resonator

belly

tension hoop

sleeve protector

tailpiece

tension screw

Mandolin

paired strings

shell plate

belly

Appalachian Dulcimer

tuning pegs

sound box

Electric Guitar and Synthesizer

The electric guitar has a *solid body* rather than the *hollow* or *semi-hollow body* of an acoustic guitar. *Special-effects pedals,* among them *fuzz, fuzz-phaser, wah-wah* and *distortion,* can be linked to the amplifier. *Pre-amplifiers,* which serve to magnify weak signals, can also be hooked up to the amplifier.

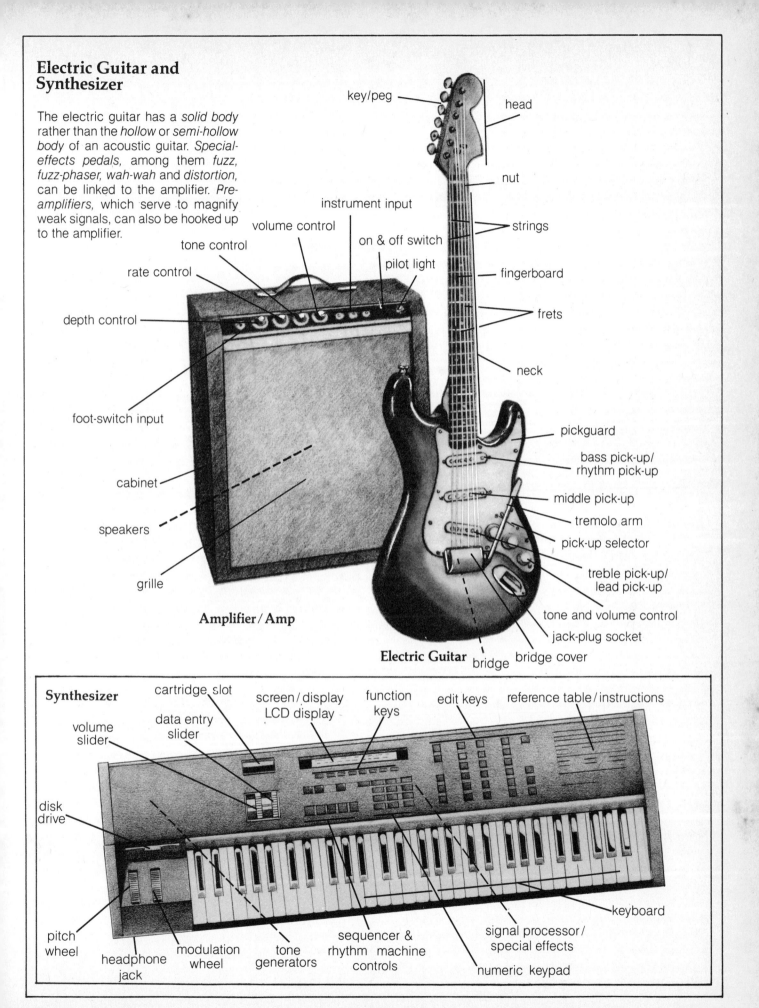

key/peg
head
nut
strings
fingerboard
frets
neck

instrument input
volume control
on & off switch
tone control
pilot light
rate control
depth control

foot-switch input

cabinet

speakers

grille

Amplifier / Amp

pickguard
bass pick-up/ rhythm pick-up
middle pick-up
tremolo arm
pick-up selector
treble pick-up/ lead pick-up
tone and volume control
jack-plug socket
bridge cover

Electric Guitar bridge

Synthesizer

cartridge slot
volume slider
data entry slider
screen/display LCD display
function keys
edit keys
reference table/instructions

disk drive

pitch wheel
headphone jack
modulation wheel
tone generators
sequencer & rhythm machine controls
signal processor/ special effects
numeric keypad
keyboard

Drums

Drums, or *membranophones*, in a *drum set* such as the one shown here, are played with *drumsticks*, *mallets* or *brushes*. A *gong* is struck with a *beater*. Adjustable metal, nylon or gut strings, called *snares*, are stretched across the bottom head, or *snare head*, of a snare drum. Timpani can be adjusted by screws or pedals to produce sounds of different pitches.

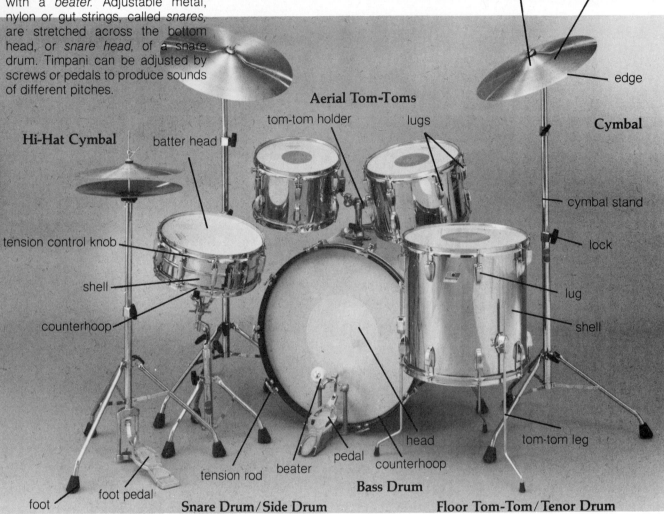

bell

bow

edge

Cymbal

cymbal stand

lock

lug

shell

tom-tom leg

Aerial Tom-Toms

tom-tom holder

lugs

Hi-Hat Cymbal

batter head

tension control knob

shell

counterhoop

foot

foot pedal

tension rod

beater

pedal

Bass Drum

head

counterhoop

Snare Drum/Side Drum

Floor Tom-Tom/Tenor Drum

Bongos

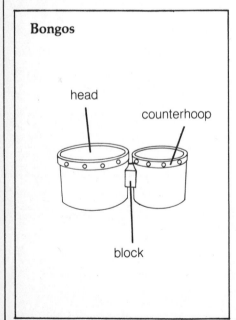

head

counterhoop

block

Tambourine

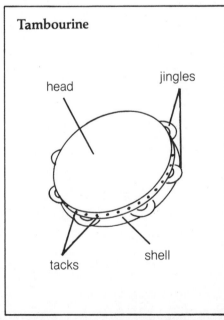

head

jingles

tacks

shell

Kettledrum/Timpano

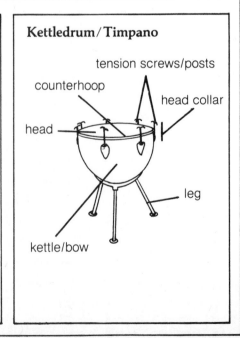

tension screws/posts

counterhoop

head collar

head

leg

kettle/bow

Bagpipe

A *drone reed*, or *double-reed*, held in-side the chanter by a *tenon*, creates music when air is blown into the *pipes* by a *bagpiper* or by pumping *bellows* strapped to the *piper's* body. The melody is played on the eight *open holes* in the chanter. The *leather bag* is usually covered with a decorative *bag cover*.

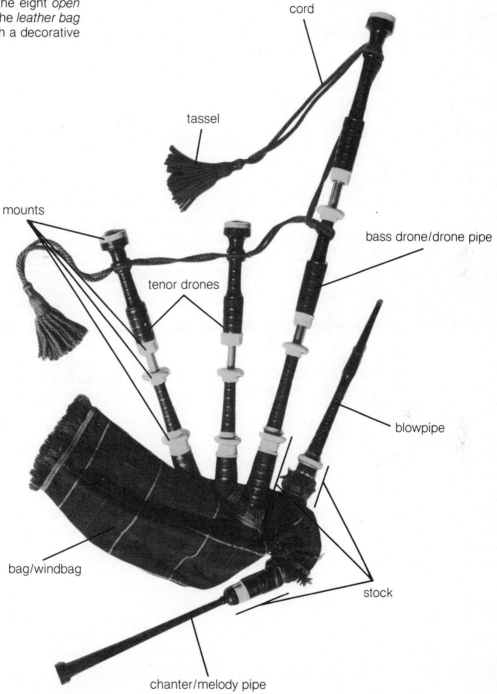

cord

tassel

mounts

tenor drones

bass drone/drone pipe

blowpipe

bag/windbag

stock

chanter/melody pipe

Folk Instruments

Like the harmonica, the accordion, or *piano-accordion,* is a *free-reed instrument.* Many accordions have *treble* and *bass register buttons* which allow the *accordionist* to change the tone of the instrument.

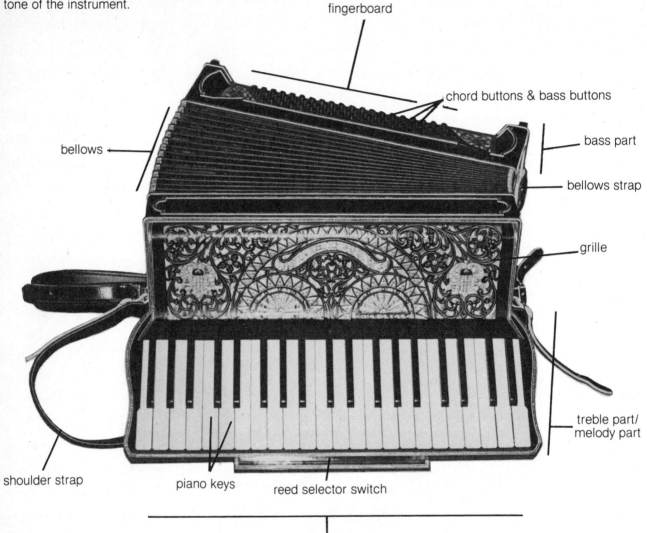

fingerboard

chord buttons & bass buttons

bass part

bellows

bellows strap

grille

treble part/ melody part

shoulder strap

piano keys

reed selector switch

keyboard

Accordion

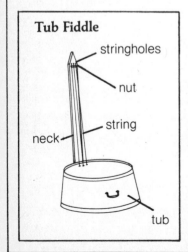

Tub Fiddle

stringholes

nut

neck

string

tub

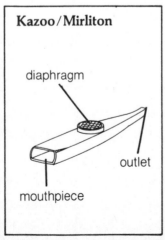

Kazoo/Mirliton

diaphragm

outlet

mouthpiece

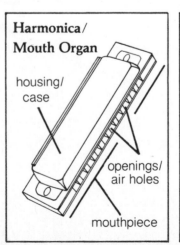

Harmonica/ Mouth Organ

housing/ case

openings/ air holes

mouthpiece

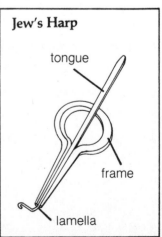

Jew's Harp

tongue

frame

lamella

Musical Accessories

A metronome, used to find the correct speed for music in beats per minute, can be spring wound or electric. A tuning fork is constructed and tempered so as to give a pure *tone* when caused to vibrate. It can be used in conjunction with a *resonance box* to amplify its sound.

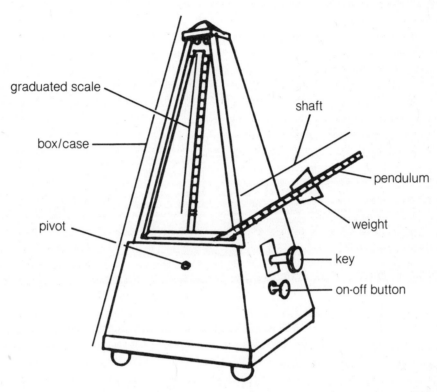

graduated scale

box/case

pivot

shaft

pendulum

weight

key

on-off button

Metronome

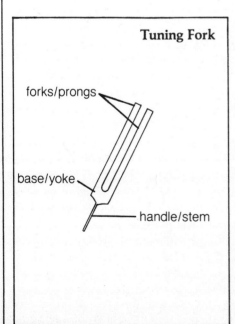

Tuning Fork

forks/prongs

base/yoke

handle/stem

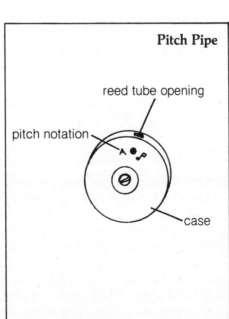

Pitch Pipe

reed tube opening

pitch notation

case

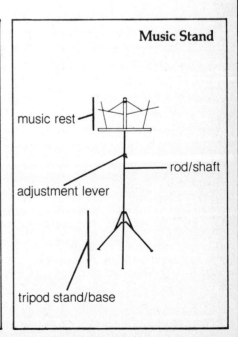

Music Stand

music rest

rod/shaft

adjustment lever

tripod stand/base

Elements of Composition

The forms of *linear perspective* illustrated here allow an artist or illustrator to show *dimension – height, width* and *depth –* on a *flat surface*. The central focus of a work of art is the *subject*. The way an artist renders a subject, which ranges from *literal rendition* to forms of *abstraction*, is called *style*.

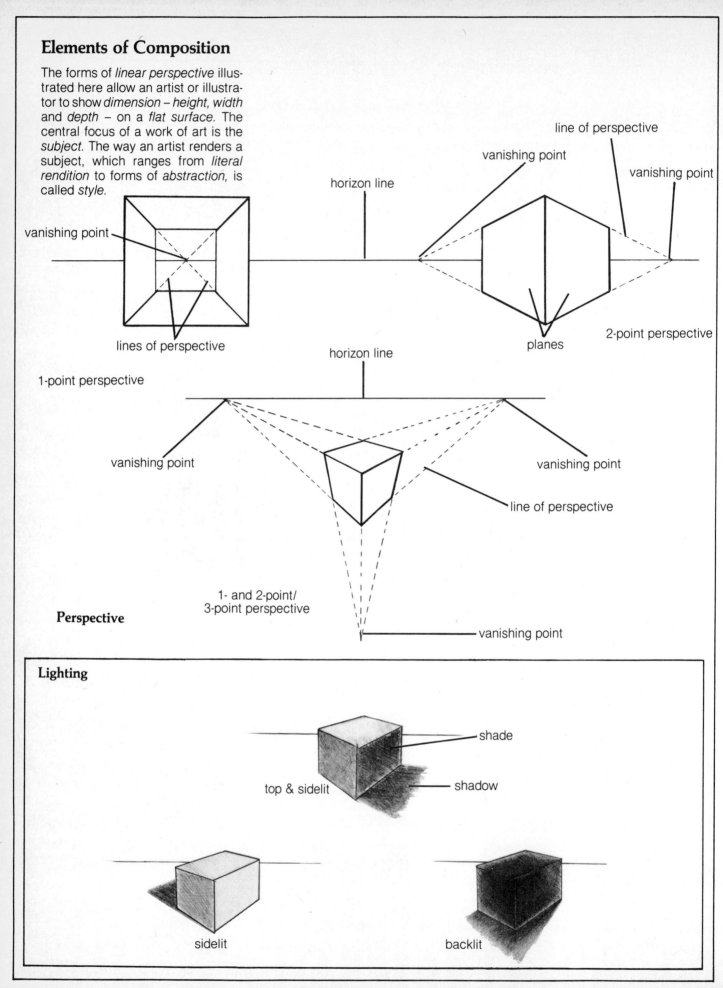

horizon line

line of perspective

vanishing point

vanishing point

vanishing point

planes

2-point perspective

vanishing point

lines of perspective

1-point perspective

horizon line

vanishing point

vanishing point

line of perspective

1- and 2-point/
3-point perspective

Perspective

vanishing point

Lighting

shade

shadow

top & sidelit

sidelit

backlit

Composition

background

light source

focal point

midground

foreground

Texture

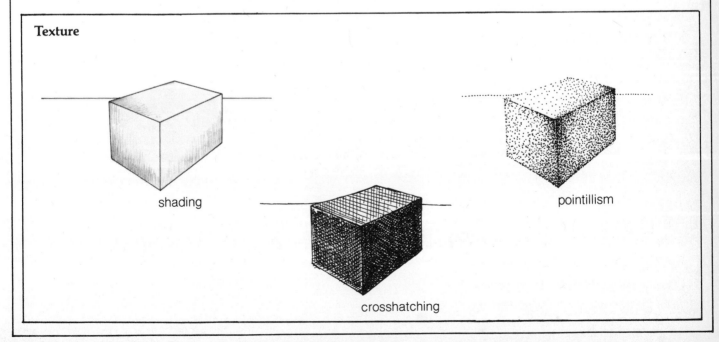

shading

crosshatching

pointillism

Painting

Before paint is applied to a *canvas* it must be drawn taut on a *stretcher* and the surface coated with *primer*, usually a substance called *gesso*. The *artist*, or *painter*, chooses a type of paint, or *medium*, in which to work, the most common of which are *tempera*, *acrylic* and *oil*. A thin blade set in a handle, used for mixing colors or applying them to a canvas, is a palette knife.

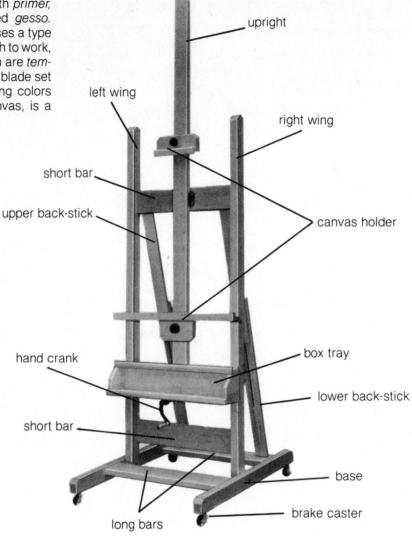

upright

left wing

right wing

short bar

upper back-stick

canvas holder

hand crank

box tray

lower back-stick

short bar

base

long bars

brake caster

Easel

Brushes

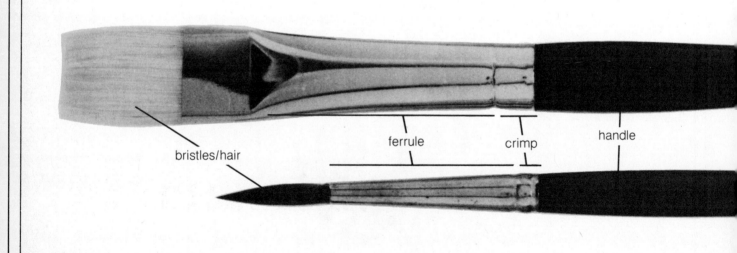

ferrule

crimp

handle

bristles/hair

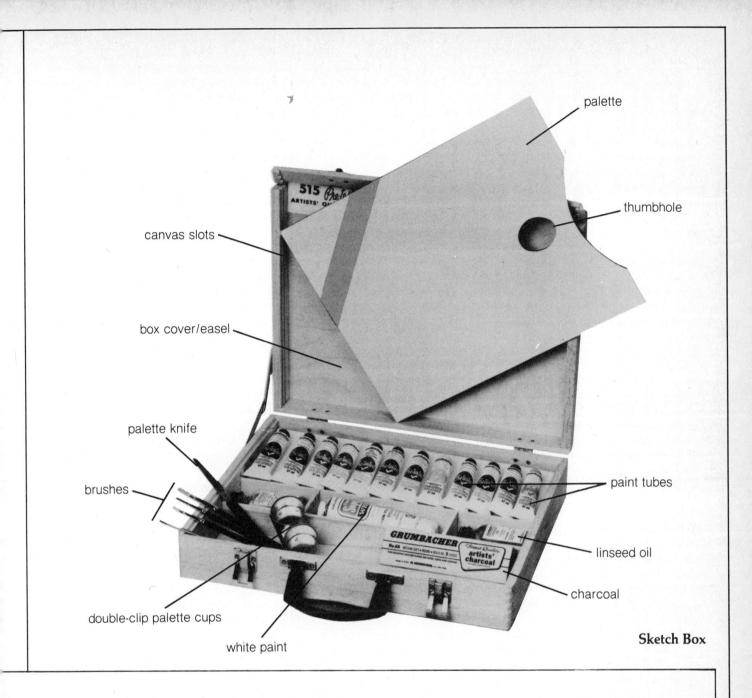

palette

thumbhole

canvas slots

box cover/easel

palette knife

brushes

paint tubes

linseed oil

charcoal

double-clip palette cups

white paint

Sketch Box

M. GRUMBACHER N.Y. 127-B U.S.A.

brush size

manufacturer

series number

M. GRUMBACHER N.Y. 977 U.S.A.

Fine Arts

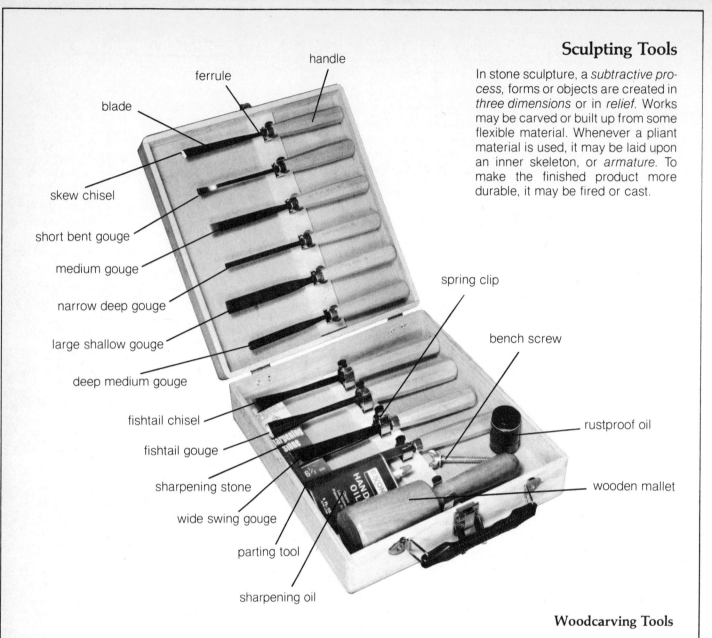

Sculpting Tools

In stone sculpture, a *subtractive process,* forms or objects are created in *three dimensions* or in *relief.* Works may be carved or built up from some flexible material. Whenever a pliant material is used, it may be laid upon an inner skeleton, or *armature.* To make the finished product more durable, it may be fired or cast.

handle

ferrule

blade

skew chisel

short bent gouge

medium gouge

narrow deep gouge

large shallow gouge

deep medium gouge

fishtail chisel

fishtail gouge

sharpening stone

wide swing gouge

parting tool

sharpening oil

spring clip

bench screw

rustproof oil

wooden mallet

Woodcarving Tools

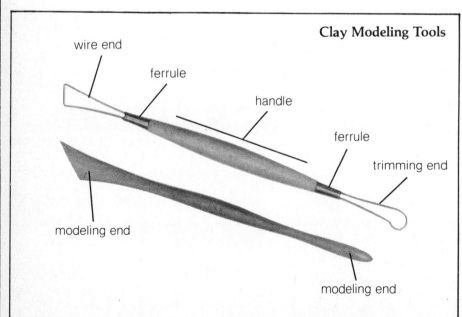

Clay Modeling Tools

wire end

ferrule

handle

ferrule

trimming end

modeling end

modeling end

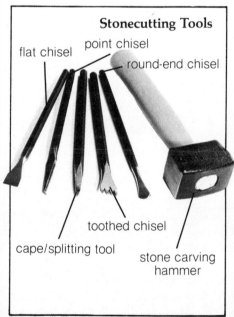

Stonecutting Tools

flat chisel

point chisel

round-end chisel

toothed chisel

cape/splitting tool

stone carving hammer

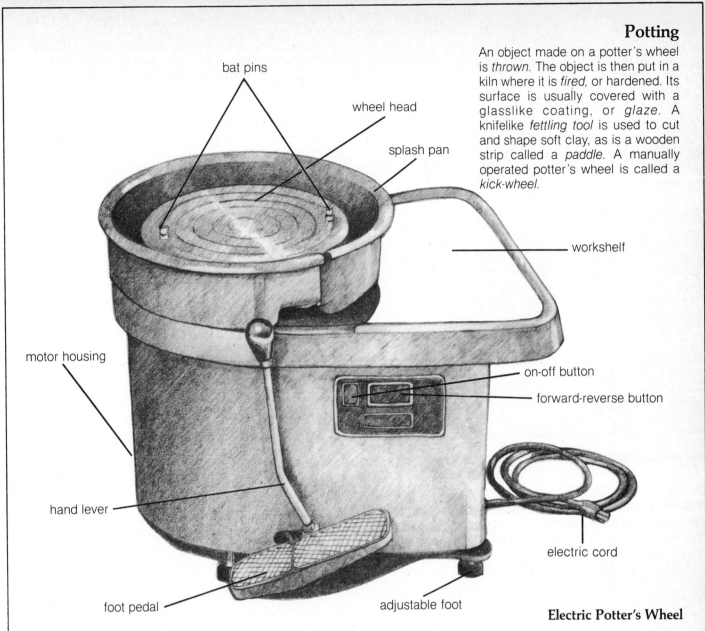

Potting

An object made on a potter's wheel is *thrown*. The object is then put in a kiln where it is *fired*, or hardened. Its surface is usually covered with a glasslike coating, or *glaze*. A knifelike *fettling tool* is used to cut and shape soft clay, as is a wooden strip called a *paddle*. A manually operated potter's wheel is called a *kick-wheel*.

bat pins

wheel head

splash pan

worksheel

motor housing

on-off button

forward-reverse button

electric cord

hand lever

foot pedal

adjustable foot

Electric Potter's Wheel

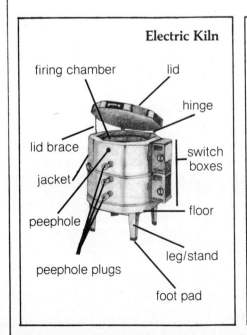

Electric Kiln

firing chamber

lid

hinge

lid brace

switch boxes

jacket

peephole

floor

leg/stand

peephole plugs

foot pad

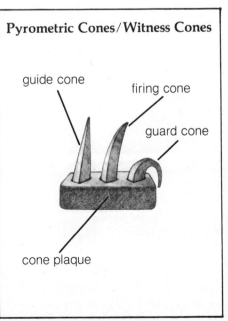

Pyrometric Cones/Witness Cones

guide cone

firing cone

guard cone

cone plaque

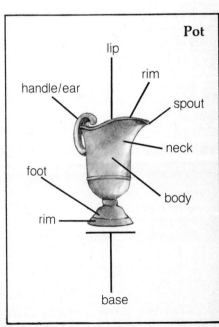

Pot

lip

rim

handle/ear

spout

neck

foot

body

rim

base

Fine Arts

Woodcut Printing

The art of making *engravings* with wooden blocks is *xylography,* and the tools used to create the designs are called *gravers.*

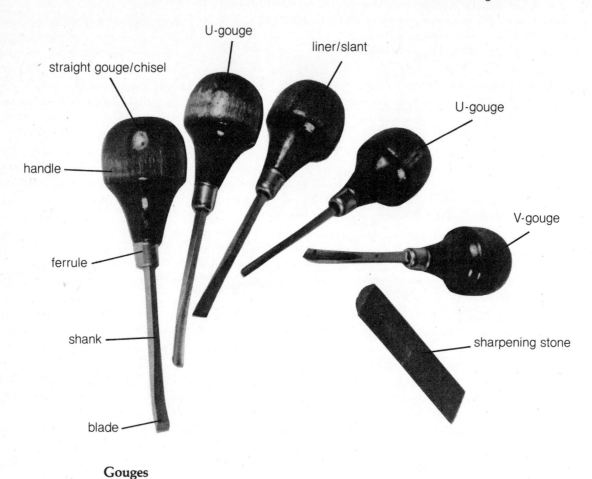

straight gouge/chisel

U-gouge

liner/slant

U-gouge

V-gouge

handle

ferrule

shank

blade

sharpening stone

Gouges

Wood Block

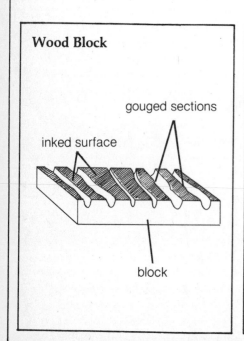

gouged sections

inked surface

block

Brayer/Roller

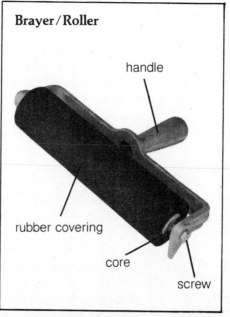

handle

rubber covering

core

screw

Baren

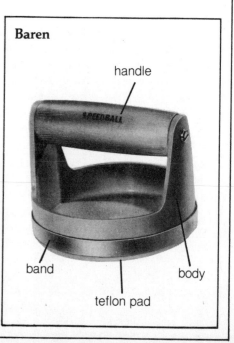

handle

band

teflon pad

body

Silk Screen and Scrimshaw

The *silk-screen printmaking process* is called *serigraphy*. A *stopping medium*, called a *resist*, blocks out or *masks* an area of the screen. Ink or paint passes through the unprotected areas of the screen to become the print. A person who does *decorative engravings* or *carvings* in *ivory* or *whalebone* is called a *scrimshander*.

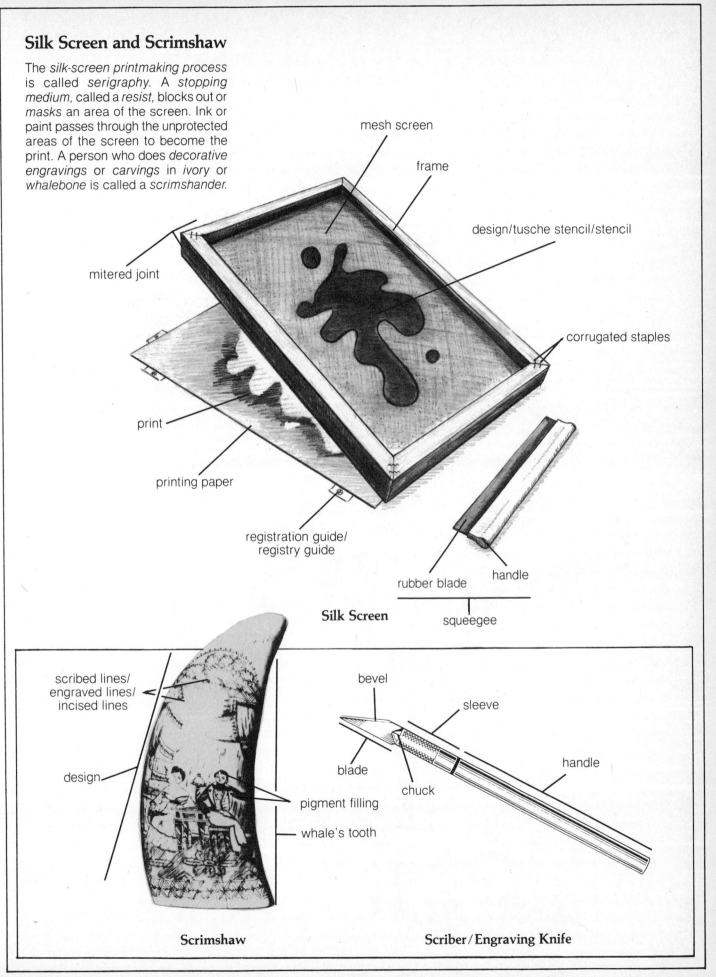

mesh screen

frame

design/tusche stencil/stencil

mitered joint

corrugated staples

print

printing paper

registration guide/
registry guide

rubber blade

handle

Silk Screen

squeegee

scribed lines/
engraved lines/
incised lines

bevel

sleeve

design

handle

blade

chuck

pigment filling

whale's tooth

Scrimshaw

Scriber/Engraving Knife

Fine Arts

Lithography

Lithography is a form of *plano-graphic printing*. The design is made on a stone, prepared, or "grained," by spinning the levigator over its surface, or on a metal *plate* with a *lithographic crayon, lithographic pencil, rubbing ink* or *asphaltum*.

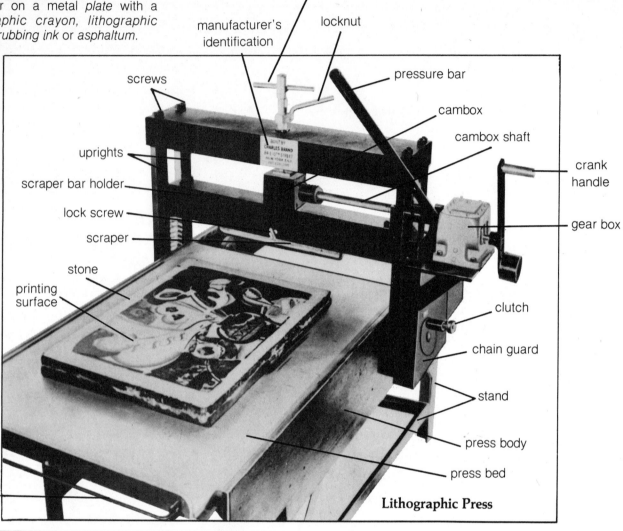

adjustment screw

manufacturer's identification

locknut

pressure bar

cambox

cambox shaft

crank handle

gear box

screws

uprights

scraper bar holder

lock screw

scraper

stone

printing surface

clutch

chain guard

stand

press body

press bed

bed handle

Lithographic Press

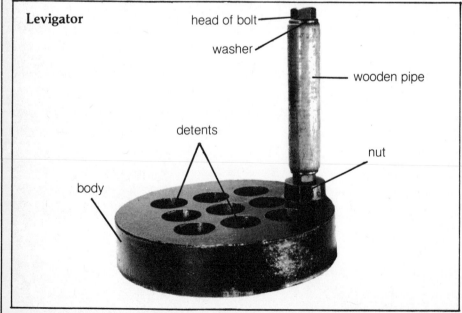

Levigator

head of bolt

washer

wooden pipe

detents

nut

body

Intaglio and Etching

Intaglio, or *incised printing,* is a type of *printmaking* in which a design is cut into a *plate* by techniques such as etching, *engraving, soft ground* or *aquatint.* A person who engraves metal is called a *chaser.*

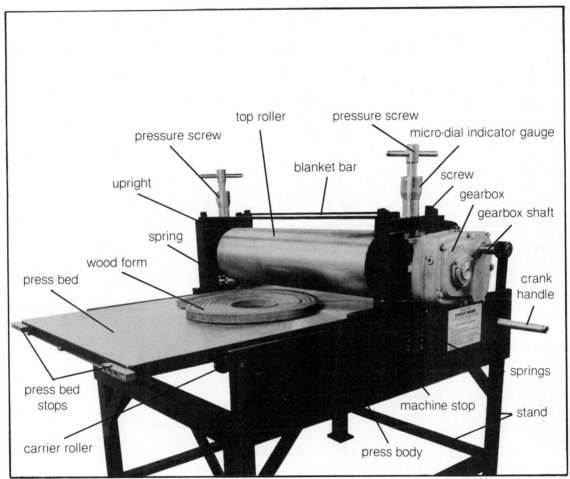

top roller

pressure screw

pressure screw

micro-dial indicator gauge

blanket bar

screw

upright

gearbox

gearbox shaft

spring

wood form

press bed

crank handle

press bed stops

springs

machine stop

stand

carrier roller

press body

Etching Press

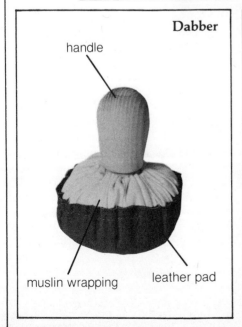

Dabber

handle

muslin wrapping

leather pad

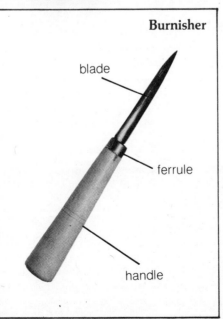

Burnisher

blade

ferrule

handle

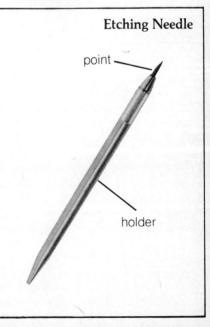

Etching Needle

point

holder

Fine Arts

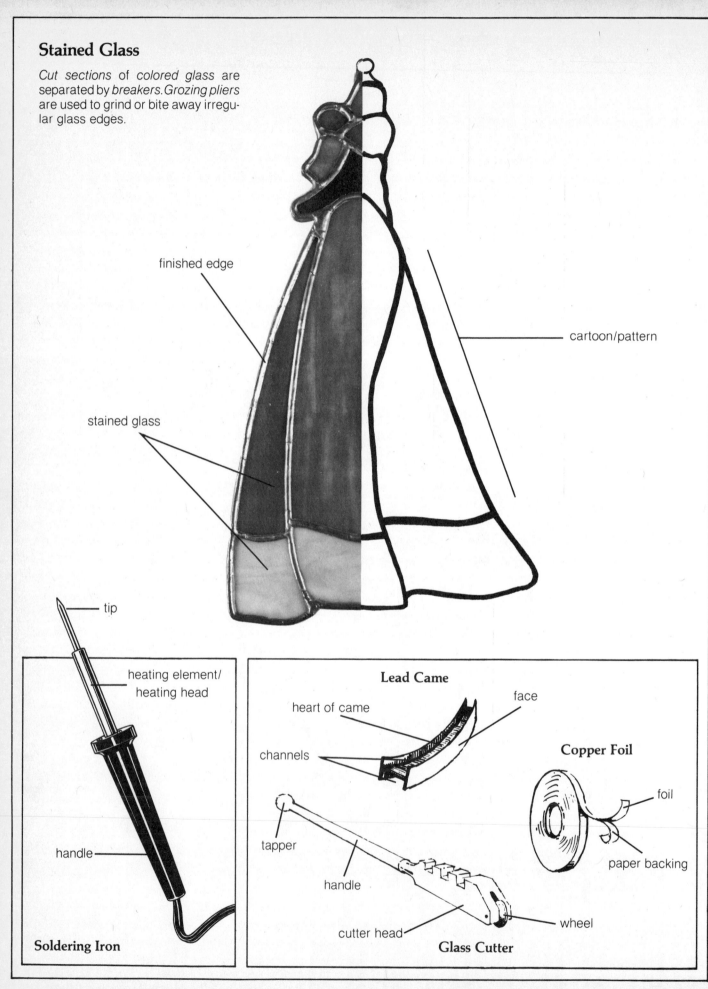

Stained Glass

Cut sections of *colored glass* are separated by *breakers. Grozing pliers* are used to grind or bite away irregular glass edges.

finished edge

cartoon/pattern

stained glass

tip

heating element/
heating head

Lead Came

heart of came

face

channels

Copper Foil

handle

foil

tapper

paper backing

Soldering Iron

handle

cutter head

wheel

Glass Cutter

Frame

The frame shown here is a long-lasting *archival frame*. The area cut out of the mat to reveal the artwork is the *mat window*. A wire hanger can be attached to L-shaped *shoulder hooks*, *picture hooks* or *nails* as well as to screw eyes. The process of permanently affixing artwork to a backing is called *mounting*. A *free-standing easel-back* or *piano frame* consists of an easel, backing and an angled support *stand*. In *passe-partout*, the framing elements are held together by strips of cloth or paper pasted over the edges.

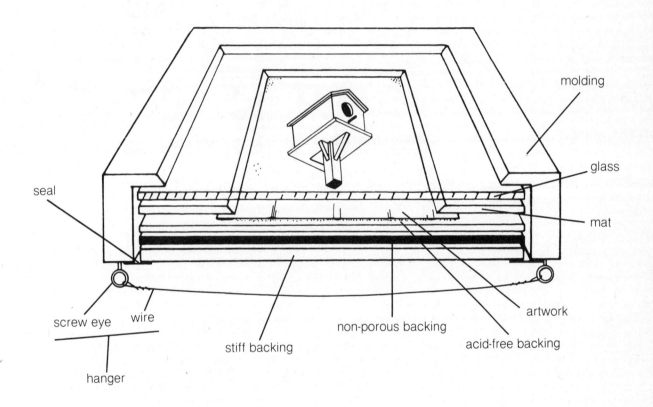

molding

glass

mat

seal

screw eye

wire

hanger

stiff backing

non-porous backing

artwork

acid-free backing

Cartooning

Many one-panel cartoons use *captions* or *labels* below the *illustration* for dialogue or explanation. Those appearing on the editorial pages of newspapers are called *editorial* or *political cartoons* and usually feature an exaggerated likeness, or *caricature,* of some well-known figure, as the main *character. Comics,* or *comic books,* use cartooning throughout. A complete *sphericasia,* or *swalloop,* is used by a *cartoonist* to depict a complete swing at an object, be it a golf ball or another person.

brick symbolia

thought balloon

agitrons

onomatopoeia

dites

ROWR!

lucaflect

staggeration

hites

briffit

vites

artist's signature

cross-hatching

Comic Strip

strip title

cartoonist

by mort walker

border

cartoon panel/frame

speech balloon

DOES ANYONE KNOW WHERE I LEFT MY...MY, UH...

...WHERE I LEFT MY, UH...

...THINGAMAJIG?

Cartooning

Fireworks

Fireworks makers, *pyrotechnists*, work in concrete block buildings called *magazines. Display rockets, aerial bombs, pin wheels* or *Catherine wheels*, and *fountains* derive their explosive force from a combination of *saltpeter, sulfur* and *charcoal.* Explosive *M-80s* and *cherry bombs* are now banned.

chrysanthemums

aerial flash

titanium salute

firing smoke

Grand Finale

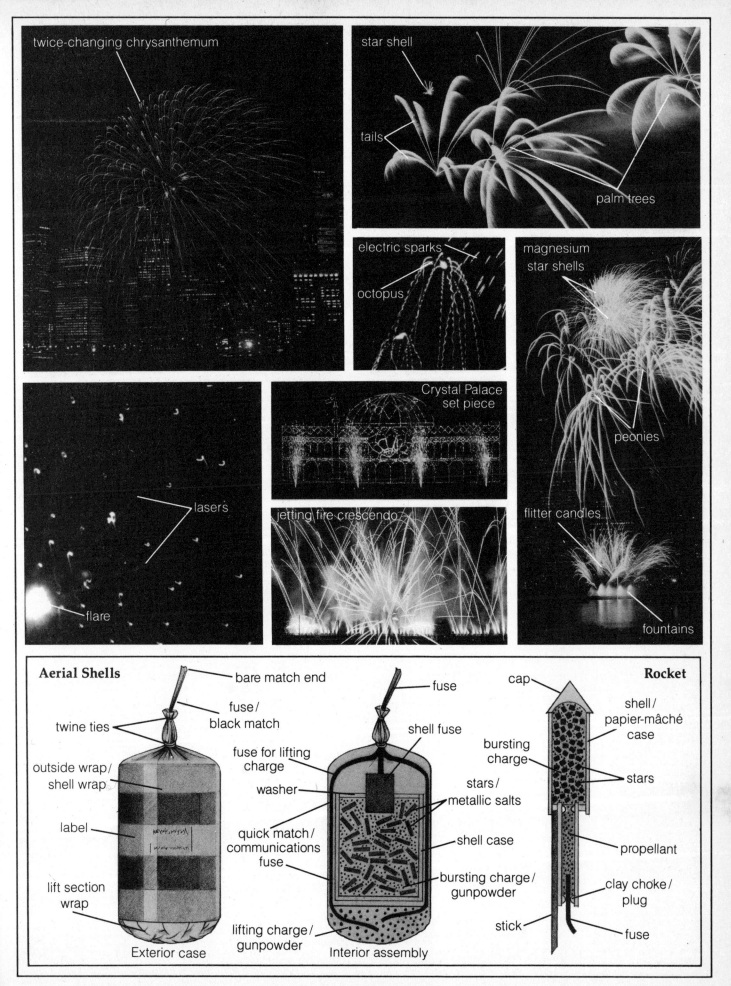

twice-changing chrysanthemum

star shell

tails

palm trees

electric sparks

octopus

magnesium star shells

Crystal Palace set piece

peonies

lasers

jetting fire crescendo

flitter candles

flare

fountains

Aerial Shells

bare match end

fuse/ black match

twine ties

fuse

shell fuse

Rocket

cap

shell/ papier-mâché case

outside wrap/ shell wrap

fuse for lifting charge

washer

bursting charge

stars

label

quick match/ communications fuse

stars/ metallic salts

shell case

propellant

lift section wrap

bursting charge/ gunpowder

clay choke/ plug

stick

fuse

lifting charge/ gunpowder

Exterior case

Interior assembly

Sewing

Each in-and-out movement of a threaded needle produces a *stitch*. A scissor's *bite* is the distance it cuts into a fabric on a single stroke. A small cushion into which pins or most-used needles are stuck until needed is called a *pincushion*.

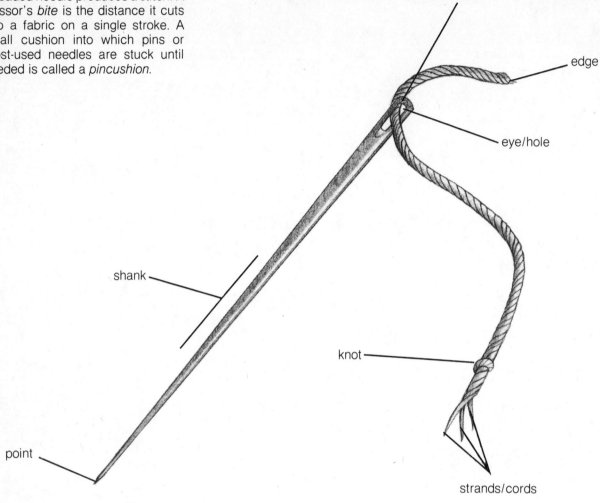

crown

edge

eye/hole

shank

knot

point

strands/cords

Needle and Thread

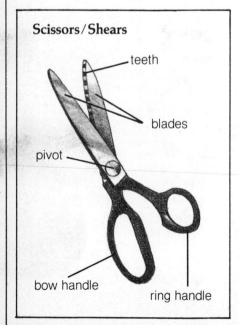

Scissors/Shears

teeth

blades

pivot

bow handle

ring handle

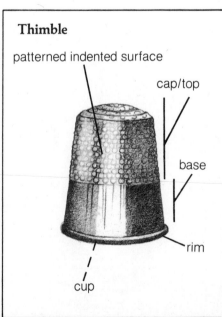

Thimble

patterned indented surface

cap/top

base

rim

cup

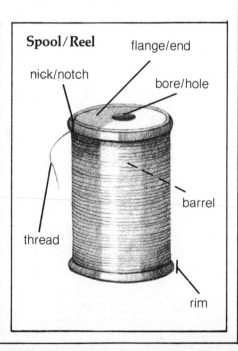

Spool/Reel

flange/end

nick/notch

bore/hole

barrel

thread

rim

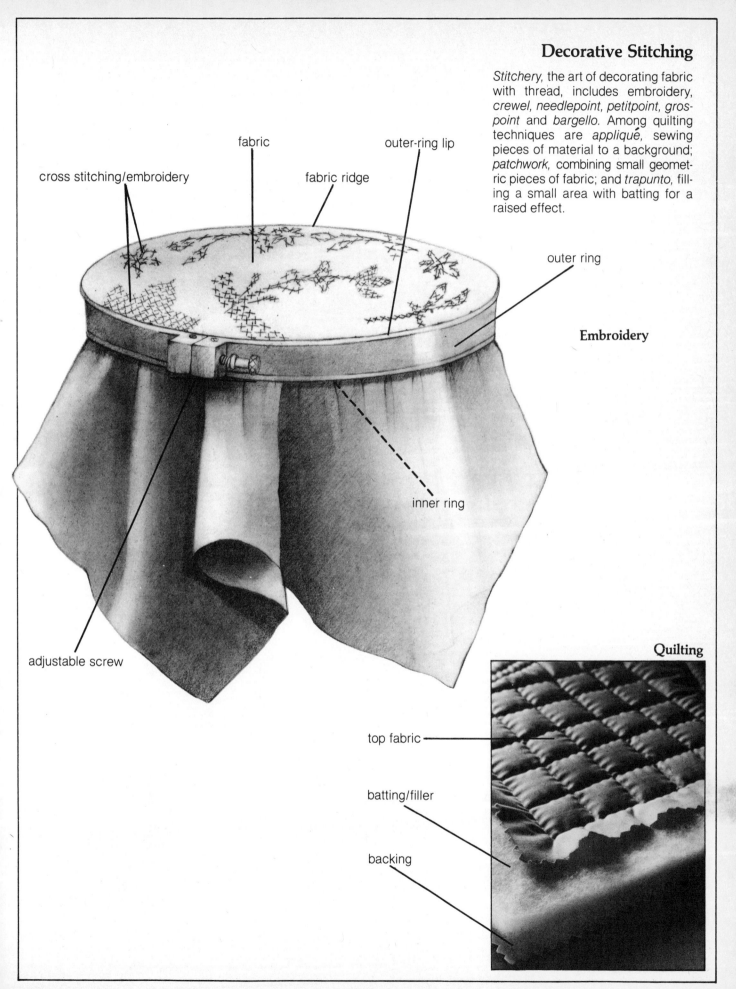

Decorative Stitching

Stitchery, the art of decorating fabric with thread, includes embroidery, *crewel, needlepoint, petitpoint, grospoint* and *bargello.* Among quilting techniques are *appliqué,* sewing pieces of material to a background; *patchwork,* combining small geometric pieces of fabric; and *trapunto,* filling a small area with batting for a raised effect.

cross stitching/embroidery

fabric

fabric ridge

outer-ring lip

outer ring

Embroidery

inner ring

adjustable screw

Quilting

top fabric

batting/filler

backing

Crafts

Knitting

Knitting is the interlacing of *loops*. The main stitches are the *knit stitch*, or *stitch*, and the *purl stitch*, or *purl*. *Crocheting* is a form of *needlework* done by looping thread with a *crochet needle*. *Macrame* is knotting, and *tatting* is done by looping and knotting with a single cotton thread and a small shuttle.

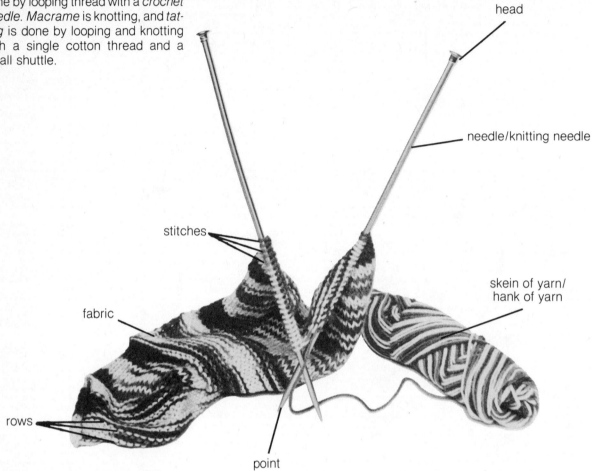

head

needle/knitting needle

stitches

skein of yarn/
hank of yarn

fabric

rows

point

Hand Knitting

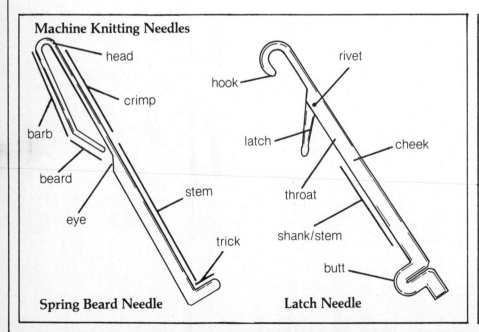

Machine Knitting Needles

head

crimp

barb

beard

eye

stem

trick

Spring Beard Needle

hook

rivet

latch

cheek

throat

shank/stem

butt

Latch Needle

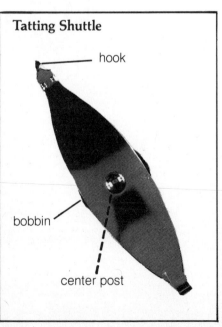

Tatting Shuttle

hook

bobbin

center post

Weaving

The lengthwise (front to back) *yarn* or *threads* on a loom are called the warp. Threads taken together which run from side to side, or from *selvage* to selvage, are called the *weft*. The weft is also often called the *woof,* although more correctly, the woof is the same as the *web,* or finished *fabric.*

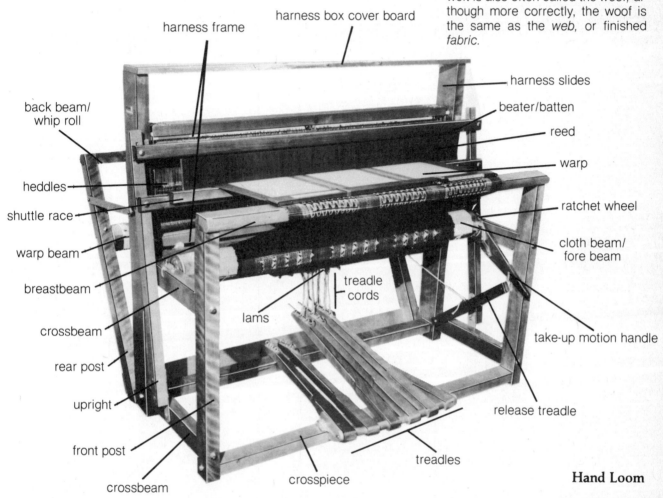

harness frame

harness box cover board

harness slides

back beam/ whip roll

beater/batten

reed

warp

heddles

ratchet wheel

shuttle race

cloth beam/ fore beam

warp beam

breastbeam

treadle cords

crossbeam

lams

take-up motion handle

rear post

upright

front post

release treadle

crossbeam

crosspiece

treadles

Hand Loom

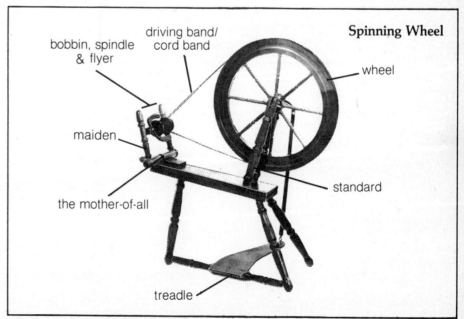

Spinning Wheel

driving band/ cord band

bobbin, spindle & flyer

wheel

maiden

the mother-of-all

standard

treadle

Sewing Pattern

A roll of fabric of a specified length is called a *bolt*. A sample of a fabric is a *swatch*. Fabrics sold at lengths specified by the customer are called *piece goods* or *yard goods*.

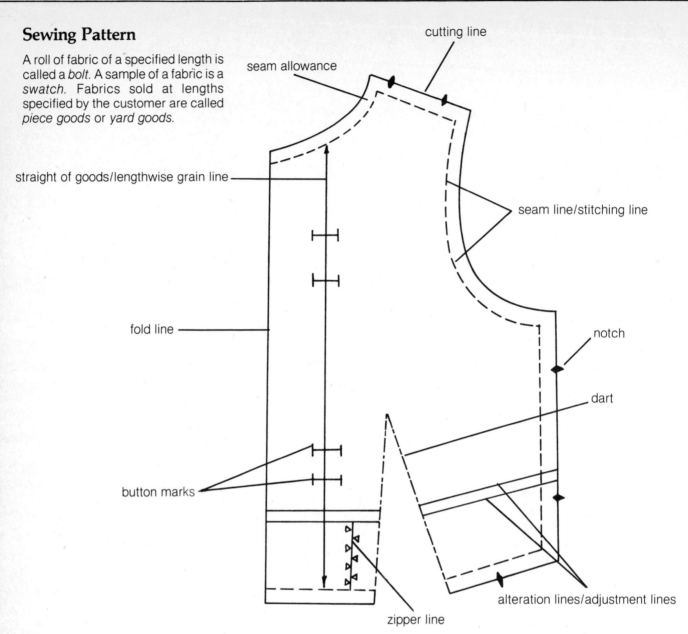

cutting line

seam allowance

seam line/stitching line

straight of goods/lengthwise grain line

fold line

notch

dart

button marks

alteration lines/adjustment lines

zipper line

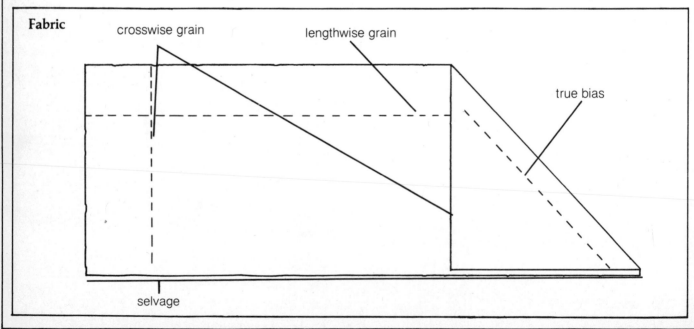

Fabric

crosswise grain

lengthwise grain

true bias

selvage

Machinery, Tools and Weapons

Except for office and industrial equipment, which is outside the scope of this book, this section covers all the man-made equipment one is likely to encounter in everyday life, daily reading or classroom learning. It includes basic power systems and offshoots, everything from a nuclear power plant to an electrical plug, equipment used to control temperature in a house, and components of various engines.

Considerable space has been devoted to illustrating the parts of tools used around the home and in the yard while not ignoring the basic gear used by ranchers, trappers, farmers, scientists and doctors. Even penal equipment used for capital punishment has been included.

The weaponry subsection traces the names and parts of articles used in warfare from medieval times to objects used today. Thus, a student reading about King Arthur for the first time will be able to identify the parts of a sword as easily as a newspaper reader is able to identify the parts of a modern missile.

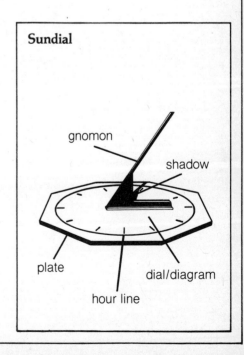

Sundial

gnomon

shadow

plate

hour line

dial/diagram

Wind Systems

The cloth sail on this *smock mill* is in a *first reef*, or *curled*, position, as opposed to *sword point*, *dagger point* or *full sail*. Sails or *shutters* on a fantail are called *vanes*. Some mills have *petticoats*, or vertical boards, below the cap, to provide protection where cap and tower meet, and *beards*, or decorated boards behind the cannister.

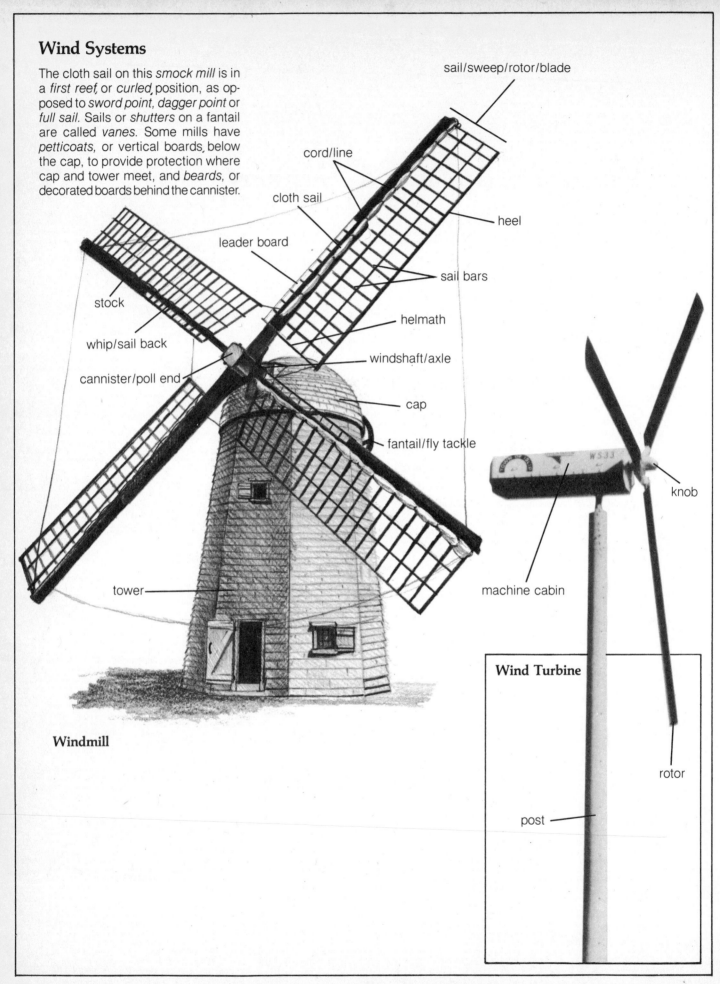

sail/sweep/rotor/blade

cord/line

cloth sail

heel

leader board

sail bars

helmath

stock

windshaft/axle

whip/sail back

cap

cannister/poll end

fantail/fly tackle

tower

knob

machine cabin

Windmill

Wind Turbine

post

rotor

Solar Power System

Solar energy can be collected by systems such as the one shown here, which operate like *radiators* working in reverse to produce hot water. The sun's energy can also be converted directly into *electricity* by *solar cells*. *Concentrating solar collectors* use *lenses* or *reflecting sufaces* to direct sunlight on a trough-type collector to produce large amounts of heat which can be converted into electricity.

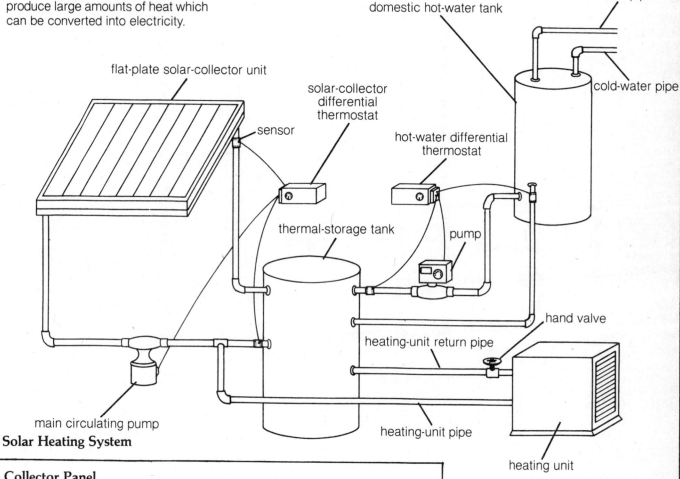

flat-plate solar-collector unit

solar-collector differential thermostat

sensor

hot-water pipe

domestic hot-water tank

cold-water pipe

hot-water differential thermostat

thermal-storage tank

pump

hand valve

heating-unit return pipe

heating-unit pipe

main circulating pump

heating unit

Solar Heating System

Collector Panel

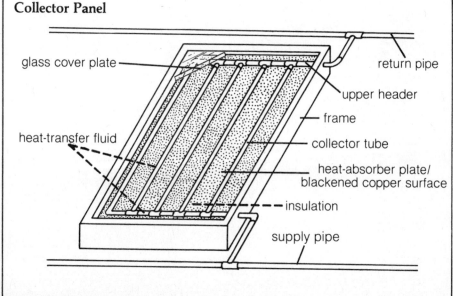

glass cover plate

heat-transfer fluid

return pipe

upper header

frame

collector tube

heat-absorber plate/ blackened copper surface

insulation

supply pipe

Power Systems

Nuclear Power Reactor

In order to generate *electricity* by using the heat produced by *fission,* the *chain reaction* must be slowed down and controlled. To control the reaction rate in a reactor, or *pile, rods* of neutron-absorbing material are moved in and out as required. The smallest amount of *fissionable material* in which fission is self-sustaining is called the *critical mass.* If more fissionable material is produced than consumed, the reactor is called a *breeder reactor.*

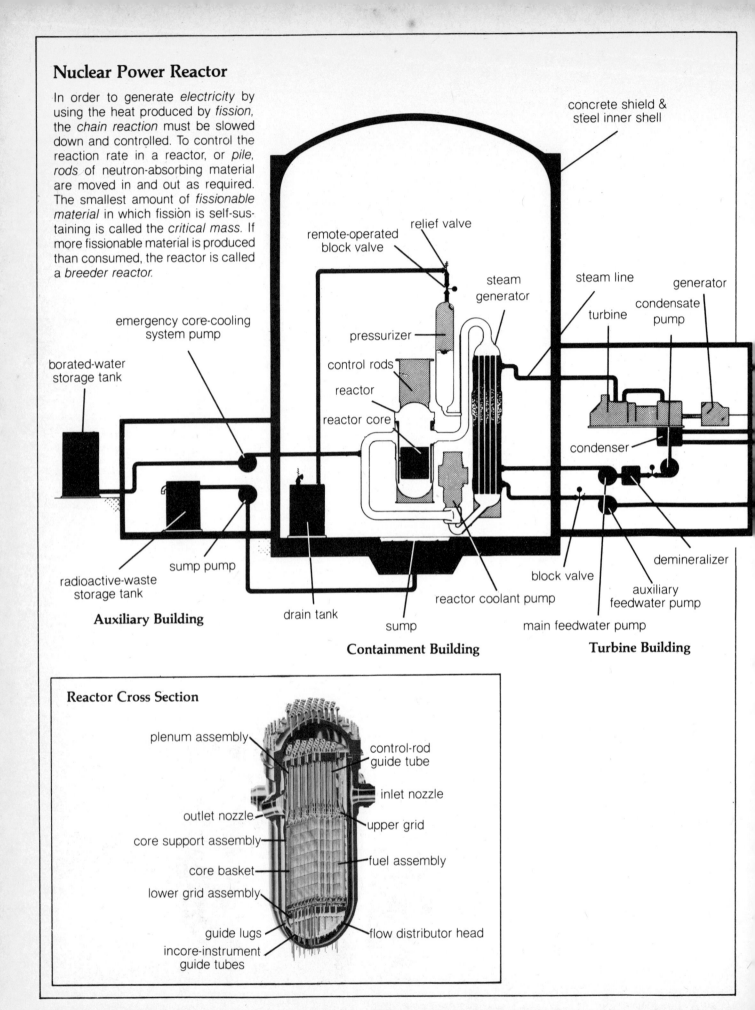

relief valve

remote-operated block valve

concrete shield & steel inner shell

steam generator

steam line

generator

turbine

condensate pump

pressurizer

control rods

reactor

reactor core

emergency core-cooling system pump

borated-water storage tank

condenser

radioactive-waste storage tank

sump pump

demineralizer

block valve

auxiliary feedwater pump

Auxiliary Building

drain tank

sump

reactor coolant pump

main feedwater pump

reactor coolant pump

Containment Building

Turbine Building

Reactor Cross Section

plenum assembly

control-rod guide tube

inlet nozzle

outlet nozzle

upper grid

core support assembly

fuel assembly

core basket

lower grid assembly

guide lugs

flow distributor head

incore-instrument guide tubes

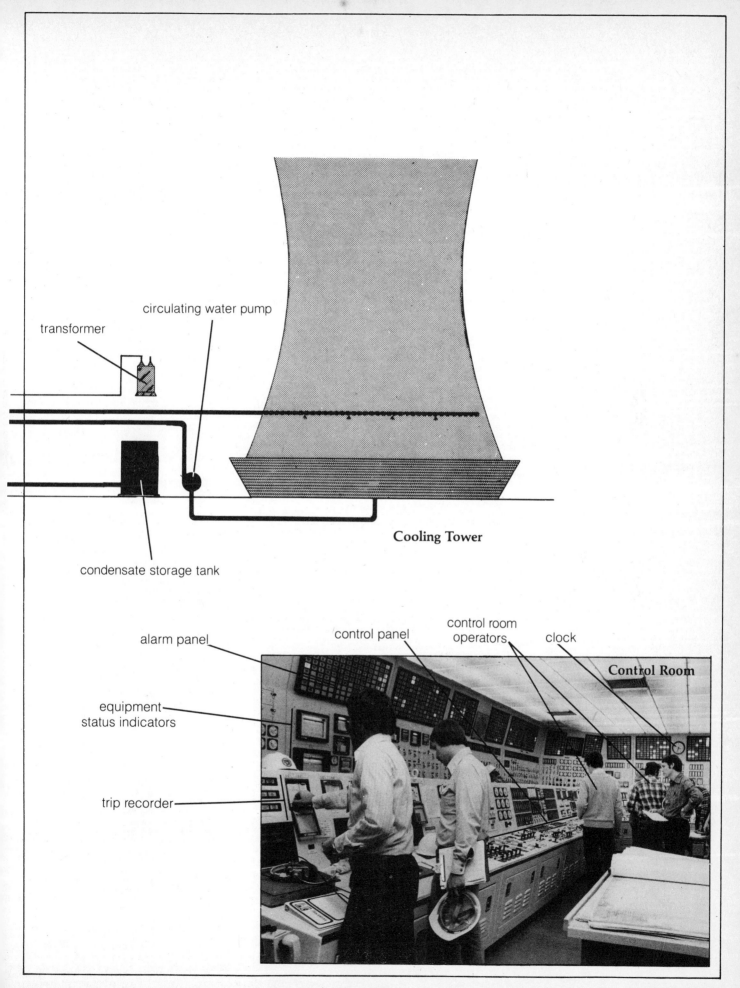

transformer

circulating water pump

condensate storage tank

Cooling Tower

alarm panel

control panel

control room operators

clock

Control Room

equipment status indicators

trip recorder

393

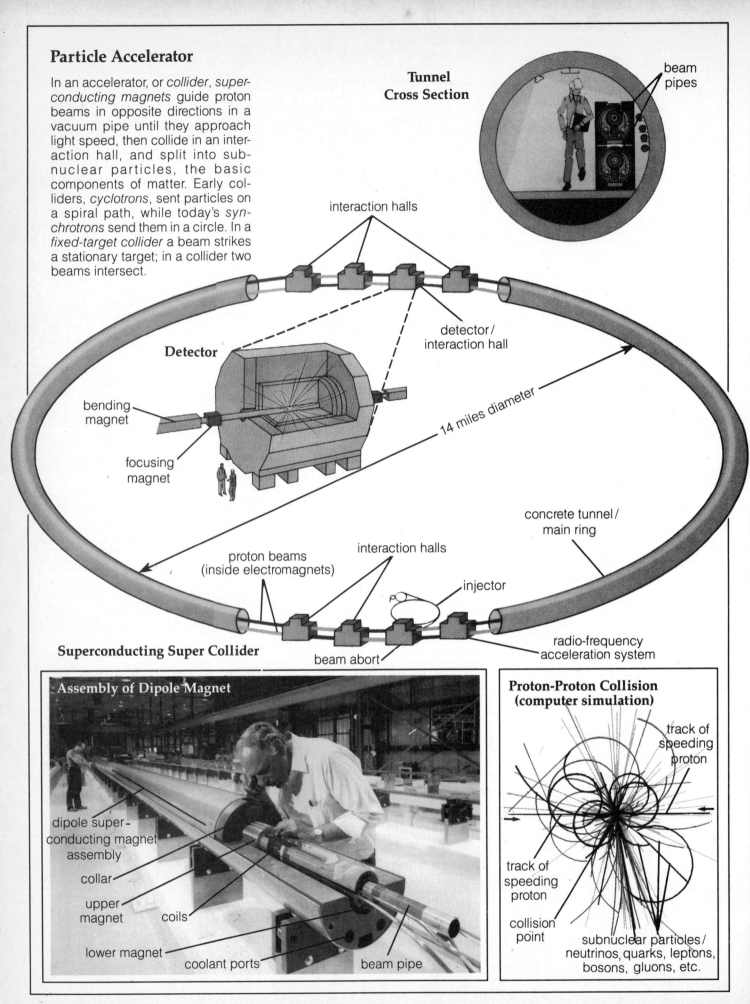

Particle Accelerator

In an accelerator, or *collider*, *super-conducting magnets* guide proton beams in opposite directions in a vacuum pipe until they approach light speed, then collide in an interaction hall, and split into subnuclear particles, the basic components of matter. Early colliders, *cyclotrons*, sent particles on a spiral path, while today's *synchrotrons* send them in a circle. In a *fixed-target collider* a beam strikes a stationary target; in a collider two beams intersect.

Tunnel Cross Section

beam pipes

interaction halls

detector / interaction hall

Detector

bending magnet

focusing magnet

14 miles diameter

concrete tunnel / main ring

proton beams (inside electromagnets)

interaction halls

injector

beam abort

radio-frequency acceleration system

Superconducting Super Collider

Assembly of Dipole Magnet

dipole superconducting magnet assembly

collar

upper magnet

coils

lower magnet

coolant ports

beam pipe

Proton-Proton Collision (computer simulation)

track of speeding proton

track of speeding proton

collision point

subnuclear particles / neutrinos, quarks, leptons, bosons, gluons, etc.

Lasers and Holography

Laser, an acronym for Light Amplification by Stimulated Emission of Radiation, is a device that produces intense light from a laser tube, or *resonator*. Photons in a laser light race along a narrow, "coherent" *beam* in which all the rays are vibrating together, on exactly the same *wavelength* and at exactly the same phase. In holography, a laser's beam is split in two, the object beam, which lights the subject, and the reference beam, which goes to a film plate. In the resulting hologram, the image appears to be *three-dimensional*.

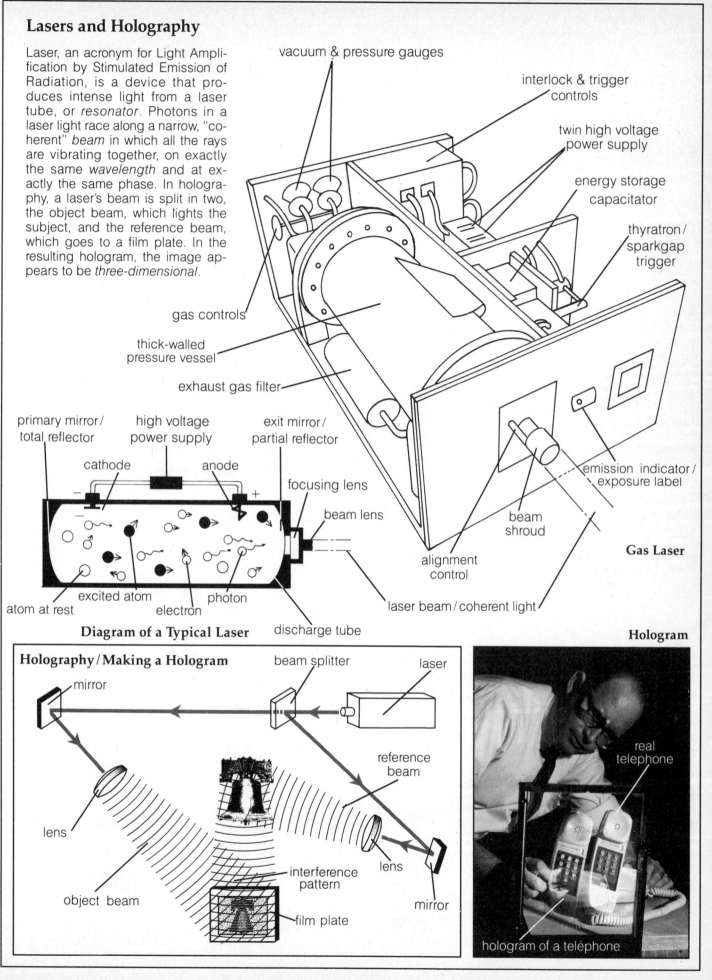

vacuum & pressure gauges

interlock & trigger controls

twin high voltage power supply

energy storage capacitator

thyratron/ sparkgap trigger

gas controls

thick-walled pressure vessel

exhaust gas filter

emission indicator / exposure label

beam shroud

Gas Laser

primary mirror / total reflector

high voltage power supply

exit mirror / partial reflector

cathode

anode

focusing lens

beam lens

excited atom

photon

atom at rest

electron

alignment control

laser beam / coherent light

Diagram of a Typical Laser

discharge tube

Hologram

Holography / Making a Hologram

beam splitter

laser

mirror

reference beam

real telephone

lens

interference pattern

lens

object beam

mirror

film plate

hologram of a telephone

Power Line, Vacuum Tube and Transistor

An *overhead line support, lattice-work tower* or *double-circuit tower* transmits high-voltage electrical power from *generating plants* to various parts of a *power network.* A transistor consists of a small block of a *semiconductor* with at least three *electrodes.*

strain insulator/protective sleeve

drip loop

pole

primary cable

secondary cable

crossarm/
traverse arm

tower

Overhead Power Line

Transistor Chip

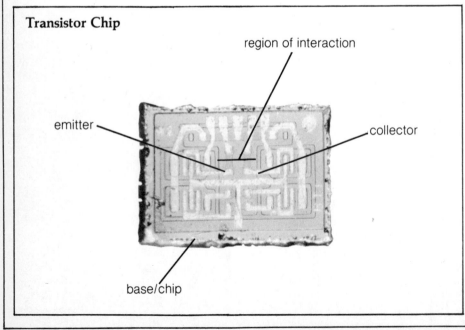

region of interaction

emitter

collector

base/chip

Vacuum Tube / Electron Tube

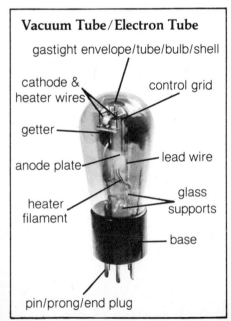

gastight envelope/tube/bulb/shell

cathode &
heater wires

control grid

getter

anode plate

lead wire

heater
filament

glass
supports

base

pin/prong/end plug

Battery

Batteries are marked with *polarity symbols*, + identifying the positive terminal, − the negative. *Secondary cells* can be recharged, while *primary cells* cannot.

cell compartments

positive terminal/post

vent cap

negative terminal/post

cover

case

Lead Acid Battery

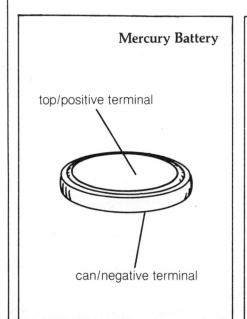

Mercury Battery

top/positive terminal

can/negative terminal

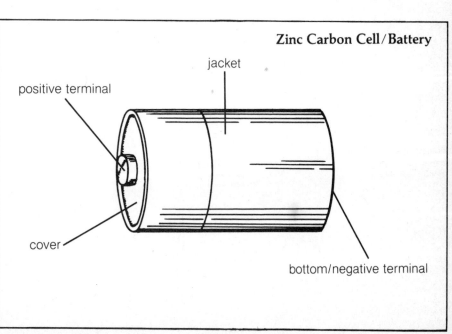

Zinc Carbon Cell/Battery

jacket

positive terminal

cover

bottom/negative terminal

Switch, Receptacle and Plug

A wall switch conducts *electrical current* only when it is in the up, or *on position,* as opposed to the down, or *off position.* Ground wires are located inside the junction box. *Attachment plugs,* or *"dead front" plugs,* such as the one shown here, have no exposed current-carrying parts except prongs, blades or *pins.* A *male plug* is fitted into a *female receptacle.*

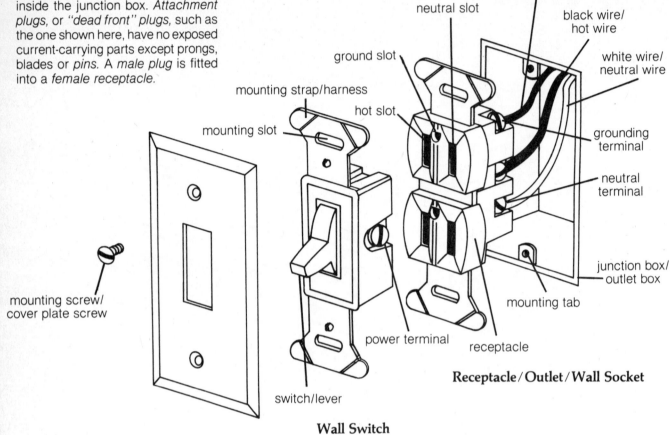

Wall Switch

Cover Plate/Switch Plate

mounting screw/ cover plate screw

mounting slot

mounting strap/harness

ground slot

hot slot

switch/lever

power terminal

neutral slot

green wire/ grounding wire

black wire/ hot wire

white wire/ neutral wire

grounding terminal

neutral terminal

junction box/ outlet box

mounting tab

receptacle

Receptacle/Outlet/Wall Socket

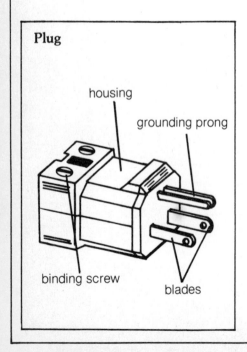

Plug

housing

grounding prong

binding screw

blades

Fuses "blow" and circuit breakers "trip" when there is too much current in the wires of a particular *circuit*. The fuse or circuit breaker acts as a safety device to keep fire from starting by heat caused by an *overload* or by a *short circuit*.

usage registers

shaft

KILOWATT HOURS

glass casing

primary cell

SINGLE-PHASE WATTHOUR METER TYPE I-30-A
15 AMPERES   115-120 VOLTS
K₀=1.5   60 CYCLES   3-WIRE
MODEL AC10.3

18 690 382

specifications

electrical connection

LINE   LOAD

Electric Meter

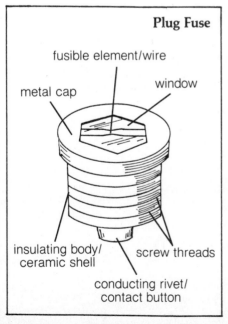

Plug Fuse

fusible element/wire

metal cap

window

insulating body/
ceramic shell

screw threads

conducting rivet/
contact button

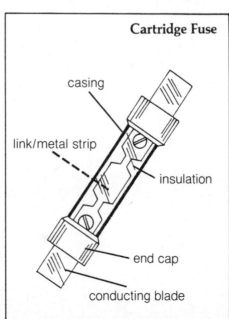

Cartridge Fuse

casing

link/metal strip

insulation

end cap

conducting blade

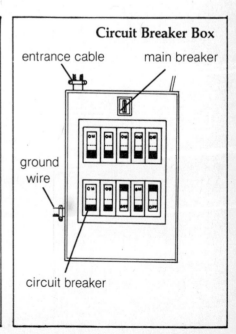

Circuit Breaker Box

entrance cable

main breaker

ground
wire

circuit breaker

Furnace

The furnace shown in this schematic illustration provides *steam heat* to radiators located in various parts of a building.

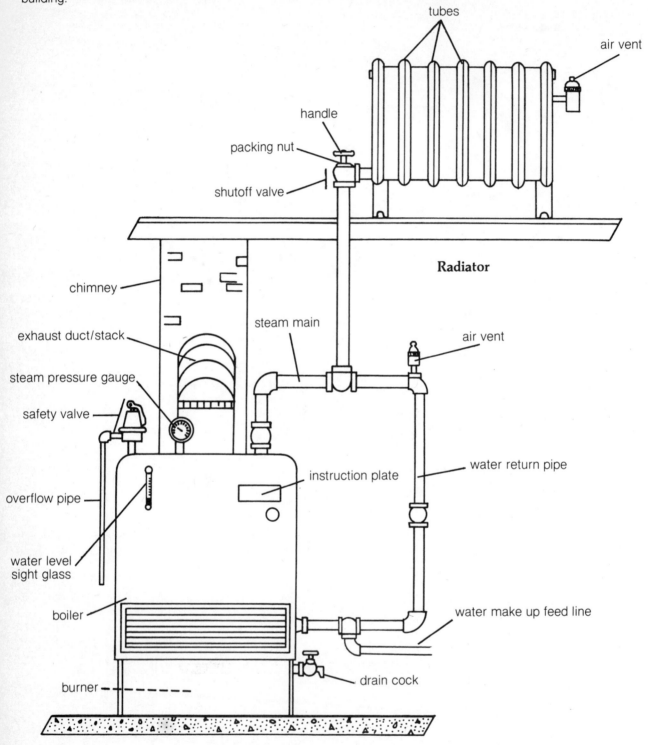

tubes

air vent

handle

packing nut

shutoff valve

Radiator

chimney

exhaust duct/stack

steam main

air vent

steam pressure gauge

safety valve

instruction plate

water return pipe

overflow pipe

water level sight glass

boiler

water make up feed line

burner

drain cock

Furnace

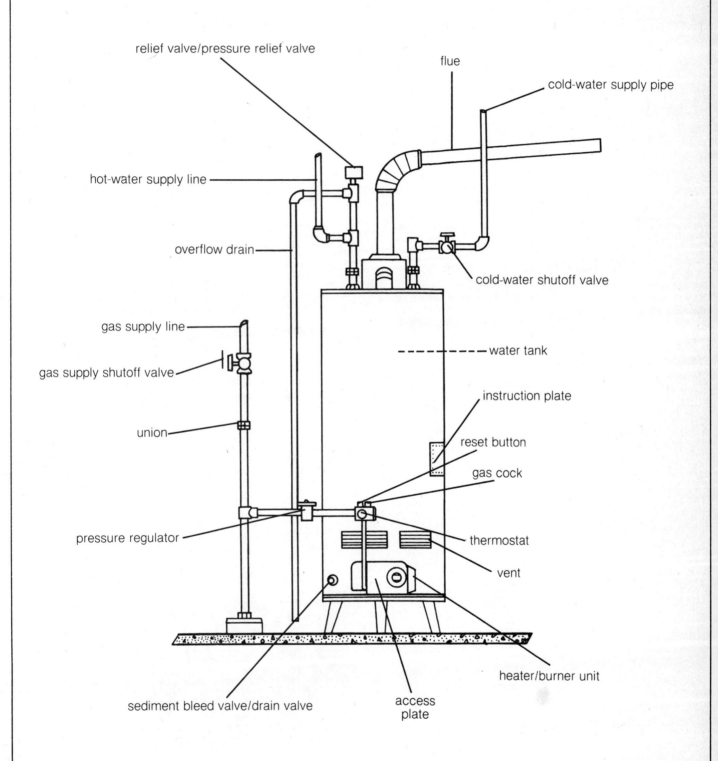

Hot Water Heater

The unit shown here is *gas-fired*. Other models include *electric water heaters* and *oil water heaters*.

relief valve/pressure relief valve

flue

cold-water supply pipe

hot-water supply line

overflow drain

cold-water shutoff valve

gas supply line

water tank

gas supply shutoff valve

instruction plate

reset button

union

gas cock

pressure regulator

thermostat

vent

heater/burner unit

sediment bleed valve/drain valve

access plate

Climate Control Units

Air Conditioning

An air conditioner's *front grille* has *louvers* which allow cooled air to be directed to any part of a room. *Condenser coils* in the rear of the unit discharge heat outdoors. Hand-held *folding fans*, *overhead fans* and *rotary fans* circulate air without actually cooling it. A *dehumidifier* removes moisture from the air, whereas a humidifier adds moisture to it.

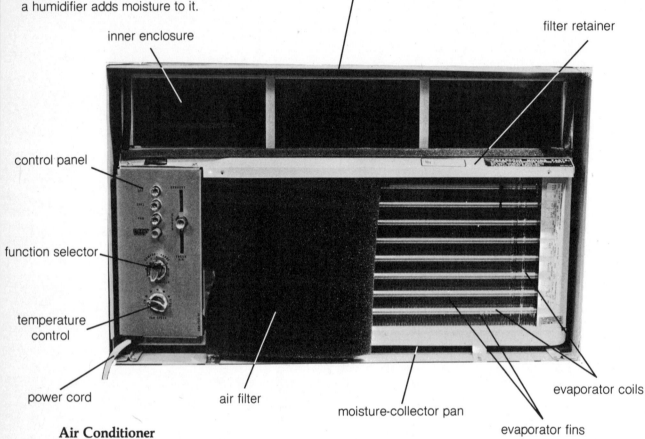

cabinet

inner enclosure

filter retainer

control panel

function selector

temperature control

power cord

air filter

moisture-collector pan

evaporator fins

evaporator coils

Air Conditioner

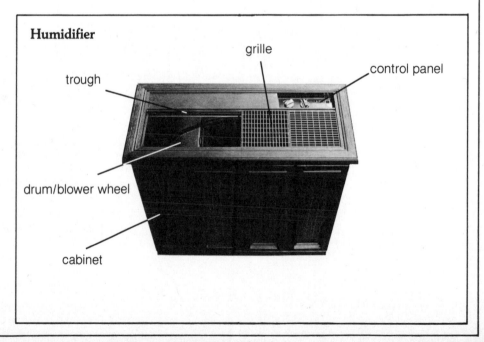

Humidifier

grille

control panel

trough

drum/blower wheel

cabinet

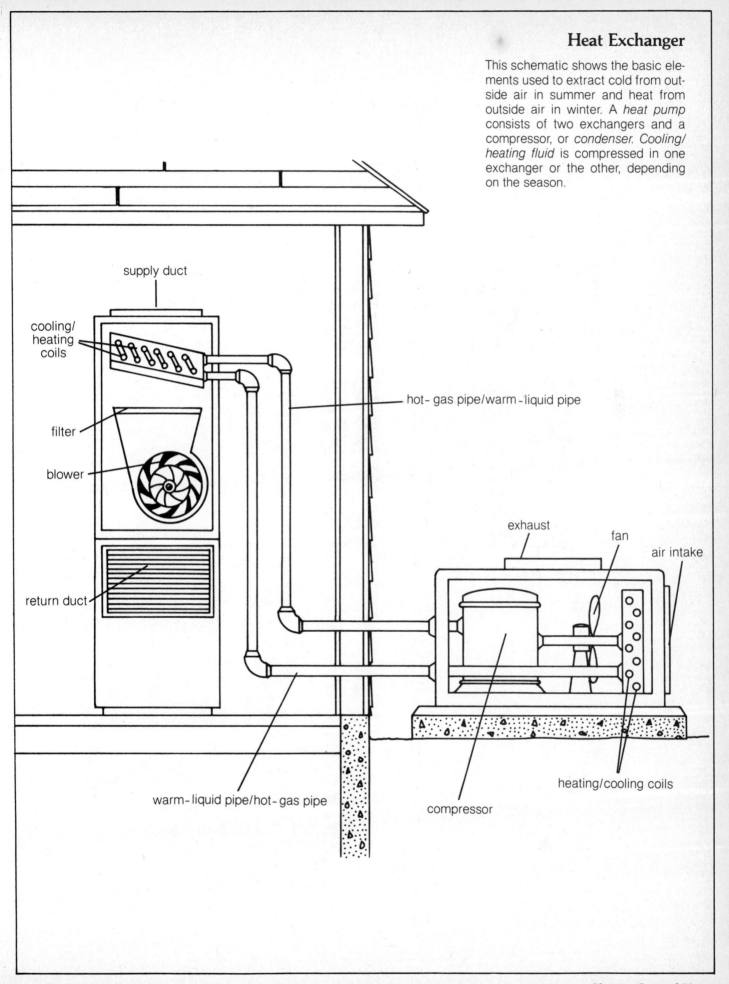

Heat Exchanger

This schematic shows the basic elements used to extract cold from outside air in summer and heat from outside air in winter. A *heat pump* consists of two exchangers and a compressor, or *condenser. Cooling/ heating fluid* is compressed in one exchanger or the other, depending on the season.

supply duct

cooling/ heating coils

filter

blower

return duct

hot- gas pipe/warm -liquid pipe

exhaust

fan

air intake

heating/cooling coils

warm- liquid pipe/hot- gas pipe

compressor

Climate Control Units

Woodburning Stove

When the *stove damper* is closed, interior *baffles* direct air into the *secondary combustion chamber,* then through the *smoke path* until it exits through the flue collar. A stovepipe led through a wall is attached to a *thimble.* The original *Franklin stove* was built into the wall, but three sides extended into the room to radiate heat.

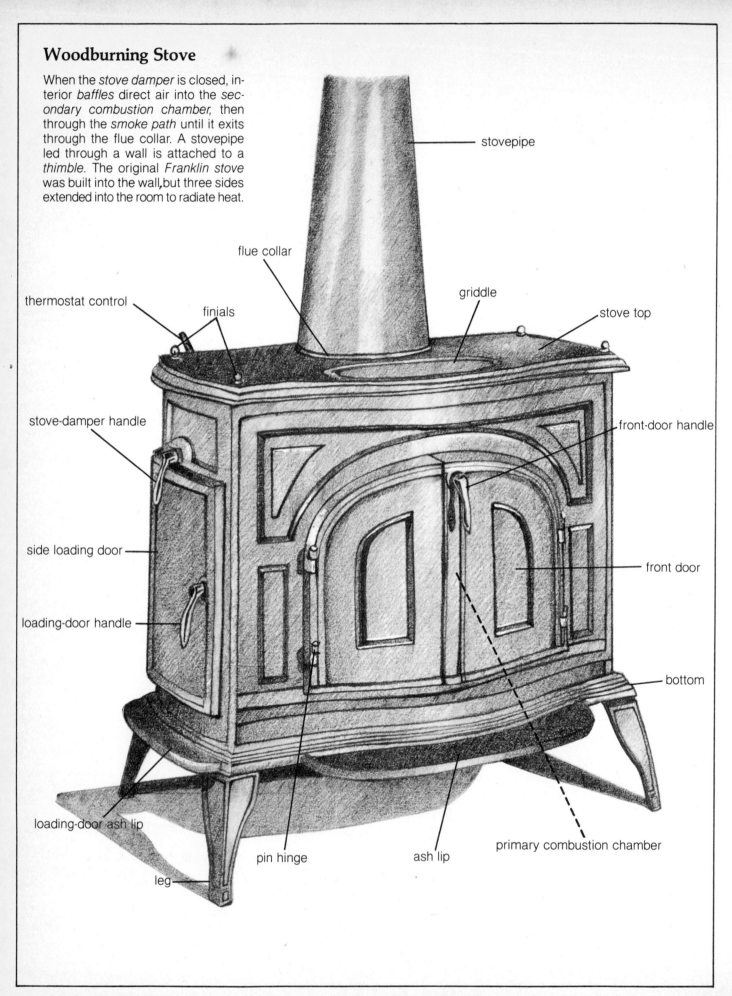

stovepipe

flue collar

griddle

thermostat control

finials

stove top

stove-damper handle

front-door handle

side loading door

front door

loading-door handle

bottom

loading-door ash lip

pin hinge

ash lip

primary combustion chamber

leg

The steam engine was used to generate *mechanical power* from *thermal energy*. A *piston* inside the steam cylinder, or *engine cylinder*, was driven by *high-pressure steam*. It moved the crankshaft to provide *rotational motion*.

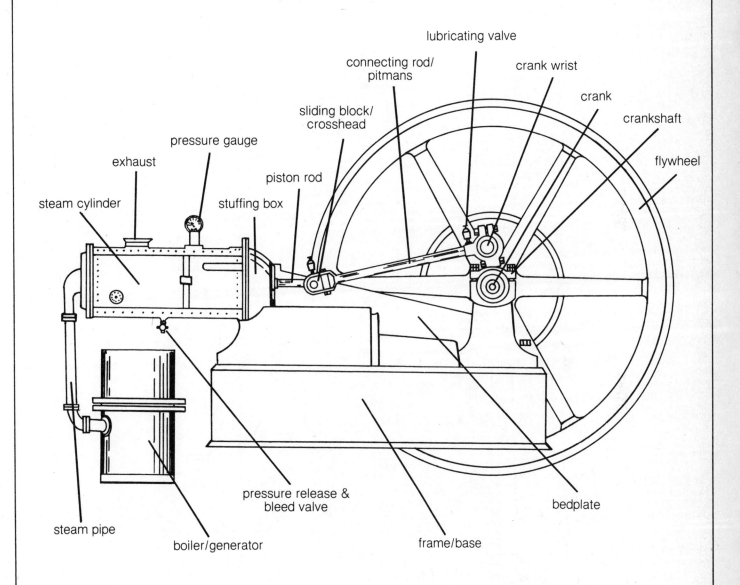

lubricating valve

connecting rod/ pitmans

crank wrist

crank

sliding block/ crosshead

crankshaft

flywheel

pressure gauge

exhaust

piston rod

steam cylinder

stuffing box

pressure release & bleed valve

bedplate

steam pipe

boiler/generator

frame/base

Internal Combustion Engine

The internal combustion engine is one in which combustion of fuel takes place within the *cylinder*, the product of which is measured in *horsepower*. Engines are *two-cycle*, *four-cycle*, or *Otto cycle*; *gas-* or *diesel-fueled*; *air-cooled* or *liquid-cooled*.

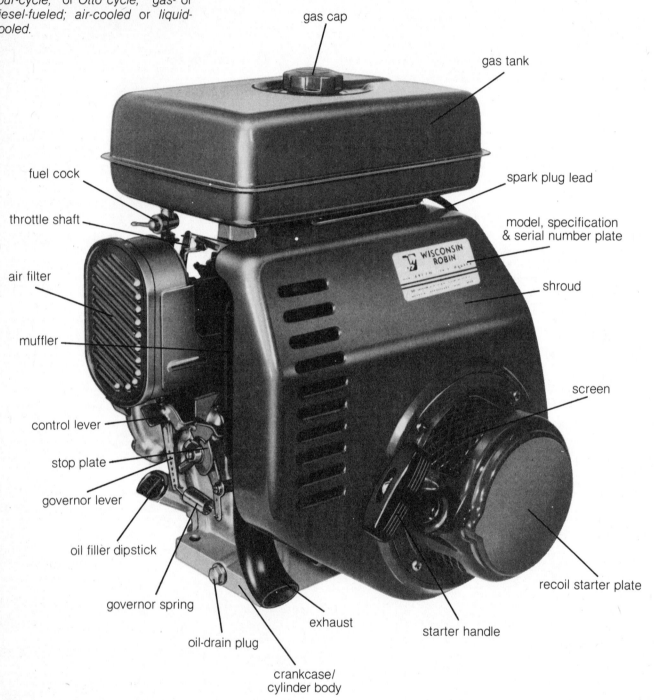

gas cap

gas tank

fuel cock

throttle shaft

air filter

muffler

control lever

stop plate

governor lever

oil filler dipstick

governor spring

oil-drain plug

crankcase/cylinder body

exhaust

starter handle

spark plug lead

model, specification & serial number plate

shroud

screen

recoil starter plate

WISCONSIN ROBIN

Jet Engines

A *turboprop engine* is like a combustion jet engine or *turbofan jet,* except that its turbine wheel is attached to a *crankshaft* that turns a *propeller.* Unlike a rocket, a *ramjet,* or *flying stovepipe,* combines compressed incoming air with fuel injection and ignition for propulsion.

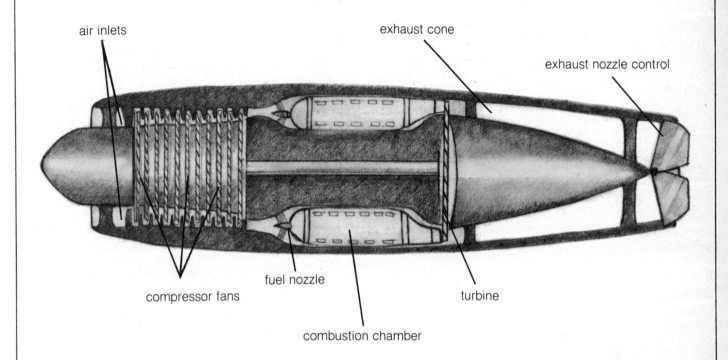

air inlets

exhaust cone

exhaust nozzle control

compressor fans

fuel nozzle

turbine

combustion chamber

Combustion Jet Engine

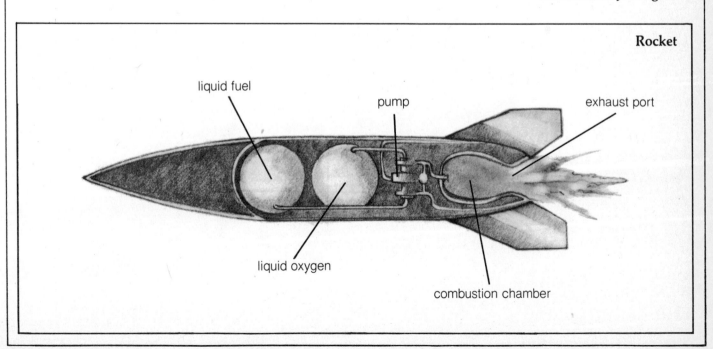

Rocket

liquid fuel

pump

exhaust port

liquid oxygen

combustion chamber

Engines

Workbench

A *machinist's vise* has two parallel iron *jaws* with a wide *throat opening* to allow as much working room as possible. A *vise dog* is a steel pin in a vise which can be raised to hold materials between the vise and the bench dogs. A *backstop* is a raised portion at the rear of a workbench.

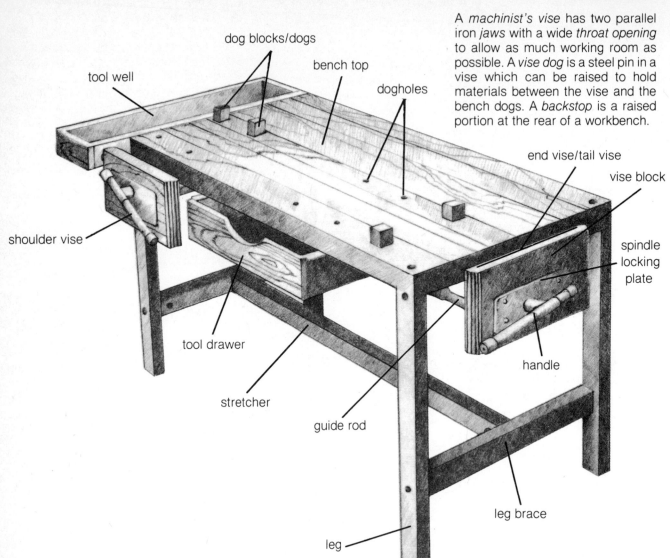

dog blocks/dogs

tool well

bench top

dogholes

end vise/tail vise

vise block

shoulder vise

spindle

locking plate

tool drawer

handle

stretcher

guide rod

leg brace

leg

Sawhorse/Sawbuck

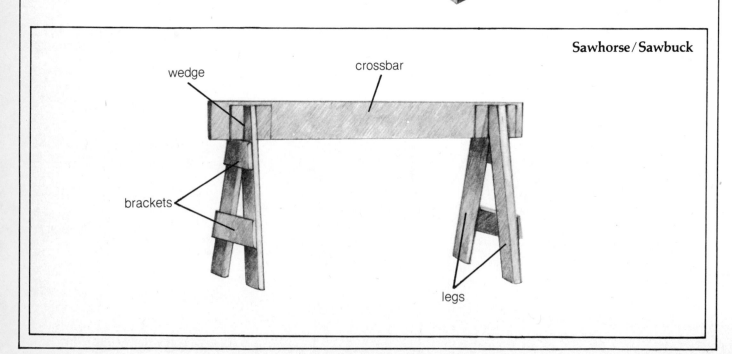

wedge

crossbar

brackets

legs

Clamps

In addition to the *holding tools* shown here, there are *hand screws, bar clamps, miter clamps, band clamps* and *spring clamps*. A *woodworking vise* is similar to a *metalworking vise* except that its jaws are padded in order to hold lumber without marring it. In wood clamps, the steel screws operate through *pivots* so that the jaws can be set at any required angle. *Adjustable C-clamps,* also known as *short bar clamps,* have an adjustable jaw that slides along a flat metal bar to the desired position.

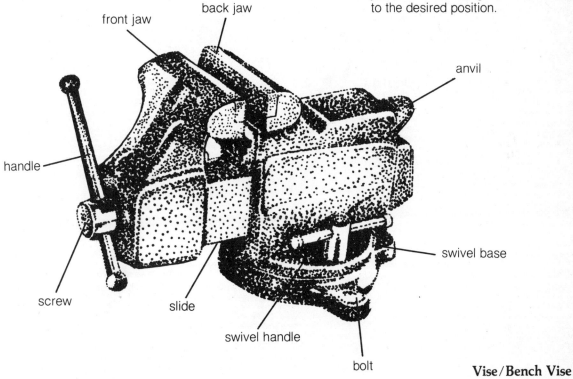

front jaw

back jaw

anvil

handle

swivel base

screw

slide

swivel handle

bolt

Vise / Bench Vise

Hand-Screw Clamp / Wood Clamp

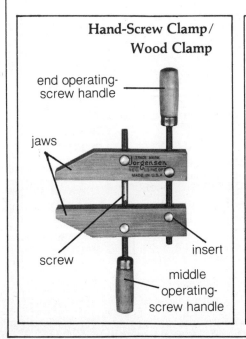

end operating-screw handle

jaws

screw

insert

middle operating-screw handle

C-Clamp

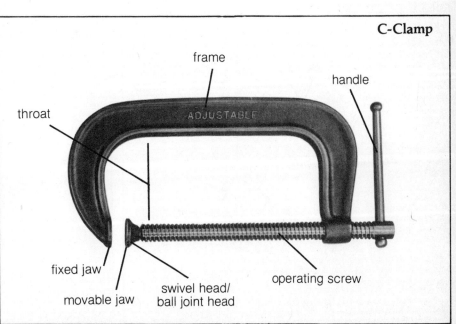

frame

handle

throat

ADJUSTABLE

fixed jaw

swivel head / ball joint head

movable jaw

operating screw

Household Tools

Nails and Screws

A nail is measured in *penny sizes*. A *brad* is a thin *finishing nail* with a tiny *nailhead* used mainly in cabinetwork. *Spikes* are large, heavy nails. The small hole drilled prior to driving a screw is called a *pilot hole*.

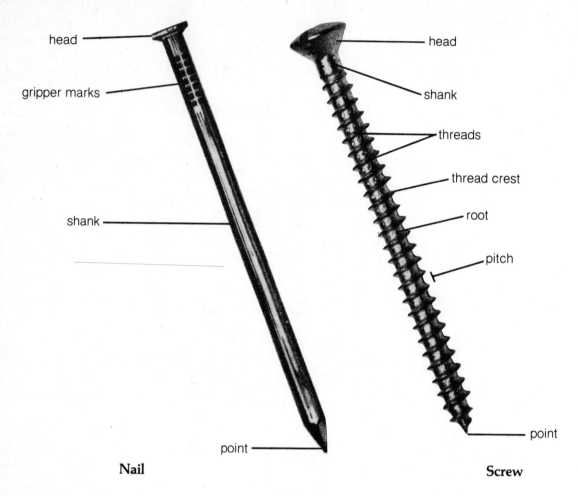

head
gripper marks
shank
point

Nail

head
shank
threads
thread crest
root
pitch
point

Screw

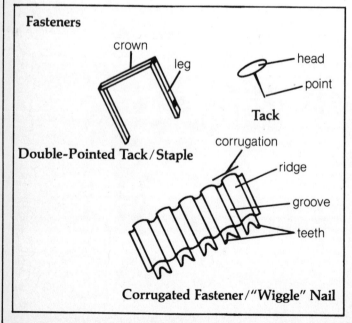

Fasteners

crown
leg

head
point

Tack

Double-Pointed Tack/Staple

corrugation
ridge
groove
teeth

Corrugated Fastener/"Wiggle" Nail

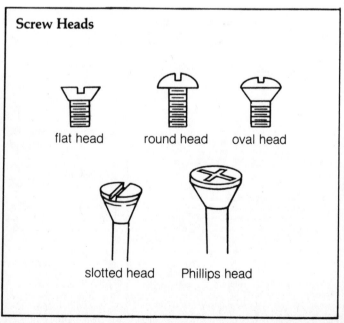

Screw Heads

flat head   round head   oval head

slotted head   Phillips head

Nuts and Bolts

Some bolts have small *collars* below the head to prevent them from turning in a piece of wood. *Washers,* flat discs with a hole in the center, are used to prevent nutheads or bolts from digging into wooden surfaces. *Eyebolts* have rounded tops that enable them to anchor string or rope.

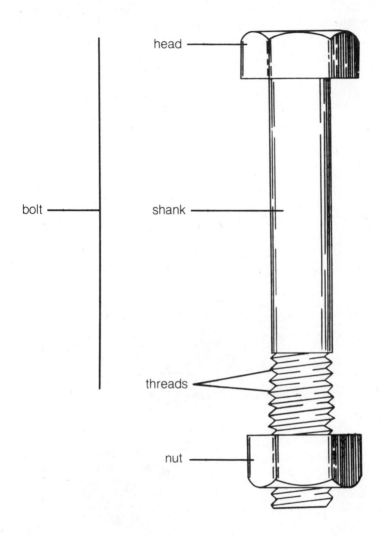

bolt

head

shank

threads

nut

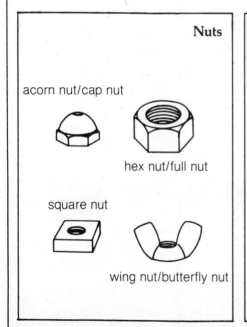

Nuts

acorn nut/cap nut

hex nut/full nut

square nut

wing nut/butterfly nut

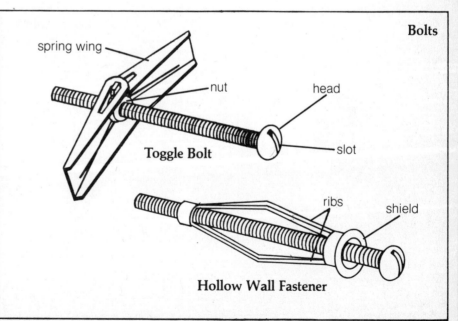

Bolts

spring wing

nut

head

slot

Toggle Bolt

ribs

shield

Hollow Wall Fastener

Household Tools

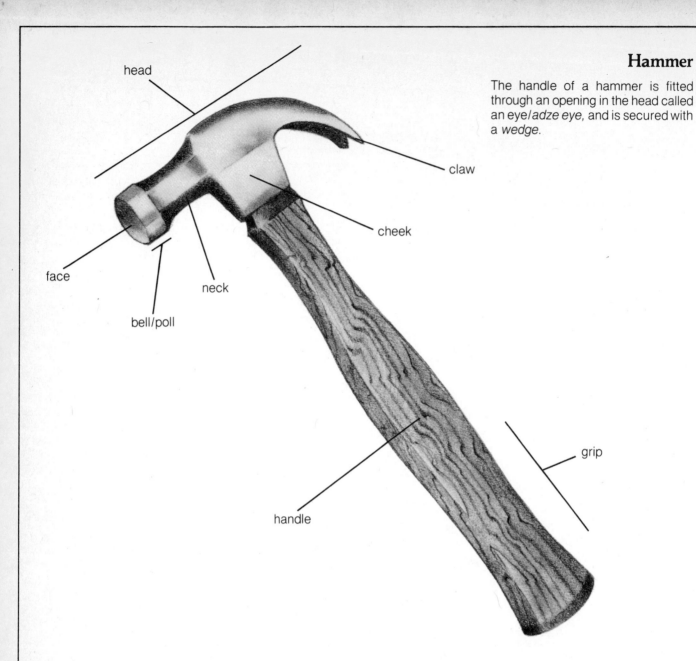

Hammer

head

claw

cheek

face

neck

bell/poll

grip

handle

The handle of a hammer is fitted through an opening in the head called an eye/*adze eye*, and is secured with a *wedge*.

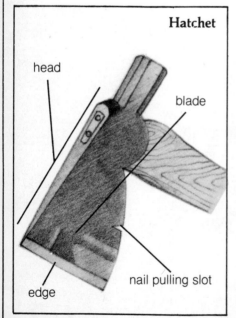

Hatchet

head

blade

edge

nail pulling slot

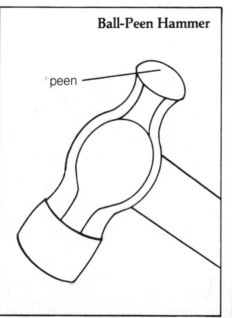

Ball-Peen Hammer

peen

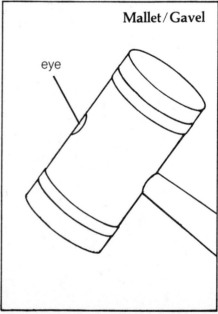

Mallet/Gavel

eye

Screwdriver

Screwdrivers are specified by the length of the blade and the width of the tip. Some have a *ferrule* where the blade meets the handle. *Offset screwdrivers* are used when working in tight areas where a regular screwdriver will not fit. The *standard ratchet screwdriver* is the predecessor to the spiral ratchet screwdriver. It has a *ratcheting mechanism* in the handle.

head

handle

flute

round shank

blade

square shank

tip

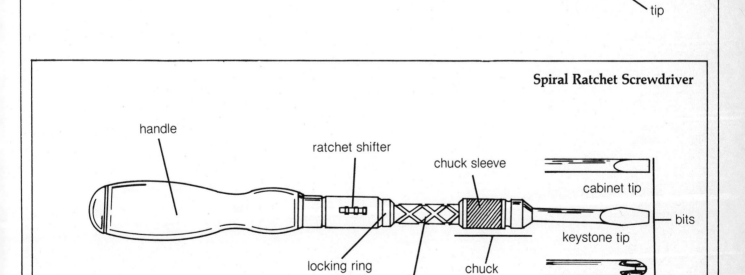

Spiral Ratchet Screwdriver

handle

ratchet shifter

chuck sleeve

cabinet tip

bits

locking ring

chuck

keystone tip

spiral groove spindle

Phillips head tip

Household Tools

Pliers

In addition to the pliers seen here, there are heavy-duty *bolt cutters; midget pliers* and *needle-nose pliers,* often used for jewelry work or electrical jobs; *music wire pliers,* used for cutting piano wire; and *duckbill pliers,* used primarily by telephone workers and weavers.

nose

curved jaw

straight jaw

teeth

nest

wire cutter

slip joint/pivot

handle

Combination Pliers / Slip-Joint Pliers

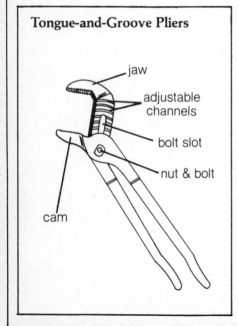

Tongue-and-Groove Pliers

jaw

adjustable channels

bolt slot

nut & bolt

cam

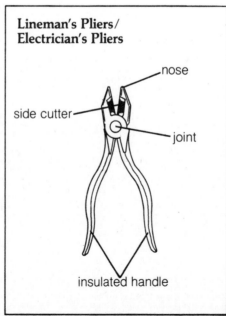

Lineman's Pliers / Electrician's Pliers

nose

side cutter

joint

insulated handle

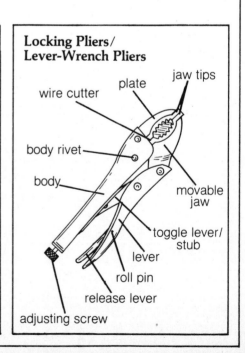

Locking Pliers / Lever-Wrench Pliers

jaw tips

plate

wire cutter

body rivet

body

movable jaw

toggle lever/ stub

lever

roll pin

release lever

adjusting screw

Wrench

Adjustable wrenches come in two styles, *locking* and *non-locking*. A *"cheater"* is a handle extension used to increase leverage. Some wrenches have *offset handles* to provide clearance over obstructions. *Socket wrenches* combine an offset handle with a male *drive piece* which has a spring-loaded *bearing* to lock on various sized *sockets*. Many socket wrenches also have a *ratchet handle* so that reversing is possible.

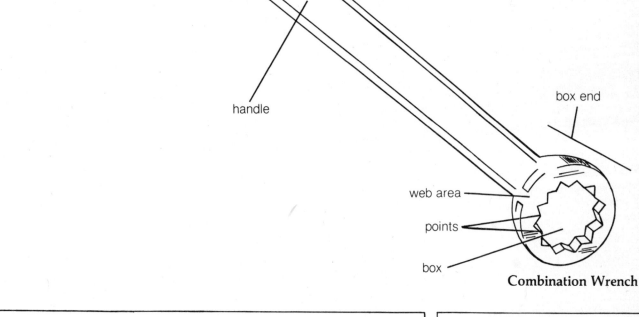

jaws

web area

open end

handle

box end

web area

points

box

Combination Wrench

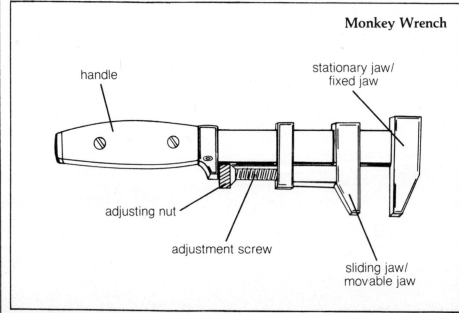

Monkey Wrench

handle

stationary jaw/
fixed jaw

adjusting nut

adjustment screw

sliding jaw/
movable jaw

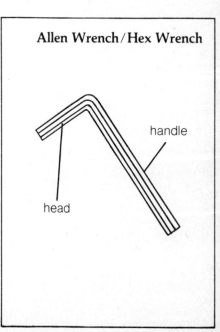

Allen Wrench/Hex Wrench

handle

head

Household Tools

Handsaws

The cut or incision made by a saw blade is the *kerf*. The carpenter's saw, shown here, occurs in two major varieties, the *ripsaw* (used for cutting with the grain) and the *crosscut saw* (for cutting across the grain). A *skewback handsaw* has an inwardly curved back. On a coping saw, the distance from the blade to the frame is the *throat* or *throat clearance*. A coping saw with a particularly long throat is called a *deep throat*.

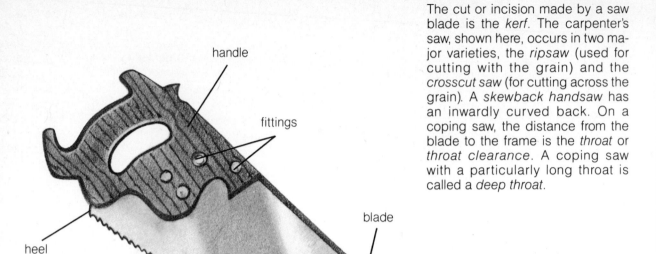

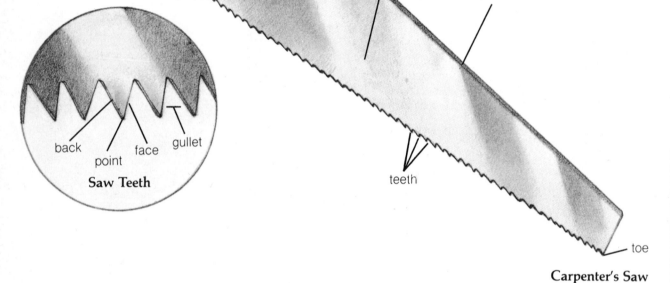

handle

fittings

heel

blade

back

teeth

toe

Carpenter's Saw

back
point
face
gullet

Saw Teeth

Coping Saw

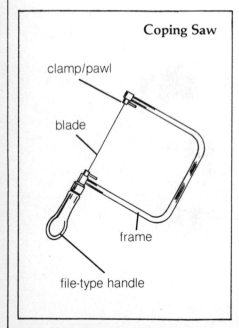

clamp/pawl

blade

frame

file-type handle

Hacksaw

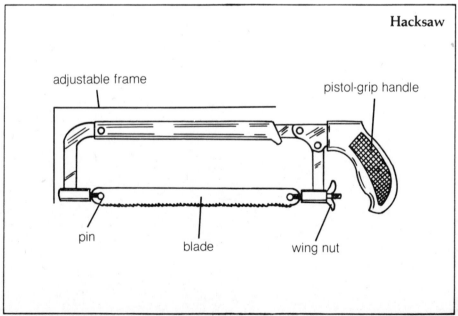

adjustable frame

pistol-grip handle

pin

blade

wing nut

Power Saw

The round blades used in table and circular saws have either *crosscut teeth* or *rip teeth*. Circular saws can be equipped with a *rip guide* and an *ejector chute*, which routes sawdust to the rear or side. Saber units include *variable-speed controls* and a *roller support* behind the blade. The *band saw* derives its name from the fact that its blade is a continuous band revolving on two wheels.

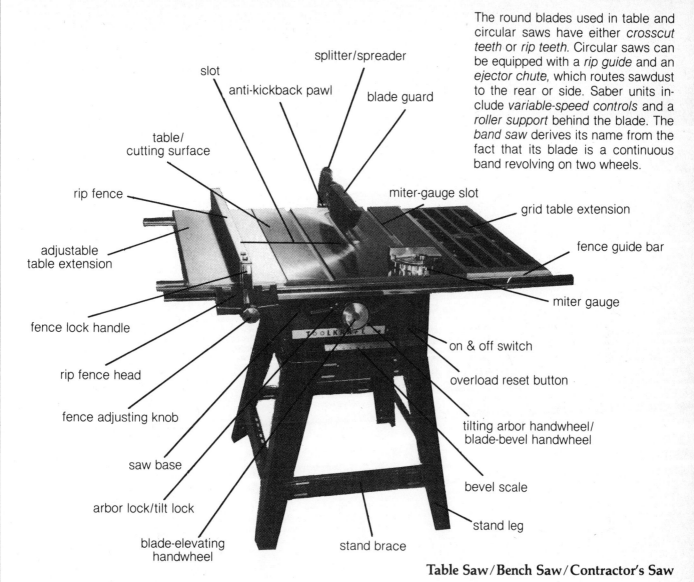

splitter/spreader

slot

anti-kickback pawl

blade guard

table/ cutting surface

rip fence

miter-gauge slot

grid table extension

fence guide bar

adjustable table extension

fence lock handle

miter gauge

rip fence head

on & off switch

overload reset button

fence adjusting knob

tilting arbor handwheel/ blade-bevel handwheel

saw base

arbor lock/tilt lock

bevel scale

blade-elevating handwheel

stand brace

stand leg

Table Saw/Bench Saw/Contractor's Saw

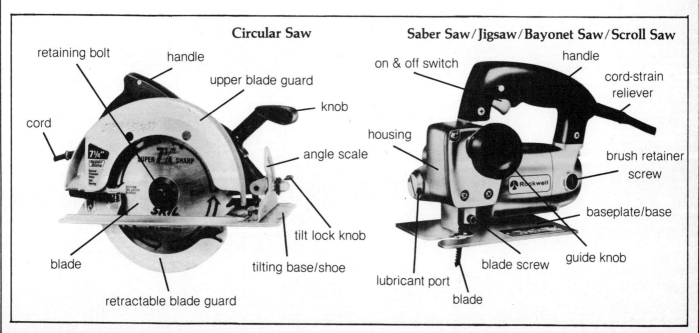

Circular Saw

retaining bolt

handle

upper blade guard

cord

knob

angle scale

7¼"

blade

tilt lock knob

tilting base/shoe

retractable blade guard

Saber Saw/Jigsaw/Bayonet Saw/Scroll Saw

on & off switch

handle

cord-strain reliever

housing

brush retainer screw

baseplate/base

blade screw

guide knob

lubricant port

blade

Household Tools

Manual Drill

Drilling accessories include a *bit gage, reamer, auger bits, dowel bits, expanding bits, screwdriver bits, countersink bits, twist drill bits, spade bits* and *power bore bits.* The circle described by turning the handle of a brace is called the *sweep.*

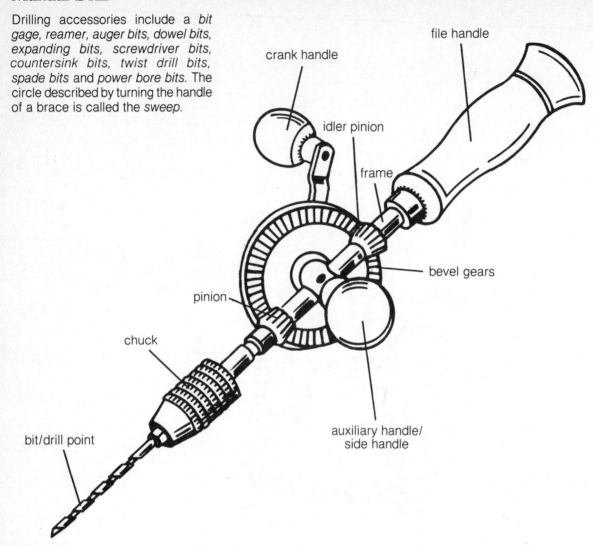

crank handle

file handle

idler pinion

frame

bevel gears

pinion

chuck

bit/drill point

auxiliary handle/ side handle

Hand Drill

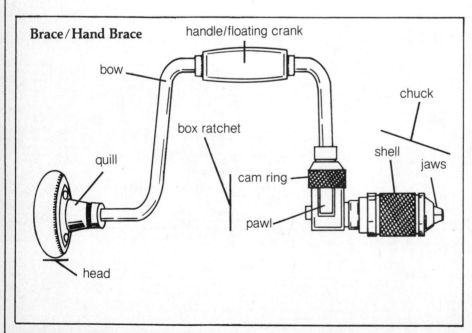

Brace/Hand Brace

handle/floating crank

bow

box ratchet

quill

cam ring

pawl

chuck

shell

jaws

head

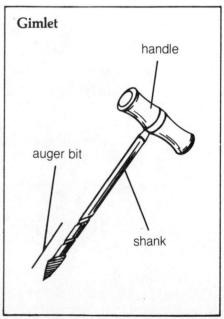

Gimlet

handle

auger bit

shank

Power Drills

A regular bit, or *drill*, consists of a *point, body* and shank. Some bits have specially configured *tangs* at the end of the shank. If a drill has a *geared key chuck*, the bit is locked in place with a key. Holes can be drilled to predetermined depths by clamping an *adjustable bit gauge* to the bit shank. A drill is classified by the largest bit its chuck will accept. Some drills have *reversible motors*.

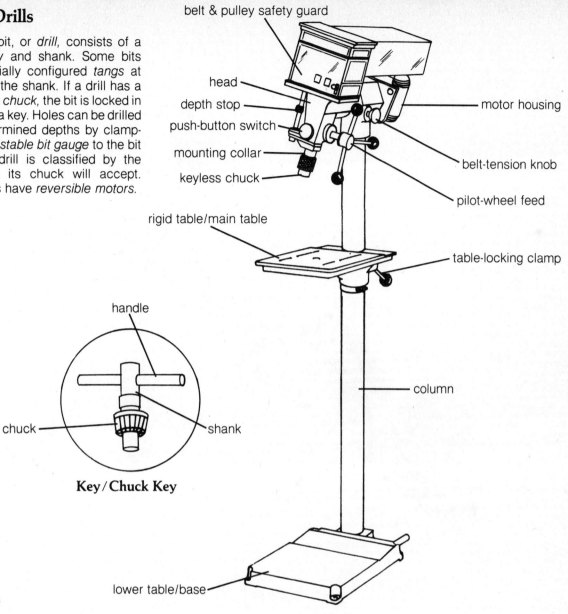

belt & pulley safety guard

head

depth stop

push-button switch

mounting collar

keyless chuck

motor housing

belt-tension knob

pilot-wheel feed

rigid table/main table

table-locking clamp

column

handle

chuck

shank

Key/Chuck Key

lower table/base

Drill Press

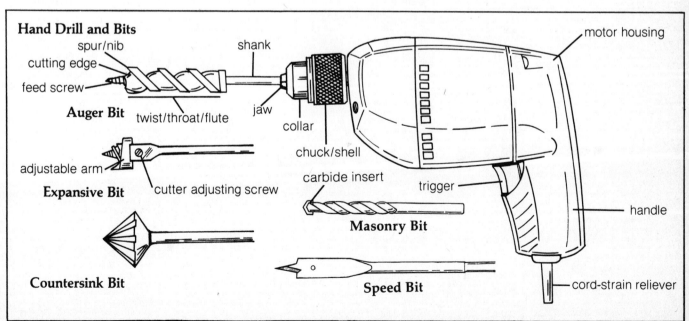

Hand Drill and Bits

spur/nib

cutting edge

feed screw

Auger Bit

twist/throat/flute

shank

jaw

collar

chuck/shell

motor housing

adjustable arm

Expansive Bit

cutter adjusting screw

carbide insert

trigger

handle

Masonry Bit

Countersink Bit

Speed Bit

cord-strain reliever

Household Tools

Planing and Shaping Tools

The body of a plane is the *frame*. The angle of the blade is the *pitch*. The flat side of a chisel is its *back*. *Cold chisels* are designed to cut metal and have no handles. *Gouges* are either *in-cannel*, with the bevel ground on the inside of the curved blade, or *out-cannel*, with the bevel ground on the outside. The rough side of a rasp or file is the *face*. The smooth side is called the *"safe" side*.

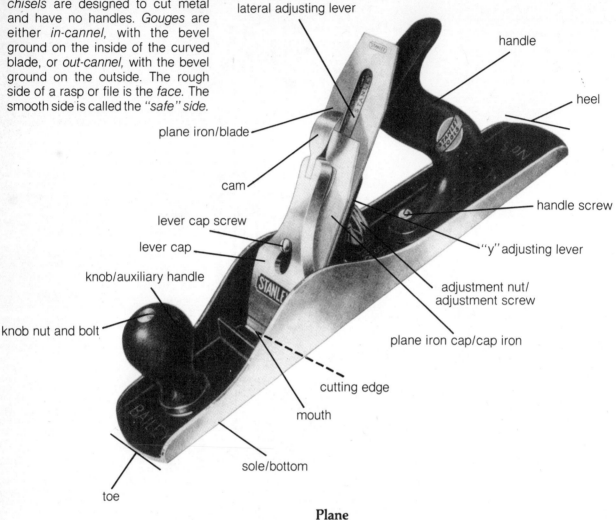

lateral adjusting lever

handle

heel

plane iron/blade

cam

handle screw

lever cap screw

"y" adjusting lever

lever cap

knob/auxiliary handle

adjustment nut/ adjustment screw

knob nut and bolt

plane iron cap/cap iron

cutting edge

mouth

sole/bottom

toe

Plane

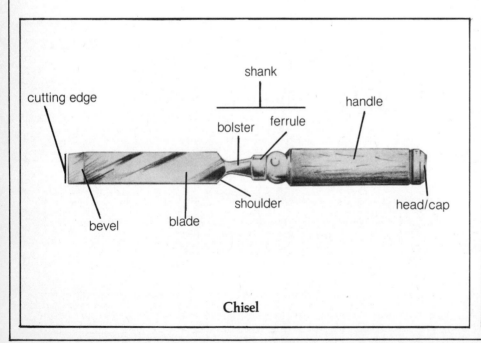

cutting edge

shank

handle

bolster

ferrule

knob/auxiliary handle

shoulder

head/cap

bevel

blade

Chisel

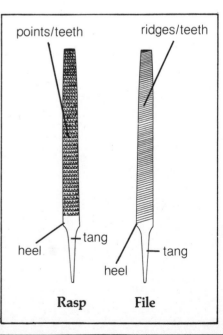

points/teeth

ridges/teeth

heel

tang

heel

tang

heel

Rasp   **File**

Sander

In a finishing, or *straight-line*, sander, the pad moves back and forth, whereas in the similar-looking *orbital sander*, the pad moves in a small orbital pattern. *Belt sanders* use a continuous *belt* of either *natural* or *artificial abrasive material*, and are available with or without *dust bags*. Sandpaper has either an *open* or *closed coat*, depending on spacing between *grains*.

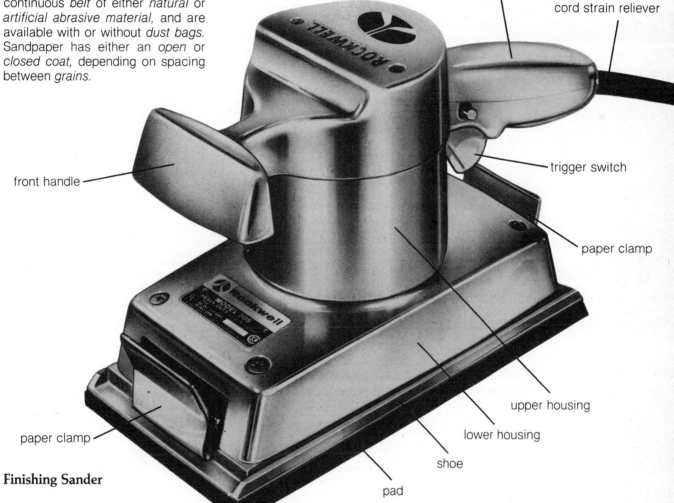

handle

cord strain reliever

trigger switch

paper clamp

front handle

upper housing

lower housing

shoe

paper clamp

pad

Finishing Sander

Sandpaper

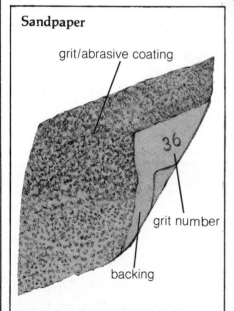

grit/abrasive coating

36

grit number

backing

Belt Sander

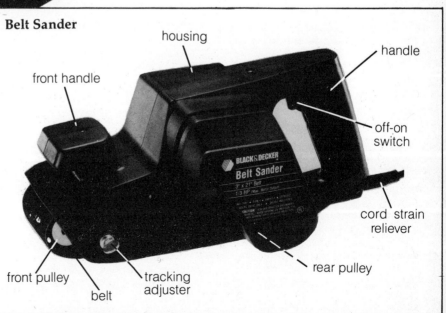

housing

front handle

handle

off-on switch

BLACK & DECKER
Belt Sander
3" x 21" Belt
1/3 HP (Max. Motor Output)

cord strain reliever

rear pulley

front pulley

belt

tracking adjuster

Household Tools

Plumbing Tools

In addition to the basic plumbing tools shown here, there are *tubing*, or *pipe cutters*, some of which have built-in *polishers; reamers* for removing *burrs* inside cut *pipe;* and *flaring tools*, used to spread the ends of copper *tubing* for *flare fittings*. In *sweat soldering, flux* and *solder* are used. When working with *threaded pipe*, a *pipe threader* (which consists of a *die, diestock* and *handles*) and *joint-sealing tape* or *compound* are used. Other basic plumbing tools are *hacksaws* and *pipe wrenches*.

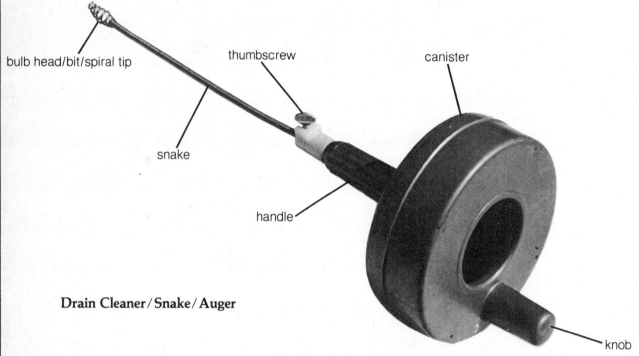

bulb head/bit/spiral tip

thumbscrew

canister

snake

handle

knob

Drain Cleaner / Snake / Auger

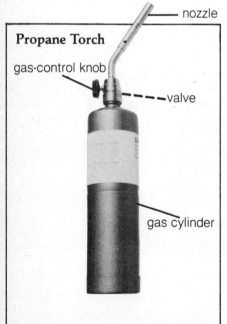

nozzle

Propane Torch

gas-control knob

valve

gas cylinder

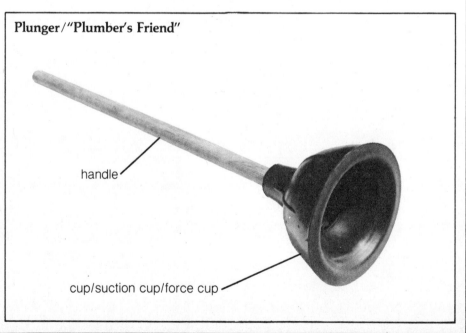

Plunger / "Plumber's Friend"

handle

cup/suction cup/force cup

Electrician's Tools

A volt-ohm meter, also known as a *multimeter* or *volt-ohm-milliammeter*, is used with test *leads* and *jacks* attached to needle-type *probes* or *alligator clips*. The markings on the sheath of a wire describe *wire size*, number of *conductors*, the existence of a ground wire and cable type.

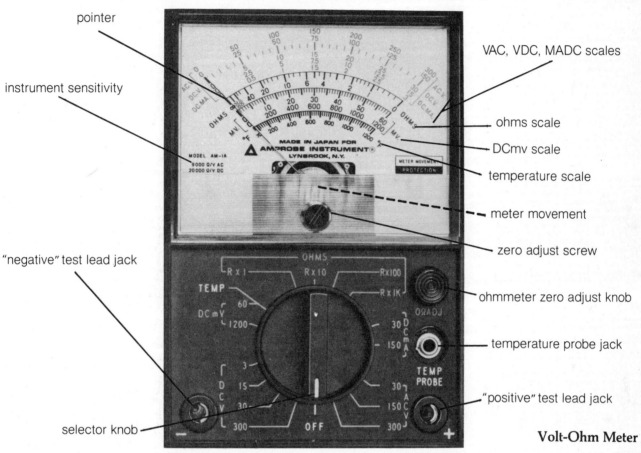

pointer

instrument sensitivity

VAC, VDC, MADC scales

ohms scale

DCmv scale

temperature scale

meter movement

zero adjust screw

"negative" test lead jack

ohmmeter zero adjust knob

temperature probe jack

"positive" test lead jack

selector knob

Volt-Ohm Meter

Wire Stripper and Crimper/Multipurpose Tool

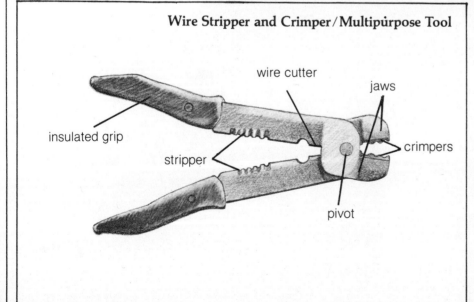

wire cutter

jaws

insulated grip

stripper

crimpers

pivot

Wire/Cable/Cord

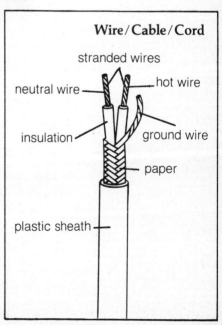

stranded wires

neutral wire

hot wire

insulation

ground wire

paper

plastic sheath

Household Tools

Measuring Tools

The basic measuring tool is the one-piece *bench rule,* or *ruler.* Tape measures also come in *reels* which can be manually rewound. An *L-shaped square* has two *arms* set at right angles. The longer arm is the *blade,* the shorter one is the *tongue.* They meet at the *heel.* A *combination square* substitutes for *try squares, depth gauges* and *marking gauges.* When the *air bubble* in a monovial stops between *marks,* the level is on the desired *plane.*

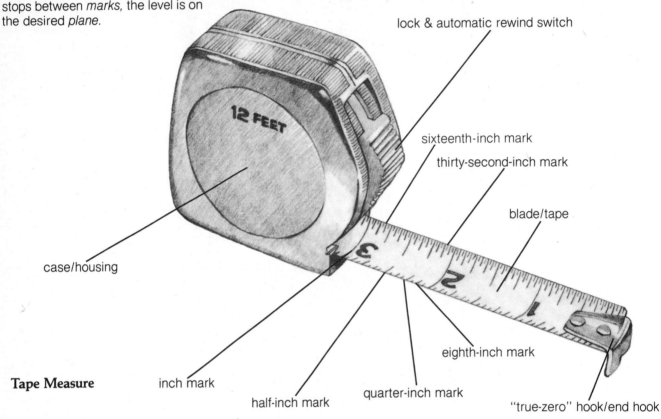

lock & automatic rewind switch

sixteenth-inch mark

thirty-second-inch mark

blade/tape

case/housing

eighth-inch mark

Tape Measure

inch mark

half-inch mark

quarter-inch mark

"true-zero" hook/end hook

Combination Square

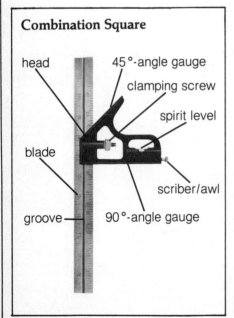

head

45°-angle gauge

clamping screw

spirit level

blade

scriber/awl

groove

90°-angle gauge

Folding Rule/Zigzag Rule

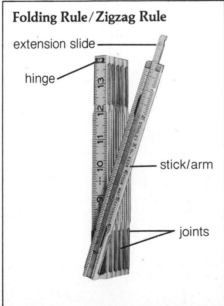

extension slide

hinge

stick/arm

joints

Carpenter's Level

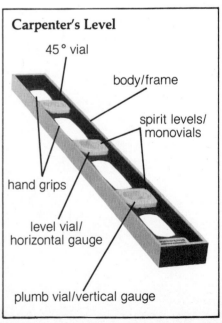

45° vial

body/frame

spirit levels/monovials

hand grips

level vial/horizontal gauge

plumb vial/vertical gauge

Painting Tools

A regular *paint brush* has *bristles* with *split,* or *flagged,* *ends.* The *heel* section of a brush is where the *butt ends* of bristles fit into a *ferrule* attached to the handle. Other paint-application tools include *pressure brushes, foam brushes* and *pad applicators.* Accessories include *pot* and *brush holders* and *brush spinners.* Paint rollers may have *threaded handles* to accommodate *extenders.* *Tack cloth* is used to clean surfaces to be painted, and a *drop cloth* protects objects and areas against paint spills.

housing

high-pressure pump

control knob

venthole

trigger

handle

nozzle

safety guard

container cover

container

plug

Paint Spray Gun

Tray and Roller

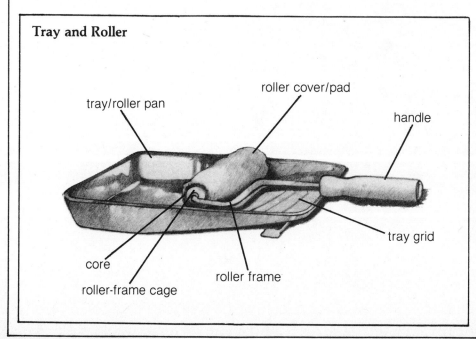

roller cover/pad

tray/roller pan

handle

core

roller-frame cage

roller frame

tray grid

Ladder / Stepladder

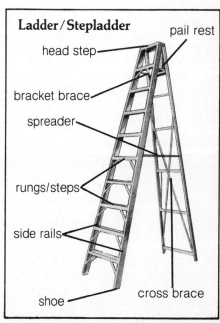

pail rest

head step

bracket brace

spreader

rungs/steps

side rails

shoe

cross brace

Swiss Army Knife

The *dividers* in the *handle* of a *jack-knife*, pocketknife or *camping knife* keep each blade or *tool* separate.

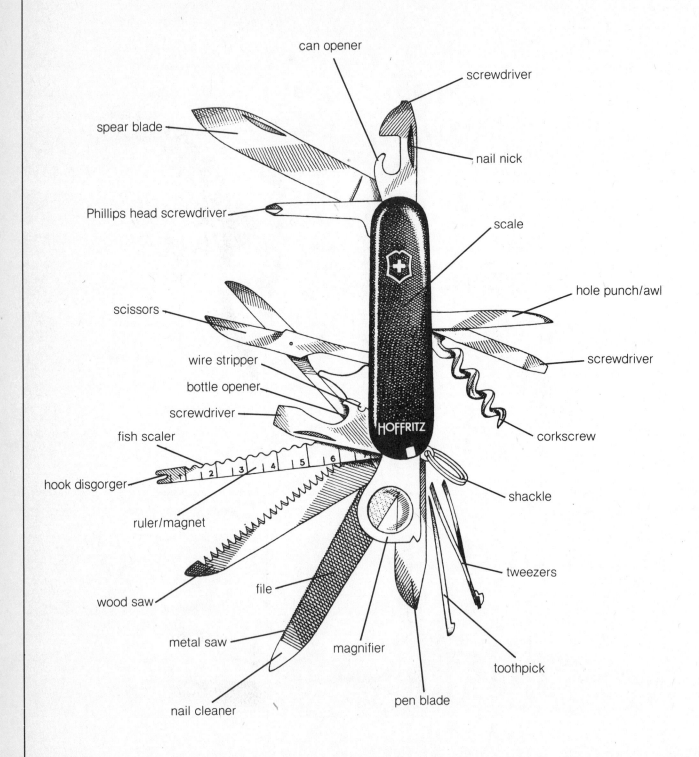

can opener

screwdriver

spear blade

nail nick

Phillips head screwdriver

scale

hole punch/awl

scissors

screwdriver

wire stripper

bottle opener

corkscrew

screwdriver

fish scaler

shackle

hook disgorger

ruler/magnet

tweezers

wood saw

file

metal saw

magnifier

toothpick

nail cleaner

pen blade

HOFFRITZ

Gardening Implements

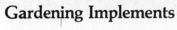

A hand tool with a small scooped blade used for potting and planting is a *trowel*. A *spading fork* is used for turning soil. Shears are generally of two types: *anvil,* in which a blade cuts through a branch and stops against an anvil, and *by-pass,* which uses a shearing action to cut.

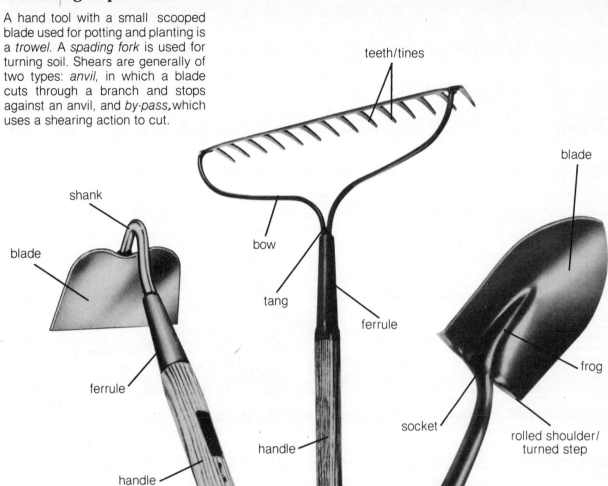

teeth/tines

shank

blade

blade

bow

tang

ferrule

frog

ferrule

socket

rolled shoulder/
turned step

handle

handle

handle

Hoe   **Rake**   **Shovel/Spade**

Shears/Clippers

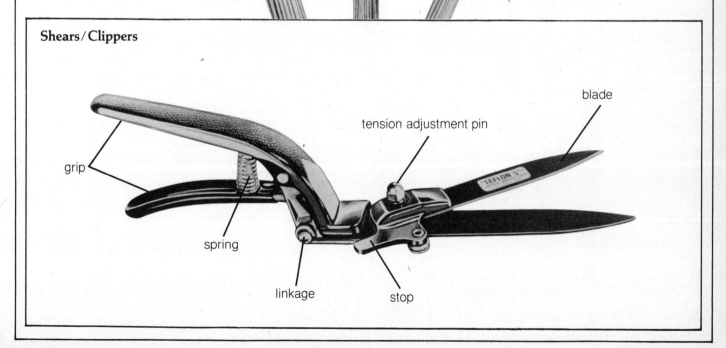

blade

tension adjustment pin

grip

spring

linkage   stop

Gardening Tools

Sprinkler and Nozzles

Revolving sprinklers have rotating *arms* that spray water through nozzles at each end. An inverted Y-shaped *coupling*, or *siamese*, makes it possible to connect two *hoses* to a single *faucet*. In making a *hose connection*, the larger *female coupling* is fitted over the *male coupling* and turned until the connection is made fast. *Washers* inside couplings make seals watertight.

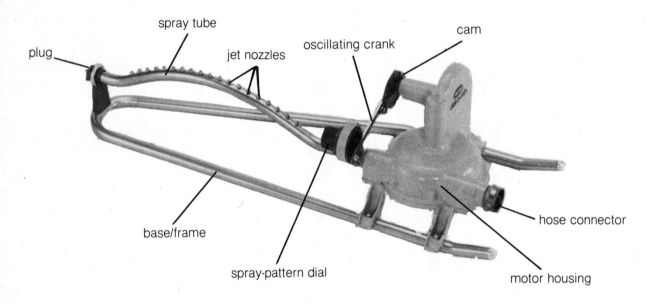

plug

spray tube

jet nozzles

oscillating crank

cam

hose connector

base/frame

spray-pattern dial

motor housing

Oscillating Lawn Sprinkler

Hose Nozzle

threaded fitting/socket

adjustable barrel/stem

standard/ screw nozzle

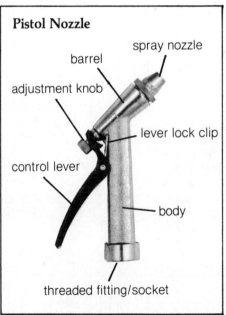

Pistol Nozzle

spray nozzle

barrel

adjustment knob

lever lock clip

control lever

body

threaded fitting/socket

Lawn Mower

Rotary mowers, such as the one shown here, use a single *blade* to slice off grass, as does a *scythe*. *Reel mowers*, such as the *sickle-bar mower*, use multiple blades, called a *reel*, to push grass against a stationary *bed knife* at the base of the mower. Cut grass is contained in a bag called a *grass-catcher*. With a *mulching mower*, bagging is unnecessary. A *lawn sweeper* uses a rotating sweeping action to pick up cuttings and leaves. *Lawn edgers* and *trimmers* are used to cut grass in areas where mowers cannot.

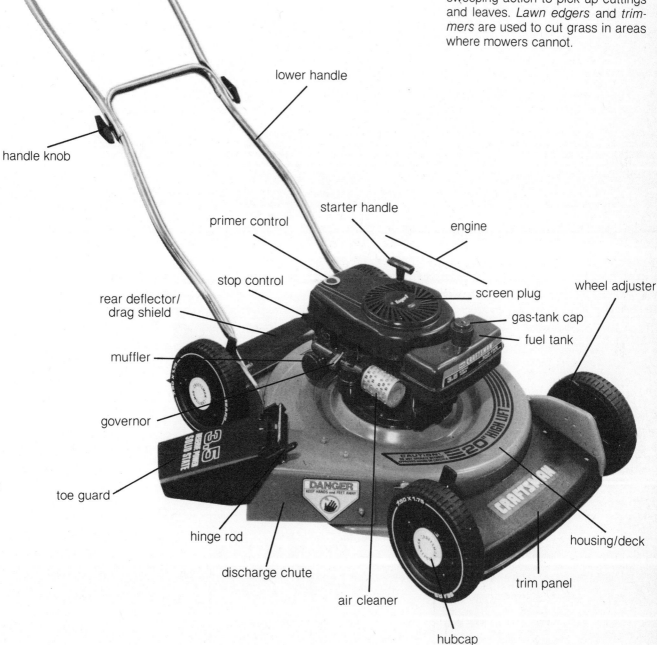

upper handle

lower handle

handle knob

starter handle

primer control

engine

stop control

screen plug

rear deflector/drag shield

wheel adjuster

gas-tank cap

muffler

fuel tank

governor

toe guard

hinge rod

housing/deck

discharge chute

trim panel

air cleaner

hubcap

DANGER KEEP HANDS and FEET AWAY

Power Mower

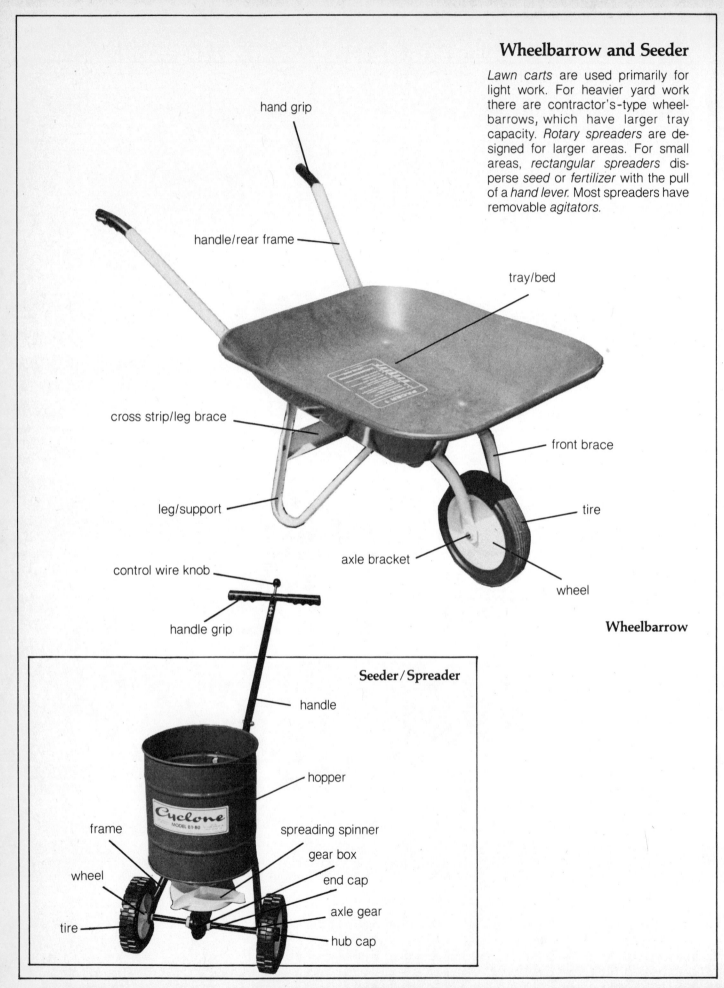

Wheelbarrow and Seeder

Lawn carts are used primarily for light work. For heavier yard work there are contractor's-type wheelbarrows, which have larger tray capacity. *Rotary spreaders* are designed for larger areas. For small areas, *rectangular spreaders* disperse *seed* or *fertilizer* with the pull of a *hand lever*. Most spreaders have removable *agitators*.

hand grip

handle/rear frame

tray/bed

cross strip/leg brace

front brace

leg/support

tire

axle bracket

wheel

Wheelbarrow

control wire knob

handle grip

Seeder / Spreader

handle

hopper

frame

spreading spinner

gear box

wheel

end cap

tire

axle gear

hub cap

Chain Saw

Chain saws are either gasoline- or electric-powered. Power output is measured in cubic inches of *piston displacement* in the *power head* rather than in horsepower. The *cutting head* may be *direct drive* or *gear drive*. A *sprocket-tip cutting bar* increases cutting speed because it eliminates most of the friction around the *bar tip*. Safety devices include a *chain brake* intended to stop the moving chain when the saw begins to kick back, *throttle latches* for safer starting, *safety triggers* to prevent accidental acceleration, *muffler shields,* and *chain catchers* designed to protect the operator from a broken or slipped chain.

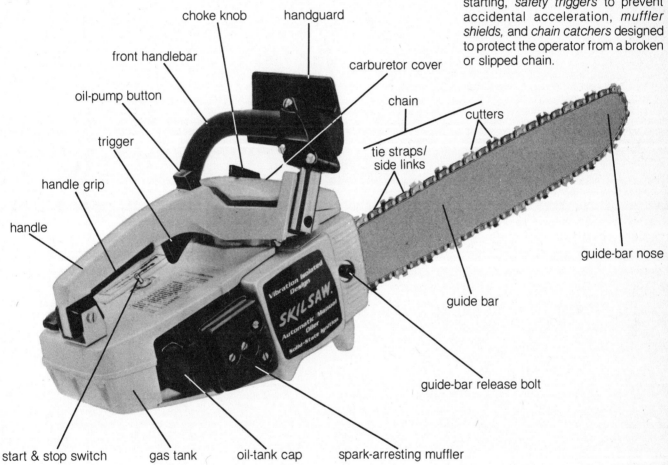

choke knob

handguard

front handlebar

carburetor cover

oil-pump button

chain

cutters

trigger

tie straps/ side links

handle grip

handle

guide-bar nose

guide bar

guide-bar release bolt

start & stop switch   gas tank   oil-tank cap   spark-arresting muffler

Gardening Tools

Ranching Gear

In the days of cattle ranching, *ketch hands* would rope *calves,* or "critters," an *iron man* would brand them, and, in some instances, a *knife man* would cut an additional identifying notch, or *earmark,* in their ears. A *tally man* would record the operation.

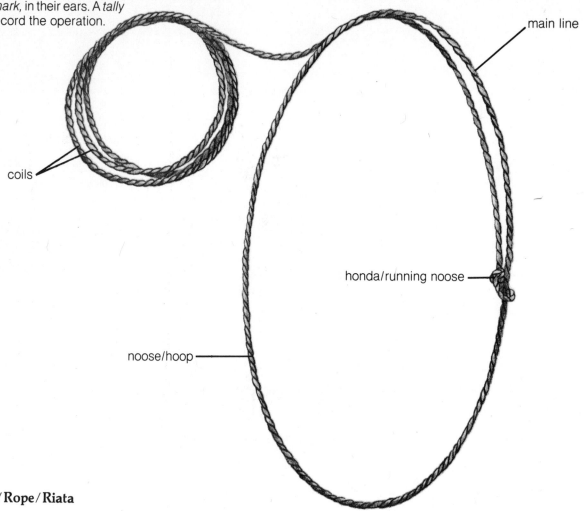

main line

coils

honda/running noose

noose/hoop

Lasso/Lariat/Rope/Riata

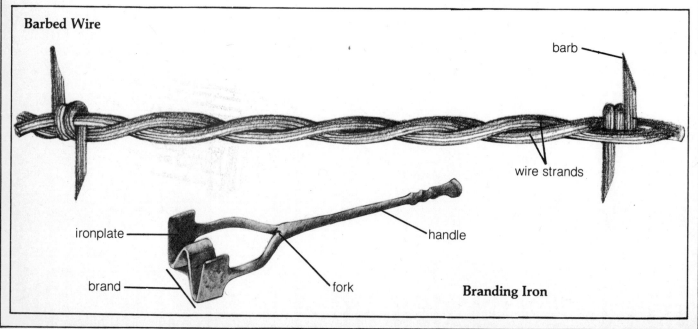

Barbed Wire

barb

wire strands

ironplate

handle

brand

fork

Branding Iron

Traps

Enclosing traps catch animals without hurting them. *Arresting traps,* such as the bear trap shown here, catch and hold animals in their teeth. *Killing traps* destroy animals and rodents.

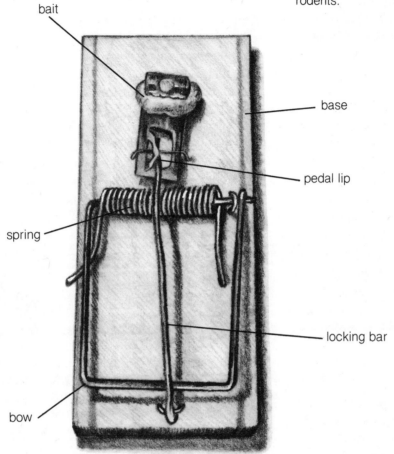

bait

base

pedal lip

spring

locking bar

bow

Mousetrap

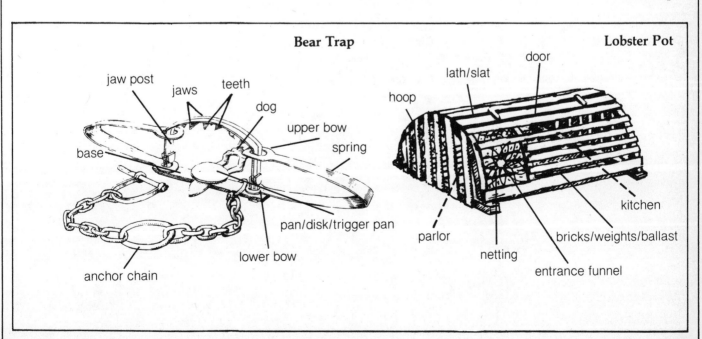

Bear Trap

jaw post

jaws

teeth

dog

upper bow

spring

base

pan/disk/trigger pan

lower bow

anchor chain

Lobster Pot

door

lath/slat

hoop

kitchen

parlor

bricks/weights/ballast

netting

entrance funnel

Trapping Devices

Tractor

Plows, reapers, cultivators, like the harrow seen here, and various *planting machines* are coupled to a tractor to work the land. The operating speed of attachments is controlled by a *power takeoff.* Optional *outboard planetaries* with *adjustable wheel treads* and *add-on segment weights* help boost traction.

front windows

cab

muffler

warning light

headlamp/ headlight

hood

air filter

grille

fender

front-end weights

rear axle

adapter plate

frame

wide tire

side panel

steps

Hitch and Harrow

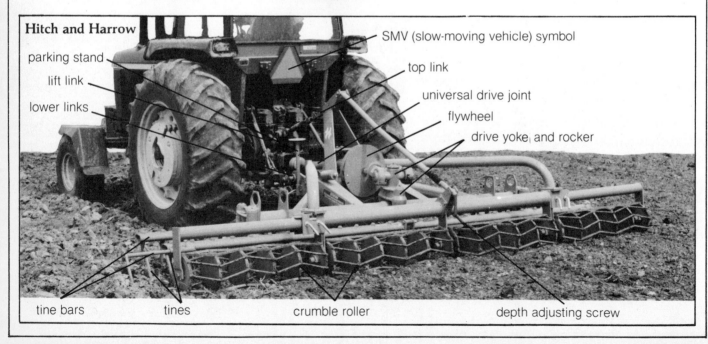

SMV (slow-moving vehicle) symbol

parking stand

top link

lift link

universal drive joint

lower links

flywheel

drive yoke and rocker

tine bars   tines   crumble roller   depth adjusting screw

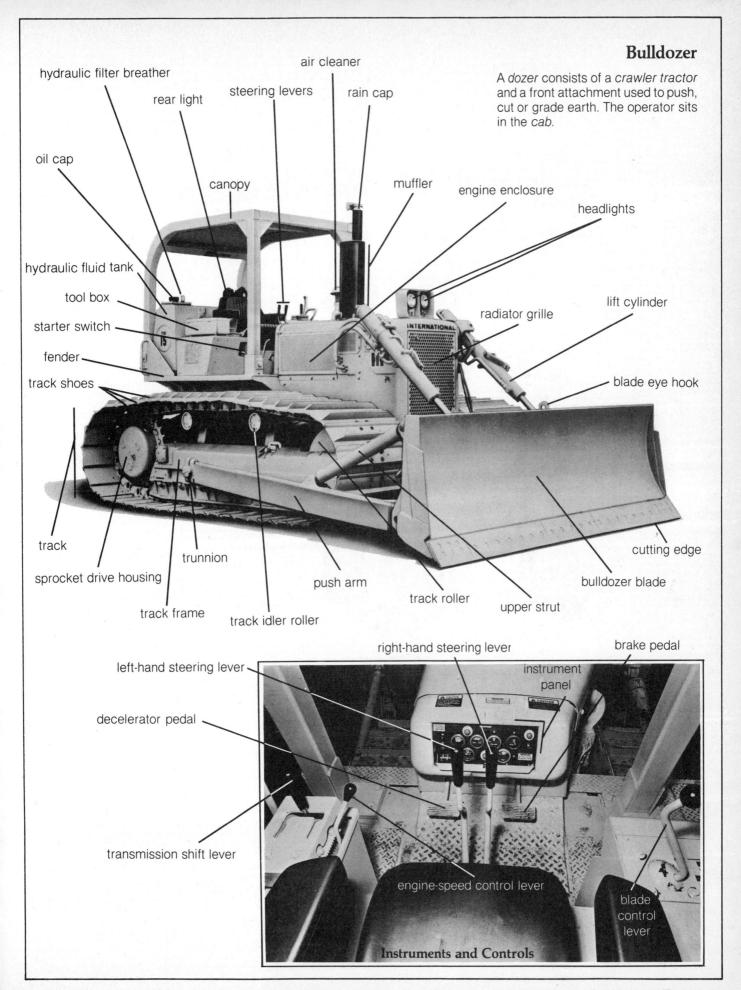

Bulldozer

A *dozer* consists of a *crawler tractor* and a front attachment used to push, cut or grade earth. The operator sits in the *cab*.

hydraulic filter breather

rear light

steering levers

air cleaner

rain cap

oil cap

canopy

muffler

engine enclosure

headlights

hydraulic fluid tank

tool box

starter switch

radiator grille

lift cylinder

fender

blade eye hook

track shoes

track

sprocket drive housing

trunnion

track frame

track idler roller

push arm

track roller

upper strut

bulldozer blade

cutting edge

left-hand steering lever

decelerator pedal

transmission shift lever

right-hand steering lever

instrument panel

brake pedal

engine-speed control lever

blade control lever

Instruments and Controls

435

Construction Equipment

Transit and Jackhammer

A transit is used by *engineers* and *surveyors* to determine *angles, bearings* and *levels*. It is mounted on a three-legged stand called a *tripod*. A weight, known as a *plumb* or *plumb bob*, is suspended directly below the telescope to determine *true vertical*.

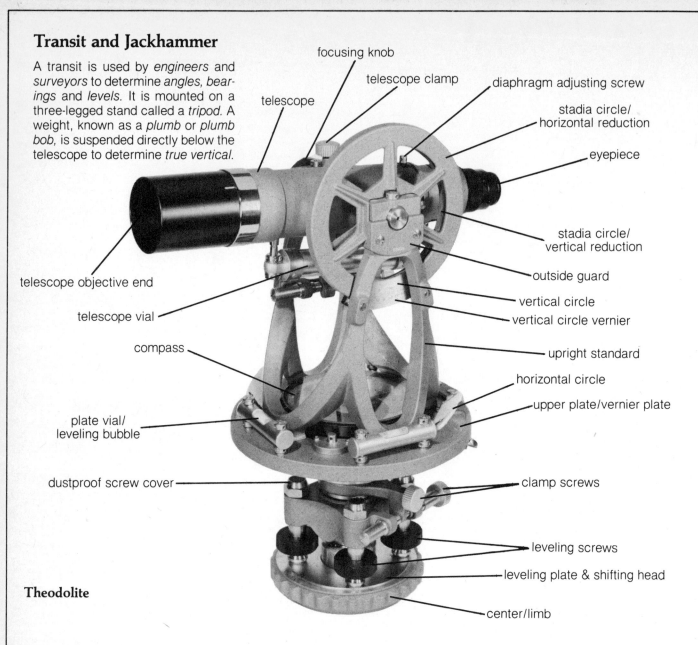

focusing knob

telescope clamp

diaphragm adjusting screw

stadia circle/ horizontal reduction

eyepiece

telescope

stadia circle/ vertical reduction

outside guard

vertical circle

vertical circle vernier

telescope objective end

telescope vial

compass

upright standard

horizontal circle

upper plate/vernier plate

plate vial/ leveling bubble

dustproof screw cover

clamp screws

leveling screws

leveling plate & shifting head

center/limb

Theodolite

Jackhammer/Breaker Hammer

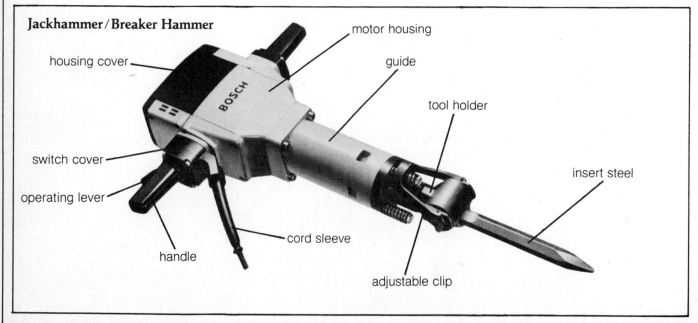

housing cover

motor housing

guide

tool holder

BOSCH

switch cover

operating lever

insert steel

cord sleeve

handle

adjustable clip

Voting Booth

Voting booths, or *mechanized voting machines,* are located at *polling places,* or *polls.* An *x-indication* appears next to a candidate's name when a lever is pressed. When a *voter* presses levers for every candidate of a single political party, it is called voting a *straight ticket.* Any variation is a *split ballot.*

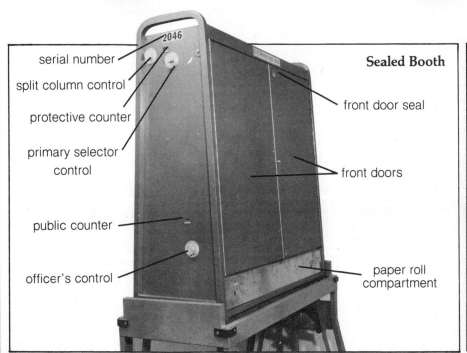

R. F. Shoup corp. 10-35

- light
- question index column
- office index column
- candidate's name column
- selection levers/ individual voting levers
- curtain
- personal choice/ write-in
- voter handle
- ballot/face
- custodian's seal
- officer's lock & seal
- poll's open & closed indicator

Mechanical Voting Booth

Electronic Voting System

Sealed Booth

- 2046
- serial number
- split column control
- protective counter
- primary selector control
- public counter
- officer's control
- front door seal
- front doors
- paper roll compartment
- ballot layout
- privacy curtain
- electronic touch button voting positions
- console door

Computing Tools

Computer Workstation

A workstation uses the computer's problem solving ability to generate drawings or perform complex design analyses. It is made up of a *central processing unit*, or *CPU*, and a *display monitor* and keypad, all of which is referred to as *hardware*. *Application packages*, or *software*, come on *digital tapes* and both *hard and floppy disks*. Within the CPU, data and files are stored in *random access memory*, or *RAM*, and *read only memory*, or *ROM*.

cathode ray tube/CRT

monitor/high-resolution display

Mexico, Central America
& The West Indies

floppy disk drive

function keys

alpha-numeric
keypad

keyboard

numeric
keypad

cursor control/puck

reset switch

circuit boards/
central processing
unit/CPU

hard disk drive

tablet/menu/
graphics functions
selector

adjustable platform/
ergostand

data file server/
deskside electronics cabinet

pedestal

movable base

Computer Aided Design System/CAD

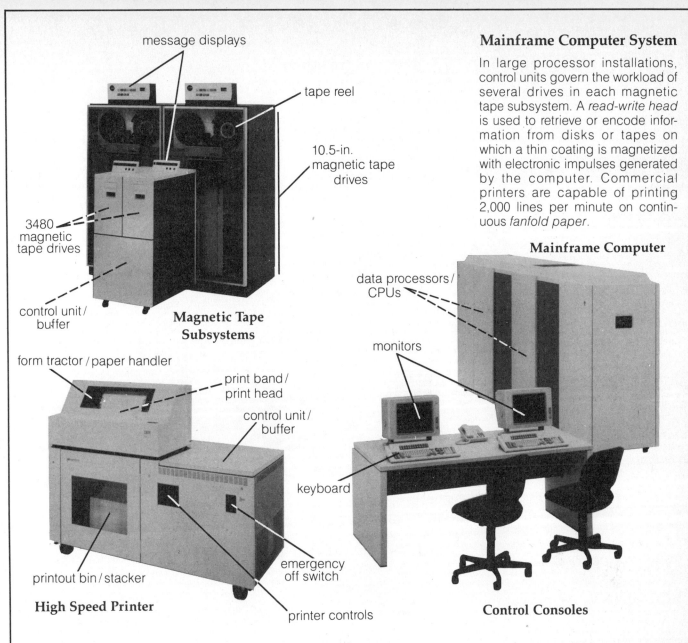

message displays

tape reel

10.5-in.
magnetic tape
drives

3480
magnetic
tape drives

control unit /
buffer

**Magnetic Tape
Subsystems**

Mainframe Computer System

In large processor installations, control units govern the workload of several drives in each magnetic tape subsystem. A *read-write head* is used to retrieve or encode information from disks or tapes on which a thin coating is magnetized with electronic impulses generated by the computer. Commercial printers are capable of printing 2,000 lines per minute on continuous *fanfold paper*.

Mainframe Computer

data processors /
CPUs

monitors

keyboard

Control Consoles

form tractor / paper handler

print band /
print head

control unit /
buffer

printout bin / stacker

emergency
off switch

High Speed Printer

printer controls

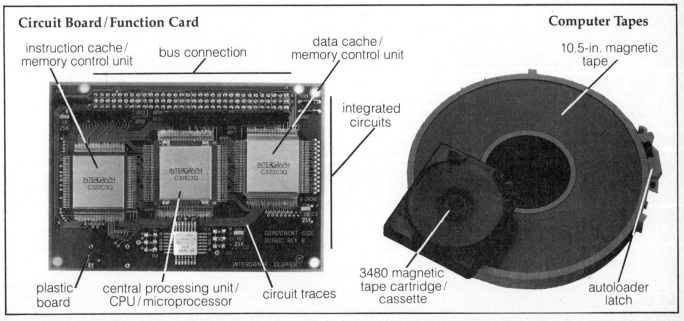

Circuit Board / Function Card

Computer Tapes

instruction cache /
memory control unit

bus connection

data cache /
memory control unit

10.5-in. magnetic
tape

integrated
circuits

plastic
board

central processing unit /
CPU / microprocessor

circuit traces

3480 magnetic
tape cartridge /
cassette

autoloader
latch

Computing Tools

Cash Register

The money drawer of a cash register is the *cash box,* or *till.* A roll of coins put up in paper is a *rouleau.* A *checkout center,* such as the one shown here, is sometimes equipped with a penlike optical *scanner* that translates information on the Universal Product Code, or *UPC label,* into a *cash register receipt* or *item-by-item tape.* It can also feed data to a *central inventory control unit.*

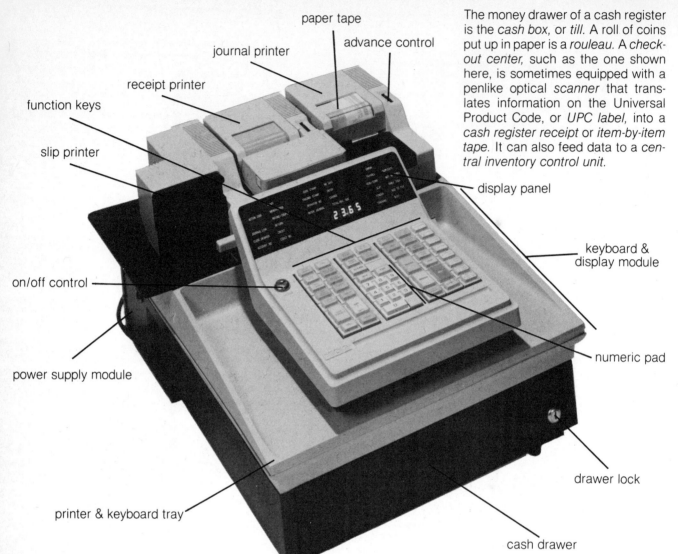

- paper tape
- advance control
- journal printer
- receipt printer
- function keys
- slip printer
- display panel
- on/off control
- keyboard & display module
- power supply module
- numeric pad
- printer & keyboard tray
- drawer lock
- cash drawer

Universal Product Code

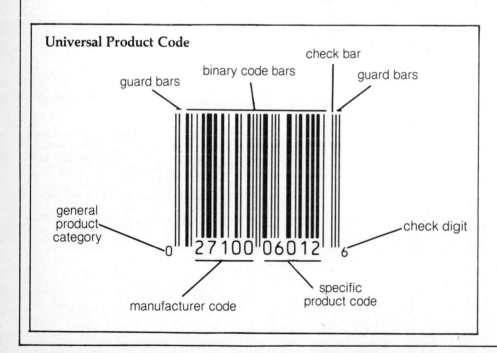

- guard bars
- binary code bars
- check bar
- guard bars
- general product category
- check digit
- manufacturer code
- specific product code

0 27100 06012 6

Calculators

The electronic calculator has generally replaced the *adding machine* today. The linear slide rule, seen here, often has scales on both sides. A *circular slide rule* can only be used for *multiplication* and *division*. A *cylindrical slide rule* is a series of long scales wound around a cylinder like a screw thread. The abacus is an ancient calculator used for solving problems of *addition*, *subtraction*, *multiplication* and *division*, all by the movement of beads. Other early devices include *counting rods*, or "*bones*."

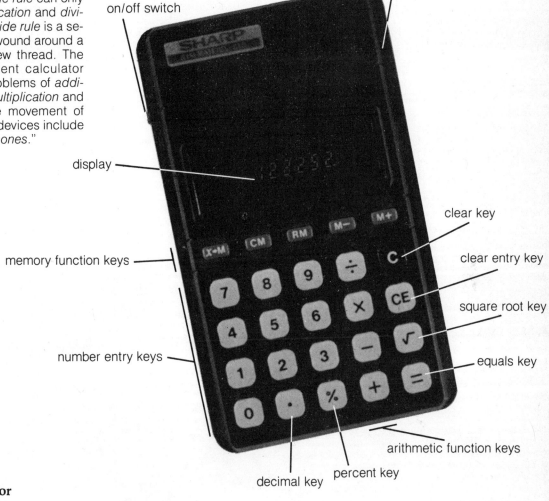

casing

on/off switch

display

memory function keys

number entry keys

clear key

clear entry key

square root key

equals key

arithmetic function keys

decimal key

percent key

Electronic Calculator

Linear Slide Rule

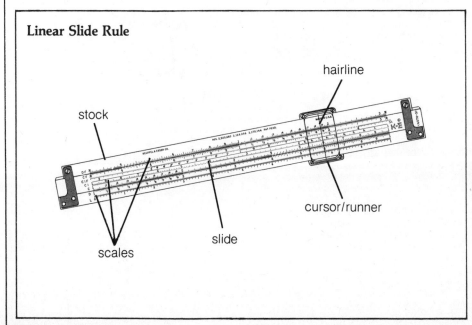

hairline

stock

scales

slide

cursor/runner

Abacus

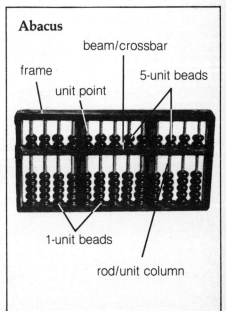

beam/crossbar

frame

unit point

5-unit beads

1-unit beads

rod/unit column

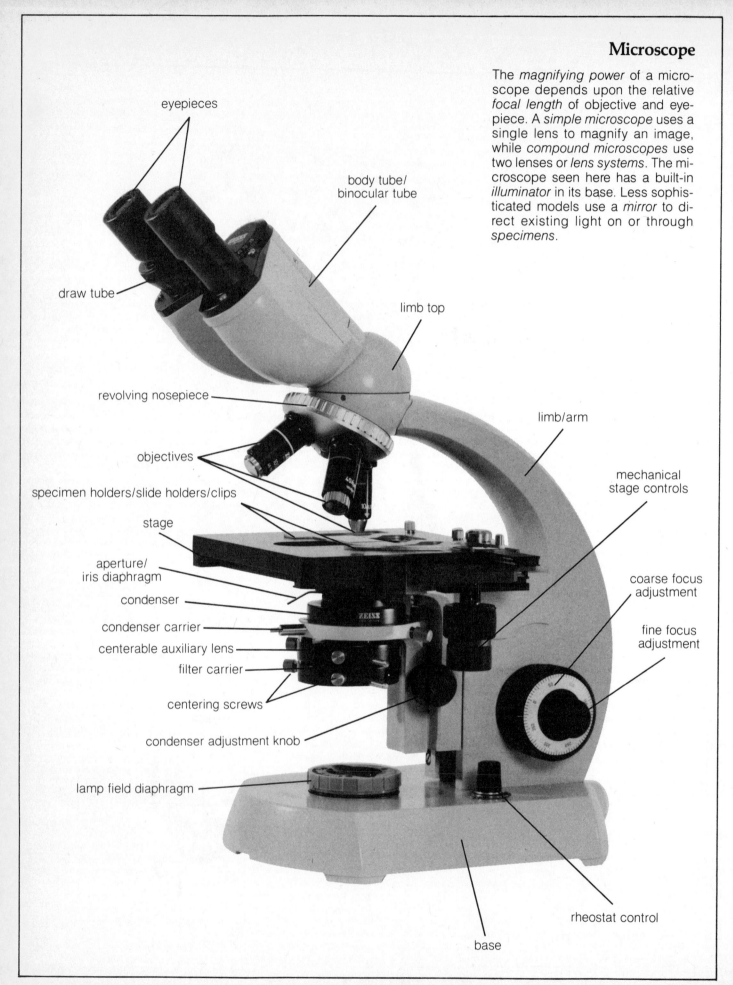

Microscope

The *magnifying power* of a microscope depends upon the relative *focal length* of objective and eyepiece. A *simple microscope* uses a single lens to magnify an image, while *compound microscopes* use two lenses or *lens systems*. The microscope seen here has a built-in *illuminator* in its base. Less sophisticated models use a *mirror* to direct existing light on or through *specimens*.

eyepieces

body tube/ binocular tube

draw tube

limb top

revolving nosepiece

limb/arm

objectives

mechanical stage controls

specimen holders/slide holders/clips

stage

aperture/ iris diaphragm

coarse focus adjustment

condenser

fine focus adjustment

condenser carrier

centerable auxiliary lens

filter carrier

centering screws

condenser adjustment knob

lamp field diaphragm

rheostat control

base

Telescope & Binoculars

A *refracting telescope,* such as the one seen here, relies on the objective lens to concentrate incoming light. A *reflecting telescope* employs a *concave mirror* to do the same task. Binoculars are composed of two similar telescopes, one for each eye. *Field glasses* are lightweight binoculars that employ *erecting telescopes* of the *spyglass* type, while *opera glasses,* designed for use inside, use *Galilean telescopes.*

objective outer cell

objective lens

telescope maintube

dewcap/sunshade

cradle

altitude coarse-motion clamp

viewfinder/guide scope

slow-motion control knobs

viewfinder collimating screw

azimuth coarse-motion clamp

eyepiece

altazimuth mounting

focus knob

star diagonal

fine focus sleeve

drawtube

eyepiece holder

tripod leg

tripod accessories shelf

shelf mount

Binoculars

central focusing drive

eyecup

eyepiece

ocular lens

hinge

body/frame

objective lens

Telescope

Scientific Tools

Radar and Sonar

The cursor on a radar display unit is used to determine the *relative bearings* of *targets*. Most units come with a *viewing hood* and *magnifying lens*. Sonar, formerly known as *asdic*, uses a trainable *transducer* housed in a *soundome* beneath a vessel's hull.

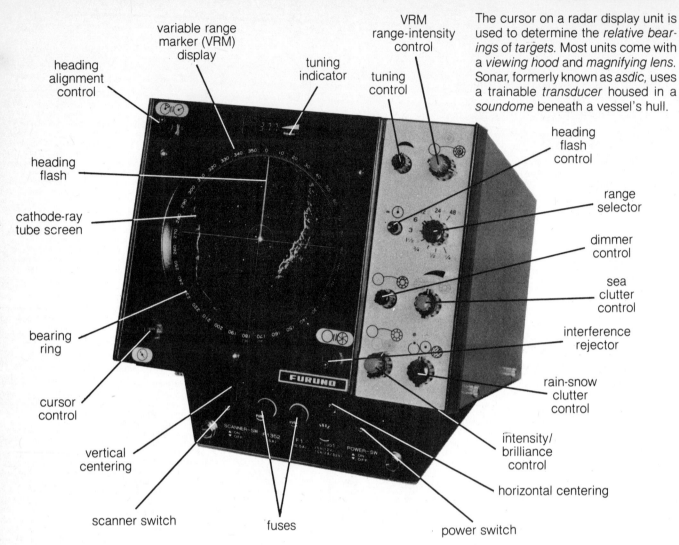

heading alignment control

variable range marker (VRM) display

tuning indicator

VRM range-intensity control

tuning control

heading flash control

heading flash

range selector

cathode-ray tube screen

dimmer control

sea clutter control

bearing ring

interference rejector

cursor control

rain-snow clutter control

vertical centering

intensity/ brilliance control

scanner switch

fuses

horizontal centering

power switch

Radar Display Unit

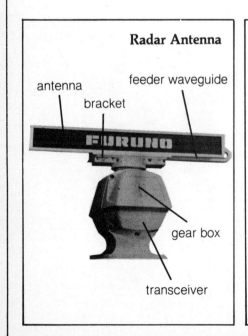

Radar Antenna

antenna

feeder waveguide

bracket

FURUNO

gear box

transceiver

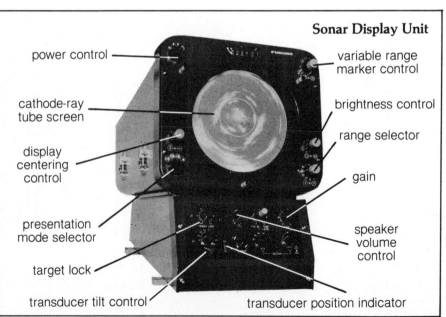

Sonar Display Unit

power control

variable range marker control

cathode-ray tube screen

brightness control

range selector

display centering control

gain

presentation mode selector

speaker volume control

target lock

transducer tilt control

transducer position indicator

Sensing Devices

444

Detectors

A *metal locator* works by subtracting a frequency produced by an *oscillator* from a frequency produced by internal circuitry. When the *search coil* is near a metal object, this produces an audio frequency in the speaker or headphones.

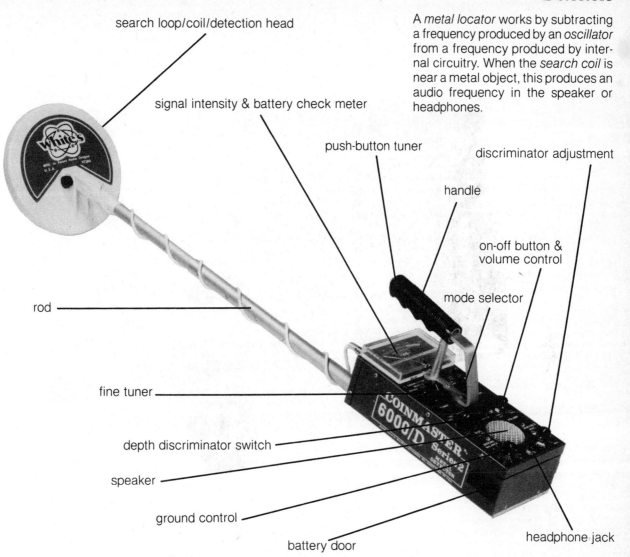

search loop/coil/detection head

signal intensity & battery check meter

push-button tuner

discriminator adjustment

handle

on-off button & volume control

mode selector

rod

fine tuner

depth discriminator switch

speaker

ground control

battery door

headphone jack

Metal and Mineral Detector

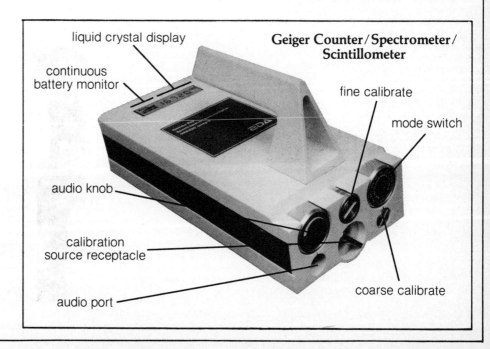

liquid crystal display

Geiger Counter/Spectrometer/ Scintillometer

continuous battery monitor

fine calibrate

mode switch

audio knob

calibration source receptacle

coarse calibrate

audio port

Sensing Devices

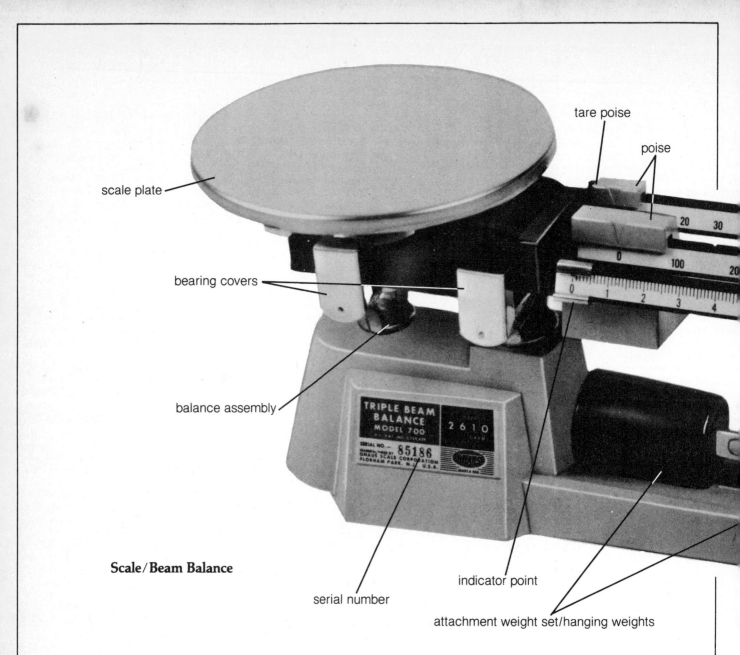

scale plate

tare poise

poise

bearing covers

balance assembly

TRIPLE BEAM BALANCE
MODEL 700

2610

SERIAL NO. — 85186
OHAUS SCALE CORPORATION
FLORHAM PARK, N.J. U.S.A.

20   30

0

100   20

0   1   2   3   4

Scale/Beam Balance

serial number

indicator point

attachment weight set/hanging weights

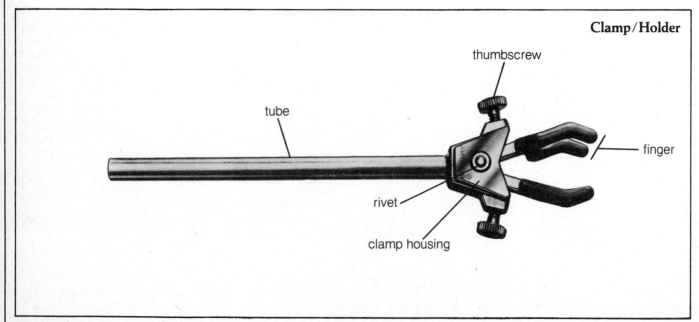

Clamp/Holder

thumbscrew

tube

finger

rivet

clamp housing

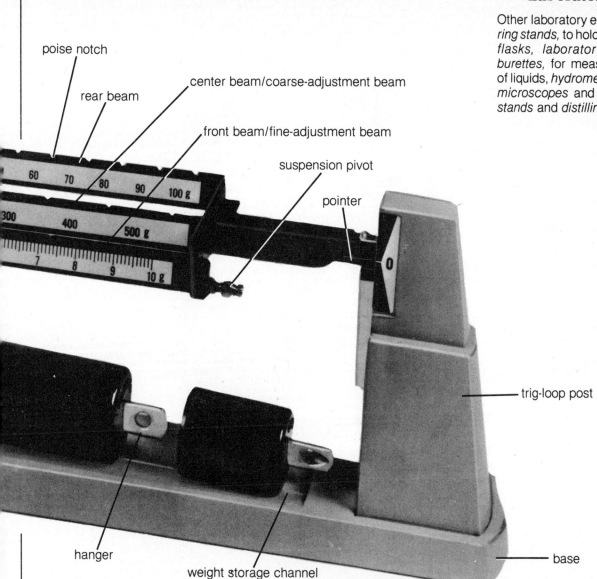

Other laboratory equipment includes *ring stands,* to hold various cylinders, *flasks, laboratory thermometers, burettes,* for measuring the volume of liquids, *hydrometers, vacuum jars, microscopes* and *slides, adjustable stands* and *distilling equipment.*

poise notch

rear beam

center beam/coarse-adjustment beam

front beam/fine-adjustment beam

suspension pivot

pointer

60 70 80 90 100 g

300 400 500 g

7 8 9 10 g

0

trig-loop post

hanger

weight storage channel

base

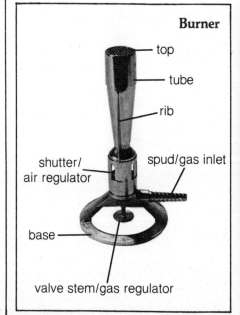

Burner

top

tube

rib

shutter/
air regulator

spud/gas inlet

base

valve stem/gas regulator

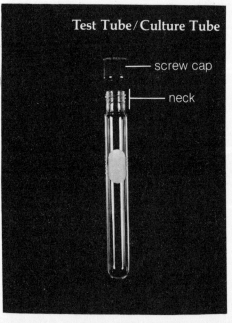

Test Tube/Culture Tube

screw cap

neck

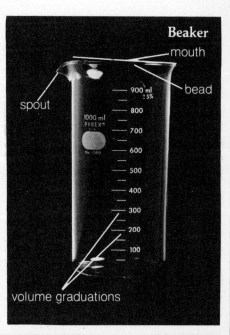

Beaker

mouth

bead

spout

900 ml ±5%

800

1000 ml
PYREX®

700

No. 1060

600

500

400

300

200

100

volume graduations

Examination Equipment

The scopes seen below are used by *Eye, Ear, Nose and Throat Doctors,* or *EENT specialists.* The speculum is used by *gynecologists* and *obstetricians.* *Headlights* mounted on headbands provide a light source for doctors.

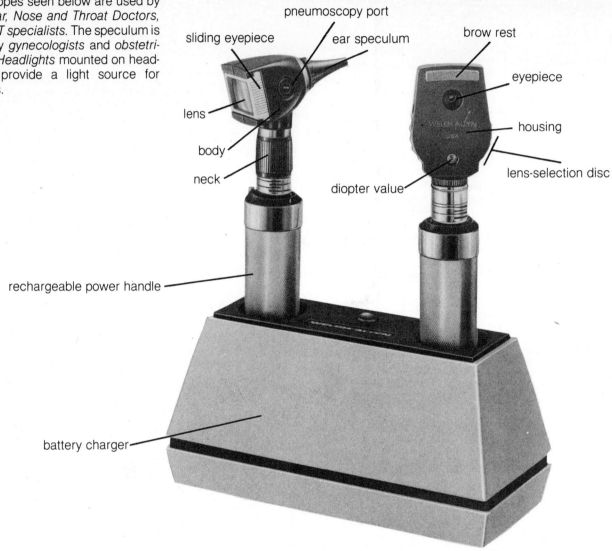

pneumoscopy port

sliding eyepiece

ear speculum

brow rest

eyepiece

lens

housing

body

diopter value

lens-selection disc

neck

rechargeable power handle

battery charger

Ear Scope/Otoscope

Eye Scope/Ophthalmoscope

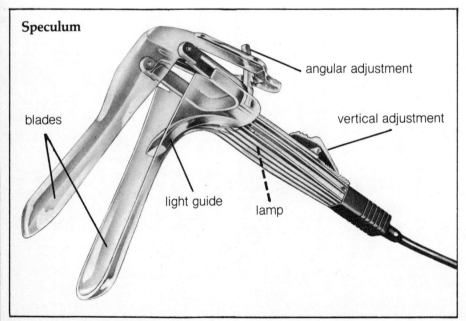

Speculum

angular adjustment

blades

vertical adjustment

light guide

lamp

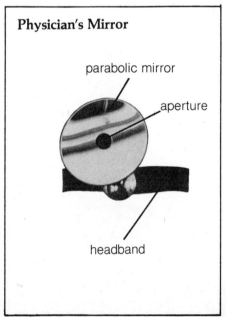

Physician's Mirror

parabolic mirror

aperture

headband

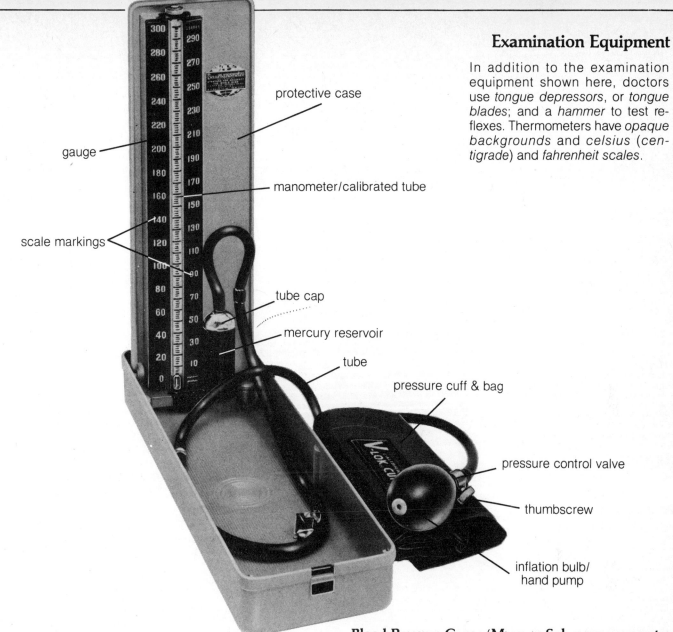

Examination Equipment

In addition to the examination equipment shown here, doctors use *tongue depressors*, or *tongue blades*; and a *hammer* to test reflexes. Thermometers have *opaque backgrounds* and *celsius (centigrade)* and *fahrenheit scales*.

gauge

protective case

manometer/calibrated tube

scale markings

tube cap

mercury reservoir

tube

pressure cuff & bag

pressure control valve

thumbscrew

inflation bulb/ hand pump

Blood Pressure Gauge/Mercury Sphygmomanometer

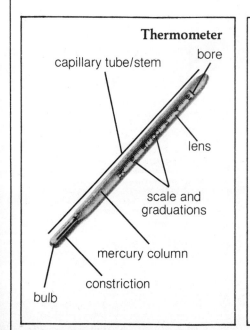

Thermometer

capillary tube/stem

bore

lens

scale and graduations

mercury column

constriction

bulb

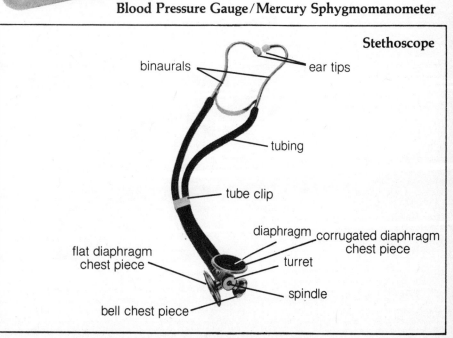

Stethoscope

binaurals

ear tips

tubing

tube clip

diaphragm

corrugated diaphragm chest piece

flat diaphragm chest piece

turret

spindle

bell chest piece

Medical Tools

Medical Tables

Surgical, or *operating room, tables,* have built-in *channels* for holding *x-ray cassettes.* Among the accessories that can be attached to them are *intravenous,* or *IV, equipment,* arm- and *footboard extensions, crutch sockets* for holding legs in position, and buckle-type *body-restraint straps.*

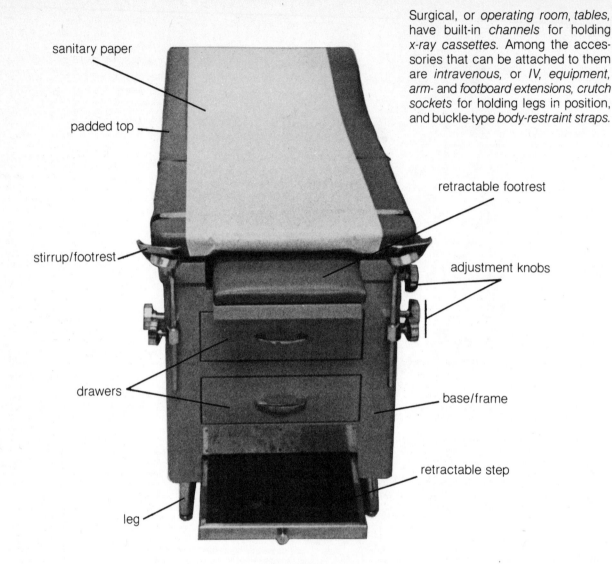

sanitary paper

padded top

retractable footrest

stirrup/footrest

adjustment knobs

drawers

base/frame

retractable step

leg

Examination Table

Surgical Table / Operating Table

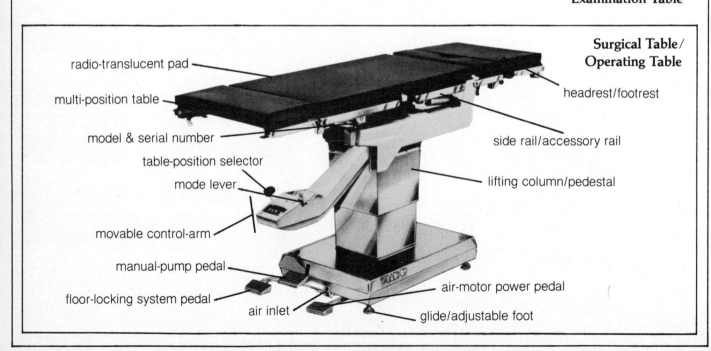

radio-translucent pad

multi-position table

model & serial number

table-position selector

mode lever

movable control-arm

manual-pump pedal

floor-locking system pedal

air inlet

headrest/footrest

side rail/accessory rail

lifting column/pedestal

air-motor power pedal

glide/adjustable foot

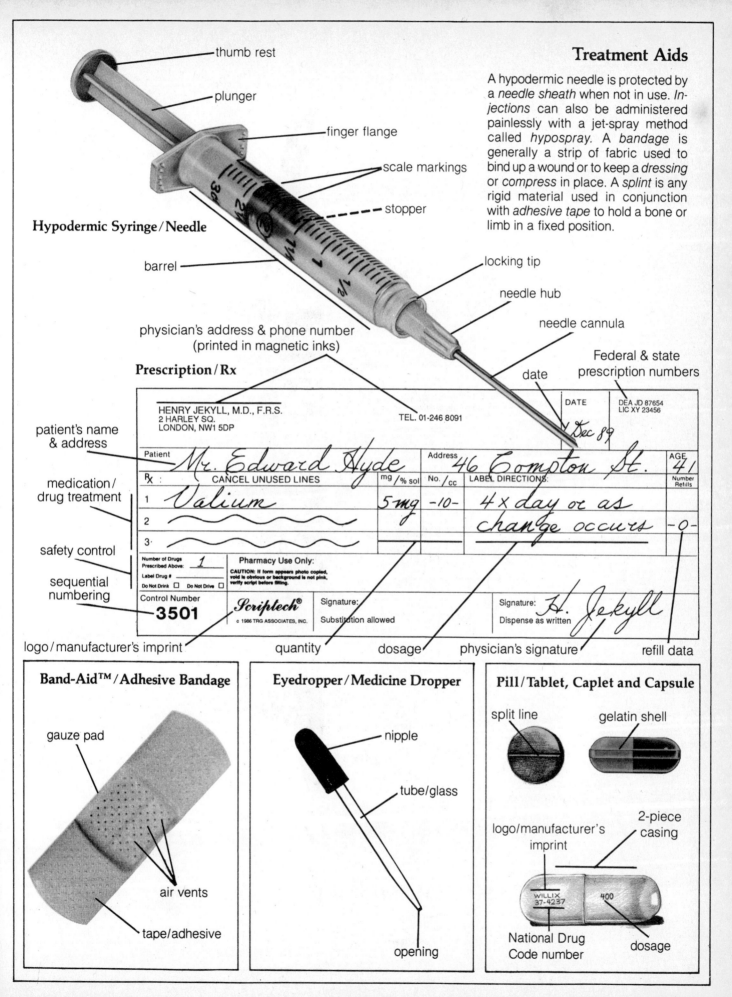

thumb rest

plunger

finger flange

scale markings

stopper

Treatment Aids

A hypodermic needle is protected by a *needle sheath* when not in use. *Injections* can also be administered painlessly with a jet-spray method called *hypospray*. A *bandage* is generally a strip of fabric used to bind up a wound or to keep a *dressing* or *compress* in place. A *splint* is any rigid material used in conjunction with *adhesive tape* to hold a bone or limb in a fixed position.

Hypodermic Syringe / Needle

barrel

locking tip

needle hub

needle cannula

physician's address & phone number
(printed in magnetic inks)

date

Federal & state
prescription numbers

Prescription / Rx

patient's name
& address

medication/
drug treatment

safety control

sequential
numbering

logo/manufacturer's imprint

HENRY JEKYLL, M.D., F.R.S.
2 HARLEY SQ.
LONDON, NW1 5DP

TEL. 01-246 8091

DATE	DEA JD 87654 LIC XY 23456
1 Dec 89	

Patient	*Mr. Edward Hyde*	Address	*46 Compton St.*	AGE *41*
Rx : CANCEL UNUSED LINES		mg / % sol	No. / cc	LABEL DIRECTIONS:	Number Refills
1	*Valium*	5 *mg*	–10–	*4 x day or as*	
2				*change occurs*	–0–
3·					

Number of Drugs Prescribed Above: *1*	Pharmacy Use Only:	Signature:		Signature: *H. Jekyll*
Label Drug #	CAUTION: If form appears photo copied, void is obvious or background is not pink, verify script before filling.			Dispense as written
Do Not Drink ☐ Do Not Drive ☐				
Control Number **3501**	*Scriptech*® © 1986 TRG ASSOCIATES, INC.	Substitution allowed		

quantity

dosage

physician's signature

refill data

Band-Aid™/Adhesive Bandage

gauze pad

air vents

tape/adhesive

Eyedropper/Medicine Dropper

nipple

tube/glass

opening

Pill/Tablet, Caplet and Capsule

split line

gelatin shell

logo/manufacturer's
imprint

2-piece
casing

WILLIX
37-4237

400

National Drug
Code number

dosage

Supportive Devices

Battery-powered *electric chairs* provide mobility for totally handicapped people. For minor leg and foot injuries, a *cane,* or *walking stick,* is used. Other supportive devices include *dialysis machines, iron lungs, oxygen tents, decompression chambers,* and *braces* of various kinds.

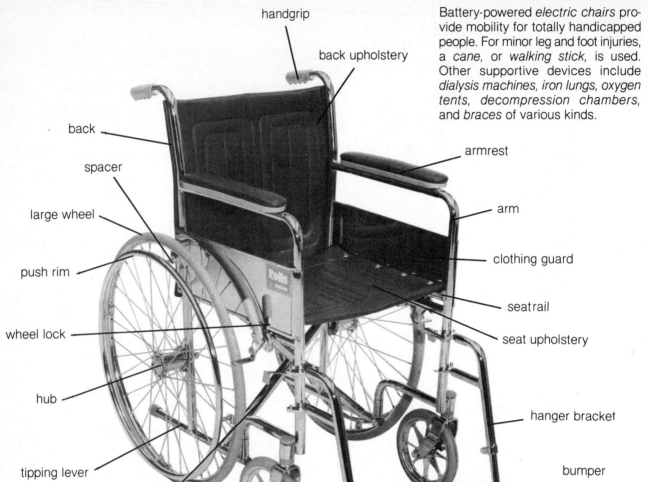

handgrip

back upholstery

back

spacer

large wheel

push rim

wheel lock

hub

tipping lever

cross brace

caster

axle bolt

armrest

arm

clothing guard

seat rail

seat upholstery

hanger bracket

bumper

heel loop

footplate

Wheelchair

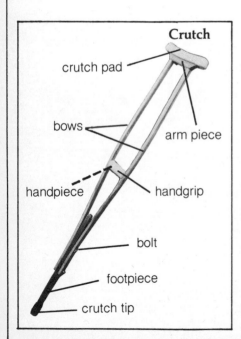

Crutch

crutch pad

bows

arm piece

handpiece

handgrip

bolt

footpiece

crutch tip

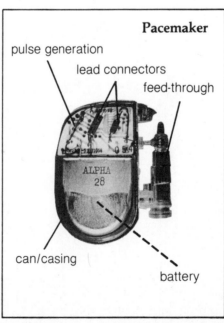

Pacemaker

pulse generation

lead connectors

feed-through

ALPHA 28

can/casing

battery

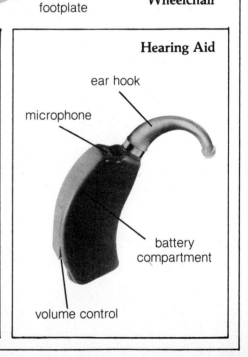

Hearing Aid

ear hook

microphone

battery compartment

volume control

Dental Corrective Devices

A *bridge* consists of one or more false teeth anchored between abutment teeth. The portion of the bridge that actually replaces the missing tooth or teeth is the *pontic*. A *crown* or *jacket crown* covers that part of the tooth normally protected by enamel. In *orthodontia*, the correction of the position of teeth, a *band* or *wire* is inserted in the slot and held in place by *rubber bands* looped over the tie wings.

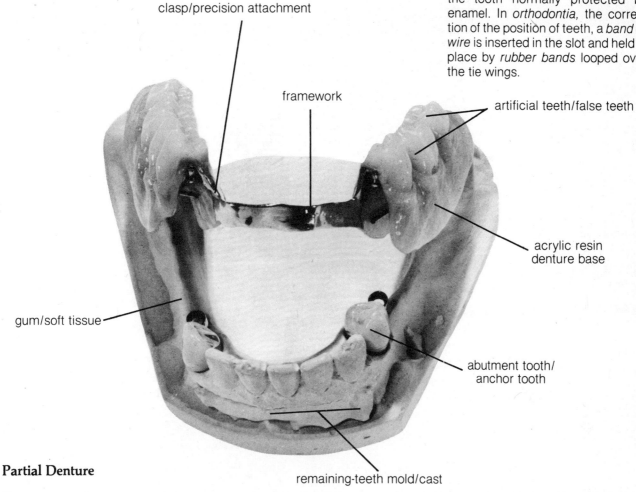

clasp/precision attachment

framework

artificial teeth/false teeth

acrylic resin denture base

gum/soft tissue

abutment tooth/ anchor tooth

Partial Denture

remaining-teeth mold/cast

Full Denture

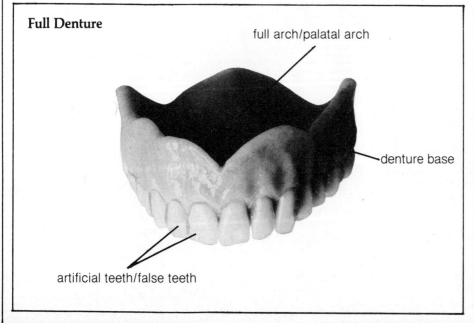

full arch/palatal arch

denture base

artificial teeth/false teeth

Braces/Orthodontic Bracket

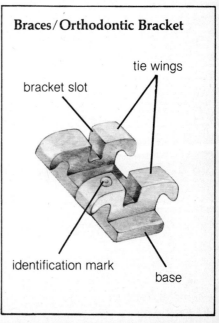

tie wings

bracket slot

identification mark

base

Dental Unit

A high-intensity *dental light* is usually attached to a dental unit, or *dental island*. Instrument trays may be attached to a *drift-free arm*, such as the one shown here, or to a *post-mounted arm*.

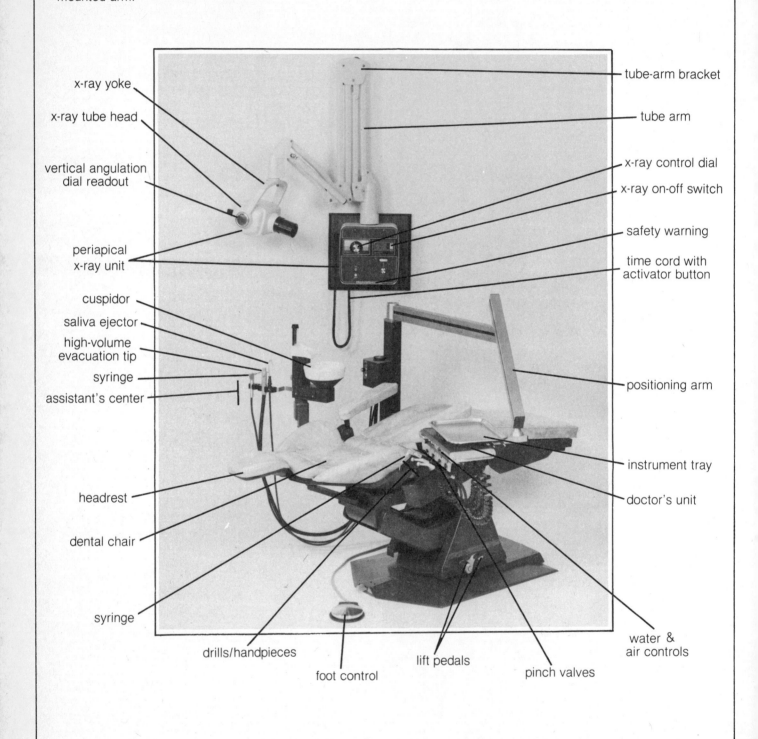

x-ray yoke

x-ray tube head

vertical angulation dial readout

periapical x-ray unit

cuspidor

saliva ejector

high-volume evacuation tip

syringe

assistant's center

headrest

dental chair

syringe

drills/handpieces

foot control

lift pedals

pinch valves

tube-arm bracket

tube arm

x-ray control dial

x-ray on-off switch

safety warning

time cord with activator button

positioning arm

instrument tray

doctor's unit

water & air controls

Dental Equipment

Fillings of *silver amalgam* or *inlays*, *cast restorations* of *gold, synthetic porcelain* or *acrylic resins*, are used to fill *cavities*. Teeth can also be fitted with *crowns* or *caps*.

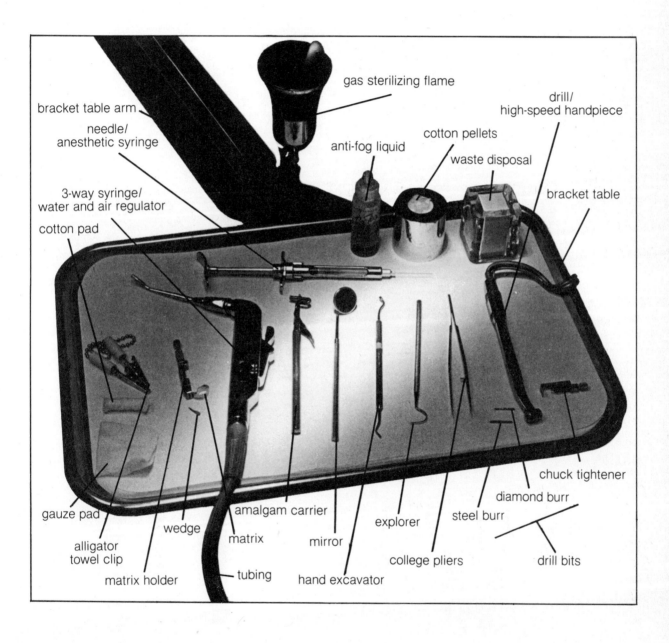

gas sterilizing flame

bracket table arm

needle/ anesthetic syringe

3-way syringe/ water and air regulator

cotton pad

anti-fog liquid

cotton pellets

waste disposal

drill/ high-speed handpiece

bracket table

chuck tightener

diamond burr

gauze pad

alligator towel clip

wedge

matrix

matrix holder

tubing

amalgam carrier

mirror

hand excavator

explorer

college pliers

steel burr

drill bits

Teeth

Each tooth has one or two *neighbors* and a biting *partner* in the opposite jaw. Teeth fit into *sockets*. The first set of teeth are *baby teeth*, or *milk teeth*, replaced in time by permanent teeth. A person with a fondness for sugary edibles is said to have a *sweet tooth*.

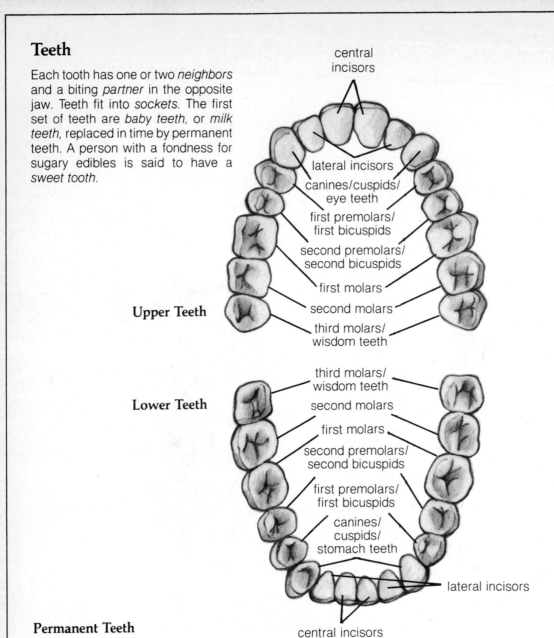

central incisors

lateral incisors

canines/cuspids/ eye teeth

first premolars/ first bicuspids

second premolars/ second bicuspids

first molars

second molars

third molars/ wisdom teeth

Upper Teeth

Lower Teeth

third molars/ wisdom teeth

second molars

first molars

second premolars/ second bicuspids

first premolars/ first bicuspids

canines/ cuspids/ stomach teeth

lateral incisors

central incisors

Permanent Teeth

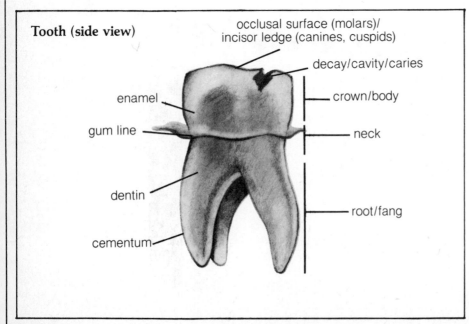

Tooth (side view)

occlusal surface (molars)/ incisor ledge (canines, cuspids)

decay/cavity/caries

enamel

crown/body

gum line

neck

dentin

root/fang

cementum

Tooth (top view)

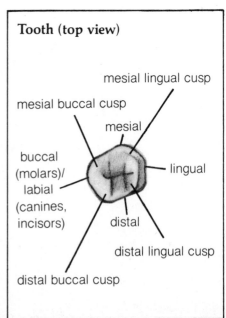

mesial lingual cusp

mesial buccal cusp

mesial

buccal (molars)/ labial (canines, incisors)

lingual

distal

distal lingual cusp

distal buccal cusp

Vault and Safe

Vaults are connected to *alarm systems*, which include *bells* and *silent alarms*. *Time locks* open safes or vaults at a predetermined time and prevent their being opened otherwise. A *strongbox* is a stoutly made box or chest for preserving valuable possessions. Most safes are insulated to protect against fire as well as theft. A home *money box*, *coin bank* or *piggy bank* is opened at the bottom or with a hammer.

door jamb

architrave

door hinge

bolt-retracting gears

primary combination dial

vault door

locking bolts

door handle

bolt-activating gear rings

bolt guide ring

safe deposit boxes

day gate

bolt holes

vestibule

bridge

timelock/movement dial

bolt linkage

dust cover/ bolt cover

Vault

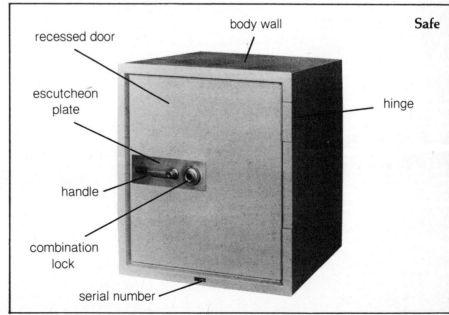

body wall

Safe

recessed door

escutcheon plate

hinge

handle

combination lock

serial number

Security Devices

Door Locks

Many mortise locks have two *buttons* below the latch bolt which allow the *outside knob* to be independently locked or unlocked. Bolts fit into a *striker plate,* attached to the door frame. A *latch* is a device which holds a door closed, but cannot be locked. A *catch* holds lightweight doors, such as cabinet doors, closed. A *lockset* has the features of a lock and a catch.

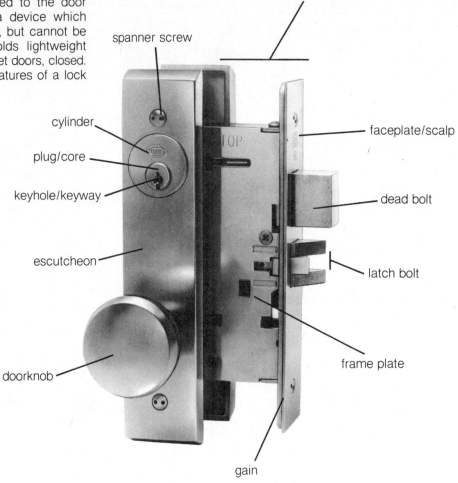

latch assembly

spanner screw

cylinder

plug/core

keyhole/keyway

escutcheon

doorknob

faceplate/scalp

dead bolt

latch bolt

frame plate

gain

Mortise Lock

Chain Lock/Door Bolt

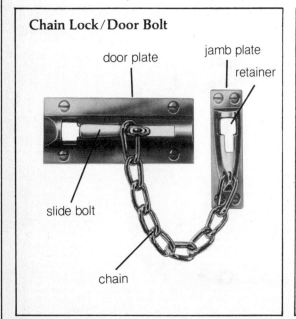

door plate

jamb plate

retainer

slide bolt

chain

Inter-grip Rim Lock

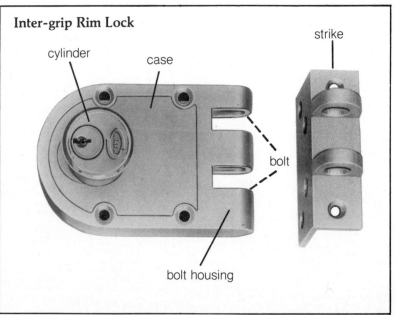

cylinder

case

strike

bolt

bolt housing

Key and Padlock

A key is inserted into a lock's cylinder via a *keyway*. The angled serrations, or *cuts*, on a key blade correspond to different sized *pin-tumblers*, or *pins*, within the lock cylinder. A key that has not yet been configured to any particular lock is a *blank*. A key used to open many common locks is a *skeleton key*.

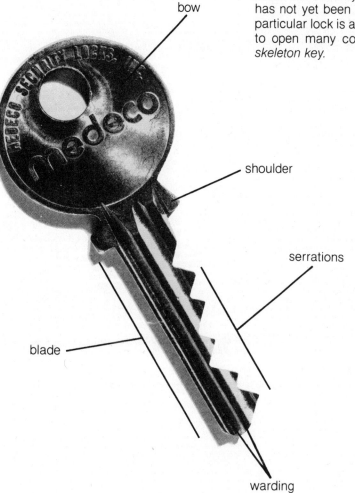

bow

shoulder

serrations

blade

warding

Key

Padlock

shackle

cylinder/plug

case/body

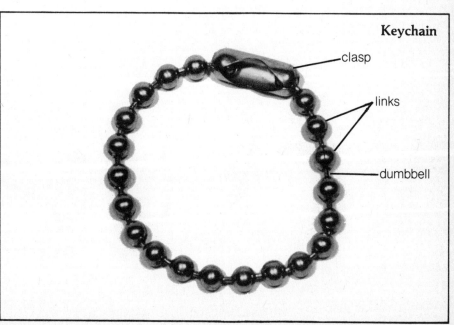

Keychain

clasp

links

dumbbell

Security Devices

Hinge and Hasp

In addition to the *butt hinge,* seen here, there are *pivot hinges, full-surface hinges, half-surface hinges, spring hinges, strap hinges* and *continuous hinges.* Hinge pivot pins or *fixed pins,* used on smaller hinges, are available in a variety of ornamental *heads,* or *caps,* such as the ball tip seen here. A *safety hasp* is secured with a padlock or pin.

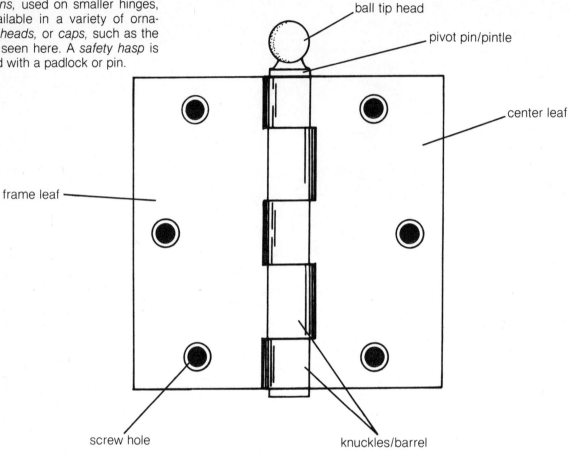

ball tip head

pivot pin/pintle

center leaf

frame leaf

screw hole

knuckles/barrel

Hinge

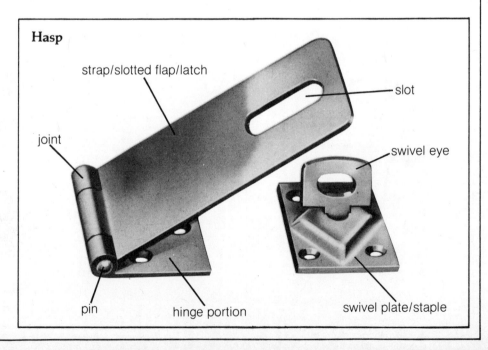

Hasp

strap/slotted flap/latch

slot

joint

swivel eye

pin

hinge portion

swivel plate/staple

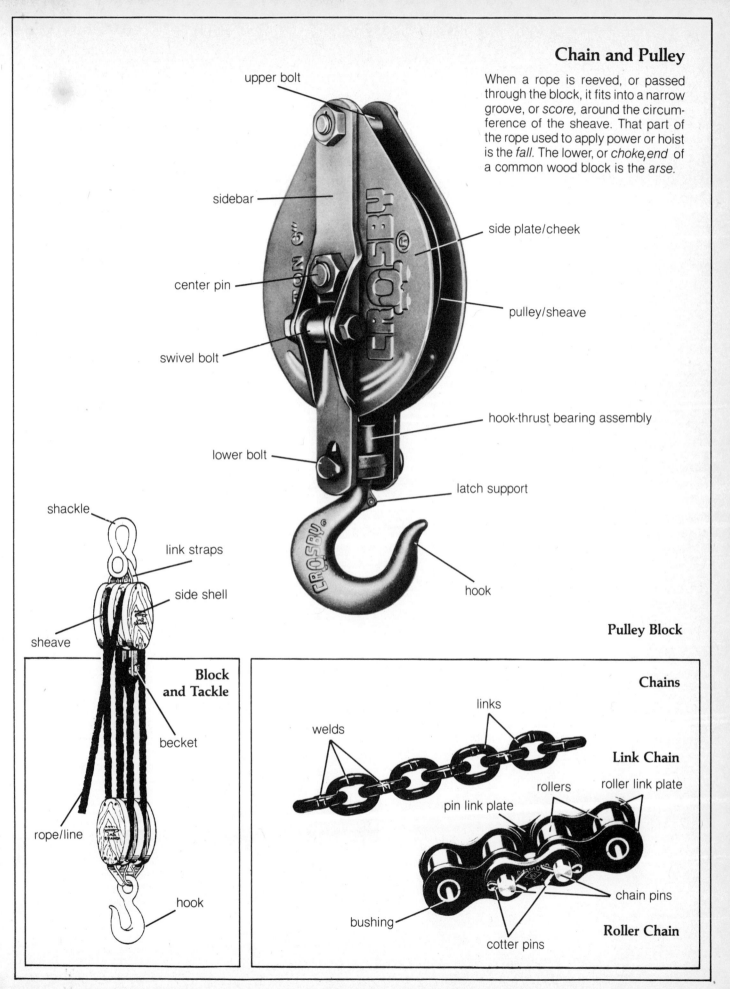

Chain and Pulley

When a rope is reeved, or passed through the block, it fits into a narrow groove, or *score,* around the circumference of the sheave. That part of the rope used to apply power or hoist is the *fall.* The lower, or *choke,end* of a common wood block is the *arse.*

upper bolt

sidebar

side plate/cheek

center pin

pulley/sheave

swivel bolt

hook-thrust bearing assembly

lower bolt

latch support

shackle

link straps

side shell

sheave

Block and Tackle

becket

rope/line

hook

hook

hook

Pulley Block

Chains

links

welds

Link Chain

rollers

roller link plate

pin link plate

chain pins

bushing

cotter pins

Roller Chain

Execution Devices

The blade on the guillotine is released by a *release cord* or *release button.* The Italian *mannaia* and the Scottish *maiden* were variations of the French guillotine. A *gibbet,* similar to a gallows, has a single, horizontal arm from which the noose was hung. On an electric chair, electrodes are attached to the prisoner's head and leg to complete the circuit. A *tumbrel* is any vehicle used to bring condemned people to the place of execution.

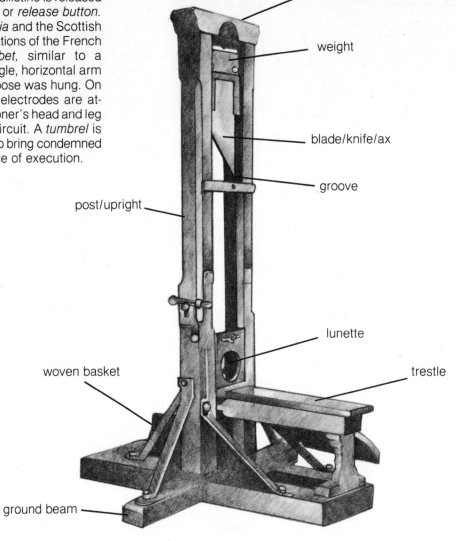

crossbeam

weight

blade/knife/ax

groove

post/upright

lunette

woven basket

trestle

ground beam

Guillotine

Gallows

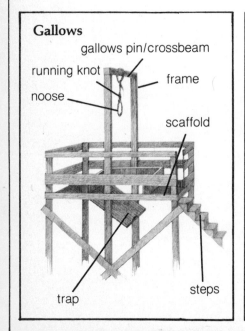

gallows pin/crossbeam

running knot

frame

noose

scaffold

trap

steps

Electric Chair

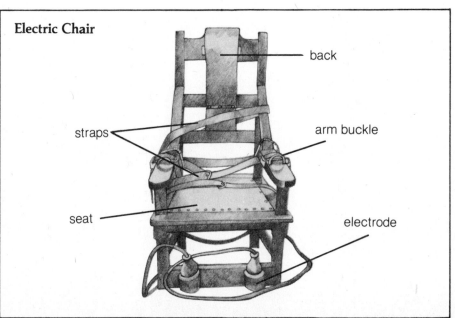

back

straps

arm buckle

seat

electrode

Thrusting and Cutting Weapons

A knife or sword is stored in a *sheath*. The handle fits over the *tang*, a projection from the upper end of the blade.

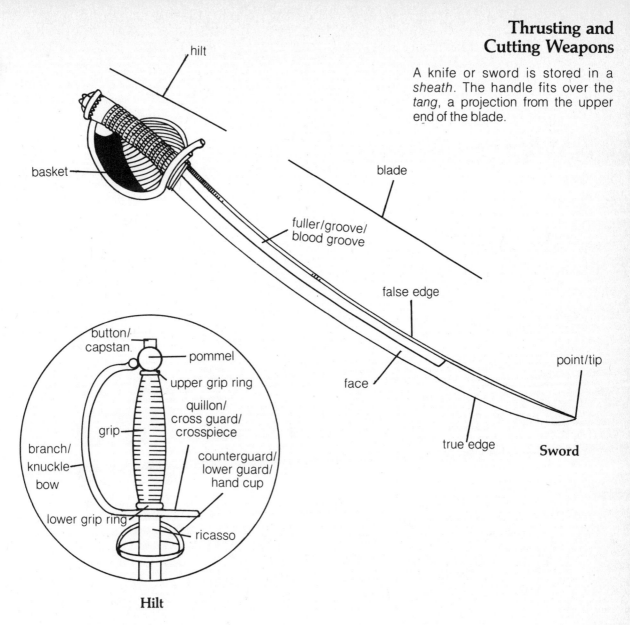

hilt

basket

blade

fuller/groove/
blood groove

false edge

face

point/tip

true edge

Sword

button/
capstan

pommel

upper grip ring

quillon/
cross guard/
crosspiece

grip

branch/
knuckle
bow

counterguard/
lower guard/
hand cup

lower grip ring

ricasso

Hilt

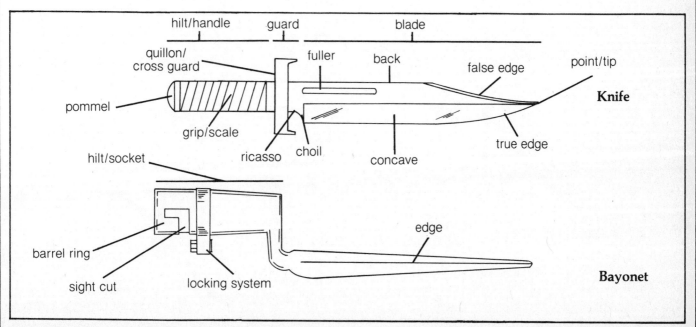

hilt/handle

guard

blade

quillon/
cross guard

fuller

back

false edge

point/tip

Knife

pommel

grip/scale

ricasso

choil

concave

true edge

hilt/socket

barrel ring

edge

sight cut

locking system

Bayonet

Medieval Arms

A round shield held at arm's length is called a *buckler,* while a shield held across the body by straps or handles called *enarmes* is a *target.* A shield offering protection during a siege is a *pavise.* Cutouts on the sides of a shield for holding spears to be thrown are called *bouches.* A shafted weapon having a *spear blade* and a pair of curved *lobes* at the base of the *spearhead* is a *partisan.*

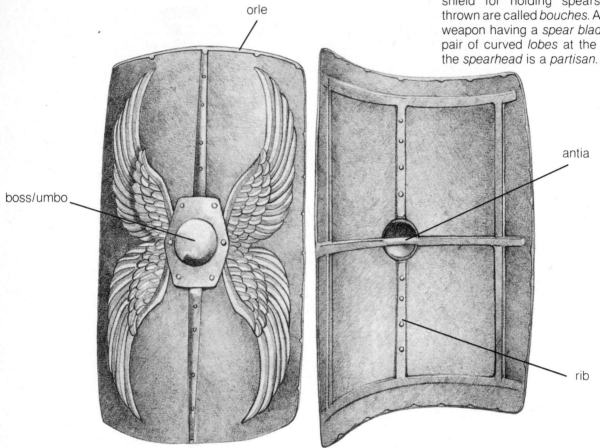

orle

boss/umbo

antia

rib

Shield

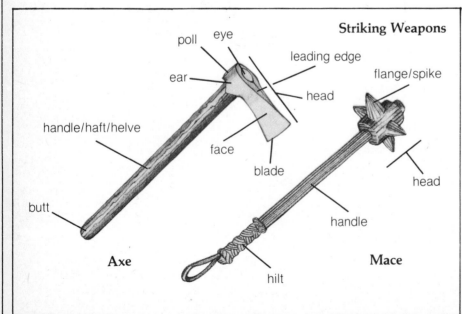

Striking Weapons

poll
eye
ear
leading edge
head
handle/haft/helve
face
blade
butt
flange/spike
head
handle
hilt

Axe

Mace

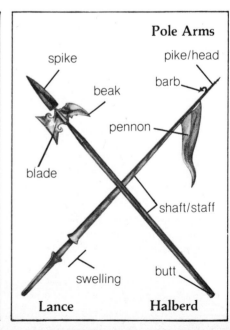

Pole Arms

spike
pike/head
beak
barb
pennon
blade
shaft/staff
swelling
butt

Lance

Halberd

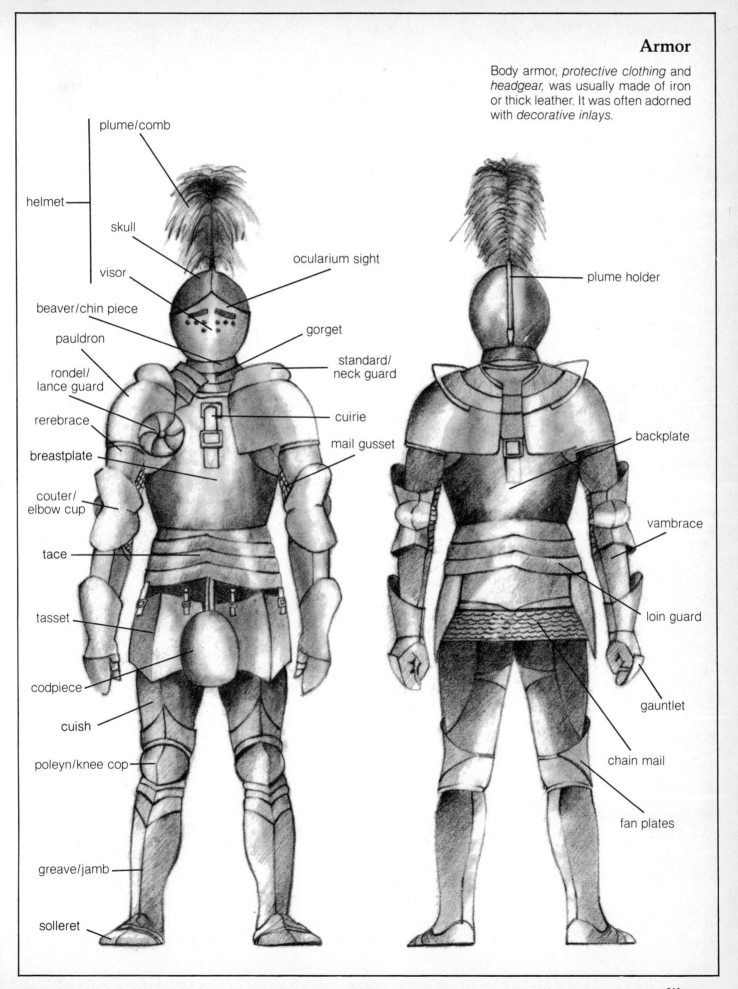

Armor

Body armor, *protective clothing* and *headgear*, was usually made of iron or thick leather. It was often adorned with *decorative inlays*.

plume/comb

helmet

skull

visor

beaver/chin piece

pauldron

rondel/
lance guard

rerebrace

breastplate

couter/
elbow cup

tace

tasset

codpiece

cuish

poleyn/knee cop

greave/jamb

solleret

ocularium sight

gorget

standard/
neck guard

cuirie

mail gusset

plume holder

backplate

vambrace

loin guard

gauntlet

chain mail

fan plates

Weapons

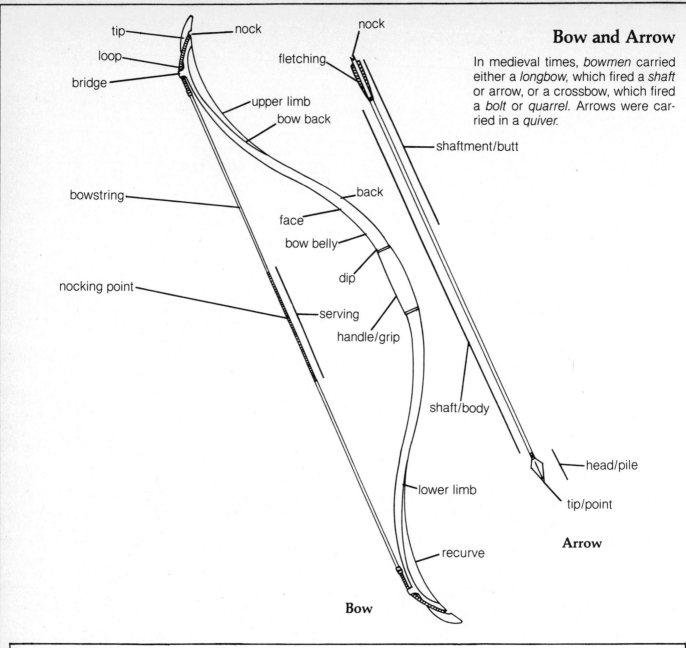

Bow and Arrow

In medieval times, *bowmen* carried either a *longbow,* which fired a *shaft* or arrow, or a crossbow, which fired a *bolt* or *quarrel.* Arrows were carried in a *quiver.*

tip

nock

loop

bridge

nock

fletching

upper limb

bow back

shaftment/butt

bowstring

back

face

bow belly

dip

nocking point

serving

handle/grip

shaft/body

head/pile

lower limb

tip/point

Arrow

recurve

Bow

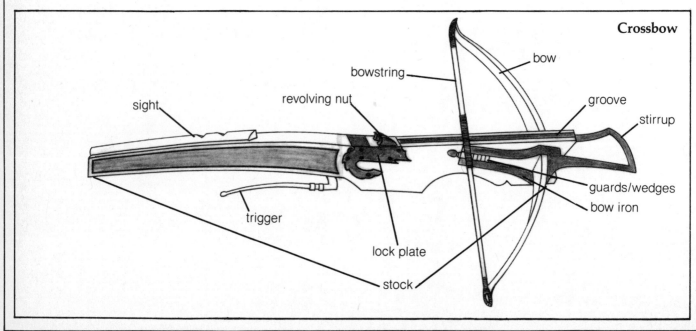

Crossbow

bow

bowstring

groove

stirrup

sight

revolving nut

trigger

guards/wedges

bow iron

lock plate

stock

Cannon and Catapult

Cannonballs fired by *muzzle-loaders* were transported in *caissons* and stacked in trays called *monkeys*. *Loaders* used a *swab* or *sponge* to get rid of residue, a *worm* to remove obstructions, and a *rammer* to drive the *projectile* into the *bore* at the muzzle, or *mouth,* of the cannon. Catapults were used to fire javelinlike shafts a quarter of a mile or more. Ballistas, using the same system of hurling, were employed to heave heavy stones short distances.

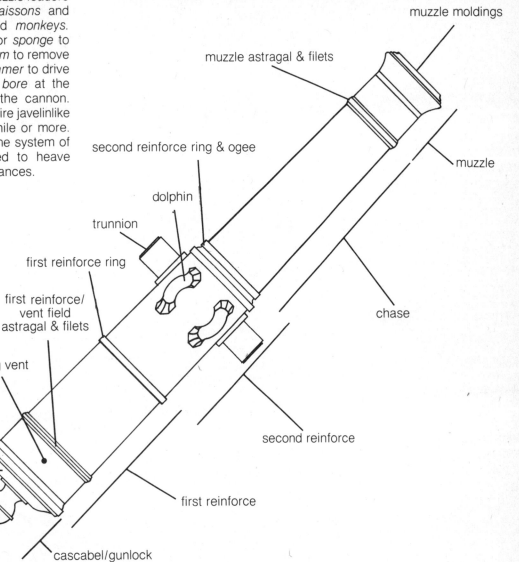

muzzle moldings

muzzle astragal & filets

second reinforce ring & ogee

dolphin

trunnion

first reinforce ring

first reinforce/ vent field astragal & filets

firing vent

base ring

breech

button/knob

muzzle

chase

second reinforce

first reinforce

cascabel/gunlock

Cannon Barrel

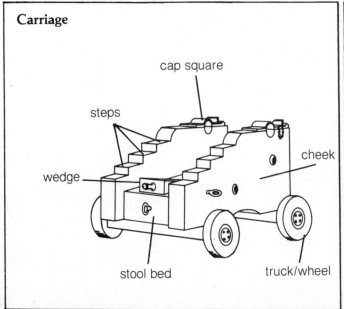

Carriage

cap square

steps

wedge

cheek

stool bed

truck/wheel

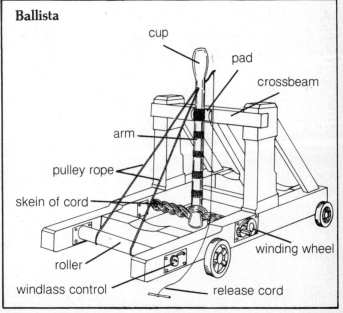

Ballista

cup

pad

crossbeam

arm

pulley rope

skein of cord

roller

winding wheel

windlass control

release cord

Shotgun and Rifle

A shotgun fires small *pellets* through a *smooth bore*, while a rifle fires *bullets* through a *rifled barrel*. Shotgun barrels are usually tapered, or *choked*, to constrict the *shot pattern*. Rifles may be carried across the shoulder on a beltlike *sling* connected to the weapon by *sling swivels* and adjusted with bucklelike *claws*.

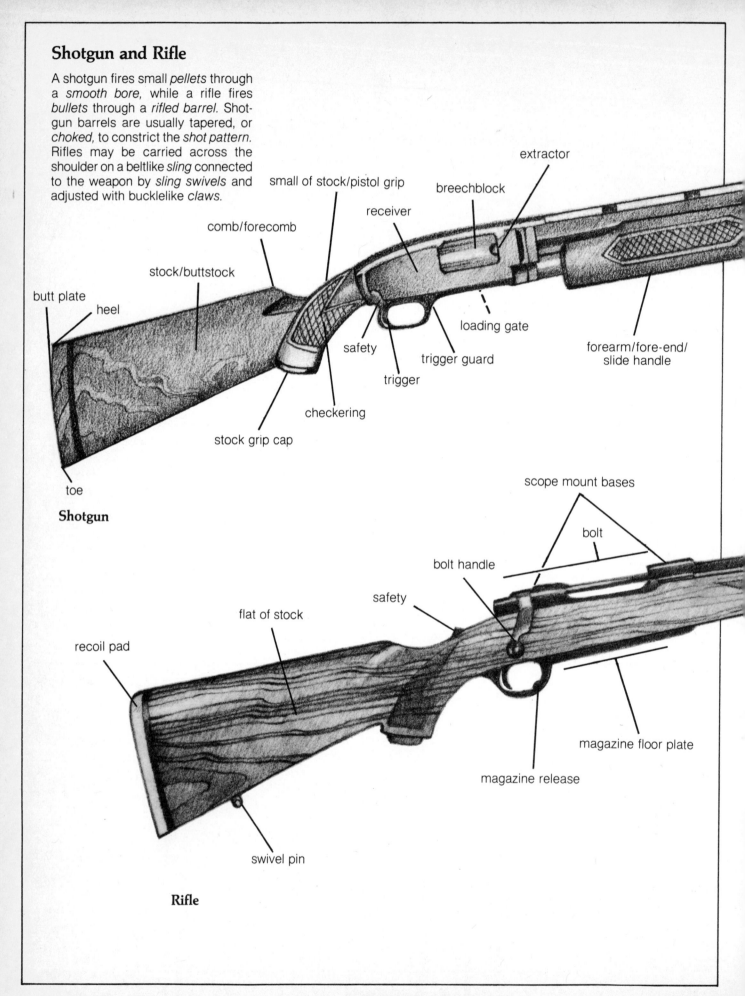

extractor

small of stock/pistol grip

breechblock

receiver

comb/forecomb

stock/buttstock

butt plate

heel

loading gate

safety

trigger guard

forearm/fore-end/
slide handle

trigger

checkering

stock grip cap

toe

Shotgun

scope mount bases

bolt

bolt handle

safety

flat of stock

recoil pad

magazine floor plate

magazine release

swivel pin

Rifle

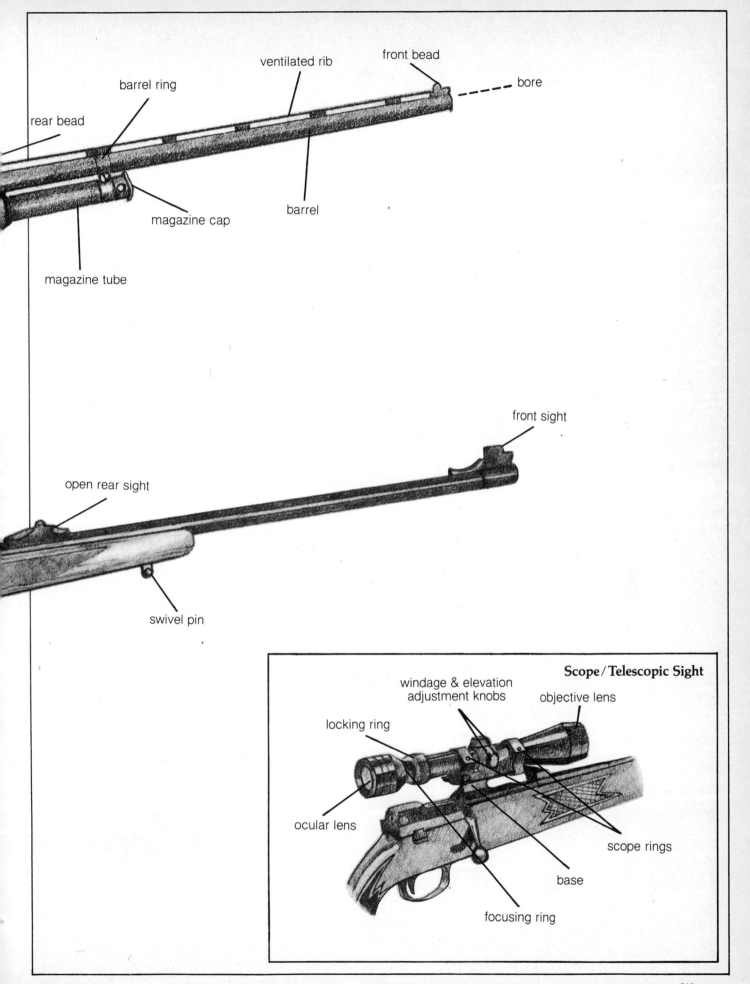

rear bead

barrel ring

ventilated rib

front bead

bore

magazine cap

barrel

magazine tube

open rear sight

front sight

swivel pin

Scope/Telescopic Sight

windage & elevation
adjustment knobs

objective lens

locking ring

ocular lens

scope rings

base

focusing ring

469

Weapons

Handguns

A *gun,* or *side arm,* is *fired* when a *firing pin* in the *breech* strikes the cartridge primer. A *silencer* dampens the sound of a gun's *discharge.* Grooves in the barrel, called *rifling,* cause a fired bullet to spiral for stability in flight. Cartridges are measured in *calibers,* their diameters in hundredths or thousandths of an inch written in a decimal fraction, or in *millimeters.* Handguns are carried in *holsters.*

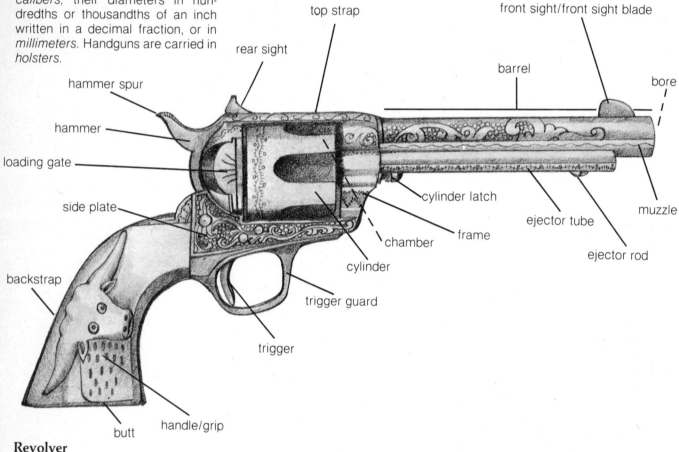

top strap

front sight/front sight blade

rear sight

barrel

bore

hammer spur

hammer

loading gate

side plate

cylinder latch

frame

ejector tube

muzzle

backstrap

chamber

ejector rod

cylinder

trigger guard

butt

handle/grip

trigger

Revolver

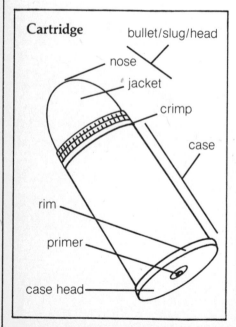

Cartridge

bullet/slug/head

nose

jacket

crimp

case

rim

primer

case head

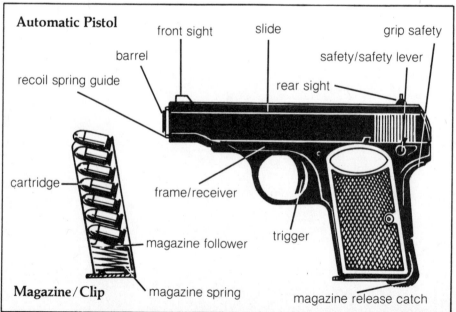

Automatic Pistol

front sight

slide

grip safety

barrel

safety/safety lever

recoil spring guide

rear sight

cartridge

frame/receiver

trigger

magazine follower

Magazine/Clip

magazine spring

magazine release catch

Automatic Weapons

Multi-shot automatic weapons are grouped by weight: light, medium and heavy. The *air-cooled,* medium-weight machine gun shown here can be handled by one man on the ground or on a vehicle when mounted on *pintle mounts.* The light, hand-held automatic rifle is also able to deliver a rapid burst of continuous fire as long as the trigger is depressed. *Ammunition* is fed to it from *handle clips* or *banana clips.*

front sight

flash suppressor

barrel

forearm

cocking handle

chassis plate

rear sight

carrying handle

grips

feed plate

trigger/firing lever

operating rod

height adjustment control

tripod/tripod mount

cartridge

feed belt

cartridge box

Machine Gun

Ammunition Can

Automatic Rifle

rear sight/ receiver sight

receiver

carrying handle/ upper receiver

cocking piece

bolt

breech

handguard liner

front sight housing

heel

comb

barrel

flash suppressor

butt

handguard

slip ring

muzzle

barrel extension

safety

stock

barrel nut

handguard cap

butt plate

trigger

pistol grip

magazine/cartridge clip

trigger guard

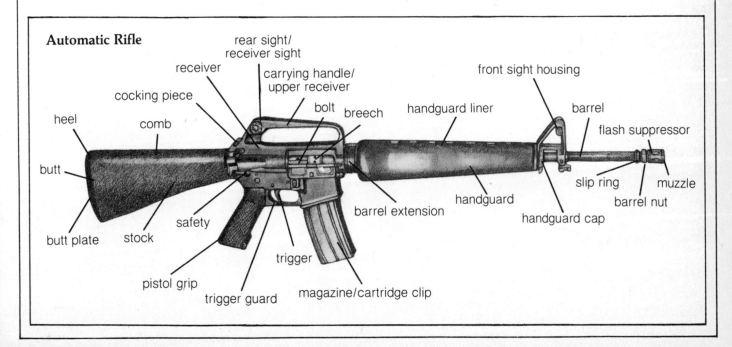

Mortar and Bazooka

A mortar is a *muzzle-loading cannon*, or *midget howitzer*, used to throw *finned projectiles* at high angles. A bazooka is a portable shoulder weapon with an *open-breech smoothbore firing tube* that fires several types of *rockets*.

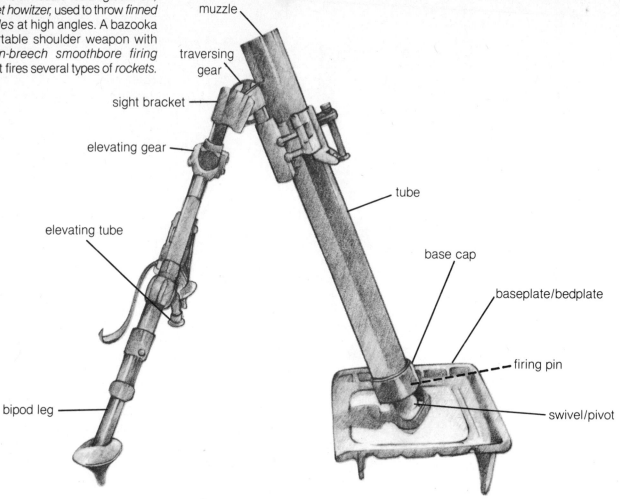

muzzle

traversing gear

sight bracket

elevating gear

elevating tube

bipod leg

tube

base cap

baseplate/bedplate

firing pin

swivel/pivot

Mortar

Bazooka/Rocket Launcher

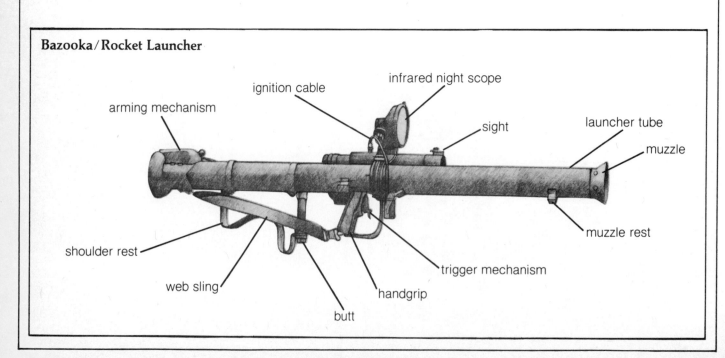

ignition cable

infrared night scope

arming mechanism

sight

launcher tube

muzzle

shoulder rest

muzzle rest

web sling

trigger mechanism

handgrip

butt

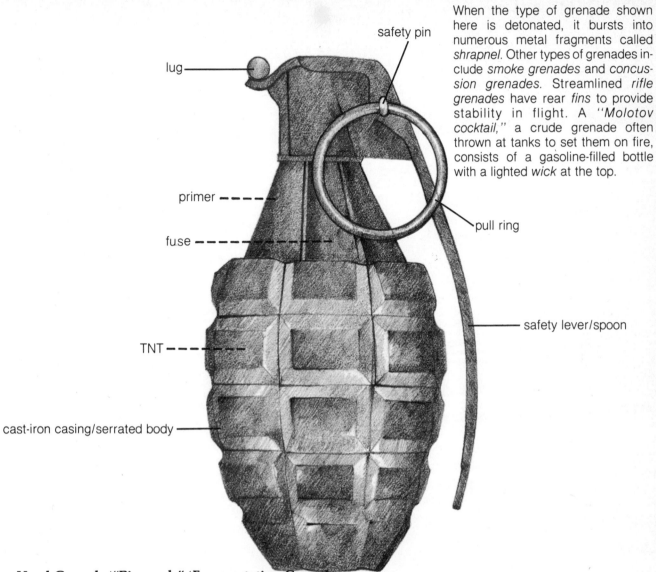

Grenade and Mine

When the type of grenade shown here is detonated, it bursts into numerous metal fragments called *shrapnel*. Other types of grenades include *smoke grenades* and *concussion grenades*. Streamlined *rifle grenades* have rear *fins* to provide stability in flight. A *"Molotov cocktail,"* a crude grenade often thrown at tanks to set them on fire, consists of a gasoline-filled bottle with a lighted *wick* at the top.

safety pin

lug

primer

fuse

TNT

cast-iron casing/serrated body

pull ring

safety lever/spoon

Hand Grenade/"Pineapple"/Fragmentation Grenade

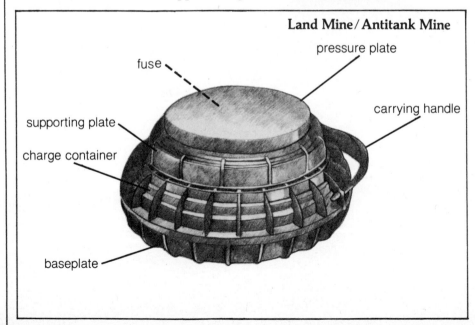

Land Mine/Antitank Mine

pressure plate

fuse

carrying handle

supporting plate

charge container

baseplate

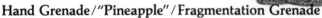

Weapons

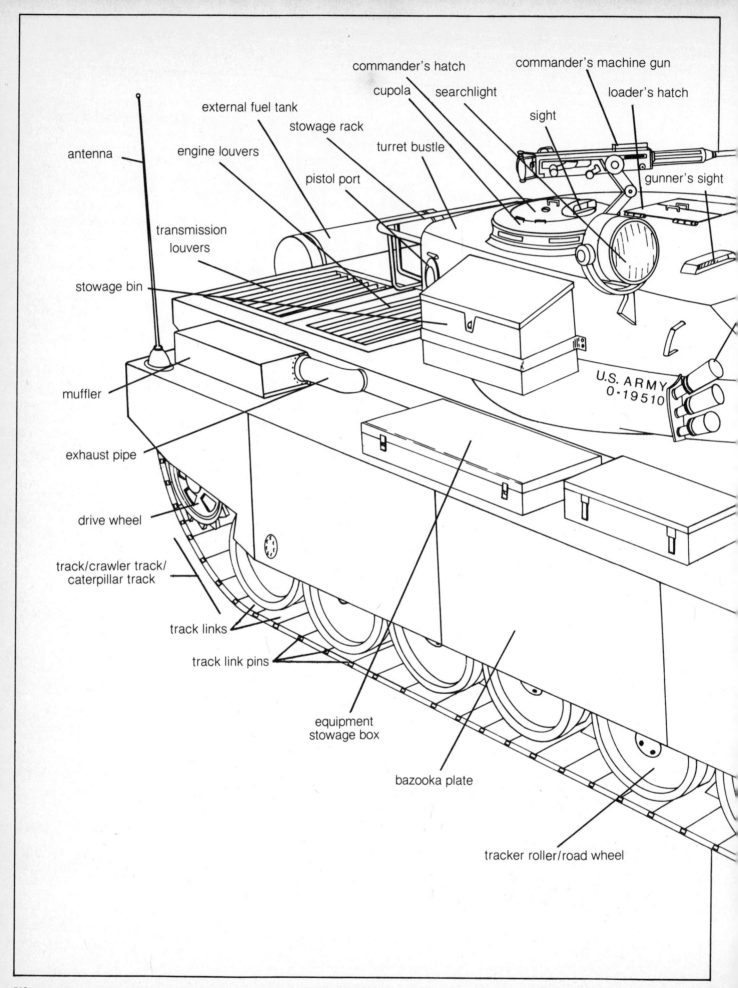

antenna

external fuel tank

commander's hatch

commander's machine gun

cupola

searchlight

loader's hatch

sight

engine louvers

stowage rack

turret bustle

transmission
louvers

pistol port

gunner's sight

stowage bin

U.S. ARMY
0·19510

muffler

exhaust pipe

drive wheel

track/crawler track/
caterpillar track

track links

track link pins

equipment
stowage box

bazooka plate

tracker roller/road wheel

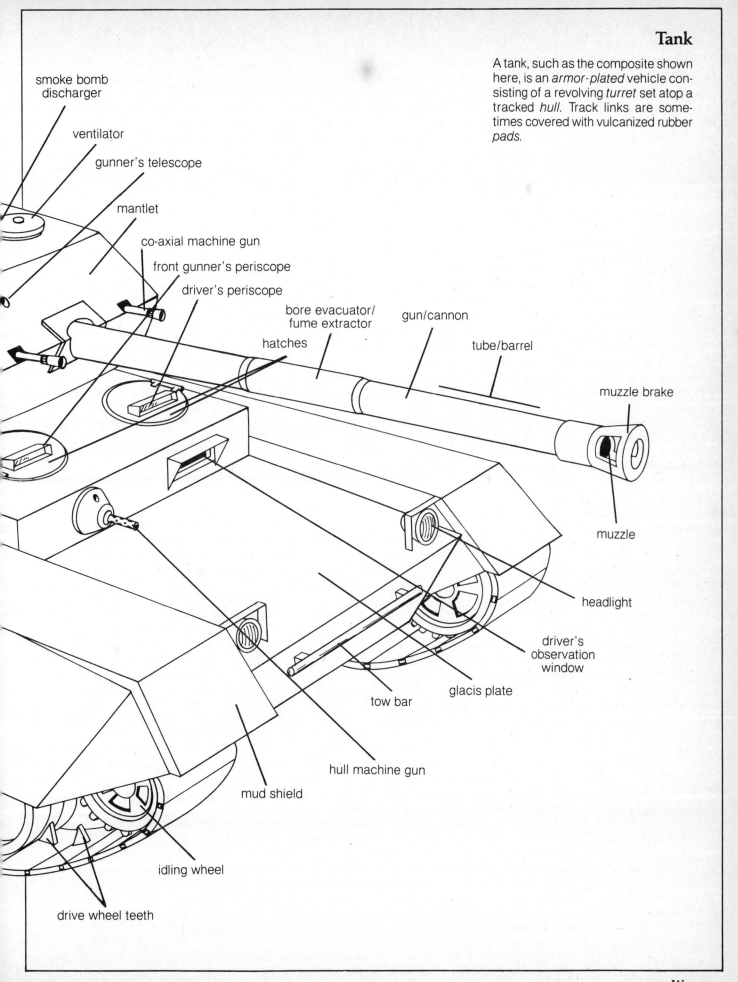

Tank

A tank, such as the composite shown here, is an *armor-plated* vehicle consisting of a revolving *turret* set atop a tracked *hull.* Track links are sometimes covered with vulcanized rubber *pads.*

smoke bomb discharger

ventilator

gunner's telescope

mantlet

co-axial machine gun

front gunner's periscope

driver's periscope

bore evacuator/ fume extractor

gun/cannon

tube/barrel

hatches

muzzle brake

muzzle

headlight

driver's observation window

glacis plate

tow bar

hull machine gun

mud shield

idling wheel

drive wheel teeth

Surface Fighting Ship

Beginning with *dreadnoughts*, or *battleships*, modern surface *warships*, such as this *destroyer*, or *tin can*, have the capability to protect *shipping lanes*, deter invasions or support military operations on land. Today military vessels carry *surface-to-air missiles* and *surface-to-surface missiles*, as well as a range of *defensive guided weapons*. Many are *nuclear-powered*.

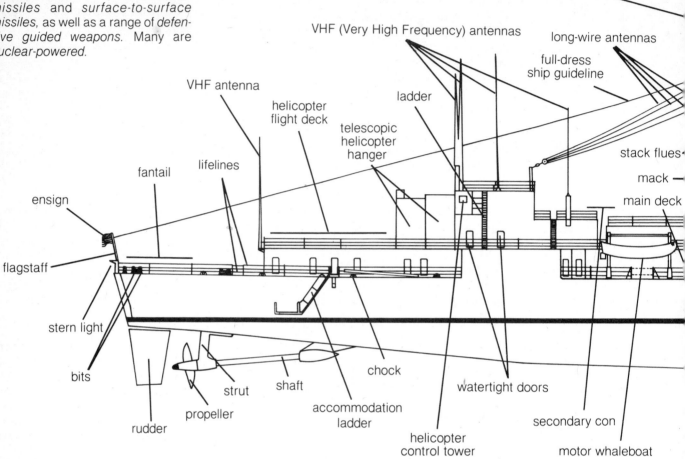

TACAN antenna

VHF (Very High Frequency) antennas

long-wire antennas

full-dress ship guideline

stack flues

mack

main deck

VHF antenna

helicopter flight deck

telescopic helicopter hanger

ladder

fantail

lifelines

ensign

flagstaff

stern light

bits

rudder

propeller

strut

shaft

chock

accommodation ladder

watertight doors

helicopter control tower

secondary con

motor whaleboat

Fighting Ship Types

scale 1:2,600

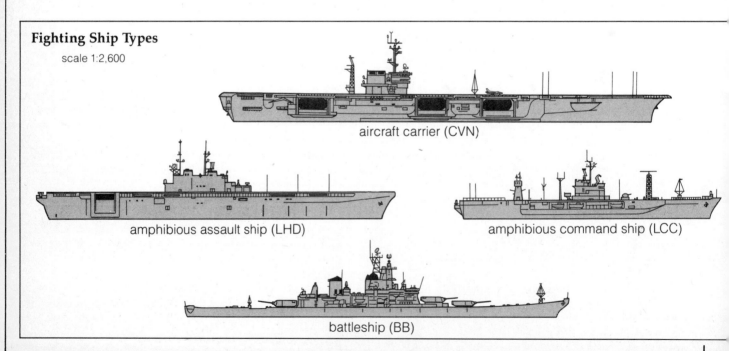

aircraft carrier (CVN)

amphibious assault ship (LHD)

amphibious command ship (LCC)

battleship (BB)

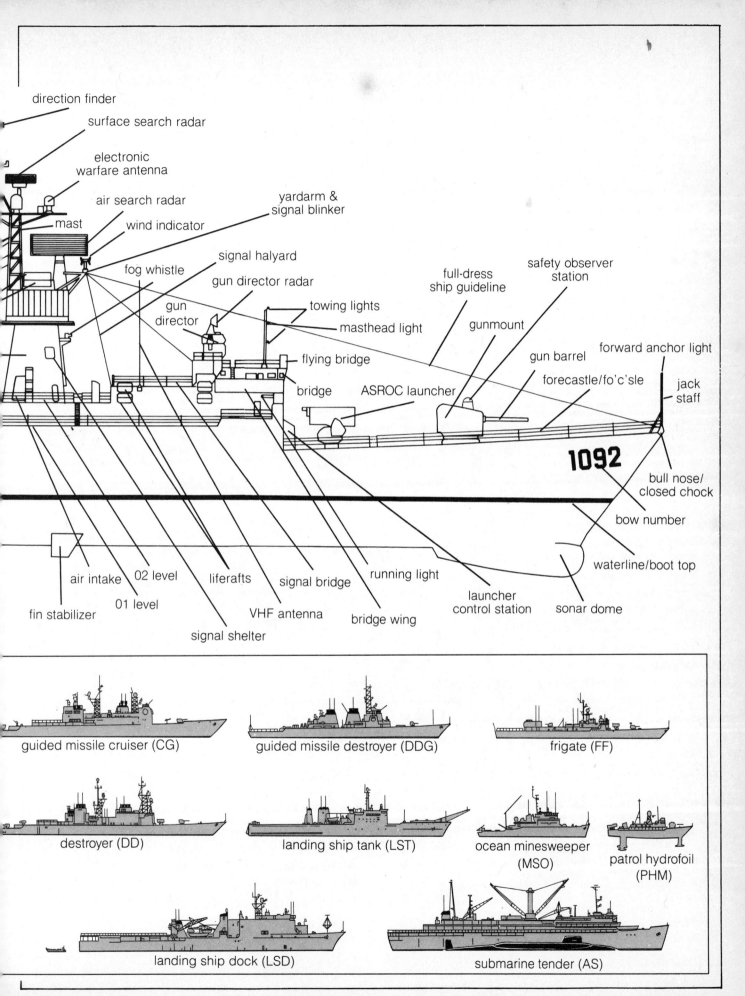

direction finder

surface search radar

electronic
warfare antenna

air search radar

yardarm &
signal blinker

mast

wind indicator

signal halyard

fog whistle

gun director radar

safety observer
station

full-dress
ship guideline

gunmount

gun
director

towing lights

masthead light

gun barrel

forward anchor light

flying bridge

forecastle/fo'c'sle

jack
staff

bridge

ASROC launcher

1092

bull nose/
closed chock

bow number

waterline/boot top

air intake

02 level

liferafts

signal bridge

running light

fin stabilizer

01 level

VHF antenna

bridge wing

launcher
control station

sonar dome

signal shelter

signal shelter

guided missile cruiser (CG)

guided missile destroyer (DDG)

frigate (FF)

destroyer (DD)

landing ship tank (LST)

ocean minesweeper
(MSO)

patrol hydrofoil
(PHM)

landing ship dock (LSD)

submarine tender (AS)

Fighting Ships

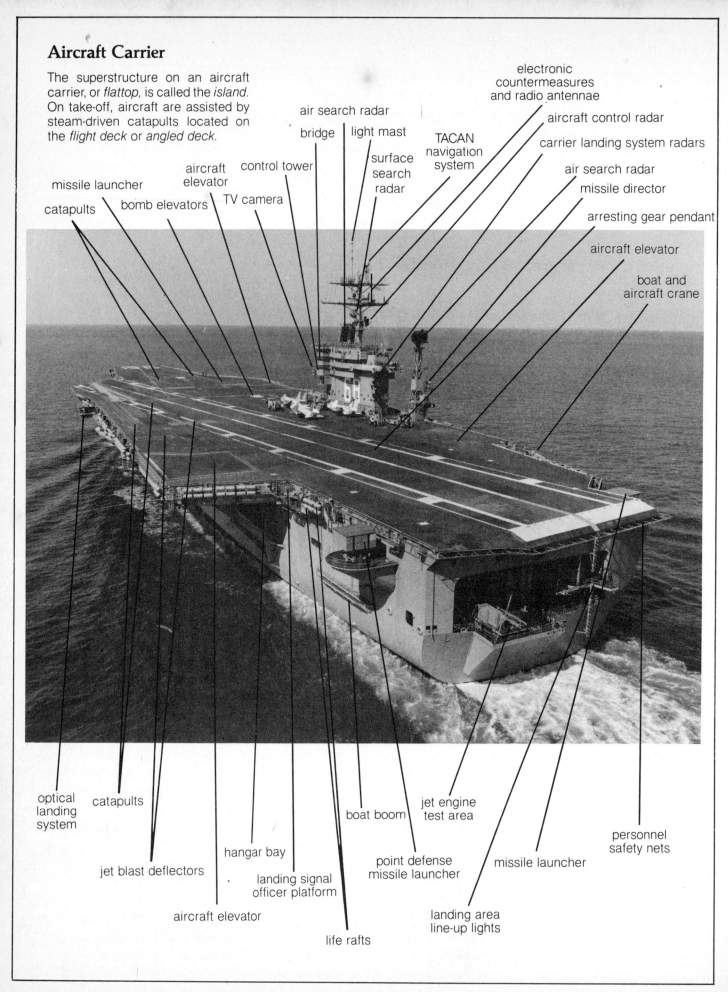

Aircraft Carrier

The superstructure on an aircraft carrier, or *flattop,* is called the *island.* On take-off, aircraft are assisted by steam-driven catapults located on the *flight deck* or *angled deck.*

electronic countermeasures and radio antennae

air search radar

bridge   light mast

TACAN navigation system

aircraft control radar

carrier landing system radars

air search radar

missile director

arresting gear pendant

aircraft elevator

boat and aircraft crane

control tower

surface search radar

aircraft elevator

bomb elevators

TV camera

missile launcher

catapults

optical landing system

catapults

jet blast deflectors

hangar bay

aircraft elevator

landing signal officer platform

boat boom

jet engine test area

point defense missile launcher

landing area line-up lights

missile launcher

personnel safety nets

life rafts

Submarine

Submarines, formerly called *U-boats* or *pigboats,* have thick inner *pressure hulls* and lighter *outer hulls.* The space between hulls is divided into several *ballast tanks,* used to control the vessel's buoyancy and trim. The conning tower contains *radio* and *radar antennas* and various *periscopes,* used for observation and navigation. In older submarines the sail also contained a *snorkel tube.* Navigation underwater is accomplished by means of an *inertial guidance system.* In addition to missiles, submarines can carry *torpedoes.*

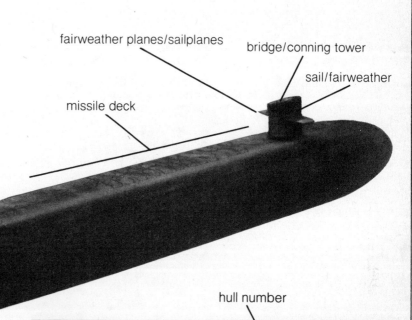

fairweather planes/sailplanes

bridge/conning tower

sail/fairweather

missile deck

rudder

propeller   diving plane

Fleet Ballistic Missile Submarine

hull number

Nuclear-Powered Attack Submarine

Torpedo

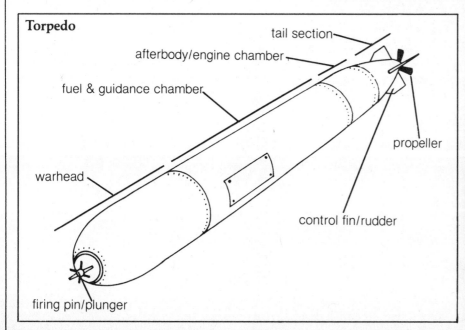

tail section

afterbody/engine chamber

fuel & guidance chamber

propeller

warhead

control fin/rudder

firing pin/plunger

Ballistic Missiles Launch Deck

hatch covers

launch tubes/silos

Combat Aircraft

A fighter, such as the one shown here, has an advanced *airframe* with a *variable sweep wing* and a *long-range weapon system*. It is flown at speeds in excess of the speed of sound, or *mach speeds*.

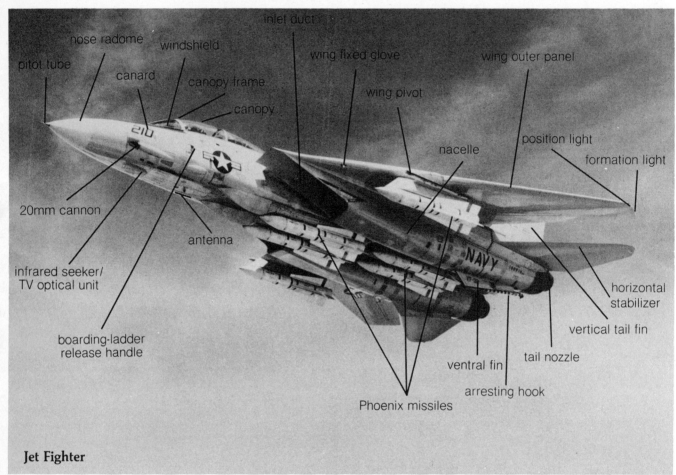

pitot tube
nose radome
canard
windshield
canopy frame
canopy
inlet duct
wing fixed glove
wing pivot
wing outer panel
nacelle
position light
formation light
20mm cannon
antenna
infrared seeker/ TV optical unit
boarding-ladder release handle
Phoenix missiles
ventral fin
arresting hook
tail nozzle
vertical tail fin
horizontal stabilizer

Jet Fighter

Combat Aircraft Wing Types

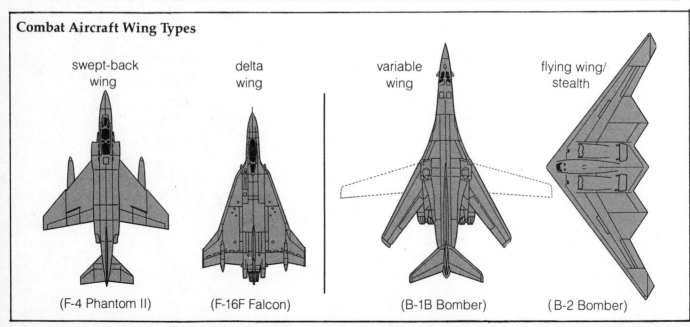

swept-back wing

delta wing

variable wing

flying wing/ stealth

(F-4 Phantom II)

(F-16F Falcon)

(B-1B Bomber)

(B-2 Bomber)

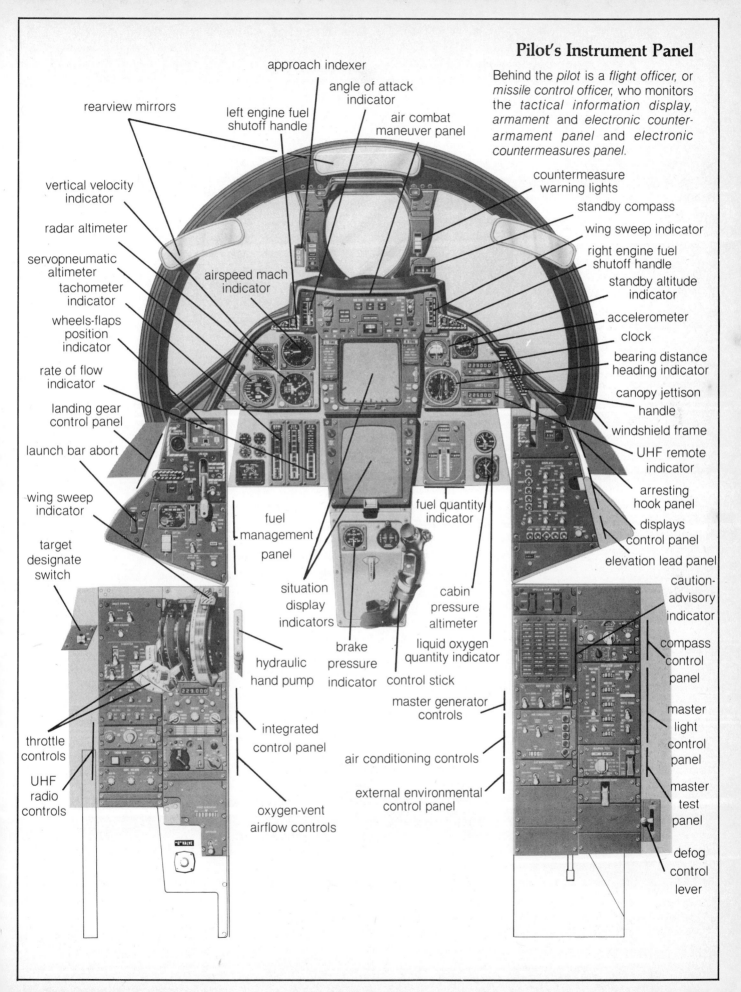

Pilot's Instrument Panel

Behind the *pilot* is a *flight officer*, or *missile control officer*, who monitors the *tactical information display, armament* and *electronic counter-armament panel* and *electronic countermeasures panel*.

approach indexer

angle of attack indicator

air combat maneuver panel

rearview mirrors

left engine fuel shutoff handle

vertical velocity indicator

radar altimeter

servopneumatic altimeter

tachometer indicator

airspeed mach indicator

wheels-flaps position indicator

rate of flow indicator

landing gear control panel

launch bar abort

wing sweep indicator

target designate switch

throttle controls

UHF radio controls

fuel management panel

situation display indicators

hydraulic hand pump

integrated control panel

oxygen-vent airflow controls

brake pressure indicator

control stick

master generator controls

air conditioning controls

external environmental control panel

fuel quantity indicator

cabin pressure altimeter

liquid oxygen quantity indicator

countermeasure warning lights

standby compass

wing sweep indicator

right engine fuel shutoff handle

standby altitude indicator

accelerometer

clock

bearing distance heading indicator

canopy jettison handle

windshield frame

UHF remote indicator

arresting hook panel

displays control panel

elevation lead panel

caution-advisory indicator

compass control panel

master light control panel

master test panel

defog control lever

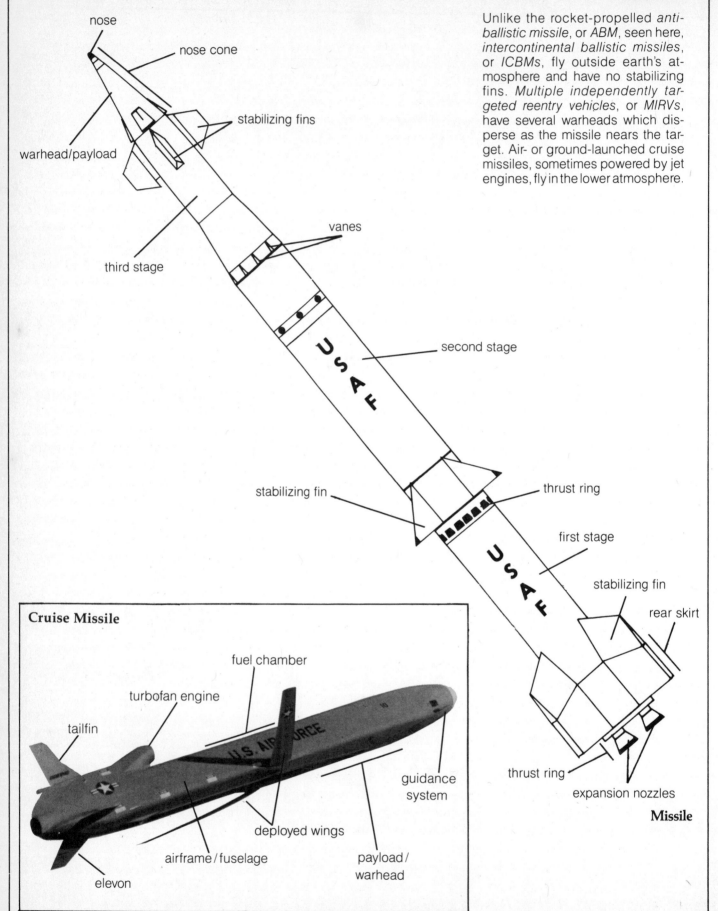

Missiles

Unlike the rocket-propelled *antiballistic missile*, or *ABM*, seen here, *intercontinental ballistic missiles*, or *ICBMs*, fly outside earth's atmosphere and have no stabilizing fins. *Multiple independently targeted reentry vehicles*, or *MIRVs*, have several warheads which disperse as the missile nears the target. Air- or ground-launched cruise missiles, sometimes powered by jet engines, fly in the lower atmosphere.

nose

nose cone

stabilizing fins

warhead/payload

vanes

third stage

second stage

stabilizing fin

thrust ring

first stage

stabilizing fin

rear skirt

USAF

USAF

thrust ring

expansion nozzles

Missile

Cruise Missile

fuel chamber

turbofan engine

tailfin

U.S. AIR FORCE

guidance system

deployed wings

airframe/fuselage

elevon

payload/warhead

Uniforms, Costumes and Ceremonial Attire

The attire presented in this section ranges from vestments and formal dress used on special occasions to dress of distinctive design or fashion worn by members of particular groups. The parts of military or municipal attire, for example, serve to identify not only branch of service but rank and distinction as well.

Garb can be highly stylized or informal. Manchu Court dress, for example, was worn only on formal occasions, whereas the clothes commonly worn by cowboys, dictated by the demands of the profession, was casual.

In addition to the trappings that have come to typify characters in history— a general, pirate, miser, magician—this section also includes clothing used by performers such as clowns, ballet dancers and drum majorettes.

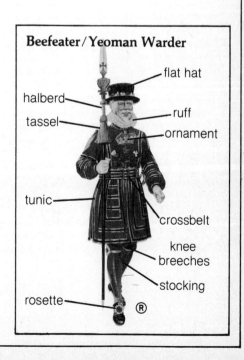

Beefeater / Yeoman Warder

halberd — tassel — flat hat — ruff — ornament — tunic — crossbelt — knee breeches — stocking — rosette

483

Royal Regalia

In coronations and investitures, a king wears a blunted sword called a *curtein* on his sash. Among a queen's foundation garments, or *underpinnings,* are a *corset, corselet, chemise* and *pantaloons.*

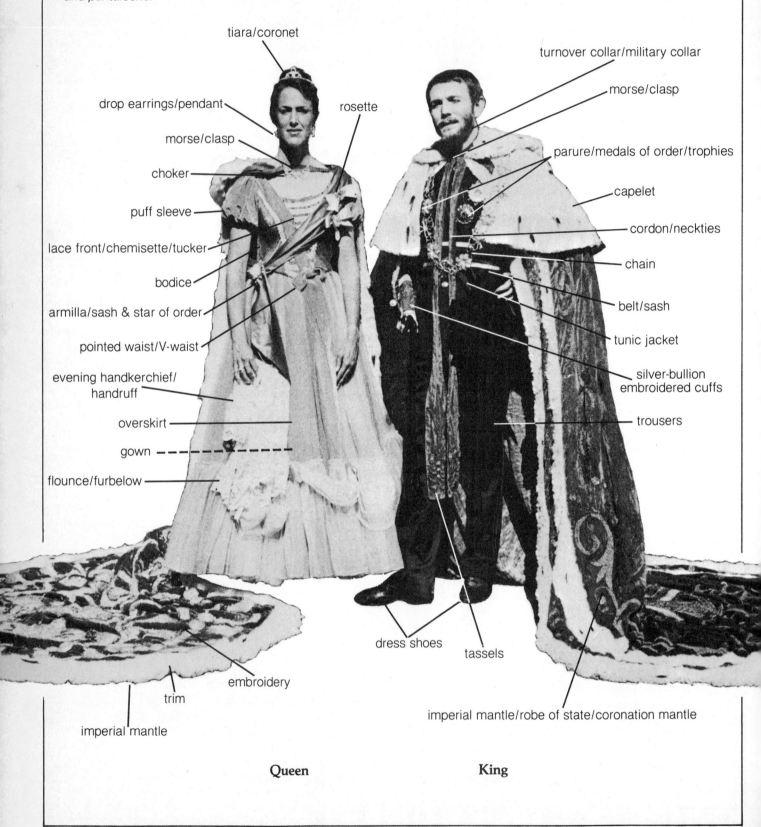

tiara/coronet

turnover collar/military collar

morse/clasp

drop earrings/pendant

rosette

morse/clasp

parure/medals of order/trophies

choker

capelet

puff sleeve

cordon/neckties

lace front/chemisette/tucker

chain

bodice

belt/sash

armilla/sash & star of order

tunic jacket

pointed waist/V-waist

silver-bullion embroidered cuffs

evening handkerchief/ handruff

overskirt

trousers

gown

flounce/furbelow

dress shoes

tassels

embroidery

trim

imperial mantle/robe of state/coronation mantle

imperial mantle

Queen

King

Royal Regalia

A *coronet* is a small crown worn by royalty ranking below the reigning monarch. A *tiara* is a royal head-piece, usually consisting of a *diadem,* or band, tied around the forehead, supporting several tiers of ornaments. A wreath, or circlet of leaves, worn as a crown or collar is a *garland.*

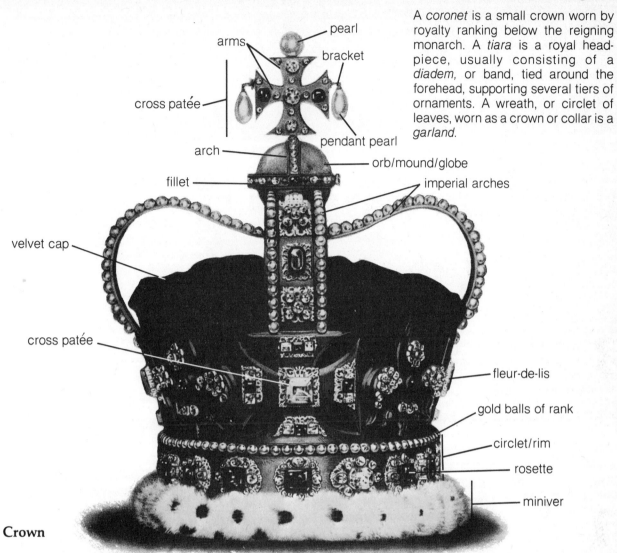

pearl
arms
bracket
cross patée
pendant pearl
arch
orb/mound/globe
fillet
imperial arches
velvet cap
cross patée
fleur-de-lis
gold balls of rank
circlet/rim
rosette
miniver

Crown

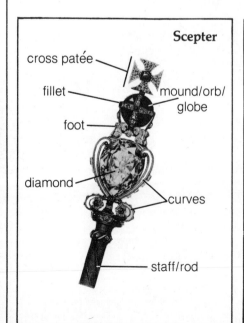

Scepter

cross patée
fillet
mound/orb/globe
foot
diamond
curves
staff/rod

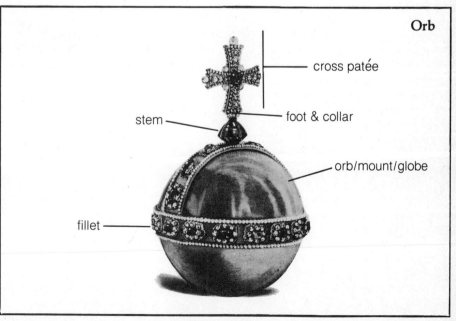

Orb

cross patée
stem
foot & collar
orb/mount/globe
fillet

Royal Vestments

Jewish Ritual Items

During regular service in a *Temple,* or *Synagogue,* excerpts are read by the *Rabbi,* who is assisted in leading the service by a *Cantor,* who sings the liturgy. Their vestments are the same as the rest of the congregation. During morning prayer, a *shel rosh,* similar to the tefillin, is worn on the forehead. Some Jews hang a *mezuzah,* a decorative box containing passages from the Torah, on the doorpost of their homes.

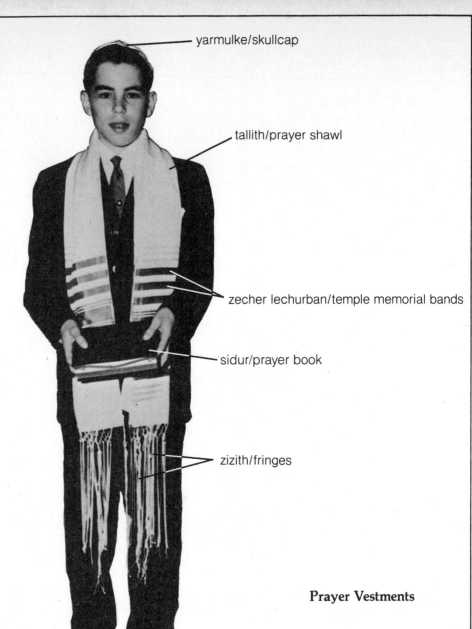

yarmulke/skullcap

tallith/prayer shawl

zecher lechurban/temple memorial bands

sidur/prayer book

zizith/fringes

Prayer Vestments

Ner Tamid/eternal light

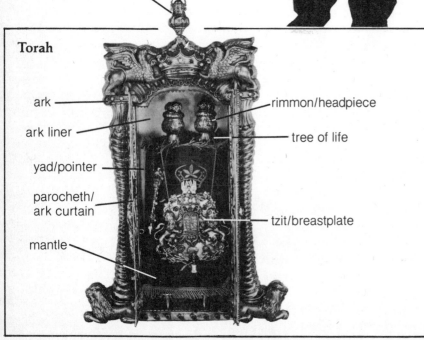

Torah

ark

ark liner

rimmon/headpiece

tree of life

yad/pointer

parocheth/ark curtain

tzit/breastplate

mantle

Tefillin/Phylacteries

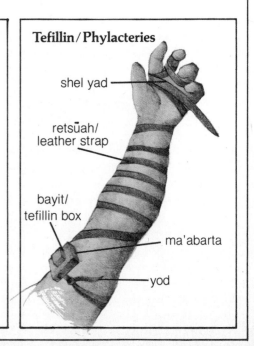

shel yad

retsūah/leather strap

bayit/tefillin box

ma'abarta

yod

Religious Vestments

The small square cap with three corners worn by Roman Catholic clergy is a *biretta*. Ropes, belts or sashes used to keep vestments closed are *cinctures*. Traditionally, the white band worn by nuns to encircle their faces is a *wimple*, while the wide cloth worn below it to cover their necks and shoulders is a *guimpe*. The ring worn by the Pope is the *Ring of the Fisherman*.

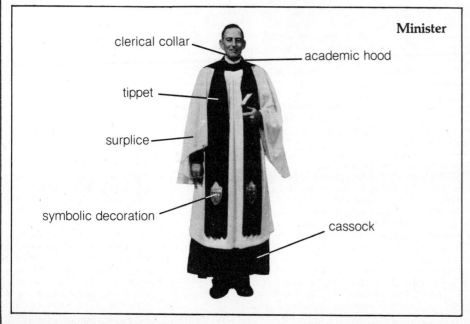

simple miter

precious miter

lappet

Roman collar

crosier/pastoral staff

pectoral cross

dalmatic

stole

Episcopal ring

cope

chasuble

cope piping

rochet

alb

cassock

cassock

Bishop　　**Cardinal**

Minister

clerical collar

academic hood

tippet

surplice

symbolic decoration

cassock

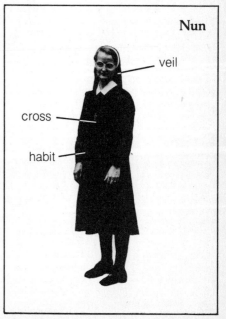

Nun

veil

cross

habit

Bride and Groom

The bride, wearing white to symbolize purity, and a veil, symbol of modesty, is carrying a fan rather than the more traditional *wedding*, or *bridal*, *bouquet*, or *nosegay*. Some grooms wear semiformal evening dress at weddings: *tuxedos*, or *tuxes*, which are worn with *cummerbunds*, broad *waistbands*, *pleated* or *ruffled shirts* with *studs*, and *bow ties*.

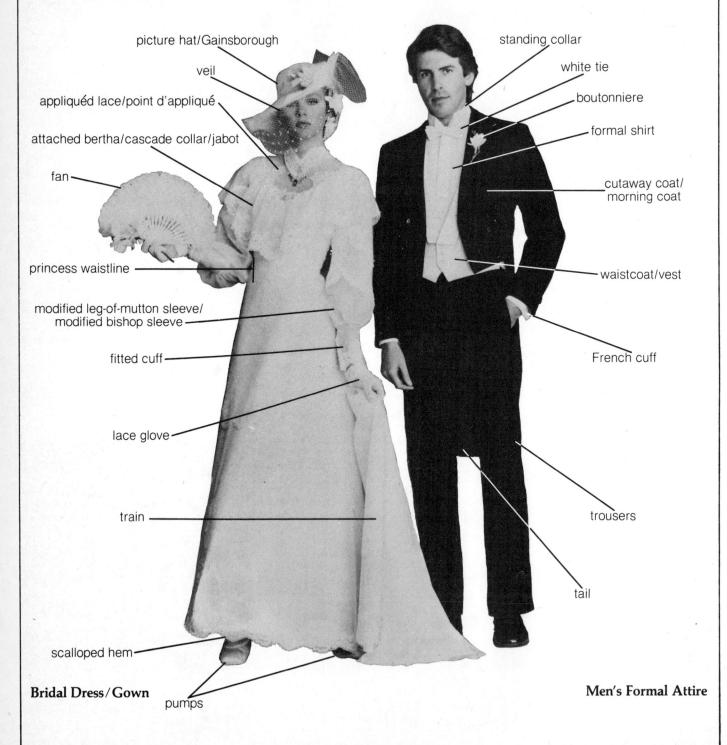

picture hat/Gainsborough

veil

appliquéd lace/point d'appliqué

attached bertha/cascade collar/jabot

fan

princess waistline

modified leg-of-mutton sleeve/
modified bishop sleeve

fitted cuff

lace glove

train

scalloped hem

standing collar

white tie

boutonniere

formal shirt

cutaway coat/
morning coat

waistcoat/vest

French cuff

trousers

tail

Bridal Dress/Gown

pumps

Men's Formal Attire

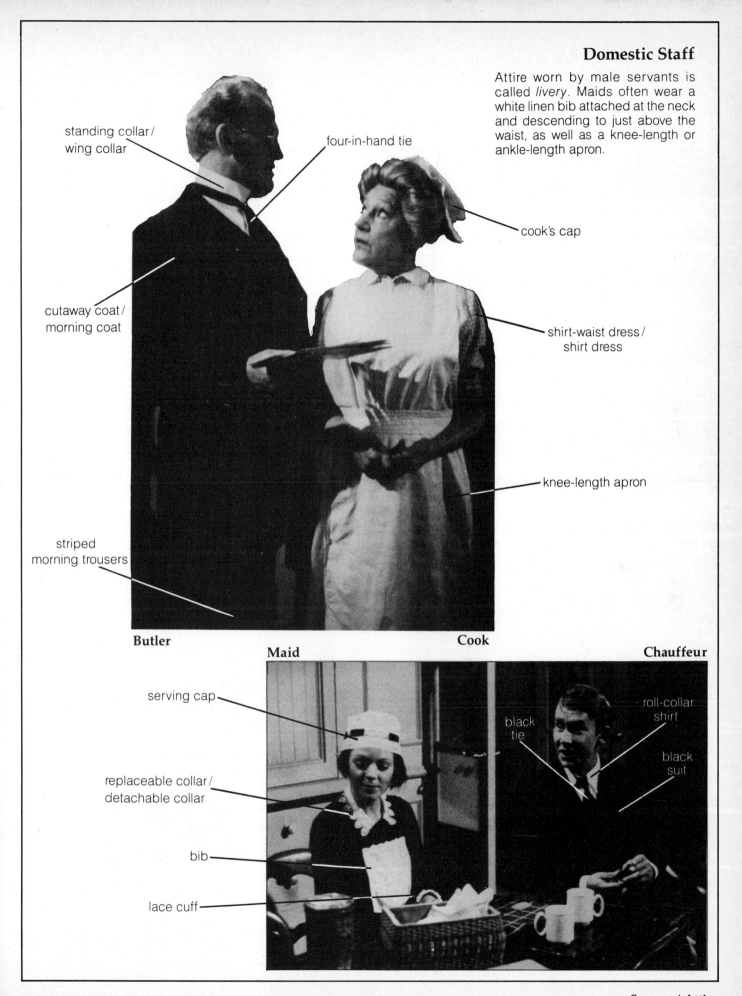

Domestic Staff

Attire worn by male servants is called *livery*. Maids often wear a white linen bib attached at the neck and descending to just above the waist, as well as a knee-length or ankle-length apron.

standing collar/
wing collar

four-in-hand tie

cook's cap

cutaway coat/
morning coat

shirt-waist dress/
shirt dress

knee-length apron

striped
morning trousers

Butler

Cook

Maid

Chauffeur

serving cap

roll-collar
shirt

black
tie

black
suit

replaceable collar/
detachable collar

bib

lace cuff

Servants' Attire

Cowboy and Indian

On the range, cowboys, *cow punchers,* or *buckaroos,* carried *oilskin slickers,* a *tarp,* and heavy cotton or wool quilts to make up a *bedroll, crumb incubator, shakedown,* or *fleatrap.* Bullets, carried in *loops* on *cartridge belts,* were known as *blue whistlers* or *lead plums.* A cowboy's *ten-gallon hat* was held in place in a wind by buckskin thongs known as *bonnet strings.*

Members of most Indian tribes wore *leggings* and *moccasins.* Many decorated their faces with *war paint* prior to battle. Indians in the East shaved their heads except for a ridge of hair in the middle called a *roach.*

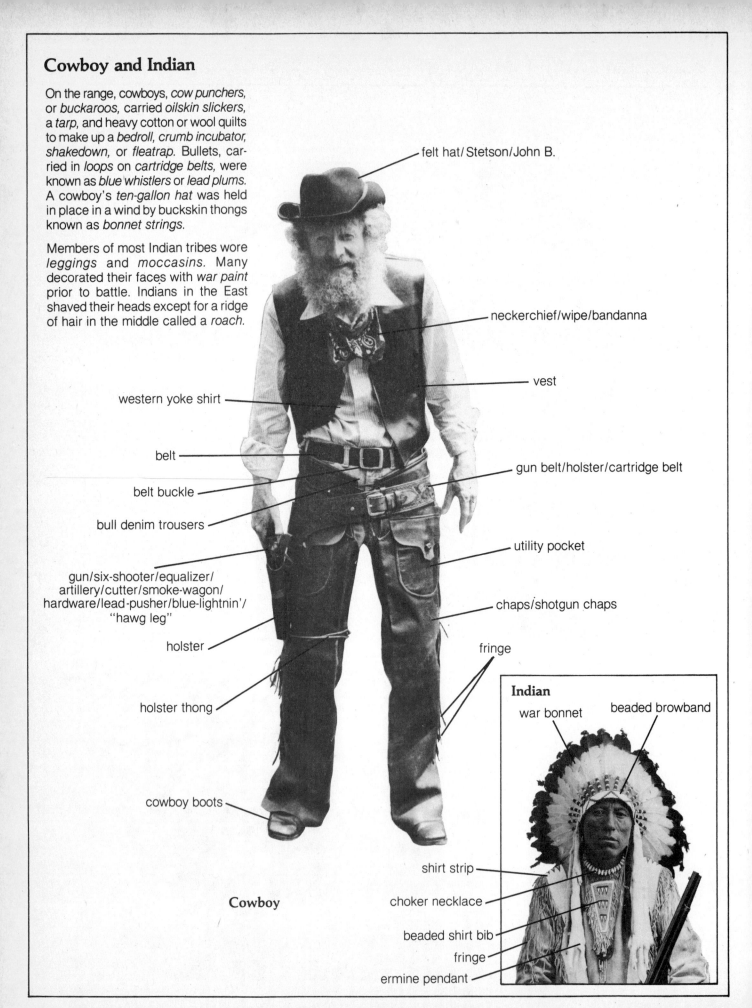

felt hat/Stetson/John B.

neckerchief/wipe/bandanna

vest

western yoke shirt

belt

gun belt/holster/cartridge belt

belt buckle

bull denim trousers

utility pocket

gun/six-shooter/equalizer/
artillery/cutter/smoke-wagon/
hardware/lead-pusher/blue-lightnin'/
"hawg leg"

chaps/shotgun chaps

holster

fringe

holster thong

cowboy boots

Cowboy

Indian

war bonnet

beaded browband

shirt strip

choker necklace

beaded shirt bib

fringe

ermine pendant

Native Dress

Romans wore full-length, loose-fitting robes called *togas.* East Indian women wear *sarongs,* but Indian (Hindu) women wear *saris.* An ankle-length Middle East garment with long sleeves and a waist sash is called a *caftan.* The loose-fitting, sleeveless robes worn by Arabs are called *abas.*

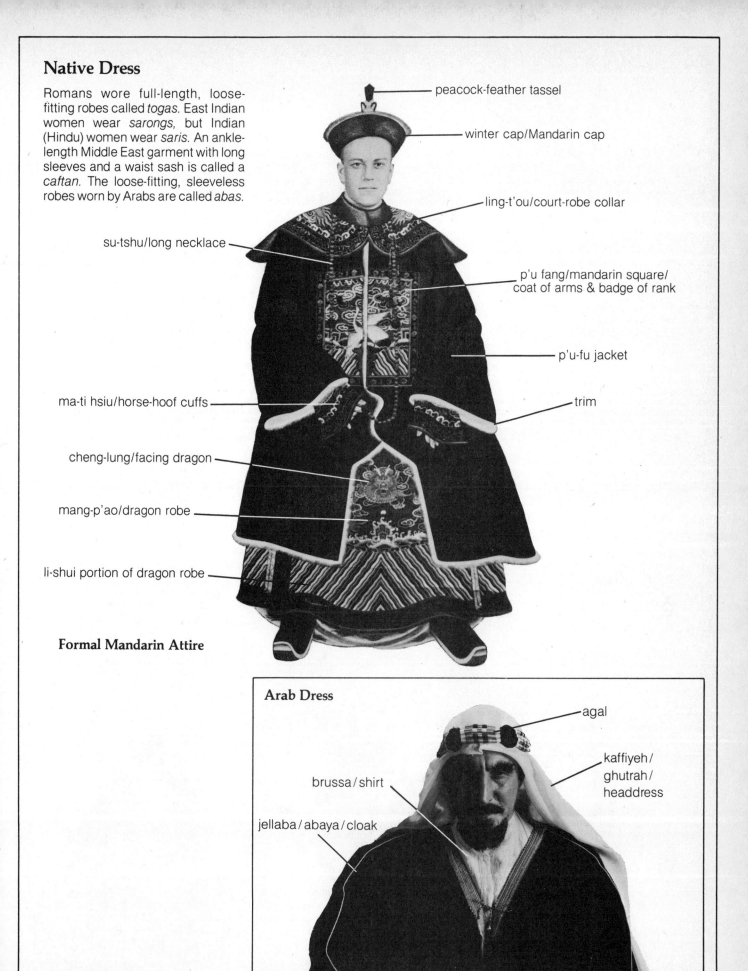

peacock-feather tassel

winter cap/Mandarin cap

ling-t'ou/court-robe collar

su-tshu/long necklace

p'u fang/mandarin square/ coat of arms & badge of rank

p'u-fu jacket

ma-ti hsiu/horse-hoof cuffs

trim

cheng-lung/facing dragon

mang-p'ao/dragon robe

li-shui portion of dragon robe

Formal Mandarin Attire

Arab Dress

agal

kaffiyeh/ ghutrah/ headdress

brussa/shirt

jellaba/abaya/cloak

Bill Ashe photo

Native Attire

Historical Costumes

Many characters in popular lore and history have become identified or associated with the clothing they wear. Other military attire worn by *Revolutionary* officers included a tunic, a plain jacket with a stiff collar, and a particularly heavy overcoat called a *greatcoat*.

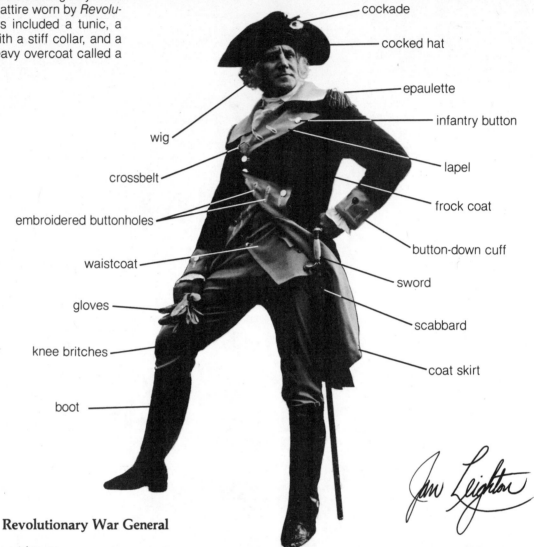

- cockade
- cocked hat
- epaulette
- infantry button
- lapel
- frock coat
- button-down cuff
- sword
- scabbard
- coat skirt
- wig
- crossbelt
- embroidered buttonholes
- waistcoat
- gloves
- knee britches
- boot

Jan Leighton

Revolutionary War General

- eyepatch
- tricorne
- crossbelt
- scarf
- pistol

Pirate

photo by BODI

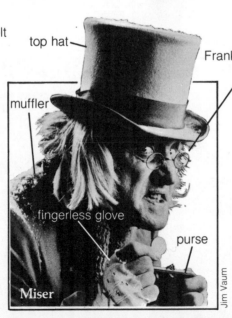

- top hat
- Franklin glasses
- muffler
- fingerless glove
- purse

Miser

Jim Vaum

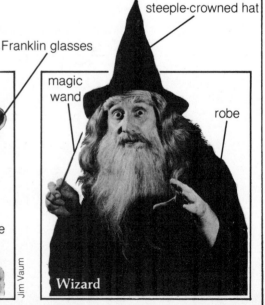

- steeple-crowned hat
- magic wand
- robe

Wizard

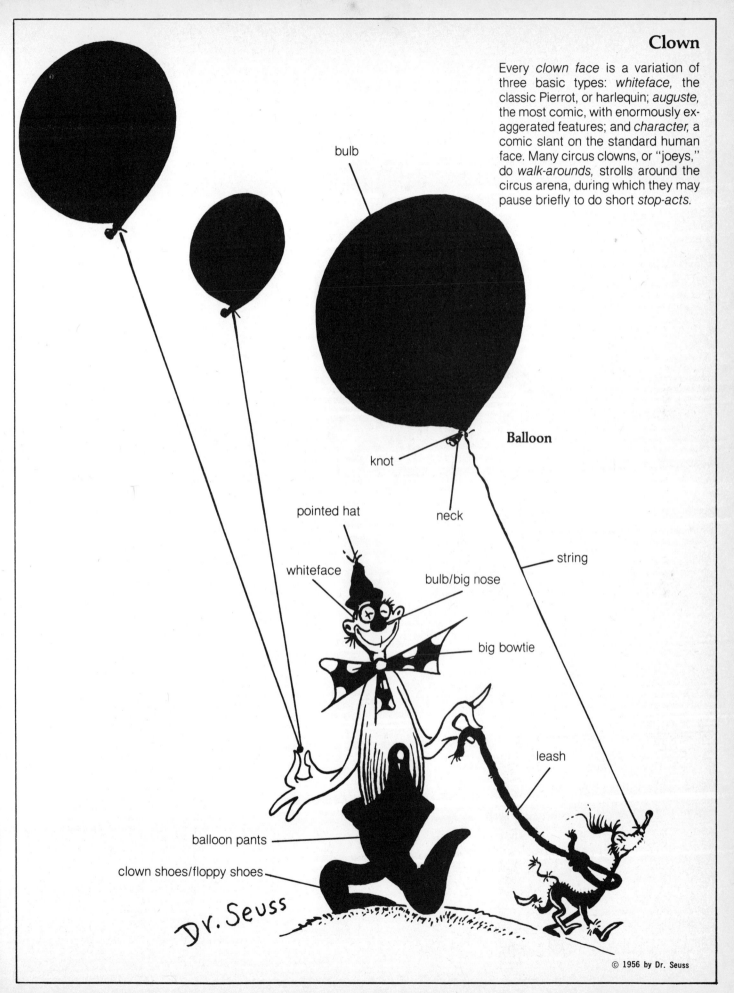

Clown

Every *clown face* is a variation of three basic types: *whiteface,* the classic Pierrot, or harlequin; *auguste,* the most comic, with enormously exaggerated features; and *character,* a comic slant on the standard human face. Many circus clowns, or "joeys," do *walk-arounds,* strolls around the circus arena, during which they may pause briefly to do short *stop-acts.*

bulb

Balloon

knot

pointed hat

neck

whiteface

bulb/big nose

string

big bowtie

leash

balloon pants

clown shoes/floppy shoes

Dr. Seuss

© 1956 by Dr. Seuss

Performers' Costumes

Ballet Dancer

The toeshoes worn by this *ballerina* are satin covered. Cloth mache has replaced wooden box toes. A short skirt of layered net often worn by female dancers is called a *tutu*.

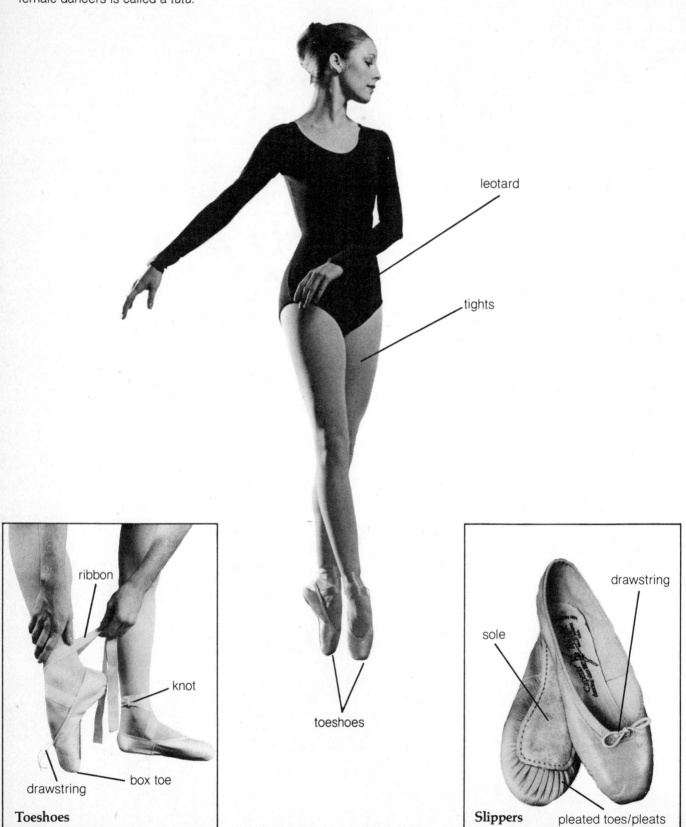

leotard

tights

toeshoes

Toeshoes

ribbon

knot

drawstring

box toe

Slippers

sole

drawstring

pleated toes/pleats

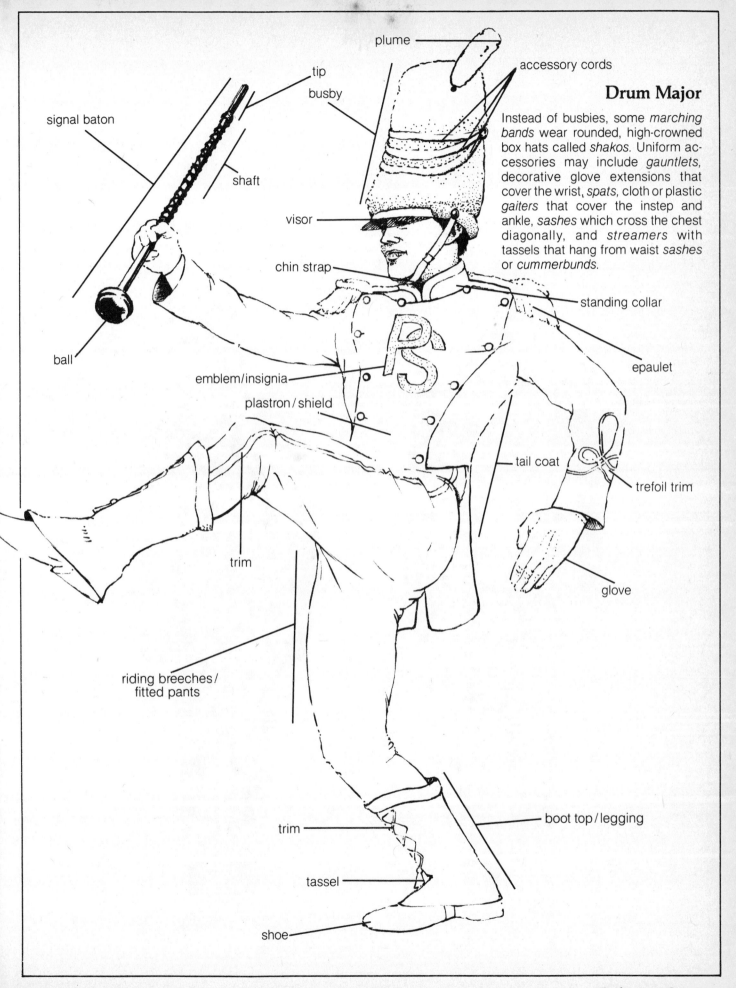

plume

accessory cords

tip

busby

signal baton

shaft

Drum Major

Instead of busbies, some *marching bands* wear rounded, high-crowned box hats called *shakos*. Uniform accessories may include *gauntlets*, decorative glove extensions that cover the wrist, *spats*, cloth or plastic *gaiters* that cover the instep and ankle, *sashes* which cross the chest diagonally, and *streamers* with tassels that hang from waist *sashes* or *cummerbunds*.

visor

chin strap

standing collar

epaulet

ball

emblem/insignia

plastron / shield

tail coat

trefoil trim

trim

glove

riding breeches / fitted pants

boot top/legging

trim

tassel

shoe

495

Military Uniforms

The *uniform of the day* is worn for the season, day or occasion. A cloth band worn around the arm above the elbow, such as the one worn by *Military Police,* or *MPs,* is a *brassard.* A leather belt for a dress uniform is a *Sam Browne, or garrison, belt.* Service ribbons are worn on a *ribbon bar.* The only *neck decoration* awarded to members of the armed services is the *Medal of Honor.*

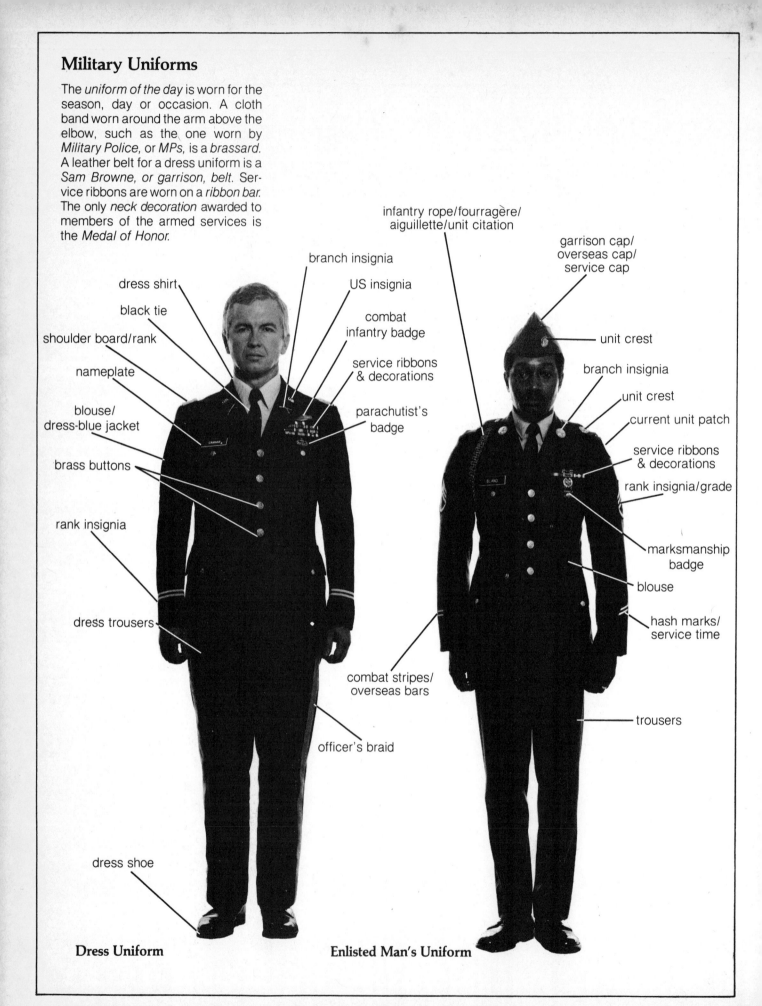

infantry rope/fourragère/ aiguillette/unit citation

branch insignia

US insignia

combat infantry badge

service ribbons & decorations

parachutist's badge

dress shirt

black tie

shoulder board/rank

nameplate

blouse/ dress-blue jacket

brass buttons

rank insignia

dress trousers

combat stripes/ overseas bars

officer's braid

dress shoe

garrison cap/ overseas cap/ service cap

unit crest

branch insignia

unit crest

current unit patch

service ribbons & decorations

rank insignia/grade

marksmanship badge

blouse

hash marks/ service time

trousers

Dress Uniform

Enlisted Man's Uniform

Military Uniforms

An *infantryman*, or "grunt," carries a *rain poncho* on his ammunition belt. A sailor, "swab," or "gob," may wear a *watch cap, leggings* and a *jersey* instead of a jumper. Sailors aboard ship keep their clothing in *seabags*.

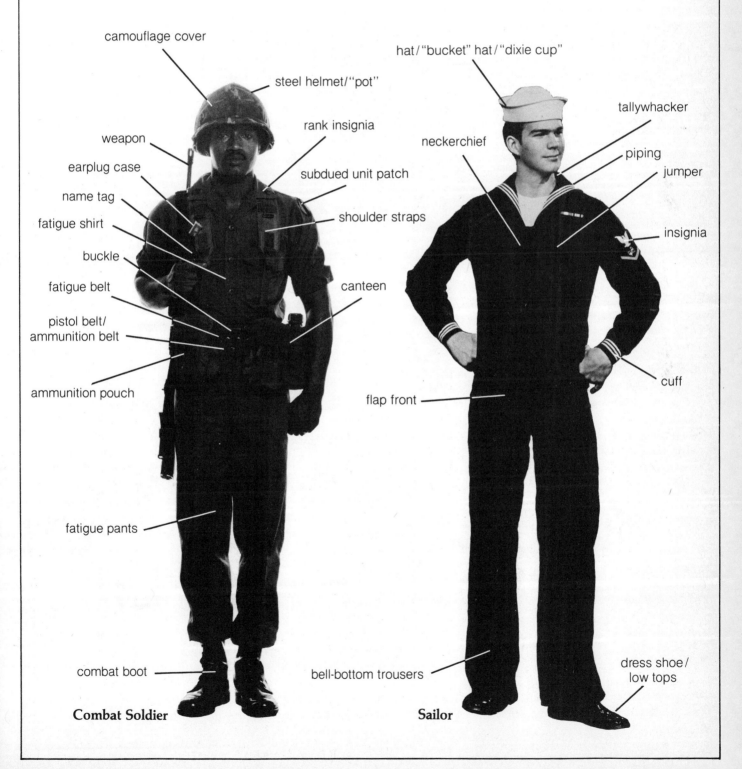

Combat Soldier

- camouflage cover
- steel helmet/"pot"
- weapon
- rank insignia
- earplug case
- subdued unit patch
- name tag
- shoulder straps
- fatigue shirt
- buckle
- fatigue belt
- pistol belt/ ammunition belt
- canteen
- ammunition pouch
- fatigue pants
- combat boot

Sailor

- hat/"bucket" hat/"dixie cup"
- tallywhacker
- neckerchief
- piping
- jumper
- insignia
- cuff
- flap front
- bell-bottom trousers
- dress shoe/ low tops

Military Attire

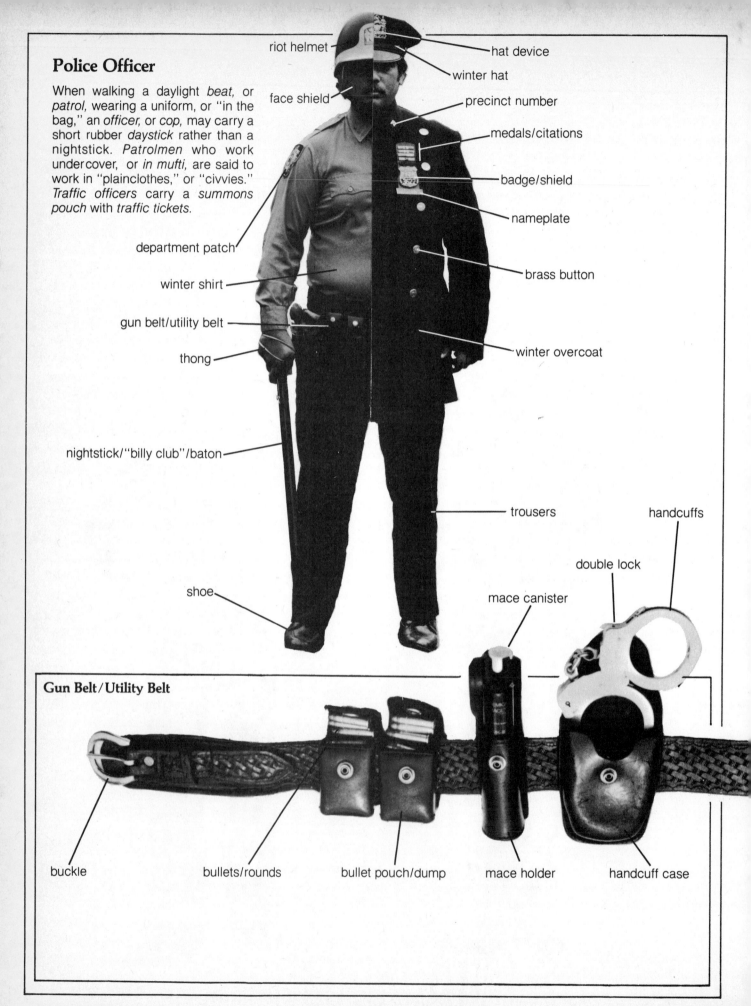

Police Officer

When walking a daylight *beat,* or *patrol,* wearing a uniform, or "in the bag," an *officer,* or *cop,* may carry a short rubber *daystick* rather than a nightstick. *Patrolmen* who work undercover, or *in mufti,* are said to work in "plainclothes," or "civvies." *Traffic officers* carry a *summons pouch* with *traffic tickets.*

riot helmet

face shield

hat device

winter hat

precinct number

medals/citations

badge/shield

nameplate

department patch

brass button

winter shirt

gun belt/utility belt

winter overcoat

thong

nightstick/"billy club"/baton

trousers

handcuffs

double lock

mace canister

shoe

Gun Belt/Utility Belt

buckle

bullets/rounds

bullet pouch/dump

mace holder

handcuff case

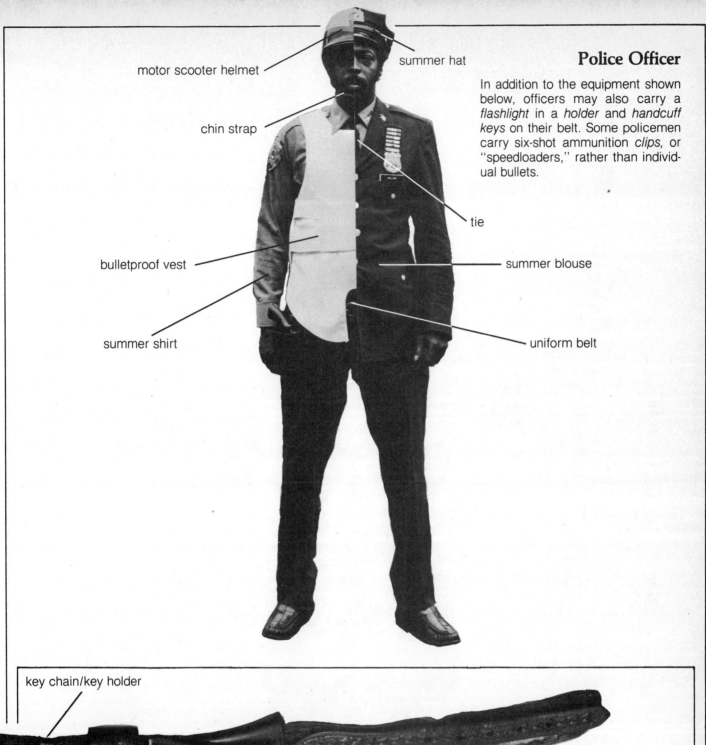

motor scooter helmet

summer hat

chin strap

Police Officer

In addition to the equipment shown below, officers may also carry a *flashlight* in a *holder* and *handcuff keys* on their belt. Some policemen carry six-shot ammunition *clips*, or "speedloaders," rather than individual bullets.

tie

bulletproof vest

summer blouse

summer shirt

uniform belt

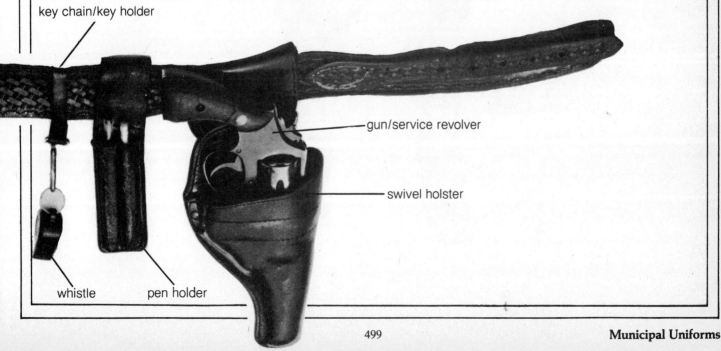

key chain/key holder

gun/service revolver

swivel holster

whistle

pen holder

Municipal Uniforms

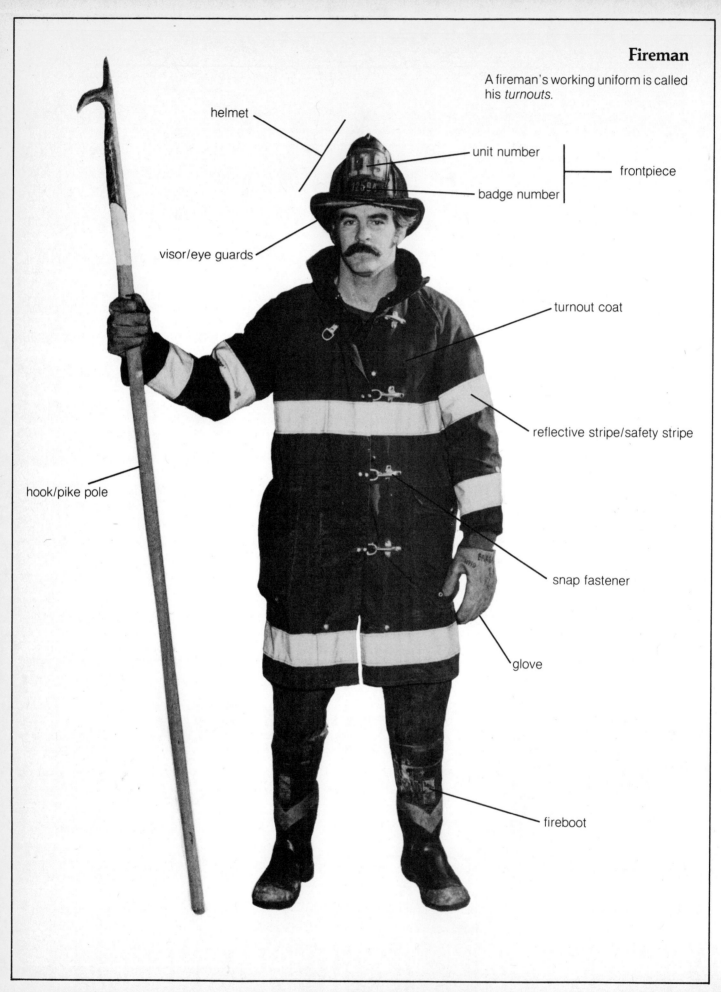

Fireman

A fireman's working uniform is called his *turnouts*.

helmet

unit number

badge number

frontpiece

visor/eye guards

turnout coat

reflective stripe/safety stripe

hook/pike pole

snap fastener

glove

fireboot

Signs and Symbols

While signs and symbols take the place of language or are used to represent meaning, either by suggestion, relationship or association, many have parts for which there are proper names. A flag is used as a sign of a nation, for example, or as a symbol of patriotism, yet it has distinctive components which are identifiable.

Other signs, such as editing and proofreading marks, also included in this section, are used to convey instructions, while sign language is a set of gestures used as a substitute for words or letters.

The fields of science, business and industry have all devised signs whose meanings have legal as well as instructional implications, and the world of transportation is largely controlled by traffic signs. Even hobos, whose pictographs appear here, use pictorial signs instead of written language to communicate messages.

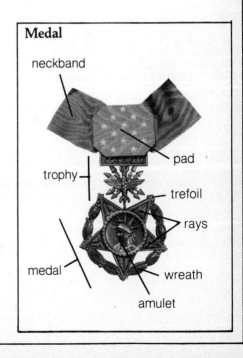

Medal

neckband

trophy

medal

pad

trefoil

rays

wreath

amulet

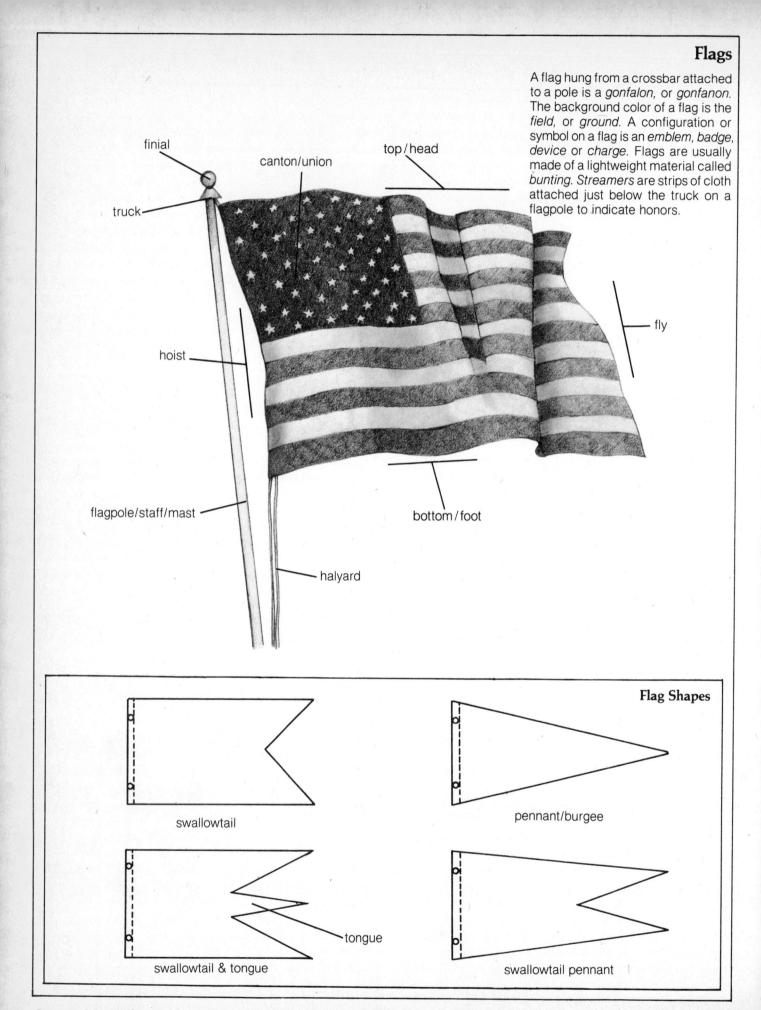

Flags

A flag hung from a crossbar attached to a pole is a *gonfalon,* or *gonfanon.* The background color of a flag is the *field,* or *ground.* A configuration or symbol on a flag is an *emblem, badge, device* or *charge.* Flags are usually made of a lightweight material called *bunting. Streamers* are strips of cloth attached just below the truck on a flagpole to indicate honors.

finial

canton/union

top / head

truck

fly

hoist

flagpole/staff/mast

bottom / foot

halyard

Flag Shapes

swallowtail

pennant/burgee

tongue

swallowtail & tongue

swallowtail pennant

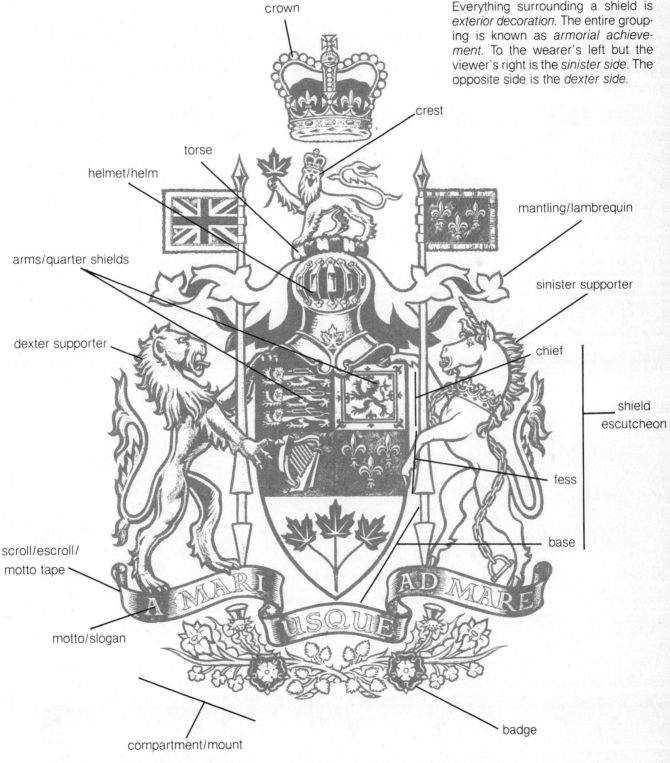

Coat of Arms

Technically, a coat of arms, or *achievement of arms*, consists only of a shield, the surface of which is called the *field*. Everything surrounding a shield is *exterior decoration*. The entire grouping is known as *armorial achievement*. To the wearer's left but the viewer's right is the *sinister side*. The opposite side is the *dexter side*.

crown

crest

torse

helmet/helm

mantling/lambrequin

arms/quarter shields

sinister supporter

dexter supporter

chief

shield
escutcheon

fess

base

scroll/escroll/
motto tape

motto/slogan

badge

compartment/mount

A MARI

USQUE

AD MARE

stop	yield	one way	one-way traffic/ do not enter	railroad crossing

no bicycles	no trucks	no U turn	no right turn	no left turn

interstate route	U.S. route	state route	trail	bike route

picnic area	camping	trailer park	hospital	telephone

Signs and Symbols

Road Signs

With the exception of *route signs,* which are different shapes and colors, road signs are color-coded: red signs are *prohibit movement signs;* yellow are *warning signs;* white are *regulatory signs;* orange are *construction signs;* blue are *service signs;* green are *guide signs.* Octagonal red signs are used exclusively for *stop signs.* Rectangular signs with white letters on a green background are *destination signs.*

signal ahead	two-way traffic	no-passing zone	divided highway ends	merge

merge left	winding road	slippery when wet	hill	school crossing
pedestrian crossing	bicycle crossing	farm machinery	cattle crossing	deer crossing

Signs and Symbols

Public Signs

Pasigraphy is a universal written language that uses signs and symbols rather than words, whereas *pictographs* can represent an object as well as a thought. A symbol or character that represents a word, syllable or phoneme is a *phonogram*. A symbolic representation of an idea rather than a word is an *ideogram* or *ideograph*.

 first aid

 information

 handicapped

 hotel/motel

 restaurant

 coffee shop

 bar

 no smoking

 toilets

 taxi stand

 bus transportation

 air transportation

 car rental

 rail transportation

 elevator

 baggage check-in

 baggage claim

 customs

 lost and found

 telephone

 mail

 gas station

 no parking

 parking

 mechanic

 picnic area

 campfires

 bicycle trail

 hiking trail

 playground

 launching ramp

 horse trail

 no entry

Signs and Symbols

A gesture, the movement of the head, arm, hand or body to express reaction, emotion, opinion or a concept, can be one of friendship (as in a kiss, a hug, nose rubbing, back slapping) or one of anger (with a clenched fist or a raised middle finger).

approval   disapproval

everything's OK / perfection

you're out / hitch-hiking

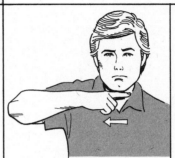

for good luck

the end / cut it / "throat-cutting"

blunder / faux pas

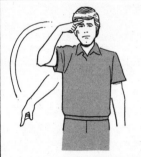

close escape / close call

no money

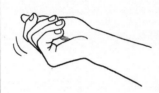

money / "pay up"

good luck / knock-on-wood

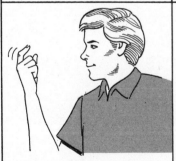

beckoning / come here

excessive talk / "yackety-yak"

self-congratulation

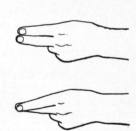

close relationship

derision / mockery

victory / V-sign

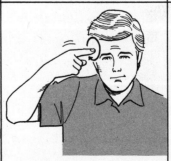

odd / foolish / "crazy"

annoyance / exasperation

Signs and Symbols

Religious Symbols

The symbols shown here represent beliefs and religions such as Christianity, Judaism, Islam, Shinto, as well as Chinese philosophy. The ankh was an ancient Egyptian *symbol of life,* and the gammadion was an eon-old Oriental and Indian *good luck symbol.*

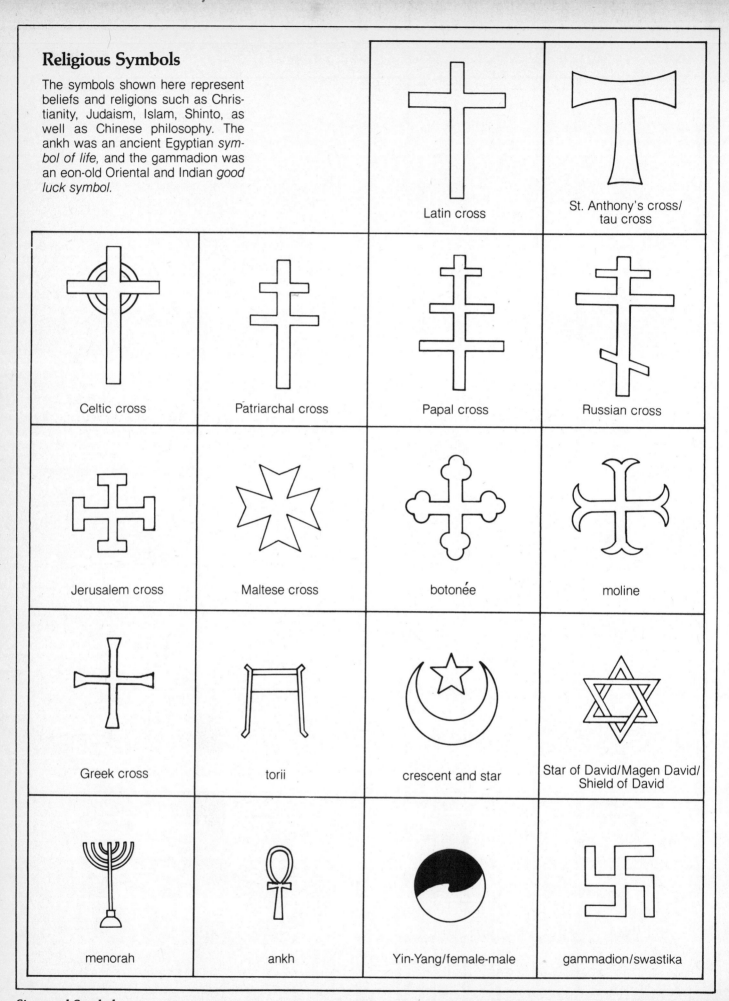

Latin cross

St. Anthony's cross/ tau cross

Celtic cross

Patriarchal cross

Papal cross

Russian cross

Jerusalem cross

Maltese cross

botonée

moline

Greek cross

torii

crescent and star

Star of David/Magen David/ Shield of David

menorah

ankh

Yin-Yang/female-male

gammadion/swastika

Signs of the Zodiac

The *zodiac* is an imaginary belt in the heavens divided into twelve parts named for constellations, called *houses*. A *horoscope*, drawn by an *astrologer*, foretells the influence of these heavenly bodies on human affairs.

Spring Signs

Aries — The Ram
March 21—April 20

Taurus. — The Bull
April 21—May 21

Gemini — The Twins
May 22—June 21

Summer Signs

Cancer — The Crab
June 22—July 22

Leo — The Lion
July 23—August 23

Virgo — The Virgin
August 24—September 23

Autumn Signs

Libra — The Balance
September 24—October 23

Scorpio — The Scorpion
October 24—November 22

Sagittarius — The Archer
November 23—December 21

Winter Signs

Capricorn — The Goat
December 22—January 20

Aquarius — The Water Bearer
January 21—February 19

Pisces — The Fish
February 20—March 20

Signs and Symbols

Symbols of Science, Business and Commerce

The symbols shown here are used in the medical and pharmaceutical fields, in chemistry, engineering and electronics, in mathematics and business, and by currency-exchange centers and banks. Also included are miscellaneous symbols used in other walks of life.

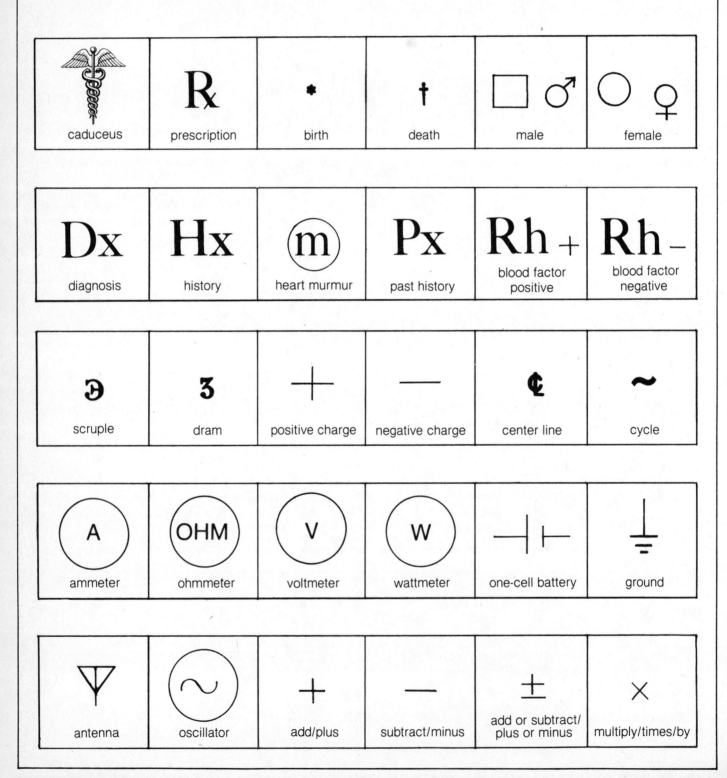

caduceus	prescription	birth	death	male	female
diagnosis	history	heart murmur	past history	blood factor positive	blood factor negative
scruple	dram	positive charge	negative charge	center line	cycle
ammeter	ohmmeter	voltmeter	wattmeter	one-cell battery	ground
antenna	oscillator	add/plus	subtract/minus	add or subtract/plus or minus	multiply/times/by

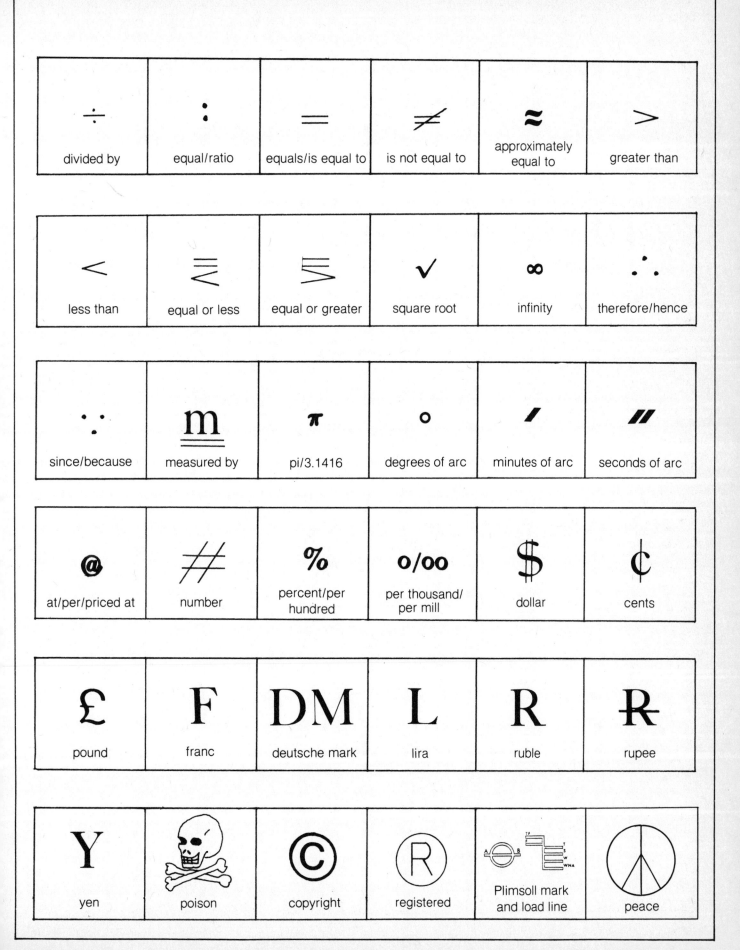

÷	:	=	≠	≈	>
divided by	equal/ratio	equals/is equal to	is not equal to	approximately equal to	greater than

<	≦	≧	√	∞	∴
less than	equal or less	equal or greater	square root	infinity	therefore/hence

∵	m	π	°	′	″
since/because	measured by	pi/3.1416	degrees of arc	minutes of arc	seconds of arc

@	#	%	o/oo	$	¢
at/per/priced at	number	percent/per hundred	per thousand/ per mill	dollar	cents

£	F	DM	L	R	₨
pound	franc	deutsche mark	lira	ruble	rupee

Y		©	®		
yen	poison	copyright	registered	Plimsoll mark and load line	peace

511

Signs and Symbols

Symbolic Language

Sign language, used by deaf-mutes, substitutes *gestures* for spoken words. Embossed *dots* are used by blind people to read by touch. *Semaphore* and *wigwag* are systems of signalling by hand-held flags.

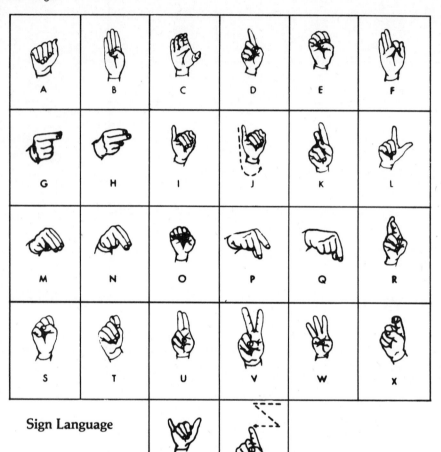

Sign Language

Braille

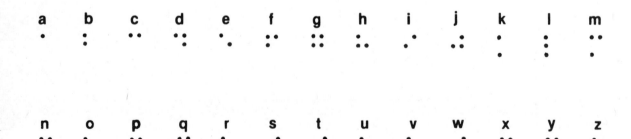

In addition to these *punctuation*, *diacritic* and *pronunciation symbols*, there are *phonetic symbols*, *abbreviations* and *contractions*.

'a' single quotation marks	**"a"** quotation marks	**′** foot/minute/prime	**″** inch/second/ double prime	**a'** apostrophe
(a) parentheses	**[a]** brackets/crotchets	**a-a** hyphen	**a—a** dash	**a/a** virgule/ slant/slash
, comma	**;** semicolon	**:** colon	**&** ampersand	***** asterisk
• period/full point	**•••** ellipsis/marks of omission	**!** exclamation point/ bang/ecphoneme	**?** question mark/ eroteme	**‽** interrobang/ interabang
a̲ underline/ underscore	**sh** ligature	**é** acute accent	**à** grave accent	**â** circumflex accent/ doghouse
ñ tilde	**ç** cedilla	**ā** macron	**ă** breve	**äi** dieresis/umlaut

Proofreader's Marks

The marks illustrated below are used for the purpose of standardizing the transmittal of corrections and queries between *editors* and/or *proofreaders* and *typesetters* and/or *printers*. When the corrected *copy* is set in *type* it is *proved*, or *proofed*, and additional marks are then made on the *galley proofs*. The first *impressions* of the corrected galleys are called *page proofs*.

Mark

Enter HAMLET.

Ham. To be, or not to be: that is the question:

Whether 't is nobler in the mind to suffer

The slings and arrows of outrageous fortune

Or to take arms against a sea of troubles,

And end by opposing them? To die: to sleep:

No More; and by a sleep to say we end

The heart-ache and the 1000 natural shocks

That flesh is heir to 't is a consummation

Devoutly to be wish'd. To die, to sleep;

To sleep: perchance to dream: ay, there's

□□□ the rub;

For in that sleep of death what dreams may come

When we have shuffled off this mortal coil,

Must give us pause. There's the res pect

That makes calamity of soo long life;

For who would bear the whips and scorns of time,

The oppressor's wrong, the proud mans contumely,

The pings of disprized love, the law's delay,

The ins°lence of office, and the spurns

That patient merit of the unworthy takes,

When he himself might his quietus make

With a bare bodkin who would fardels bear,

to grunt and sweat under a weary life,

But that the dread of something death,

Symbol — Meaning

Symbol	Meaning
ital	set in italics
¶	begin a paragraph
(G?)	grammar?
⧣	close up partly/less space/take out space
]	move right/flush left
tr	transpose
lc	set in lower case
(sp)	spell out
⌃	insert comma
eq. #	equalize space
[	move left/square up
[	move left—indent 3 ems
⎵	move down
au?	query author
⌢	close up completely/take out space
⟍	delete
#	insert space/insert lead
∨	insert apostrophe
a/	substitute letter
⎓	straighten type horizontally
rom	set in roman type
stet	let it stand
?	insert question mark
cap	set in capitals
after	insert/insert omitted matter

Hobo Signs

Symbols, inscriptions, phrases and signatures drawn in public places are collectively called graffiti. Those shown here are used among tramps and vagrants.

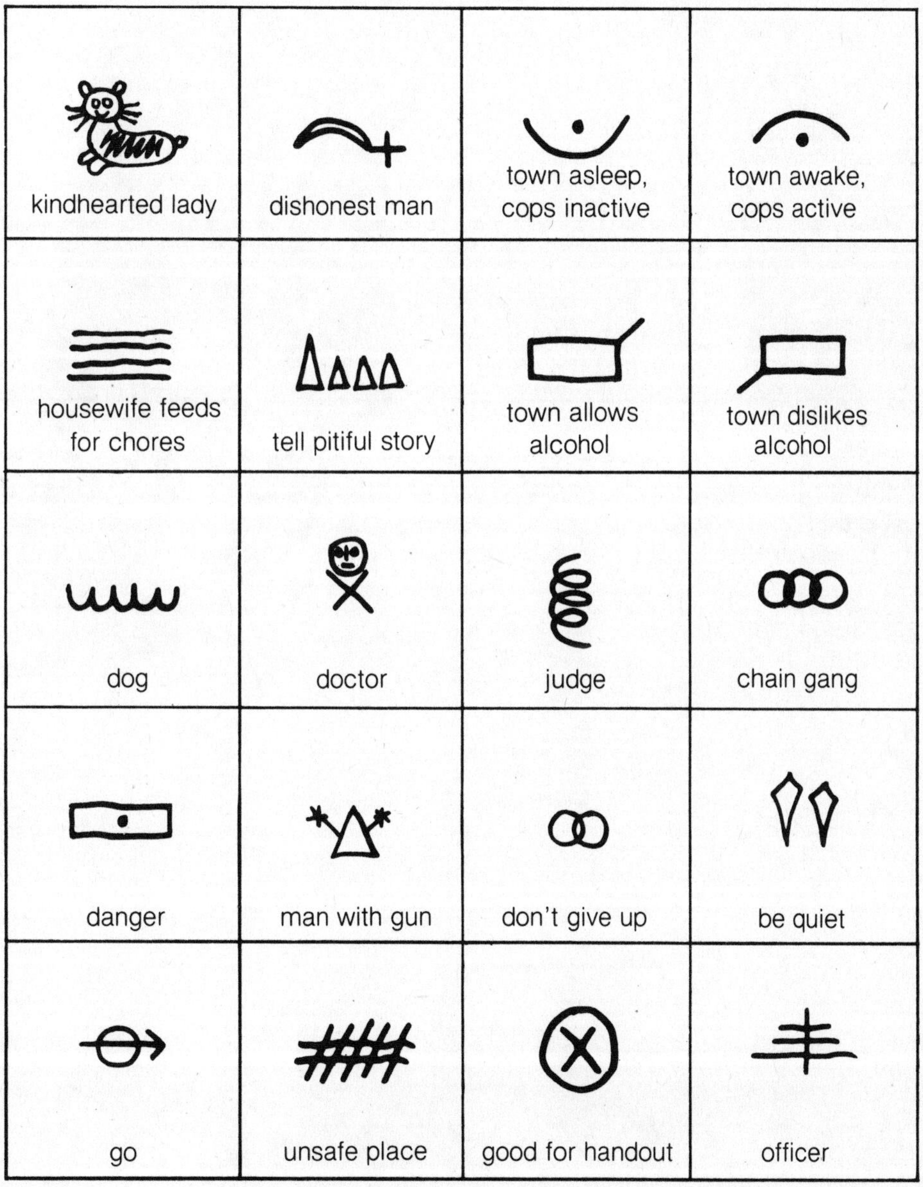

kindhearted lady	dishonest man	town asleep, cops inactive	town awake, cops active
housewife feeds for chores	tell pitiful story	town allows alcohol	town dislikes alcohol
dog	doctor	judge	chain gang
danger	man with gun	don't give up	be quiet
go	unsafe place	good for handout	officer

Signs and Symbols

Tombstone and Coffin

A stone placed at the foot of a grave is a *footstone*. *Crypts,* or *vaults,* are wholly or partly underground *burial chambers*. *Mausoleums* are large aboveground *tombs*.

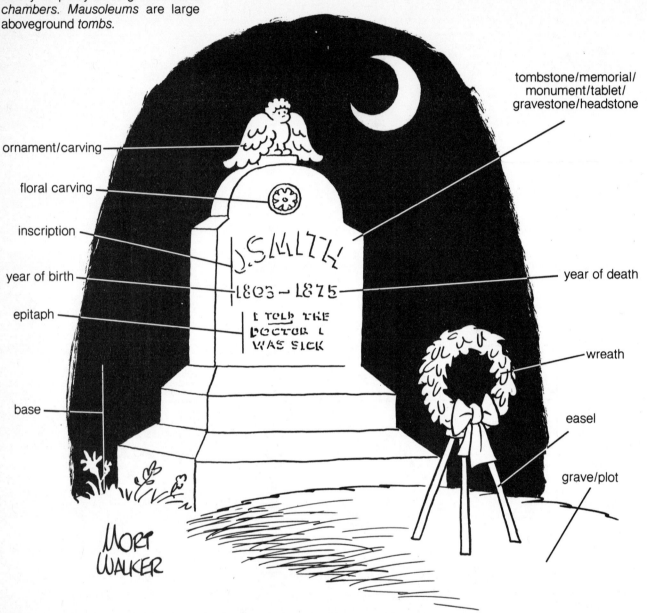

ornament/carving

floral carving

inscription

year of birth

epitaph

base

tombstone/memorial/
monument/tablet/
gravestone/headstone

J.SMITH
1803 – 1875
I TOLD THE
DOCTOR I
WAS SICK

year of death

wreath

easel

grave/plot

MORT
WALKER

Coffin/Casket

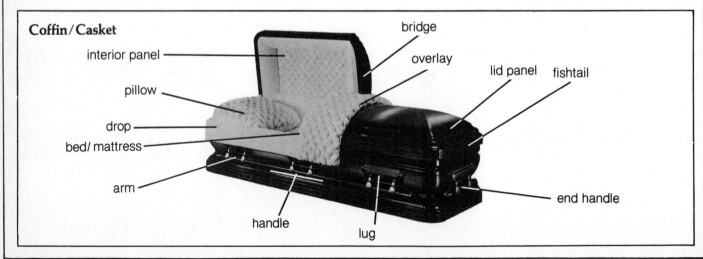

interior panel

pillow

drop

bed/mattress

arm

handle

lug

bridge

overlay

lid panel

fishtail

end handle

Index

73; vault, 457; White House, 75
archival frame, 379
arch-stones, arch, 72
arco, stringed instrument, 355
area code, telephone, 180
area rug, 246
A recreation yard, prison, 76
arena, circus, 90
areole, cactus, 56
arête: glacier, 12; mountain, 9
Argine, playing card queen, 348
Aries, zodiac, 509
arithmetic function key calculator, 441
ark, synagogue, 88
arm: anchor, 132; automobile, 161, 166; ballista, 467; bobby pin, 214; cactus, 56; candelabrum, 237; chaise longue, 288; clothes hanger, 281; coffin, 516; corkscrew, 251; dental, 454, 455; dishwasher, 250; dog, 36; drill bit, 419; fishing reel, 340; folding rule, 424; frog, 44; gas pump price-poster, 112; guitar, 363; hand shower, 274; human, 24, 25; jellyfish, 46; lamp, 239; launch pad, 152; lounger, 235; L-shaped square, 424; lyre, 355; microscope, 442; movie projector, 175; octopus, 46; outboard engine, 137; organ, 360; overhead power line, 396; phonograph turntable, 178; piano, 361; revolving sprinkler, 428; rocking chair, 234; sewing machine, 278; sextant, 137; shower, 274; slot machine, 346; sofa, 236; starfish, 46; toilet, 275; toll booth gate, 114; traffic light, 113; type, 165; wheelchair, 452; see also arms
armament countermeasure panel, 481
armament panel, pilot's, 481
armature, sculpture, 372
armboard extension, operating table, 450
arm buckle, electric chair, 462
armed guard, prison, 76
arm grip, phonograph turntable, 178
armhole: jacket, 188, 196; undershirt, 194
armhole seam, blouse, 197
armilla, queen's regalia, 484
arming mechanism, bazooka, 472
armlet, jewelry, 219
armoire, 272
armor, 465
armored cord, pay phone, 180
armorial achievement, coat of arms, 503
armor-plated vehicle, 474-475
armory, castle, 81
arm pad, lounger, 235
arm piece, crutch, 452
armpit: frog, 44; human, 24
arm post, rocking chair, 234
arm protector, ice hockey goalie, 294
armrail, commuter bus, 118
armrest: Jacuzzi, 274; lounger, 235; rocking chair, 234; sofa, 236; wheelchair, 452
arms: church, 87; coat of, 503; Manchu coat dress, 491; medieval, 464; royal crown, 485; see also arm
aro, jai alai cesta, 314
arrester, fireplace sparks, 232

arresting gear pendant, aircraft carrier, 478
arresting hook, jet fighter, 480
arresting hook panel, pilot's instrument panel, 481
arresting trap, 433
arrow, 466; bowling lane, 317; road map, 20
arrowhead, weather vane, 19
arrow loop, castle, 80
arse, wood block, 461
art: book jacket, 167; composition, 368-369; in frame, 379; magazine, 169, 170, 171; newspaper, 168
arteriole, human, 28
artery, human, 27, 28
article, magazine, 169, 170
artificial abrasive material, sander, 421
artificial teeth, denture, 453
artificial turf, baseball field, 291
artillery, cowboy, 490
artist: cartoon, 380; circus, 90; painting, 370; phonograph record, 178
ASA-DIN exposure index, light meter, 176
ascender, type, 165
ascent air-data system, space shuttle, 152
ascent stage, lunar lander, 154
ascot, 193
asdic, 444
ash: cigar and cigarette, 228; volcano, 10
A sharp, piano keyboard octave, 361
ash catcher, grill, 288
ash dump, fireplace, 232
ash lip, woodburning stove, 404
ashpit, fireplace, 232
ashtray, car, 110
asparagus, 54
asphaltum, 376
ASROC launcher, destroyer, 477
assembly: backyard equipment, 287; lamp, 239; pulley block, 461; scale, 446
assigned weight, flat racing entry, 336
assistance telephone, automatic teller machine, 226
assistant quartermaster, frontier fort, 82
assistant's center, dental unit, 454
assist handle, truck tractor, 120
association football, 297
asterisk, grammatical symbol, 513
asteroid, Milky Way, 2
astragal: cannon barrel, 467; column, 73
A string, double bass, 355
astrologer, 509
asymmetrical closing, jacket, 196
at, symbol, 511
athletic sock, 207
athletic supporter, 194
athwartships, boat, 132
Atlantic Drift, ocean, 6
Atlantic North Equatorial Current, ocean, 6
Atlantic South Equatorial Current, ocean, 6
ATM, 226
atmosphere, earth, 4
atom smasher, 394
attaché case, 285
attached bertha, bridal gown, 488

attaching point, inflatable, 133
attaching socket, movie camera, 174
attachment: denture, 453; vacuum cleaner, 283
attachment loop, basketball backstop, 296
attachment plug, electrical, 398
attachment screw thread, camera, 172
attachment weight set, scale, 446
attack indicator, pilot's instrument panel, 481
attack line, volleyball court, 319
attackman, lacrosse position, 298
attic, house, 62, 63
attitude indicator, space shuttle, 153
audience, circus, 91
audio control, police car, 122
audio-input, movie projector, 175
audio knob, Geiger counter, 445
audio port, Geiger counter, 445
audio power status, space shuttle, 153
audio system, 179
auditorium, prison, 76
auditory canal, 30
auger, 422
auger bit, drill, 418, 419
auguste face, clown, 493
auricle, 30
auricular, bird, 39
author: book, 167; magazine, 169; music, 352
authorized signature, traveler's check, 227
autofeed bin, laser printer, 163
autofocus 35 mm camera, 172
auto gate, toll booth, 114
auto inflation, hose, skin diving, 331
autoloader latch, computer tape, 439
automatic choke, automobile, 111
automatic citrus juicer, 255
automatic cue, phonograph turntable, 178
automatic direction finder: helicopter, 146; 747 cockpit, 150
automatic inflator, skin diving, 331
automatic line finder, typewriter, 161
automatic music sensor, compact disc player, 178
automatic noise limiter, CB radio, 183
automatic nozzle, gas pump, 112
automatic pilot disengage, 747 cockpit, 151
automatic pistol, 470
automatic rewind switch, tape measure, 424
automatic rifle, 471
automatic teller machine, 226
automatic teller machine card, 226
automatic temperature probe, microwave oven, 248
automatic timer, coffee maker, 252
automatic weapons, 471
automobile: cutaway, 108-109; drag racing, 339; engine, 111; exterior, 106-107; Grand Prix racer, 338; interior, 110; police, 122; see also car

autopilot display, space shuttle, 153
autopilot engage switch, 747 cockpit, 150
auto redial, cellular telephone, 181
auto-reverse, portable radio/cassette player, 182
auxiliary attaching socket, movie camera, 174
auxiliary building, nuclear reactor, 392
auxiliary car-station panel, elevator car, 78
auxiliary contact, movie camera, 174
auxiliary counterweight, lift bridge, 97
auxiliary feedwater pump, nuclear reactor, 392
auxiliary handle: hand drill, 418; plane, 420
auxiliary instruments arm, dental, 454
auxiliary lens, microscope, 442
auxiliary power feed, Walkman, 182
auxiliary selector, movie camera, 174
auxiliary tank, truck, 121
avalanche area, mountain, 9
aven, cave, 11
aviation light, bridge, 97
aviation lens, eyeglasses, 221
awards, résumé, 160
awl: combination square, 424; knife, 426
awn, grass, 58
awning: barn, 104; tent, 342
ax: guillotine, 462; ice climbing, 334; medieval, 464
axilla, frog, 44
axillary bud, tree, 50
axis: fern, 57; peeler, 256
axle: automobile, 109; bicycle, 128; child's wagon, 287; Ferris wheel, 93; Hansom cab, 131; roller skate, 324; stroller, 286; tractor, 434; wheelbarrow, 430; wheelchair, 452; windmill, 390
axle gear, seeder, 430
axle hole, tire, 105
azimuth coarse-motion clamp, telescope, 443

B

B: braille, 512; music notation, 353; piano keyboard octave, 361; sign language, 512
B-1B Bomber, 480
B-2 Bomber, 480
baby carriage, 286
baby chair, 286
baby teeth, 456
baccarat, 346
back: bird, 39; bow, 466; carpenter's saw, 416; cat, 37; chaise longue, 288; chicken, 35; chisel, 420; coin, 225; dog, 36; easel, 370; electric chair, 462; horse, 38; human, 24, 25; knife, 256, 463; playing card, 348; polo position, 299; rocking chair, 234; saw tooth, 416; shank button, 209; sheep, 33; sofa, 236; stringed instrument, 355; wave, 14 wheelchair, 452
back arch, English saddle, 335
back beam, hand loom, 387
backboard, basketball backstop, 296
backbone, hardback book, 167
back boundary line, badminton court, 319

hurdle, 304; juice extractor, 255; laboratory burner, 447; laboratory scale, 447; lantern, 342; lawn sprinkler, 428; leaf, 52; light bulb, 238; makeup, 216; medical examination table, 450; microscope, 442; minaret, 70; mortar cap, 472; mousetrap, 433; music stand, 367; onion, 54; parallel bars, 306; pedestal table, 242; pencil sharpener, 277; percolator brewing basket, 252; phonograph turntable, 178; pole vault pole, 305; pommel horse, 307; pot, 373; power saw, 417; pyramid, 71; refrigerator grille, 249; rifle scope, 468, 469; sandwich cookie, 264; stapler, 277; steam engine, 405; telephone, 180; television, 185; thimble, 384; tombstone, 516; transistor chip, 396; trimline phone, 180; trophy, 289; tuning fork, 367; vacuum tube, 396; vise, 409; White House, 75
baseball, 290-291; darts, 322
baseboard, and carpet, 246
baseline: baseball field, 291; Ping-Pong table, 321; shuffleboard court, 319; tennis court, 312; type, 165
basement, house, 60, 63
basepath, baseball field, 291
baseplate: land mine, 473; mortar, 472; railroad track, 115; saber saw, 417; sewing machine, 278
base unit, cordless phone, 180
basin: ambulance, 123; dam, 100; river, 13; sink, 273
basin compartment, sink, 247
basket: basketball, 296; bee, 41; coffee maker, 252; container, 266; deep frying, 260; garbage disposal, 247; guillotine, 462; hot air balloon, 332; jai alai, 314; juice extractor, 255; refrigerator, 249; sink, 247; ski pole, 326; sword, 463; toll booth, 114; typewriter type, 161; washing machine, 280
basketball, 296
basket-release handle, garbage disposal, 247
bass: accordion, 366; bagpipe drone, 365; bassoon joint, 357; fiddle, 354, 355; guitar, 363; music clef, 353; phonograph dial, 179
bass and guitar, double-neck, 363
bass clarinet, 354
bass display, portable radio/cassette player, 182
bass drum, 354, 364
bass fiddle, 354, 355
bassinet, 286
bass neck, double-neck bass and guitar, 363
bassoon, 354, 357
bass speaker, portable radio/cassette player, 182
basting brush, 259
basting ladle, 259
bastion: castle, 80, 81; permanent fort, 83
bat: badminton, 319; baseball, 291; brick wall, 69; flat racing, 336; Ping-Pong, 321
bateau neck, sweater, 199
bath, 274

bath oil, 217
batholith, volcano, 10
bathtub, 274
baton: drum major, 495; police, 498
bat pin, potter's wheel, 373
batten: hand loom, 387; stage, 350
batten pocket, mainsail, 136
batter, baseball, 290
batter head, snare drum, 364
batter's box, baseball, 291
batter's circle, baseball, 291
battery, 397; automobile, 108; buoy, 132; electronic flash, 176; Geiger counter, 445; hearing aid, 452; intercity bus, 118; lunar rover, 155; metal detector, 445; movie camera, 174; pacemaker, 452; tape recorder, 177; truck, 120, 121
battery charger: medical examination equipment, 448; tow truck, 126
battery holder, camera, 172
battery jumper cable, tow truck, 126
battery pack: cellular telephone, 181; video camera, 184; video-still camera adaptor, 173
battery-powered tape recorder, 177
battery recharge contact, cordless phone, 180
batting, quilting, 385
batting glove, baseball, 290
batting helmet, baseball, 290
battlement, castle, 80
battleship, 476
bat weight, baseball, 290
bay: aircraft carrier, 478; barn, 104; coastline, 7, 15; space shuttle, 152
bay bar, 15
bay barrier, 15
bayit, tefillin, 486
baymouth, bar, 15
bayonet, 463
bayonet saw, 417
bay window, house, 62, 63
bazooka, 472
bazooka plate, tank, 474
B cell block, prison, 76
BC inflator mouthpiece, skin diving, 331
beach, 14, 15
beacon: helicopter, 146; police car, 122; single engine airplane, 147
bead: abacus, 441; beaker, 447; cowboy hat, 202; shotgun, 469
beading: attaché case, 285; Indian attire, 490
bead line, bell, iv
beak: bird, 39; chicken, 35; clam, 47; dolphin, 45; halberd, 464; turtle, 43; type, 165
beaker: coffee maker, 252; laboratory, 447
beam: abacus, 441; automobile, 106; boat, 132; bus, 118; drag racing, 339; guillotine, 462; gymnastic, 306; hand loom, 387; house, 61; incline track, 92; laboratory scale, 447; laser, 395; lumber, 68; skyscraper, 77; subway car, 119; tow truck bed, 126
beam abort, super collider, 394
beam balance, laboratory, 446-447
beam lens, laser, 395
beam pipe, super collider, 394

beam shroud, gas laser, 395
beam splitter, holography, 395
beanie cap, space shuttle, 152
beard: man's, 211; spring beard needle, 386; turkey, 35; type, 166; ultimate beast, 49; windmill, 390
bearing: airport runway, 94; fishing reel, 340; laboratory scale, 446; radar, 444; roller skate, 324; skateboard, 324; socket wrench, 415; transit, 436
bearing distance heading indicator, pilot's instrument panel, 481
bearing edge, horse's foot, 38
bearing line, compass, 136
bearing rail, bureau, 272
bearing ring, radar, 444
bearing surface, brick, 68
bearpaw shoe, snowshoe, 327
bear trap, 433
bear trap binding, ski, 326
beat, police, 498
beater: bass drum, 364; kitchen tool, 258; vacuum cleaner, 283
beauty products, 217
beauty salon, passenger ship, 142
beaver, armor, 465
because, symbol, 511
becket, block and tackle, 461
beckoning, gesture, 507
bed, 270-271; brick, 68; cannon carriage, 467; child's wagon, 287; coffin, 516; etching press, 377; hammock, 288; highway, 114; lithographic press, 376; railroad track, 115; river, 13; slide, 287; tower, ladder, 124; trampoline, 308; wheelbarrow, 430
bed cloth, pool table, 320
bedcover, 271
bedding, 270-271
bed handle, lithographic press, 376
bed joint, brick wall, 69
bed knife, sickle-bar mower, 429
bed mold, column entablature, 73
bedplate: mortar, 472; steam engine, 405
bedrail, 270
bedroll: backpacking, 343; cowboy, 490
bedspread, 271
bee, 41
beef, 32
Beefeater, 483
beehive, woman's hair, 213
begin paragraph, proofreader's mark, 514
belfry, church, 86
bell, iv; bassoon, 357; boxing, 309; buoy, 132; candle snuffer, 237; clarinet, 356; cymbal, 364; fire engine, 124, 125; foil mounting, 315; hammer, 412; jellyfish, 46; slot machine, 346; steam locomotive, 116; telephone, 180; trombone, 358, 359; vault, 457
bell boot, harness racing pacer 337
bell-bottom trousers, 191, 497
bell brace, trombone, 358
bell buoy, nautical chart, 22
bell chest piece, stethoscope, 449
bell cord, commuter bus, 118
bellows: accordion, 366;

bagpipe, 365; fireplace, 232; organ, 360; paper bag, 266
bellows pocket, parka, 201
bellows strap, accordion, 366
bell plug, fencing foil, 315
bell rim, bugle, 359
bell shade, lamp, 238
bell wire, trumpet, 359
belly: baluster, 73; banjo, 362; cat, 37; horse, 38; human, 25; jumbo jet, 149; mandolin, 362; type, 166; violin, 355
bellybutton, 25
belowdeck storage entrance, tanker, 140
belt: automobile engine, 111; backpack, 343; belt sander, 421; cardigan sweater, 199; cowboy, 490; drag racing driver, 339; dress, 198; football uniform, 292; ice hockey player, 294; jewelry, 219; king's regalia, 484; machine gun ammunition, 471; man's, 190; military, 496, 497; Milky Way, 3; mountain climbing, 334; police, 498-499; sander, 421; shoulder bag, 222; skirt, 197; time, 5; trench coat, 200; trousers, 191; waterskiing vest, 329
belt carrier, trousers, 191
belted waistband, woman's pants, 196
belt safety guard, drill press, 419
belt sander, 421
belt-tension knob, drill press, 419
bench: baseball field, 291; basketball court, 296; courtroom, 89; football field, 293; ice hockey rink, 295; sled, 328; toboggan, 328
bench rule, 424
bench saw, 417
benchseat, powerboat, 139
bench screw, woodcarving, 372
bench top, workbench, 408
bench vise, 409
bend: fishhook, 341; paper clip, 277; tuba, 358
bending magnet, super collider, 394
Benguela Current, ocean, 6
bent, roller coaster, 92
bent gouge, woodcarving, 372
bent side, grand piano, 361
beret, 202
berg, glacier, 12
bergschrund, mountain, 9
bergy bit, glacier, 12
berm: permanent fort, 83; shoreline, 14
berry, tomato, 54
berth, sailboat, 135
berta, bridal gown, 488
berthing hawser, passenger ship, 142
besom, skirt, 197
beta rod, radio antenna, 183
betting: jai alai, 314; odds, flat racing, 336
bevel: chisel, 420; scriber, 375
bevel gear, hand drill, 418
bevel scale, table saw, 417
bezel: pendant, 219; watch, 220, 304
bezel facet, cut gemstone, 218
B flat, piano keyboard octave, 361
bias, fabric, 388
bias switch, tape recorder, 177
bias tape, garment seam, 196
bib: fencing mask, 315; Indian

crescent moon, 4
crest: coat of arms, 503; dam, 100; dog, 36; enlisted men's uniform, 496; grandfather clock, 233; horse, 38; human, 25; iceberg, 12; mountain, 9; rocking chair, 234; screw thread, 410; wave, 14
crest fringe, lizard, 43
crest rail, sofa, 236
crevasse, mountain, 9
crevice, mountain, 9
crevice tool, vacuum cleaner, 283
crew compartment, lunar lander, 154
crewel, stitchery, 385
crew neck sweater, 199
crew's quarters, passenger ship, 142
cricket, darts, 322
crier, and minaret, 70
crimp: cartridge, 470; painting brush, 370; spring board needle, 386
crimper, electrician's wire stripper, 423
cringle, mainsail, 136
cripples, house, 61
crisper, refrigerator, 249
critical mass, nuclear power, 392
crocheting, 386
crocket, church, 86
crockpot, 257
crocodile, 42
crocodilians, 42
crook: of arm, 25; bassoon, 357; brasses, 358, 359
crop: cow, 32; flat racing, 336; masonry gate post, 67
croquet, 318
crosier, cardinal, 487
cross, 86, 487; symbol, 508
crossarm: power line, 396; railroad crossing signal, 115; weather station, 18
crossbar: abacus, 441; bicycle, 128; football goalpost, 293; hand glider, 333; ice hockey goal, 294; lyre, 355; pole vault, 305; sawhorse, 408; snowshoe, 327; suit hanger, 281; weather vane, 19
crossbeam: ballista, 467; gallows, 462; guillotine, 462; hand loom, 387
crossbelt, 483, 492
crossbow, 466
cross brace: ladder, 47; wheelchair, 452
crossbuck, railroad crossing signal, 115
cross-country skiing, 327
crosscut saw, 416, 417
crosse, 298
cross guard, knife, 463
crosshatching: cartoon, 380; and texture, composition, 369
crosshead, steam engine, 405
crossing: church, 87; railroad, 115
cross joint, brick wall, 69
crossknot, bow tie, 192
Cross of Christ, church, 87
crossover, railroad yard, 96
cross patée, royal regalia, 485
crosspiece: bow tie, 192; hand loom, 387; kite, 323; rocking chair, 234; sword hilt, 463; torii, 71
cross section: cave, 11; coral polyp, 46; fireplace, 232; frame, 379; hurricane, 17; insulated window, 65; lumber, 68; permanent fort,

83; river, 13; stage, 350; tree trunk, 50; tunnel, 98; volcano, 10
cross stitching, 385
cross straps, overnight bag, 285
cross strings, tennis racket, 312
cross strip: kite, 323; wheelbarrow, 430
cross support, pool table, 320
crosstie, railroad track, 115
crosswise grain, fabric, 388
crotch: underpants, 194; trousers, 191
crotchet: grammatical symbol, 513; music, 352
crotch strap: child's car seat, 286; drag racing driver's belt, 339
croup: dog, 36; horse, 38; pommel horse, 307
croupier, roulette, 346
crown: anchor, 132; arch, 72; bell, iv; bird, 39; cactus, 56; coat of arms, 503; croquet wicket, 318; cut gemstone, 218; human, 25; incline track, 92; man's hair, 211; man's hat, 202; needle, 384; palm, 52; pineapple, 55; royal, 485; staple, 410; tennis racket, 312; tooth, 453, 455, 456; tree, 50; watch, 220, 304; woman's hat, 203
crown cap opener, 251
crowning pavilion, minaret, 70
crown stabilizer, football helmet, 292
crow's nest: tanker, 140; train caboose, 117
CRT: computer workstation, 438; personal computer, 162; television, 185
crucifix, church, 87
cruise missile, 482
crumb, bread, 263
crumb incubator, cowboy's, 490
crumble roller, hitch and harrow, 434
crumb tray, toaster, 253
crupper, harness racing, 337
crusher claw, lobster, 47
crust: earth, 4; prepared food, 263, 265
crustacean, 47
crutch, 452
crutch socket, operating table, 450
crypt: burial chamber, 516; Capitol, 74
crystal, watch, 220
Crystal Palace set piece, fireworks, 383
crystal pool, cave, 11
C sharp, piano keyboard octave, 361
C-strap, motorcycle, 129
cubbyhole, sailboat, 135
cube: backgammon, 345; slide projector, 175
cucumber, 54
cue: billiards, 320; cassette tape recorder, button, 177; phonograph turntable, 178; shuffleboard, 318
cuff: blood pressure gauge, 449; blouse, 197; bridal gown, 488; fencing glove, 315; golf bag, 311; ice hockey goalie's glove, 294; jacket, 196; king's regalia, 484; Manchu court dress, 491; paramedic, 123; parka, 201; Revolutionary War general, 492; sailor, 497; shirt, 189, 488; ski boot, 326;

327; sweater, 199; trousers, 191
cuff checklist, spacesuit, 155
cuff link, 218
cuirie, armor, 465
cuish, armor, 465
cuissard, fencing, 315
culet, cut gemstone, 218
cull, lobster, 47
culm, grass, 58
cultivator, 434
culture tube, laboratory, 447
cummerbund, 488, 495
cumulonimbus cloud, 16, 17
cumulus congestus cloud, 16
cup: armor, 465; athletic supporter, 194; ballista, 467; baseball catcher, 290; brassiere, 195; bugle, 359; citrus juicer, 255; Communion, 87; coral polyp, 46; golf course, 311; measuring, 258; plumber's plunger, 422; seed, 51; sketch box, 371; table setting, 245; thimble, 384; trombone, 358; weather station, 18
cupboard, 243
cup level scale, coffee maker, 252
cupola: barn, 104; Capitol, 74; kokoshniki, 70; mosque, 70, 71; tank, 474; train caboose, 117
curbside sidewall, truck van, 121
curb window, bus, 118
curd, cheese, 263
curfew, fireplace, 232
curl: pail, 284; wave, 14; woman's hair, 213
curled position, windmill, 390
curling iron, 214
currency pocket, wallet, 223
current: electrical, 398; ocean, 6
current temperature, thermometer, 19
current unit patch, enlisted man's uniform, 496
curriculum vitae, 160
cursor: linear slide rule, 441; radar, 444
cursor control: computer workstation, 438; personal computer, 162
cursor keypad, portable word processor, 162
curtain: cave, 11; four-poster bed, 270; living room, 240; overnight bag, 285; permanent fort, 83; shower, 274; stage, 350; stagecoach, 131; theatre, 351; Torah, 486; voting booth, 437
curtain rod, 240
curtain wall: castle, 81; skyscraper, 77
curtein, king's regalia, 484
curve, royal scepter, 485
curved jaw, combination pliers, 414
curved slat, rocking chair, 234
cushion: bowling lane, 317; boxing ring, 309; chaise longue, 288; dog, 36; jai alai cancha, 314; lounger, 235; phonograph headphone, 179; pool table, 320; roller skate, 324; sofa, 236
cusp, tooth, 456
cuspid, 456
cuspidor, dental unit, 454
custodian's seal, voting booth, 437
customized automobile, 106-107

customs, public sign, 506
cut: book, 167; key blade, 459; label, 268; magazine, 170
cutaway coat: butler's uniform, 489; man's formal attire, 488
cut gemstone, 218
cuticle: human fingernail, 31; leaf, 52
cut it, gesture, 507
cut line, newspaper, 168
cutoff rule, magazine, 171
cutout switch, 747 cockpit, 151
cut section, stained glass, 378
cutter: can opener, 251; chain saw chain, 431; cigar, 228; cowboy, 490; electric razor, 210; glass, 378; juice extractor, 255; kitchen tool, 261; pencil sharpener, 277; pliers, 414; wirestripper, 423
cutter adjusting-screw, expansive bit, 419
cutting board, 261; barbecue grill, 288
cutting edge: auger bit, 419; bulldozer, 435; chisel, 420; nail clippers, 215; plane, 420
cutting line, sewing pattern, 388
cutting surface, table saw, 417
cutting teeth, lobster, 47
cwm, mountain, 8
cyc, stage, 350
cyc flood, stage, 350
cycle: internal combustion engine, 406; symbol, 510
cycle selector: clothes dryer, 281; dishwasher, 250; washing machine, 280
cyclorama, stage, 350
cyclorama floodlight, stage, 350
cyclotron, 394
cylinder: ambulance, 123; automobile, 108, 111; fire extinguisher, 284; internal combustion engine, 406; letterpress, 166; lock, 458; locomotive, 116; offset-lithography, 166; padlock, 459; propane torch, 422; revolver, 470; rotogravure, 166; skin diving, 331; steam engine, 405
cylinder desk, 276
cylinder model, vacuum cleaner, 283
cylindrical buoy, nautical chart, 22
cylindrical slide rule, 441
cymatium, column entablature, 73
cymbal, 354, 364
cytoplasm, animal cell, 23

D

D: braille, 512; music notation, 353: piano keyboard octave, 341; sign language, 512
dabber, 377
dado, column pedestal, 73
daggerboard, windsurfer, 330
dagger point position, windmill, 390
dairy department, supermarket, 102
daisy-wheel printer, 163
daiwa, torii, 71
dalmatic, cardinal, 487
dal segno sign, music, 353
dam, 100; cave, 11; horse, 38, 336
dampening roller, offset-lithography, 166
damper: fireplace, 232; grill, 288; woodburning stove, 404

534

536

hand drill, 418, 419
hand excavator, dental, 455
hand flexor, body building, 344
hand grenade, 473
handgrip: bazooka, 472; body building, 344; carpenter's level, 424; crutch, 452; Jacuzzi, 274; motorcycle, 129; movie camera, 174; pole vault pole, 305; rocking chair, 234; swimming pool, 316; video camera, 184; wheelbarrow, 430; wheelchair, 452
handguard, automatic rifle, 471; chain saw, 431
handgun, 470
handhold: harness racing driver, 337; lunar rover, 155
handicap: drag racing, 339; flat racing entry, 336
handicapped, public sign, 506
handkerchief, queen's regalia, 484
handkerchief pocket, jacket, 188
hand knitting, 386
handle: attaché case, 285; automobile door, 107; ax, 464; barbecue grill, 288; baren, 374; baseball bat, 291; basket, 266; blender, 254; bow, 466; brace, 418; branding iron, 432; brayer, 374; broom, 282; burnisher, 377; candle snuffer, 237; can opener, 251; C-clamp, 409; cellular telephone, 181; chafing dish, 245; cheese plane, 256; chest pull, 344; child's wagon, 287; chisel, 420; citrus juicer, 255; clay modeling tool, 372; clothespin, 280; coffee maker, 252; coffin, 516; croquet mallet, 318; dabber, 377; drain cleaner, 422; drill, 418, 419; ear scope, 448; etching press, 377; faucet, 273; field events hammer, 303; finishing sander, 421; fire engine, 125; fire extinguisher, 284; fishing reel, 340; fishing rod, 340; foil mounting, 315; food mill, 260; food processor, 254; garbage disposal, 247; garbage truck, 127; gimlet, 418; glass cutter, 378; gouge, 374; hair dryer, 212; hammer, 412; handbag, 222; hand loom, 387; hand shower, 274; hoe, 427; hot air balloon, 332; ice hammer, 334; internal combustion engine, 406; iron, 279; jackhammer, 436; jet fighter, 480; jump rope, 344; knife, 244, 256, 463; lacrosse stick, 298; land mine, 473; lithographic press, 376; lorgnette, 221; mace, 464; mailbox, 231; metal detector, 445; microwave oven, 248; mower, 429; outboard engine, 137; pail, 284; painting brush, 370; paint roller, 425; paint spray gun, 425; paper bag, 266; parking meter, 113; peeler, 256; pencil sharpener, 277; pilot's instrument panel, 481; Ping-Pong racket, 321; plane, 420; playpen, 286; pliers, 414; plumber's plunger, 422; pocket knife,

426; pommel horse, 307; portable radio/cassette player, 182; pots and pans, 257; projector, 175; radiator, 400; rake, 427; razor, 210; refrigerator door, 249; revolver, 470; rifle, 471; safe, 457; scissors, 384; saw, 416, 417, 431; screen, 175; screwdriver, 413; scriber, 375; seeder, 430; 747 cockpit, 150, 151; sewing machine, 278; sextant, 137; sharpening steel, 256; shaver, 210; shotgun, 468; shovel, 427; silk screen squeegee, 375; single engine airplane, 147; sink, 247, 273; soldering iron, 378; sponge mop, 282; squash racket, 313; stove, 342, 248, 404; stroller, 286; tea kettle, 245; tennis racket, 312; thrown pot, 373; toilet, 275; toothbrush, 215; tuning fork, 367; umbrella, 230; vacuum cleaner, 283; vault, 457; video camera, 184; vise, 408, 409; voting booth, 437; waterskiing towline, 329; wheelbarrow, 430; woodcarving tool, 372; wrench, 415
handlebar: bicycle, 128; chain saw, 431; snowmobile, 130
handlebar mustache, 211
handle grip: chain saw, 431; seeder, 430; stroller, 286; vacuum cleaner, 283
handler, boxing, 309
handle release pedal, vacuum cleaner, 283
handle screw, plane, 420
hand lever: potter's wheel, 373; spreader, 430
hand loom, 387
hand pad, football uniform, 292
handpiece: crutch, 452; dental, 454, 455
hand protector, waterskiing towline, 329
hand pump: blood pressure gauge, 449; pilot's instrument panel, 481
handrail: bus, 118; elevator car, 78; escalator, 79; locomotive, 116, 117; lunar lander, 154; powerboat, 139; roller coaster, 92; sled, 328; staircase, 66; subway car, 119
hand rope, racing sled, 328
handruff, queen's regalia, 484
handsaw, 416
hand screw, 409
handset, desk phone, 180; cellular telephone, 181
hand shower, 274
hand slide, trombone, 359
handstrap: bus, 118; subway car, 119; video-still camera, 173
hand throttle, car, 110
hand valve, solar heating system, 391
hand warming slot, parka, 201
handwheel: sewing machine, 278; table saw, 417
hangar, airport, 95
hangar bay, aircraft carrier, 478
hanger: dress, 198; fishing plug, 341; frame, 379; harness racing, 337; laboratory scale weight, 447; lamp, 239; screen, 175; swing, 287

hanger bracket, wheelchair, 452
hang glider, 333
hang hole: blister card, 268; dustpan, 282
hanging glacier, mountain, 8
hanging locker, sailboat, 135
hanging ring: can opener, 251; skillet, 359
hanging strip, window shutters, 241
hanging weight, laboratory scale, 446
hang ring, hair dryer, 212
hang-up hole, toothbrush, 215
hank, knitting yarn, 386
Hansom cab, 131
hardback book, 167
hard copy, computer printer, 163
hardcover book, 167
hard disk, computer, 438
hard-hat diving, 331 ·
hardness, pencil lead, 158
hard suction connection hose, pumper, 125
hardware: bureau, 272; computer workstation, 438; cowboy, 498, 499; shoulder bag, 222; sideboard, 243
hardware sling, mountain climbing, 334
hard-way bets, craps table, 347
hare traction splint, paramedic equipment, 123
harmonica, 366
harness: drag racing driver, 339; electrical wall switch, 398; hang glider, 333; harness racing, 337; mountain climbing, 334; parachute, 333; skin diving tank, 331
harness frame, hand loom, 387
harness racing, 336, 337
harp: orchestra, 354; table lamp, 238
harrow, tractor, 434
hash mark: enlisted man's uniform, 496; football field, 293
hassock, lounger, 235
hasp, 460
hat: automobile engine, 111; Beefeater, 483; circus ringmaster, 90; clown, 493; cowboy, 490; miser, 492; pirate, 492; police, 498, 499; Revolutionary War general, 492; sailor, 497; skiing, 327; wizard, 492; woman's, 203
hatband, 202, 203
hat bow, beret, 202
hatch: bus, 118; fireboat, 144; lunar lander, 154; sailboat, 134; tank, 474, 475; tanker, 141; tugboat, 144
hatchback, passenger car, 109
hatch cover, ballistic missile launch deck, 479
hatchet, 412
hatmaker, 202
hat pin, woman's hat, 203
hatter, men's hats, 202
haunch: arch, 72; human, 25
hawg leg, cowboy, 490
hawsehole: fireboat, 144; passenger ship, 142, 143
hawser: and canal lock, 99; passenger ship, 142; tugboat, 144
hay door, barn, 104
hay scale, frontier fort, 82
hay yard, frontier fort, 82
hazard, golf course, 310-311
head: Allen wrench, 415; anchor, 132; arrow, 466; automobile engine, 111; ax,

464; badminton shuttlecock, 319; barrel, 267; bell, iv; billiard bridge, 320; bolt, 411; book page, iv, 167; bowling lane, 317; brace, 418; cartridge, 470; C-clamp, 409; chain saw, 431; chisel, 420; cigar, 228; coin, 225; combination square, 424; comet, 3; croquet mallet, 318; dental x-ray tube, 454; dispenser, 267; drain cleaner, 422; drill press, 419; drum, 364; electric razor, 210; electronic flash, 176; field events hammer, 303; fish, 45; fishing jig, 341; flag, 502; golf club, 310; grasshopper, 41; guitar, 362, 363; hammer, 412; hatchet, 412; helicopter rotor, 146; hinge fixed pin, 460; human, 24; javelin, 302; knee kicker, 246; knitting needle, 386; lacrosse stick, 298; lance, 464; lettuce, 262; levigator bolt, 376; mace, 464; magazine, 170, 171; mainsail, 136; match, 228; mechanical sweeper gutter broom, 127; movie camera microphone, 174; music note, 353; nail, 410; newspaper, 168; octopus, 46; pelt, 201; pin, 208; polo mallet, 299; saddle, 335; sailboat, 135; screw, 410; screwdriver, 413; shower, 274; shuffleboard court, 318; soldering iron, 378; spring beard needle, 386; squash racket, 313; stemware, 244; tambourine, 364; table saw, 417; tack, 410; tape recorder, 177; tennis racket, 312; theodolite, 436; toothbrush, 215; venetian blinds, 241
headband: hair ornament, 214; hardback book, 167; headphone, 179, 182; physician's mirror, 448; ski hat, 327
headboard: four-poster bed, 270; mainsail, 136
head box, venetian blind, 241
head channel, venetian blind, 241
head collar, kettledrum, 364
head cover, golf club, 311
headdress, Arab dress, 491
header: brick wall, 69; drag racing dragster, 339; house, 60, 61; solar collector panel, 391
headgear: armor, 465; boxing, 309
headguard, boxing, 309
heading: book page, iv; draperies, 240; letter, 159; radar, 444
heading alignment control, radar, 444
head jamb, window, 65
head joint: brick wall, 69; flute, 357
headlight: automobile, 106; bulldozer, 435; bus, 118; locomotive, 116, 117; medical examination equipment, 448; motorcycle, 129; snowmobile, 130; tank, 475; tractor, 434; truck, 120
headlight controls, car, 110
headline: human hand, 31; magazine, 170; newspaper, 168
head lock, camera tripod, 176
head lug, bicycle, 128

546

547

missile launcher, aircraft carrier, 478
mission specialist, space shuttle, 153
mistigris, playing cards, 348
miter: bishop, 487; cardinal, 487
miter clamp, 409
mitered joint, silk screen, 375
miter gauge, table saw, 417
mitochondrion, animal cell, 23
mitt, baseball, 290, 291
mitten, 200; ski clothes, 327
mixer, kitchen sink, 247
mixing blades, food processor, 254
mixing bowl, 258
mixing tools, kitchen, 258
moat: castle, 80, 81; mountain, 9; permanent fort, 83
mobile platform, space shuttle, 152
moccasin: Indian, 490; man's shoe, 204
mockery, gesture, 507
mode control, microwave oven, 248
mode display window, laser printer, 163
mode indicator, VCR, 184
model: baseball glove, 291; internal combustion engine, 406
mode lever, surgical table, 450
modeling end, clay modeling tool, 372
model number: phonograph speaker, 179; surgical table, 450
mode mute, phonograph receiver, 179
moderately loud, music, 352
mode selection control, police car, 122
mode selector: metal detector, 445; 747 cockpit, 151; sonar, 444
modesty panel, desk, 276
mode switch, Geiger counter, 445
modified bishop sleeve, bridal gown, 488
modified leg-of-mutton sleeve, bridal gown, 488
modulation indicator, CB radio, 183
modulation wheel, synthesizer, 363
module, jumbo jet gallery, 148; 149
moisture collector pan, air conditioner, 402
moisturizer, beauty product, 217
molar, tooth, 456
mold: church, 86; denture, 453
molding: automobile, 106, 107; church, 86; cupboard, 243; escalator, 79; frame, 379; grandfather clock, 233; minaret, 70
molding scoop, cooking utensil, 259
moline, symbol, 508
Molotov cocktail, 473
molten material, volcano, 10
money, 224-225; gesture, 507
money box, 457
money slot, blackjack, 347
money totalizer, gas pump, 112
monitor, 184; computer, 439; computer workstation, 438; fireboat, 144; movie projector, 175; personal computer, 162; portable word processor, 162; prison, 76; space shuttle, 153;

tanker, 141; tape recorder, 177; television, 185
monkey, caisson, 467
monkey bars, backyard equipment, 287
monkey board, oil drilling platform, 101
monkey ear, ultimate beast, 48
monkey wrench, 415
monocle, 221
monocoque chassis, racing car, 338
monorial, carpenter's level, 424
Monroe Room, White House, 75
monsoon, 6
montgolfier hot air balloon, 332
month, lunar, 4
monthly statement, credit card, 227
monticule, 7
monument, tombstone, 516
moon, 3; phases, 4
moon buggy, 155
moon dial, grandfather clock, 233
moon roof, automobile, 106
mooring mast: airship, 156; skyscraper, 77
mooring winch, tanker, 140
moose antler, ultimate beast, 48
mop, 282
moraine, 8, 9, 12
morning coat: butler's uniform, 489; man's formal attire, 488
morning line, flat racing entry, 336
morse, royal regalia, 484
mortar, 472; kitchen tool, 261
mortar joint, brick wall, 69
mortice hole, stagecoach, 131
mortise, label, 269
mortise lock, 458
mosque, 70
mosquito, 41
mosquito netting screen, tent, 342
mother, flat racing entry, 336
mother-in-law, bowling pin, 317
mother-of-all, spinning wheel, 387
motion, steam engine, 405
motion compensator, oil drilling platform, 101
motor: automobile, 108; automobile engine starter, 111; power drill, 419
motor cruiser, 133
motorcycle, 129
motor home, 130
motor housing: blender, 254; can opener, 251; food processor, 254; hair dryer, 212; jackhammer, 436; juice extractor, 255; lawn sprinkler, 428; potter's wheel, 373; power drill, 419; vacuum cleaner, 283
motorman's cab, subway, 119
motor mount, automobile engine, 111
motor nerve, human, 29
motor scooter helmet, police, 498
motor whaleboat, destroyer, 476
motto: coat of arms, 503; money, 224
mound: baseball field, 291; royal regalia, 485
mount: automobile engine, 111; bagpipe, 365; castle, 80, 81; coat of arms, 503; film

slide, 172; fire engine, 124; fishing reel, 340; machine gun tripod, 471; pencil sharpener, 277; polo, 299
mountain, 8-9; peak, 7
mountain climbing, 334
Mountain Time, 5
mount base, rifle scope, 468
mounting: ballpoint pen, 158; bicycle caliper brake, 128; drill press, 419; electrical receptacle, 398; electrical wall switch, 398; electronic flash, 176; fencing foil, 315; frame, 379; lamp, 239; mailbox, 231; ski binding, 326; telescope, 443
mouse, personal computer, 162
mousetrap, 433
mouth: beaker, 447; bell, iv; bottle, 267; cannon, 467; coral polyp, 46; fish, 45; frog, 44; hot air balloon, 332; human, 24, 30; jellyfish, 46; plane, 420; river, 7, 13; starfish, 46; suspenders, 190; tadpole, 44
mouth organ, 366
mouthpiece: boxing, 309; clarinet, 357; French horn, 358; harmonica, 366; kazoo, 366; pipe, 229; skin diving, 331; trombone, 358; trumpet, 359; tuba, 358
mouthpiece key, saxophone, 357
movable base, computer workstation, 438
movable bridge, 97 *
movable control-arm, surgical table, 450
movable fret, sitar, 362
movable jaw: C-clamp, 409; locking pliers, 414; monkey wrench, 415
move down, proofreader's mark, 514
move left, proofreader's mark, 514
movement, clock, 233
movement dial, vault, 457
move right, proofreader's mark, 514
movie camera, 174
movie projector, 174
movie film, 174
moving gate, racing, 336
moving sidewalk, 79
mower, lawn, 429
MP, uniform, 496
mucoprotein coat, animal cell, 23
mud: hogan, 84; nautical chart, 22
mud flap, truck, 120, 121, 126
mud shield, tank, 475
muezzin, and minaret, 70
muffler: automobile, 109; bulldozer, 435; internal combustion engine, 406; miser, 492; motorcycle, 129; power mower, 429; tank, 474; tractor, 434
muffler shield, chain saw, 431
mufti, police, 498
mug, shaving, 210
mulching lawn mower, 429
mule, canal lock, 99
Mulligan, darts, 322
mullion, church, 86
multifoil window, church, 86
multimeter, 423
multi-picture key, television, 185
multiple fruit, 55
multiple independently

targeted reentry vehicle (MIRV), 482
multiplication, with slide rule, 441
multiply, symbol, 510
multi-position surgical table, 450
multipurpose electrician's tool, 423
multipurpose vacuum cleaner brush, 283
muntins, window, 65
muscle: human, 26; scallop, 47
mushroom, 57
music: accessories, 367; notation, 352
music arch, organ, 360
music desk, grand piano, 361
music ensemble, 354
musician, orchestra, 354
music selection button, compact disc player, 178
music selection window, compact disc player, 178
music selector, tape recorder, 177
music stand, 367
music wire pliers, 414
Muslim temple, 70-71
muslin wrapping, dabber, 377
mussel, 47
mustache, 211
mustard, and frankfurter, 265
mute, phonograph receiver, 179
mutton, 33
muttonchop whiskers, 211
muzzle: automatic rifle, 471; bazooka, 472; cannon barrel, 467; cat, 37; cow, 32; dog, 36; horse, 38; mortar, 472; neck, 267; revolver, 470; sheep, 33; tank gun, 475
muzzle-loading cannon, 472
mycelium, mushroom, 57
mystery gas cloud, Milky Way, 3

N

N: braille, 512; sign language, 512
nacelle, jet fighter, 480
nail, 410; bird, 39; frame, 379; human hand, 31
nail cleaner: clippers, 215; pocket knife, 426
nail clippers, 215
nail crease, horseshoe, 38
nail file, 215
nail hole, horseshoe, 38
nail nick: corkscrew, 251; pocket knife, 426
nail polish, 217
nail pulling slot, hatchet, 412
name: business card, 160; credit card, 227; flat racing entry, 336; label, 268; letter, 159; magazine mailing label, 169; paper money, 225; passenger ship, 142; pencil brand, 158; political map, 20; résumé, 160; tugboat, 144
name column, voting booth, 437
nameplate: automobile, 107; can opener, 251; fireboat, 144; military uniform, 496; newspaper, 168; police uniform, 498
name tag, soldier's uniform, 497
nap, tennis ball, 312
nape: bird, 39; cat, 37; human, 25
napkin, 244
nare, nose, 30

108; helicopter, 146; windmill, 390; wind turbine, 390
rotunda, Capitol, 74
rouge, 216, 217
rough, golf course, 310-311
roughneck, oil drilling, 101
rough sill, house, 61
rouleau, 440
roulette wheel, 346
round: beef, 32; boxing, 309; police ammunition, 498
round-bottom hull, powerboat, 138
round-end chisel, stonecutting, 372
round head, screw, 410
roundhouse, railroad yard, 96
rounding board, merry-go-round, 93
round pin, window shade roller, 241
round shank, screwdriver, 413
round-the-clock, darts, 322
roustabout, circus, 90
route: bus, 118; road map, 20; subway, 119
route sign, road, 505
routing number, check, 226
row, hand knitting, 386
rowboat, 133
rowel, spur, 335
row house, 63
royal regalia, 484-485
rubber: baseball pitcher, 291; shoe accessory, 207
rubber band, dental, 453
rubber blade, silkscreen squeegee, 375
rubber bumper, knee kicker, 246
rubber covering, brayer, 374
rubber face, Ping-Pong racket, 321
rubber foot, food processor, 254
rubber mat, phonograph turntable, 178
rubber plug, sink, 273
rubber-soled shoe, jai alai player, 314
rubber tip, bobby pin, 214
rubbing ink, 376
ruble, symbol, 511
rub rail: powerboat, 138; truck platform, 121
ruching, bonnet, 203
rucksack: backpacking, 343; ski touring, 327
rudder: blimp, 156; destroyer, 476; glider, 147; jumbo jet, 149; sailboat, 134; single engine airplane, 147; space shuttle, 152; submarine, 479
rudder pedal, 747 cockpit, 150
rudimentary root, 51
ruff, Beefeater, 483
ruffled shirt, man's, 488
rug, 246; hairpiece, 211
rule: magazine, 170, 171; measuring, 424
ruler, 424; pocket knife, 426
rumble seat, automobile, 106
rump: beef, 134; bird, 39; cat, 37; dog, 36; horse, 38; pelt, 201; sheep, 33
run: step tread, 66; track and field, 300
run and lock switch, movie camera, 174
rung: ladder, 425; rocking chair, 234
run light, movie camera, 174
runner: grass, 58; ice skates, 325; rug, 246; running shoe, 302; skate, 295; sled, 328; slide rule, 441; umbrella, 230

running board, automobile, 107
running foot: book page, **iv**; magazine, 171
running knot, gallows, 462
running light: camper, 130; destroyer, 477; fireboat, 144; single engine airplane, 147; tow truck, 126; tugboat, 144
running mold, church, 86
running noose, lasso, 432
running ornament, church, 86
running rigging, sailboat, 134
running shoe, 302
running title, magazine, 170
running track, 300
run number: bus, 118; paper money, 225
runway: airport, 94; bowling lane, 317; javelin throw, 301; pole vault, 305; stage, 351
rupee, symbol, 511
rural mailbox, 231
Russian Cross, symbol, 508
rustproof oil, woodcarving, 372
Rx, prescription symbol, 451

S

S: braille, 512; sign language, 512
saber saw, 417
sabot, blackjack, 347
sabre, 315
sabre and épée warning line, fencing strip, 315
sac: flower stamen, 53; octopus, 46
sacral hump, frog, 44
sacristy, church, 87
sacrum, human, 26
saddle: bicycle, 128; door, 64; guitar, 362; horse, 335, 336, 337; matchbook, 228; motorcycle, 129; mountain, 8; pipe, 229; polo, 299; pommel horse, 307; screen, 175
saddlebag, 335; motorcycle, 129
saddle blanket, polo, 299
saddle feather, chicken, 35
saddle head, dispenser, 267
saddle plate, iron, 279
safe, 457
safe deposit box, 457
safe side, file, 420
safety: elevator shaft, 78; weapon, 468, 470, 471
safety bar, Ferris wheel, 93
safety belt: car, 110; lunar rover, 155
safety binding, ski, 326
safety cable, elevator, 78
safety cable tension sheave, elevator, 78
safety cage, hammer throw, 301
safety catch, revolver, 218
safety-chain hole, tow truck bed, 126
safety control data, prescription, 451
safety cool tip, curling iron, 214
safety dome, train tank car, 116
safety edge, elevator door, 78
safety guard: drill press, 419; paint spray gun, 425
safety guardrail, slide, 287
safety hasp, 460
safety jacket, waterskiing, 329
safety ladder, Ferris wheel, 93
safety lever: hand grenade, 473; pistol, 470
safety line, inflatable, 133
safety loop, circus aerialist, 90

safety lug, cassette tape, 177
safety matches, 228
safety mirror, mechanical sweeper, 127
safety net: aircraft carrier, 478; circus aerialist, 90
safety observer station, destroyer, 477
safety pad, trampoline, 308
safety padding, football goalpost, 293
safety pin, 208; hand grenade, 473
safety rail: bathtub, 274; bridge, 97; powerboat, 139
safety razor, 210
safety rope, roller coaster, 92
safety shield, child's car seat, 286
safety shut-off, Jacuzzi, 274
safety stripe, fireman's coat, 500
safety trigger, chain saw, 431
safety valve, furnace, 400
safety warning, dental x-ray unit, 454
safety zone, polo grounds, 299
Sagittarius, zodiac, 509
sail, 134, 136; hang glider, 333; submarine, 479; windmill, 390; windsurfer, 330
sailboard, 330
sailboat, 134-135
sailing thwart, rowboat, 133
sailor, uniform, 497
sailplane, 147; submarine, 479
St. Anthony's cross, symbol, 508
salad bowl, 245
salad fork, 244
salad plate, 245
salad shaker, 260
salamander, 44
salient angle, 83
saline, paramedic equipment, 123
saliva ejector, dental unit, 454
sally port, frontier fort, 82
salon, sailboat, 135
salt shaker, 261
salutation, letter, 159
Sam Browne belt, 496
same name differentiation code, magazine mailing label, 169
same scale extension inset, political map, 21
sample bag dispenser, lunar rover, 155
sanctuary: church, 87; mosque, 70-71
sand, hourglass, 233
sandal, 206
sand area, topographic map, 22
sandbag: ambulance, 123; hot air balloon, 332
sandbar: coastline, 14, 15; river, 13
sandbox: backyard, 287; locomotive, 116, 117
sander, 421
sandglass, 233
sandhill, nautical chart, 22
sandpaper, 421
sand shoe, truck van, 121
sand tower, railroad yard, 96
sand trap, golf course, 311
sand wedge, golf club, 310
sandwich, 263
sandwich cookie, 264
sanitary hose: baseball, 290; football uniform, 292
sanitary paper, medical examination table, 450
sanitation vehicle, 127
sanman, 127

sans serif type, 165
sapwood, tree, 50
sari, 491
sarong, 491
sartorius, human, 26
satellite, 3, 186
Saturn, planet, 3
sauce, sundae, 264
saucepan, 257
saucer, 245
sauerkraut, and frankfurter, 265
sauna, passenger ship, 143
saurischian, dinosaur, 43
sausage, pizza, 265
saw, 416, 417; pocket knife, 426
sawbuck, 408
sawhorse, 408
saxophone, 357
S-band antenna, lunar lander, 154
S bend, tuba, 358
scabbard, Revolutionary War general, 492
scaffold, gallows, 462
scaffolding web, spider, 40
scale: bird foot, 39; blood pressure gauge, 449; camera, 174; coffee maker, 252; electronic flash, 176; fish, 45; frontier fort, 82; house blueprint, 62; hypodermic syringe, 451; kitchen, 258; knife, 426, 463; laboratory, 446-447; lettuce, 262; light meter, 176; metronome, 367; nautical chart, 22; pine cone, 52; political map, 21; saw, 417; sewing machine, 278; slide rule, 441; snake, 42; thermometer, 18, 449; typewriter, 161; volt-ohm meter, 423
scallop, 47; bridal gown hem, 488; curtain, 240
scalp, 211; mortise lock, 458
scalper, harness racing pacer, 337
scanner: cash register, 440; fax machine, 164; hovercraft, 145; radar, 444
scapha, outer ear, 30
scaphoid pad, sandal, 206
scapula, human, 26
scapular, bird, 39
scapular region, salamander, 44
scarf, pirate, 492
scarp, fort, 83
scend, wave, 14
scenery, stage, 350
scenic overlook, highway, 114
scent, 217
scepter, royal, 485
school: fish, 45; prison, 76
school crossing, road sign, 505
sciatic nerve, human, 29
scimitar antenna, lunar lander, 154
scintillometer, 445
scissor grip, body building, 344
scissors, 384; pocket knife, 426
sclera, eye, 30
scoop: ice cream cone, 265; kitchen tool, 258, 259; lacrosse stick, 298; pipe tool, 229
scoop stretcher, ambulance, 123
scooter car, amusement park, 92
scooter helmet, police, 499

Credits

pages 2-3, illustration by Neal Adams; **5**, time zone map courtesy of Hammond Incorporated, Maplewood, NJ; **8-9**, illustration by Dee Molenaar; **18**, photo courtesy of Science Associates Inc.; **20-21**, Japan map courtesy of Hammond Inc., thematic map of "Number of Irish Foreign Born 1930" courtesy of Carnegie Institution of Washington; **28, 29, 30**, anatomy cross sections courtesy of Hammond Inc.; **60-61**, illustrations courtesy of American Plywood Assoc.; **62**, illustration by Charles Addams, blueprint by Carl Hribar; **74-75**, photos by David Burnett, courtesy of Contact Press Images, Inc.; **76**, photo courtesy of State of N.Y. Dept. of Correctional Services; **77**, top photo courtesy of The Port Authority of New York & New Jersey, lower photo courtesy of Empire State Building; **78**, elevator shaft illustration courtesy of Westinghouse Elevator, elevator car illustration courtesy of Williamsburg Steel Products, Co.; **80**, photo courtesy of British Information Service; **86-87**, illustrations courtesy of Cathedral Church of St. John the Divine, N.Y.C.; **88**, courtesy of Temple Emanuel, N.Y.C.; **90-91**, courtesy of Ringling Brothers and Barnum & Bailey; **92-93**, roller coaster courtesy of Magic Mountain Amusement Park, Ferris wheel and merry-go-round courtesy of Rye Playland; **94-95**, airport photo courtesy of American Airlines; **96**, photo courtesy of Association of American Railroads; **97**, photos courtesy of Triborough Bridge and Tunnel Authority; **101**, photo by Carroll S. Grevemberg, Grevy Photography, New Orleans, LA; **102-103**, supermarket plan courtesy of *Progressive Grocer*, coupon courtesy of Folger's Coffee; **106-107**, AnyCar photos courtesy of Manufacturers Hanover Trust, N.Y.C.; **108-109**, photo courtesy of Buick Division, General Motors Corp.; **110**, photo courtesy of Alfa Romeo; **111**, photo courtesy of Bradford La Riviera Inc.; **114**, courtesy of Triborough Bridge & Tunnel Authority; **116-117**, steam locomotive photo courtesy of Association of American Railroads, turbine engine photo courtesy of National Railroad Passenger Corporation, panels courtesy of The Train Shop, Ltd.; **118**, coach courtesy of American Eagle, commuter bus interior courtesy of NY Metropolitan Transit Authority; **119**, courtesy of NY Metropolitan Transit Authority Museum; **120-121**, photos courtesy of Mack Trucks Corp.; **124-125**, photos courtesy of New York City Fire Department; **126**, tow truck courtesy of LST Towing, N.Y.C.; **127**, courtesy of NYC Department of Sanitation; **129**, photo courtesy of Kawasaki Motorcycles; **130**, camper photo courtesy of Winnebago Industries, Inc., snowmobile photo courtesy of Yamaha Motor Corp.; **131**, stagecoach courtesy of Wells Fargo Bank History Dept., hansom cab courtesy of The New-York Historical Society; **133**, photo courtesy of Dyer Jones, Warren, RI; **134-135**, illustrations courtesy of CSY Yacht Corp., Tampa, FL; **136**, compass photo courtesy of Aqua Meter Instrument Corp., Roseland, NJ; **137**, outboard photo courtesy of Mariner Outboards, Fond du Lac, WI, sextant photo courtesy of Weems & Plath, Annapolis, MD; **138-139**, illustration courtesy of Bertram Yachts, Miami, FL; **142-143**, illustration courtesy of Cunard Line Ltd., N.Y.C.; **144**, tugboat courtesy of Moran, fireboat courtesy of NYC Fire Department; **145**, hovercraft photo courtesy of British Hovercraft Corp. Ltd.; **146**, photo courtesy of Sikorsky; **147**, airplane photo courtesy of Piper Aircraft Corp.; **148-149**, illustration courtesy of Boeing; **150-151**, photo courtesy of Boeing; **152-153**, photo and illustration courtesy of NASA; **154-155**, illustrations courtesy of NASA; **156**, photo courtesy of Goodyear; **159**, calligraphy by Melissa, text by Sean Kelly; **161**, manual typewriter photo courtesy of Royal Business Machines, Inc.; **162**, top photo courtesy of Apple Computer Inc., bottom right photo courtesy of Sharp Electronics Corp.; **163**, top photo courtesy of Fujitsu America, San Jose, CA, bottom illustration after NEC Information Systems, Inc.; **164**, fax machine and copier photos courtesy of Sharp Electronics Corp.; **166**, illustrations courtesy of International Paper Company; **168**, courtesy of *The New York Times*, N.Y.C.; **169**, *Time* cover reprinted by permission from *Time* The Weekly Newsmagazine, copyright Time Inc., 1980, contents page reprinted courtesy of *Sports Illustrated* from the March 3, 1980 issue, copyright (c) 1980, Time, Inc.; **170-171**, prepared by *New York* Magazine, N.Y.C.; **172**, zoom lens photo courtesy of Tokina Optical Ltd.; **173**, video still camera photo courtesy of Sony; **174**, photo courtesy of Minolta Camera Co., Ltd.; **175**, movie projector photo courtesy of Minolta, slide projector photo courtesy of Kodak, screen courtesy of Da-Lite Screen Co.; **176**, light meter courtesy of Gossen-Luna Pro, electronic flash courtesy of Vivitar Corp., tripod courtesy of E. Leitz Inc.; **177**, reel-to-reel recorder photo courtesy of Pioneer Electronics, cassette tape photo courtesy of Sony; **178**, turntable photo courtesy of Pioneer Electronics Corp.; **179**, audio photos courtesy of Pioneer Electronics Corp.; **181**, cellular telephone photo courtesy of Panasonic, answering machine photo courtesy of Sony; **182**, bottom photo courtesy of Sharp Electronics Corp.; **183**, photo courtesy of Radio Shack; **184**, VCR photo courtesy of Panasonic, video camera courtesy of Sharp Electronics; **185**, television photo courtesy of Sony; **186**, illustration courtesy of NASA; **195**, panty hose photo courtesy of Hanes Corp.; **196-197**, illustrations by Calvin Klein; **201**, fur photo courtesy of Rosette, NY; **205**, courtesy of Andy Warhol; **207**, sock photo courtesy of Alexander Lee Wallan Inc.; **209**, photo courtesy of Velcro USA; **210**, electric razor photo courtesy of Sunbeam Corp.; **212**, hair dryer photo courtesy of Conair; **214**, curling iron photo courtesy of Conair; **216-217**, products courtesy of Avon Products, Inc., make-up by Tom Gearhard; **218-219**, ring and pendant illustrations courtesy of Jane Evans; **220**, wristwatch courtesy of Chronosport Inc., Rowayton, CT; **227**, traveler's check courtesy of Barclay's Bank, N.Y.C.; **237**, candle snuffer courtesy of Fortunoff Department Store, N.Y.C.; **244**, place setting courtesy of Rosenthal China Co.; **245**, dessert setting courtesy of Rosenthal China, panels courtesy of Gorham Division of Textron Inc.; **247**, sink courtesy of Elkay Manufacturing Co., disposal unit courtesy of Hobart Co.; **248**, stove and microwave oven photos courtesy of General Electric Co.; **251**, electric opener courtesy of Oster Corp., can piercer courtesy of Ekco Industries; **255**, vegetable juicer courtesy of Hamilton Beach, automatic juicer courtesy of Oster Corp., manual juicer courtesy of Acme Juicer Mfg. Corp.; **257**, pressure cooker courtesy of National Presto Industries, electric wok courtesy of Farberware; **258-261**, courtesy of H&P Mayer Corp.; **267**, pump dispenser courtesy of Calmar Division/Diamond Int'l.; **268-269**, illustration by The Schecter Group; **278**, courtesy of Viking Sewing Machine Co.; **279**, courtesy of Proctor-Silex; **281**, dryer courtesy of General Electric; **283**, vacuum cleaner courtesy of Hoover Co., minivacuum courtesy of Black & Decker; **284**, fire extinguisher courtesy of Amerex Corp., smoke alarm courtesy of General Electric; **286**, stroller courtesy of Perego/Pines, Milan, Italy, playpen and car seat courtesy of Century Products, Los Angeles, CA; **287**, wagon illustration courtesy of Flexible Flyer; **288**, barbecue courtesy of King Seeley Co.; **290**, models: Rod Carew, California Angels (batter), Ossie Virgil Jr., Philadelphia Phillies (catcher); **291**, glove courtesy of Rawlings Sporting Goods; **292**, model: James Ramey, New York Jets, helmet courtesy of Bike Athletic Co.; **294-295**, models: Ken Morrow (defenseman) and Billy Smith (goalie), New York Islanders; **296**, model: Mike Glenn, New York Knickerbockers; **298**, photos courtesy of STX Company; **299**, photo courtesy of *Polo* Magazine; **302**, running shoe courtesy of Adidas; **306-307**, photos courtesy of Nissen/Walter Kidde & Co.; **309**, model: Wendal Newton; **310-311**, equipment photos courtesy of Northwestern Golf Co.; **314**, courtesy of Bridgeport, Conn., Jai Alai, model: Donald Mazza; **315**, piste courtesy of George Santelli Fencing School, N.Y.C.; **320**, photo courtesy of Brunswick Corp.; **322**, courtesy of Darts Unlimited, N.Y.C.; **324**, photo courtesy of Chicago Roller Skates Inc.; **326**, equipment courtesy of Scandinavian Ski Shop; **327**, cross-country equipment courtesy of Scandinavian Ski Shop, snowshoe courtesy of The Snowcraft Corp.; **329**, ski courtesy of Connelly Skis, Inc.; **331**, equipment courtesy of Atlantic Divers World, NY; **332**, photo courtesy of The Balloon Works, Statesville, NC; **333**, parachute courtesy of Para-Flite Inc., US Parachuting Assoc., hang glider courtesy of United States Hang Gliding Assoc.; **334**, photos courtesy of George Willig, Topanga, CA; **335**, Western saddle courtesy of H. Kauffman and Sons, Inc., English saddle by Crosby, courtesy of Millers, N.Y.C.; **336**, program entry courtesy of Pimlico Race Track; **337**, Meadowlands Racetrack, East Rutherford, NJ, model: Courtney Foos; **338**, illustration by Jack Lane, courtesy of L'Art et L'Automobile Gallery, 354 E. 66th Street, N.Y.C., Jacques Vaucher; **339**, photos courtesy of National Hot Rod Association; **340-341**, fishing reel photo courtesy of Penn Reels, rod photo courtesy of Shakespeare Fishing Rods; **342**, photos courtesy of Coleman Co.; **343**, backpack photo courtesy of Johnson/ Camp Trails; **344**, universal gym photo courtesy of Nissen; **346-347**, courtesy of Mr. Lucky Equipment, Rosedale, NY; **349**, ticket courtesy of Globe Ticket Co.; **351**, photo of the Bardavon Theatre courtesy of Robert Paul Molay; **352-353**, *Theme From What's What® Book* written by John Hill, John Hill Music Inc.; **354**, illustration and photo courtesy of Chicago Symphony Orchestra; **360**, photo courtesy of Rodgers Organ, N.Y.C.; **365**, bagpipes courtesy of Larry Cole; **366**, accordion courtesy of Stuyvesant Music; **369**, painting courtesy of the Metropolitan Museum of Art, N.Y.C.; **370-371**, painting equipment courtesy of Grumbacher; **372**, Sculpture House, N.Y.C.; **374**, equipment courtesy of Rembrant Graphic Arts, NJ; **376-377**, courtesy of Rembrant Graphic Arts, NJ and Charles Brand Machinery Inc., NY; **378**, equipment courtesy of Glassmaster Guild; **380-381**, cartoon by Mike Witte, comic strip by Mort Walker, copyright 1978 King Features Syndicate, Inc.; **382**, photo courtesy of Fireworks By Grucci Inc., Brookhaven, NY; **383**, top and bottom right photos courtesy of Fireworks By Grucci Inc., Brookhaven, NY, center and bottom left photos courtesy of Zambelli Fireworks Mfg. Co., Inc., New Castle, PA; **385**, quilt courtesy of Fairfield Processing; **386**, shuttle courtesy of C.J. Bates & Son, Inc.; **387**, loom courtesy of LaClerc Weaving Looms; **390**, wind turbine photo courtesy of Grumman Corp.; **394**, super collider illustrations and photo courtesy of Universities Research Assoc., Washington, DC; **395**, gas laser diagram after *Lumonics*, hologram photo courtesy of AT&T Archives; **396**, transistor photo courtesy of Bell Laboratories; **402**, courtesy of Hampton Sales; **406**, courtesy of Teledyne Wisconsin Motor; **409**, photos courtesy of Adjustable Clamp Co.; **417**, table saw photo courtesy of ToolKraft, circular saw photo courtesy of Ski, saber saw photo courtesy of Rockwell International; **421**, sander photo courtesy of Rockwell International, belt sander courtesy of Black & Decker; **423**, voltmeter courtesy of Amprobe Instruments; **424**, folding rule courtesy of Stanley Tools, carpenter's level courtesy of ToolKraft; **425**, spray painter courtesy of Spray Tech Corp.; **426**, photo courtesy of Hoffritz; **427**, courtesy of Douglas Products; **428**, photos courtesy of L.R. Nelson Corp.; **429**, photo courtesy of Sears, Roebuck & Company; **430**, wheelbarrow courtesy of Jackson Mfg. Co., seeder courtesy of Cyclone Seeder Co., Inc.; **431**, chainsaw photo courtesy of Ski Corp.; **434**, tractor photo courtesy of J.I. Case; **436**, theodolite courtesy of Dietzgen Corp., jackhammer courtesy of Bosch Power Tools; **437**, photos courtesy of R.F. Shoup Corp., Radnor, PA; **438**, computer workstation photo courtesy of Intergraph Corp., Huntsville, AL; **439**, computer system and computer tapes photos courtesy of IBM Corp., White Plains, NY, circuit board photo courtesy of Intergraph Corp.; **440**, courtesy of NCR Corporation; **442**, photo courtesy of Carl Zeiss Inc.; **443**, telescope photo courtesy of Unitron Instruments Inc., binoculars photo courtesy of Minolta Camera Co., Ltd.; **444**, photos courtesy of Furuno U.S.A., Inc.; **445**, metal detector photo courtesy of White Electronics Inc., geiger counter photo courtesy of EDA Instruments; **446-447**, burner courtesy of Fisher Scientific Co., scale courtesy of Ohaus Scale Corp.; **448**, photos courtesy of Welch Allyn, Skaneateles Falls, NY; **449**, photos courtesy of Sybron Corp.; **450**, courtesy of Affiliated Hospital Products; **451**, prescription form courtesy of Scriptech; **452**, wheelchair photo courtesy of Invacare Corp., hearing aid photo courtesy of Dahlberg Electronics, pacemaker photo courtesy of Medtronic, Inc.; **453**, denture photo courtesy of Sterndent Corp., braces bracket photo courtesy of 'A' Company, Inc.; **454**, courtesy of Ritter Dental Corp.; **455**, courtesy of Dr. Herbert Spasser; **457**, photos courtesy of Mosler Safe Co.; **458**, Safe Hardware Corporation, Emhart Industries Inc.; **459**, lock photo courtesy of Medico Security Locks Inc.; **460**, hasp courtesy of Lawrence Brothers, Inc.; **461**, chains courtesy of Diamond Chain Co., block and pulley courtesy of The Crosby Group; **476-477**, illustration of DE 1092 courtesy of officers and men of *USS Thomas C. Hart*, drawings of ship types after *Jane's Fighting Ships*; **478-479**, photos courtesy of US Navy Department; **480-481**, fighter aircraft photos courtesy of Grumman; **482**, cruise missile photo courtesy of Boeing Aerospace; **483**, illustration courtesy of James Burrough Ltd., N.Y.C.; **484**, costumes courtesy of Eaves-Brooks Costume Co.; **486**, photo courtesy of Irving Fisher; **487**, minister photo courtesy of The Very Reverend Francis B. Sayre; **488**, photo courtesy of After Six Formal Wear; **489**, photos courtesy of Masterpiece Theatre, LWT, N.Y.C.; **490**, costume courtesy of Eaves-Brooks Costume Co., Indian courtesy of the Museum of the American Indian, N.Y.C.; **491**, Manchu Court Dress courtesy of Reginald Bragonier, Arab dress courtesy of Bill Ashe, model: Jan Leighton; **492**, model: Jan Leighton, pirate photograph by BODI, miser photograph by Michael Weiss; **493**, illustration by Ted Geisel; **494**, photo courtesy of Lois Greenfield/Capezio Ballet Makers; **496-497**, photos by Phil Koenig, soldiers courtesy of US Army, sailor courtesy of US Navy; **500**, photo courtesy of New York City Fire Department; **503**, courtesy of Government of Canada; **506**, symbols courtesy of *Handbook of Pictorial Symbols*, Rudolph Modley, Dover Publications, Inc., N.Y.C.; **514**, courtesy of Mary Grace and Maria Maggi; **516**, casket courtesy of Simmons Casket Co./ Gulf and Western Casket Co.

Acknowledgements

The editors wish to express their special appreciation to the late Hugh Johnson for his friendship and support. Without him, WHAT'S WHAT® would not exist.

Harold Adler, Adler Monument and Granite Works; Roslyn Alexander, librarian, Charles Evans Hughes High School; Jack Arnoff; Dave Lipsky, Juana Torres and Frank Coppinger, Army Corps of Engineers; Martin Bacheller, Hammond Inc.; Gwen Baker, Hammond Inc.; Roberta Baker, *Life* Magazine; Barney's Clothing Store; Sandy Bartram; Susan Bates Inc.; David Baxley, Triborough Bridge & Tunnel Authority; Mitch Becker, Globe Ticket Corp.; Paul Berkovitz, Algoma Net Company; Randy Black, Bike Athletic Corp.; Mitchell and George Tepper, Bond Street Suspender Inc.; Bonny Products; Carol Boswell and Gina Frantz, Boswell-Frantz Public Relations; Jerry Boxer, Abraham Boxer and Sons; Lee Bracy, Westinghouse Elevator Inc.; Benjamin Bragonier; Dana Bragonier; queen model Penelope Bragonier; Bill and Betty Brennan; Andreas Brown, Gotham Book Store; Donna Grucci Butler, Grucci Inc.; Cadillac Meat Company; Camrod Motorcycles; Carez Health Care Corp.; cross-country skiing model Catherine Carlen; Zack Carr, Calvin Klein Ltd.; Celeste Champagn, LWT Int'l.; Robert E. Lewis and William S. DeArment, Channellock Corp.; Betty Charak, Personality Hanger Inc.; Jerry Charles, Hollco Tools Coats and Clark, Inc.; accordion supplied by Larry Cole; Phil Colicchio, Oreo Cookies; Dita Comacho; Nancy Conforti, H & P Mayer Inc.; H. C. Cook, Inc., Division of Gem Products; Ron Coplon, Rubin Gloves Inc.; Richard Curtis, Richard Curtis Associates; Elmer Danch and Elaine Harr, Da-Lite Movie Screen Company; Frank Davis; John and Jessica Dorfman; Rose Dreger; Alfred Dunhill Inc.; Alex Dupuy, Columbia Computer Lab; Blaise Dupuy, The Box Studio; Ken Durst, Rawlings Inc.; John Edelmann, EKCO Housewares Corp.; Lt. Juan Torres and Ray Florida, NYC Emergency Medical Service; Lee Entwistle, Eaves-Brooks Costumes Inc.; Herbert Eskelson, Para-Flite Inc.; Eye Center Inc.; Penny Farber, Foxmore Inc.; staff of Fashion Institute of Technology library; Arthur Ferguson, Metropolitan Transit Authority; Steve Fineberg, Feinberg Associates; Ira Finke, Ira Finke Photography; Nini Finkelstein, Ringling Brothers and Barnum & Bailey Circus; Irving and Sylvia Fisher; Anthony Forgione, Consolidated Wafer and Cone Corp.; Joann Forster, International School of Harness Racing at Roosevelt Raceway; William Free Advertising Agency; Bill Freeman, The Gill Track and Field Equipment Company; Steve Friedman; Lois Fry, Shakespeare Fishing Equipment; Fuller Brush Corp.; Louise Gaither, Executive Services Advertising; Gary Galante, Museum of the American Indian; cosmetic model make-up by Tom Gearhard; Irv Goldfinger, Forsyth Monument Works; Matthew Goldman; Bob Goldstein, M & F Hanger; Brian Goodman; Mary Grace; Kathy Graham, Bridgeport, Conn., Jai Alai; Thomas Grasso, Kay Jeep Eagle; J. F. Grgula, Structo Division, King-Seeley Thermos Co.; John Growth, School of Visual Arts; Mike Gue, Ethics Automobile Racing; Walter Guslawski, Williamsburg Steel Products; Stephen A. Halls, Jr., Digital Equipment Corp.; Dana Hammond, Hammond Inc.; Dean Hammond, President, Hammond Inc.; Kathy Hammond, Hammond Inc.; Stuart Hammond, Hammond Inc.; management and staff of Hampton Sales; Harvey Sound Corp.; Irving Heiberger, Marshall Clark Inc.; Joyce Heiberger, JBH Advertising; Kenneth Heinz, Welch-Allyn Corporation; Paul Heller, International Creative Management; Katharine Hill; Hoffritz Inc.; Ernst Hofmann, Hammond Inc.; Anne S. Hopkins, *Time* Magazine; Edward Irrizarry; Chris Jones, Hammond Inc.; Edward M. Kalail, Diebold Inc.; PO Ken Kaufman, NYPD, coauthor of *The Incredible Scooter Cops*; Scrooge's letter by Sean Kelly, former editor of *The National Lampoon*; Chris Kelly; Jessie O. Kempter, IBM; cowboy model by William Ketchum, Jr., author of *Western Memorabilia*; George Klauber, George Klauber Graphic Arts Studio; Morris and Ruth Kleinman; Drew Kuber, Hammond Inc.; Barbara Lach, Fermilab; Richard and Elyse Langsam; Larry Letizia, Joyson Motors; Leaf Tent and Sail Inc.; Charles Leib; Leland-Penn; Patricia Lewis; Robert Lewis, Chrysler Corporation; Teresa Longhitano; Mel and Cheryl London, authors of *Bread Winners*; Lionel V. Lorona, New York Public Library; Candace Love; Donald A. Macaulay; Joseph W. Maresca, Jr., SRI Institute; Daniel Mazzarella, Science Associates Inc.; Ken McAdams; Kay McDowell, US Postal Data Center; Frank 'Tug' McGraw, Philadelphia Phillies; Dave McNamara, Wilson Sporting Goods, Inc.; The Meadowlands Racetrack management; Jennifer Meyer, Hammond Inc.; John Meyers, Fisher Scientific Company; Ray Miller, VISA; Mr. Lucky School of Gambling; Macmillan Publishing Corp.; Captain Don Mitchell, Eastern Airlines; Jenny Moradfar; Ruth Grevey and Larry Osterman, Mosler Safe Corp.; Edward J. Murphy, Edward J. Murphy Corp.; Neckwear Association of America; Steve Nesbitt, Mark Hess, Tom Jacqua, NASA; New York Jets; New York Knickerbockers; New York Yankees; Don Morris and Suzanne Eagle, *New York* Magazine; PO George Legas and Steve Berenhaus, NYPD; John Nicholson; C. Michael Oldenberg, Centennial Management Corp.; Joan Rubin and Christine Martorana, Omega Fashions Ltd.; John Pace, National Cash Register; Shirley Palmer, *Progressive Grocer*; Rolando Pena; Arthur and Lois Perschetz, LTC Gerald Perschetz, U.S. Army (Ret.); Clarence Peskac, Dietzgen Corp.; Allen Petersen, Petersen Manufacturing Co., Inc.; Robert Pledge, Contact Press Images; Brigit Polk, The Factory; Marian Powers, *Time* Magazine; Andrew W. Prescott, Hammond Inc.; Donald Quest, Southwest Texas Drilling Co.; James Ramey, New York Jets; Jim Ramsey, Rodgers Organ Corp.; Mitch Rapaport, Scriptech; Mark Resnick, Hammond Inc.; Malcolm Ritter, Associated Press; Rock of Ages Corp.; Rosemary Rodgers, John Hill Music, Inc.; Linda Rosenblatt, R.D.H.; Joan Evanish, Judith Johnson and Canon West, Cathedral Church of St. John the Divine; Teddi Sann, Avon Products, Inc.; Gene Sayet, Executive Recording Ltd.; Frank and Harriet Sayre; Rosette Schecter, Furs by Rosette; Leslie Schwartz, Hammond Inc.; Deputy Police Commissioner 'Mickey' Schwartz, NYPD; Ann Scott, *Sports Illustrated*; Elizabeth Scott, Chicago Symphony Orchestra; Ray Scroggins, Wisconsin-Teledyne; Esther R. Selby, Zambelli Fireworks Mfg. Co.; Dr. John H. Seward, MD EENT; Joel Shaffer, Hammond Inc.; J. Ronald Shumate, Association of American Railroads; Craig Siebert; Harold Silver, Caldwell Button Corp.; Robert Simon, Wan, Simon and Black; Robert Smith; NY-NJ Port Authority; Dr. Herbert Spasser, D.D.S.; cosmetics model Tina Stahle; Stappers Equipment Corp.; Stuyvesant Music; Tom Szobe, Paragon Sporting Goods; Bob Taylor, Hedstrom Baby Furniture; Technigraph Studio; Marilyn Tempkins, Vivitar Inc.; calligraphy letterhead on Scrooge's letter by Melissa Topping; Tower Manufacturing; Paul Schulhaus, Russ Levin, Train Shop Ltd.; Bobbie Tupper, Park West Chapel; Helen Turi, General Motors Corp.; Helen Tutt, American Eagle; Tina T. Underwood, Intergraph; Universal Fastenings Inc.; Anna Urband, US Navy Public Relations; officers and men of the *USS Thomas C. Hart* (DE 1092); Jacques Vaucher, L'Art et L'Automobile Gallery; Ossie Virgil, Jr., Philadelphia Phillies; Dan Walden, Consolidated Edison Corp.; John Wanamaker; Sam Weinstein, Color Group; Western Union Corp.; Janet L. Wetmore, AT&T Archives; George Willig; king model Robert Wills; PO 'Scooter' Joe Wins, NYPD, coauthor of *The Incredible Scooter Cops*; John Wisdom; Laurie Wolford; Janet Wygall; Will Yolin, author of *The Complete Book of Kites and Kite Flying*; Richard Ziskin, American Umbrella Co.; Roger Zissu, Cowan, Liebowitz & Latman; Nell Znamierowski, Fashion Institute of Technology; and special thanks to the Hammond staff for their numerous contributions and assistance in producing this book.

Afterword

When we first created WHAT'S WHAT® in 1981, it was
a major new undertaking, the first visual glossary
to appear in more than a century. While we were
confident that our research was meticulous, we also
recognized that errors were bound to creep into such
an ambitious project. So we asked readers to share
their special knowledge and observations with us.
Hundreds did. Most of the mail was embarrassing in
its flattery, much of it was touching. Letters from
parents of deaf children or children with learning
disabilities, for example, described the benefits and
pleasures derived by a very special reading audience.
Dozens of other letters proffered thoughtful criticism
that proved extremely valuable in preparing this
revision. We are indebted to all who wrote, and we
invite you to correspond with us in the future, for
whatever reason.

David Fisher
WHAT'S WHAT®
357 West 19th St.
New York, N.Y., 10011